THE HANDY POLITICS ANSWER BOOK

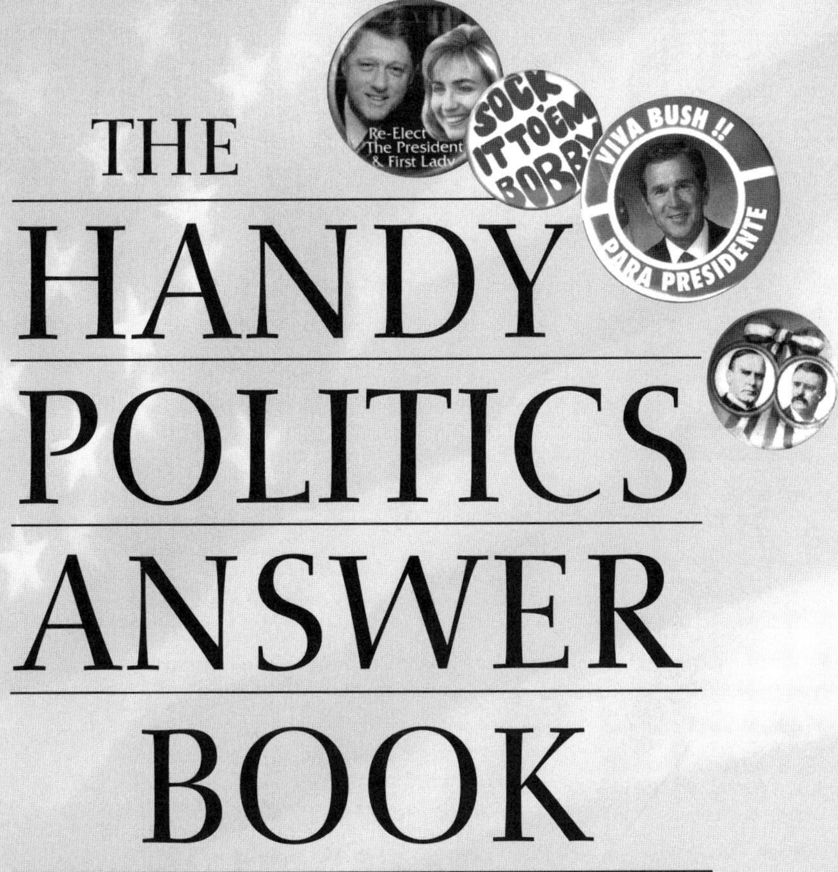

THE HANDY POLITICS ANSWER BOOK

GINA MISIROGLU

Detroit

The Handy Politics Answer Book™

Photo Credits

AP WideWorld: pages 1, 3, 10, 23, 27, 31, 34, 37, 44, 49, 59, 67, 73, 77, 79, 104, 93, 94, , 96, 102, 108, 112, 136, 141, 148, 167, 173, 176, 196, 199, 200, 203, 206, 215, 218, 219, 200, 224, 226, 231, 243, 246, 252, 255, 257, 258, 260, 261, 263, 266, 273, 275, 279, 295, 297, 302, 304, 322, 325, 329, 330, 332, 339, 356, 373, 374, 382, 389, 390, 395, 398, 399, 507.

Hulton Archive: pages 13, 29, 41, 82, 90, 92, 111, 127, 129, 143, 160, 161, 164, 166, 168, 179, 180, 182, 223, 237, 242, 247, 307, 308, 312, 405, 406, 412, 415, 416, 417, 426, 435, 439, 441, 449, 452, 456, 457, 459, 461, 462, 465, 466, 463, 468, 470, 479.

Visible Ink Press®
43311 Joy Road #414
Canton, MI 48187

Visible Ink Press and The Handy Politics Answer Book are trademarks of Visible Ink Press LLC.

Most Visible Ink Press books are available at special quantity discounts when purchased in bulk by corporations, organizations, or groups. Customized printings, special imprints, messages, and excerpts can be produced to meet your needs. For more information, contact Special Markets Director, Visible Ink Press, at www.visibleink.com or (734) 667-3211.

Art Director: Mary Claire Krzewinski
Typesetting: Graphix Group

ISBN 1-57859-139-2

Library of Congress Cataloging-in-Publication Data

Misiroglu, Gina Renâee.
The handy politics answer book / Gina Misiroglu.
p. cm.
Includes bibliographical references and index.
ISBN 1-57859-139-2 (alk. paper)
1. United States--Politics and government--Miscellanea. I. Title.
JK276 .M63 2003

2002012885

Printed in the United States of America

10 9 8 7 6 5 4 3 2

"The essential principles of our Government ... form the bright constellation which has gone before us and guided our steps through an age of revolution and reformation. The wisdom of our sages and blood of our heroes have been devoted to their attainment. They should be the creed of our political faith, the text of civic instruction, the touchstone by which to try the services of those we trust; and should we wander from them in moments of error or of alarm, let us hasten to retrace our steps and to regain the road which alone leads to peace, liberty and safety."

—Thomas Jefferson, First Inaugural Address, 1801

The Handy Answer Book™ Series

The Handy Answer Book for Kids (and Parents)
The Handy Bug Answer Book
The Handy Dinosaur Answer Book
The Handy Geography Answer Book
The Handy History Answer Book
The Handy Ocean Answer Book
The Handy Physics Answer Book
The Handy Politics Answer Book
The Handy Religion Answer Book
The Handy Science Answer Book
The Handy Space Answer Book
The Handy Sports Answer Book
The Handy Weather Answer Book

Contents

POLITICAL BEHAVIOR AND POLICY

GOVERNMENT INSTITUTIONS

APPENDICES AND INDEX

Introduction

"What is government itself, but the greatest of all reflections on human nature? If men were angels, no government would be necessary. If angels were to govern men, neither external nor internal controls on government would be necessary." Although James Madison wrote these words in *The Federalist* No. 51 more than two centuries ago, his words are for today.

Recent events like the national election debacle of 2000, the tragedy of September 11 and its aftermath, the heated climate of the Middle East, and the effect of big money on political decision making and its relationship to the various corporate financial scandals have forced people to take pause and consider realities that our Founding Fathers never dreamed of. Clarification is not easily obtained; television, radio, and newspapers, those repositories of America's basic freedom to express opinions, however misinformed, frequently mean to seduce with spin and sell product rather than serve anything resembling truth. Yet in the midst of the overheated rhetoric of the moment, Americans are responsibly rethinking their role in history and their place as citizens in a free democracy. In the twenty-first century, people across the political spectrum are seeking a better understanding of international issues such as terrorism and national issues like campaign finance reform. They are turning to their leaders and asking them hard questions about how they are going to govern our land and relate to the unprecedented situations of this fast-changing, crisis-dominated world.

The Handy Politics Answer Book is set against this political backdrop. It is meant to answer basic questions about how our very complex government operates and what it promises, thereby removing a barrier to understanding current political drama. Its straightforward, easily understood question-and-answer format addresses contemporary issues as well as the fundamental basics of government and politics in the United States. It traces the historic development of the government and demystifies the departmental labyrinth, providing clear and concise definitions of who does what and why. Meant to inform and entertain, this at-a-glance resource is for those who want to revisit the best snippets of their high school civics class, as well as those who desire a more detailed background on today's headlines. Organized into easily accessible, topic-oriented chapters, over 1,000 most-asked, potentially useful questions are presented. Interspersed are trivia-oriented and off-the-cuff questions that you might not have considered since you last watched *Jeopardy*. In sum, the book presents an overarching look at government and politics, its key players, and notable events since the time of the early republic.

The book begins with a general look at today's political culture. You'll find out why trust in government has declined, what Americans think of their president, and what the average citizen can do to get involved in government. Questions like Why should I vote? Is government responsive to public opinion? and What is the history of women in government and politics? kick off the book. What follows is an intricate look at civil liberties, those fundamental freedoms so many Americans feel are slipping away in these tenuous times. In 1755 Benjamin Franklin said, "Those who would give up essential liberty, to purchase a little temporary safety, deserve neither liberty nor safety." Civil liberties are under fire in this age of unprecedented wiretapping, data collection, Internet regulation, microchip implants, and increased federal law enforcement powers. Read about these issues and more—why there is so much controversy over school prayer, whether random drug tests for student athletes violate their right to privacy, if burning the American flag is considered free speech, and how September 11 ushered in a new era of restricted freedoms.

Political behavior and political policy—in short, the way government acts—make up the bulk of the book. Readers glean little-known facts about political parties, campaigns and elections, how the media works, the nuances of economic, social, and foreign policy, and the way our government functions in times of crisis. You'll come away of with a solid understanding of everything from détente to the newly created Office of Homeland Security, as much as some of these elusive entities can be understood. The most thought-provoking questions—from What is the dirtiest presidential campaign on record? to What is the war on terrorism, exactly?—cover topics as varied as the federal budget, the national debt, war in the Middle East, campaign finance, the electoral college, the origins of the Republican and Democratic parties, how liberals and conservatives differ, and what public interest groups do to gain influence. Terms like Know-Nothings, NAFTA, split-ticket voting, front-loading, PAC, whitewash, Whitewater, dollar diplomacy, MAD, neoconservative, New Deal, and bioterrorism are defined and made easy to understand.

Even government and politics aficionados can use some brushing up on how the three branches of the government interact with one another and work to serve the American people. The executive, legislative, and judicial branches are rigorously covered. Related concepts, such as democracy, limited government, bureaucracy, separation of powers, and check and balances, are examined. What is the president's job description? How does a bill become a law? What is a quorum? A whip? A pocket veto? A filibuster? Logrolling? How do Supreme Court justices interpret the Constitution? How does a case reach the Supreme Court?

Finally, the origins of American government are explored. From early colonial governments to the Revolutionary War and the Declaration of Independence, the red, white, and blue shines through in these chapters. You'll be reminded why the English philosopher John Locke's ideas were inspiration for the new republic, who founded the early colonies, and how an emerging spirit of independence changed the shape of a tenuous America and laid the foundation for a national government. A careful look at the Constitution, our Founding Fathers, the issues of federalism, and state government conclude this section of the book.

No work of this kind would be whole without acknowledging the numerous resources available to those who want to learn more about the workings of American government and current political trends. For this reason, the concluding pages of the book function as their own mini-resource section—complete with original documents like the Constitution and the Declaration of Independence. Here you'll find recommended reading lists and lists of web sites for further study, as well as profiles of prominent political personalities, political journals, and politically active organizations.

"The best political community is formed by citizens of the middle class," said Aristotle, a citizen of an early democracy. An informed citizenry is the best defense against political and corporate chicanery, and an active electorate presents the greatest opportunity for democracy to flourish. *The Handy Politics Answer Book* provides some basic illumination in that quest.

Acknowledgments

I am indebted to all the scholars, political scientists, Washington think tanks, and government agencies that have made their work and ideas available. Although they are too numerous to mention here, a list of resources in the back of the book provides those names and organizations that offer myriad perspectives on government and politics today. My deepest appreciation goes to the wonderful team of people at Visible Ink Press, without whom this book would not have been realized. Martin Connors, the press's publisher and visionary of the Handy Answer Book series, has provided unwavering support throughout the creative process. Terri Schell, the book's project manager, is a dream of a craftsman with whom any author would be proud to work. Deserved thanks go to Roger Janecke, VIP's director of marketing; Christa Brelin, the press's managing editor; Mary Claire Krzewinski, the book's designer; Jeff Hermann, photo researcher and permissions expert; Robert J. Huffman, imager; Amy Lucas, researcher and proofreader extraordinaire; Mark Schell, researcher; Marco Di Vita of Graphix Group, typesetter; Mark Berger, chart and graphs; Larry Baker, indexer; and Brad Morgan and the other proofreaders whose watchful eyes saved the book from errors.

On a personal note, I thank my family, whose abundant care made writing time possible.

—Gina Misiroglu

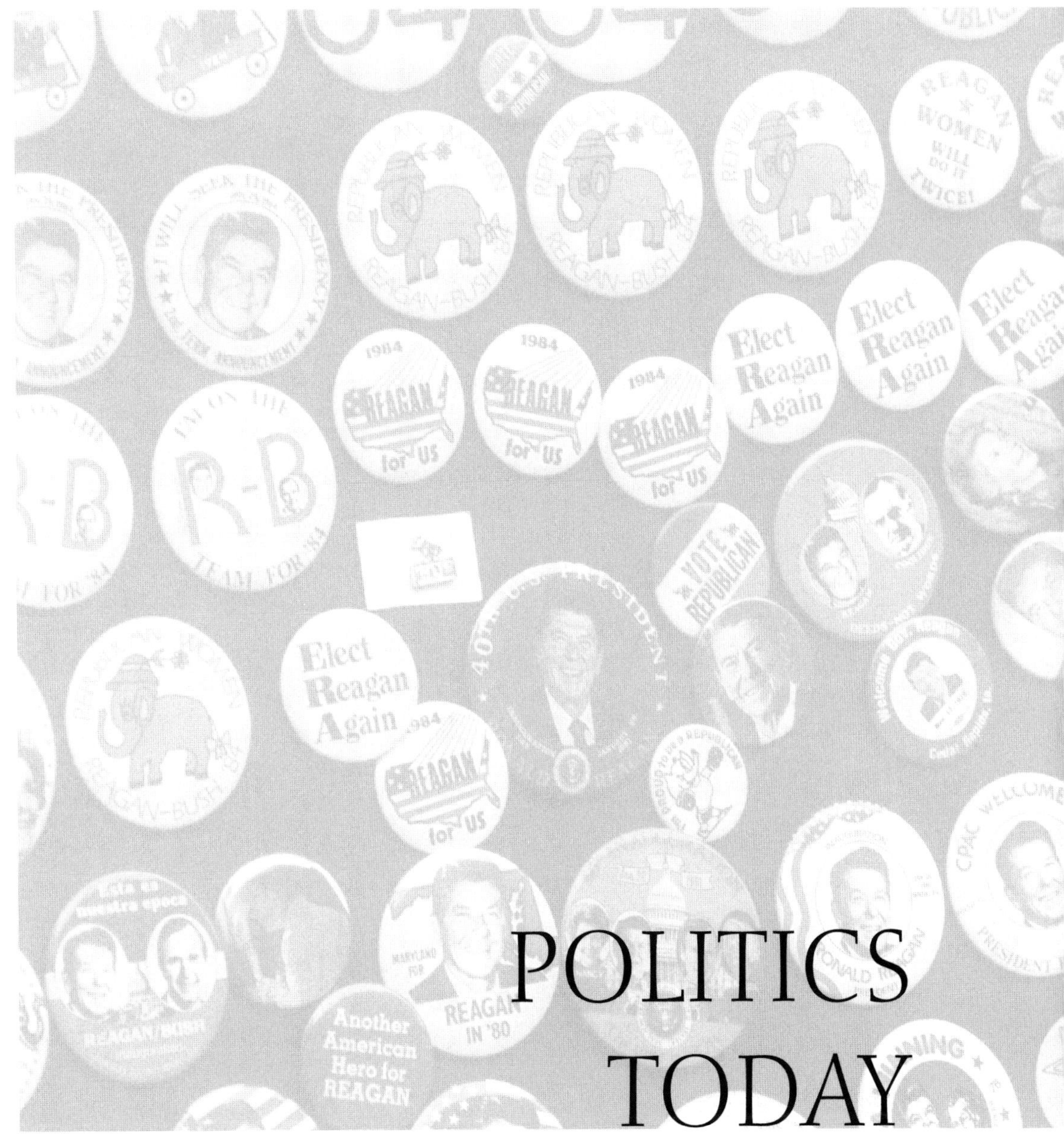

POLITICS TODAY

AMERICAN POLITICAL CULTURE

TODAY'S CULTURE AND CLIMATE

What is **political culture**?

In its broadest sense, political culture is the political atmosphere or climate of a nation's government as it is perceived by its people. It is based upon a shared identity or belief system in the government and its functions. Although a wide variety of responses might come from people who are asked, "What do you think of your government?" few people would disagree that the American political culture embraces values such as democracy, equality, independence, and liberty.

How does **political culture** differ from **political ideology**?

How Americans live in a democracy and resolve conflicts depends upon their ideology; that is, the ideas and beliefs an individual has about the role of government and its purpose, scope, and power. Traditionally, Americans have defined their personal political ideology in terms of liberal or conservative, and often frame their discussions of political ideology in the context of these two points of view. Although these definitions have changed over the years, in their simplest form a conservative generally believes that the best form of government is one that governs least, and that a "hands-on" government only hinders individual and economic rights; a liberal tends to favor active government involvement in the economy and the dispersal of social services.

What do **Americans think about their government**?

While opinion about the government of the United States is as varied as its citizens, overall there are two major trends that indicate how Americans perceive the federal government: in recent years, the public's trust in government has declined, and the average person feels that there is little he or she can do to influence the government. For example, 66 percent of Americans said that government officials don't really care what people think, according to a recent poll.

According to a 1995 joint survey by Democratic and Republican pollsters, three out of four Americans indicated they distrust government. The bipartisan poll stated 76 percent of the people questioned said that they rarely or never trust "government to do what is right." This statement surpasses polls dating back to the late 1950s that showed dramatic discontent in times of political crisis—61 percent were distrustful in 1974 after the Watergate scandal, 69 percent in 1980 after the Iran hostage crisis, and 62 percent in 1990 following the Iran-Contra affair.

Why has **trust in the government declined**?

Americans' trust in their government is closely tied to their perception of the government and its performance. According to public opinion polls and expert opinion, Americans may not trust the government for the following reasons: they believe that the government does not always tell the truth; they feel that the government has become too big and nonresponsive to citizens' needs; there are few benefits that can be obtained from the government; and the government is too intrusive in matters of privacy. According to various reports, there is also a public sense that the government has spent large sums of money on problems that have not improved, thus fueling the public's distrust of the government in general.

Under what circumstances does **Americans' trust in government** tend to improve?

Certain events, such as the bombings of the World Trade Center and the Pentagon in September 2001 and the United States' subsequent war on terrorism, have mustered up an unprecedented sense of patriotism, unity, and confidence in America. According to a select nationwide November 2001 *Los Angeles Times* telephone poll, when asked, "How much of the time do you think you can trust the government in Washington to do what is right?" 43 percent of Americans responded, "Most of the time." In addition, 86 percent of Americans expressed overwhelming approval of President George W. Bush's job performance, earning him the highest presidential job approval rating ever recorded in a *Times* poll. (The *Times* survey began during President Jimmy Carter's administration.) Polls taken months after the attacks consistently showed that two-thirds of the public now trust their government, a figure analysts report had not been seen since the pre–Vietnam War era. Although Americans' confidence in government appears to be strong during times of crisis, it's unclear if this trend will continue as the new challenges arise for the nation.

Why is it important that Americans understand they can **influence the government**?

The main reason Americans need to know they can influence the government is because in a very real sense Americans *are* the government. The preamble of the Constitution opens with the statement, "We the People of the United States...." Because the United States government is a constitutional democracy, created "of, by, and for the people," Americans have an inherent right to actively participate in their government. In fact, this clause regards "the people"—that is, you and me—as superior to any one ruler or governmental system. Additionally, the democratic form of government assumes that people are politically equal, and as equal persons we should all participate in the decision-making process.

How Do Americans Feel About the U.S. Government?

Attitudes toward government divide Americans into four categories:

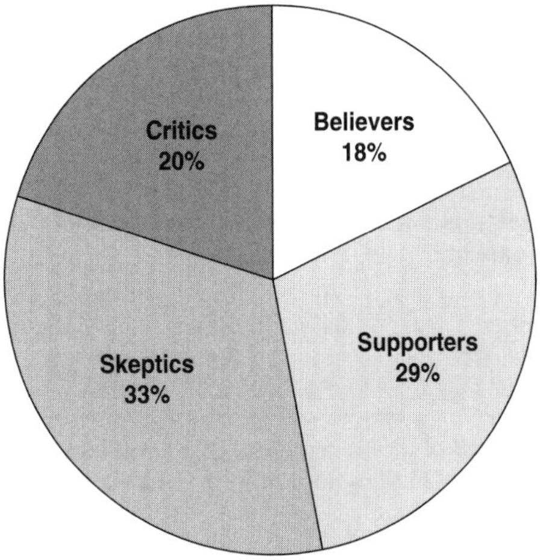

Believers feel the government helps them achieve American dream; they have confidence in all levels of government.

Supporters have some confidence in federal government; they feel government has helped them.

Skeptics are the least politically active; they don't believe government has helped them.

Critics have no confidence in any part of government; they are very critical of elected officials.

NOTE: Survey was conducted for the Council for Excellence in Government by the firms of Peter D. Hart and Robert M. Teeter. Results are based on interviews conducted Feb. 20-24, 1997, with 1,003 randomly selected adults and have a margin of sampling error of plus or minus 3 percentage points.

The majority of Americans have attitudes toward government that can be categorized as ranging from skeptical to critical, although the number considered to be believers and supporters is significant.

What can **Americans do to influence their government**?

Findings from several 1998 studies suggest citizen participation in their local communities through volunteerism and civic education is the best way to restore people's faith in the state and federal governments. More involvement by houses of worship, corporations, foundations, the media, public officials, and individuals would lead to increased activism and revitalized communities. Likewise, taking personal responsibility for community issues by volunteering and making charitable contributions can increase citizens' feelings of empowerment. According to a report by the National Commission on Civic Renewal,

Post–September 11 Opinions on President George W. Bush

Do you approve or disapprove of the way George W. Bush is handling...

	Approve	Disapprove
...his job as president	86%	10%
...the war in Afghanistan?	83%	11%
...the economy?	66%	25%

Is Bush a stronger or weaker leader than you expected him to be, or is his leadership about what you expect?

	All	Dem.	Indep.	Repub.
Stronger	54%	53%	55%	56%
What I expected	40%	39%	40%	40%
Weaker	4%	6%	5%	1%

How much of the time do you think you can trust the government in Washington to do what is right?

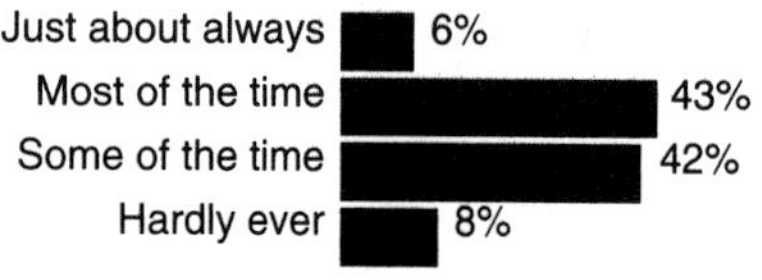

Notes: Among all U.S. adults unless otherwise indicated. Numbers may not total 100% where "don't know" responses are not shown.

Source: *Los Angeles Times* poll of 1,995 Americans nationwide conducted Nov. 10-13, 2001. Margin of error is plus or minus 3 percentage points.

Surveys conducted by many media outlets after the September 11, 2001, terrorist attacks indicated significant increases in support and trust in President George W. Bush and the actions of the government.

"This idea—citizens freely working together—is at the heart of the American conception of civic liberty, through which citizens take responsibility for improving the condition of their lives. Civic liberty offers citizens the power to act, and it strengthens their conviction that they can make a difference." Another way that Americans can stay involved in the political process is to vote. Voting can provide people with a sense of purpose and empowerment because it is a direct, physical action that has a very specific outcome.

How can the **average person get involved in the government**?

The average person can get involved in government by first educating him- or herself about current issues. This can be done through reading the newspaper daily, reading a weekly newsmagazine, or watching the evening news. In order to make a difference, a person needs to have a working understanding of government in this country; indeed, a democratic system of government assumes there is a knowledgeable, interested public body of citizens. Next to education, other very practical methods of involvement include volunteering at a local politician's office, working with voter registration drives, or registering to vote. Activities of a more political nature might include attending a local district or county meeting of a chosen political party, calling or writing legislators to voice an opinion, and participating in nonviolent protest demonstrations or marches.

How is **distrust in government** linked to **voter turnout**?

Experts say declined trust in the government (specifically cynicism concerning the political process), coupled with a sense that a person's vote does not really matter, is

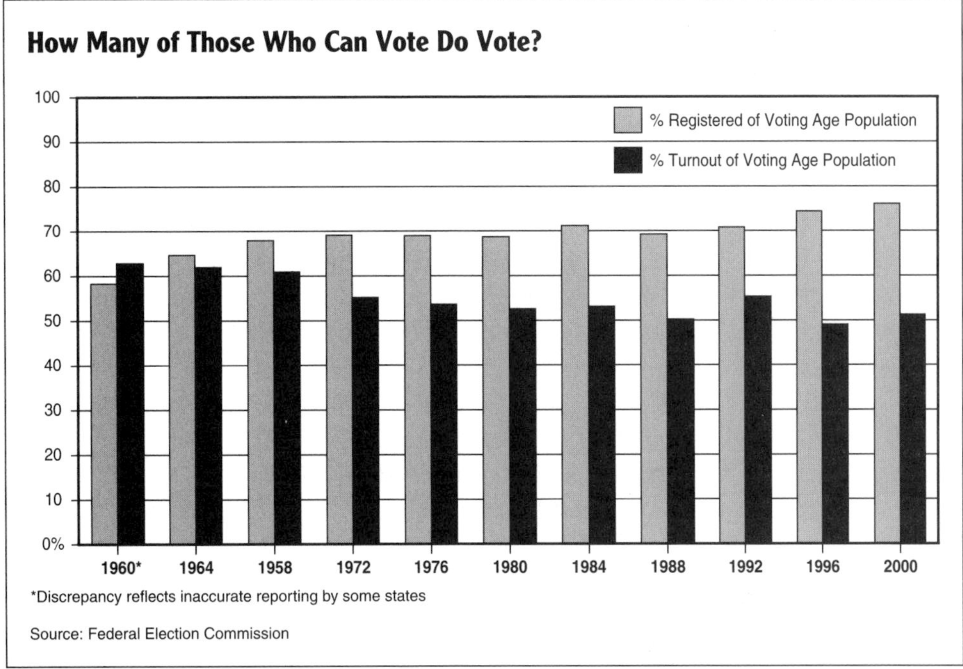

While the number of those of voting age who are registered remained steady during the last half of the twentieth century, voter turnout has steadily declined.

one of the primary reasons that fewer and fewer voters are showing up at the polls. The inconvenience of polling locations and times is another reason cited by some. Furthermore, the fact that voting rights are taken for granted by many Americans and the feeling among some citizens that they are uninformed about issues and thus "unqualified" to vote also contribute to decreased voter turnout. In addition, because the 2000 presidential election was won with a majority of electoral, rather than popular, votes, citizens may have lost faith in the voting process.

Who **votes**?

Statistics reveal that only about half of the U.S. citizens in this country vote. In the 1996 presidential primaries, voter turnout fell to 49 percent; voter turnout scores were well below the 50 percent mark during congressional elections. Although over 105 million Americans cast their vote during the 2000 Bush-Gore presidential race, the 2000 elections only represented a 10 percent increase in voters, bringing that year's turnout to 51 percent. Beyond this general statistic, studies on voter demographics reveal the following specifics: Whites are more likely to vote than minorities, although there is not much difference in voter turnout between whites and African Americans; college graduates are much more likely to vote than people with less than eight years of education; senior citizens are much more likely to vote than people in the 18 to 24 age category; and higher income groups are more likely to vote. Although America is seen as one of the most treasured democracies compared to other societies, its citizens are not as likely to vote.

Why should I **vote**?

If half the people in the United States vote, can it be said that the government truly represents "the people"? And are the people of the United States active citizens if they don't vote? What are the policy consequences if America's people don't vote? Democratic governments such as the United States cannot disregard the interests of a voting population, but if the citizens of this country do not vote, then politicians do not necessarily need to heed their interests. It is necessary for the people of a democratic country to constitutionally voice their opinions as to which political party best supports the overall interests of the nation, and ultimately themselves. One of the most effective ways to represent oneself is to vote; choosing not to vote can be equated with not voicing one's opinion. Not voting also adds to the increasing sense of political alienation already prevalent in this country, and when members of a particular demographic (such as those in a low income bracket or a certain age group) don't vote, they become more powerless because the don't have the voice to influence social policy. In order for citizens to have a say in the nation's future, voting is imperative.

How do Americans form **political opinions**?

People form political opinions, that is, attitudes or perspectives about political events, circumstances, or people, in a variety of ways and from a variety of sources. Inherent factors such as race, gender, age, and religion help shape people's belief systems and political opinions, as do the external factors of economic and social position, education, family origin, social groups, political leaders, peer pressure, and the mass communications media. The government itself also strives to manage public opinion, although the results of this have been mixed throughout history. In an openly democratic country like the United States, private groups and the government compete to shape opinion—often showcasing their positions through the media. A person's political opinions on certain issues, events, and leaders are formed as he or she evaluates the details of the issue at hand according to his or her belief system and/or political ideology.

How is **public opinion** measured?

There are a number of ways in which public opinion is measured. While consumer behavior and group demographics play a role in measuring public opinion, researchers and politicians rely on public opinion polls—sampling techniques used to understand the attitudes or opinions of voters on significant political issues—to help them with a myriad of decisions. Polls are used to obtain information about voters' attitudes toward issues and candidates, to profile candidates with winning potential, to plan campaigns, and to forecast voting patterns.

The process of polling in general has met with some skepticism from the public who fail to see how polling a limited number of people could represent the views of the majority. Further, many Americans have been soured by experiencing a technique called "push polling" (asking a participant what he or she perceives to be a "loaded" question in order to illicit a certain response) and thus have become ambivalent about participating in polls and surveys. Experts say that, when analyzing poll data, politicians should bear in mind that that public opinion on a given topic cannot be understood simply through the polling process, and that alternate methods of measuring public opinion—such as monitoring citizen behavior and garnering public opinion directly from the people—should also be considered. In addition, the misinterpretation of specific trends in public opinion or biases about the public adds to the challenge of measuring public opinion.

Is measuring public opinion a new phenomena in politics?

Although early politicians often tried to gauge public opinion by the turnout at an event or the roar of a crowd, the systematic measurement of mass public attitudes is a twentieth-century development. Although occasionally opinion polls were conducted before the 1930s, they were neither systematic nor scientific. Public opinion polling improved in the 1930s when business and educational organizations began to develop methods that allowed the relatively unbiased selection of respondents and the systematic gathering of data from a wide cross-section of the public. Among the pioneers was statistician George H. Gallup, who in 1935 created the Gallup Poll, which is still widely used to assess public opinion today. The Harris Survey, which began in 1956, and the Gallup Poll are probably the two best-known polling organizations. Nonprofit polling organizations include the Princeton Office of Public Opinion Research (1940), the National Opinion Research Center (1941), and the National Council of Public Polls (1968).

What landmark event "forced" **polling techniques** to improve?

A well-publicized 1948 political event encouraged polling agencies to further refine their methods. In that year's presidential election, most polls mistakenly predicted a victory for the Republican candidate Thomas E. Dewey over President Harry Truman, primarily because voters with a lower income level were underrepresented and also because the polling agencies missed last-minute attitude changes among the voting public. Since 1948 techniques of public opinion research and polling have improved considerably, but there is still not a foolproof method for gauging public opinion. Politicians use public opinion polls to assess voting trends, determine values among

President Harry Truman holds up a newspaper with a headline mistakenly declaring victory for his Republican opponent Thomas E. Dewey after the 1948 presidential election. Since then, polling techniques have greatly improved.

the voting population, decide how to target their campaigns, and help determine how to vote on certain legislation. Even today, the media publishes polls reflecting candidate popularity to predict which candidates will win certain elections.

Is the government responsive to **public opinion**?

In a democracy, where the government operates according to the consent of the people, it is the leaders' obligation to attend to public opinion, and recent survey results suggest that they do. Major shifts in policy changes tend to occur when major shifts in public opinion occur, and generally both the president and Congress respond to public preferences, such as those for more or less government regulation, more or less government spending, foreign policy issues, welfare reform, and issues affecting the environment, as examples. Because often public opinion is not specific, and ways of measuring public opinion are not always accurate, the government can take leeway in the way that it responds to public opinion. The prominence of public interest groups that represent the voice of select population groups has evolved in order to meet this challenge.

What are **Americans' core political values**?

Although Americans have a vast array of political opinions, at the heart of these are the fundamental ideals of democracy, liberty, equality, and individualism, upon which this country's government was established.

Where do these **core political values** come from?

The political values and beliefs that Americans hold dear are rooted in a philosophical tradition known as classical liberalism, an ideology that influenced the founders of the early republic and which continues to play a part in democratic movements around the world today. Classic liberalism emphasizes the importance of the individual and individual freedom, equality, private property, limited government, and popular consent.

Does the **political system uphold America's political values**?

Over the course of America's history, gaps between the values of equality, liberty, and democracy and the application of these ideals have surfaced. The most obvious example of contradiction can be found in the concept of equality. While the words "all men are created equal" appear in the Declaration of Independence, our nation has a long history of slavery, segregation, and discrimination. Not until after the Civil War, when the Fourteenth Amendment was adopted, did the Constitution expressly provide for equal protection against discrimination. In fact, many people argue that the United States did not become a full democracy until 1965, when African Americans were treated as equal citizens and guaranteed the right to vote through the passage of the Voting Rights Act.

The concept of liberty has also evolved over the nation's history, as the scope of personal liberties has expanded and individuals have fought rigorously to defend their individual freedoms; today, far fewer limitations exist on the press, political speech, and individual moral behavior than ever before in this nation's history, although issues of personal liberties and what they mean continue to be debated.

Are **politics and political values ever in conflict**?

Many of the political debates and events that have occurred over history involve conflict over the nation's values and what words like liberty, equality, and justice mean. Events such as the Civil War, the civil rights movement, the history of suffrage, and the assassination of presidents reflect this conflict. Additionally, there is conflict within the system of government itself. Because of the separation of powers that exists between the three branches of government and the checks and balances system that keeps each branch's actions accountable to the other, often political values are in conflict and cannot be worked out in cases wherein one major party represents the presidency and another major party controls the Congress. With power divided between the legislative and executive branches, it can take months to arrive at agreement, and often branches of the government are operating on different policies.

Is **patriotism** a political value?

Patriotism, or love for one's country, is considered a citizen trait more than it is considered an inherent political value. Most recently, patriotism came to the nation's forefront when the September 2001 terrorist attacks triggered an outpouring of nationalist sentiment on a scale not engaged in since Word War II. Symbols of patriotism—including images of the national flag, song lyrics from "The Star Spangled Banner," the recitation of the Pledge of Allegiance, and phrases such as "United We Stand"—flooded the national consciousness in the months following the attacks. Whether patriotism will affect such things as citizen's involvement in government or voter turnout for future elections is yet to be seen.

FUNDAMENTALS OF GOVERNMENT

What is **government,** and how does it differ from **politics**?

To govern means "to rule." Generally, government is the word used to describe the formal institutions through which a land and its people are ruled. Americans live in a constitutional democracy: limits are placed on what the government can do and how it can do it. The term politics, however, refers to conflicts over the character, leadership, membership, and policies of a government. The goal of politics is to have a voice or representation in the government's leadership, organization, and policy-making, because this representation leads to political power or influence. Political activities include things like raising funds for candidates, lobbying, or attempting to influence public opinion. Americans are given access to their government through political participation, whereby they can debate and remedy the issues of leadership, structure, and policy of the government that arise.

What is the difference between **politics** and **political science**?

Politics refers to the conduct of government, especially the making of government policies and government organization. Political science is the academic study of political systems and theories.

How are **various governments** classified?

There are several basic features that are used to classify governments. They include: the geographic distribution of power, which divides the definitions of government between unitary, federal, or confederate; the relationship between the legislative and executive branches, which defines government as presidential or parliamentary; and the number of people who take part in the governing process, which yields the definitions of autocracy, oligarchy, and democracy.

What are the **different forms** a government can take?

The ideas of English philosopher John Locke (1632–1704) formed the foundation for America's democratic system of government.

The three general forms of government, based upon who rules, are divided between (1) those in which the authority is vested in one single person; (2) those dominated by several people; and (3) those controlled by many. In some nations, governing is done by a single individual, such as a king, queen, or dictator. This form of government is known as an *autocracy*. A government is called an *oligarchy* if a small group, such as landowners, military officers, or wealthy merchants, make up the government. If the country's people make up the government and contribute to its decision-making process, that nation's government is known as a *democracy*.

There are also several ways in which governments do their governing. Limited governments, such as the United States and most countries in Western Europe, are known as *constitutional governments,* since these governments are limited as to what they are permitted to control and how they go about enforcing their control. In other words, they have limited power, and this limited power is enforced by a separation of powers. Most of these nations have constitutions that define the scope of governmental power. In contrast to a constitutional government, a government is called *authoritarian* when it has no formal limits; the government is limited by other political and social institutions in the land, such as churches, labor unions, and political parties. While these governments are sometimes responsive to these entities of limitation, there is no *formal* obligation for the government to consult its citizens. An example of a recent authoritarian government is that of Spain from 1936 to 1975 under General Francisco Franco. *Totalitarian* governments attempt to control every area of political, economic, and social life and are usually associated with dictators who seek to eliminate other social institutions that might challenge the government's complete, or total, power. Some examples of totalitarian governments might include Nazi Germany from 1933 to 1945 under dictator Adolf Hitler and the Soviet Union from 1928 to 1953 under dictator Joseph Stalin.

Why does **government exist**?

Governments exist for many reasons. A thread that is common to all governments is the desire to provide a sense of order to the land. All governments tax, penalize, restrict, and regulate their people. A democracy exists to give voice to the people and to protect their inalienable rights, as English philosopher John Locke (1632–1704) suggested it should. In contrast, a totalitarian government exists to benefit the state or those in charge, and this type of government empowers its leaders to rule in any way they see fit. In this type of government, the people's personal freedom is not recognized. In the United States, the purpose of the government is outlined in the preamble of the Constitution: to form a more perfect union; to establish justice; to insure domestic tranquility; to provide for the common defense; to promote the general welfare; and to secure the blessings of liberty. In sum, our government provides us with an organized system by which we can live as a nation in peace.

Do all governments have **constitutions**?

No. A constitution, which serves to outline the fundamental laws that establish government organization, determine the roles and duties of segments of the government, and clarify the relationship between the people and their government, is a characteristic of a democracy. The U.S. Constitution was created in 1787 and ratified in 1788.

What are the **major concepts of American government**?

Three major concepts define American government. First, it is *a representative democratic* type of government, outlined in and enforced by the Constitution of the United States, that serves the will of the people and gives them direct access to their government through the political process. Second, it is *federal,* with the powers divided between a central government and several local governments. Third, it is *limited* in nature, in that the government does not have ultimate authority over the people, and each individual has certain rights that the government cannot take away. Associated with its limited nature is the government's power distribution, which is divided among its three branches and kept in place by a system of checks and balances. Together these concepts ensure that the American government lies in the hands of the people.

What is meant by **separation of powers**?

The cornerstone of the U.S. government wherein power is divided among its three branches—the executive, legislative, and judicial—is called the separation of powers. Officials of each branch are selected differently, have different responsibilities, and serve different terms. By distributing the essential business of government among three separate but interdependent branches, the framers of the Constitution ensured that the government's powers were not concentrated in any one branch. The separation of power is not absolute, however, because of the system of checks and balances, which says that these branches must cooperate with one another, oversee one another, and enforce and support one another's decisions according to established rules. For example, Congress's authority to make laws can be "checked" by presidential veto; the president has the authority of commander in chief of the armed forces, but only Congress can declare war; and the Supreme Court has the authority to "check" on both the legislative and executive branches by declaring their acts unconstitutional.

Why is America's **democratic system** considered so precious?

Although Americans have their own reasons why they treasure democracy, there are several underlying concepts that make a democracy a valued system of government. First, there is a respect for the fundamental worth of the individual, which allows for each person to be viewed as a separate and distinct human being. Second, a democracy stresses the equality of all individuals as it relates to equality of opportunity and equality before the law. Third, it is the will of the people and not the will of a select ruling leadership that determines public policy. This is most commonly referred to as "majority rule and minority rights." Fourth, a democracy holds the concept of individual freedom key to its society, while recognizing that there must be balance between the rights of the individual and the rights of the society at large. Finally, a democracy upholds individual decision making, both in one's private life and in government participation; that is, people in a democracy make their own decisions because, according to the definition, people who cannot choose for themselves are not really free.

What does the concept **"majority rule with minority rights"** mean?

In a democracy, decision making is done by majority rule, with each person having one vote equal to that of his or her neighbor. It is the will of the people and not the dictate of a select ruling leadership that determines public policy. The process of majority rule does not seek to come up with the "right" answers, but instead seeks satisfactory solutions to public issues and problems. So, although the majority's decisions are not always right, majority rule means that all people have an equal say in decisions that affect them. Because majority rule, if unchecked, has the potential to destroy its opposition (and, hence, the democratic process), democracy upholds majority rule restrained by minority rights. This means that the majority must always recognize the rights of the minority and be willing to hear their voice.

What does **government** do?

Since the government is the institution through which a land or a society is ruled, the government is the institution that enforces the land's public policies. In it simplest sense, public policies are all the things that the government decides to do, such as impose an income tax, service its armed forces, protect the environment, and hold businesses to certain standards. In a democratic United States, the people elect representatives to the government to enact the popular will. The people who exercise the powers of the government include: legislators, who make the law; executives and administrators, who administer and enforce those laws; and judges, who interpret the law. Each year, Congress enacts approximately 500 laws and the state legislatures enact about 25,000 laws; local governments enact countless ordinances.

What is the **federal government**?

The federal government is the national government of the United States of America under the Constitution, including the executive, legislative, and judicial branches, as opposed to state or local governments. The executive branch is responsible for enforcing the laws of the United States. Its main components include the president, the vice president, the various government departments, and the independent agencies. The president is leader of the country and commander in chief of the armed forces; the vice president is president of the Senate and first in line for the presidency should the president be unable to serve; the departments and their heads (called Cabinet members) advise the president on policy issues and help execute those policies; and the independent agencies also assist in executing policy and provide special services. The legislative branch is the lawmaking branch of the federal government. It is made up of a bicameral (or two-chamber) Congress: the Senate and the House of Representatives. The judicial branch, made up of the Supreme Court and other federal courts, is responsible for interpreting the meaning of laws, how they are applied, and whether or not they violate the Constitution.

How did **limited government** develop?

The concept of limited government is relatively rare today, and still, in the scope of history, relatively new. Starting in the seventeenth century, select Western nations began to accept formal limits to their power, and a few governments began to provide their citizens with a voice through the vote. During the nineteenth century, liberalism emerged, the hallmarks of which were equality and liberty. Liberals believed in individual rights, participation in government or republicanism, and freedom of thought and religion. Liberals were mainly members of the middle class, or bourgeoisie, who had the most to gain from changing the old order of conservatism. They called for constitutions that redistributed power so that more fell into their hands, mainly through the creation of parliaments and voting rights. At first, most were not democrats, because they believed only educated property owners were entitled to vote. Gradually, however, liberalism embraced democracy, and equality and liberty for all people. In the eighteenth century liberal revolutions burst out over much of Western Europe, with the sentiment that all change was possible. It was from this cultural milieu that the introduction of many of the principles that are foundational to individual liberty, such as free speech, free assembly, and free conscience, were born. In this nation, the concept of a limited government and power in the hands of the people were key to the American Revolution of 1776.

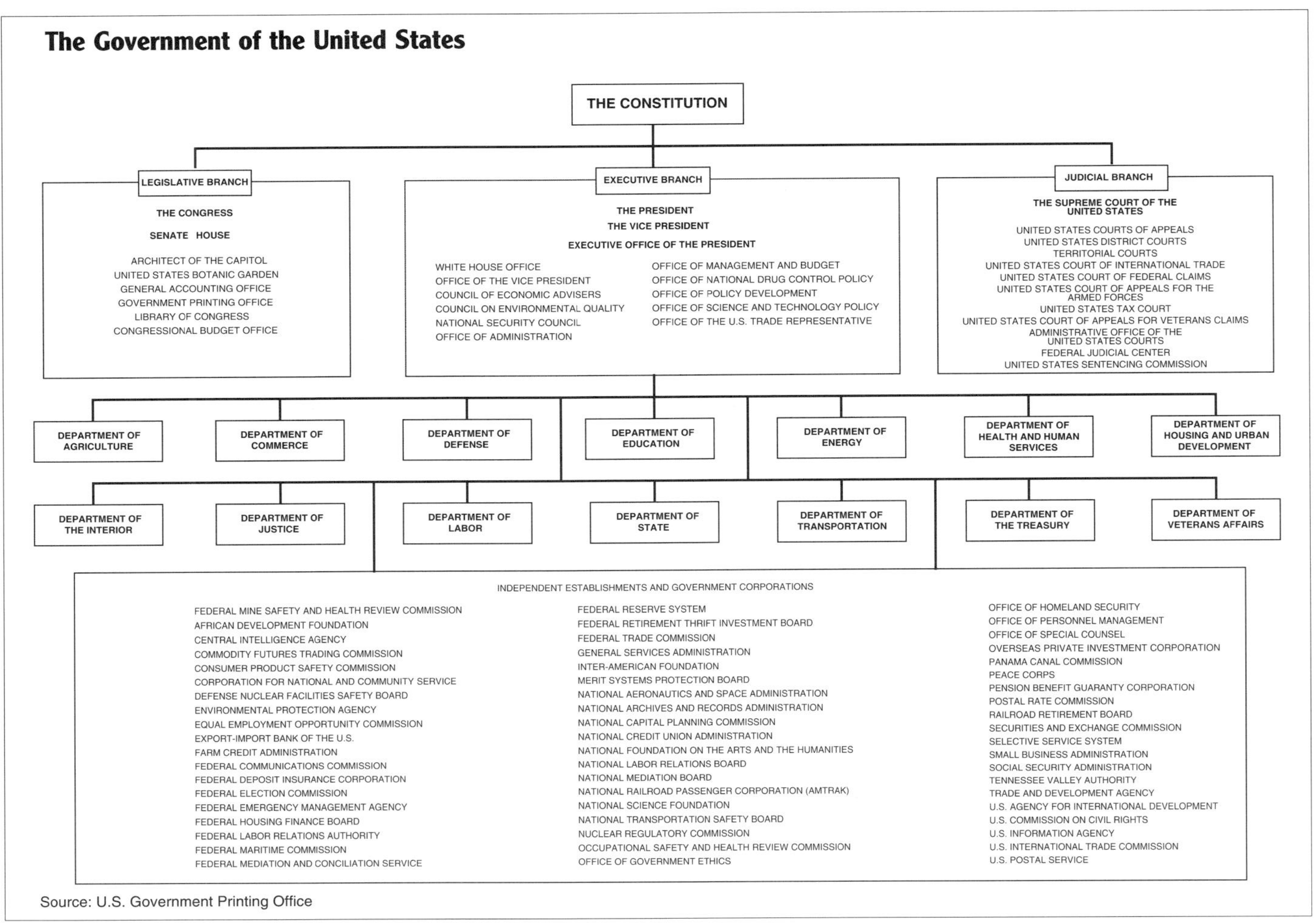

Source: U.S. Government Printing Office

Is there a **philosophical basis to limited government**?

The philosophical basis of a government that has limitations upon its power and that gives a voice to its people can be traced back to the ideas of English philosophers John Locke (1632–1704) and John Stuart Mill (1806–1873) and author Adam Smith (1723–1790). Locke challenged the concept of a king's divine right to rule, and instead introduced the concept of the "social contract" of government. He believed that government should only exist with the consent of the people, and that the only legitimate reason for its existence is to preserve and protect the inalienable rights that people possess.

Fellow philosopher John Stuart Mill believed passionately in the importance of individual freedom against the power of the state. He also came to believe that one of the goals of society should be to offer all its citizens economic security. Today his name is most associated with a philosophical school called utilitarianism, the main tenant of which is that we should make our ethical decisions on the basis of which action will bring the greatest amount of happiness to the greatest number of people.

When the 13 American colonies of Great Britain declared their independence from their mother country in 1776, Adam Smith published *The Wealth of Nations*, considered the first true work of economics and believed to be the most important book in the development of capitalism ever written. In the book, Smith champions a free market economy and proposes that supply and demand (instead of government laws) are the best regulators of an economic system. Together, these three men represent the early philosophical thought that lead to the concept of limited government in the United States.

Did the United States government actually **evolve**?

Over a sequence of events that took place between 1775 and 1787, the government of the United States actually evolved to become the system we know today. When the Revolutionary War began there was no central American government established by law. The only thing that existed was the Continental Congress, a group of men who believed in independence from Great Britain. In July 1776 they declared the colonies independent and began the initial step of developing a government. To replace the outdated colonial regimes, each of the former colonies called conventions that wrote state constitutions that were ratified by the citizens of each of the states. They established republics, and each of the 13 new states elected governors and representative assemblies.

In an effort to coordinate the war effort and establish a representative voice, the Continental Congress took the next step of establishing an overall government. The states accepted this reluctantly, however, believing that the only way to insure freedom from oppressive rule was to remain as independent states. Therefore, the first government established under the Articles of Confederation in 1781 was very restricted in its authority. While it consisted of a Congress composed of representatives from the states, there was no well-defined overarching system of justice to which the states were accountable. While this early government resulted in two legacies—it adopted a system of government for the territories that would eventually become states and permanently established a republican form of government—its weakness outweighed its strengths. Recognizing that a new government was necessary if the United States was to become a strong, independent nation, the Founding Fathers formulated a new document, the Constitution of the United States, at the Philadelphia Convention in 1787. It is this document that enhanced the powers of the national government, and it provides the framework by which America governs today.

What is a **state**?

A state is a body of people, occupying a specific geographic location, that organize into a political unit. States can also refer to the smaller geographic and political units that make up a larger state. In U.S. politics, state is generally used to refer to one of the 50 states that make up the union, but in international politics nations and governments are often called states.

How is a **nation** defined?

A nation is a large group of people united by bonds of geography, language, customs, and shared collective experiences. Some nations that have developed governmental systems are also referred to as states.

What does the word democracy mean?

The word democracy comes from the ancient Greek word *demokratia*. *Demo* means "the people" and *kratia* means "to rule." A democracy, then, is a form of government in which the people rule. The power lies in the hands of the people, who may either govern directly or govern indirectly by electing representatives. The American government is a democracy, and the Constitution of the United States ensures this. Under this "social contract" the people of the United States established a government, endowed it with powers, placed upon it certain limitations, set up the administrative structure, and provided the means of control over it. At the heart of democracy lies the concept of "popular sovereignty"—that is, the idea that the people are the supreme authority, or sovereignty, and that sovereignty rests in the body of citizens, not one supreme ruler.

What is the difference between **representative democracy** and **direct democracy**?

A system of government that provides its citizens with a regular and ongoing opportunity to elect top government officials is known as a representative democracy. A system that allows citizens to vote directly on laws and policies is termed a direct democracy. The government of the United States is a representative democracy at the national level, since citizens vote for government officials but do not vote on legislation. Certain states, however, allow for direct legislation through popular referendum. In these states, the voters decide on state legislation through the voting process.

Are **democracy** and **limited government** the same thing?

The concept of democracy embodies the concept of limited government almost inherently, in that a government created "by and for the people" puts the power in the hands of many, versus in the hands of one. Guarding against the abuse of powers was so important to the Founding Fathers (who had just claimed independence from tyrannical England) that when they created the Constitution they established a system of separation of powers in order to keep the federal government limited in scope and authority. The separation of powers is kept in effect by a system of checks and balances, whereby each of three branches of government—executive, legislative, and judicial—is able to participate in and have influence over the activities of the other branches. Examples of this include the president's veto power over congressional legislation; the Senate's power to approve presidential appointments; and Supreme Court's power to review congressional enactments.

What are the essential differences between a **presidential system** of democracy and a **parliamentary system** of democracy?

When governments are viewed through the relationship between their legislative and executive agencies, they can be called either presidential or parliamentary. A presidential government, such as exists in the United States, has a separation of powers between the executive and legislative branches. The executive branch is that of the president, while the legislative branch is that of the Congress, which is made up of the Senate and the House of Representatives. While the branches are independent of one another and equal in weight, each must be accountable to the other, and thus a system of checks and balances ensures that each branch can restrain actions of the other branch.

In a parliamentary government, such as that of the United Kingdom and most other European nations, the executive branch is made up of a prime minister or a premier and that official's cabinet. They are members of the legislative branch, which is called the parliament. The prime minister is the leader of the majority party in parliament and is chosen by that party, making him or her a part of the legislature, and subject to its control. There is no checks and balances system, because the chief executive is responsible to and holds office in the legislature.

Is one system **better** than another?

Many scholars argue that the parliamentary form of government is more expeditious because it does not have one of the major problems that a presidential government has: there is no conflict and deadlock on issues between the executive and legislative branches, who may not always see eye-to-eye on issues. Under the parliamentary system there is never an instance of a "divided government" as has occurred in the United States, when one of the major political parties holds the presidency and another major political party controls the Congress. Although the American system of government works best when the same party controls its executive and legislative branches, the separation of powers and independent spirit that a democracy ensures does not always guarantee this situation. However, the parliamentary system does not have a system of checks and balances in place, thus increasing the possibility of abuse of power.

What is **liberty**?

Since the founding of America, perhaps the most fundamental ideal expressed has been that of liberty. It is found in all of the early documents of this country: The Declaration of Independence outlined "Life, Liberty, and the pursuit of Happiness" as the three inalienable rights of the people of this country, and the Bill of Rights was created to preserve individual liberties. Because the concept of democracy recognizes a fundamental worth of the individual, liberties are the personal freedoms to which we are entitled as human beings. Personal freedom also means freedom from government control, and all democratic governments minimize the role that government plays in lives of its people.

What is **laissez-faire capitalism** and how does it relate to government?

Closely related to the idea of personal liberty, or personal freedom, is the concept of economic freedom. Since the origin of this country, economic freedom has been associated with the concepts of capitalism, free competition, and the protection of private property. *Laissez-faire*, which is translated "to let do" and interpreted as "to let [people] do [as they choose]" is a concept that opposes governmental influence in economic affairs beyond the minimum amount necessary to maintain peace and property rights. Laissez-faire capitalism was the economic philosophy introduced during this country's formation to encourage minimal government involvement in business affairs in order to maximize individual freedom of choice and expression. Americans continue to value economic freedom, recognizing that state and federal governments need to extend certain business restrictions to protect the public, including health and safety laws, environmental protection laws, and regulations in the workplace. Born out of the Industrial Revolution and the Progressive movement, the concept of what industry can and cannot do at the expense of the individual continues to be fine-tuned as government laws are enacted.

What is **equality**?

Few people fail to recognize the statement in the Declaration of Independence that "all men are created equal." Democracy is based upon a fundamental belief in the individual as a unique human being. Under the democratic concept of equality, all people are inherently equal, and because of this are entitled to both equality of opportunity and equality before the law. The concept of liberty embodies the limits of the government so that personal freedom can be recognized. The concept of equality, by contrast, implies an obligation of the government to the people. Democracy maintains that each person's worth must be recognized by both other individuals and the society as a whole, and no person should be limited for reasons such as race, religion, or gender. While not every race, nationality, or gender has realized full equality before the law over the course of this country's history, the United States has made great strides in the areas of civil liberties and civil rights to ensure the ideal of full equality can be achieved.

What is **political equality**?

Closely tied to the concept of individual equality is the concept of political equality, in which each person has the right to participate in politics on equal terms. The political community, which began with this nation's forefathers as white male property-owners, now encompasses all races and genders. The Voting Rights Act of 1965 made racial discrimination in voting illegal, and specifically sought to provide a remedy to the number of African Americans who were being kept from participating in the voting process due to various forms of racial discrimination taking place in certain southern states. The ideal of political equality in this country has come to be known by the phrase, "one person, one vote," underlying the concept that the right to participate in the voting process is available to all.

What are considered the three **defining eras of American government**?

The three defining eras in the transformation of the American government are years leading up to and including the Revolutionary War (1750s–1783), the Civil War period (1854–1865), and the FDR era (1933–1945). The Revolutionary period of American history was marked by the growing desire of the American colonists to break away from their mother country England and establish their independence. America became a new nation at the end of the Revolutionary War, and a new government based upon the principles of democracy, liberty, and equality was birthed. The principles of the Constitution and the portion of the Declaration of Independence that upholds "all men are created equal" were challenged during the Civil War era, when Northerners protested and went to war to end (among other things) the enslavement of blacks in the South. The concept of federalism was also threatened, as Southerners demanded to run their states without the interference of the federal government, and began to secede from the union. The issues of basic human freedom and states' rights have never been so amplified as during this period in American history.

The administration of Franklin D. Roosevelt and his depression-era New Deal ushered in one of most powerful economic forces of the twentieth century, and challenged the concept of laissez-faire capitalism, that is, how much the government should interfere with the economics of the country. With the passing of 15 major legislative bills into law, this period introduced large-scale federal oversight of the economy: It forced the development of bureaucratic procedures in business administration; revolutionized public finance; pioneered a mixed economy; and erected the welfare state. The economic philosophies and techniques of financial management that arose from the administration dominated American business life from 1945 to 1980.

Thomas Jefferson (1743–1826) was the principle author of the Declaration of Independence, which emphasized the belief that all individuals are endowed with certain fundamental rights.

What is **individualism**?

In the Declaration of Independence, Thomas Jefferson (1743–1826) stated that all individuals are endowed with certain inalienable, or fundamental, inalterable rights. Our Founding Fathers placed great value on the individual in an American democracy, and believed strongly in the concept of individualism, which dictates that the primary function of government is to enable the individual person to achieve his or her highest potential, making the interests of the individual more important than those of the state. Since the early republic a concern for upholding individual freedom, and the limits that have been placed on individual freedom, have been at the heart of political debate, canvassing such topics as censorship, legalized abortion, homosexual rights, and affirmative action programs.

CITIZENSHIP

What is **citizenship**?

Although the words "citizen" and "citizenship" are used loosely to refer to anyone involved in the political community, that is not an accurate definition. As early as the ancient Greeks, the term citizenship has meant "membership in one's community." Today, the term has come to be defined as an "informed and active membership in a political community." But there are legalities tied to citizenship, and just because a person is active in the political community does not make him or her a citizen of the United States.

What does it mean to be a **citizen of the United States**?

The original Constitution did not supply a definition of citizenship nor specify exactly whom it considered citizens, although the term is used several times. When the Fourteenth Amendment was added in 1868, an authoritative definition was established. According to this amendment, "All persons born or naturalized in the United States, and subject to the jurisdiction thereof, are citizens of the United States and the state wherein they reside." Here, two types of citizenship are mentioned—national and state. State citizenship follows national citizenship automatically; however certain states require a period of residence before granting certain political privileges.

How does a **citizen differ from an alien**?

In the United States, a citizen holds all the rights, privileges, and immunities as outlined by the Constitution. By contrast, an "alien," or foreign national, is a citizen of another national state. However, aliens are obligated to obey local laws and must pay taxes. They may own property, engage in business, access the court system, and attend public schools. The civil rights guaranteed to citizens by the Constitution apply to aliens as well, and the equal protection clause of the Fourteenth Amendment protects them from unreasonable discrimination by the states. However, aliens cannot vote, nor can they hold an American passport. In order to become citizens, aliens must naturalize, or follow a specific set of requirements in order to establish their citizenship. When an alien because naturalized as a citizen, he or she is granted all the rights and privileges that are part of citizenship; and in turn agrees to accept all of the responsibilities of being a citizen.

What is the difference between a **citizen's rights** and a **citizen's obligations**?

Citizens in the United States have many *rights*. According to the First Amendment of the Constitution, freedom of speech is the primary right of American citizenship. Other rights and liberties outlined in the Bill of Rights, that is, the first 10 amendments to the Constitution, include freedom of religion, the right to keep and bear arms, various rights in criminal proceedings, and the right to elect a president and vice president. Technically, citizens do not have any *obligations* to the government from a constitutional standpoint, other than to obey the laws of the government.

What might some **citizen obligations** include?

Many scholars maintain that in order to be called a *true citizen,* a person has several obligations. Citizens have a responsibility to participate in the political process by voting in elections and serving on a jury. Additionally, a citizen must have the knowledge necessary to engage in political debate. He or she must have a working knowledge of government and politics as well as an understanding of one's own political rights and the democratic principles upon which the American political system is based. Responsible citizens are obligated to understand these principles so that they can effect their interests and know when to defend them. Also, many believe that tolerance for differences is a responsibility of citizenship, since America becomes stronger when all its citizens respect the various opinions, cultures, and ethnic groups found in this country. A final obligation of citizenship involves becoming an active member of one's community.

What is the **new citizenship** movement?

The "new citizenship" movement is the term given to grassroots-level politics that take place in local communities and cities, where broad-ranging coalitions of citizens and interest groups come together to join in civic discussion to arrive at solutions to local problems. Participants include environmental activists, civil rights advocates, grassroots community organizations, progressive churches, ethical businesses, and public officials. Birthed in the mid-1990s, the new citizenship movement's underlying premise is that citizens "must reclaim responsibility for and power over the nation's public affairs." Drawing on grassroots political methods, these groups include the League of Women Voters, which has created new partnerships among citizens, businesses, and regulatory agencies; the Common Ground Network for Life and Choice, which has helped bring together both sides in the highly polarized abortion debate; the Common Enterprise, which uses collaborative strategies in a several cities to address issues such as censorship in public schools; and a broad range of nonprofit service organizations, such as the YMCA and National Easter Seals, which have begun to redefine their missions as helping to develop the skills of diverse communities to problem solve together.

How is **citizenship** acquired?

Citizenship can be acquired in three ways: (1) by birth in the United States of America; (2) by birth abroad to either one or two United States citizens; or (3) through the process of naturalization. Naturalization laws are administered by the Immigration and

Naturalization Service (INS) through the government's Department of Justice. Although there are a number of details involved in the naturalization process, eligibility requirements generally include: residing in the United States for five years; reading, writing, and speaking English; and passing an exam and taking an oath of allegiance to the United States. According to the INS, in fiscal year 1999 almost 840,000 people became naturalized citizens of the United States. This figure is down from just a few years ago; the INS reported a figure of 1.1 million naturalized citizens for fiscal year 1996.

What is **naturalization**?

Naturalization is the legal process by which an alien becomes a citizen. An individual who is at least 18 years old may become a U.S. citizen after meeting certain qualifications.

Do I need to know anything about the government to become a **naturalized citizen**?

Yes. If a person applies for citizenship through the naturalization process governed by the Immigration and Naturalization Service, the citizen exam asks many questions about the U.S. government. Some of these questions include: What kind of government does the U.S. have? Whose rights are guaranteed by the Constitution? Who controls the government in the United States? How? In which branch of the federal government do the president and vice president work? Name one qualification of the presidency. What is the purpose of primary elections in choosing a president? What are some possible differences between the U.S. Constitution and state constitutions? How many branches do all state governments have, and what are they called? Why are amendments added to the Constitution? Name two precedents set by the first president. Name one result of the War of 1812. Name two issues that helped to cause the Civil War. What important event took place at Pearl Harbor in 1941?

How is **citizenship lost**?

Whether a native-born or naturalized, every citizen has the right to voluntarily "expatriate," or renounce his or her citizenship. The Constitution prohibits automatic expatriation, so Congress cannot take away a person's citizenship for something he or she has done, such as commit a crime. However, naturalized citizens can lose their citizenship through the process of denaturalization, but only when it has been proven that a person became a citizen fraudulently. A person cannot gain or lose citizenship by marriage.

Who are **illegal immigrants**?

An illegal immigrant is a person who comes from another country to live in the United States without applying for entrance or completing the appropriate immigration documents.

New citizens are sworn in during a ceremony after meeting all of the requirements of the naturalization process. Approximately 1 million people become naturalized citizens of the United States each year.

What is the difference between **illegal immigrants** and **refugees**?

According to the Immigration and Naturalization Service, a refugee is "any person who is outside his or her country of nationality who is unable or unwilling to return to that country because of persecution or a well-founded fear of persecution. Persecution or the fear thereof must be based on the alien's race, religion, nationality, membership in a particular social group, or political opinion." Refugee numbers are subject to ceilings by geographic area set annually by the president of the United States in consultation with Congress and are eligible to adjust to lawful permanent resident status after one year of continuous presence in the United States.

AMERICAN POLITICAL COMMUNITY

What is meant by the **political community**?

The political community is defined by its members. In the case of the United States, it is the citizenship and its various races and ethnic groups (as opposed to a specific ideology or set of beliefs) that makes up the political community.

How has **race, ethnicity, gender, or class** affected a group of people's right to participate in politics?

By not allowing a certain nationality or gender to vote, the law restricts these groups' full participation in politics. The Declaration of Independence states that "all men are created equal"; however, when Thomas Jefferson penned that phrase in 1776, blacks were enslaved and women were not recognized as full citizens. "Political equality" applied to white, male property owners, who were the only segment of the population granted suffrage. The Thirteenth, Fourteenth, and Fifteenth Amendments to the Constitution, passed during Reconstruction (1865–1878), made some gains in granting African Americans the right to vote, but it would not be until the Voting Rights Act of 1965 that legal protection of voting rights would be extended to African Americans and other minority groups. Women were given the right to vote by the Nineteenth Amendment (1920).

What is the history of **women** in government and politics?

"We hold these truths to be self-evident, that all men and women are created equal...." These words, written in 1848 at the first Women's Rights Convention held at Seneca Falls, New York, announced the opening of a new American revolution in which the goal was to overthrow masculine "tyranny" and to establish political, social, and economic equality between the sexes. Although the campaign for the vote created the greatest public outcry, it was one facet of the larger struggle of women to enter the professions, to own property, and to enjoy the same legal rights as men. It would be 72 years from the Seneca Falls convention before the Nineteenth Amendment to the Constitution universally gave women the right to vote, which they first exercised in the 1920 presidential election. Other rights of equality would come over the next 150 years, but more slowly.

What role did the **Equal Rights Amendment** play in women's political history?

The introduction and failure of the Equal Rights Amendment (ERA), which stated that legal rights could not be denied or changed based on a person's gender, had perhaps the most profound political effects upon women's lives of any event. While it was several states short of its required three-fourths majority to become law, the campaign to pass the ERA placed women's issues on the political agenda. It tripled membership in the National Organization for Women, making it a powerful advocacy group for women's rights. It prompted some states to pass their own ERAs or to interpret statutes in a manner more favorable to women. Finally, it encouraged women on both sides of the issue to participate more in politics and to run for local, state, and national offices. The "year of the woman" election in 1993 brought an increase in the num-

Suffragettes march in the Women of All Nations Parade in New York City in May 1916, using the event to further the cause of national voting rights for women.

ber of women represented in the House of Representatives, and in 1998 women's representation in the House increased again.

What was the breakdown of **women serving in the 107th Congress**?

While women represent 52 percent of the adult population, they only represented 13 percent of the Senate and 13.8 percent of the House after the 2000 election. There were a total of 74 women serving in the 107th Congress, 13 of which were senators and 20 of which were women of color. Although this number represents the greatest number of women to have ever served in Congress, 23 states had no women serving in the 107th Congress. Six states—Alaska, Delaware, Iowa, Mississippi, New Hampshire, and Vermont—have never sent a woman to the U.S. Congress.

What is the history of **women in the executive branch**?

Since the cabinet was established in 1789 there have been 29 female cabinet members, less than 6 percent of the 498 individuals who have served. The first woman to serve in the cabinet was Frances Perkins, appointed by President Franklin D. Roosevelt as secretary of labor in 1933. More recently, upon taking office in 2001, President George W. Bush appointed five women to his cabinet: Elaine Chao (Department of Labor), Gale Norton (Department of the Interior), Condoleezza Rice (National Security Advisor),

Ann Veneman (Department of Agriculture), and Christine Todd Whitman (Environmental Protection Agency).

What is the history of **African Americans** in government and politics?

The course of the African American in government and politics has a multifaceted history, with issues of equality, suffrage, civil rights, and full political participation at its heart. During the years that followed Reconstruction and in the first decade of the twentieth century (particularly in the late 1890s and early 1900s), African Americans were systematically stripped of their political and civil rights throughout the southern United States. While the Fifteenth Amendment was intended to secure the vote for African American men, it took Congress almost 90 years to pass the laws necessary to make the amendment applicable. The Civil Rights Act of 1960 strengthened voting rights by providing federal supervision of voter registration, but it was the Voting Rights Act of 1965 that truly made the amendment effective.

Because of the struggle involved in African Americans realizing their full political and civil rights, few have held office over the nation's history. While the number of black representatives in local and state governments totaled more than 1,500 in 1870, it would be close to 100 years before African Americans were again represented in significant numbers in local, state, and national governments.

What "firsts" did **African Americans** make in government positions in the last half of the twentieth century?

In the later half of the 1900s, African Americans in public office achieved three significant milestones. In 1990 Douglas Wilder of Virginia was sworn in as the first African-American elected governor in U.S history. In 1966 Edward Brooke of Massachusetts became the first African American senator of the century. And in 1969 Shirley Chisholm became the first black woman in U.S. history to sit in the House of Representatives.

What was the breakdown of **African Americans serving in the 107th Congress**?

Although African Americans comprise approximately 12 percent of the U.S. population, they made up approximately 7 percent of Congress after the 2000 elections. In the 107th Congress, there were 38 African Americans serving in the House of Representatives, and no African American senators.

Have the people of the United States ever elected an **African American to the Senate**?

Yes, in the Senate's history, there have been four African Americans: Hiram R. Revels

(R–MS), who served from 1870 to 1871; Blanche K. Bruce (R–MS), 1875–1881; Edward W. Brooke (R–MA), 1967–1979; and, most recently, Carol Moseley-Braun (D–IL), 1993–1999.

Democrat Shirley Chisholm of New York became the first African American woman elected to the House of Representatives in 1968.

What is the status of **Hispanics** in government and politics?

Census data show that the Hispanic population (Mexican Americans, Puerto Ricans, Cubans, and other people of Spanish-speaking descent) has grown faster than the overall U.S. population since 1990 and is projected to become the largest U.S. minority group by 2005. However, the political power of Mexican Americans, the nation's largest Hispanic group, does not yet equal their population percentage. Recent achievements by Hispanics in politics include the appointment of Aida Alvarez as head of the Small Business Administration in 1997 (making her the first Hispanic woman and the first person of Puerto Rican heritage to hold a position in the president's cabinet) and the appointment of Henry Cisneros, former mayor of San Antonio, as secretary of housing and urban development in President Clinton's administration.

What was the breakdown of **Hispanics serving in the 107th Congress**?

Hispanics constitute 12 percent of the total U.S. population, yet Hispanic representatives only accounted for less than 4 percent of Congress after the 2000 elections. In the 107th Congress, 21 Hispanic Americans served in the House, including two delegates, one from Guam and one from Puerto Rico. None of the senators were of Hispanic origin.

Have the American people ever elected a **Hispanic to the Senate**?

Yes, there have been three Hispanic American senators in U.S. History: Octaviano Larrazolo (R–NM), who served from 1928 to 1929; Dennis Chavez (D–NM), 1935–1962; and Joseph M. Montoya (D–NM), 1964–1977.

Do many Hispanic Americans vote?

Although their voter turnout remains lower than that of other ethnic groups in the United States, in the 1998 midterm elections Hispanic voters turned out in record numbers and had a noticeable influence on the vote in heavily Hispanic-populated states such as California. And according to a 1998 article in the *Dallas Morning News*, Hispanics represent the largest growing segment of the Democratic Party. Special interest groups, such as the National Council of La Raza (NCLR), are working to ensure that the Hispanic vote remains a force in developing policy and that the Hispanics' civil and human rights are advanced. Hispanic advocacy groups achieved a victory in 1998 when President Clinton allocated $600 million for an action plan that would address Hispanic education issues.

What is the role of **Asian Americans** in government and politics?

The 10.2 million Asian Americans living in the United States have established a growing presence in this country. Advocacy groups who represent this population are working toward advancing their civil rights, supporting immigration policies that benefit Asian Americans living in the United States, and encouraging bilingual education programs for Asian Americans.

The November 1996 elections were viewed as historically significant for Asian Americans because of the election of a number of Asian Americans throughout the country. The most notable was the election of Gary Locke as the governor of the state of Washington, the first Chinese American to capture a state's top post, as well as the first Asian American to become governor outside of Hawaii. In California, the election of Mike Honda of San Jose to the California Assembly was hailed a major political achievement because he became only the second Asian American in the 120-member California legislature. According to UCLA's Asian American Studies Center, in 1998–1999 there were nearly 2,000 Asian American and Pacific Islander elected and appointed officials across the nation. One of the lowest rates of voter turnout, however, is found among the Asian American population in general. Various studies of California voter demographics in the 1980s and early 1990s, for example, found that Asian American citizens turned out for elections at rates that were 10 to 15 percent lower than that of whites and African Americans. Advocacy and public interest groups are working to increase voter participation for the November 2004 elections.

What was the breakdown of **Asian Americans in the 107th Congress**?

While Asian Americans represent approximately 4 percent of the total U.S. population, in the 107th Congress, eight members were of Asian or Native Hawaiian/Pacific Islander descent, including the delegate from Guam, who is also Hispanic. Two Asian Americans, Daniel K. Akaka and Daniel K. Inouye (both D–HI), served in the Senate.

How have **Native Americans** gained prominence in government and politics?

Since the arrival of the first Europeans to this land, American Indians have experienced issues of invasion, military defeat, and land concessions. Political focus over history has been in the areas of protecting religious freedom, securing sacred sites, reclaiming cultural identity, protecting treaty rights, and reestablishing sovereignty and self-determination among Indian peoples. As an advocate for American Indian concerns, the National Congress of American Indians (NCAI) provides tribal feedback to legislators seeking an American Indian perspective on issues that range from treaty disputes over land and resources to the protection of American Indian religious freedom and sacred sites. Groups like the Association on American Indian Affairs (AAIA) track federal legislation, keep members informed on policies that affect Indian communities, lobby for Indian interests and federal and state levels, and draft legislation. They have seen some successes toward these goals: in 1996, President Bill Clinton issued an executive order calling for federal agencies to respect sacred areas and to allow Indians ceremonial access to them, but no legislation has been formed along these lines.

What was the breakdown of **Native Americans in the 107th Congress**?

Native Americans were not well represented in Congress after the 2000 elections. In the 107th Congress, there was one Native American representative, Brad Carson (D–OK), and one Native American senator, Ben Nighthorse Campbell (R–CO).

What is the history of **homosexuals** in government?

Like other minorities, homosexuals have initiated political activity to lobby for their interests and achieve their goals. Political pressure from the gay community has brought about many social and policy changes in recent years, at both the local and federal level—from city ordinances that prohibit housing and employment discrimination to Congressional legislation that has allocated billions of dollars to AIDS research. It has also generated intense political debate over issues such as homosexual marriage and participation in military service. While the 2000 Census reported an increase in the number of same-sex couples sharing households (for example, more than 3,500 same-sex couples live in Washington, D.C., a 66 percent increase from the figures reported in 1990), these figures do not yet translate into government positions at the federal level.

Ben Nighthorse Campbell (R–CO) is the only Native American currently serving in the Senate.

Analysts also note that the Employment Non-Discrimination Act, the main piece of federal homosexual rights legislation, appears to be years away from passage.

What was the breakdown of **homosexuals serving in the 107th Congress**?

In the 107th Congress, three representatives of the House acknowledged being homosexual: Jim Kolbe (R–AZ); Barney Frank (D–MA), and Tammy Baldwin (D–WI), who in 1998 became the first woman elected to Congress from Wisconsin and the first proclaimed lesbian elected to the House. There were no openly homosexual senators serving in the 107th Congress.

What methods did these groups use to gain access to the **political process**?

There are a number of ways that groups have realized their right to participate in the political process, including holding demonstrations and marches, lobbying, testifying at congressional hearings, and commenting on policy. Leaders such as Dr. Martin Luther King Jr. paved the way for unique methods of participation. King shaped 13 years of civil rights activities with his philosophy of nonviolent social action and peace marches. Activists like Cesar Chavez and Dolores Huerta followed suit on behalf of farm workers, women, and Hispanic Americans. Feminists Betty Friedan and Gloria Steinem launched a nationwide grassroots campaign in the 1970s to pass an Equal

Rights Amendment (ERA) to the Constitution. Many people form public interest groups in an effort to unite for a common cause and attempt to influence public policy. In fact, many argue that the real impact of equal rights and greater political participation for these groups took place—at continues to take place—at the local level. Through grassroots movements, and through their own labor organizations, volunteer groups, and pressure groups, women, homosexuals, and people of color have won broader and greater rights for themselves and future generations.

How are the **youth** represented in the political community?

According to experts and young adults themselves, there is widespread cynicism about the political community among many 18- to 29-year-olds, and much uncertainty as to how many will bother to vote in upcoming elections. A recent poll conducted for the Pew Research Center for the People and the Press revealed that 55 percent of 18- to 29-year-olds are registered to vote. In the 1996 presidential election, voters under 30 years of age made up about 28 percent of total participants; in the 1998 midterm elections, those aged 18 to 24 made up just 12 percent of the voter population, while only 8 percent of those aged 18 to 21 voted. Further, the 2000 U.S. Census reported that among 18- to 24-year-old African Americans, 62.4 percent were not registered to vote in November 1998. The percentage of nonregistered citizens of voting age for other races is high as well, with the 18- to 24-year-old age group topping the charts with the most eligible voters who are not registered. Experts cite busy schedules, disillusionment with the government, apathy, a highly individualistic nature, and lack of trust in the political process as the reasons fewer and fewer young people are turning out at the polls.

How has **immigration** affected the American political community?

The United States is a nation made of immigrants, and the belief systems and values that the diverse cultures hold have greatly affected the American political culture. According to the U.S. Census Bureau's Center for Immigration Studies, as of the year 2000, 28.4 million immigrants lived in the United States, the largest number ever recorded in the nation's history and a 43 percent increase since 1990. As a percentage of the population, immigrants account for more than 1 in 10 residents, the highest percentage in 70 years. Half of today's immigrants to the United States come from 10 countries: Mexico, China, the Philippines, the Dominican Republic, Vietnam, India, Poland, the Ukraine, El Salvador, and Ireland. This influx of diverse peoples makes for a rich political community with a wide array of interests, needs, and concerns. Today, the "politics" of immigration center on both cultural and economic conflicts: policy makers are divided over whether to preserve language and cultural differences in this country, and economists debate the economic impact of immigration. Furthermore, the immigration policies enacted after the September 11, 2001, terrorist attacks—including limited and carefully scrutinized immigration entry—fuel the immigration discussion.

How has **social class** played a role in political participation?

Certain early voting requirements kept the vote in the hands of wealthier citizens and away from various ethnic groups. Early in this nation's history, property ownership was a common suffrage requirement. The poll tax was a tax payment required by some states before a person could vote, and it was still in effect in certain southern states until the Twenty-fourth Amendment outlawed the tax in 1964. Certain states required literacy in order to vote, and used that to discourage poorer groups, and African Americans in the South, from voting. Even in southern states where the poll tax was no longer used, closed registration lists and straightforward intimidation were used to prevent blacks and the poor from voting.

What does the **2000 Census** have to do with the political community?

The accuracy of the U.S. Census is of great concern to many public interest groups and their multicultural members. The national census, conducted every 10 years, is the constitutionally required count of all people in the United States. Data from the census is used to determine the U.S. representatives from each state, draw the boundaries of congressional districts, and allocate hundreds of billions of dollars in federal grant money. Historically, the census has tended to undercount minorities, meaning that the regions in which they live tend to receive less representation in government and less federal funding.

CIVIL LIBERTIES

CIVIL RIGHTS AND LIBERTIES

What are **civil liberties**?

Civil liberties are those fundamental freedoms that together guarantee the rights of free people, and are the protections of the people from improper government actions against them. The specific rights that together make up the civil liberties of the people of the United States are written in the Bill of Rights, the first 10 amendments to the Constitution. Examples of civil liberties include freedom of religion, freedom of speech, freedom of the press, and the guarantee of a fair, unbiased trial.

What are **substantive liberties**?

Some of the restraints put on the government are substantive liberties, which limit what the government shall and shall not have the power to do, including establish a religion, quarter troops in private homes without consent, or seize private property without just compensation.

How do **civil liberties** differ from **civil rights**?

Although these two terms are often used interchangeably, scholars generally agree that *civil liberties* are those liberties that protect people from the government, that is, those that guarantee the safety of people, their opinions, and their property from the government as listed in the Constitution. The term *civil rights*, on the other hand, is generally used to refer to *acts* of government that make constitutional guarantees real for all people, ensuring that they receive equal treatment under the law, as outlined by the "equal protection" clause of the Fourteenth Amendment. Landmark civil rights legislation is found in the Civil Rights Act of 1964, which prohibits discrimination based on race or sex.

Does the Constitution **grant** Americans their civil rights and liberties?

No, it doesn't grant them, it only guarantees them. According to the Ninth Amendment, "The enumeration in the Constitution, of certain rights, shall not be construed to deny or disparage others retained by the people." The people of America had all their rights and liberties before they wrote the Constitution. The Constitution was formed, among other purposes, to *secure* the people's liberties—not only against foreign attack tbut also against oppression by their own government. The First Amendment to the Constitution, for example, does not "give" freedom of religion or speech to the people; rather, it prohibits Congress from passing any law interfering with freedom of religion, speech, and peaceful assembly.

What are some of the **rights** established in the original Constitution?

The Constitution strives to meet several core democratic principles, one of which is the protection of individual rights and civil liberties. Thus, individual rights are at the heart of the Constitution, as expressed by the framers in the document's preamble with key phrases like "to establish Justice" and "to secure the Blessings of Liberty to ourselves and our Posterity." To establish justice, the Constitution makes no distinction as to the wealth or status of any person; all are equal before the law, and all are equally subject to judgment and punishment when they violate the law. The same holds true for civil disputes involving property, legal agreements, and business arrangements. The emphasis on personal liberty is one of the main features of the Constitution, and the framers were careful to protect the rights of all people by limiting the powers of the national and state governments. As a result, Americans are free to move from place to place; make their own decisions about jobs, religion, and political beliefs; and go to court for justice and protection when they feel these rights have been violated.

What are **unalienable rights**?

Because the American Revolution was fought to preserve and expand the rights of the individual against the government, America's Founding Fathers made sure that they boldly proclaimed these rights in the opening of the Declaration of Independence: "We hold these truths to be self-evident, that all men are created equal, that they are endowed by their Creator with certain unalienable Rights, that among these are Life, Liberty, and the pursuit of Happiness." In this document, the authors expressed their belief in certain unalienable, God-given rights that all people are inherently created with and entitled to enjoy simply because they are human beings, including the rights to life, liberty, and the pursuit of happiness. These rights are not destroyed when civil society is created, and neither society nor government can remove or "alienate" them. Most democratic societies agree that unalienable rights include freedom of speech and expression, freedom of religion and conscience, freedom of assembly, and the right to equal protection before the law. Since these rights exist independently of government, these rights cannot be taken away by legislation, nor are they subject to the whim of an electoral majority.

THE BILL OF RIGHTS

What is the **Bill of Rights**?

The Bill of Rights—collectively, the first 10 amendments to the U.S. Constitution—guarantees rights and liberties to the American people. These amendments were proposed by Congress on September 25, 1789, and ratified as a block by three-fourths (11) of the states on December 15, 1791, thereby officially becoming part of the Constitution. The first eight amendments outline substantive and procedural individual rights guaranteed to all people, while the Ninth and Tenth Amendments are general rules of interpretation of the relationship among the people, the state governments, and the federal government. Although the Bill of Rights was originally written to restrict the national government, the Supreme Court has nationalized the Bill of Rights by upholding that most of the provisions also apply to the states, as outlined by the Fourteenth Amendment's due process clause.

How does the Bill of Rights **protect individual liberties**?

The Bill of Rights limits the ability of government to intrude upon certain individual liberties, guaranteeing freedom of speech, press, assembly, and religion to all people. Nearly two-thirds of the Bill of Rights was written to safeguard the rights of those suspected or accused of crime, providing for due process of law, fair trials, freedom from self-incrimination and from cruel and unusual punishment, and protection against being held twice in jeopardy for the same crime. In short, the Bill of Rights places certain liberties beyond the reach of those in power on the premise that depriving citizens of fundamental rights diminishes their civil standing and ultimately their humanity. Since the adoption of the Bill of Rights, only 17 additional amendments have been added to the Constitution. While a number of these amendments revised how the federal government is structured and operates, many followed precedent established by the Bill of Rights and expanded individual rights and freedoms.

How do the **Ninth and Tenth Amendments** relate to **individual rights**?

The Ninth and Tenth Amendments contain very broad statements of constitutional authority. The Ninth Amendment declares that the listing of individual rights is not meant to be comprehensive; that the people have other rights not specifically mentioned in the Constitution. The Tenth Amendment provides that powers not delegated by the Constitution to the federal government nor withheld by it from the states are reserved to the states or the people.

Why was the **Bill of Rights** written?

Although the Constitution, as it was originally written, contained a number of important guarantees in Articles I and III, it did not include a general list of the rights of the people. One explanation for this omission is that the framers assumed that the powers of the newly created national government were so carefully limited that individual rights really required no additional protections. Nevertheless, the states contested this omission so strongly that several refused to ratify the Constitution until they were promised by the Continental Congress that a Bill of Rights would be added.

One of the loudest proponents for the inclusion of a bill of rights was George Mason, the author of the Declaration of Rights of Virginia. As a delegate to the Constitutional Convention, Mason refused to sign the Constitution, and his opposition almost blocked ratification by Virginia. Because of similar sentiment in Massachusetts, that state conditioned its ratification on the addition of specific guarantees of individual rights. By the time the first Congress convened, agreement for adoption of such amendments was nearly unanimous, and the Congress began to draft the Bill of Rights.

How are a person's individual rights **relative**?

While the Constitution guarantees a number of rights, all people can only exercise those rights as long as they do not infringe on the rights of others. For example, while everyone in the United States enjoys a right to free speech, no one has *absolute* freedom of speech. A person can be convicted under the law for using obscene language, or for using words in a manner that cause another person to commit a crime, as seen in the example of rioting. Recently, the relativity of individual rights was exemplified in *Apollo Media Corporation v. United States* (1999), where the U.S. Supreme Court upheld a federal law that makes it illegal for anyone to send obscene e-mail over the Internet.

Does the Bill of Rights **apply to all people**?

Most constitutional rights are extended to all people of the United States. The Supreme Court has oftentimes determined that the word "persons" as it appears in the Constitution includes both aliens, or foreign-born residents, and citizens. However, certain rights, such as the right to travel freely as guaranteed by the two privileges and immunities clauses (found in Article IV and the Fourteenth Amendment), are only guaranteed to citizens.

Does the Bill of Rights only **limit the national government**?

No. One of the most far-reaching amendments to the Constitution is the Fourteenth Amendment, ratified in 1868, which establishes a simple definition of citizenship and guarantees equal treatment to all persons under the law. With the words, "No State shall ... deprive any person of life, liberty or property, without due process of law," in essence the Fourteenth Amendment requires the states to abide by the protections of the Bill of Rights, thereby applying those rights to more than just the national government. It wasn't until the 1960s, however, that most of the civil liberties outlined in the Bill of Rights were applied to the states.

George Mason (1725–1792) authored a bill of rights and a constitution for the state of Virginia. His work served as a model for the Declaration of Independence and the first 10 amendments to the U.S. Constitution.

How and when did the **Supreme Court nationalize the Bill of Rights**?

While the Supreme Court ruled in 1833 that the Bill of Rights limited only the national government, the Court slowly expanded Bill of Rights protections to the states. For example, in 1897, the Court used the Fourteenth Amendment to prohibit states from taking private property for public use without just compensation to the original owner. It wasn't until 1925, in *Gitlow v. New York*, that the Supreme Court applied the Bill of Rights to states in protecting individual liberties by ruling that freedom of speech is protected at the state level.

However, despite these milestones, as late as 1937 the Court held that only certain parts of the Bill of Rights applied to the states. Starting in 1961, most of the important provisions of the Bill of Rights were incorporated into the Fourteenth Amendment and were legally mandated for the states, one by one. During this decade, for example, the Supreme Court applied the Fourteenth Amendment to several important cases, including: *Robinson v. California* (1962), applying the Eighth Amendment's right against cruel and unusual punishment to the state of California; *Klopfer v. North Carolina*

(1967), applying the Sixth Amendment's right to a speedy trial to the state of North Carolina; and *Duncan v. Louisiana* (1968), applying the Sixth Amendment's right to a trial by jury to the state of Louisiana. Today, the Fourteenth Amendment imposes all the Bill of Rights provisions on the states, except those of the Second, Third, Seventh, and Tenth Amendments, and the grand jury requirements of the Fifth Amendment.

What is meant by **"selective incorporation"**?

"Selective incorporation" is the term used to refer to the Supreme Court's decision to selectively incorporate each provision of the Bill of Rights into the due process clause of the Fourteenth Amendment.

Could the **Supreme Court reverse the nationalization of the Bill of Rights**?

In theory, yes. Some scholars are quick to point out that since none of the decisions made in the 1960s that nationalized most of the Bill of Rights clauses have actually been reversed, a reversal is unlikely. However, other scholars disagree, maintaining that because in the 1980s and 1990s the Supreme Court ruled narrower and more restrictive interpretations of some of its earlier decisions, a reversal may be possible. Specifically, they cite the narrowing of abortion rights, noting *Webster v. Reproductive Health Services* (1989), in which the Court narrowly ruled that restrictions on the use of public medical facilities for abortion are constitutional, and *Planned Parenthood v. Casey* (1992), which narrowed the scope of the landmark *Roe v. Wade* (1973) decision, which upheld a woman's right to privacy through her right to have an abortion. In the 1990s, state power over capital punishment was extended when the Supreme Court severely limited repeated habeas corpus petitions from state prisoners, which would have required that they be brought before a judge to decide the legality of their detention.

The terms **"substantive restraints"** and **"procedural restraints"** are both used in the Bill of Rights. What's the difference?

Substantive restraints limit what the government has the power to do, such as restricting freedom of speech, religion, or the press. Procedural restraints limit how the government can act, and are usually grouped under the general category of due process of law. For example, citizens are guaranteed due process of law when they are charged with a crime, and the government may not infringe upon this basic civil liberty.

Have our **basic civil liberties changed** over the years?

No. Since the addition of the Bill of Rights, no amendments have been added to the Constitution to alter the civil liberties guaranteed by these first 10. After the Supreme

The Bill of Rights

Amendment I
Congress shall make no law respecting an establishment of religion, or prohibiting the free exercise thereof; or abridging the freedom of speech, or of the press; or the right of the people peaceably to assemble, and to petition the government for a redress of grievances.

Amendment II
A well regulated militia, being necessary to the security of a free state, the right of the people to keep and bear arms, shall not be infringed.

Amendment III
No soldier shall, in time of peace be quartered in any house, without the consent of the owner, nor in time of war, but in a manner to be prescribed by law.

Amendment IV
The right of the people to be secure in their persons, houses, papers, and effects, against unreasonable searches and seizures, shall not be violated, and no warrants shall issue, but upon probable cause, supported by oath or affirmation, and particularly describing the place to be searched, and the persons or things to be seized.

Amendment V
No person shall be held to answer for a capital, or otherwise infamous crime, unless on a presentment or indictment of a grand jury, except in cases arising in the land or naval forces, or in the militia, when in actual service in time of war or public danger; nor shall any person be subject for the same offense to be twice put in jeopardy of life or limb; nor shall be compelled in any criminal case to be a witness against himself, nor be deprived of life, liberty, or property, without due process of law; nor shall private property be taken for public use, without just compensation.

Amendment VI
In all criminal prosecutions, the accused shall enjoy the right to a speedy and public trial, by an impartial jury of the state and district wherein the crime shall have been committed, which district shall have been previously ascertained by law, and to be informed of the nature and cause of the accusation; to be confronted with the witnesses against him; to have compulsory process for obtaining witnesses in his favor, and to have the assistance of counsel for his defense.

Amendment VII
In suits at common law, where the value in controversy shall exceed twenty dollars, the right of trial by jury shall be preserved, and no fact tried by a jury, shall be otherwise reexamined in any court of the United States, than according to the rules of the common law.

Amendment VIII
Excessive bail shall not be required, nor excessive fines imposed, nor cruel and unusual punishments inflicted.

Amendment IX
The enumeration in the Constitution, of certain rights, shall not be construed to deny or disparage others retained by the people.

Amendment X
The powers not delegated to the United States by the Constitution, nor prohibited by it to the states, are reserved to the states respectively, or to the people.

Although considered offensive by some, burning the American flag is an act protected by the Constitution as an expression of free speech.

Court ruled in *Texas v. Johnson* (1989) that flag burning was an expression of free speech and overturned the conviction of Gregory Johnson, who was arrested for torching the American flag in 1984, many citizens rallied to add a constitutional amendment that would ban flag burning. This proposal resurfaced in the 1990s, although reluctance to alter the First Amendment eventually won over, and no amendment has been added to date. The Christian Coalition's 1995 Contract with the American Family set out to alter many civil liberties, including passing legislation that would place limits on second-trimester abortions and instituting the Religious Equality Amendment to allow prayer in public schools. Although no amendment has been passed, state legislation to restore school prayer has been ignited in Pennsylvania, South Carolina, and Florida, and certain legislators support an amendment that would permit students to pray aloud in schools, marking a growing trend toward increasing religious expression in school.

How have **civil liberties been threatened** throughout U.S. history?

Since the late 1700s, the United States has witnessed actions by Congress or the president that have either restricted civil liberties or led to controversies about those rights. For example, in 1861 President Abraham Lincoln suspended the writ of habeas corpus in several states before extending the suspension to all states in 1863, thus denying those accused of crimes the right to be brought before a judge to consider whether the charges are valid; and in 1942 President Franklin D. Roosevelt signed an executive order that resulted in the internment of more than 120,000 Japanese Americans at "war relocation" camps in America during World War II. Although in 1944 the Supreme Court upheld the forced evacuation as a necessary wartime act, the action has been strongly criticized. The twentieth century saw additional threats as well. The cold war era passage of the 1950 Internal Security Act made it illegal for a "Communist-action" organization in the United States to hold any nonelective office, become employed in a defense organization, or apply for or use a passport. The 1978 Foreign

Intelligence Surveillance Act allows for electronic eavesdropping and wiretapping when collecting "foreign intelligence" information. And the 1996 Antiterrorism and Effective Death Penalty Act established membership in a terrorist organization as grounds for denying noncitizens entry into the United States, and allows federal officers to use wiretapping when investigating immigration offenses.

What are some examples of how **civil liberties have been threatened since the September 11, 2001, terrorist attacks** on the World Trade Center and the Pentagon?

Historians agree that many threats to civil liberties arise in times of war or during threats of terrorism. Most recently, many criticize the USA Patriot Act—which eases search-warrant requirements to allow the Federal Bureau of Investigation (FBI) to monitor certain Internet activity and allows the agency to search any phone line a suspect uses despite the Fourth Amendment's requirement that a search warrant specifically describe the place being searched—because the increased protection from terrorists comes at the cost of privacy, a basic civil liberty. The Justice Department's new policy of monitoring communications between terrorist suspects and their lawyers has been sharply criticized, primarily because of its limitation on the Constitutional right to legal representation. Critics say the policy violates both the Sixth Amendment, which grants a criminal defendant the right "to have the assistance of counsel for his defense," and the Fourth Amendment, which relieves citizens from "unreasonable searches and seizures." In addition, the USA Patriot Act has been criticized by the American Civil Liberties Union (ACLU) because it significantly increases the government's law enforcement powers while continuing a trend to decrease the checks and balances that Americans have traditionally relied on to protect individual liberty. Specifically, the act expands the ability of the government to conduct secret searches; grants the FBI broad access to sensitive business records about individuals without having to show evidence of a crime; and provides for large-scale investigations of American citizens for "intelligence" purposes.

In fact, in the wake of the October 2001 passage of antiterrorism legislation, many have criticized the Bush administration's extended detention of hundreds of unnamed suspects associated with the September 11 terrorist attacks without charging them with specific crimes, as well as its plans to try suspected terrorists before military tribunals, which prohibits judicial review and replaces public criminal trials guaranteed by the Sixth Amendment. Further, many constitutional safeguards provided to U.S. criminals would not apply to those being tried: Suspects would not be advised that they can remain silent, and evidence would most likely not be challenged because of the circumstances under which it was gathered. Although the Constitution makes provision for certain tribunals, the United States has generally opposed them in other nations because they fail to provide adequate due process.

CIVIL LIBERTIES AT RISK

In turbulent or threatening times throughout U.S. history, the government has frequently responded with measures to ensure domestic security. These measures, however, have often been at the expense of civil liberties. Among the most controversial actions:

1798: Passed in response to the threat of war with France, the Alien Enemy Act allows for the deportation of "alien enemy males" aged 14 and older in the case of declared war or invasion.

1861: Insisting the action is necessary to put down insurrection in the South that threatened the Union, President Lincoln suspends the writ of habeas corpus in four states (extending the suspension to the remaining states two years later), thus allowing for the indefinite detainment of those suspected of sympathizing with or supporting the Southern cause. Habeas corpus, which is guaranteed by the Constitution, dictates that someone accused of a crime will be brought before a court to decide the legality of the charges against him or her.

1918: As the U.S. becomes involved in World War I, the Entry and Departure Controls Act is passed, giving the president, "during times of war or national emergency," the power to control the movement in and out of the country of noncitizens considered to be a threat to public security.

1940: The Alien Registration Act mandates that all noncitizens register with the government, which includes the fingerprinting of those over the age of 14. The act makes it unlawful for anyone in the United States to advocate or support the overthrow of the U.S. government. The act is passed in an effort to undermine the Communist Party and other left-wing political entities deemed a threat to the country.

1942: Issued by President Franklin D. Roosevelt, Executive Order 9066 restricts access to "military areas" any persons not considered to be "necessary or desirable." This action results in the forcible relocation of over 100,000 Japanese Americans to internment camps throughout the remainder of World War II, which Roosevelt justifies on the grounds that "war requires every possible protection against espionage and against sabotage to national-defense material, national-defense premises and national-defense utilities."

1950: The Internal Security Act is passed, preventing members of "Communist-action" groups from being employed by the government, from working at defense facilities, and from applying for or using a passport. A part of the act that called for members of the Communist Party to register with the government was found unconstitutional in 1965, thereby nullifying the entire act.

1973: President Richard Nixon comes under the scrutiny of the American Civil Liberties Union, which makes a case for his impeachment based upon charges that he violated a range of civil liberties, laws, and constitutional mandates. The ACLU accuses Nixon of authorizing the illegal surveillance of political enemies, establishing a "secret police" to carry out these actions, assuming war-making powers reserved for Congress in his execution of the Vietnam War, and obstructing the Watergate investigation.

1978: The Foreign Intelligence Surveillance Act is passed, permitting the use of electronic eavesdropping technology and wiretaps to gain "foreign intelligence" information upon the permission of a special group of federal judges.

1994: The Foreign Intelligence Surveillance Act is extended to allow for secret physical searches conducted to gain "foreign intelligence" information. All types of searches under this act can be executed in some cases without a court order.

1996: The Antiterrorism and Effective Death Penalty Act is passed, allowing the government to keep noncitizens who are members of terrorist organizations from entering the United States, deport noncitizens already in the United States who are members of terrorist organizations, and use wiretaps to investigate the possible violation of immigration laws, including those involving identification fraud.

2001: The USA Patriot Act, passed in the wake of the September 11 terrorist attacks and the subsequent war on terrorism, grants the executive branch increased powers to conduct surveillance and collect intelligence (especially involving telecommunications and computer activity and business records) and gives the government broader authority to detain immigrants suspected of or connected to terrorist activities.

Finally, the USA Patriot Act and new immigration legislation authorizes U.S. authorities to jail and deport any noncitizen whom the attorney general considers a threat under the new definitions of terrorists groups, allows the deportation of suspicious legal U.S. residents, and broadens the grounds on which foreigners may be denied entry to the United States. Because the tightening immigration policies expand the government's power to detail and expel residents, civil libertarians are concerned that these newfound powers might be used against minorities and other disenfranchised people to compromise their civil liberties.

What is the relationship between **individual liberties** and **national security** since September 11, 2001?

The issue of balancing civil liberties and national security has again come to the forefront of American discussion since the Bush administration first proposed its recent antiterrorist legislation. Since its passage, many civil libertarians have expressed fear that the hasty adoption of sweeping limitations on personal freedom comes at a cost that ultimately reaches beyond the present administration. While acknowledging that recent terrorist activities require attention in order to maintain national security, the Antiterrorism Act is ultimately too threatening to civil liberties because it greatly expands the investigative authority of government agencies and the conduct of surveillance and intelligence gathering organizations. Civil libertarians argue that the administration and Congress could have struck a better balance between national security and civil liberties—for example, modifying statutes perceived as restricting law enforcement officials to make exceptions only for terrorist investigations, and better determining how to share a narrow class of information relating to terrorist activities with the intelligence community.

THE FIRST AMENDMENT: FREEDOM OF RELIGION, SPEECH, PRESS, ASSEMBLY, AND PETITION

What is **"freedom of religion"**?

Guaranteed by the First Amendment, freedom of religion—or more broadly, freedom of conscience—means that no person should be required to profess any religion or other belief against his or her desires. Additionally, because a person's religious faith is a profoundly personal matter, no one should be penalized in any way because he or she chooses one religion over another, or chooses no religion at all. With nine out of

10 Americans expressing some religious preference, and approximately 70 percent holding membership to religious congregations, America has long been a country comprised of a variety of religious faiths, and one that upholds religious tolerance. The First Amendment forbids Congress to set up or in any way provide for an established church. In addition, Congress may not pass laws limiting worship, speech, or the press, or preventing people from meeting peacefully.

Muslims pray at a place of worship in Queens, New York. Freedom of religion is a right guaranteed by the Constitution.

What is the **establishment clause**?

The First Amendment phrase "Congress shall make no law respecting an establishment of religion" is referred to as the establishment clause. Simply put, it prohibits the national government from establishing a national religion. However, the establishment clause does not prevent government from meeting the needs of religious groups, although the Supreme Court has often interpreted the clause to forbid government endorsement of or aid to religious doctrines.

What is the **free exercise clause**?

The second clause of the First Amendment, "or prohibiting the free exercise thereof," is known as the free exercise clause, which prohibits the national government from interfering with an American's rights to practice his or her religion.

What does the phrase **"separation of church and state"** mean?

Ordained by the First Amendment, separation of church and state provides in part that "Congress shall make no law respecting an establishment of religion, or prohibiting the free exercise thereof...." Thomas Jefferson declared that this clause in essence creates a "wall of separation" between church and state, or between the government and any religious activity. Although there are situations where this "wall" has been lowered—for example, each session of Congress opens with prayer, but it is illegal for public schools to begin their day this way—the doctrine of the separation of church and state has been applied stringently by the Supreme Court to most types of state-supported religious activity. As a result of the separation of church and state, students in public schools may not pray aloud publicly as part of the school day; they may not study the Bible as a sacred text, and they may not celebrate religious holidays. Furthermore, cities may not display a Christmas crèche on certain public property, such as a courthouse, and students may not receive federal grants or loans specifically to attend religious elementary or secondary schools.

What is the **Lemon test**?

Although the Supreme Court has historically debated how to interpret the establishment clause and measure the constitutionality of state laws that appear to further religion, the Supreme Court decision *Lemon v. Kurtzman* (1971) established a "test" by which to measure the constitutionality of these types of laws. Thus, under what is commonly referred to as the Lemon test, a law or practice dealing with church/state issues must: (1) have a secular legislative purpose; (2) have a primary effect that neither advances nor inhibits religion; and (3) not propel an excessive government entanglement with religion. In *Lemon v. Kurtzman*, state funding of parochial school teachers' salaries failed this test and is therefore prohibited by the Constitution. A decade later the Lemon test was applied to a Kentucky law that required the posting of the Ten Commandments in public school classrooms, and invalidated that law because the Court ruled the posting had no "secular legislative purpose." Since this time, the Supreme Court has ruled more flexibly where issues of church and state are concerned, as long as the hot button—school prayer—has not been pushed. Consistently, the Court has ruled for a strict separation of church and state with school prayer.

Why is there so much **controversy over school prayer**?

Perhaps no aspect of the church/state controversy creates more discussion than the subject of prayer in public schools—primarily because this topic cuts right to the core of what Americans think religious freedom constitutes. The First Amendment protects both advocates and critics of school prayer by mandating government neutrality between religious belief and nonbelief. At the heart of the school-prayer debate is the intense conflict between the establishment clause and the free exercise clause. The Supreme Court has ruled that it is unconstitutional for the government—through the educators who run public schools—to lead children in prayer or force them to pray a certain way. However, all children have the right to pray voluntarily before, during, or after school, and students have the right to discuss their religious views with their peers so long as they are not disruptive. Because the establishment clause does not apply to purely private speech, students have the right to read their Bibles or other scriptures, say grace before meals, and pray before tests.

Despite these rights, some proponents of school prayer rally for increased religious freedom in school, and advocate amending the Constitution so that the government would legally sponsor the activity of prayer. A majority of the American public say they support such an amendment, Republican presidential candidates have generally agreed with such an amendment's adoption. In its 1990 decision *Board of Education v. Mergens*, the Supreme Court lessened the ban on prayer in school a bit by saying that students may form Bible-reading or school-prayer clubs as long as they are not exclusive, since banning religious groups while allowing secular ones to meet impedes students' right to free exercise of religion as guaranteed by the First Amendment. However, despite these and other examples of leniency, the Supreme Court ruled in *Lee v. Weisman* (1992) that even nonsectarian prayer at public school graduation ceremonies violated the establishment clause of the Constitution both because of its inevitably coercive effect on students and because it conveyed a message of government endorsement of religion. Because of varying Supreme Court decisions, rich arguments on both sides, and the time-consuming and often difficult nature of signing an amendment into law, it's likely the school-prayer controversy will remain alive for some time to come.

What role do **school vouchers** play in the freedom of religion debate?

School voucher programs, which are being used in several states and give parents of school-aged children yearly stipends to pay for their children's tuition at the school of their choosing, including private religious schools, have not—as of 2002—been deemed either constitutional or unconstitutional by the Supreme Court. Although proponents of school-voucher programs maintain that the main purpose of vouchers is educational, not religious, and that vouchers are in accordance with the free exercise of religion clause because they allow families to choose the religious environment in which their children will be raised, other feel differently. Those critics of school vouchers argue that they violate the establishment clause because they allow parents to use state-provided stipends to pay for religious education, in essence mandating government financial support of religious institutions, thus breaching the wall of separation and state.

How are issues of **religion** and **politics** tied?

The most controversial aspect of religion in the United States today is probably its role in politics. In recent decades some Americans have come to believe that separation of church and state has been interpreted in ways hostile to religion. Religious conservatives and fundamentalists have joined forces to become a powerful political movement known as the Christian Right. Among their goals is to overturn, by law or constitutional amendment, Supreme Court decisions allowing abortion and banning prayer in public schools. Ralph Reed, former executive director of the Christian Coalition, estimates that one-third of the delegates to the 1996 Republican Convention were members of this or similar conservative Christian groups, an indication of the increased involvement of religion in politics.

What does **"freedom of speech"** mean?

"Congress shall make no law ... abridging the freedom of speech, or of the press." Freedom of speech and expression is the lifeblood of any democracy. Actions such as debating and voting, assembling and protesting, and worshipping rely upon the unrestricted flow of speech and information. In contrast to authoritarian states, democratic governments do not control, dictate, or judge the content of written and verbal speech, and thus the First Amendment guarantees this basic civil liberty. A democratic nation depends upon a literate, knowledgeable citizenry whose access to the broadest possible range of information enables it to participate as fully as possible in the public life of their society, and democracy can only thrive when it is supported by citizens who enjoy a free flow of ideas and opinions.

What are the **limits on free speech**?

Although free speech is guaranteed by the First Amendment, not *all* speech is free from government control. Specifically, three types of speech—commercial speech, libel and slander, and obscenity—are not protected under the First Amendment and may be regulated. Commercial speech includes advertising or other speech made for business purposes, including print, radio, and television advertising. Libel is a false statement made about another made in print, while slander involves the spoken use of malicious words—both have the intent of injuring a person's character or reputation. Obscenity includes publicly offensive language or images of no social value. Whether pornography is considered "obscene" depends upon whether it is deemed to have some artistic or literary value. According to the Supreme Court's 1942 decision *Chaplinsky v. New Hampshire*, obscenity, lewdness, libel, and "fighting words" are not protected because "such expressions are no essential part of any exposition of ideas."

What is meant by **"prior restraint"**?

The origins of freedom of speech find their place in the early colonial period of American history, where speech and press were governed by the doctrine of prior restraint, which maintained that the government could not censor written materials before they were published. This doctrine still holds true today, and legally people have the right to publish material of their choosing without being required to submit the material beforehand to a government censor. Further, the government cannot block publication of materials, as upheld by the Supreme Court in the famous Pentagon Papers case. This 1971 ruling maintained that the U.S. government could not block the publication of Defense Department documents illegally given to the *New York Times* by anti–Vietnam War activists.

What is **strict judicial scrutiny**?

The Supreme Court has adhered to the Constitution's underlying premise that certain rights are essential to individual liberty in America society by deeming them worthy of "strict judicial scrutiny." These include the liberties found in the Bill of Rights, and specifically the First Amendment. Thus, when a case comes before the Supreme Court that deals with civil liberties issues, the Court assesses that case in terms of its "real and appreciable impact on, or a significant interference with the exercise of the fundamental right" and applies the strict scrutiny doctrine, meaning it provides a close or rigid reading and interpretation of the law.

How does the phrase "clear and present danger" relate to freedom of speech?

The phrase arose out of the Supreme Court case *Schenck v. United States* (1919), in which the Court was asked to review a World War I soldier's conviction for espionage after he printed and mailed antiwar leaflets to draft-age men. In that decision the Court upheld the clear and present danger doctrine, which states that people should have complete freedom of speech unless their language presents a "clear and present danger" to the nation or instigates "evils that Congress has a right to prevent." Although the Court upheld Schenck's conviction, it marked the first time the Court limited the regulation of speech with a definite standard.

How does the popular phrase **"Them's fightin' words"** relate to freedom of speech?

In *Chaplinsky v. New Hampshire* (1942), the Supreme Court utilized the fighting words doctrine to maintain that some words constitute violent acts. In that case they upheld a Jehovah's Witness's conviction because he had used words against a police officer that were considered threatening and "by their very utterance inflect injury or intend to incite an immediate breach of peace." Prior to this decision, the Court protected most speech under the clear and present danger doctrine.

Is a **symbol** "speech"?

In addition to the protection guaranteed to pure, spoken speech, the Supreme Court has generally extended the First Amendment to cover other means of expression called symbolic speech, including symbols, logos, and signs, as well as to activities such as picketing, sit-ins, and demonstrations. Although the Court has historically been sympathetic toward symbolic speech—as in instances of flag desecration and the wearing of symbols, such as armbands to protest the Vietnam War as seen in the historic *Tinker v. Des Moines* (1969)—it has not given blanket First Amendment coverage to symbolic speech. Thus, what some have maintained is symbolic speech, such as burning draft cards, hasn't held up under Supreme Court scrutiny.

What is meant by the term **"speech plus"**?

Communicating political, social, and other views is not accomplished solely by one-on-one, direct speech, through web pages, or in newspaper editorials, but often reaches into the area of "speech plus," which includes picketing and marching, distributing leaflets and pamphlets, addressing public audiences, soliciting door-to-door, and conducting many forms of sit-ins. However, because all of these means of expression involve action rather than mere speech, they are much more subject to regulation and restriction by the government than straightforward speech. While the First Amendment protects some forms of "speech plus," the Supreme Court does not extend that coverage to all.

What is **confidentiality**?

Many federal courts have rejected the news media's argument of their right to confidentiality, that is, their right to refuse to testify in court to reveal their sources and other confidential information. In fact, the Supreme Court ruled in *Branzenburg v. Hayes* (1972) that reporters, like other citizens, must "respond to relevant questions put to them in the course of a valid grand jury investigation or criminal trial." Despite this ruling, approximately 30 states have passed "shield laws," giving news journalists some protection against disclosing their sources in those states.

What are **speech codes**?

Meant to advocate what is sometimes called "politically correct" speech, speech codes are those speech impositions adopted by universities and colleges that have attempted to ban what they consider to be offensive speech—usually racial epithets and comments regarding sexual orientation. Since 1989, more than 200 colleges and universities across the United States have adopted speech codes that prohibit racial comments directed at minorities. In recent years the American Civil Liberties Union (ACLU), which maintains that speech codes violate the First Amendment's guarantee of free speech, has been active in defending those students accused of violating their university speech codes, and continually and aggressively seeks their appeal.

How is **saluting the flag** related to freedom of speech?

In the twentieth century, the relationship between church and state evolved into a conflict between civic duty and individual conscience, as seen in a number of Supreme Court rulings. In *West Virginia State Board of Education v. Barnette* (1943), certain members of the Jehovah's Witness religion refused to salute the American flag during the school day, as commanded by state law. Because their religion forbade such pledges of loyalty, the Jehovah's Witnesses argued they were being forced to violate their consciences. The justices determined that saluting the flag was considered to be a symbol of speech, which the state could not force its residents to perform. In 1985 it upheld its decision that burning the American flag is a form of symbolic protected speech in *Texas v. Johnson* by overturning the conviction of Gregory Johnson, who had been found guilty of setting fire to an American flag during the 1984 Republican National Convention.

How is the **banning of books in schools** related to freedom of speech?

Because banning books involves restricting and/or censoring materials by an individual or group who feels that the books' opinions are unorthodox or unpopular, it cuts to the heart of freedom of expression as guaranteed by the First Amendment. Challenges to books in schools or libraries are often motivated by a desire to protect children from "inappropriate" sexual content or "offensive" language; however, censorship by librarians or school officials of constitutionally protected speech, even if for a child's protection, violates the First Amendment. According to Herbert N. Foerstel's *Banned in the U.S.A.*, frequently challenged books of the 1990s included *Of Mice and Men* by John Steinbeck, *The Catcher in the Rye* by J. D. Salinger, *I Know Why the Caged Bird Sings* by Maya Angelou, *Lord of the Flies* by William Golding, *Slaughterhouse-Five* by Kurt Vonnegut, and *The Color Purple* by Alice Walker.

How do **freedom of speech** and **freedom of the press** relate?

Of all the liberties listed in the Bill of Rights, scholars and civil libertarians maintain that there is a "trio of rights" that are so closely related they are often discussed together as one: freedom of speech, freedom of the press, and freedom of assembly. In a democratic society, if free speech is to have an effect, then it must be disseminated through a free media. An audience must also have the freedom to gather to listen to a speaker who is communicating his or her ideas in order for a free exchange of thought and information to be possible. Because democracy involves public debate and open decision-making, the communication of ideas, opinions, and information is essential, both through the spoken and printed word. Newspapers, magazines, radio, and television serve both as both forums for debate and sources of information on which decisions can be based.

What are the **limits on free press**?

Under the First Amendment, the press—which is also referred to as mass media and includes all print and electronic media—is protected, although different constitutional rules apply to each kind of media. Besides issues of copyright infringement and libel, the print media are for the most part unregulated; the electronic media—radio, television, and the Internet—are subject to limited regulation based on the Federal Communications Act of 1934, administered by the Federal Communications Commission (FCC). Because radio and television use public airwaves to broadcast their programs, they must do so with the public's permission, and thus have a license to broadcast that is subject to FCC renewal. While the FCC cannot censor program content, it can prohibit the use of indecent language. In general, cable programming has received broader First Amendment freedom than traditional television by the Supreme Court.

Although the Supreme Court has determined that "liberty of expression" through motion pictures in guaranteed by the First and Fourteenth Amendments, state or local governments are within their constitutional rights to ban an obscene film (as states like Massachusetts and Maryland have in times past), but only under a law that mandates a judicial hearing where the government must prove obscenity. Today, local review boards are rare, having been replaced with a rating system created by the movie industry that most viewers respect.

What is the **equal time rule**?

The Federal Communications Commission (FCC) enforces the Communication Act of 1934's "equal time doctrine," which says that broadcast media must grant equal access to air time to like parties. Thus, if a television network grants air time to one political candidate, it must offer equal time to all other political candidates running for that office.

How does the **Internet** factor into the discussion of free speech?

Much concern over Internet regulation—including communications that contain indecent words or pictures that can easily be accessed by minors, and child pornography sites—arose during the Clinton administration, leading to the passage of the 1996 Communications Decency Act. In a landmark 1997 decision, the Supreme Court ruled that the Communications Decency Act violated the First Amendment's guarantee of freedom of speech, deeming the Internet a unique medium entitled to the highest protection under the Constitution's free-speech protections. The ruling in effect gave the Internet the same free-speech protection as print, making it the first electronic media to enjoy this privilege primarily because of its unique construction, including low barriers to access, abundance of sites, and the variety of perspectives and opinions disseminated.

Is **rap music** protected under freedom of speech?

Yes. Although rap groups and other performers of popular music came under increased scrutiny in the 1990s by concerned parent groups and child advocates such as Tipper Gore, wife of former vice president Al Gore and author of *Raising PG Kids in an X-Rated Society*, rap artists have cited First Amendment protection when called on to defend their controversial lyrics, considered by some to be degrading and violent. Women's groups and even police departments have objected to what is known as "gangsta rap" for its sexually explicit and anarchistic lyrics; their arguments, however, consistently lose out to these expressive artists and their music labels, who maintain that their viewpoint is unique and protected by the free speech provisions of the Constitution.

What is **"freedom of assembly"**?

The corollary to freedom of speech is the right of the people to assemble and peacefully demand that the government hear their grievances. Without this right to gather and be heard, freedom of speech would be devalued. For this reason, freedom of speech is considered closely linked to, if not inseparable from, the right to gather, protest, and demand change. Democratic governments can legitimately regulate the time and place of political rallies and marches to maintain the peace, but they cannot use that authority to suppress protest or to prevent groups from making their voices heard.

What are **"time, place, and manner"** regulations?

According to several Supreme Court rulings, the government can make and enforce reasonable, precisely defined, and fairly administered laws regarding the time, place, and manner of public assemblies, including, for example, city ordinances that prohibit making noise or causing disturbances near schools or state laws that forbid parades near courthouses when they are intended to influence court proceedings. Because these laws must also be neutral in content, meaning they cannot regulate assemblies based on what might be said in that location, the Supreme Court has been careful in its review of ordinances that are vague or attempt to pinpoint a particular group of people.

What are people's rights regarding **demonstrations on public property**?

Although it is within a person's constitutional rights to freely assemble and petition in public, the Supreme Court has often upheld laws that, seeking to avoid unnecessary violence and conflict, require advanced notice and permits for demonstrations in public places. Public forums include streets, sidewalks, parks, and other public places people naturally assemble. Other kinds of public property, such as rooms in a city hall or classrooms in public schools used for after-hours activities, are known as limited public forums, and thus are available only for limited use of assembly and speech. In the 1990s, the most controversial demonstrations have been those held by anti-abortion groups such as Operation Rescue. Although these groups have the right to assemble outside of abortion clinics, in 1994 the Supreme Court ruled that it was well within the domain of a Florida judge—whose order drew a 36-foot neutral zone around the clinic—to direct protestors not to block access to abortion clinics in that state. Congress responded by passing the Freedom of Access to Clinic Entrances Act later that year, which makes it a federal offense to threaten or interfere with anyone providing or receiving abortions, and allows abortion clinic employees or patients to sue for damages and seek federal injunctions against violators.

Can **public schools ban political protests**?

Yes. The Supreme Court determined that although public facilities like libraries, schools, and government offices are open to the public, they are not public forums. Schools, for example, have the right to exclude those who engage in activities other than those for which the school was created. Students, parents, and visitors have no right to interfere with educational programs or inhabit facilities in order to further a political goal or stage a political protest. Even if their actions are peaceful, because they occur on what the Court has called nonpublic property they are not constitutionally protected.

What is **freedom of association**?

The constitutional guarantee of freedom of association is enveloped in the right to assemble and petition, meaning that a person has the right to freely associate with others to promote political or social issues. Although it is not explicitly referred to in the Constitution, the Supreme Court deemed freedom of association one of the guarantees of free expression in its 1958 ruling *National Association for the Advancement of Colored People v. Alabama*, by saying, "freedom to engage in association for the advancement of beliefs and ideas is an inseparable aspect of 'liberty' assured by the due process clause of the Fourteenth Amendment which embraces freedom of speech." Freedom of association applies to state and congressional regulation of the amount of money candidates and political parties can raise and spend for their interests. Although the Court ruled that there are limits on the amount of money people may contribute to candidates, it struck down limits on the amounts people may contribute to associations created to support or oppose ballot measures. Further, the government cannot set limits on the amounts that people, including candidates, *spend* on politics—as seen with presidential candidates Ross Perot in 1992 and Steve Forbes in 1996, and New York City mayor Michael Bloomberg in 2001, all of whom used their personal fortunes to finance their political candidacies.

THE SECOND, FOURTH, FIFTH, SIXTH, AND EIGHTH AMENDMENTS: FROM THE RIGHT TO BEAR ARMS TO THE RIGHTS OF THE CRIMINALLY ACCUSED

What is the **"right to bear arms"**?

The Second Amendment was originally adopted so that Congress could not disarm a state militia, thus the Second Amendment prohibits only the national government

President Bill Clinton signs the Brady Bill, which instituted a 72-hour waiting period before the purchase of handguns, in November 1993. James Brady, the former White House press secretary who was shot and paralyzed in the 1981 assassination attempt against President Ronald Reagan and for whom the bill was named, is seated at left.

from limiting the right to carry weapons. At its heart was the preservation of the "citizen-soldier"; however, it does not guarantee a citizens' right to keep and bear arms free from government restriction. Because the Supreme Court has never found the Second Amendment to be within the meaning of the Fourteenth Amendment's due process clause, each state has the authority to limit its citizens' rights to keep and bear arms.

Is the right to bear arms **restricted** in any way?

Yes. Each state imposes its own limits on its citizens' rights to keep and bear arms. While the Brady Law imposes a 72-hour waiting period before gun purchases, many states have adopted longer waiting periods, and some states have banned so-called "Saturday night specials," inexpensive guns that can be easily concealed. States have also implemented laws that bar the possession of handguns by those under 18 years of age; require adults to use a gun-locking device or store guns in a place that is not accessible to minors; and require permits to purchase and carry firearms, firearm registration, and licensing by owners. Permit, registration, and licensing laws break down the types of guns these laws apply to—for example, rifles and shotguns versus handguns. California, a gun control–conscious state, enacted a one-handgun-per-month law and a stricter assault weapons ban. Maryland, which limits the carrying of concealed weapons, has a one-handgun-per-month law and a strong juvenile possession law, and enforces its child access prevention law. In 1999 Connecticut adopted a groundbreaking law that gives law enforcement and the courts the authority under limited conditions to remove guns from the homes of those who are found to pose a significant threat to the community. States with more permissive gun-control laws include Kentucky, Louisiana, Maine, Montana, and Wyoming.

Why is the issue of **gun control** so controversial?

As violence and murder rates escalated in America throughout the 1980s and 1990s, the issue of gun control enjoyed much heated debate. After the attempted assassination of President Ronald Reagan in 1981, gun-control legislation was on the forefront of Congress's agenda, but it wouldn't be until 1994—with the passage of the Brady Handgun Violence Prevention Act, or Brady Law, which mandates a 72-hour waiting period on the purchase of handguns, and the Violent Crime Control and Law Enforcement Act, which bans the manufacture, sale, or possession of nineteen kinds of semiautomatic assault weapons—that any substantial gun-control laws would take effect. In opposition to these laws stand the National Rifle Association (NRA) and other groups that maintain that the Second Amendment forbids the federal government from obstructing the right to bear arms and that laws that attempt to do so are therefore unconstitutional.

A central question in the gun control debate is whether or not there is an *individual* right to keep and bear arms under the Second Amendment, or whether the amendment guarantees only the right of individual states to have their own militias, making it a community right. Groups like the NRA view the Second Amendment as recognizing a right to be armed for individual as well as community protection, and the right of the states to have militias. These groups also maintain that regulation should stay where it belongs, in the hands of the states. Because the Supreme Court has ruled on only a handful of cases regarding the Second Amendment, and because the wording of the Second Amendment is vague and subject to interpretation, it is unlikely that the gun control debate will be settled anytime soon.

What does the **Fifth Amendment** allow for?

The Fifth Amendment covers a lot of ground. According to this amendment, a capital crime is punishable by death, while an infamous (serious) crime is punishable by death or imprisonment. This amendment guarantees that no one has to stand trial for such a federal crime unless indicted by a grand jury. Further, a person cannot be put in double jeopardy, or tried twice, for the same offense by the same government. The amendment also guarantees that a person cannot be forced to testify against him- or herself, and forbids the government from taking a person's property for public use without fair payment. Finally, this amendment deals with the "due process of law," for which is it is probably best known.

What does **"due process of law"** mean?

The statement that no person shall "be deprived of life, liberty, or property without due process of law" expresses one of the most important tenets of the Constitution. These words of the Fifth Amendment uphold the idea that a person's life, liberty, and property are not subject to the uncontrolled power of the government, but rather can be limited only through a due course of legal action. This concept has its roots in the Magna Carta, a thirteenth-century British charter that provided that the king could not imprison or harm a person "except by the lawful judgment of his peers or by the law of the land." The Fourth, Fifth, Sixth, and Eighth Amendments provide a number of procedural guarantees for those accused of crimes, and those guarantees are often called *due process rights*. Language found in the Fifth Amendment is repeated in the Fourteenth Amendment as restrictions on the power of the states.

However, due process is a vague clause, and the Supreme Court has applied it to widely different cases. Until the mid-1900s, the court used the due process clause to strike down laws that prevented people from using their property as they wished; for instance, in *Dred Scott v. Sandford* (1857), the Court overturned the Missouri Compromise, which regulated the extention of slavery in the U.S. territories. The Court upheld that the compromise unjustly prevented slave owners from taking slaves—their property—into the territories. Today, the courts use the due process rule to strike down laws that interfere with a person's civil liberties.

How do the **Fourth, Fifth, Sixth, and Eighth Amendments** provide for due process of law?

Taken together, these amendments provide for due process of law by protecting those accused of a crime. The Fourth Amendment says that federal law enforcement officials may not arrest people or search their homes without a search warrant that describes the location to be searched and/or the items to be removed. The Fifth Amendment safeguards the rights of people accused of those crimes that may result in the death penalty. The Sixth Amendment guarantees those who are arrested a speedy, public trial by jury. And the Eighth Amendment prohibits courts from setting excessive bail and fines and forbids cruel and unusual punishment.

What is a **writ of habeas corpus**?

From the Latin *habeas corpus*, meaning "you should have the body," a writ of habeas corpus, also referred to as a writ of liberty, was written into Article I, Section 9 of the Constitution to prevent unjust arrests and imprisonments. As a court order that is directed to an officer holding a prisoner, it mandates that the prisoner be brought before the court and that the officer show cause why the prisoner should not be released. The writ challenges only whether a prisoner has been accorded due process of law, not whether he or she is guilty or innocent. Today the most common usage of the writ is to appeal state criminal convictions to the federal courts in cases where the petitioner believes his or her constitutional rights were violated by state judicial procedure.

Because the colonists regarded this writ as fundamental to their rights and the wrongful refusal to issue it was one of their grievances leading up to the American Revolution, the framers of the Constitution provided that "the privilege of the Writ of Habeas Corpus shall not be suspended, unless when, in cases of rebellion or invasion, the public safety may require it." Although President Lincoln suspended habeas corpus at the beginning of the Civil War, since that time the writ has only been suspended once (in Hawaii during World War II), and the Supreme Court ruled that action illegal, based on its decision in 1866 that neither Congress nor the president can legally suspend the writ where there is no actual fighting. While the Supreme Court's liberal decisions regarding prisoners' rights in the 1950s and 1960s encouraged many inmates to file writs challenging their convictions, the late twentieth century witnessed the Court refusing to allow multiple habeas corpus filings, primarily from death row.

What is the takings clause and how does it relate to eminent domain?

The takings clause of the Fifth Amendment states that private property cannot be taken by the government for public use without just compensation to the property owner. The drafters of the Bill of Rights included a takings clause to address outright physical appropriations of private property, such as government expropriation of private land for the paving of roads, since colonial governments often confiscated private property for public projects without paying (or justly paying) its owners. Today the government uses its right of eminent domain to acquire land for highways, schools, and other public facilities, but constitutionally it must always pay a "fair" price for its acquisition.

What are the **rights of an accused criminal** from the time of arrest until the time of trial?

Until the time that suspects are proved guilty of crimes, they are constitutionally allowed full respect for their individual rights. The Fourth Amendment safeguards against illegal search and seizure, and illegally collected evidence cannot be introduced in court. In most cases, law enforcement officers must have a court-ordered search warrant obtained with probable cause before searching property, and arrests cannot be made without probable cause. The Fifth Amendment provides that no person in a criminal case is compelled to be a witness against him- or herself. As a result, police are required to advise a suspect of his or her right to remain silent and the right to have an attorney present during any questioning. Further, no one may be tried twice for the same crime. The Sixth Amendment allows for the right to a speedy and public trial by an impartial jury of one's peers and the right to counsel; the Eighth Amendment puts a limit on the amount of bail imposed and guards against cruel and unusual punishment. In totality, the rights outlined in the Bill of Rights are meant to place the burden of proof on the government, rather than on the accused, who is presumed innocent until proven guilty.

What is the **right to remain silent**?

Because certain seventeenth-century English courts forced confessions of heresy from religious dissenters, the framers of the Bill of Rights were careful to include in the Fifth Amendment the provision that a person has the right to remain silent, and shall not be compelled to testify against him- or herself in a criminal prosecution. Although the provision for self-incrimination applies to criminal prosecutions, it has also been interpreted to protect anyone questioned by a government agency, including a congressional committee.

What does it mean to **"mirandize"** someone?

In *Miranda v. Arizona* (1966), the Supreme Court declared that no federal or state conviction could stand in court if evidence introduced at the trial had been obtained by the police during interrogation *unless* the suspects have been (1) notified that they are free to remain silent; (2) told that what they say may be used against them in court; (3) told that they have the right to have attorneys present at the time of questioning; (4) told that attorneys will be provided for them in the event that they cannot afford to hire their own attorneys; and (5) allowed to terminate any stage of a police interrogation. Known as the *Miranda* warning, this announcement is read to a suspect by a police officer before questioning him or her. If the police officer fails to read a suspect his or her *Miranda* rights, charges against the suspect can be dropped and convictions reversed, even if there is enough evidence to establish the suspect's guilt. If a suspect answers questions without an attorney present, then the burden of proof is on the prosecution to demonstrate that the suspect knowingly and willingly gave up his or her right to remain silent and have an attorney present.

Where did the phrase **"I'll take the Fifth"** come from?

The phrase comes from the Fifth Amendment's provision that a person cannot be forced to testify against him- or herself. Made familiar to the public through motion-picture screenplays and Court TV, "I'll take the Fifth" has often been cited as a catchall phrase used by defendants on trial to avoid answering questions that might incriminate them. Recently, Kenneth Lay, former chairman and CEO of Enron Corporation, exercised this right when he refused to testify in a Senate hearing regarding investigations into the company's wrongdoings.

What does the term **"double jeopardy"** mean?

According to the Fifth Amendment, double jeopardy means that a person cannot be tried twice for the same crime by the same government. However, he or she may be tried a second time if a jury cannot agree on a verdict, if a mistrial is declared for some other reason, or if he or she requests a new trial.

What is a speedy and public trial?

According to the Sixth Amendment, a person accused of crime must have a prompt, public trial by an open-minded jury. The requirement for a speedy and public trial grew out of the fact that some political trials in England had been delayed for years and then were held in secret. Accused individuals must be informed of the charges against them and must be allowed to meet the witnesses against them face to face. Otherwise, innocent persons may be punished if a court allows the testimony of unknown witnesses to be used as evidence. Further, the Sixth Amendment guarantees that individuals on trial can face and cross-examine those who have accused them. Finally, accused persons must have a lawyer to defend them if they want one. If a criminal defendant is unable to afford a lawyer, the Supreme Court has held that one must be appointed by the government to represent the accused individual.

What is the **right to counsel**?

The Supreme Court decision *Gideon v. Wainwright* (1963) established that all persons accused of serious crimes are constitutionally entitled to legal representation per the Sixth Amendment, and that if the accused cannot afford to hire an attorney the court must assign one. This is known as a person's right to counsel. Most states have established an office of the public defender, an attorney who is responsible for providing the defense of impoverished criminal suspects.

What is an **indictment**?

An indictment refers to a formal complaint that is presented before a grand jury by the prosecutor charging an accused person with one or more crimes.

What is the role of the **grand jury**?

The grand jury determines whether a person can be tried for a crime. Guaranteed by the Fifth Amendment, the right to a grand jury is meant to protect the accused from unjust prosecutors. In federal cases, the grand jury consists of between 16 and 23 people drawn from the area of the federal district court that it serves. When an indictment comes before the grand jury, at least 12 jurors must agree that there is enough evidence to return an indictment and allow for the case to be heard in court. If the grand jury determines that there is enough evidence to warrant a trial, the accused is then held for prosecution. If there is not enough evidence to warrant a trial, then the charge(s) is dropped. Because the grand jury's proceedings are not a trial, their sessions are not publicized, and only the prosecution is present.

What is **trial by jury**?

The framers of the Constitution considered the right to jury trial so important that in the Sixth Amendment they provided for jury trials in criminal cases. In the Seventh Amendment, they provided for such trials in civil suits where the amount contested exceeds $20. The amendment applies only to federal courts, but most state constitutions also call for jury trials in civil cases. Not all criminal prosecutions require a jury trial, and the Supreme Court has consistently excluded "petty offenses," so called because of their punishment or the nature of the offense, from the right to a trial by jury. In both state and federal courts, an accused person may waive the right to a trial by jury in exchange for a bench trial before a judge.

What are **bills of attainder**?

A bill of attainder refers to a legislative act that targets an individual or group for punishment without a trial. According to Article I, Sections 9 and 10 of the Constitution, neither Congress nor the states can pass such laws. While they can pass laws that define crime and set appropriate penalties, it is unconstitutional for them to decide whether or not a person is guilty of that crime and then impose punishment for that crime.

What are **ex post facto laws**?

From the Latin phrase *ex post facto*, meaning "after the fact," ex post facto laws are those laws that define a crime or provide for its punishment that are then applied to an act committed before the law was passed, and clearly work to the disadvantage of those accused. For example, a law making it a crime to sell narcotics cannot be applied to a person who sold narcotics before the law was passed. According to the Constitution, these laws may not be enacted by either Congress or the states. However, ex post facto laws only apply to criminal law; retroactive civil laws, on the other hand, are not unconstitutional.

What factors have led to **increased public cynicism about jury trials**?

Although it's hard to cite all the factors that have led to increased public cynicism about jury trials, many commentators have noted that the sensational newspaper and television coverage of trials of the 1990s, coupled with questionable convictions or acquittals for what appear to be obvious crimes, has lead the public to be cynical about the jury process overall. Trials criticized for what some perceive as blatant injustice include the 1992 acquittal of Los Angeles police officers after the extended beating, captured on videotape, of Rodney King; the 1990s trials of Lyle and Eric Menendez, who confessed to killing their parents but whose first trials resulted in "hung juries" that could not come to a consensus about the exact nature of their crime; and the highly debated 1995 acquittal of O. J. Simpson at his criminal trial for the murder of his ex-wife, Nicole Brown Simpson, and Ronald Goldman. Although questions of racial equality and justice were paramount in the Simpson debate, many also criticized jury trial procedures and called for their overhaul.

What is a **plea bargain** and how does it relate to the **"three strikes"** law?

In an effort to speed up the criminal justice process, defenders and prosecutors have established the plea bargain, which is referred to as an agreement between the prosecution and defense that the accused person will admit a plea of guilty to a crime, provided that other charges are dropped and a reduced sentence is recommended to the judge. While the Supreme Court has approved of plea bargaining in general, extensive use of this tactic has been an issue with many politicians who mandate that those convicted should serve longer sentences. In response, they proposed the "three strikes" law (adapted from the baseball phrase "three strikes and you're out"), which says that after having been convicted of three felonies, a convict must receive a mandatory life sentence, whether or not a plea bargain has been struck. The three-strikes concept came to the forefront of national attention in 1994 when California voters approved the law, which also doubles minimum terms for second-time offenders, and Congress passed its federal version. Between 1993 and 1995, 25 other states besides California adopted three-strikes statutes.

How does the **Eighth Amendment** relate to **capital punishment**?

The Eighth Amendment states, "Excessive bail shall not be required, nor excessive fines imposed, nor cruel and unusual punishments inflicted." Simply put, bails, fines, and punishments must be fair and humane. In the case of *Furman v. Georgia* (1972), the Supreme Court ruled that capital punishment, as it was then imposed, violated this amendment. Because it was deemed "arbitrary and capricious," and not applied fairly and uniformly across the states, the Court held that the death penalty was "cruel and unusual punishment" in violation of the Eighth Amendment and the due process guarantees of the Fourteenth Amendment. After that decision, many states adopted new capital punishment laws designed to meet the Supreme Court's objections. The Court has since ruled that the death penalty may be imposed if certain standards are applied to guard against arbitrary results in capital cases.

How many states have the **death penalty**?

While more than 100 countries have abolished the death penalty, over the twentieth century the United States increased its rate of executions and the number of crimes

Although the Supreme Court has ruled the death penalty, when administered according to specific standards, is not in violation of the Eighth Amendment guarantee against cruel and unusual punishment, it remains the target of protest and controversy.

punishable by death. Currently, 38 states exercise the death penalty, and 24 of them allow capital punishment for crimes committed by the prosecuted when they were children. Twelve states have no death penalty. According to the U.S. Department of Justice, in 2000 there were 85 executions in the United States, a decrease of 13 percent from 1999. Fourteen of the states with the death penalty used it in 2000. Texas had the most executions in 2000 (20), and Oklahoma was second with 11. Six states with the death penalty, including California, used it once in 2000. Of the 85 persons executed, 51 percent were white, 40 percent black, and 9 percent Latino or Native American.

Which **crimes** has capital punishment been used for?

Under the federal system of the United States, most serious crimes such as murder are tried by individual states, not by the federal government. However, the U.S. government and the U.S. military have also employed capital punishment for certain federal offenses, primarily murder or crimes resulting in murder. However, since the federal death penalty was first used on June 25, 1790, convictions for piracy, rape, rioting, kidnapping, and spying and espionage have resulted in federal executions. The states reserve the penalty for the most brutal crimes, which are not subject to review by the president, although they can be appealed to the U.S. Supreme Court. Although the states can seek the death penalty for several different serious crimes, such as terrorism, in practice it is only used in cases of first-degree murder.

Do Americans **support the death penalty**?

A February 2000 Gallup Poll found that 66 percent of Americans support the death penalty, a decline of 14 percent from 1994. However, while most Americans favor the death penalty many have expressed reservations about whether all prisoners on death row have received fair trials. In January 2000 the governor of Illinois, George Ryan, declared a moratorium on further executions in that state in an effort to study why there had been a high number of errors found in recent death-penalty cases, and to ensure that no innocent person would face the death penalty. And in 2002, the Supre-meme Court ruled that the execution of mentally retarded criminals was unconstitutional, thus limiting the scope of capital punishment.

THE RIGHT TO PRIVACY

What is the **"right to privacy"**?

The right of privacy is generally referred to as a person's right to be free of government interference in those area's of one's personal life that do not affect other citizens. The Supreme Court justice Louis Brandeis defined it as "the right to be let alone." Although the word "privacy" doesn't appear in either the Constitution or the Bill of Rights, nor is it directly addressed in the Federalist Papers, the Ninth Amendment allows for this right by stating, "The enumeration in the Constitution, of certain rights, shall not be construed to deny or disparage others retained by the people." In other words, there are some rights that people may retain even though they are not spelled out specifically in the Constitution, and the Supreme Court has held that the right of privacy is one such right.

How is the **right to privacy** enveloped in the First, Third, Fourth, Fifth, and Ninth Amendments?

Although not explicitly mentioned in the Bill of Rights, the Supreme Court has found defense for a right to privacy in the First, Third, Fourth, Fifth, and Ninth Amendments. Since the late 1950s, the Supreme Court has upheld a series of privacy interests under the First Amendment and due process clause, for example, "associational privacy," "political privacy," and the "right to anonymity in public expression." However, many constitutional scholars acknowledge that it wasn't until the Supreme Court case *Griswold v. Connecticut* (1965), when a statute prohibiting the use of contraceptives was struck down as an infringement of the right of marital privacy, that privacy was defined by the Court. In this landmark case the Court defined a "zone of privacy" to be embedded in the Constitution. There, the Court maintained that the First Amendment's right of association, the Third Amendment's prohibition against quartering soldiers in citizens' homes, the Fourth Amendment's protection against illegal searches and seizures, the Fifth Amendment's protection against self-incrimination, and the Ninth Amendment's guarantee that individuals are entitled to rights not specifically defined in the Constitution, in combination, create the "penumbra" of a right to privacy.

How are the **right to privacy** and the **right to an abortion** tied?

Although the Supreme Court has not been specific with regard to the range of sexual acts covered under one's right to privacy, in *Roe v. Wade* (1973) it ruled that the right to privacy includes a woman's right to have a safe and legal abortion. The court argued that the right of privacy was "founded in the Fourteenth Amendment's concept of personal liberty and restrictions on State action." This landmark decision spurred the "right to life," or "pro-life," movement, which upholds that human life begins at conception and thus abortion is comparable to infanticide, and its "pro-choice" counterpart, which maintains that a woman's right to choose how to use her own body is intrinsically connected to her constitutional right of privacy. Although the Supreme Court has reacted to these two groups and various political pressures by declaring certain restrictions on abortion as constitutional and severely limiting Roe's scope since the early 1970s, it has yet to overturn the decision completely. As late as 2001, the Supreme Court upheld its position on privacy and abortion, ruling that states could not ban what is commonly referred to as partial-birth abortion. The access to a safe and legal abortion is still fundamentally a privacy issue and constitutionally guaranteed, although many scholars agree the Court no longer gives abortion the same measure of constitutional scrutiny it once did. Indeed, over the years the composition of the Supreme Court, the partisan composition of Congress, and the views of the president (in terms of legislation he will support or justices he will nominate) have all played a role in the evolving abortion issue.

How are **sexual orientation rights** and the **right to privacy** related?

Sexual relations between members of the same sex has been deemed constitutional under the banner of the right to privacy since the Supreme Court overturned Georgia's sodomy law in 1998. A little more than a decade earlier, however, the Court had ruled in *Bowers v. Hardwick* (1986) that Georgia's antisodomy law was constitutional in that privacy rights did not extend to homosexual couples. Since that time, state courts—including those in Louisiana and Maryland—have overturned antisodomy laws because they interfere with the right to privacy; today 13 states have antisodomy laws, and only three of the homosexual-specific statutes still stand. For that same reason, the Vermont legislature ruled to legalize civil unions between same-sex couples (colloquially referred to as "gay marriage") in April 2000, and voted to provide comprehensive legal status to lesbian and gay couples, allowing them to share all the protections and benefits of marriage under state law. However, partly because of the 1996 Defense of Marriage Act and overwhelming public opinion—a January 2000 Gallup poll found that 62 percent of Americans believe marriages between homosexuals should not be recognized by the law—other states have been slow to legalize civil unions between same-sex couples. Proponents of gay marriage include the American Civil Liberties Union, which argues that keeping gay marriage illegal violates the due process clause of the Fifth Amendment, in that it discriminates on the basis of sex because it makes one's ability to marry depend on one's gender. Further, numerous activist groups maintain that gay marriage embodies civil liberties issues, in that the legal union allows for basic marriage rights afforded same-sex couples, including tax exemptions, Social Security benefits, inheritance rights, and property rights.

Do **random drug tests for students** violate their right to privacy?

The move toward drug testing comes in an era of school safety crackdown that many say has restricted student freedom and infringed upon their civil liberties. In the 1995 Supreme Court ruling *Vernonia School District v. Acton*, the Supreme Court upheld random drug testing of student athletes and ruled that it does not violate the student athletes' right to privacy primarily because they are subject to more regulations than other students and thus cannot be guaranteed the same level of privacy. Hundreds of school districts responded by adopting drug testing policies, but several state courts struck down broader programs that test nonathletes, based on their invasion of the students' right to privacy. In March 2001, for example, a federal judge rejected mandatory drug testing for all seventh- through twelfth-grade students in Lockney, Texas, and state courts in Indiana, New Jersey, Oregon, and Pennsylvania have expressed similar objections to like policies. However, in June 2002, the Supreme Court extended its opinion to cover nonathletes, voting to uphold drug testing of students involved in extracurricular activities—even those not suspected of drug use. The Court reasoned that the importance of detecting and preventing drug use by "reasonable means" outweighed an individual's right to privacy.

Does **wiretapping** violate a person's **right to privacy**?

Citing the right to privacy as a basic citizen right, state laws prohibit the interception or recording of a private conversation without all those involved in the conversation first giving their permission, and federal statutes prohibit the same and similar activities. In *Olmstead v. United States* (1928) the Supreme Court ruled, "Whenever a telephone line is tapped, the privacy of the persons at both ends of the line is invaded, and all conversations between them upon any subject, and although proper, confidential, and privileged, may be overheard." However, special monitoring of communications between citizens are granted to the federal government, which exercised increased wiretapping and other forms of electronic surveillance at the hands of the FBI during the Clinton administration. In an effort to aid the Federal Bureau of Investigation (FBI) in doing its job, Congress passed the controversial 1994 Communications Assistance for Law Enforcement Act (CALEA), which requires the telecommunications industry to design its systems in compliance with FBI technical requirements to facilitate electronic surveillance. In addition, increased wiretapping privileges were granted to the federal government under President George W. Bush's antiterrorism legislation. However, many civil libertarians are concerned with the far-reaching surveillance rights the FBI has been granted, and have asked Congress to remedy this situation by adopting legislation that would uphold the Fourth Amendment's protection against unwarranted searches and maintain a citizen's right to privacy.

How has the **right to privacy** been compromised in the Information Age?

Many civil libertarians purport that an individual's right to privacy has been compromised in this Age of Information, where technology makes it easier to access a person's private information—from web sites that allow customers to uncover information about people's financial profiles to the government-sponsored global communications system "Echelon," which many say monitors worldwide satellite, microwave, cellular, and fiber-optic communications for suspicious or "antigovernment" language. While the benefits of an electronic age provide for higher productivity and sheer convenience, advances in technology make it possible to collect, store, analyze, and retrieve information in ways that were previously impossible—and that are clear infringements on a person's right to privacy. Both Intel and Microsoft have been criticized for creating software that transmits unique identification numbers whenever a personal computer user logs on to the Internet. One company, Acxiom Corporation in Conway, Arkansas, has a database combining public and consumer information for more than 95 percent of American households. A 1997 survey by the American Management Association revealed that nearly two-thirds of large companies admitted to some form of electronic surveillance of their workers. In fact, a May 1999 issue of the *Economist* asks, "The power to gather and disseminate data electronically is growing so fast that it raises an even more unsettling question: in 20 years' time, will there be any privacy left to protect?"

Does the **implantation of ID chips** infringe upon the right to privacy?

Developers of an identification chip implanted in the skin of Alzheimer's patients claim their chip will make health professionals' and patients' lives easier. However, this ground-breaking act—implanting a microchip that emits an identification number inside the human body, much like a human barcode—has civil libertarians and other concerned citizens objecting on grounds of privacy. By scanning the radio-frequency identification (RFID) chip, medical personnel can access a wealth of information at their fingertips—a person's name, address, and medical profile. The maker of the VeriChip is only just beginning to develop more sophisticated chips, among them one that is able to receive satellite signals that transmit a person's location. Although the process is voluntary, critics say the precedent lays groundwork for others getting implanted, possibly involuntarily, including entire groups of people, such as prisoners, teenagers, or aging parents. Along with national identification cards and citizen-tracking databases, ID chips represent one of the most substantial threats that technology proposes to individual liberties.

CIVIL RIGHTS AND AFFIRMATIVE ACTION

How did the post–World War II era bring about **greater civil rights for African Americans**?

The postwar era marked a period of unprecedented energy against discrimination experienced by African Americans in many parts of the United States. Resistance to racial segregation and discrimination came through strategies such as civil disobedience, nonviolent resistance, marches, protests, and boycotts—all of which received national attention as the media documented the struggle to end racial inequality—and court cases that heard the pleas of African Americans legally challenging segregation. Both Supreme Court decisions and legislation—specifically the *Brown v. Board of Education of Topeka* decision in 1954, the Civil Rights Act of 1964, and the Voting Rights Act of 1965—helped bring about greater civil rights for African Americans. While civil libertarians agree there is more to achieve in ending discrimination, major milestones in civil rights laws were passed to ensure African Americans' basic civil liberties, including regulating equal access to public accommodations, establishing equal justice before the law, and mandating equal employment, education, and housing opportunities. The black struggle for civil rights also inspired rights movements for other disenfranchised groups who recognized their interests were not being held up by law, including those of Native Americans, Latinos, and women.

What is **affirmative action**?

Although the Civil Rights Act of 1964 is probably the most important piece of legislation outlawing discrimination in Americans' lives by establishing that discriminatory

Dr. Martin Luther King (center, right arm raised) leads the March on Washington in August 1963, one of the landmark events in the civil rights movement.

practices based on race, color, national origin, or sex are illegal, discriminatory practices still occur. In response to this, in 1965 the federal government adopted a policy of affirmative action, which requires that employers take positive steps to remedy the effects of past discrimination by having a multiethnic workforce. Affirmative action programs vary is scope, ranging from targeting advertising and recruitment techniques to factoring a person's race or sex into hiring or admissions decisions. The most aggressive form of affirmative action involves establishing a quota, or specified number of positions, for members of minority groups. Affirmative action applies to all federal government agencies, the states, and all private employers who sell goods or services to the federal government.

How does **affirmative action** relate to the politics of **civil rights**, and why has it come under scrutiny?

Because affirmative action programs involve race- and sex-based criteria, critics of the policy uphold that these programs are unconstitutional, in effect, guaranteeing a kind of reverse discrimination against the majority because of female and nonwhite preference. The landmark *Regents of the University of California v. Bakke* (1978) set the standard for reverse discrimination by maintaining that the decision to deny a white medical student admission to the university's medical school because the school had set aside a number of admissions for nonwhite students was unconstitutional and violated the Fourteenth Amendment's equal protection clause. In the 1980s and 1990s, however, the Supreme Court made it more difficult for those charging discrimination to win their cases.

One recent affirmative action case, *Adarand Constructors v. Pena* (1995), marks a major departure from the Court's previous rulings. In that case, the Court held that whenever the government provides any preferential treatment based on race or sex that it is in almost all cases unconstitutional, even when the result is intended to have a beneficial effect, such as righting past wrongs for minority groups. That same year the University of California Board of Regents voted to end its affirmative action policies, a decision that was followed by the passage of Proposition 209, in which the state of California added an amendment to its constitution that bans affirmative action. Voters in Washington State passed a similar measure, and in 1997 a federal court ordered Texas to drop its affirmative action policy from its state university admissions requirements. Both 2000 presidential candidates George W. Bush and Al Gore expressed their opposition to affirmative action, reflecting a trend of national ambivalence toward this policy.

How have **Latinos, Asian Americans, and Native Americans** fought for civil rights?

Many efforts by disenfranchised and minority groups to achieve civil rights parallel African American efforts. Neither the 1964 or 1965 civil rights legislation identified any ethnic groups other than African Americans as deserving affirmative action, however because the civil rights movement stirred the issue of equal protection under the Constitution other ethnic groups have made similar civil rights claims, and Congress has given them the recognition they lobbied for through voting rights legislation. Since the 1960s, Latinos, Asian Americans, and Native Americans have all had various successes in receiving recognition under the law, depending upon how effectively each group has been able to mobilize its members in elections. Latinos have been very active in this area; for example, George P. Bush, whose mother is of Mexican descent, campaigned for his uncle George W. Bush during the 2000 presidential primaries in order to help secure the Latino vote for Bush.

Latinos have become increasingly active in securing their civil rights, primarily through groups such as the Mexican American Legal Defense and Education Fund (MALDEF), which has focused on voting and immigration issues. MALDEF argued that English-language ballots and voter registration materials discriminated against Latinos, to which Congress responded in 1982 by requiring that these materials be printed in the language of any minority group that constitutes more than 5 percent of a county's population, in effect protecting not only Latinos from discrimination but Asian Americans and Native Americans as well. In 1994 the Latino community rallied to the opposition of California's Proposition 187, which if passed would have denied illegal aliens state and local public services. Although Asian Americans are only beginning to rally in national electoral politics, their biggest victory came in the area of civil rights, where they mandated that compensation be paid to Japanese Americans who were relocated by the U.S. government to internment camps during World War II.

In contrast to these two ethnic groups, Native Americans' rights and liberties are not protected under the Bill of Rights—since at the time of its writing Native Americans were considered members of a foreign nation—but rather under Congressional laws and treaties signed between United States and American Indian tribes. However, despite this exclusion, members of these tribes have been granted special rights, such as the right of Pacific Northwest tribes to fish for salmon, and through congressional legislation have been guaranteed the civil liberties applicable to other groups under the Bill of Rights. Recent tribal rights recognized in the late twentieth century include the right to provide commercial gambling on tribal property and tribal religious freedom, provided for by the 1978 American Indian Religious Freedom Resolution.

POLITICAL BEHAVIOR AND POLICY

PARTIES, CAMPAIGNS, AND ELECTIONS

POLITICAL PARTIES

What is a **political party**?

A political party is a group of people, made up of political office holders and candidates, activists, and voters, who identify with a group name and platform and seek to elect to office those who share their identity. Although party members are diverse and not always of one mind, a party shares in the common goal of coming together to get its candidates elected to office.

What are the **major responsibilities of political parties**?

While political parties perform a variety of functions, they are mainly involved in nominations and elections. Their major responsibilities include: recruiting candidates for local, state, and national office; nominating candidates through caucuses, conventions, and primary elections; "getting out the vote" for their candidates and providing voters with information about candidates and their parties; and facilitating mass electoral choice—that is, helping voters recognize their options and encouraging electoral competition. In addition, they influence the institutions of national government and the policy-making process. For example, Congress is organized around the two-party system, and the Speaker of the House position is a party office. Parties determine the makeup of congressional committees, including those who chair the committees, whose positions are no longer based solely on seniority.

How are **political parties organized**?

Political parties are organized on national, state, and local levels. At the national level, the national committee is directly in charge of the national party; for example, the

Democratic National Committee and the Republican National Committee are the two committees that run the Democratic and Republican Parties, respectively. The national party chair is the committee's top official, formally elected by the national committee but at the selection of the presidential candidate. Chairs play a major role in running the national campaign and planning the presidential nominating convention, and after the election serve as a liaison between the party and the White House. As the primary spokesperson for the committee, the chair tries to manage party factionalism, negotiate disputes between candidates, raise money, and prepare for the next presidential election. The national committee usually elects a new chair after every electoral defeat. While winning the White House is the major goal of the national party committee, winning congressional elections is the goal of the congressional and senatorial campaign committees, which are composed of senators and representatives chosen for two-year terms by their fellow party members in the Senate and House. Their party leadership appoints the chairs of these committees.

Parties at the state and local levels are organized much like they are at national level, although state law determines how committees are structured and run. Each state committee is headed by a chair who is normally elected by the committee, although approximately 25 percent of state chairs are chosen at state conventions. Members of the state committees are usually elected from local areas, and are usually dominated by governors, senators, or a coalition of local business leaders. Today's trend is toward stronger state organizations, most of which run independently of the national party. Republicans are typically better funded than other parties at the state level. Below state committees are county committees, which vary widely in scope. Their key job is to recruit candidates for offices such as county commissioner, sheriff, and treasurer, but they perform a variety of other functions as well—distributing campaign literature, organizing telephone campaigns, distributing posters and lawn signs for their candidates, and soliciting door-to-door. Party committees also appear at the city, town, and village level.

What is **electoral realignment**?

In the United States, party politics have taken an interesting course of control, generally referred to by political scientists as "electoral realignment." Typically, one party has dominated the national electoral arena for a period of approximately 30 years, after which a new party supplants the dominant party. This electoral realignment is usually followed by a long period in which the new party is the dominant political force, not necessarily winning every election but maintaining control of the Congress and the White House. At least five such realignments have taken place since the founding of the American Republic: (1) in 1800, when the Jeffersonian Republicans defeated the Federalists, thus becoming American politics' dominant force; (2) in 1828, when the Jacksonian Democrats gained control of both the White House and Congress; (3) in 1860, when Abraham Lincoln's newly founded Republican Party usurped the Whig Party, which had formerly been one of the country's major parties; (4) in 1896, when the Republicans gained control of the national government; and (5) between 1932 and 1936, when Franklin D. Roosevelt's Democratic Party took control of the White House and Congress, where the party remained dominant through the 1960s. Since the 1960s, party politics in the United States have been primarily characterized by the term "divided government."

What is the concept of **divided government**?

A divided government refers to a government in which the president is a member of one political party and at least one chamber of Congress, either the Senate or the House of Representatives, is controlled by the opposite party. While this term is generally applied to the federal government, it can also be applied at the state level, when one party controls the governor's office and another controls the state legislature. Divided government is a frequent historical occurrence, meant to dissuade radical changes in policy and to motivate politicians of both parties to compromise on proposed legislation. In the post–World War II era, 17 of 28 national elections produced a divided government, and rarely has the United States seen administrations where the White House and Congress were aligned with the same party. Divided government has also increased at the state level in the postwar era.

Is the **administration of George W. Bush a divided government**?

As of November 2002, yes. George W. Bush and his vice president, Dick Cheney, are Republicans, while the Senate is in the control of the Democrats. This occurred when Senator James Jeffords of Vermont announced his switch from Republican to Independent status, effective June 6, 2001. Jeffords announced that he would caucus with the Democrats, changing control of the evenly divided Senate from the Republicans to the Democrats. The House of Representatives is Republican-controlled.

How do the **differences between liberals and conservatives** affect Congress and policymaking?

Divided government influences which issues are on the congressional agenda as well as the outcome of proposed legislation. To the extent that the president and members of the majority party in Congress promote some issues instead of others, more issues arise when control of government is divided rather than unified, often leading to a high level of partisan conflict and the stunting of proposed legislation. For example, throughout most of the 1990s, divided party control of the government caused incessant conflict between President Bill Clinton, a Democrat, and the Republican-controlled Congress. Both the congressional Republicans and Democrats exhibited sharp policy variations and an unusually high level of unity within their individual parties. This atmosphere is contrasted with that of a unified government: when the president's party controls both houses of Congress, it is likely to introduce, consider, and pass bills that are on the president's agenda.

Louisiana governor and senator Huey "Kingfish" Long (1893–1935) was the head of a political machine that dominated Louisiana politics in the 1920s and 1930s.

What are **political machines**?

Throughout history political parties have sometimes failed to maintain transparency and integrity in their pursuit of elected office. In American politics some regional or local political party organizations have been called "political machines," the "machine" being that part of the political party that operates like a well-oiled mechanism, headed by a boss, or small group of autocratic leaders, whose orders are carried out by a small group of loyal members. In some cases, the machines are simply extensions of the politician himself. In the nineteenth and early twentieth century, these machines were known for their unethical methods of sustaining their positions in elected office, including relying on bribery, patronage, control over nominations, and election rigging. The power of these political machines was greatly reduced by the introduction of primaries to select a party's candidate, as well as citizen activism that pressed to restore government accountability.

Infamous political machines include Tammany Hall, led by William "Boss" Tweed in New York City in the 1860s, which was accused of defrauding New York City of between $75 million and $200 million in an effort to control city politics. Huey "Kingfish" Long's Louisiana machine helped him obtain the governorship in 1928, after which he controlled every level of Louisiana state politics until his election to the Senate in 1930. James Michael Curley, intermittent mayor of Boston between 1914 and 1950 and governor of Massachusetts in the mid-1930s, was known for his leadership of Boston's Democratic political machine. Tom Pendergast and his Kansas City machine suggested that Harry Truman run for Senate and provided the backing of his machine in Truman's successful 1934 primary and general election races. And Mayor Richard J. Daley's Chicago political machine single-handedly ruled the city for three decades of the mid-twentieth century.

What is **partisanship**?

Partisanship refers to a person's or candidate's loyalty to a particular political party.

THE TWO-PARTY SYSTEM

What is the **"two-party system"** in American politics?

Political parties were not envisioned by America's Founding Fathers, but they gradually took hold as the electorate expanded. By the late 1820s, two political parties, the Democrats and the Whigs, dominated the U.S. political system. During the 1850s, a third political party, the Republicans, gained widespread popularity because of its opposition to slavery, and since 1852 every U.S. president has been either a Republican or a Democrat. These two parties continue to volley at the forefront of the U.S. political system, known as a "two-party system," in contrast to most of the world's other democracies, which are sustained by multiple parties.

Approximately two-thirds of Americans today consider themselves to be Republicans or Democrats. Even those citizens who maintain they are independents (not subscribing to any party) generally have partisan leanings and show high levels of partisan loyalty. On average, 75 percent of those independents who leaned either toward the Republicans or the Democrats voted for their preferred party's presidential candidate in the five presidential elections held between 1980 and 1996.

What is the **Democratic Party**?

The Democratic Party of the United States is one of the nation's two major political parties. It is represented by the Democratic National Committee (DNC), which serves as the national party organization for the Democrats. The DNC plans the party's quadrennial presidential nominating convention; promotes election of party candidates with technical and financial support; and works with national, state, and local party organizations, elected officials, candidates, and constituencies to respond to the needs and views of the Democratic electorate and the nation. Often referred to as "the party of the people," the Democratic Party has traditionally been associated with its commitment to support immigrants, blue-collar workers, women, and minorities—a reputation due in part to President Franklin D. Roosevelt and his New Deal social programs. Democrats tend to take a more liberal stand on society's issues, and believe that the federal government should take a more active role in people's lives, particularly the disenfranchised.

What is the **Republican Party**?

The Republican Party is the other major political party in the United States. It is represented by the Republican National Committee (RNC), which is the national party organization for the Republicans. The RNC functions as DNC's counterpart, and accomplishes many of the same functions. The Republican Party is also referred to as the GOP, although the acronym's meaning has changed with time. In 1875, GOP stood for the "Gallant Old Party," 1876 references called it the "Grand Old Party," and during the 1964 presidential campaign, "Go-Party" was briefly used as the meaning behind the acronym. The Republican Party tends to take a more conservative stand on issues, maintaining that the federal government should not play a major role in individuals' lives. Most Republicans favor lower taxes and less government spending on social programs, as well as less government intervention in business and the economy.

What are the **historical origins** of each party?

The Democratic Party was founded by Thomas Jefferson in 1792 as a congressional caucus to fight for the Bill of Rights and against the elitist Federalist Party. Known at the time as the Jeffersonian Republicans, in 1798 the "party of the common man" was officially named the Democratic-Republican Party and in 1800 elected Jefferson as the first Democratic president of the United States. In 1830, the name was shortened to the Democratic Party. In 1848, the party's national convention established the Democratic National Committee, now the longest-running political organization in the world, and charged it with "promoting the Democratic cause."

The Republican Party was formed in the early 1850s by antislavery activists and individuals who believed that government should grant western lands to settlers free of charge. The first official Republican meeting took place on July 6, 1854, in Jackson, Michigan, during which the name "Republican" was chosen because it alluded to equality and reminded individuals of Thomas Jefferson's Democratic-Republican Party. At the Jackson convention, the new party adopted a platform and nominated candidates for office in Michigan. In 1856, the Republicans became a national party when John C. Frémont was nominated for president. Even though they were considered a "third party" because the Democrats and Whigs constituted the two-party system at the time, it wasn't long before they usurped the Whigs. In the 1865, Abraham Lincoln became the first Republican to assume the White House.

Where do the party symbols of the **donkey and the elephant** come from?

The symbol of the Democratic Party is the donkey, while the symbol of the Republican Party is the elephant. During the midterm elections of 1874, Democrats tried to convince voters that Republican president Ulysses S. Grant would seek an unprecedented third term. Thomas Nast, a cartoonist for *Harper's Weekly*, depicted a Democratic jackass trying to scare a Republican elephant—and both symbols have stuck to this day.

What is the link between the **Civil War** and an **era of one-party domination**?

The Civil War era is closely tied to the Republicans and their strength as a party. In 1861 the fledgling Republican Party was a coalition of men who had belonged to groups as diverse as Whigs, Anti-Slavery Democrats, Free-Soilers, Know-Nothings, and Abolitionists. By the outbreak of the Civil War, these parties had melded into three basic factions—conservatives, moderates, and radicals—and it was President Abraham Lincoln's job to shape these factions into a government that could win the war without politically and economically destroying the South. The most aggressive and eventually most influential of the three was the Radical Republican faction, which vehemently opposed slavery. Although they weren't a majority within the Republican Party, the Radicals dominated the other factions because of their commitment to their cause and the steadfastness of their members—some of whom chaired key committees in Congress—coming to the forefront of such issues and legislation as the Confiscation Acts, emancipation, the enlistment of blacks in the war, the Thirteenth Amendment, and Reconstruction policies. The Union victory and the destruction of slavery did not end the Radical agenda, and with Lincoln's assassination and Andrew Johnson's succession the Radicals' domination of the Republican Party and Congress increased. These committed politicians would shape the reconstruction of the nation and continue to play an active role in politics through Johnson's presidency.

Which administrations were **Republican**, and which administrations were **Democrat**?

Presidents during most of the late nineteenth century and the early part of the twentieth century were Republicans. While the Democrats and Franklin D. Roosevelt tended to dominate American politics in the 1930s and 1940s, for 28 of the 40 years from 1952 through 1992 the White House was in Republican hands. The following presidents were Republican: Abraham Lincoln (1861–1865); Ulysses Grant (1869–1877); Rutherford Hayes (1877–1881); James Garfield (1881); Chester Arthur (1881–1885); Benjamin Harrison (1889–1893); William McKinley (1897–1901); Theodore Roosevelt

(1901–1909); William Howard Taft (1909–1913); Warren Harding (1921–1923); Calvin Coolidge (1923–1929); Herbert Hoover (1929–1933); Dwight Eisenhower (1953–1961); Richard Nixon (1969–1974); Gerald Ford (1974–1977); Ronald Reagan (1981–1989); George Bush (1989–1993); and George W. Bush (2001–).

The following presidents were Democrats: Andrew Jackson (1829–1837); Martin Van Buren (1837–1841); James Polk (1845–1849); Franklin Pierce (1853–1857); James Buchanan (1857–1861); Andrew Johnson (1865–1869); Grover Cleveland (1885–1889; 1893–1897); Woodrow Wilson (1913–1921); Franklin D. Roosevelt (1933–1945); Harry Truman (1945–1953); John F. Kennedy (1961–1963); Lyndon Johnson (1963–1969); Jimmy Carter (1977–1981); and Bill Clinton (1993–2001).

When did the **first presidential election with two dominant parties** take place?

The first election featuring two dominant parties was in 1796. Federalist John Adams was elected president and Republican Thomas Jefferson was elected vice president, prompting Congress to pass in 1804 the Twelfth Amendment, which prevented the election of a president and vice president from two different parties.

What is a liberal?

Liberal is the term given to those politicians or supporters who are "Left" of center, supporting the preservation of the existing order, favoring civil liberties, and supporting the use of public resources to promote social change in a free-market society. "Political" liberals tend to favor greater federal power to remedy social inequities, while "cultural" liberals tend to support feminist causes, homosexual rights, and similar freedoms of personal choice and behavior. Modern American political liberalism is widely perceived to support affirmative action programs; abortion rights; government social programs such as welfare, national health care, unemployment benefits, and retirement programs; strong environmental regulations; trade unions and strong regulation of business; and animal rights. Of the two main political parties, the Democrats are considered to be more liberal.

What is a **conservative**?

Conservative is the term given to those politicians or supporters whose political opinions fall to the "right" of center. Conservatism, often referred to as mainstream conservatism, has at least two important aspects: "Political" conservatives generally support free-market economic principles and low taxes, and tend to distrust federal, as opposed to state and local, government power. "Social" or "cultural" conservatives tend to stand for traditional values, such as those associated with family, church, and morality, and support governmental restrictions on personal behavior with an aim of upholding traditional values. Modern American political conservatism is widely perceived to support personal responsibility; Judeo-Christian religious and moral values; strong law enforcement and strong penalties for crimes; restraint in taxation and regulation of businesses; a strong military; and well-defended protected borders with regulated immigration. Conservatives tend to oppose gun control laws; many social programs such as welfare and national health care (although many favor the country's mandatory user-funded retirement benefits system); and policies such as affirmative action and multilingual education, which they believe can be perceived as government favoritism of minority groups. The Republican Party is most closely associated with conservatism.

What is a neoconservative?

In general, neoconservatives believe in the economic and political beliefs associated with classical liberalism of the early nineteenth century. Generally, classical liberalism maintains that unregulated free markets are the best means to allocate productive resources and distribute goods and services to society, and that government intervention in society should be minimal. The philosophy of neoconservatism, made popular in the 1990s and early twenty-first century by the writings of *Wall Street Journal* columnist Irving Kristol and *Washington Post* columnist Charles Krauthammer, among others, includes the acceptance of an unregulated market economy; the belief in limited government, particularly with regard to its intervention in public policy; a general distrust toward the welfare state; and a commitment to individualism. While the positions of neoconservatives continue to evolve, neoconservatives generally emphasize traditional values and institutions. Some hold positions consistent with New Deal liberalism, while others identify themselves with more mainstream conservatives. Many neoconservatives have been associated with the magazines *Commentary* and *The Public Interest*.

How do **libertarians** differ from **conservatives**?

In general, libertarians emphasize limited government more than conservatives and believe the sole legitimate purpose of government is the protection of property rights against force. According to Jim Kalb of Yale University, who frequently writes on the subject of conservatism, because of this underlying philosophical difference, libertarians usually consider legal restrictions on such things as immigration, drug use, and prostitution to be illegitimate violations of personal liberty. Some, but not all, libertarians hold a position that might be described as economically right (that is, antisocialist) and culturally left (opposed to "cultural repressiveness," racism, sexism, and homophobia), and tend to attribute to state intervention the survival of things the cultural Left dislikes. In addition, libertarians tend to believe in rigid individualism and absolute and universally valid human rights, while conservatives are less likely to have that commitment, tending instead to understand rights within the context of particular societies and their norms.

What is meant by George W. Bush's philosophy of **"compassionate conservatism"**?

The philosophy of George W. Bush's public policies is called "compassionate conservatism." Rather than having big government pay for all of society's ills, the philosophy suggests that social problems are better solved by the private sector, namely churches, faith-based institutions, volunteers, and civic-minded corporations. Based on the writings of key conservative thinkers, the philosophy maintains that an overreliance on government and Democratic excesses that began the 1960s created an enormous underclass excessively reliant on welfare and other social programs. Authors like Marvin Olasky, who wrote *The Tragedy of American Compassion* and *Compassionate Conservatism*, pushed for a return to a more moral way of living—"a return to a day when people helped themselves—and when neighbors helped one another" as an April 2000 article in the *Dallas Morning News* put it.

Defending his philosophy, Bush has said, "[Government] must act in the common good, and that good is not common until it is shared by those in need." Bush maintains that while the government has a responsibility to help needy Americans, government best serves the people when its programs emphasize personal responsibility and self-reliance. "Compassionate conservatism means providing vigorous and thorough support for those in need, while preserving the dignity of the individual and fostering personal responsibility." To that end, his first term in office included dedicating $8 billion to provide tax incentives for charitable giving, and to support faith-based charities and other private institutions. His Office of Faith-Based and Community Initiatives works to identify barriers to such efforts, to serve as a national clearinghouse for information, and to assist faith-based and community groups needing help with federal action. President Bush also created Centers of Faith-Based and Community Initiatives within the Departments of Education, Health and Human Services, Justice, Labor, and Housing and Urban Development.

What is a **moderate**?

In general, a moderate supports democratically authored changes that are not excessive or extreme from either conservative or liberal viewpoints, tending to take a "middle-of-the-road" stand on many issues. Moderate conservatives tend to support prudent, cautious, traditionally aligned conservative changes in society, while moderate liberals tend to support broad-minded, tolerant, traditionally aligned liberal changes in society.

Who are the **New Democrats**?

New Democrats are most closely associated with the Clinton administration and its policies. The New Democratic, or Third Way, philosophy touts three fundamental principles: the idea that government should promote equal opportunity for all while granting special privilege for none; an ethic of mutual responsibility that equally rejects the politics of entitlement and the politics of social abandonment; and a new approach to governing that empowers citizens to act for themselves. Some New Democrat ideas that have become law include national service, work-based welfare reform, charter schools, community policing, an expanded earned-income tax credit, and market incentives for environmental protection. According to the Democratic Leadership Council, which leads the movement, "The Third Way approach to economic opportunity and security stresses technological innovation, competitive enterprise, and education rather than top-down redistribution or laissez faire. On questions of values, it embraces 'tolerant traditionalism,' honoring traditional moral and family values while resisting attempts to impose them on others. It favors an enabling rather than a bureaucratic government, expanding choices for citizens, using market means to achieve public ends and encouraging civic and community institutions to play a larger role in public life."

THIRD PARTIES

Are there **other political parties**?

Yes, any political party that is not Republican or Democratic, receives a base of support, and plays a role in influencing the outcome of an election is referred to a minor party or "third party." Today's third parties include the American Independent Party, the Reform Party, the Libertarian Party, the Socialist Labor Party, the Communist Party USA, the Peace and Freedom Party, and the USA Green Party. Third parties are often formed to voice a protest vote against one or both of the major parties—for example, Theodore Roosevelt's Bull Moose Party in 1912 and George Wallace's American Independent Party in 1968.

Who were the **National Republicans**?

The National Republicans comprised the administration party during John Quincy Adams' presidency (1825–1829). Adams' supporters adopted the name National Republicans because they favored strong economic nationalism, much like the former Federalist Party. The National Republicans stood in opposition to Andrew Jackson's Democratic-Republican Party, which favored a limited national government and opposed economic aristocracy. As the National Republicans dissolved in the mid-1830s, the Whigs emerged.

Who were the **Anti-Masonics**?

Formed in New York in 1828, the Anti-Masonic Party was the first third party to appear in American national politics. It was formed primarily in response to America's

The administration of John Quincy Adams (1767–1848), above, sixth president of the United States, was dominated by the National Republican Party, which favored strong economic nationalism and opposed Andrew Jackson's Democratic-Republican Party.

suspicion of secret societies like the Masons and in reaction to what some perceived as a Masonic threat to public institutions at that time. The Anti-Masonic Party was the first party to hold a nominating convention and the first to announce a platform, nominating William Wirt of Maryland for president and Amos Ellmaker of Pennsylvania as his running mate in September 1831. However, the political effect of the first-time entrance of a third party into a United States presidential election siphoned support from presidential contender Henry Clay and helped then-President Andrew Jackson, who was a Mason, win reelection by a wide margin. Although the Anti-Masonics enjoyed some success (Vermont elected an Anti-Masonic governor, William A. Palmer), after the elections of 1836 the Anti-Masonic party declined and was eventually absorbed into the Whig Party.

Who were the **Whigs**?

The Whig Party was formed during the second quarter of the nineteenth century to oppose President Andrew Jackson and the Democratic Party. The term "Whig" came into popular parlance in 1834 and continued until the party disbanded after the presidential election of 1856. The anti-Jackson group drew upon the political history of two revolutions—the American Revolution and seventeenth-century English Glorious Revolution, for its name; during the latter, the opposition to the king had called themselves Whigs. The party's leading figures, Henry Clay of Kentucky and Daniel Webster of Massachusetts, supported a nationalistic economic policy called the "American System," which entailed a program of tariff protection, federally sponsored communication projects (internal improvements), continuation of the national bank, and a conservative public land sales policy, the essence of which harkened back to Alexander Hamilton's Federalist economic policy of 1791. Although they enjoyed some successes, ultimately they were hindered by the rising power of the Jacksonians, who were thereafter called Democrats.

Who were the Know-Nothings?

The Know-Nothing Party, more formally known as the American Party, was founded in New York City in 1849. It was organized to oppose the large influx of immigrants who entered the United States after 1846. Because Know-Nothings believed that these primarily Irish and Roman Catholic immigrants threatened to destroy America, the party strove to use government power to uphold their vision of an Anglo-Saxon Protestant society. Their platform outlined a limited immigration policy, proposed that only native-born Americans could hold public office, and advocated a 21-year mandatory waiting period for immigrants before they were granted citizenship and voting rights. They also sought to limit the sale of liquor, restrict public-school teaching to Protestants, and allow only the Protestant version of the Bible to be read daily in classrooms. Despite their strength and appeal, the Know-Nothings declined as a national party when many members defected to the Republican Party. Although their numbers remained strong in several northern states in the late 1850s, the party had eroded as a national presence before the election of 1860.

What was the **Populist Party**?

Also known as the People's Party, the Populist Party was formed by a group of small farmers and sharecroppers to oppose large-scale commercial agriculture that they feared would put them out of work. The national party was officially founded in 1892 through a merger of the Farmers' Alliance and the Knights of Labor. That year the Populist presidential candidate, James B. Weaver, won over 1 million votes. Between 1892 and 1896, however, the party failed to make further gains, in part because of fraud and intimidation from southern Democrats.

Populists advocated federally regulated communication, transportation, and banking systems to offset the economic depression and prevent poverty among working-class families. Progressive Republican Theodore Roosevelt resurrected many Populist ideas and recast them in new forms as he expanded the federal regulation of business corporations, and addressed many People's Party concerns in his Progressive Party. Other Populist planks—particularly those calling for aid to farmers and employment on public works project in times of economic depression—became reality during the 1930s under the New Deal administrations of President Franklin D. Roosevelt, a Democrat.

Former Republican president Theodore Roosevelt formed the Progressive Party in 1912 as an alternative party for many liberal Republicans.

What was the **Progressive Party**?

Also known as the Bull Moose Party, the Progressive Party was formed in 1912 by former Republican president Theodore Roosevelt. Progressives supported women's suffrage, environmental conservation, tariff reform, stricter regulation of industrial combinations, and prohibition of child labor. Many liberal Republicans went to the new party, which nominated Roosevelt for president and Hiram W. Johnson for vice president. Although the Progressives greatly outpolled Republicans in the election, the net result was a victory for the Democratic candidate, Woodrow Wilson. Progressive candidates for state and local offices did poorly, and the party disappeared in 1916 when Roosevelt returned to the Republican Party. Presidential candidates Robert La Follette and Henry Wallace briefly resurrected their own versions of the Progressive Party, and the party officially disbanded after the 1952 presidential election.

Who were the **Dixiecrats**?

Also known as the States' Rights Party, the Dixiecrats were a small group of southern Democrats in the elections of 1948 who opposed President Harry Truman's civil rights program and revolted against the civil rights plank adopted at the Democratic National Convention. A group of states' rights leaders then met in Birmingham, Alabama, and suggested Governor Strom Thurmond of South Carolina for president, hoping to force the election into the House of Representatives by preventing either Truman or his Republican opponent, Thomas E. Dewey, from obtaining a majority of the electoral votes. However, their plan failed (Thurmond garnered only 39 electoral votes and 1.1 million popular votes), and many Dixiecrats became Republicans.

In 1992, Texas billionaire Ross Perot ran for president as the nominee of United We Stand America, the precursor to the Reform Party, which has been the most successful third party in recent years.

Which **third-party presidential bids** have been noteworthy in the post–World War II era?

No third-party candidate has ever come close to winning the presidency, and only eight minor parties have managed to win a single state's electoral votes. However, historians agree that there have been four noteworthy third-party presidential bids since World War II, where third-party or independent candidates have garnered more than 7 percent of the popular vote: In 1948, two independent candidates for president challenged the Republican candidate, Thomas E. Dewey, and the Democratic contender, then-President Harry Truman. On the right, Strom Thurmond—then a Republican senator from South Carolina—ran as the nominee of the Dixiecrats or States' Rights Party, a group of dissident Democrats in favor of racial segregation. On the left, Henry Wallace, a former vice president under Franklin D. Roosevelt, ran as the nominee of the Progressive Party. Thurmond won 22 percent of the vote in the South, the only area of the country in which he campaigned; Wallace garnered slightly more than 2 percent of the vote.

In 1968, George Wallace, the pro-segregation governor of Alabama, ran as the presidential nominee of the American Independent Party. Wallace, who won 13.8 percent of the vote, was thought to have taken votes away from both major-party candidates, Democrat Hubert Humphrey and Republican Richard Nixon. In 1980, Illinois congressman John Anderson ran as the presidential nominee of the National Unity Movement. It was assumed that Anderson, a moderate, would take votes away from both the Democratic nominee, President Jimmy Carter, and the Republican nominee, Ronald Reagan. In the end, Anderson won 7 percent of the vote, which hardly dampened Reagan's landslide victory. The most recent example involves Ross Perot, who in 1992 ran as the presidential nominee of United We Stand America, the precursor of the Reform Party. Political commentators argue that Perot's strong garnering of 19 percent of the vote probably hurt the Republican candidate, President George Bush, while helping elect Democratic nominee Bill Clinton. And some could argue that Ralph Nader's presence in the 2000 presidential race siphoned votes from Democratic candidate Al Gore, who despite gaining the majority of popular votes lost the electoral vote to George W. Bush.

Jesse Ventura's election as governor of Minnesota in 1998 marked the first time a candidate of the Reform Party, founded by Texas businessman Ross Perot, won a statewide office.

What were some **third-party issues that changed America**?

Many of American politician's ideas about social issues and reform had their roots in the fledgling campaigns of third-party politicians. Although they were eventually adopted by a major political party and quickly became part of the public political debate, movements advocating prohibition (introduced by the Prohibition Party in the late 1800s), women's suffrage (advocated by the Prohibition and Socialist Parties before being supported by both major parties in 1916), prohibition of child labor (a backbone of the Socialist Party), unemployment insurance (another social issue advocated by the Socialist Party), and a tough stance on crime (advocated by the American Independent Party in 1968 and adopted by the Republican Party) had humble beginnings with third-party platforms.

What is the **Reform Party**?

The most successful third party in recent years has been the Reform Party, founded by billionaire Texan Ross Perot, who enjoyed a fair measure of success in the presidential election of 1992 as an independent and again in 1996 under his newly formed party. In the 1992 elections, Perot garnered 19 percent of the popular vote (the largest percentage of the popular vote by a third-party candidate since Theodore Roosevelt on his Progressive ticket) and 9 percent in 1996. In fact, no other third-party presidential candidate in history has ever received more than 5 percent of the popular vote in two consecutive elections. After Perot's presidential campaigns, grassroots efforts continued to mount in the 50 states in which the party established itself; however, typical of many third-party experiences, attempts to reach voters were quickly blocked. For example, in 1997 when Perot attempted to buy air time for an infomercial regarding campaign finance reform, the networks rejected him. During the 1996 presidential campaign, Perot was kept out of the presidential debates. Still active today, Reformists seek to limit the power of special interest groups and return political power back to the people. They have advocated term limits for members of Congress, campaign reform, and the creation of a new federal tax system. Jesse Ventura became the first Reform Party candidate to win statewide office when he was elected governor of Minnesota in 1998.

Why are **third parties considered unsuccessful** in America's political system?

The recent elections of Reform Party candidate–turned–Minnesota governor Jesse Ventura and Green Party candidate–turned–state legislator Audie Bock of California have brought to the forefront of American consciousness the role of third-party and independent candidates in American politics. Although a number of political parties exist, and some have been somewhat effective at certain times over the course of American political history, Stephen Rockwood, author of *American Third Parties Since the Civil War*, cites several reasons why third parties have not been successful in the United States. First, the U.S. election system outcome is based on "winner-takes-all" voting, rather than proportional representation (granting legislative seats in proportion to the number of votes received). Second, the historic tradition in which the two parties act as umbrella groups for a variety of interests inhibits the voice of third parties; in essence, third parties have a hard time succeeding because one or both of the major parties often adopt their most popular issues, and thus their voters. Finally, the media tends to concentrate on the Republicans and Democrats, rather than giving air time to smaller parties.

In addition, most states have laws that require third parties to secure their place on the ballot by submitting large numbers of voter signatures, in contrast to the Democrats and Republicans, who are given automatic ballot access. Further, in the state legislatures both the Democrats and Republicans strive to keep the political agenda limited to two parties, fearing increased conflict and stress with the addition of a third party. Finally, the public funding of campaigns is much more supportive of the two main parties, and at the national level third-party presidential candidates receive funds after the general election (as opposed to the major party candidates, who receive funds after their summer nominations), and only if they have received more than 5 percent of the vote. Many third-party and independent candidates and their supporters complain about these aspects of the campaign system, upholding that the process is so biased against them that they are automatically pushed to the fringe of elections. Nevertheless, even when they don't win, these candidates can play an important part in raising issues, mobilizing new voters, introducing campaign innovations, and tipping elections from one major party candidate to another.

Green Party presidential nominee Ralph Nader's presence on the 2000 ballot is considered by some to have drawn votes away from Vice President Al Gore, perhaps costing Gore the election.

What is an **independent candidate** and **has one ever won a presidential election**?

An independent candidate is one who has no party affiliation, choosing to run for office independent of the Democratic or Republican Party, or any third party for that matter. An independent candidate gets on the ballot by petition. Key independent candidates include Ross Perot in his 1992 presidential campaign and John B. Anderson in his 1980 campaign. Three independent candidates had ballot status in the 2000 presidential elections: Cathy Gordon Brown of Tennessee, liberal political activist Randall Venson of Tennessee, and Louie Youngkeit of Utah, although none received any newsworthy attention nor the support of the popular vote to any notable degree. In fact, no independent candidate has ever won a presidential election, and less than a handful have received 5 percent or more of the popular vote. Rarely does an independent candidate garner any electoral votes.

Why do some people think **Ralph Nader** cost Al Gore the 2000 election?

Because of the presence of third-party candidates, 40 percent of the presidents elected since 1840 lacked a popular-vote majority, greatly affecting their terms in office. In the 2000 presidential elections, consumer advocate and Green Party nominee Ralph Nader appeared to be a significant factor in garnering votes in states that had close races between Democratic candidate Al Gore and Republican candidate George W. Bush, ultimately keeping Gore from winning the popular vote in those states. According to the Associated Press, exit polls in states including Colorado, Florida, Nevada, New Hampshire, Oregon, Washington State, and Wisconsin suggested that at least half the Nader voters would have voted for Gore if it had been a two-way race. In many of those states, it was enough to throw the state to Bush. While obviously not all of Nader's supporters would have instead voted for Gore, according to ABC's "This Week," prior to the election 56 percent of Nader's supporters said that if Nader wasn't running they'd pick Gore, 23 percent would pick Bush, and the rest wouldn't vote. Despite Democratic Party accusations that "a vote for Nader is a vote for Bush," Nader maintained that he was a viable third-party candidate, and "did not run for president to help elect one or the other of the two major candidates." Even though he may not have had a real chance at winning the White House, if Nader had received over 5 percent of the vote it would have entitled the Green Party to get millions of dollars in federal matching funds in the 2004 elections.

THE ELECTION PROCESS

What is the difference between **elections in the United States versus those in authoritarian and totalitarian states**?

In a democracy like the United States, elections are considered free and fair. For an election to be free and fair, certain civil liberties such as freedoms of speech, association, and assembly are required. Democratic elections are characterized by political parties and civic groups who mobilize and organize supporters and share alternative platforms with the public. Elections are competitive and their results considered to reflect the will of an informed citizenry. Democratic elections are competitive, periodic, inclusive of all citizens, and definitive. Quite the opposite is true of totalitarian states. Although right-wing dictatorships, Marxist regimes, and single-party governments stage elections, they are often held to give the aura of legitimacy, but are really void of opposition parties and fair and free voting methods. Suffrage in totalitarian and authoritarian states is the expression of the force of the state rather than of the free choice of the citizens. Often, because the act of abstaining from the vote might be interpreted as an expression of hostility toward the government in power, election results are generally heavily skewed in favor of the government. These scenarios are typical of authoritarian/totalitarian regimes today, including those in Iran, North Korea, and Cuba.

In recent years, elections have been a prime vehicle for democratization, as authoritarian governments have increasingly conceded to democratic principles. By the close of the twentieth century electoral democracies clearly predominated the world, including much of the post-Communist world, Latin America, and parts of Asia and Africa. According to Freedom House, a nonpartisan organization that monitors political rights and civil liberties around the world, electoral democracies—political systems whose leaders are elected in competitive multiparty and multicandidate processes in which opposition parties have a legitimate chance of attaining power—now constitute 120 of the 192 existing countries and represent 62.5 percent of the world's population.

What are the **types of elections**?

In the United States, there are generally three types of elections: presidential elections, congressional elections, and regional or local government elections. Within these three general types, there are primary elections, which are either open or closed and whose main function is to decide which candidates will represent their parties in the general election; and general elections, during which voters decide which candidates will actually fill public offices. Primaries are contests between candidates within each party, whereas general elections are contests between candidates of opposing parties. In addition, there are three other types of elections: initiative, which gives citizens an opportunity to propose legislation and present it to the state electorate for popular vote; referendum, which allows the state legislature to submit proposed legislation to the state's voters for their approval; and recall, which is an election to remove a politician from office by popular vote.

What is the process of electing the president of the United States?

The process of electing the president is usually divided into four main stages: (1) the prenomination stage, during which candidates compete in state primary elections and caucuses for delegates to the national party conventions; (2) the national conventions themselves, held in the summer of the election year, in which the two major parties nominate candidates for president and vice president and ratify a platform of the parties' policy positions and goals; (3) the general election campaign, during which the major party nominees and independent candidates compete for votes from the entire electorate, culminating with the popular vote on election day in November; and (4) the electoral college phase, in which the president and the vice president are officially elected.

How does the **presidential election process of the twenty-first century** differ from the **election process of a century ago**?

Today's presidential elections differ in many ways from those held earlier in America's history. First, voter participation today is a major factor in determining who the party nominees will be. In recent years the political parties have given a much greater role to party voters in the states (versus party leaders) when determining nominees. Secondly, in the twenty-first century's technically advanced society, the media (and more recently the Internet) plays a large role in conveying information to voters and shaping the course of the campaign. Finally, the financing of presidential campaigns is substantially governed in the various election phases by a system of public funding enacted in the 1970s as a result of increasing campaign costs and the fundraising pressures on candidates.

How often are **presidential elections** held?

The president and vice president of the United States are elected every four years, in even-numbered years divisible by the number four, by a majority vote of presidential electors who are elected by popular vote in each state.

How often are **Senate and House elections** held?

Both Senate and House of Representative elections occur during the midterm election season, the second year into a president's four-year term. They occur on the first Tuesday after the first Monday in November of even-numbered years.

What are **midterm elections**?

Midterm elections are those elections for seats in the Senate and House of Representatives that take place two years into a four-year presidential term. Midterm elections determine some members of the Senate and all members of the House of Representatives, as well as may state and local officials, but the results are sometimes interpreted as a popular referendum on the president's performance during the first two years of his term.

What is a **nonpartisan election**?

A nonpartisan election is a contest in which candidates campaign and run for office without formal identification or association with a particular political party.

What is a **primary**?

A primary is an electoral contest held to determine each political party's candidate for a particular office. In primary elections, voters decide which political candidates within a party will represent that party in the general election. Primaries are held at all levels of government, including local contests for mayor, district races for the House of Representatives, statewide elections for governor or U.S. senator, and presidential elections. The most publicized primary is the presidential primary, which is the state-run election held for the purpose of nominating presidential party candidates. Presidential primaries perform this function indirectly, primarily because voters do not directly select presidential nominees, but rather choose delegates from their respective states who will attend a national party convention to nominate a presidential candidate for their party. Most states restrict voting in a primary to party members, and these are called *closed primary* states. In contrast, *open primary* states allow voters to choose either party's ballot in the voting booth on primary day. None of the open primary states require voter registration by party. Some states, such as Massachusetts, hold semi-closed primaries, which means that independents can participate; one state, Louisiana, holds completely nonpartisan elections. In 2000, 39 Democratic and 42 Republican primaries took place in the states and the District of Columbia.

What is the main **advantage and disadvantage of open primaries and closed primaries**?

Advocates of open primaries argue that voters should be able to choose which primary they will vote in at each election, which ultimately increases voter participation and is the most democratic form of election. Party organizations prefer closed primaries because they promote party unity and keep those with no allegiance to the party from influencing its choice, as happens in "crossover voting," when members of rival parties vote for the weakest candidate in the opposition's primary.

When is the **official primary season**?

Although the increasingly earlier dates that mark the beginning of primary season make it harder to set an "official" time period for the season, based on the 2000 primaries the season usually begins in February and ends in June. In 2000, New Hampshire kicked off the primary season—as it traditionally does—with a February 1 date, with the largest group of states (California, Connecticut, Georgia, Maine, Maryland, Massachusetts, Missouri, New York, Ohio, Rhode Island, and Vermont) holding their primaries on March 7. The last date of the primary season was June 6, when a handful of states held their primaries. However, both the Republican and the Democratic Parties have decided to allow states to hold their presidential primaries more than a month earlier in 2004 than they did in 2000.

What is **Super Tuesday**, and why did both major parties support its development?

Widespread use of the phrase "Super Tuesday" dates from 1988, when on March 9 of that year a group of southern states came together to hold the first large and effective regional group of primaries in order to increase the importance of southern states in the presidential nomination process and lessen the impact of early votes in the New Hampshire primary and Iowa caucuses. Super Tuesday does not fall on a particular date, however, and the term has since become muddied, largely because during the presidential primary season there may be several groups of state primaries in various regions of the United States falling on one or more Tuesdays. For the 2000 election, a large number of states (including California and New York) held their primary election on March 7, one week before the dates usually associated with Super Tuesday. However, major parties support these regional or multiregional elections because, as so many convention delegates are selected at once, the weight of such a large, simultaneous vote tends to make or break would-be presidential nominees.

What is **"front loading"**?

"Front loading" refers to the process of states pushing up the dates of their presidential primaries in hopes of gaining influence over the nomination process. In 2000, approximately three-quarters of the parties' national delegates were chosen in the six weeks between February 1 and March 14. This trend toward an early, condensed primary season has been criticized by those politicians and observers who say it discourages candidates who are not able to raise sufficient campaign funds early enough in the campaign process.

What is a **political caucus**?

In the most general sense, a caucus is a meeting of people who gather to effect political or organizational change. In American presidential politics the term political caucus has come to mean a meeting of each party's local political activists, party members, and leaders to select nominees for public office and conduct other business. In the presidential nominating process, the caucus is often used in combination with a state convention to elect delegates to the national nominating convention. In what is referred to as a layered caucus system, local party activists work at the precinct level to select delegates to county meetings, who in turn select delegates to state meetings. The state-level conventions select delegates to their party's national nominating convention, thus indicating which presidential candidate is preferred by each states party's members. The overall effect of the political caucus is to democratize presidential nominations by determining candidate preference at the precinct level and then moving them forward. In the 2000 presidential election, both state parties in nine states selected delegates using the caucus process; Democrats scheduled caucuses in three additional states.

Do people ever argue that a **primary is a more democratic type of election than a caucus**?

Yes. The main argument for the primary as a presidential selection vehicle is that it is open to everyone who wants to vote, not just party activists. Representatives of a wide variety of groups are in theory eligible to win the presidency, and primaries are the most representative means by which to nominate presidential candidates because they both measure a candidate's popularity and challenge the candidate to display under pressure his or her leadership and communication skills. Advocates of caucuses argue that, although primaries attract more participants than caucuses, caucus participation allows for more time with the candidates: Attendants spend several hours learning about the political process and the goals of the party, listening to candidate speeches, and summing up party leaders and elected officials in ways that aren't possible in the fast-paced primary atmosphere. Because primaries tend to get extensive media coverage, voters can easily be swayed in opinion. Further, critics of primaries also argue that the way they are scheduled unfairly affects their outcome; New Hampshire, simply by virtue of being the first state to hold its primary, receives much more media attention than the other states. Although arguments for *regional primaries*—where the nation is divided into five or six distinct geographical regions who all hold their primary elections on the same day—occasionally surface, at present the primary is the preferred preconvention contest of a majority of the states.

What is a **platform**?

A platform is a political party's formal written statement of its principles and goals, which is put together and issued during the presidential nomination process.

Vice President Al Gore and his running mate Joe Lieberman, the first person of Jewish descent to run on a major-party ticket, acknowledge the support of the crowd at the 2000 Democratic National Convention in Los Angeles, California.

How does the party **nominate political candidates**?

Party conventions are the ratifying bodies that confer the nomination upon the candidate who won it in state contests during the primary season. The primary season gradually reduces the playing field of major-party candidates, as the accelerated pace of the primary winnows out candidates who fall short of expectations and thus find it difficult to raise the money they need to sustain their runs. The reforms of the past 30 years have changed the dynamics of the nominating process by closely tying the allocation of delegates to electoral performance. In years past a candidate could compete in a select number of primaries to demonstrate his or her popular appeal; today, however, the nomination goes to the candidate who holds a majority of delegates in the primaries and caucuses.

Has the **vice presidential candidate always been the choice of the presidential candidate**?

No. While current practice maintains that the choice of a vice presidential nominee remains the prerogative of the presidential candidate (Franklin D. Roosevelt is generally regarded as the first president who was able to impose his personal vice presidential choice), this was not always the case. Prior to this precedent, party leaders usually chose the vice presidential nominee, often an unsuccessful presidential candidate who had wide support, or who was perceived as adding geographical balance to the ticket.

What is the concept of **ticket balance**?

An active ingredient in contemporary vice presidential nominations, ticket balance refers to matching the presidential candidate with a vice presidential nominee whose geographical support, age, and political ideology are different from the presidential candidate, thus maximizing the diversity of the ticket. For example, a presidential nominee perceived as liberal will often choose a more conservative running mate. In the interest of continuity, incumbent presidents seeking reelection usually select their current vice presidents as running mates, although there have been exceptions. In 1956, for example, Republican leaders unsuccessfully urged President Dwight Eisenhower to replace Vice President Richard Nixon, and in 1976 Vice President Nelson Rockefeller announced that he would not seek the nomination, widely interpreted by political analysts as an effort to allow a more conservative candidate to take his place in order to bolster President Gerald Ford's candidacy. In the November 2000 presidential elections Al Gore broke new ground by nominating Connecticut senator Joseph Lieberman as his vice presidential running mate, marking the first time a person of Jewish descent ran on major-party ticket.

THE NATIONAL CONVENTION

What happens at the **national convention**?

The spring of an election year is characterized by vigorous campaigning for primaries and caucuses nationwide, climaxing at the national conventions of the political parties. The national conventions are said to "jump start" the general election campaign for the presidential candidates. Once at the national party conventions, the delegates from the states cast votes for the person who will represent the political party in the November general election. In order to secure a party's nomination, a candidate must receive a majority of the votes from the delegates. It is not unusual for delegates to vote several times before one candidate secures the majority of the votes and officially becomes that party's candidate for the presidential election. If a president is running for reelection, this nomination process still must be completed. Even if the president does not face any opposition from within his own political party, the national convention still takes place.

How are **delegates to the national convention chosen**?

There are significant differences from state to state in the way national convention delegates are chosen. Many states even have different rules for choosing Democratic and Republican delegates. Some states award delegates to candidates on a "winner-

Confetti and balloons add to the festive atmosphere of the delegates gathered at the 2000 Republican National Convention in Philadelphia, Pennsylvania.

take-all" basis, meaning that the candidate with the most votes in a state is awarded all of that state's delegates. Other states award delegates in proportion to each candidate's share of the primary vote. Some delegates are office-holders of state party organizations, but many others are chosen in primary elections held in most states to select delegates. In addition, delegates can "pledge" or "unpledge" to vote for the same candidate the voters in his or her state or district supported in the primary, and these rules vary widely by state. Despite their composition and various methods of selection, the number of delegates has risen over the years. In 2000 the Democratic National Convention was composed of 4,337 delegates and 610 alternates, while the Republican selected 2,066 delegates and an equal number of alternates.

What are **super delegates**?

"Super delegates" is the term given to party leaders and party-affiliated elected officials.

When was the **first national nominating convention**?

The Anti-Masonic Party was the first to hold a national convention, meeting in Baltimore, Maryland, in September 1831 to choose William Wirt as its candidate; the Democrats and National Republicans each held national conventions the following year. By 1840 the Democrats and Whigs had adopted the national convention as the standing nominating devise, which the major parties have used without exception ever since.

What was so special about the **Convention of 1832**?

The election of 1824 brought an end to the use of a congressional caucus as a nominating devise, but a brief transitional period followed in which state legislative caucuses and conventions and various other methods were used to nominate presidential candidates. In 1832 the three parties contesting the election—Anti-Masonic, Democratic, and National Republican—used their respective national conventions as vehicles for nominating their presidential tickets for the first time. The use of nominating conventions reflected the growing trend toward greater democratic participation that characterized the Jackson era.

Is there such as thing as **"convention rules"**?

Yes. At the national convention, each party establishes rules for the party as well as the convention. In addition, this is when the party's platform—an outline of its philosophy and priorities—is adopted.

What is the **two-thirds rule**?

In the days when national conventions were often unruly and strongly contested gatherings, various party rules and political practices were in effect. One such rule was the so-called "two-thirds rule," a Democratic Party requirement adopted at the 1832 convention (but not abandoned until 1936) mandating that the party's nominee receive a two-thirds majority of delegate votes. The record for the number of ballots cast is held by the Democrats, who required 103 ballots to nominate John W. Davis in the 1924 national convention.

What was a "dark horse" candidate?

Fear of deadlock among the most widely known candidates led to the occasional emergence of a "dark horse" candidate, a minor candidate or party figure who had not originally been considered as a candidate, as a compromise choice. Historians often cite James K. Polk of Tennessee, nominated by the Democrats in 1844, as the first dark horse candidate to win nomination. In 1936 the Democrats enacted rule changes that required only a simple majority for nomination, which largely ended the lengthy ballots that had once resulted in the selection of dark horse candidates.

What was the **"smoke-filled room"**?

Convention deadlock was not unknown among Republicans, despite the fact that they required only a simple majority to nominate their candidates. At their 1920 convention, Ohio senator Warren Harding emerged as a compromise nominee. According to various stories, Harding's nomination was created at a secret late-night meeting of party leaders held in a hotel suite, establishing the image of presidential nominees being selected in the "smoke-filled room." The term came to imply choice of a nominee by a small group of party leaders meeting out of view of public scrutiny.

Who are **"favorite sons"**?

The "favorite son" candidacy is another historical device that is less frequently seen in contemporary national conventions. Favorite sons were political figures such as governors or senators who ran for the presidency, usually campaigning only in their home states, for the purpose of retaining control of state delegations. Once at the national convention, the favorite son typically used his delegates as bargaining chips to influence the party platform, help secure the nomination for a preferred candidate, seek future political favors, or enhance his own prospects as a vice presidential nominee. A 1972 rule change required that candidates garner pledges of support from at least 50 delegates, not more than 20 of whom can be from one state. This rule, which essentially required candidates to obtain a modest level of support from a geographically diverse base, helped reduce the number of names placed in nomination at subsequent conventions. Current Republican Party rules require that candidates obtain the support of a majority of delegates from five or more states in order to have their names placed in nomination.

Which national convention was a **symbol of national disunity**?

The 1968 Democratic National Convention, held in Chicago, was less notable for its politics than for its televised account of social unrest and national disunity. Recent events, including the assassinations of Martin Luther King Jr. and Robert Kennedy and the loss of young lives in the Vietnam War, triggered war protestors to barrage the convention and voice their concerns to the Democratic Party and its presidential candidate, Hubert Humphrey. Chicago mayor Richard Daley met the protestors with 12,000 police officers and the Illinois National Guard, resulting in a bloody riot that led to hundreds of arrests and injuries. Captured by television cameras and broadcast across the nation, the convention doomed Humphrey's candidacy and intensified the revolutionary protests against the Vietnam War.

Which was the **longest national convention**?

The 1924 Democratic National Convention in New York, which lasted 17 days and required 103 ballots to select conservative lawyer John W. Davis as the presidential nominee, was one of the longest in American history. Catholic New Yorker Al Smith and Protestant prohibitionist William McAdoo of California were the two candidates with most support, but they were also the two candidates who were most disliked among the convention crowd. It took 17 days of compromise before candidate John W. Davis was nominated for the Democratic ticket.

When was the last major convention held in which the **nomination was still in doubt** and had to be decided at the convention?

The 1976 Republican National Convention was the most recent convention in America's history at which the identity of a major party's nominee was in question before the nominating ballots were cast. That year, President Gerald Ford fended off a strong challenge from former California governor Ronald Reagan to secure the nomination.

THE ELECTION CAMPAIGN

What are the factors in a **successful election campaign**?

Political scientists and scholars agree that campaigning for an office such as the presidency, a governorship, or Senate seat is an art, involving many layers of activity that must come together successfully in order for a candidate to win office. First, there is a very personal aspect to campaigning, as the candidate and his supporters make appearances, meet voters, conduct press conferences, and give speeches around the nation; here the candidate's diplomatic skill is tested, and the issues of the campaign challenged to strike a balance between reaching everyday voters as well as leaders of various groups and voting "blocs," such as business, labor, and key ethnic populations. There is also an organizational aspect, which involves planning sophisticated mass mailings, coordinating electronic telephone banks to reach voters, reaching special interest groups for money and endorsements, and raising money to support the campaign. The media aspect involves both running paid advertisements and soliciting the press in an effort to gain the maximum campaign coverage possible, as well as managing the art of "damage control," that is, responding to and turning around any form of controversial or negative press.

Who are the **key players** in a candidate's election campaign?

Depending on the candidate's level of office, an organizational staff consisting of anywhere from a dozen volunteers to hundreds of paid specialists carry out the day-to-day work of the campaign. In presidential campaigns, literally tens of thousands of volunteers are at work, directed by a paid staff of hundreds, including lawyers, accountants, and a variety of consultants. The campaign manager and a few political consultants run the campaign, providing both the strategy and the hands-on plan to carry the strategy out. The key consultants include the media consultant, who is the chief liaison with the press; the pollster, who manages the public opinion surveys critical to the direction of the campaign; and the direct mailer, who oversees direct-mail fundraising efforts. Most argue that the most valuable player is the finance chair—directly responsible for soliciting and garnering the large contributions that pay the staff and keep the campaign running—because without adequate finances a campaign comes to a grinding halt.

Prominent political consultant and campaign manager James Carville is largely credited as the force behind Bill Clinton's election as president in 1992.

How are **presidential campaigns generally managed**?

Recent presidential campaigns have been managed by separate candidate-centered organizations, ad-hoc groups assembled for the specific purpose of winning the election. After the conventions, these committees are usually expanded from the nominee's primary organization to include key staff from the campaigns of rival contenders for the nomination. The campaign organization prepares the campaign plan, schedules appearances for the campaigners, conducts opposition and survey research, manages the national media campaign, and conducts both voter registration and get-out-the-vote drives. Campaigns are organized on the national, state, and local levels, overlapping existing party structures, especially at the local level. One of the campaign organization's main goals is to broaden the candidate's appeal, bringing his or her message to the largest number of independent voters possible and to disgruntled members of the other party in order to win votes.

What is the **campaign plan**?

The campaign plan outlines the strategy and tactics that the campaign organizations and candidates hope will bring a winning combination of electoral and popular votes in the general election. The plan details the issues the nominees will emphasize, and aspects of the candidates' personal images they hope to convey to voters. Specific points include a "plan of attack" on the platform, issues, and candidates of the opposition; methods for targeting socioeconomic, ethnic, and religious groups the campaign organization feels will most likely accept the campaign message; an assessment of the ticket's strengths and weaknesses in various states; and geographic areas the candidates should target in order to secure an electoral college majority.

How long is a presidential election campaign?

Presidential candidates begin organizing their campaigns and raising money a year or more before the primary season. While the length of the nominating season has remained unchanged, the pre-election maneuvering by candidates usually begins shortly after the previous presidential election, and exploratory committees are often in operation one or two years before the election. For the 2000 presidential election, six candidates announced their desire to run by the end of April 1999, and all 12 major party candidates had announced their candidacies by September.

Why are political campaigns sometimes called **"horse races"**?

The term "horse race" is sometimes used as a metaphor for an election campaign because it conveys the feeling of excitement that people experience when they watch a horse race or other sporting event. The term has also been applied to media coverage of campaigns, which frequently emphasizes the candidates' standings in public opinion polls as if they were horses in a race, rather than the candidates' positions on the issues.

What is the **"coattail effect"**?

The "coattail effect" refers to the ability of a popular officeholder or candidate, on the strength of his or her own popularity, to increase the chances for victory of other candidates of the same political party. The candidate carries others to victory "on his coattails."

When was the **first presidential public debate held**? What about the **first televised debate**?

The year 1948 saw the first public debate among presidential candidates Thomas E. Dewey and Harold Stassen, which was held as a radio broadcast in connection with the Oregon Republican presidential primary. The first televised debate took place in 1956, between contestants for the Democratic presidential nomination Adlai Stevenson and Estes Kefauver.

Have the **number of debates increased** and what does this phenomenon have to do with the **"straw poll"**?

Yes, campaign debates have become an increasingly important aspect of the nominating process, and an unprecedented number occurred during the 1988 primarily season: approximately 60 debates, virtually all televised, were held among presidential candidates of one or both parties. According to the Alliance for Better Campaigns, for the 2000 presidential election cycle, 19 debates between Democratic or Republican candidates were held between October 1999 and February 2000. In general, the increase in debates coincided with a decrease in the number of "straw poll" elections before and during the nominating season. Straw polls measure the candidate popularity among party activists at state conventions, but have no influence on the selection of delegates. To some extent, candidate debates offset one of the most frequently criticized aspects of the election process: The idea that the combined influence of the media and the back-to-back primaries seem to promote an emphasis on candidate image over substantive issues.

What is the **League of Women Voters** and what do they have to do with the debate system currently followed during national campaigns?

The League of Women Voters (LWV) is a nonpartisan political organization that, according to its mission statement, "encourages the informed and active participation of citizens in government, works to increase understanding of major public policy issues, and influences public policy through education and advocacy." The organization's involvement in the debating process dates to 1952, when a joint televised appearance before the LWV national convention, the precursor to the modern televised debate, included several presidential candidates or their representatives discussing the issues. Because candidate debates are a key component of a political campaign, the LWV often sponsors or cosponsors presidential debates, as it did in 1977 (when it sponsored a series of three presidential debates between nominees Jimmy Carter and Gerald Ford) and in 1992 with cosponsor CNN.

What is the **dirtiest presidential campaign on record**?

In his book *Presidential Campaigns*, author Paul F. Boller, Jr., remarks, "Presidential campaigns are a lot nicer today than they used to be. What respectable person today would think of calling one of the candidates for the highest office in the land a carbuncled-faced old drunkard? Or a howling atheist? Or a pickpocket, thief, traitor, lecher, syphilitic, gorilla, crook, anarchist, murderer? Yet such charges were regular features of American presidential contests in the 19th century." Although many early campaigns contained their share of derogatory remarks, historians agree that the 1828 presidential campaign between Andrew Jackson and incumbent president John Quincy Adams was probably history's dirtiest. Having its roots in the 1824 election between the same two candidates, in which Jackson had won the popular and electoral vote but due to the House decision Adams had won the presidency, mudslinging ranged from accusations of adultery against Andrew and Rachel Jackson to suggestions that President Adams had spent thousands of federal dollars to stock the White House with gambling equipment. Attacks against Jackson included criticism of his leadership abilities, name calling involving his mother and wife, and allegations that he was involved in dueling and brawling. Words used to describe him included "slave trader," "gambler," and "promoter of cock fights and horse races." Despite this unprecedented attack on the candidates' personalities, the campaign resulted in Jackson's landslide victory, the revival of a two-party system, and the creation of a new national party, the Democratic Party of the United States.

Who is repeatedly cited as one of the **most colorful campaigners** in America's political history?

The 1928 Democratic presidential candidate Alfred E. Smith is often cited for his commanding personality, razor-sharp wit, and ability to launch impromptu speeches laden with humor. A New York Catholic and longtime member of the Tammany Hall machine, Smith's history and upbringing made it difficult for him to appeal to a wide electorate. He is most remembered for his trademarks: a brown derby hat, an upbeat campaign song ("The Sidewalks of New York"), and his habit of pronouncing "radio" as "raddio."

Considered one of the most colorful campaigners in America's political history, prominent New York politician Alfred E. Smith ran unsuccessfully for president in 1928.

Which vice presidential and presidential candidates **successfully hid illnesses during their campaigns**?

Franklin D. Roosevelt kept his deteriorating heart condition quiet during his 1944 reelection campaign (Roosevelt's personal physician himself asserting that there was "nothing wrong organically with him at all.... He's perfectly okay"). During the 1960 presidential campaign, John F. Kennedy successfully hid his long-rumored and publicly denied struggle with Addison's disease, a failure of the adrenal glands for which the Massachusetts senator received injections of cortisone and other medications. Edmund Muskie, an early 1972 Democratic hopeful who was being treated for depression, was considered unfit to hold office after he allegedly cried in public. George McGovern's 1972 running mate, Missouri senator Tom Eagleton, was forced to quit the ticket within a month of the Democratic National Convention after the media revealed allegations of electroshock therapy as treatment for his clinical depression. While in times past the media often went along with not publicizing candidates' or incumbents' health conditions, today the media makes much of presidential hopefuls' health status, as witnessed by its coverage of Bill Bradley's irregular heartbeat and John McCain's recurring skin cancer during the 2000 campaign.

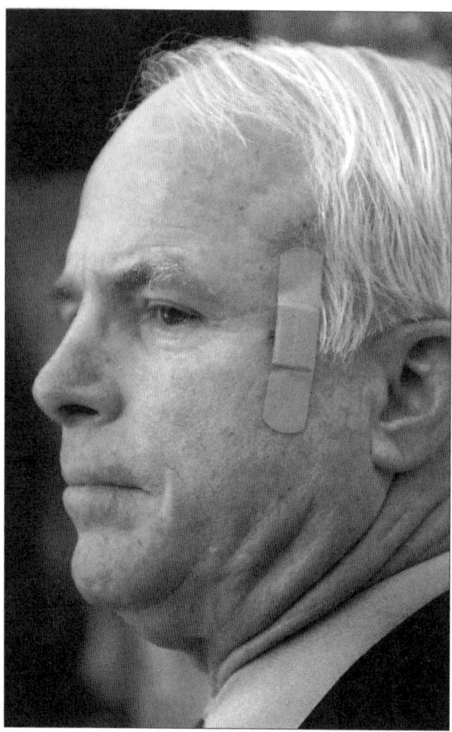

Senator and Republican presidential hopeful John McCain's treatment for skin cancer made headlines during the 2000 campaign, an example of how politicians' health issues are subject to media scrutiny.

Which presidential candidates sought a place on the national ballot at least three times in their political career, **but never won office**?

It is not unusual for a candidate to make several unsuccessful runs for political office, including the presidency. Consider these unlucky candidates: Henry Clay, who was nominated as a Democratic Republican in 1824, as a National Republican in 1832, and as a Whig in 1844 (he also ran two other times without a nomination, as a Whig in 1840 and 1848); William Jennings Bryan, who ran as a Democrat in 1896, 1900, and 1908; Eugene Debs, who ran on the Socialist ticket five times, in 1900, 1904, 1908, 1912, and 1920; and Gus Hall, who ran on the Communist Party ticket in 1972, 1976, 1980, and 1984. However, the candidate who probably holds the record for the most unsuccessful runs for presidential nomination is Republican his party's nomination for Harold Stassen, who sought the executive office nine times between the years 1944 and 1992.

CAMPAIGN FINANCE

Who **pays for the campaigns** of candidates?

Most of the funding for federal candidates comes from voluntary contributions by individuals, groups, and political parties. Since 1976, presidential candidates have also had the option of public funding for their campaigns, which is supported by taxpayer designations against their tax liability of $3.00. Public funding is not available to candidates running for Congress.

In the 1980s and 1990s, usually the money given to presidential campaigns came in the form of "soft money"—unlimited financial contributions made to the political parties by corporations, labor unions, and wealthy individuals. During the 1998 election, for example, the parties raised $172.5 million in soft-money contributions, Philip Morris being the largest single contributor of soft money to the political parties with its donations totaling $1.7 million. In addition, businesses and labor groups spend large sums on what are termed "independent expenditures," such as media campaigns to endorse or oppose specific candidates, and the political parties themselves can also make campaign expenditures, as long as they are independent of their own candidates. In addition, candidates may spend unlimited amounts of their own personal funds on their campaigns. Presidential and vice presidential candidates who accept public funds cannot spend more than $50,000 from personal and immediate family funds.

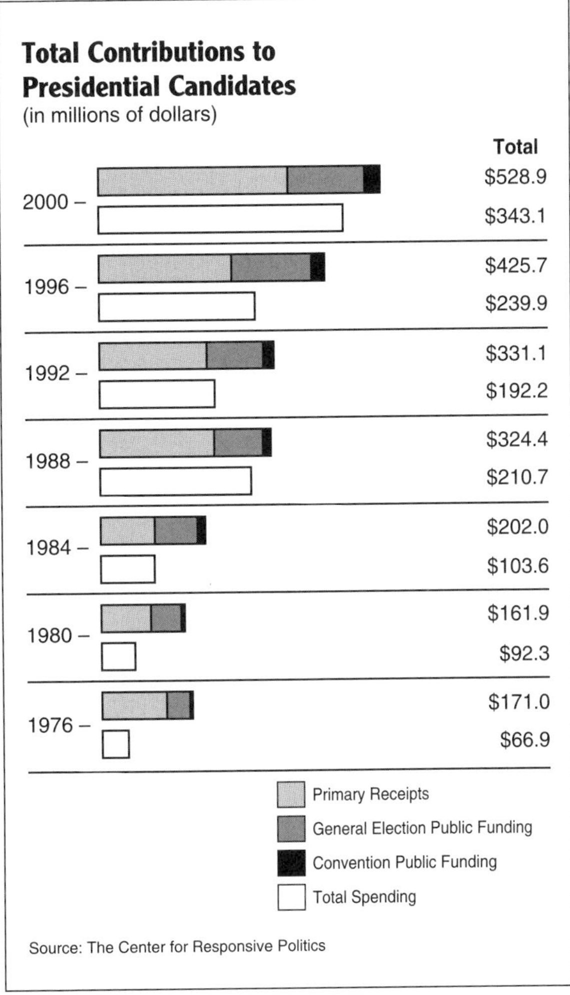

Running a presidential campaign is an expensive undertaking, and candidates earn funding, which has grown significantly since 1976, from several sources.

The Shays-Meehan/McCain-Feingold campaign finance reform bill, passed by Congress in March 2002 and signed into law by President George W. Bush as the Bipartisan Campaign Finance Reform Act, changed the terms of soft-money contributions. The bill prohibits national political parties from raising or spending soft money, and also disallows state and local parties from spending soft money on federal elections, with one exception: The bill allows parties to collect up to $10,000 per donor annually in those states that allow soft money, but that money can only be utilized for voter registration and turnout efforts.

What do the terms **"hard money"** and **"soft money"** mean?

These two terms are used to differentiate between campaign funding that is and is not regulated by campaign finance law. "Hard money" refers to money that is regulated by the Federal Elections Commission and that can be used to influence the outcome of federal elections because it supports the election of a specific candidate. In contrast, "soft money" is the term used for those funds raised and spent by political parties, corporations, labor unions, and other groups that are not regulated by law and can only be spent on activities that do not affect the election of candidates for national offices. These activities include voter registration drives, party-building events, and administrative costs for state and local candidates. In the 1990s, the term "soft money" came to be synonymous with unlimited financial contributions from influential labor and business groups. The most significant component of the Bipartisan Campaign Finance Reform Act involves its clamp on soft-money contributions: The act makes it illegal for national political parties to raise or spend soft money, and bans states and local parties from spending soft money on federal elections, with the exception of voter registration and turnout efforts.

Was there an increase in the **amount of soft money raised** in the 1990s?

Yes. Republicans raised $138.2 million in soft money in the 1996 presidential election cycle, a 178 percent increase over 1992. During that same time, Democrats raised $123.9 million, a 242 percent increase over 1992. In the 1998 midterm election cycle, Republicans raised $93.7 million, a 144 percent increase over the funds they raised in 1994; Democrats raised $78.8 million, an 84 percent increase of their 1994 fundraising. This skyrocketing in soft money contributions led, in part, to the passage of the Bipartisan Campaign Finance Reform Act. Effective November 6, 2002, the act prohibits national political parties from raising or spending soft money.

How did **incumbents have the advantage** during the 1990s?

An overwhelming proportion of special-interest contributions went to candidates already in office, especially those whose seniority and influence were highly regarded by special interest groups. In the 1996 general election contests, Republican incumbents in the House of Representatives outspent their challengers by nearly an eight-to-one margin; for Democrats, the margin was four to one. Critics of the system were very vocal in maintaining that this process limited competition and intimidated those potential challengers who couldn't afford the television time they needed to become known among voters. The incumbent advantage had a particularly detrimental effect on the candidacies of minorities and women seeking to break through the political barriers that traditionally have stood in the way of their political involvement.

How much can **individuals donate** to a particular candidate?

As a result of the Bipartisan Campaign Finance Reform Act, individuals can contribute up to $2,000 per candidate per election, with primary and general elections counted separately. Individuals can give $5,000 per year to a political action committee (PAC); $25,000

Top 20 Campaign Contributors by Industry, 1999–2000

Industry	Amount	Dems.	Repubs.	Contributions Tilt
Lawyers/Law Firms	$112,751,467	69%	30%	Strongly Democratic
Retired	$101,938,557	30%	68%	Strongly Republican
Securities/Invest.	$92,199,600	45%	55%	On the Fence
Real Estate	$79,870,628	45%	55%	On the Fence
Health Professionals	$45,773,302	42%	57%	Leans Republican
Insurance	$40,887,556	34%	66%	Leans Republican
Computer Equip./Svcs.	$40,052,004	52%	46%	On the Fence
TV/Movies/Music	$37,821,890	64%	35%	Leans Democratic
Oil & Gas	$33,880,094	20%	78%	Strongly Republican
Business Services	$31,622,038	52%	47%	On the Fence
Misc. Mfg./Distrib.	$30,292,279	30%	69%	Strongly Republican
Pharm./Health Prod.	$26,405,263	31%	69%	Strongly Republican
Commercial Banks	$24,717,454	37%	63%	Leans Republican
Public Sector Unions	$22,153,437	93%	7%	Solidly Democratic
Retail Sales	$20,503,958	34%	65%	Leans Republican
General Contractors	$19,961,528	30%	69%	Strongly Republican
Air Transport	$19,814,665	38%	62%	Leans Republican
Leadership PACs	$19,470,658	37%	63%	Leans Republican
Automotive	$18,829,097	20%	79%	Strongly Republican
Telephone Utilities	$18,702,504	41%	59%	Leans Republican

METHODOLOGY: The numbers on this page are based on contributions from PACs, soft money donors, and individuals giving $200 or more. All donations took place during the 1999–2000 election cycle and were released by the Federal Election Commission.

Source: The Center for Responsive Politics

Industries make significant contributions to the campaigns of candidates who can influence policy that affects their interests.

per national party committee per year; and $10,000 per state or local party committee per year. In addition, the act increases the aggregate limit on individual contributions from $25,000 per year to $95,000 per two-year election cycle, of which only $37,500 may be contributed to candidates over the two years. The two-year election cycle starts on January 1 of odd-numbered years and extends to December 31 of even-numbered years.

Where does the money go when I **check off the box on my income tax form to donate to a campaign fund**?

Under the taxpayer "check off" system, a mechanism whereby U.S. taxpayers can choose to contribute $3.00 of their annual federal income tax payment to a public

Top 20 Individual Campaign Contributors, 1999–2000

Contributor	Total Contributions	To Dems	To Repubs	Contributions Tilt
Abraham, S. Daniel & Ewa Slim-Fast Foods, West Palm Beach, FL	$1,618,500	100%	0%	Solidly Democratic
Schwartz, Bernard L. & Irene Loral Spacecom, New York, NY	$1,362,000	99%	0%	Solidly Democratic
Buttenwieser, Peter/Marek, Terry Buttenwieser & Assoc., Philadelphia, PA	$1,349,700	98%	0%	Solidly Democratic
Gilo, Davidi & Shamaya Vyyo Inc., Woodside, CA	$1,311,000	100%	0%	Solidly Democratic
Saban, Haim & Cheryl Saban Entertainment, Los Angeles, CA	$1,250,500	99%	0%	Solidly Democratic
Lindner, Carl H. & Edyth B. American Financial Group, Cincinnati, OH	$1,218,000	52%	48%	On the Fence
Milstein, Constance Milstein Properties, New York, NY	$959,515	100%	0%	Solidly Democratic
Angelo, Peter G. & Georgia K. Angelos Law Offices/Baltimore Orioles, Baltimore, MD	$959,500	97%	3%	Solidly Democratic
Eychaner, Fred Newsweb Corp., Chicago, IL	$946,000	99%	0%	Solidly Democratic
Quinn, John M. O'Quinn & Laminack, Houston, TX	$840,250	100%	0%	Solidly Democratic
Caspersen, Finn M. W. & Barbara M. Knickerbocker Management, Gladstone, NJ	$808,000	27%	73%	Strongly Republican
Bing, Stephen L. & Helen L. Writer/Producer, Los Angeles, CA	$760,500	100%	0%	Solidly Democratic
Shimmon, David J. Kinetics Group, Los Altos Hills, CA	$727,000	100%	0%	Solidly Democratic
Farmer, Richard T. & Joyce E. Cintas Corp., Cincinnati, OH	$721,000	0%	100%	Solidly Republican
DeVos, Richard M. & Helen J. Amway Corp., Grand Rapids, MI	$706,000	0%	97%	Solidly Republican
Watanabe, Terry K. Oriental Trading Co., Omaha, NE	$704,700	100%	0%	Solidly Democratic
Shorenstein, Walter H. & Lydia Shorenstein Co., San Francisco, CA	$670,148	99%	0%	Solidly Democratic
Childs, John W. & Marlene I. JW Childs Assoc., Chestnut Hill, MA	$670,000	0%	100%	Solidly Republican
Kirsch, Steve T. & Michele Propel, Los Altos Hills, CA	$655,000	100%	0%	Solidly Democratic
Steiner, David S. & Sylvia L. Steiner Equities Group, West Orange, NJ	$651,150	95%	0%	Solidly Democratic

Source: The Center for Responsive Politics

Prior to campaign finance reform measures enacted in 2002, top individual contributors—who tend to support Democratic candidates—donated several million dollars to political campaigns.

fund for financing presidential elections, taxpayers simply check a box on their tax return that indicates they want to participate. By doing so, the individual deposits $3.00 of the tax payment into the presidential election campaign fund. The money is drawn from a fund maintained by the U.S. Treasury, consisting of moneys that are exclusively given by the voluntary contributions made by U.S. taxpayers.

What does the **Bipartisan Campaign Finance Reform Act of 2002** do, specifically?

The Shays-Meehan/McCain-Feingold campaign finance reform bill, the brainchild of Congressmen Christopher Shays (R–CO) and Marty Meehan (D–MA) and Senators John McCain (R–AZ) and Russ Feingold (D–WI), is the first bill since the Watergate era to seriously rein in the large donations of soft money that characterized national party fundraising efforts of the 1980s and 1990s. Signed into law by President George W. Bush as the Bipartisan Campaign Finance Reform Act of 2002, the law prohibits the national political parties from raising or spending the unlimited financial donations from labor unions, corporations, and wealthy individuals known as soft money. It also bans state and local parties from spending soft money on federal elections, with one exception: It allows parties to collect up to $10,000 per donor annually in those states that allow soft money. However, the money can only be used for one purpose: Voter registration and turnout. To balance this soft money cut at federal and state levels, the act increases individual hard money contribution limits. It doubles individual contributions to candidates running for president and Congress, so that individuals can donate $2,000 to candidates per election, for a total of $95,000 to parties and candidates every two years. The bill eases contribution limits even further for federal candidates who run against wealthy, self-financed opponents.

In addition, the bill prohibits special interest groups from using their general funds to finance ads for radio or television that target a federal candidate one month before a primary election and two months before a general election. Contribution limits for political action committees (PACs) remain unchanged. Most of the bill takes effect on November 6, 2002; the hard money limitations take effect January 1, 2003. Analysts uphold that the act's most predictable impact on the campaign finance world will involve an increase in the influence of corporations, trade associations, and other organizations with large hard-money PACs, while decreasing the influence of those that have relied primarily on large soft-money contributions. It should alleviate the pressure many corporations and wealthy individuals feel to make large donations to the political parties in response to requests from members of Congress and White House officials. In contrast, pressure for smaller donations of hard dollars from individuals will increase.

What are some of the issues surrounding **campaign finance reform**?

Advocates of campaign finance reform maintain that campaign spending is a self-serving system spun out of control. In 1996, for example, congressional candidates spent more than $765 million on their races, a 5 percent increase over the record-breaking 1994 elections. According to reform advocates, unlimited campaign spending contributed to a number of problems in the 1990s, including an increasing reliance by candidates on special-interest dollars to cover skyrocketing campaign costs; a tendency among incumbents to spend large amounts of their time raising funds rather than serving the people; and frustration among potential candidates who were dismayed at having to raise exorbitant amounts of money in order for their candidacies to have a chance at succeeding. In addition, campaign donations from political action committees (PACs) can be directly linked to the way elected officials vote on issues once they reach public office.

Advocates of campaign finance reform argued that the methods of financing political campaigns should enable candidates to compete more equitably for public office, allow maximum citizen participation in the political process, and combat corruption and undue influence. Specific suggestions for campaign finance reform included placing additional limits on contributions, which led mavericks like Congressman Christopher Shays (R–CT) and Senator John McCain (R–AZ) to sponsor the Shays-Meehan/McCain-Feingold campaign finance reform bill. Other suggestions continue to be discussed, including encouraging citizens to make voluntary limits on spending; introducing measures to close loopholes in the current law; encouraging the public financing of campaigns; and introducing new disclosure and reporting requirements.

Can the government **regulate campaign spending**?

Yes. By putting caps on donations and the amount of money that candidates can spend, the government regulates campaign spending. In addition, money used to communicate with voters independent of a candidate's campaign is subject to federal regulation only if the message contains express advocacy (i.e., with terms like "vote for Jones"). If an ad campaign or other media communication contains express advocacy and has not been made in coordination with the candidate, it is considered an independent expenditure under the Federal Election Campaign Act, and there are no limits on the amounts that may be spent on these types of communications. If a media communication does not contain express advocacy, but rather discusses a candidate's actions, voting record, or position on an issue, courts have generally held that funding for these messages are not subject to federal contribution limits, primarily because such speech is protected under the First Amendment. The Bipartisan Campaign Finance Reform Act of 2002 prohibits special interest groups from using their general funds to pay for radio or television ads that target a federal candidate one month before a primary election and two months before a general election.

What did the **Federal Election Campaign Act** do?

Known colloquially as FECA, this 1971 law, which was amended in 1974, 1976, and 1979, governs the financing of federal elections. The law requires candidates and political committees to disclose the sources of their funding and how they spend their money; regulates the contributions received and expenditures made during federal election campaigns; and governs the public funding of presidential elections. The provisions of the Bipartisan Campaign Finance Reform Act of 2002 amend the Federal Election Campaign Act.

What is the role of the **Federal Election Commission**?

The Federal Election Commission (FEC) in an independent regulatory agency charged with administering and enforcing federal campaign finance law. Established by Congress in 1975, the duties of the FEC are to disclose campaign finance information, to enforce the provisions of the law such as the limits and prohibitions on contributions, and to oversee the public funding of presidential elections. The commission is made up of six members, each of whom is appointed by the president and confirmed by the Senate. Each member serves a six-year term, and two seats are subject to appointment every two years. By law, no more than three commissioners can be members of the same political party, and at least four votes are required for any official commission action.

PUBLIC INTEREST GROUPS

What is a **public interest group**?

Although public interest groups are often referred to by a variety of names—special interest groups, organized interest groups, pressure groups, and lobby groups—their common denominator is that the group is a formally or informally organized association of people with common interests and demands that attempts to influence public policy.

What **different kinds of interests are represented** by public interest groups?

Interests groups are defined by the causes and issues they represent; therefore there are as many groups as there are interests: Property rights groups, states' rights groups, civil rights and civil liberties groups, environmental groups, animal rights groups, children's advocacy groups, peace groups, right-to-carry-arms groups, right-to-life groups, and church groups, to name a few. They include good-government groups like Common Cause and Public Citizen, Inc., civil liberties groups like the American Civil Liberties Union, environmental groups like Greenpeace USA and the Sierra Club, and religious groups, such as the Christian Coalition. Some, such as the AFL-CIO—the umbrella organization for 78 labor unions in the United States—represent more than one issue. Public interest groups that have received widespread attention for their lobbying efforts include the American Association of Retired Persons (AARP), Amnesty International, the National Rifle Association (NRA), and the National Right to Life Committee. Others that are dedicated to representing the needs of certain ethnic groups include the National Association for the Advancement of Colored People (NAACP), the Mexican American Legal Defense and Education Fund, and the Native American Rights Fund.

What are some examples of **conservative interest groups**?

Conservative interest groups dominated the political landscape in the Bush and Clinton administrations, and have grown ever since, fueled by factors such as the growth of conservative talk radio and the desire of some Americans to return to the moral foundations of the mid–twentieth century. Examples include the 2-million-member Christian Coalition, a dominant force in the pro-life debate; the National Taxpayers Union; the Home School Legal Defense Association; and the National Federation of Independent Business, to name a few. Conservative groups have been able to pressure the national government into considering their agenda and have become a substantial presence at the state and local levels—introducing property rights and gun-owner rights legislation in a large number of states.

What do public interest groups do to **gain influence**?

Interest groups represent the interests of their members to policy makers at all levels of state and national government. Thus, the elderly play a lead role in pushing the government to adapt affordable health care legislation and Social Security programs, people with disabilities fight for improved access to public buildings, and right-to-life groups press for increased protection for the unborn. While increasing public awareness about their issues and helping to set the public agenda, most public interest groups lobby the government directly to put pressure on the lawmaking process—including shaping the government's agenda by raising new issues or calling attention to previously ignored problems. Besides lobbying Congress, regulatory agencies, and the courts, many engage in protest activities, such as marches and demonstrations. Many also become more directly involved in the electoral process, through endorsing candidates, evaluating candidates or office holders, even creating political parties.

What are the **benefits of joining a public interest group**?

Interest groups allow like-minded individuals to come together and take their claims directly to the government, and thus fill the void left by traditional political parties. Interest groups provide a vehicle for the unrepresented or underrepresented to have their voices and positions heard, thereby making the policy-making process more representatives of diverse populations and varying perspectives. As an organized effort, public interest groups provide a support mechanism for the individual, often making headway into political policy in ways no individual could.

How are **public interest groups organized**?

Interests groups vary in the way that they are organized, depending primarily on their size and scope. Most of the established groups have state affiliates and numerous local chapters. All groups have a leader who mobilizes members and acts to a certain extent as the group's public voice, such as Marian Wright Edelman of the Children's Defense Fund, Pat Robertson (and more recently Roberta Combs) of the Christian Coalition of America, and Nadine Strossen of the American Civil Liberties Union. Membership can range from anywhere in the low hundreds to the many tens of thousands. Funding of the groups primarily comes from membership contributions, dues, and fundraising activities.

What is the **"New Politics"** movement?

Formed during the 1960s in opposition to the Vietnam War, the New Politics movement is a coalition of citizens that has rallied for such issues as environmental protection, women and children's rights, and nuclear disarmament. The movement has been called the number-one contributor to the expansion of interest group activity in the late twentieth century because many of its constituents created the public interest groups that are so prominent today, such as Common Cause, the Sierra Club, the National Organization for Women, and the Environmental Defense Fund, as well as several of consumer activist Ralph Nader's organizations. They applied the term "public interest group" to themselves in order to be distinguished from other business groups and to suggest that their issues were "public," rather than self-serving. Because in the 1960s and 1970s these groups were particularly effective in laying the groundwork for influencing Congress and the courts and securing various consumer and safety legislation, they spawned the interest-group activity that is so prevalent today.

What does the concept of **pluralism** have to do with interest groups?

Pluralism, or the theory that all interests are and should be free to compete for influence in the government, is the underlying philosophy of public interest groups. Numerous groups competing for their agendas at the national, state, and local levels ensures balance and compromise in public policy.

What does it mean to **lobby**?

Public interest groups use the process of lobbying to assert their influence over the policy process. A lobbyist is any person who attempts to influence a policy member through what are known as lobbying techniques, such as testifying at court hearings, contacting government officials directly to present a certain point of view, presenting research results to back a certain position, entering into coalitions with other organizations to shape the implementation of policies, soliciting the media to advance a particular cause, consulting with government officials to plan legislative strategy, even helping to draft legislation. Lobbyists inspire letter-writing campaigns, undertake grassroots lobbying efforts, and engage in fundraising projects. While some public interest groups, such as Common Cause, Mothers Against Drunk Driving, and the National Coalition for the Homeless, maintain permanent lobbies in Washington and in state capitals, others—such as colleges and trade associations—hire lobbying firms who are adept at navigating Congress and the bureaucratic maze.

Who is a **lobbyist**?

Most estimates place the number of lobbyists in Washington, DC, at close to 20,000, more than 35 for each of the 535 members of the 107th Congress. According to the 1995 Lobbying Disclosure Act, a lobbyist must spend at least 20 percent of his or her time lobbying Congressional members or executive branch officials or their staffs. Because lobbying plays such an important role in passing Congressional legislation, many lobbyists are those who know the system inside out: former members of Congress, former staff aides, former White House officials, and former Cabinet officers.

What is **grassroots lobbying**?

Grassroots lobbying is a form of political lobbying that strives to involve ordinary citizens in a special interest group's campaign. It involves door-to-door informational drives to the public, mass mailings, and print ads, in an effort to persuade voters to act as advocates for a special interest group's agenda—urging them to write or call their representatives or members of Congress with their support. Beyond knocking on doors, interest groups have grown savvy in their use of the Internet and computerized fax machines to recruit thousands of Americans at the grassroots level.

How do public interest groups **use the media to their advantage**?

Solicitation of the media is one of the most powerful tools that can be used in grassroots lobbying. Because the media has a large and powerful influence over the government and its agenda, the more media attention that a cause receives, the more likely that Congress is going to act upon it. Public interest groups gain media attention by courting reporters and keeping them up-to-date on the nuances of their issues, writing stories themselves for newspapers and magazines, discussing their issues on television talk shows, and buying ad space in newspapers, in special interest magazines, and on billboards.

In what ways is **litigation** used by interest groups to advance their cause?

Interest groups use litigation to fight for their causes in court, with a number of interest groups, or their specially created divisions, specifically dedicated to working within the judicial system. Examples include the Pacific Legal Foundation, which was created to fight environmental protection groups in court; the Christian Legal Society, which concentrates on issues of church and state; and the U.S. Chamber of Commerce, which developed its National Chamber Litigation Center to support business interests in courts. Activities include litigating cases, demonstrating in front of courthouses, sending letters to judges, and filing *amicus curiae* (Latin for "friend of the court") legal briefs in cases in which they are not directly involved.

What is meant by the term **"iron triangle"**?

The term "iron triangle" refers to the mutually supporting, cooperative relationships that often develop between a congressional committee, an administrative agency, and one or more interest groups as these groups gain access to the decision-making powers of Congress. The relationship is referred to as triangular, since each entity represents a point in the triangle with each point supporting one another; for example, consider the close relationship that exists between members of Congress from tobacco-growing states, officials in the U.S. Department of Agriculture, and the lobbyists for the tobacco industry. Critics of the iron-triangle formula maintain that it enables the special interest groups to exert undue influence in Congress and the federal bureaucracy, citing campaign finance reform as the antidote.

What is **reverse lobbying**?

Rampant in Washington during the 1990s, reverse lobbying is a form of lobbying where government officials work with interest groups to pressure other government officials. For example, the Clinton administration formed relationships with dozens of health care reform groups in 1993 and 1994, asking them to lobby Congress on behalf of the president's ambitious health care reform package. Along those same lines, Republican House leaders in 1995 organized their "Project Relief," an ambitious coalition of over 100 trade associations formed to push regulatory reform legislation through the House and Senate through grassroots efforts.

What is a **PAC**?

PAC—which stands for political action committee—is a political committee organized for the purpose of raising and spending money to elect and defeat political candidates. The term refers to those political committees that are not the official committees of any candidate or political party, but rather are affiliated with corporations, labor unions, and public interest groups. Most PACs have specific legislative agendas and play a significant role in congressional elections, contributing large amounts of money to candidates and engaging in other election-related activities.

How do **PACs and public interest groups differ**?

Public interest groups promote their causes primarily by attempting to influence government policy, rather than by raising funds or running elections. However, like a political party, an interest group will often form a PAC, which then becomes the group's federally registered fundraising arm, making campaign contributions to candidates that the interest group supports. A well-known and powerful PAC is EMILY's List, which helps elect pro-choice Democratic women candidates to office. In 2000, EMILY's List contributed a record $9.3 million to candidates during the two-year election cycle. It is associated with many women's special interest groups, including the National Organization for Women (NOW) and the National Partnership of Women and Children.

How much can PACs **contribute to candidates' campaigns for federal office**?

PACs may contribute up to $5,000 per candidate per election. However, the PAC must meet the legal requirement for a multicandidate committee; that is, it must be a political committee that has been registered with the Federal Elections Commission for at least six months, have received contributions from more than 50 people, and have at least five federal candidates. PACs can also give up to $15,000 annually to any national party committee, and $5,000 annually to any other PAC. PACs may also receive up to $5,000 from any one individual, PAC, or party committee per calendar year.

What are some examples of **influential PACs**?

PACs have increased significantly in numbers and influence since the late twentieth century. In 1976, there were 608 PACS, but by 1998 their numbers increased to more than 4,000. Through their PACs, the following industries and companies represent the largest contributors to federal candidates: law firms; the retired; securities and investment groups; the real estate industry; pharmaceutical companies; insurance companies; computer companies; the entertainment industry; and the oil and gas industry. One of the most influential industries is the tobacco industry; since 1995, tobacco industry PACs have contributed $7.4 million to congressional candidates. In the 2000 election cycle, these PACs gave $2.4 million to candidates for federal office. The pharmaceutical industry also ranks high as an influential industry; since 1991, the companies belonging to the Pharmaceutical Research and Manufacturers of America (PHRMA), the trade group for brand-name drug makers, have given more than $18.6 million in political contributions, primarily through their PACs. The gun rights lobby

Top 20 PAC Contributors to Federal Candidates, 1999–2000*

PAC Name	Total Amount	Dem.	Repub.
National Assn. of Realtors	$3,423,441	41%	59%
Assn. of Trial Lawyers of America	$2,661,000	86%	13%
Intl. Brotherhood of Electrical Workers	$2,635,125	96%	3%
American Fedn. of St./Cnty./Munic. Employees	$2,585,074	95%	5%
Teamsters Union	$2,555,495	93%	7%
National Auto Dealers Assn.	$2,498,700	32%	68%
Laborers Union	$2,245,900	91%	9%
Machinists/Aerospace Workers Union	$2,188,138	99%	1%
United Auto Workers	$2,150,050	99%	1%
American Medical Assn.	$2,028,354	48%	52%
National Beer Wholesalers Assn.	$1,871,500	21%	79%
Service Employees International Union	$1,864,449	90%	10%
Carpenters & Joiners Union	$1,847,920	85%	15%
National Assn. of Home Builders	$1,846,099	36%	64%
United Parcel Service	$1,755,065	35%	65%
United Food & Commercial Workers Union	$1,743,652	97%	2%
National Education Assn.	$1,717,125	95%	5%
Verizon Communications	$1,677,617	33%	67%
American Bankers Assn.	$1,657,615	35%	64%
American Federation of Teachers	$1,599,555	98%	2%

*For ease of identification, the names used in this chart are those of the organization connected with the PAC, rather than the official PAC name. For example, the "Coca-Cola Company Nonpartisan Committee for Good Government" is simply listed as "Coca-Cola Co."

Source: The Center for Responsive Politics

Political action committees contribute significant funds to the campaigns of candidates who can further their interests.

gave more than $6.1 million to federal parties and candidates in PAC and individual donation money.

What are the **most generous PACs** and how much did each contribute to the 2000 presidential election campaign?

According to the Federal Elections Commission, during the 1999–2000 election campaign cycle, PACs contributed about $245 million to federal candidates (up 19 percent from the 1997–1998 cycle of $206.8 million) and just under $30 million to the political parties. Those PACs in the "Top 20" list of contributors to federal candidates include the National Association of Realtors (who gave $3.4 million); the International Brotherhood of Electrical Workers ($2.6 million); the Association of Trial Lawyers of America ($2.6 million); the Teamsters Union ($2.5 million); United Auto Workers ($2.1 million); the American Medical Association ($2 million); and the American Federation of Teachers ($1.5 million). The International Brotherhood of Electrical Workers gave the most to Democratic federal candidates ($2.5 million), and the National Association of Realtors gave the most to Republican federal candidates ($2 million). Other generous PACs include the American Federation of State, County, and Municipal Employees; the Democratic Republican Independent Voter Education Committee; the National Association of Home Builders; and the National Automobile Dealers Association.

How are PAC donations and political decisions linked?

Advocates of campaign finance reform have long held that PAC donations can be directly linked to the way elected officials vote on issues that are dear to those PACs. The League of Women Voters, for example, cites these specific examples: In the 1997–1998 midterm election cycle, tobacco-industry PACs gave $1.4 million to federal candidates; in 1998, the Senate voted against teen antismoking programs by failing to increase the Food and Drug Administration's budget. Similarly, managed health care PACs gave more than $742,000 to federal candidates; in 1998, the House of Representatives defeated regulations to guarantee greater access to necessary care. PACs associated with the gun lobby and opposed to criminal background checks distributed $889,000 to federal candidates; in 1998, the Senate passed an amendment to bar taxes on gun dealers to fund a database to search criminal records. Finally, the timber industry PACs gave $818,000 to federal candidates; in 1997, the Senate voted to continue subsidies to timber companies to build logging roads. In addition, corporations seeking to restrict the ability of the Occupational Safety and Health Administration (OSHA) to enforce worker health and safety regulations increased their political contributions when the issue came before Congress in 1995; since the early 1990s, the food industry has given more than $41 million to the campaigns of Washington lawmakers and managed to influence every bill that has promised meaningful improvement to that industry.

AT THE POLLS

VOTING IN AMERICA

Who is **eligible to vote**?

Any citizen of the United States over the age of 18, and who meets certain state requirements, may vote in federal elections. The most common state requirement is registration, although requirements for registration and registration deadlines vary from state to state. North Dakota is the only state that does not require voters to register. In addition, 30 states and the District of Columbia require that voters be residents for a period of between one and five days prior to election day, and most states bar registration and voting by convicted felons and those deemed as mentally incompetent.

How do you **register to vote**?

A citizen registers to vote by filling out a registration application, which can be obtained from either the local election official in the citizen's county or city, or through registration outreach programs sponsored by such groups as the League of Women Voters. In addition, citizens can also register to vote at state department of motor vehicles offices, state offices providing public assistance, state offices providing state-funded programs for the disabled, and armed forces recruitment offices. Many states also offer registration opportunities at public libraries, post offices, unemployment offices, and public high schools and universities.

How many **people in the United States are registered to vote**?

According to Federal Elections Commission statistics, there were over 156 million registered voters at the time of the 2000 presidential elections.

If you are a citizen, how do you **change your party affiliation**?

Each state's board of elections has specific requirements and deadlines regarding changing party affiliations. In most states, if you want to change your party affiliation you must re-register to vote. Citizens can change their party affiliation on their state's voter registration form.

How has the **right to vote been extended** since the Civil War?

Before the Civil War, only white males aged 21 years or older and some black males in certain nonslave states were eligible to vote. Since this time, through a series of constitutional amendments and legislative enactments, Congress and the states have progressively extended the right to vote to other groups. The Fifteenth Amendment (ratified in 1870) guarantees the right to vote regardless of "race, color, or previous condition of servitude"; the Seventeenth Amendment (1913) provides for direct popular election to the Senate; the Nineteenth Amendment (1920) extended the vote to women; the Twenty-third Amendment (1961) established the right to vote in presidential elections for citizens of the District of Columbia; the Twenty-fourth Amendment (1964) prohibits the payment of any tax as a prerequisite for voting in federal elections; and the Twenty-sixth Amendment (1971) extended the vote to citizens 18 years or older.

When did **women get the right to vote**?

Women received the right to vote with the ratification of the Nineteenth Amendment in 1920. However, it took many years of organized struggle for women to gain the right to vote. The women's rights convention held at Seneca Falls, New York, on July 19 and 20, 1848, was considered a historical step in gaining women the right to vote, and between that time and the ratification of the Nineteenth Amendment, certain states granted women the right to vote. After years of vigorous lobbying by suffragettes such as Elizabeth Cady Stanton, Susan B. Anthony, Lucretia Mott, and Lucy Stone, in 1893 women got the vote in Colorado, followed by Utah (1896), Idaho (1896), Washington (1910), California (1911), Arizona (1912), Kansas (1912), Oregon (1912), Illinois (1913), Nevada (1914), and Montana (1914).

When did **African Americans get the right to vote**?

Technically, African Americans received the right to vote with the Fifteenth Amendment. However, it wasn't until the 1960s—with the passage of the Civil Rights Acts of 1957, 1960, and 1964 and the Voting Rights of Act 1965, which suspended all literacy tests and similar devises that had been used to discriminate against minority groups, particularly blacks—that African Americans began to experience lessened instances of discrimination at the polls and truly gained the opportunity to exercise their voting rights. In 1975 Congress again extended the Voting Rights Act, enacting a permanent nationwide ban on the

Voters line up outside a polling station in Peachtree, Alabama, in 1966, a year after the passage of the Voting Rights Act, which extended legal protection of voting rights to African Americans and other minorities.

use of literacy test and devices, expanding the act to provide coverage for minority groups not literate in English, and requiring affected states and jurisdictions to offer certain types of bilingual assistance to voters. Although voter rights for blacks and other minorities have come a long way, as recently as the 2000 presidential election the National Association for the Advancement of Colored People (NAACP) maintained that voting irregularities plagued African American voters in Florida, charging that voters were unlawfully turned away from polls by sheriff's deputies and improperly stricken from voter rolls.

What was the purpose of the **poll tax**?

The poll tax—a capital tax levied equally on every voting adult—was enacted in the southern states between 1889 and 1910. The poll tax disenfranchised many minority groups who could not afford to pay the tax, such as blacks and poor whites, because payment of the tax was a prerequisite to voting. By the 1940s certain states had abolished these taxes; in 1964 the Twenty-fourth Amendment outlawed their use, and by 1966 this prohibition was extended to all elections in the United States by the Supreme Court, which ruled that the tax violated the equal protection clause of the Fourteenth Amendment.

What is a **referendum** and how does it differ from an **initiative**?

In many states, voters play a direct role in the lawmaking process, exercising the power of both referendum and initiative in local elections where voting on pertinent issues such as those involving businesses, schools, neighborhoods, transportation, safety or health can transform a community. If a law has been passed in the state legislature, it may be sent back to the voters to accept or reject, letting the voters decide directly if a new law should be put into effect. This is known as the power of referendum. In the process of initiative, a group of voters signs a petition asking for a specific law. If enough people have signed the petition, the qualified voters must be given a chance to vote for or against the proposed law, which will go into effect if more than half (a majority) of the votes are in favor of the law.

What is **"split-ticket"** voting?

Sometimes called ticket splitting, "split-ticket" voting refers to voting for candidates of different political parties in the same election, for example, when a citizen votes for a Republican president and a Democratic senator. Because ticket splitters do not vote for all of one party's candidates in any given election, they are said to "split" their votes between parties.

What is **"straight-ticket"** voting?

"Straight-ticket" voting refers to casting a blanket vote for all candidates of a particular party, for example, when a Republican citizen who votes only for Republican candidates in any given election. In certain states, a voter can vote for all candidates of a certain party by checking one box on the ballot.

What is a **ballot**?

A ballot is the method of voting for candidates for political office. A voter's choice may be indicated in the colored circles of the ballot form itself, on printed tickets, by voting machines, or through electronic or computerized voting.

What is a **turnout**?

Voter turnout is the amount of people who actually show up and vote at the polls. Although there were over 156 million registered voters at the time of the 2000 presidential elections, only a little over 105 million people actually cast votes for the president that year.

How are the **candidates on the ballot determined**?

Candidates for the presidency and vice presidency representing the major political parties automatically have their names placed on the general election ballot in all of the states, while minor party candidates must satisfy various state requirements, such as gaining a requisite degree of public support through petition signatures, establishing a state-mandated organizational structure, or having polled a required number of votes in the most recent statewide election. All states also provide for independent candidates to be included on the general election ballot; in almost all cases, independent candidates must submit a requisite number of petitions signed by registered voters in order to gain ballot access. Some states also provide for write-in votes for those candidates not included on the ballot. Major-party congressional candidates are given automatic ballot access in all states, while minor-party and independent candidates must meet various states requirements, such as submission of petition signatures of registered voters, in order to be placed on the general election ballot.

What is the plurality system?

Used for legislative elections in the United States, the plurality electoral system is the oldest and the most frequently used voting system in the world. Known also as the "winner-take-all" system, the plurality system is straightforward: Voters simply place a mark next to their preferred candidate, and the candidate who receives the highest number of votes wins. Its more technical term, the "single-member district plurality system," captures the two basic attributes of the plurality system: First, votes are cast in single-member districts—districts in which only one member of the legislature is elected; second, the winner is determined by who receives the most votes (or the plurality of the vote). Proponents of plurality electoral systems cite three main advantages: simplicity, stability, and constituency representation.

What is **proportional representation**?

The main rival to the single-member plurality system and the system most used by European democracies is called "proportional representation." Although there are many different forms of proportional representation, all proportional representation systems have two things in common: First, proportional representation voting systems elect people in multimember districts. Instead of one member of the legislature being elected in a small district, proportional representation uses much larger districts where five, 10, or more members are elected, resulting in multiple winners of office in each district. Second, the multiple seats are distributed according to the proportion of the vote won by particular parties or political groups. For example, if there was a 10-member proportional representation district in which the Republican candidates won 60 percent of the vote, they would receive six of those 10 seats; with 30 percent of the vote, the Democrats would win three seats, and any third party who won 10 percent of the vote would receive the remaining seat.

THE POPULAR VOTE AND THE ROLE OF THE ELECTORAL COLLEGE

Is the presidential candidate who gets the **highest number of popular votes** the winner?

No. The president and vice president of the United States not elected directly by the popular vote, but rather are elected by electors, individuals who are chosen in the November general election in presidential election years. Known collectively as the electoral college, it is this entity that votes directly for the president and vice president.

Were presidents ever **elected popularly**?

No. The electoral college was established by the Founding Fathers as a compromise between election of the president by Congress and election by popular vote. They were attempting to create a blueprint that would allow for the election of the president without political parties, without national campaigns, and without disturbing the carefully designed balance between the presidency and the Congress, and between the states and the federal government. Mandated by the Constitution and modified by the Twelfth and Twenty-Third Amendments, the "College of Electors" (as the Founders called it) has served as the nation's method for selecting its highest official for over 200 years.

What is the **electoral college** and how does it work to elect the United States president and vice president?

Each state is allocated a number of electors equal to the number of its U.S. senators plus the number of its U.S. representatives. When Americans vote for a president and vice president, they are actually voting for presidential electors, known collectively as the electoral college. It is these electors, chosen by the people, who elect the chief executive. The Constitution assigns each state a number of electors equal to the combined total of the state's Senate (always two) and House of Representatives delegation (which may change each decade according to the size of each state's population as determined in the U.S. Census); at the time of the 2000 elections, the number of electors per state ranges from 3 to 54, for a total of 538.

In each presidential election year, a group (ticket or slate) of candidates is nominated by political parties and other groupings in each state, usually at a state party convention, or by the party state committee. It is these elector-candidates, rather than the presidential and vice presidential nominees, for whom the people vote in the November election, which is held on the Tuesday after the first Monday in November. In most states, voters cast a single vote for the slate of electors pledged to the party presidential and vice presidential candidates of their choice. The slate winning the most popular votes is elected; this is known as the winner-take-all, or general ticket, system. Maine and Nebraska use the district system, under which two electors are chosen on a statewide, at-large basis, and one is elected in each congressional district. Electors assemble in their respective states on Monday after the second Wednesday in December. They are pledged and expected, but not required, to vote for the candidates they represent. Separate ballots are cast for president and vice president, after which the electoral college ceases to exist for another four years.

How are the **electoral votes tabulated**?

The electoral vote results are counted and certified by a joint session of Congress, held on January 6 of the year succeeding the election. A majority of electoral votes (currently 270 of 538) is required to win. If no candidate receives a majority, then the president is elected by the House of Representatives, and the vice president is elected by the Senate, a process known as contingent election.

Who can serve as an elector?

Aside from members of Congress and employees of the federal government, who are prohibited from serving as an elector in order to maintain the balance between the legislative and executive branches of the federal government, anyone may serve as an elector. Since electors are often selected in recognition of their service and dedication to their political party, they are often state elected officials, party leaders, or persons who have a personal or political affiliation with the presidential candidate. The process for selecting electors varies throughout the United States. Generally, the political parties nominate electors at their state party conventions or by a vote of the party's central committee in each state.

Given the electoral college procedure, **is the individual vote really meaningful**?

Yes, within his or her state, a person's vote has a great deal of significance. Under the electoral college system, the people do not elect the president and vice president through a direct nationwide vote, but a person's vote helps decide which candidate receives that state's electoral votes. It is possible that an elector could ignore the results of the popular vote, but that occurs very rarely.

How can the electoral college **defeat the will of a majority of the people** in selecting a president?

The Founding Fathers devised the electoral college system as part of their plan to share power between the states and the national government. Under the federal system adopted in the Constitution, the nationwide popular vote has no legal significance. As a result, it is possible that the electoral votes awarded on the basis of state elections could produce a different result than the nationwide popular vote. The electoral vote totals determine the winner, not the statistical plurality or majority a candidate may have in the nationwide vote totals. Forty-eight out of the 50 states award electoral votes on a winner-takes-all basis (as does the District of Columbia). For example, all 54 of California's electoral votes go to the winner of that state election, even if the vote is split 50.1 percent to 49.9 percent.

Since the nation's first presidential election in 1792 there have only been a few times when the winner of the popular vote has not won the election, or when the decision was thrown to the House of Representatives, as required by the Constitution. The first viciously contested election occurred in 1876, when Democrat Samuel Tilden won the popular vote and the electoral college by one ballot, but the ballots in three southern states were contested (Louisiana, South Carolina, and Florida), eventually throwing the election to Republican Rutherford B. Hayes. The most recently contested election was the 2000 presidential race, in which George W. Bush received less (48.4 percent) of the popular vote than opponent Al Gore (who garnered 48.6 percent), but picked up the key state of Florida, thus winning 271 electoral votes to Gore's 267.

Do electors ever **switch votes**?

Theoretically, yes, but in all probability, no. There is no constitutional provision or federal law that requires electors to vote according to the results of the popular vote in their states. Some states, however, require electors to cast their votes according to the popular vote. These pledges fall into two categories—electors bound by state law and those bound by pledges to political parties. In the twenty-first century it is rare for electors to disregard the popular vote by casting their electoral vote for someone other than their party's candidate. Electors generally hold a leadership position in their party or were chosen to recognize years of loyal service to the party. Throughout United States history, more than 99 percent of electors have voted as pledged.

Did the electoral college ever **vote unanimously** for any president?

Yes, the electoral college voted unanimously on two occasions, both for George Washington, for his terms beginning in 1789 and 1793. James Monroe just missed winning this same claim to fame, since in the presidential election of 1820 all of the electors except for one voted to reelect Monroe.

Why does this nation **still have the electoral college**?

Because the electoral college process is part of the original design of the Constitution, a constitutional amendment would need to be passed in order to change this system. While many different proposals to alter the presidential election process, such as direct nationwide election by the people, have been suggested over the years, none has been passed by Congress and sent to the states for ratification. However, the Twelfth Amendment, which deals with the expansion of voting rights and the use of the popular vote in the states as the vehicle for selecting electors, has substantially changed the electoral college process.

During a presidential election, **who is responsible in a given locality for voting procedures and counting the votes**?

Each state's secretary of state office is responsible for facilitating statewide voter registration in accordance with state laws; testing and certifying all voting systems used in state elections; preparing ballots and election forms and materials; tabulating, processing, and certifying election results; and responding to requests for advice, information, and interpretation on election laws and procedures.

What is a vote recount and when is a recount necessary?

A vote recount involves just that—recounting votes made in an election. Each state has specific procedures a candidate must follow when filing a protest that results in a recount, as well as specific procedures for conducting its recounts of paper ballots, voting machines, and electronic equipment. In general, a political candidate may choose to conduct a recount if there are reasonable grounds for alleging the count of votes at any voting station was inaccurate or the number of valid or rejected ballots was sufficient to affect election results.

In the 2000 presidential election, **how many votes were eventually not counted for either candidate in Florida**, and what was the **percentage of uncounted votes nationwide**?

Although a definitive number has not been reached, according to media sources approximately 180,000 Florida ballots were cast but not counted. On a nationwide level, a July 2001 joint study conducted by the Massachusetts Institute of Technology and California Institute of Technology revealed that 4 million to 6 million votes of the 100 million cast last November were not counted, citing faulty voting equipment, confusing ballots, voter error, and problems at polling places—including long lines, short hours, and inconvenient locations—as the main reasons. The estimate of lost votes is at least twice as high as one released earlier in July 2001 by House Democrats, who said that about 2 million votes, or nearly 2 percent of the total, had not been counted. The study also confirmed that Florida was just one of many states with ballot problems, citing Illinois, New York, South Carolina, Idaho, Wyoming, and Georgia with higher rates of spoiled, unmarked, or uncounted ballots.

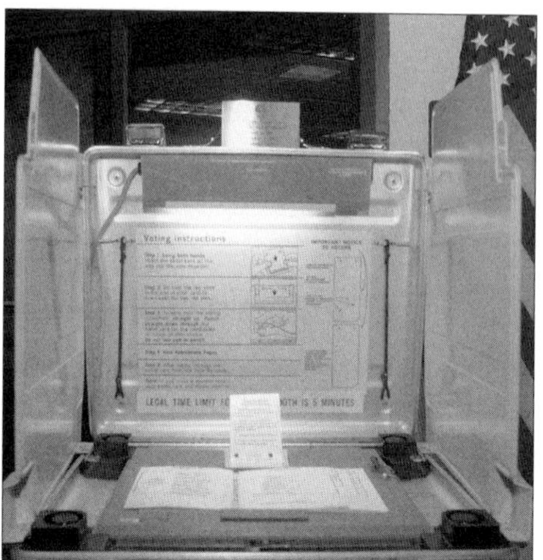

The controversy surrounding the accuracy of votes cast with the Votomatic voting machine like this one used in West Palm Beach County, Florida, during the 2000 election has led many polling sites to consider the use of computer touchscreens and other more sophisticated voting methods.

What types of **voting methods and machines** are currently used?

Counties across America vary in the voting methods and machines used, typically relying on antiquated equipment that may not count votes accurately. The oldest and simplest form of voting is the paper ballot, onto which a voter simply places a check next to the name of his or her preferred candidate, which is then counted by hand. Mechanical lever systems, which were developed in the 1890s, involve large displays of the entire ballot and small levers next to each choice; the voter flips a lever to choose a candidate and, once finished voting, pulls a large lever, which counts each vote. Developed in the 1960s, punch card systems require that voters use a stylus to punch a mark into pre-scored card perforations next to their preferred candidate's name. According to an October 2001 University of California at Berkeley study, the trend in voting equipment is away from paper, punch card, and lever systems and toward the more modern systems, including those utilizing optical scanning (in which an infrared or other scanner records the markings on a paper ballot) and computer touch-screens (voters push a button or touch the face of an ATM-type machine and choose a candidate). Many jurisdictions are replacing older voting equipment with more modern technology, and some are considering the use of vote-by-mail and Internet voting to ensure greater degrees of accuracy.

Optical scanning and electronic systems perform better than other systems, especially in large counties, and the newer versions of both systems give voters feedback that checks their selections before they submit their ballot. Touch-screen electronic voting systems allow individuals to select a ballot translated into a foreign language, and some of these systems allow disabled persons to vote by listening to recordings.

What is a **chad**, **dangling chad**, and **pregnant chad**, and how did the condition of the chad come to have such influence in the 2000 election?

In the midst of the a close presidential race, once it was announced that problems with the machine tabulations had potentially invalidated thousands of ballots, Democratic presidential nominee Al Gore demanded a recount in several Democratic counties in Florida. Gore maintained that an initial machine recount had misread thousands of punch-card ballots in the contested counties due to machine design problems: Voting machines read only those ballots that were clearly punched, and did not read those that contained a "chad," or the small tab left dangling from the punched hole, next to a candidate's name, as well as ballots with a "dangling" chad, that is, a chad hanging by one corner, or a "pregnant" chad, a swollen hole that was not clearly perforated. As the recount controversy progressed, the condition of the chad as an indicator of voter intent and the broader issue of outdated voting machines and equipment were at the heart of the debate.

What did the **Supreme Court** rule in its final decision affecting the 2000 vote?

In the Florida vote count certified on November 26, 2000, a total of 537 votes out of the more than 5.8 million cast separated Al Gore and George W. Bush. Whether additional votes from manual recounts would be counted was in litigation between the two candidates and their representatives until the evening of December 12, when the Supreme Court ruled that manual recounts could not continue on constitutional grounds because Florida's lack of uniform standards for the recounting process violated the Fourteenth Amendment's equal protection guarantees. The Court's 5 to 4 ruling thus awarded the White House to George W. Bush, based on the original certified vote.

What was the **absolute deadline for deciding the 2000 election**? If no decision had been made at that point, by law, what would have happened?

The official deadline for certifying electoral college votes was midnight, December 12, 2000. If no presidential candidate would have received a majority of the electoral college vote by that time, the election would have constitutionally been thrown to the House of Representatives—whose majority party was Republican that year—for vote. The House would have selected from among three leading candidates, with each state having one vote. If a tie occurred in the House, then the matter would have been resolved in the Senate, which is empowered by the Constitution to choose a vice president from the two leading candidates. This vice presidential choice then becomes president by order of succession. (He or she then has the authority to appoint a vice president, subject to confirmation.) If the Senate failed to select a vice president, then the order of presidential succession would have been as follows: the sitting Speaker of the House would have become provisional president, followed by the president pro tempore of the Senate (which in November 2000 was 98-year-old Republican senator Strom Thurmond of South Carolina) should the Speaker not have been able to serve.

Have the **results of any other national election ever been seriously opposed** in U.S. history?

Yes, historians generally agree on four close and disputed elections for the nineteenth century, and one for the twentieth. In the election of 1800, presidential candidates

Aaron Burr and Thomas Jefferson, both nominees of the Republican Party, tied in the electoral college vote with 73 votes each, throwing the election into the House of Representatives and triggering the passage of the Twelfth Amendment, which maintains that electoral delegates must vote separately for president and vice president. During the election of 1824, four candidates ran for the presidency, but none received either the majority of the popular vote or the majority of the electoral college; Andrew Jackson led runner-up John Quincy Adams in both popular and electoral votes but ultimately lost the presidency when the House of Representatives chose Adams. In the presidential race of 1876, Democrat Samuel Tilden won the popular vote and the electoral college by one vote against Republican Rutherford B. Hayes, but ballots contested in several southern states ultimately threw the White House to Hayes. And during the election of 1888, Democratic incumbent Grover Cleveland won the popular vote but lost in the electoral college by 65 votes to Republican Benjamin Harrison, marking the first time in history that the electoral college had denied the presidency to the clear winner of the country's national vote.

In the 1960 presidential election a little over 100,000 votes ended up separating incumbent Republican Richard Nixon and Democrat John F. Kennedy, making it one of the closest elections of the twentieth century. When it became clear that Kennedy had won the state of Illinois by approximately 8,000 popular votes, thus picking up that state's electoral votes, Nixon conceded the election. Despite these close races, no election in history has come down to such a margin as the 537-vote difference that ultimately decided the 2000 presidential contest.

How have the results of the 2000 presidential election played a role in **election reform**?

The 2000 presidential election exposed unprecedented weaknesses in America's voting systems, calling many to push for reform. Critics cited problems such as antiquated voting machines, ballot systems that confuse voters, an insufficient number of polling places, limited accessibility for people with disabilities, chaotic absentee ballot procedures, and a general lack of standardization and consistency. Under particular scrutiny was the punch-card voting system that became the focus of the Florida recount. In addition, civil rights concerns arose from the unfair application of voter identification requirements and from the fact that many of the oldest, faultiest voting machines found their way into low-income, minority neighborhoods.

Since the 2000 election fiasco, several states have implemented election overhaul measures and several others have discussed remedying their election laws. In April 2002 the Senate approved a landmark $3.5-billion bill that would require states to upgrade their voting systems over a five-year period, including replacing outdated ballot counting machines, improving access to polling places for the disabled, and increasing voter participation. The House passed its own voting reform bill in December 2001 authorizing $2.65 billion in federal aid to the states over three years. Although Congress has bickered over major election reform legislation, sponsors from both sides are optimistic that the versions can be reconciled, ensuring that some version of the legislation would become law before the 2004 presidential election. In general, lawmakers generally agree on certain areas of reform: (1) states should maintain a statewide voter registration list that is linked to local precincts; (2) voters whose names do not appear on registration list should have the right to cast a provisional ballot that would be counted if their registration is verified; and (3) in an effort to reduce the number of mistakes that occur at the polls, more time and money should be used in recruiting and training poll works and educating voters about their rights and responsibilities. In addition, many believe that uniform rules for what constitutes a valid vote should be employed, and that effective procedures for counting overseas ballots and military votes should be implemented.

Can voters expect to eventually **cast their votes online**?

Although the Internet has allowed scores of Americans to get involved in politics in unprecedented ways, only six states experimented with online voting in the November 2000 presidential election. While most of the votes were nonbinding ballots cast in experiments at Arizona and California voting stations, those who participated endorsed its ease and simplicity. (Arizona's Democratic primary in March 2000 became the nation's first binding election conducted via the Internet.) However, fears of hackers tampering with or shutting down voting sites have led most states to proceed cautiously with online voting—although it is possible to register to vote online. Critics also argue that a gap exists between connected Americans and those without the financial means to own a computer or pay for Internet service, making at-home Internet voting a viable option only for a select demographic. Optimists, however, point to the potential of the Internet to create a more democratic America by implementing a foolproof cyberspace system that soon would be available to all. Few disagree that this medium holds vast possibilities for involving the United States citizenry in the political process in the twenty-first century.

POLLING

What is a **representative sample**?

Assessments of citizen attitudes about political candidates are based on polling a "representative sample," or select portion, of the total population. Therefore, if 1,000 persons are polled, and of them 750 select candidate A as their presidential choice, then, according to pollsters, that statistic should linearly scale up to the entire population: If there are 1 million votes to be cast, then 750 x 1000, or 750,000—give or take a 5 percent or less margin of error—should select the same candidate. However, because some segments of the voting population may not be included in the "representative" sample, critics maintain that there is a larger margin of error than pollsters are willing to account for.

How is **polling done on election night** to forecast the winner?

As a routine part of election campaigns, polls are used to forecast the results of a particular election. On election night, communications companies conduct "exit polls," which, unlike electoral surveys, are not concerned with the intended vote, but are based on the answers given by voters selected at random after they have voted. Although these are not results that have already been counted and verified after the closing of the polls, they do reflect how a person says he or she has actually voted, and they are relatively reliable.

What caused the 2000 election night forecast on all the major network outlets to be so unreliable?

On election night, the networks largely based their projections on exit polling data supplied to them by the Voter News Service (VNS), a consortium funded by the networks and the Associated Press, which had produced figures predicting an Al Gore victory in Florida. Although VNS supplies the raw polling data, it is the networks' on-staff political experts who make the networks' final calls. Around 8:00 P.M. Eastern Standard Time, all of the major networks—including ABC, CBS, NBC, CNN, and Fox—called the state of Florida for Vice President Al Gore. The Associated Press and PBS followed suit. A few hours later, however, the networks began reversing themselves, as the actual counted votes did not match the projections, and the historical night of speculating which candidate would win Florida's 25 electoral votes began. According to the networks, the decision to call Florida for Gore was based on two factors: exit polls indicating a narrow Gore lead, and initial returns that may have been incorrectly entered into the networks' databases, causing their computer models to anticipate a larger Gore vote than was ultimately recorded.

Are there other instances in U.S. history in which the **predictions of major polls did not represent actual election results**?

The most notorious failure of polling was the *Literary Digest* survey of 1936 that incorrectly predicted a landslide victory for the Republican Kansas governor Alfred Landon over incumbent Democrat Franklin D. Roosevelt. Although the magazine had correctly predicted the winner of every presidential election since 1916, it incorrectly made its

Newspaper headlines the morning after the 2000 presidential election reflect the suspense, drama, and indecision surrounding the results.

prediction for Landon (who they said would garner 56 percent of the vote to Roosevelt's 44 percent) because their questionnaire of 2.4 million failed to include the poor, an ignored portion of the population who largely voted for Roosevelt in this depression era. In fact, Roosevelt ended up sweeping 62 percent of the popular vote, compared to Landon's 38 percent. In 1948, three major polls (including the Gallup Poll) incorrectly predicted that Republican New York governor Thomas Dewey would defeat incumbent Harry Truman, largely based on their improper use of quota sampling, which did not accurately reflect the voting population and hence was not totally representative. Although Gallup predicted that Dewey would win 50 percent and Truman 44 percent of the popular vote, the results were almost exactly reversed, with Truman garnering 50 percent of the popular vote, and Dewey 45 percent. (From this campaign, most remember the *Chicago Daily Tribune*'s famous headline, "Dewey Defeats Truman.") The 2000 presidential elections aside, since that time polls have correctly predicted the presidency, with the percentage of error typically at less than 4 percent.

THE MEDIA MACHINE

THE POWER OF THE PRESS

What is **public opinion**?

Public opinion is the complex collection of the opinions of many different groups of people, and represents the sum total of all of their views as they relate to matters of public affairs, namely politics and public policy. Rather than being the single, unified viewpoint of a robotic mindset, instead public opinion represents a variety of people groups, each with a differing point of view on a particular subject.

How is **mass media** defined?

Mass media is defined as the types of media that reach mass audiences; for example, television, radio, film, books, magazines, newspapers, and the Internet.

How is **public opinion measured through the media**?

The general content of public opinion can be found within a variety of media sources, including books, journals, magazine and newspaper articles and editorials, comments made on radio and television, newsletters published by special interest groups, paid advertisements (print, billboards, and commercials), letters to the editor, and e-mails to politicians. While these means of expression are often the way that politicians familiarize themselves with certain issues, because the views expressed aren't necessarily indicative of the size of the group that holds them or how strongly the opinion is held, politicians often turn to other measuring sticks, such as public opinion polls, to supplement them. Polling is also a large part of major media outlet measurements, with entities like the *New York Times* and Cable News Network (CNN) polling the public on political issues and politician approval on a regular basis.

Where do Americans get their **news**?

Americans get their news from the top four mass media outlets: television, newspapers, radio, and magazines. With at least one television set in 98 percent of the nation's homes, turned on for multiple hours each day, television is the primary vehicle for delivering the news. While television replaced newspapers as the primary source of people's political information in the 1960s, the more than 11,000 newspapers published in the United States are still a major contender for people's opinions. And because many of today's major newspapers, including the *New York Times*, the *Los Angeles Times*, the *Chicago Tribune*, and the *Washington Post*, have credible reputations for delivering in-depth coverage of national and local news, they are still a favorite among their combined 150 million readers per issue. Radio has long been a choice of those wanting to gain quick snippets of news and political information on their way to and from work, with at least one station in every major city broadcasting nothing but news. In addition, the popularity of talk radio and the many stations that cater to ethnic-specific audiences has helped this medium reach and influence an increasingly diverse public. Last but not least are the many newsmagazines that dominant the newsstands, including *Time*, *Newsweek*, and *U.S. News & World Report*, which herald a combined circulation of nearly 12 million copies each week.

Who **owns the major media** within the United States?

When America Online (AOL) announced its acquisition of Time Warner in January 2000, AOL Time Warner became the world's largest media company, valued at more than $350 billion. The merger allowed for the acquisition of Time Warner assets, then the largest media monopoly in the United States, including its magazines with a combined circulation of 130 million (*Time*, *Sports Illustrated*, *Life*, and *People*, to name a few); its cable television networks, including Cable News Network and Home Box Office (HBO); and a host of other media outlets, including Warner Books, Warner Bros. Studios, the WB Television Network, and Warner Music. Another large media giant, Viacom, is known for its broadcast and cable assets, including Music Television (MTV), Nickelodeon, VH1, Comedy Central, and Showtime Networks as well as its film production/distribution engines Paramount Pictures and Spelling Entertainment Group.

The News Corporation owns a plethora of book publishers, including HarperCollins Publishers and Morrow/Avon; television and cable companies, including the Fox Broadcasting Company and Fox Entertainment; magazines and newspapers such as *TV Guide* and the *New York Post*; and film production companies, including Twentieth Century-Fox and Fox Filmed Entertainment. Gannett is the largest newspaper group in terms of circulation, owning the Gannett News Service and national papers such as *USA Today*, as well as dozens of dailies. Knight Ridder is the second largest newspaper group in terms of circulation, owning dozens of daily state and local newspapers, as well as (with Gannett) the Detroit Newspapers. The Hearst Corporation owns the *Houston Chronicle*, the *San Francisco Chronicle*, and other notable dailies, as well as magazines as varied as *Esquire*, *Harper's Bazaar*, and *Good Housekeeping*. The Tribune Company owns a host of broadcast and cable companies, as well as the dailies the *Chicago Tribune*, the *Baltimore Sun*, and the *Los Angeles Times*. Last but not least, the New York Times Company owns the *Boston Globe* and the *New York Times*, as well as a handful of radio and television stations.

What is the **most powerful form of mass media**?

For disseminating ideas, persuading public opinion, and reaching voters, television wins hands-down as the most powerful form of mass media. With the typical American watching a minimum of three hours of television per day and the typical household running its television for seven hours per day, television attracts a large and wide-reaching audience that no other form of communication can reach. With the 1980s deregulation of the U.S. telecommunications industry and the advent of cable television, the average community in the United States receives 30 channels of television that cover every imaginable component of society. Americans can even watch the House and Senate at work on C-SPAN, something unimaginable to this country's Founding Fathers.

How has the **nature of mass media changed** in the late twentieth century?

Because media companies continue to consolidate at an ever-increasing pace, hard-and-fast rules of who owns what when have disappeared and companies are now able to offer the American public an incomparable portfolio of media and content, from the Internet and broadcast and cable television to film, music, magazines, and books. With the stamp of approval from the Federal Communications Commission, the following mergers represent the evolving culture of media today: November 1998's $4.2 billion merger of Internet giants America Online (AOL) and Netscape Corp.; AT&T's 1999 acquisition of MediaOne, creating the nation's largest cable company; Viacom and CBS's 1999 $35 billion merger, at the time the biggest in media industry history; the creation of the world's largest media business with the 2000 AOL Time Warner deal; the 2000 Time Warner and EMI Group PLC merger, creating the world's second largest music company just two weeks after Time Warner agreed to merge with America Online; and the March 2000 Tribune Co.–Times Mirror Co. $8 billion merger, the largest newspaper acquisition in U.S. history.

How is the **Internet** quickly gaining prominence as a major news outlet?

Besides revolutionizing public access to government documents and databases, public and private libraries, and archives of information, the Internet has changed public discussion of politics by allowing candidates to host web sites and solicit feedback from the public. In 1996 all major presidential candidates developed web sites to support their campaigns, and by the 2000 presidential election campaign candidates were collecting campaign contributions via the web. In addition, all major newspapers and cable and television networks have Internet sites, many of them with politics-specific components, such as CNN's allpolitics.com and the *Washington Post*'s "on politics" section of washingtonpost.com. Online magazines such as the *Drudge Report*, *Slate*, and *Salon* have made both news and gossip available to browsers at a lightening-fast pace, and a 2000 Pew Research Center for the People and the Press report has found that Americans do increasingly rely on the Internet (its major news sites and other less reliable sites alike) for news, and they *do* trust what they read. Interest groups, too, have reached new audiences and expanded their membership via the web, creating the potential for an even greater influence in Washington. And as an interactive medium, the Internet provides the ability to disseminate information quickly and readily and at the same time solicit information from its audience, giving the American public a viable outlet for voicing its opinion and talking back on important political matters.

Is the **Internet usurping more traditional print media** for the daily news?

Although Microsoft's Bill Gates predicted several years ago that the Internet would abolish print media, it hasn't happened yet—partly due to Americans' propensity to read the morning paper over a cup of coffee and the increasing exposure newspapers have gained by creating news-dedicated web sites on the Internet. However, when it comes to political news, more and more citizens are turning to the Internet for information about presidential elections and campaigns, especially as television coverage becomes more superficial. A study by the Annenberg Public Policy Center and the Alliance for Better Campaigns found that the three major network newscasts averaged 36 seconds a night of candidate discourse during the 2000 presidential primaries, "forcing" interested Americans to seek out other media sources, print and online alike, for their news. However, because many online political "front pages" provide little original reporting and not all cover a story in-depth, Internet users may just look at the day's headlines and then return to magazines and newspapers for more complete coverage.

How does the **media shape public opinion**?

Because the media is a primary vehicle for providing Americans with political information, its reporting inevitably shapes the way people think. Not only does the media set the agenda for what people will watch or read, it controls the way that content is delivered. Whether a person watches the hard facts of a live CNN report on Ground Zero or reads an editorial about Osama bin Laden written by a political scientist in a major newspaper, he or she is gathering information and forming an opinion about what he or she sees or hears. To the extent that the media reports accurately, truthfully, nonbiasedly, and nonsensationally, the public can more objectively form opinions. Conversely, to the extent that information is skewed, public opinion can also be similarly affected. Thanks to cable television, the amount of public discourse on air has increased, allowing politicians to present their case on public issues as varied as national health care, terrorism, or the size of the federal budget. So, too, has this medium allowed people to take part in public debates more knowledgably and have a more immediate impact on Congress's policymaking.

How is **media coverage** and **public perception** of current events and politics related?

How the media reports current and political events is directly linked to the public's perception of those events—whether determining a candidate's credibility and integrity, summing up the government's position on a legislative policy, or trying to make sense of a phenomenon as complex as the war on terrorism. Central to this discussion is the amount of time journalists spend editorializing during news segments by injecting their own viewpoints, and how that commentary translates to the audience. The increasing coverage the press gives to a political candidate's character, its dissemination of unsubstantiated rumor, and what it chooses to emphasize, criticize, or applaud during a presidential or congressional campaign not only affects public perception of the candidate or issue, but also the way the public acts at the polls, making or breaking legislation or a candidate's political campaign and career.

How does the media **impact the public agenda**?

Media coverage has had the ability to rally support for or create opposition to a host of national policies. The last half of the twentieth century provides dozens of examples of how the press has changed not only public opinion but public policy as well. Many cite the now-famous press coverage of the 1950s civil rights movement as the catalyst for mounting pressure on Congress to bring an end to segregation. Similarly, the media virtually single-handedly changed public opinion about the Vietnam War, projecting it as ill-fated and unwinnable, and brought pressure upon the Nixon administration to negotiate an end to the bloodshed. And few forget that the media was central to the Watergate scandal of the early 1970s, launching a series of investigations into then-President Richard Nixon's actions, which eventually led to his resignation. More recently, the press's coverage of the September 11, 2001, terrorist attacks ignited a newfound patriotism across America, and may have played a role in Americans accepting the national government's more stringent terrorist policies at the expense of hard-won civil liberties.

What role does the media play in the **coverage of political campaigns**?

In presidential campaigns, news coverage, particularly television news coverage, provides the main source of political information to voters. A January 2000 poll conducted

Fox News Channel correspondent Geraldo Rivera was one of several reporters sent to cover the war in Afghanistan from the front lines, allowing Americans to witness events on television as they unfolded.

for the Pew Research Center for the People and the Press reported that 75 percent of respondents stated that television was their main source for election campaign news. Reporting of campaigns tends to focus on the results of opinion polls, which are essentially free and have a high entertainment value because they emphasize the competitive aspect of the campaigns; nominating conventions, which, aired in a three-hour evening segment, provide compelling visuals and quotable material akin to the Emmys; and candidate advertisements, which are short "sound bites" that can work along or easily be fed into a two-minute news segment. Using these tools, reporters have a jumping-off point for portraying both candidates and the election race. Carefully worded claims that a candidate has "momentum," is a "favorite," or has "suffered a political blow" can alter the course of the election. Because politicians understand how the press works, they adapt their campaigns accordingly, sending results of their own opinion polls and copies of their advertisements to newspapers and television stations across the country in hopes of gaining coverage. Candidates are also well known for leaking their opponents' compromising histories and scandalous behavior to the press.

What role does **political advertising** play in the media and elections?

Televised political advertising today comprises the largest single expense in any presidential media campaign. In 1996, for example, more than 60 percent of the money spent by the Bill Clinton and Bob Dole general election campaigns was devoted to electronic media advertising, most all of it for television. The use of paid media in U.S. elections consists mainly of 30-second advertisements that run on both national networks (such as ABC, CBS, or NBC) and individual television stations in specific cities. However, because most candidates must woo voters at the state level, most political advertising, even in presidential campaigns, is purchased from local television outlets. Candidates focus their advertising on states where votes are split evenly between parties and their advertising dollars can be used most effectively. In hotly contested states, voters typically view six presidential advertisements for every one ad that voters in other states see. While public financing (and thus spending limits) puts the presidential candidates who accept it on an equal footing, Congressional campaigns are financed entirely through private donations. Incumbent members of the House and Senate raise and spend three dollars for every dollar raised by their challengers, thereby giving sitting members of Congress an edge in advertising their candidacies and platforms through the broadcast media.

How do Americans feel about media coverage of **elections and political campaigns**?

Given the importance of election campaigns for the political process and policymaking, it is not surprising that the media's coverage of campaigns is controversial. Overall, Americans criticize the press for being poll- and candidate-centered—providing extensive coverage on poll results as well as campaign strategy analysis—but devoting little or no attention to the discussion of public policies. According to a November 2000 Brown University study, a majority of the public felt that the media's overall coverage of the 2000 election was either "excellent or good," but 28 percent felt that media coverage was biased against an individual candidate. Critics cite the media's overemphasis on candidates' personalities and personal scandal as the reasons for turnoff. This dissatisfaction with the press coverage translates to the candidates as well: A 1999 poll by the Institute for Global Ethics indicates that Americans are bored with candidates' antics at campaign time, with more than eight in ten voters saying that attack-oriented campaigning is unethical, lowers voter turnout, and produces less-ethical elected officials. And 60 percent are "very concerned" that candidates attack each other instead of discussing the issues at campaign time.

How has the **television coverage of presidential campaigns changed** in recent years?

Political analysts cite the presidential campaign of 1992 as the event that marked a change in the power of the Big Three networks—CBS, NBC, and ABC—to dominate election coverage and campaign messages. That year the candidates turned frequently to cable TV, especially CNN as an important alternative media outlet, with Independent candidate Ross Perot announcing his availability on CNN's *Larry King Live* and

Democratic candidate Bill Clinton choosing MTV to showcase his talent as a saxophone player. As the ability of cable TV to cover a campaign 24 hours a day has become more apparent, the major networks have shifted their emphasis to interpreting and analyzing campaigns rather than trying to cover them exhaustively. Although the Big Three networks were still clearly in control in 1992 with 55 percent of the audience for evening news programs, or 22 million U.S. households, cable TV began to encroach upon these figures throughout the 1990s and have clearly provided a viable alternative for viewers in the twenty-first century.

Why do some consider the press to be too **adversarial** in its coverage of political issues?

Because the American news media is a highly competitive industry run by the private sector with very little government intervention, profits and programming choices drive the business, and the types of stories that make it onto the daily news broadcast or into special segments are often sensational stories. Reporters pride themselves in reporting thoroughly, objectively, and fairly; in their self-proclaimed role as advocates for the people they often act as investigators of the government, so to speak—"breaking" controversial stories, revealing corrupt practices, and covering scandalous behavior in an effort to gain an audience and respect among their peers. Consider for example the extraordinary amount of time that was given to the Bill Clinton-Monica Lewinsky sex scandal. While this coverage gains the station a favorable rating, it has also fed the press's reputation of being too adversarial—instigating a backlash from candidates and disproportionately shaping public opinion that ultimately reflects a lack of faith in government and public officials. Nevertheless, the public's "right to know" remains at the heart of America's free-press philosophy and governs the way the media conducts itself, particularly in relationship to the government. While some call this relationship "adversarial," others think of it as objective monitoring.

Does media's coverage of current events and politics ever **backfire** on itself?

Interestingly, how and what the media reports shapes what the public thinks about the media itself as an entity, especially in times of heightening conflict or war. During the Vietnam era, the press was criticized for its depiction of the U.S. government's role in the war. Seven weeks into the United States' war in Afghanistan, many Americans said the nation's news media was behaving irresponsibly (some said "treasonously") by providing extensive raw coverage of the event that they felt fueled the terrorists and unnecessarily alarmed U.S. citizens. By not balancing national security with the right of the American people to know the details of the conflict in Afghanistan and the larger war on terrorism, 48 percent of Americans claimed that the media was irresponsible in its coverage, according to a November 2001 *Los Angeles Times* poll. While news editors maintain that the media's duty is to inform, including reporting unpleasant or unsettling news that may bring a barrage of criticism, critics maintain that controversial breaking stories only result in leaving Americans skeptical about what they hear or read. And while many news organizations insisted that they took special care to avoid overrepresenting or being manipulated by the Taliban and their propagandists, many people objected to the repeated gruesome portrayal of their casualties, citing overstimulation and the dispersal of "too much information"—a concept inconceivable to almost any journalist—as the cause for media turnoff.

Criticism of the media in times of war is nothing new. Polls immediately following the U.S. dispatch of troops to the Caribbean island nation of Grenada in 1984 and participation in the Persian Gulf War of 1991 indicated that the American public overwhelmingly supported the restrictions by the U.S. military on media coverage of the two conflicts.

FREEDOM OF THE PRESS

What is the difference between **independent press** and an **official press**?

An independent press is one that functions free from government control or interference and without prior restraints, such as licensing requirements or content approval, and without subsequent penalties for what has been published or broadcast. An independent or free press differs from an official or government-sponsored press, which is one owned, run, and/or censored by a country's government. Although well over half of the world's nations are self-proclaimed democracies, in an effort to preserve "public stability," most of them have instituted press laws that prohibit reporting on a wide array of subjects, ranging from the internal operations of government to the private lives of government leaders. In addition, many of these countries' journalists practice self-censorship in reaction to government pressure and fear of retribution.

Why has the press been called **"the fourth branch"** of the government?

The American press has assumed the role of the watchdog of government, constantly measuring the government's ethics and practices and reporting on them. The power that comes from this role has earned the press the title "the fourth branch" of the government, after the three official (legislative, judicial, and executive) branches. A variety of court opinions have found that the press has an important function as a guardian of democracy and as a check upon governmental abuse, as echoed by U.S. Supreme Court Justice Hugo Black in his final concurring opinion in the 1971 "Pentagon Papers" case, which mandated that the *New York Times* could continue to publish the then-classified documents that outlined a Department of Defense study of American activities during the Vietnam War. Here, the government's power to censor the press was abolished so that the press would remain free to question government activities and inform the people. It this role as watchdog that prompted Founding Father Thomas Jefferson to say some 200 years ago that if he had to choose between government without newspapers or newspapers without government, he "should not hesitate a moment to prefer the latter."

What does the term **"freedom of the press"** really mean?

The Bill of Rights guarantees that Congress cannot enact a law infringing upon free speech or a free press has provided the basis for America's tradition of a free press for more than 200 years. In drafting the First Amendment, America's Founding Fathers affirmed the fundamental right of citizens to be informed about political issues without governmental interference. Belief in the importance of a press free of governmental control is the reason why the United States has remained "hands-off" when it comes to dealing with the press: Unlike other countries, there is no ministry of information that regulates the activities of journalists, no requirement that journalists be registered, and no requirement that they be members of a union.

Because of this broad constitutional protection of press freedom and similar provisions in state constitutions, few press laws exist in the United States. The ones that do exist tend to provide additional protections and legal rights for journalists; for example, the Privacy Act of 1974 regulates the collection and dissemination of personal information contained in any federal agency's files, and the Privacy Protection Act of 1980 established protection from police searches of newsrooms. There are also federal and state freedom of information and "sunshine" laws, such as the 1966 federal Freedom of Information Act, which allows executive-branch records to be reviewed by the public and press. As a result of this protection, the news media is somewhat buffered from potential backlashes from the government. For example, it is almost impossible for a public official to win a libel suit against the media, because the courts have ruled that government servants must be open to special kinds of scrutiny and accountability in a democratic system. American journalists have also won a number of court cases to protect the anonymity of news sources from government inquiry.

Can the government **restrict the press**? Is there a **difference in regulation between the print and broadcast media**?

While there is very little government interference to restrict media, regulation does exist. The print media enjoys the most freedom—there is no licensing requirement for newspapers to operate and no enforceable definition of what constitutes a legitimate news publication. The press does not require minimum standards for membership, does not issue or revoke licenses, and does not regulate professional standards, although most outlets take pains to adhere to impartial reporting and thorough news coverage. In addition, there are unofficial checks and balances against journalistic excess, including external checks such as libel laws and self-appointed press monitors and internal checks such as the appointment by some newspapers of an "ombudsman" to investigate public complaints and publish self-criticism. The broadcast media, on the other hands, requires a federal government license to operate because the space-limited airwaves it uses are deemed public property. There are, however, safeguards against political discrimination in the licensing process, although examples of political bias in issuing or revoking licenses are rare. For the most part, government decisions on broadcast licensing are aimed at ensuring competition and diversity in a free-market economy.

Under what circumstances, if any, is the government justified in **limiting access to information**? Are journalists within their rights in **publishing** such information?

Political scientists and democratic governments agree that at times, especially times of war and national strife, governments are justified in limiting access to information considered potentially harmful or too sensitive for general distribution. Likewise, however, journalists are fully justified in pursuing such information, and publishing or broadcasting such information as they deem fit. This would-be dichotomy is often called the historical struggle between two rights: that is, the government's right—some say obligation—to protect national security, and the people's right to know, based upon the journalist's right and ability to capture and disseminate the news. Certain scholars maintain that, in the journalist's view, if the publication of a story runs the risk of jeopardizing lives, then the journalist must weigh whether the decision to publish or broadcast is for the ultimate good of the people. Although this is very complex journalistic ethics, in the United States the fact remains that it is the journalist's decision alone, not the government's.

How does the press **regulate itself**?

In response to polls showing increased public distrust of the press, in the late 1970s many editors showed a renewed interest in codes of ethics and other forms of self-regulation. Journalistic codes of ethics outlining how the press should behave have been in use in the United States since 1923, when the American Society of Newspaper Editors approved the first one, revised most recently in 1975. The Society of Professional Journalists and the Associated Press Managing Editors have adopted similar codes that encourage journalists to perform with objectivity, accuracy, and fairness, and many news organization try to uphold these. In addition, some newspapers have experimented with the Scandinavian concept of an ombudsman, an individual appointed by a newspaper to investigate complaints concerning the paper's coverage and practices and to publish the results of the investigation. In 1967, the *Louisville Courier Journal* of

Louisville, Kentucky, became the first U.S. newspaper to adopt the system, with only one of the powerful dailies—the *Washington Post*—following suit. The United Kingdom's news council concept has also been adapted in the United States, beginning with the formation in 1973 of the National News Council, which acted as an alternative for libel and other judicial action by investigating complaints against media organizations in which the plaintiff agreed not to bring civil actions against the accused. Since the National News Council's funding ended in 1984, only a few news councils at the state level—most notably the Minnesota News Council—have operated successfully.

What is the role of the Federal Communications Commission?

Established by the Communications Act of 1934, the Federal Communications Commission (FCC) is an independent United States government agency, directly accountable to the U.S. Congress. The FCC is charged with regulating interstate and international communications by radio, television, wire, satellite, and cable in the nation's 50 states, the District of Columbia, and U.S. possessions. The FCC's responsibilities include processing applications for licenses and other filings, analyzing complaints, conducting investigations, developing and implementing regulatory programs, and contributing in court hearings.

What is the **equal time rule**?

The Communications Act of 1934 also established an equal opportunity, or "equal time," rule, which states that if a political candidate obtains time on a broadcast station, other candidates for the same office (or their appointed representatives) must be allowed to obtain an "equal opportunity" on that station. An equal opportunity usually includes equal time, but the term means more than equal time. For example, it means the right to obtain time in a period likely to attract approximately the same size audience as the period in which the opposing candidate appeared. News shows are exempt from the equal time rule.

What is the **fairness doctrine**?

From 1949 to 1987, the FCC also enforced a fairness doctrine that required broadcast stations to devote a reasonable percentage of time to the coverage of controversial issues and provide a reasonable opportunity for the presentations of contrasting viewpoints on such issues. It eventually extended the "right of rebuttal" to public figures who were attacked.

Why is the **Telecommunications Act of 1996** important?

In an effort to address rapid technological advances in an era of fiber optics and microwave transmissions, Congress overwhelmingly passed the Telecommunications

Act of 1996, which broke the monopolies in the telecommunications field and allowed companies to compete in areas they formerly could not by regulation or by law. A nationwide marketplace for telecommunication services was created by the bill, replacing the segmented marketplace of local and long-distance telephone service and cable television. The legislation also replaced a decades-old system based on federal and state laws and a court order that broke up AT&T, a monopoly telephone company, into a long-distance carrier and regional ("Baby Bell") telephone companies. As a result of the act's removal of previous barriers between sectors of the industry, American consumers can receive local telephone service from their cable television company, local phone service can come from a long-distance carrier, and local phone companies can provide television programming. Potentially all of these services can be provided by a single company, such as a local public utility company.

How has **regulation** changed in the last 20 years?

Deregulation of the media began wholeheartedly in the 1980s. As media choices increased during this decade, the Federal Communications Commission began to relax regulations on U.S. broadcast media, expanding the number of outlets one owner could possess and announcing it would no longer enforce the fairness doctrine. To further increase competition, in January 1994 the Clinton administration proposed eliminating restrictions that prevented cable TV and telephone companies from entering each other's markets, which eventually led to the Telecommunications Act of 1996. Despite this general trend toward deregulation, there has been an increase in the number of proposals that attempt to regulate the Internet, specifically limiting its content so that children cannot access pornographic or objectionable web sites. The privacy protections granted to users of online computer services and the Internet generally have been upheld, but are continually under debate since the 1996 federal district court panel decision to strike down the new Communications Decency Act. In this decision the court held that Internet communications are entitled to the same degree of protection as printed communications.

Why have some people argued **against cameras in courtrooms**?

The argument against having cameras in courtrooms came to light with the televised O. J. Simpson case, which many maintained left viewers with a distorted impression of the American legal system, thanks largely to selected media footage portrayed on the eleven o'clock news and the occasional play to the camera by trial participants. Although almost all the states allow camera coverage of courtroom proceedings, and have for decades, the federal courts do not. Many arguments have surfaced against their inclusion, namely that they encourage sensationalism, affect participants negatively because of undue publicity and pressure, infringe upon a person's right to privacy, and feed into the entertainment and ratings games of television stations. However, proponents of the courtroom camera uphold that responsible camera coverage is simply an extension of Americans' right to an open trial and promotes, rather than undermines, the judicial process by allowing an informed citizenry to see how the justice systems works.

MEDIA THROUGH THE ADMINISTRATIONS

Which early president first experienced a **poor press relationship**?

The administration of John Adams (1735–1826), the second president of the United States, marks the beginning of adversarial president-press relations. Although the press did not begin attacking his predecessor, George Washington, until the end of his administration, the press attacked Adams from the time of his address to Congress in May 1797 until he left the White House in March 1801. During his presidency, Federalist newspapers printed essays written by Adams' critics, most notably Federalist leader Alexander Hamilton, which accused Adams of conspiring with Republicans for peace with France. Republic newspapers called Adams a monarchist who sought a dynasty with Great Britain. Although Adams' legacy included uniting moderate Federalists and Republicans, he blamed the Federalist and Republican newspapers for his downfall, saying, "Regret nothing that you see in the papers concerning me. It is impossible that newspapers can say the truth. They would be out of their element."

When did the press start using the term **"whitewash"**?

The term "whitewash," meaning to gloss over or cover up faults, was used by the press as early as 1762 by a writer for the Boston *Evening Post*. In a political sense, the term dates to 1800, when a Philadelphia *Aurora* editorial said, "If you do not whitewash President [John] Adams speedily, the Democrats, like swarms of flies, will bespatter him all over, and make you both as speckled as a dirty wall, and as black as the devil." Since that usage the term "whitewashing" took on the meaning of a predetermined exoneration of a public official accused of wrongdoing after he has been subject to an "investigation" of a committee composed of a friendly majority.

How and when did the term **"off the record"** originate?

Long a courtroom devise, the terms "off the record" and "on the record" entered political vocabulary sometime in the late 1800s. Since 1893, when the official proceedings of Congress were first published in the *Congressional Record*, members called informal statements "off the record" and formal statements "on the record." At the 1919 Democratic National Convention President Woodrow Wilson is recorded as saying, "Personally, and just within the limits of this room, I can say very frankly that I think we ought to ..." thus ushering in an era when politicians believed they were justified in denying off-the-record statements if they were published without their consent, an ethical practice still adhered to today by many. The phrase "Let us take a look at the record" is attributed to 1928 Democratic presidential candidate Alfred E. Smith, who often used the expression to review issues.

How did a **newspaper editor's remark** actually help 1840 Whig presidential candidate William Henry Harrison of Ohio?

Even during the early nineteenth century, the press held the power to effect what the public believed. That year a Democratic newspaper editor called Harrison a poor old farmer who would be content with three things: a pension, a log cabin, and a barrel of hard cider. However, instead of having its intended effect of hurting Harrison's candidacy, the editor's comments instead rallied large numbers of westerners who found it easy to identify with a candidate who enjoyed their same lifestyle. What they didn't know was that this image—which soon caught on with the public and became the hallmark of Whig rallies and parades—was indeed just that: Harrison was very wealthy, lived in a 16-room mansion, and never drank hard cider. Although he was the exact antithesis of the editor's remarks, that image helped him build his campaign and gain voters—eventually winning him the White House.

Which nineteenth-century president was **associated with a handful of scandals** during his presidency?

While Ulysses S. Grant's administrations (1869–1877) were known for their contributions to Reconstruction policy and Indian policy, often cited are the many scandals that plagued Grant's presidency. "Black Friday" (1869) on the New York gold exchange involved Wall Street conspirators who attempted to corner the available gold supply and prevent the government from selling gold by enlisting Grant's brother-in-law as co-conspirator. In the Credit Mobilier scandal of 1872, the *New York Sun* accused Vice President Schuyler Colfax, vice presidential nominee Henry Wilson, and other prominent politicians of being involved in the operations of the Credit Mobilier Co., a corporation established by the promoters of the Union Pacific to siphon off the profits of railroad construction. In 1875 a group of corrupt officials and businessmen known as the Whiskey Ring was exposed by the *St. Louis Democrat*, ultimately compromising important Grant appointees and General Orville E. Babcock, Grant's private secretary. Finally, Secretary of War William W. Belknap was impeached in 1876 on charges of accepting bribes from Indian agents, making Belknap the first cabinet official ever impeached in the United States.

Who was **Lemonade Lucy**?

"Lemonade Lucy" was the nickname the press teasingly gave First Lady Lucy Hayes for her habit of excluding alcoholic beverages from White House functions, choosing instead to serve lemonade and fruit juices. Although the custom at the time was to serve alcohol and state functions, Hayes' custom was supported by her husband, President Rutherford B. Hayes, an ex-poker-playing, cigar-smoking drinker who gave up his vices to join the Sons of Temperance and traveled to make speeches in their behalf.

Which president introduced the phrase **"throwing the hat in the ring"**?

Theodore Roosevelt popularized the phrase in response to a reporter's question on his way to the Ohio Constitutional Convention in Columbus in 1912. Asked whether he intended to run for president again later that year, the former president drew from western sporting slang and replied, "My hat is in the ring; the fight is on and I'm stripped to the buff. You will have my answer on Monday." Since that time, the phrase "throwing the hat in the ring" has been associated with entering a political campaign or announcing one's candidacy for office.

Who coined the term **"pitiless publicity"** in response to drawing on the press to help solve political problems?

Although it was first used by poet Ralph Waldo Emerson, Woodrow Wilson coined this phrase while running for governor of New Jersey in 1910. During his campaign Wilson was asked a series of questions about how he planned to rid the state of the "boss-and-spoils system" in politics, to which he replied, "I would propose to abolish it by the reform suggested in the Democratic platform, by the election to office of men who will refuse to submit to it … and by pitiless publicity." Because the public was taken by the phrase, Wilson continued to use it, and the phrase has ever since been associated with him.

Who was the first president to make regular use of **press conferences**?

Although he disliked the media, Woodrow Wilson made many attempts to interface with it. He was the first president to hold a presidential news conference and pioneered the concept as a way of molding public opinion and rallying support for the administration. Wilson's personal appeal to the media also translated to Congress: In 1913 he broke Thomas Jefferson's precedent of submitting the then-named annual message to Congress in writing by personally delivering the address to Congress orally—thus setting a precedent for today's State of the Union Address.

Which three presidents **required the press to submit their questions in writing in advance**?

Never wanting to be taken by surprise, three presidents in succession— Warren Harding, Calvin Coolidge, and Herbert Hoover—required the press to submit their questions in writing to them or their secretaries in advance, ensuring ample time to prepare a politically advantageous response.

Which president holds the record for the **most press conferences**?

The media-savvy Franklin D. Roosevelt held 998 news conferences during his 12-year presidency. He began the trend on March 8, 1933, as soon as he was sworn into office, and continued holding press conferences steadily throughout his three terms. Unlike his predecessor, Herbert Hoover, who asked the press to prepare their questions and submit them to him prior to any press dealings, Roosevelt's off-the-cuff, frank nature established a fresh relationship with the press.

Roosevelt also holds the title of the first president to appear on television, which occurred when he spoke at the opening ceremonies of the New York World's Fair on April 30, 1939. NBC telecast the event from the Federal Building on the Exposition Grounds. Several years later Roosevelt took another "first" as the first president to broadcast in a foreign language. On November 7, 1942, Roosevelt addressed the French in their own language from Washington, D.C., in coordination with the U.S. Army's invasion of the French territorial possessions in Africa.

What **important precedent did Warren Harding set** for his successor, Calvin Coolidge?

The practice of holding biweekly press conferences throughout his term in office was set by Warren Harding and continued by Calvin Coolidge. Because of his openness and availability to the press (having held some 500 such meetings during his six years in the White House), Coolidge enjoyed great popularity among the Washington press corps.

Who was the first president to **address the nation by radio**?

Warren G. Harding was the first president to deliver a speech broadcast by radio. On June 14, 1922, his speech at the dedication of the Francis Scott Key Memorial, at Ft. McHenry in Baltimore, Maryland, was broadcast by local Baltimore station WEAR (now WFBR). Harding is frequently confused with Calvin Coolidge, who was the first president to broadcast on radio to a joint session of Congress on December 6, 1923, and also the first president to broadcast from the White House with his tribute to President Harding on February 22, 1924, which was broadcast from 42 stations from coast to coast.

Calvin Coolidge became the first president to have his annual message to Congress (later known as the State of the Union address) broadcast via radio in 1923, and was the first president to employ a full-time speech writer.

What first-time service did reporter **Judson Welliver** provide to a U.S. president?

Judson Welliver was the first person to be hired officially as a speechwriter—to President Calvin Coolidge. While even the earliest presidents had help preparing their speeches (George Washington often consulted Alexander Hamilton), Welliver was the first person employed for that sole purpose in the White House. For the last several presidencies, drafts have been prepared by full-time wordsmiths in the official Office of Speechwriting.

Beginning with the radio, how has media been used to communicate the president's annual **State of the Union address**?

Calvin Coolidge was the first president to deliver the then-named annual message to Congress via radio in 1923. With the advent of radio and television, the president's annual message expanded from a conversation between the president and Congress to an address the American people. Franklin D. Roosevelt began using the phrase "State of the Union" in 1935, which became the common name of the president's annual message from that time forward. Roosevelt's successor, Harry Truman, set a precedent in 1947 when his State of the Union speech became the first to be broadcast on television; Lyndon Johnson usurped that "first" as the first president to have his State of the Union address broadcast on all three commercial television networks. And George W. Bush broke a mold once again—his January 29, 2002, address marked the first time in

President Franklin D. Roosevelt addressed citizens in a series of radio broadcasts known as fireside chats, in which he assured Americans of the country's resilience and strength in the face of the Great Depression and World War II.

history that the president's State of the Union message was available via a live webcast originating from the White House web site.

How did **Franklin D. Roosevelt** use the media to his political advantage?

Probably one of America's most successful communicators was Franklin D. Roosevelt, who used the popular medium of the radio, by that time in over half of America's households, to his political advantage. From the room now known as the Diplomatic Reception Room of the White House, Roosevelt addressed the nation with more than 30 so-called "fireside chats"—heart-to-heart conversations he held directly with Americans about the problems they were facing during the Great Depression of the 1930s and World War II in the 1940s. These chats—for which families and friends gathered around their living-room fireplaces to listen to the president by radio—were immensely popular, primarily because Roosevelt's calming voice and everyday language assured Americans that despite the country's current crises the United States had the resiliency to survive as a nation. Their effect ultimately instilled Americans' faith in Roosevelt as president, convincing them he was working hard to correct their problems. Radio was also a means for the president to bypass the partisan newspapers that were generally critical of New Deal reforms, instead giving his administration direct access to citizens, which ultimately boosted his popularity as a leader and allowed him to move forward with his presidential agenda. Roosevelt's chats were so successful that presidents Jimmy Carter and Bill Clinton tried to replicate the technique, but with little success.

Why was **FDR's paralysis** kept quiet by the media?

When Franklin D. Roosevelt died on April 12, 1945, few Americans knew the extent of his disability and the pains he took to conceal the fact that he had polio. During his early political career, Roosevelt denied his disability in order to present himself to the public as a viable candidate, and he continued to hide his polio throughout his presidency, fearing political ramifications. Sitting mostly at his desk or at a lectern, the public did not see him in the wheelchair he used daily for two decades. Reporters and photographers followed a tacit rule to keep the disability secret, and media appearances were orchestrated with the president seated or able to reach a podium with minimal movement. Of the more than 35,000 pictures taken of Roosevelt, only two show him in a wheelchair, while political cartoonists did much to dispel the illness myth by drawing him running, jumping, or leaping. As was the trend in those times, the media emphasized the public performance and personality of the president and avoided examining his private life.

Even though **radio** was eventually usurped by television, how did it continue to have an **ongoing role in communicating the politics of the day**?

While the introduction of television in the 1950s displaced the radio as America's most popular electronic medium, radio still remained important in communicating politics. The U.S. government used radio as a cold war weapon internationally by broadcasting anti communist propaganda across the Soviet Bloc with its "Voice of America" campaign, and on the domestic front by broadcasting Senator Joseph McCarthy's infamous communist hearings. It wasn't too long before Americans enjoyed all-news radio, which remained a popular devise for gleaning national headlines throughout the rest of the twentieth century as more and more commuters tuned in on their way to work. The 1990s witnessed a rebirth in political radio programming as a series of successful talk-radio programs hosted by such conservatives as Rush Limbaugh, G. Gordon Liddy, and Oliver North informed listeners on the affairs of state.

Who was the **first president to appear on television from the White House**?

Harry Truman was the first president to appear on television from the White House when he spoke about the world food crisis on October 5, 1947. Although that speech was only seen in New York and Philadelphia, about 10 million viewers watched Truman's inauguration on TV only two years later, and more than 100 million heard it on the radio.

Why did **Harry Truman frequently get in trouble with the press**?

Critical of journalists and shy of the press, Harry Truman frequently got himself in trouble by coming unprepared to press conferences and offering impromptu answers. Truman frequently relied on his press secretary Charles Ross to brief him on trial questions and issue clarifications to any of his off-the-cuff answers, such as when he implied at a 1950 conference that he might use nuclear weapons in Korea.

What **prominent media stories did John F. Kennedy have to overcome** when he campaigned for the 1960 presidential election?

The press paid particular attention to Democratic candidate John F. Kennedy's Catholic religion, and because many voters ultimately rejected Democratic candidate Alfred E. Smith in 1928 because he too was Catholic, Kennedy fought hard to overcome this prejudice. The media also focused on his age (at 42, many citizens considered Kennedy too young to assume the White House), his extreme wealth (and charge that he and his father, who funded his campaign, were trying to buy the White House), and his mediocre congressional record as a Massachusetts senator.

Why didn't JFK's alleged affairs surface when he was president?

John F. Kennedy's presidency took place in an era when the media was more apt to be hands-off when covering a president's personal life, especially in the areas of health and sexual relations. Although the media was vaguely aware of JFK's sexual exploits, they chose not to publicize them. This is almost unimaginable to a twenty-first-century citizenry, whose public officials are barraged by the media spotlight and exposed to the press's tell-all philosophy. Prompted by the publication of a 1975 Senate committee report, journalists began linking Kennedy to various women, portraying him as a less-than-perfect husband with a penchant for extramarital affairs. Reports about Kennedy's well-disguised Addison's disease also began to surface at that time, forcing reporters to examine their responsibility to scrutinize the physical conditions and private lives of their public officials.

Why was JFK known for **courting the press**?

Kennedy always answered reporters in a respectful tone, engaging them with flattery and charm, and consistently thanking them for the facts they chose not to publish. The elite of print and television journalism considered themselves Kennedy's friends, and often mentioned their shared burden of helping Kennedy shape the country and its future. Kennedy was known for playing reporters off of one another, and for his unique way of managing to get only the most favorable stories about himself on the front page.

President John F. Kennedy, shown during a 1962 press conference, was known for his savvy and charm when dealing with the press corps.

How did **television help bring about the end of the Vietnam War**?

In 1975 Marshall McLuhan said, "Television brought the brutality of war into the comfort of the living room. Vietnam was lost in the living rooms of America—not on the battlefields of Vietnam." Few disagree with the words of this well-known social commentator, which stress that television helped bring about Americans' disillusionment with the Vietnam War as night after night viewers watched the country's young men carried off in body bags. After the media openly denounced America's involvement, Walter Cronkite, the most respected television newscaster of the era, spoke openly for a peace settlement. President Lyndon Johnson realized television's effect on the public when he responded, "If I've lost Walter, I've lost the war." Although serious negotiations to end the war did not begin until Johnson chose not seek reelection in 1968, the media attention given to the length of the war, the high number of U.S. casualties, and the exposure of U.S. involvement in war crimes provided the public pressure necessary to initiate its conclusion.

Which president signed the act that created the **Corporation for Public Broadcasting**?

Lyndon Johnson signed the Public Broadcasting Act on November 7, 1967. The act authorized $38 million for educational television and radio facilities for the next three years, created the Corporation for Public Broadcasting, and established the Commission of Instructional Technology to study instructional television and radio in United States.

Which president has appeared the most **on the cover of *Time***?

By 1994, men who served as president of the United States appeared more than 200 times on the cover of *Time* magazine. Herbert Hoover was the only occupant of the White House since *Time* began in 1923 who did not appear on its cover, although he was portrayed there before and after his presidency. Franklin D. Roosevelt appeared on the cover 9 times; Ronald Reagan was pictured on 44 covers. However, Richard Nixon appeared there 56 times, more than any other man or woman to date.

How do historians characterize **Richard Nixon's relationship with the press**?

Adversarial is the one word that defines Nixon's relationship with the press. His mannerisms, which lacked the grace of his recent predecessor John F. Kennedy, made him always appear uncomfortable before the press and the public. He carried such an unpopular public image that most of the press and public didn't trust him even before the Watergate scandal broke. Nixon himself perpetuated this image, by revealing to the press as little as possible and believing that secrecy was his prerogative as the nation's chief executive.

Presidential candidates Richard Nixon and John F. Kennedy square off in a televised debate during the 1960 campaign. Kennedy's strong camera presence, contrasted with Nixon's apparent nervousness, is said to have greatly enhanced his image among voters.

How did the **press's coverage of the Watergate scandal** usher in a new era of the power of the press?

The investigative efforts of *Washington Post* journalists Bob Woodward and Carl Bernstein exposed the tangled web of Watergate and influenced President Nixon's 1974 resignation. While both of these were groundbreaking events, the team's coverage marked a new era of investigative journalism, and forever changed the way the press would view, report on, expose, and critique presidents. Investigative reporters now viewed it as their duty to democracy to subject the presidency to intense scrutiny. Often "hands-off" on the personal details of the president's life, the press was now given permission to continue to expose the government's most corrupt practices, and by doing so altered America's consciousness with regard to the amount of privacy formerly given to government officials.

In June 2002, 30 years after they broke the Watergate story, Woodward and Bernstein spoke of journalist lessons learned from the scandal. "The lessons have to do with being careful, with using multiple sources, to putting information into context, to not being swayed by gossip, by sensationalism, by manufactured controversy," said Bernstein, who won the *Washington Post* a Pulitzer Prize for his efforts. "All of which I think have come to dominate our journalistic agenda much more in the past 30 years."

Washington Post reporters Carl Bernstein, left, and Bob Woodward led the media investigation into the Watergate scandal in the early 1970s. Their work resulted in President Richard Nixon's resignation, earned the paper a Pulitzer Prize, and ushered in a new era of investigative reporting regarding political figures.

What was the **backlash of Watergate** toward the office of president?

After the Watergate scandal and President Nixon's resignation, many people simply didn't trust the presidency. Every component of the executive office was turned inside out, from the abuse of national security and executive privilege to the misuse of large campaign donations. The willingness of a president and his aides to use respected government agencies—namely the Federal Bureau of Investigation, the Internal Revenue Service, and the Central Intelligence Agency—in unlawful and unethical ways against their "enemies" was a breach of trust between the citizenry and its leaders. As a result, Americans cited great disillusionment with the national government in general, and the presidential office in particular. In addition, Americans now welcomed viewing the life of the president and other public officials through the lens of the press's microscope—as seen with the 1988 withdrawal of Democratic Gary Hart from the presidential race after the press uncovered his relationship with Donna Rice, as well as the many allegations, extramarital and otherwise, that dogged Bill Clinton's presidency.

What was **Jimmy Carter's weakness** when it came to dealing with the press?

Political commentators often cite Jimmy Carter's inability to communicate with the press and public as his greatest weakness. Often viewed as the harbinger of bad news, Carter's non-television-friendly persona and elevated speaking style contributed to his image of an ineffectual leader who was overwhelmed by his administration's crises, including uncontrollable inflation rates at home, the hostage crisis in Iran, and the Soviet Union's invasion of Afghanistan. Carter was also apathetic toward the press, who fostered a new aggressiveness toward the executive office as a result of Watergate. Carter's crumbling relationship with the press mirrored his low approval ratings, which had dropped to 31 percent—lower than Richard Nixon's before his resignation—by the election of 1980.

Presidential candidate Gary Hart was forced to end his run for office when reports of an extramarital affair made headlines in 1988.

How did the media use **Ronald Reagan's previous career as an actor** to undermine his presidency?

While some analysts claim that Ronald Reagan's celebrity image of a Hollywood "good guy" probably helped him at the polls, the press frequently used his prior acting career to discredit his presidency, linking his weakness as a leader with a lack of qualifications. Many asserted that as president, Reagan was simply playing a role or participating in a public performance. His detractors emphasized the fact that certain administration priorities were drawn from the scripts of his most popular movies, calling attention, for example, to his proposed 1983 Strategic Defense Initiative as a copycat of the Hollywood-devised technology "the Inertia Projector" of his 1940 film *Murder in the Air.* Reagan himself did much to perpetuate his image as an actor, frequently making analogies to Hollywood when discussing his presidential responsibilities. When addressing students in Moscow during his 1988 summit meeting with Soviet leader Mikhail Gorbachev, Reagan presented his view of the presidency and role as president by comparing himself to the director of a film. He asserted that a good director makes sure that the star actors and all the bit players know their parts and comprehend the director's vision of what the film is all about.

Why were **Ronald Reagan's old films rarely shown on television** during the 1980s?

In 1976 the Federal Communications Commission ruled that rerunning old Ronald Reagan movies, even those in which he played a minor role, could be challenged by political opponents who demanded "equal time" on television. Therefore, fans were hard-pressed to find a Reagan movie on air during most of his presidency.

Which first lady captured the media's attention when she ordered over **$200,000 worth of china** for the White House?

Nancy Reagan's attempt to make the White House elegant with the purchase of $209,000 worth of new china was not well received by the public once it made headline news. Her penchant for $20,000 designer dresses and other flamboyancies were often the subject of press reports, and reporters made no bones about listing the "gifts" the Reagans acquired during their tenure in the White House, including more than $1 million worth of dresses, jewelry, shoes, and accessories.

How did the **media's sensationalism of the Clinton/Lewinsky affair** affect the public's perception of Washington?

The media's full-blown, graphic examination of President Bill Clinton's relationship with Washington intern Monica Lewinsky and Clinton's 1998 impeachment by the House of Representatives on charges of lying under oath and obstructing justice in an attempt to cover up the affair set new parameters of just how far the media is willing to go in exposing a president's sexual exploits. Entire transcripts of Clinton's testimony—including all the dirty details—were widely available to the American public. Because of the sensationalism surrounding this event, many Americans felt that Bill Clinton's actions undermined the office of the president in irreparable ways, impeachment, extramarital affairs, and Clinton's way of playing "fast and loose" with the truth having eroded the chief executive's symbolic image as the moral figurehead of the nation. Despite his actions, however, Clinton's approval ratings continued to be strong overall, although his moral character was frequently the target of Republican Party criticism. In addition, the public's perception of Clinton's exploits became an issue for Vice President Al Gore during the 2000 presidential campaign.

How did the **Clinton administration's atmosphere of scandal** reach beyond the office of the president?

The public's general lack of respect for the presidency and its fascination with scandal affected more than Bill Clinton's beleaguered public persona. Many of Clinton's aides were implicated by the media and questioned before the grand jury in Clinton's "Whitewater" investigation, and many members of Clinton's cabinet, including Agriculture Secretary Mike Espy, Interior Secretary Bruce Babbitt, and Energy Secretary Hazel O'Leary, were the subjects of their own investigations. In addition, although Clinton and his staff were found guiltless, an investigation into the Democratic Party's

1996 fundraising methods resulted in jail terms for some Democratic Party donors. Some of Clinton's rivals also felt the heat of the media's scrutiny. Republican congressman Robert Livingston was slated to become Speaker of the House until his extramarital affair became the subject of news headlines. In fact, one of the most talked-about effects of Clinton's follies was the abrupt resignation of disillusioned Republican Speaker of the House Newt Gingrich.

What was **Whitewater**?

"Whitewater" is the name of an early scandal that broke during the Clinton administration. Members of the Republican Party accused President Bill Clinton and Hillary Clinton of covering up financial misdealings with regard to his Arkansas investments prior to becoming president. The accusation centered on a failed savings and loan company operated by Clinton business associates James and Susan McDougal, who had questionable business dealings in real estate on the Whitewater River in Arkansas. McDougal was accused of wrongly using money from his failing savings and loan in the 1980s to benefit the Whitewater venture he had created with the Clintons. The scandal soon centered around the mysterious resurfacing of previously "lost" billing records from Hillary Clinton's Rose Law Firm, which could have revealed Hillary Clinton's legal work for McDougal and implicated her in the business transactions.

Once the charges of a possible cover-up were made, a special prosecutor was assigned, which after a series of events ultimately became Kenneth Starr, a conservative attorney and former federal judge who headed the Whitewater investigation as well as the resulting Paula Jones and Monica Lewinsky sex scandal investigations. By the end of 1999, no indictment or specific charges of criminal activity against the president or Hillary Clinton had resulted from the Whitewater or other Starr investigations; however, Starr did urge for the successful impeachment of Clinton related to his affair with Lewinsky. Fourteen of the Clintons' Arkansas associates were ultimately convicted and imprisoned for their Whitewater associations, including the McDougals and Jim Tucker, Clinton's replacement as governor of Arkansas.

In March 2002 the saga came to an end when the third prosecutor, independent counsel Robert Ray, issued his final report, concluding that investigators lacked insufficient evidence to prove either Bill or Hillary Clinton "knowingly participated in the criminal financial transactions used by McDougal to benefit Whitewater." According to the Associated Press, "The Clintons' lawyer called the five-volume report—the product of a $70 million, six-year investigation—the most expensive exoneration in history." Many political analysts understand that while the Clintons may have ultimately been dismissed, the Whitewater investigation caused irreparable damage to the Clinton legacy, including prompting a presidential impeachment and creating bitter divisions between Republicans and Democrats.

What **personality quirks** did the media play up in George W. Bush's campaign and early presidency?

During his campaign and early presidency, the media frequently made light of George W. Bush's inarticulate nature, inability to accurately answer questions about history and foreign policy, and vague ideas about his presidential agenda. Often called a "bumbler" who couldn't defend his proposals coherently, Bush's personal quirks, including his down-home Texas attitude, joke-cracking persona, and penchant for personally nicknaming members of his staff, were repeatedly highlighted in the press, often at the expense of his credibility.

How was **President George W. Bush perceived by the media** after his involvement in the war on terrorism?

In the aftermath of the September 11, 2001, tragedy, George W. Bush was perceived by both the American people and the media in a new light. After previously questioning his credibility and leadership at every turn, the news media exhibited a newfound respect for the president, with such notable publications as *Time* reporting that "The president is growing before our eyes," and *Newsweek* portraying him as a confident, capable leader in full command of the war against terrorism. His job approval rating averaged 89 percent in the months following the attack, and many leaders and Democratic politicians rose to compliment him as a leader. Although the news media at times criticized Bush for waging the war on terrorism at the expense of certain U.S. civil liberties and the domestic agenda, three-quarters of Americans felt the government was doing enough to protect the rights of average Americans, according to an ABC NEWS/*Washington Post* poll of December 2001. At the time of public consensus, however, Bush was less than halfway into his presidency.

What has been the role of **Voice of America** historically and how has it changed post–September 11?

In observance of its 60th anniversary, on February 25, 2002, President George W. Bush said of Voice of America (VOM), "For decades, the Voice of America has told the world the truth about America and our policies. Through a cold war—in crisis and in calm—VOA has added to the momentum of freedom." VOM is an international multimedia broadcasting service funded by the U.S. government. VOA broadcasts over 900 hours of news, informational, educational, and cultural programs every week to an audience of some 91 million worldwide. VOA programs are produced and broadcast in English and 52 other languages through radio, satellite television, and the Internet.

VOA began in response to the need of peoples in closed and war-torn societies for "a consistently reliable and authoritative source of news." While the Smith-Mundt Act of 1948 prohibits VOA from broadcasting into the United States, listeners from Albania to Thailand tune in understand United States' military actions across the globe. For example, the first VOA broadcast originated from New York City on February 24, 1942, just 79 days after the United States entered World War II. Speaking in German, announcer William Harlan Hale told his listeners, "Here speaks a voice from America. Every day at this time we will bring you the news of the war. The news may be good. The news may be bad. We shall tell you the truth." On July 12, 1976, President Gerald Ford signed the VOA Charter into law, mandating that VOA broadcasts be "accurate, objective, and comprehensive."

Many people in the Arab world have a distorted view of America in general and its role in the war on terrorism specifically. Anti-American broadcasts are the norm, especially on al-Jazeera, the Qatar-based satellite network that aired Osama bin Laden's verbal attacks against the United States. Therefore, in an effort to reach this audience, Voice of America has increased its content and invoked lively dialogue targeted to younger audiences. In addition, VOA broadcasts in Afghan languages were expanded to give opponents of the Taliban more air time. Different tactics undertaken by VOA assist in moving the Middle East away from overwhelming government-sponsored censorship toward a more independent media.

Which presidents have made **notable public speeches**?

In carrying out his roles of popular leader, chief executive, and press enthusiast, the president of the United States often makes compelling speeches in order to rally the American people around a national goal or during a time of crisis. Among the most oft-cited: George Washington's first inaugural address; George Washington's farewell address; James Monroe's state of the nation address proclaiming the Monroe Doctrine; Abraham Lincoln's Gettysburg Address; Woodrow Wilson's war message, advising Congress to declare war on Germany; Franklin D. Roosevelt's first fireside chat and third inaugural address; John F. Kennedy's inaugural address; Lyndon Johnson's state of the union address proposing the "Great Society" program; and Richard Nixon's resignation speech.

SOCIAL POLICY

PUBLIC POLICY

What is **public policy**?

In its broadest sense, public policy is a government plan of action for addressing issues that affect and involve the public. Main policy goals of the national government include making and maintaining a market economy and relieving poverty and the ills of the poor, which are instituted through economic and social policies, respectively. Because public policy is based on law, those individuals, groups, or government agencies that do not comply with the terms of the policies are subject to fines, loss of benefits, and jail terms.

What are some of the **most broadly supported public policies**?

Social polices tend to gain the most support from the public at large. These include public education, income security, medical care, sanitation and disease prevention, public housing, and children's protective services. Few disagree with a need for Social Security, a welfare program into which working Americans contribute a percentage of their income, and from which they draw cash benefits after retirement; Supplemental Security Income, which provides a minimum monthly income to eligible blind, disabled, or older participants; and Temporary Assistance to Needy Families (TANF), by which states are given federal block grants in order to create their own programs for public aid. Although economic ideals such as economic growth or low inflation receive across-the-board support, specific economic policies used to implement these ideals, including tax cuts, are open to debate, with a number of Americans questioning whether or not the national government should intervene in the nation's economy at all.

How does public policy help balance **equality and democracy**?

Public policy helps balance equality and democracy because it provides for those who would not otherwise have any means of living a healthy, balanced life, mainly the disenfranchised and the poor. By providing assistance at various economic and social levels to these groups, the government ensures that the national standard of living as a whole is raised, and that health, education, and employment standards are elevated to more equitable standards overall. If there were no such thing as Social Security, for example, more than 50 percent of all senior citizens would be living below the poverty line; this social policy guarantees a level of equality for those older adults who rely on Social Security as their only means of income. In addition, tax cuts that favor the working and middle classes help those groups gain a foothold in the American dream, and help to close the gap between various socioeconomic groups.

What kinds of **control mechanisms** does the government use to form policy?

The government uses three types of control to institute its public policies: promotional techniques, which grant benefits to the public; regulatory techniques, which directly control individual action and behavior; and redistributive techniques, which manipulate the entire economy.

How does the government use **promotional techniques** to control policy?

A promotional technique is a form of control that encourages the public to do something it otherwise might not be inclined to do, or encourages them to continue a certain action or behavior in order to promote the government's agenda. The main forms of promotional techniques used by the government are: (1) subsidies, that is, government grants of cash, goods, services, or land, such as land grants given to nineteenth-century farmers and railroad companies to encourage western settlement, or cash grants given to commercial shipbuilders to build a military fleet; (2) contracts, or agreements with people or private sector firms to purchase goods or services, as seen today, for example, with universities and research firms engaging in research and development; and (3) licenses or permits, which permit an individual or business to engage in an action that would otherwise be considered illegal, such as practicing medicine, driving a taxi, or serving alcoholic beverages.

What is **contracting power**?

Contracting power refers to the power of the government to set certain conditions on companies who want to sell goods or services to government agencies. The government uses its contracting power muscle to encourage corporations to make internal improvements, help build up entire sectors of the economy, or enforce other government goals, such as equal employment opportunity.

How does the government use **regulatory techniques**?

Regulatory techniques involve direct government control, which can be enacted in many ways: civil and criminal regulation, including fines, imprisonment, and loss of citizenship for a host of what is deemed dangerous or immoral conduct, including traffic violations, drunk driving, prostitution, or drug use; administration regulation, which involves administrative agencies who set interest rates, set standards or health (such as requiring companies to reduce pollution or adequately label the contents of food and drugs), and investigate company wrongdoings; regulatory taxation, which are those taxes on items such as liquor, gasoline, or cigarettes that are designed to keep consumption down; and expropriation, seizing private property for public use, such as public works projects and highways.

What are some **redistributive techniques** that the government uses to control policy?

Rather than regulating people directly, redistributive techniques affect the entire economy by causing the redistribution of resources, and as such are usually fiscal or monetary in nature. Fiscal techniques include the altering of the flow of money in society by changing tax laws; the use of deficit spending to pump money into the economy when it needs to be revitalized; the creation of a budget surplus, through taxes, to discourage public consumption during eras of inflation; and the changing of interest rates in order to affect the demand for money. Monetary techniques include manipulating the supply of money and credit, which is mainly achieved through the Federal Reserve System.

SOCIAL WELFARE POLICY

What is **social policy**?

Social policy is the general term given to government programs that are designed to provide people, especially low-income families, with the necessities of life, including food, health support, and educational and employment training opportunities. Specifically, they are aimed to help the working poor better their circumstances, by providing for their health, income, security, employment, and educational needs.

What is **equality of opportunity**?

Equality of opportunity means that everyone should have an equal opportunity to succeed in life—in education, employment, and housing—regardless of ethnicity, reli-

A Head Start class in San Diego, California, gives disadvantaged preschoolers the opportunity to have early learning experiences and support to boost their chances of further educational success.

gion, income, or sex. Ensuring equality of opportunity for all Americans has its roots in the Constitution and the civil rights movement of the 1960s, which brought about the Civil Rights Act, affirmative action, Title VII (which prohibits sex discrimination in employment), Title IX (which prohibits sex discrimination in education), the Fair Housing Act, and expanded rights for women and people of color. Closely aligned with the concept of equality of opportunity is what some scholars call the equality of starting conditions, which comprises much of the basis of social policy. Equality of starting conditions means that, in order for equality of opportunity to be successful, disadvantaged individuals and families must receive equal help getting started in life. It is this philosophy that created the federally funded Head Start program, which provides disadvantaged preschoolers with an equality of opportunity to learn in school and progress more on par with their more economically advantaged classmates.

Did **America's Founding Fathers** believe in equality of opportunity?

America's Founding Fathers believed in equality of opportunity enough to build its concepts into the Constitution. Although the word "equality" does not exist anywhere in the document or the amended Bill of Rights, the framers of this fundamental document believed that all men (at that time, only white men) were entitled to the inalienable rights of "life, liberty, and the pursuit of happiness." In order to assure this, they created a system of government meant to ensure man's natural, or human, rights, with the ideals that all citizens are entitled to equal protection against arbitrary treatment and to experience the liberties outlined in the Bill of Rights. While it would be years before African Americans and women fully embraced these rights, the foundations were laid with the Constitution.

How is the formation of social policy reflected in the debate over liberty, equality, and democracy?

In short, liberal policymakers believe that the national government has a responsibility to see that no one is excluded from the "American dream," stressing the importance of equality of opportunity as a fundamental tenet of both the Constitution and the national culture as a whole. Conservatives, on the other hand, believe that equality of opportunity can only be attained when individuals are free to achieve the American dream—that is, stable employment and the benefits of living a life above the poverty line—without the burden of government interference. This conservative viewpoint took hold in the mid-1990s with the Republican "Contract with America"—the Republicans' overall vision to guide legislative activity through Congress—that ignited welfare reform and shifted the ideology of welfare from pure federal assistance to partial self-sufficiency.

How does **social policy affect all citizens**?

America is a highly individualistic and capitalist nation, with wide disparities in income and class among groups of people. Rather than ensuring that all people earn the same amount of yearly income or obtain the same amount of material goods, social policy instead creates a "safety net" meant to catch anyone who might fall below a certain level and provide them with the opportunity to improve their circumstances in life. From this point of view, social policy affects all citizens, since it benefits the nation as a whole by helping to bridge this economic gap and provide better living and working conditions overall. In addition, social policy programs are paid for by the middle class through taxes, and therefore those who do not necessarily partake in all programs play a role in subsidizing them. Certain programs are meant to help not those who are poor or disenfranchised, but rather those people who might find themselves in a certain position in life one day where they would need to access these programs' benefits, namely Social Security and unemployment insurance. The middle class also benefits from Social Security by being relieved of the financial burden that would come with providing care for elderly relatives.

Who benefits from social policies?

Groups that are meant to benefit most from social policies are those individuals and families who live below the poverty line, a population that consists of more than 40 million people: the working poor, women and children, minorities, the elderly, and the disabled. According to 1996 statistics from the Population Reference Bureau, nationally about 30 percent of the working-age population living in poverty in 1994 was indeed working. Single women with children are more likely to be living in poverty, with 38 percent of those households living in poverty headed by single mothers. And while the highest number of people living in poverty in rural areas are white, poverty rates for minorities are higher in both rural and urban areas. In 1994, for example, nearly one-third of all African Americans and Hispanics were living below the poverty line. Many of the poor are elderly, and even more (about 40 percent) are children or have a work disability.

However, despite these numbers, in reality the group that receives the most benefits is the elderly, in part because Social Security is one of the most generous and strongest programs in America and because this demographic is seen as most deserving by policymakers. In addition, because many older Americans have a lot of political power (consider public interest groups such as the American Association for Retired Persons or the Gray Panthers), they can push for policies that benefit them. On the other hand, the working poor receive very little from the modern welfare state because their income excludes them from programs for which eligibility is based on means. And although the nonworking poor are provided assistance through the state-run TANF (Temporary Assistance for Needy Families) program, many states have cut benefits; thus, the benefit levels fail to provide an income above the defined poverty level.

What are some examples of **public interest groups** that work in the **social welfare arena**?

A host of special interest groups serve the needs and address the issues of low-income and disenfranchised individuals and families, including: the National Coalition against Domestic Violence, which works to empower battered women and their children while eliminating personal and societal violence in America; the Children's Defense Fund, dedicated to improving the lives of American children, particularly poor, minority, and disabled children; Disabled American Veterans, which seeks to build better lives for America's disabled veterans; the Gray Panthers, who advocate for health care, Social Security, housing, and education for both America's elderly and the nation's youth; the National Coalition for the Homeless, engaged in public education, policy advocacy, and grassroots organizing in an effort to end homelessness in America; and the National Committee to Preserve Social Security and Medicare, which works to ensure the preservation of Social Security and Medicare and lobbies members of Congress on issues related to seniors.

BEGINNINGS OF SOCIAL WELFARE

What kind of a **welfare system was in place prior to the 1930s**?

Until the early twentieth century, few programs existed to help those in need. When assistance was available, it was haphazardly distributed by state and local government and private charitable organizations. The states almost always placed the duty to provide relief on local governments, the funding for which came from local property taxes. Social welfare efforts of the national government were extremely limited, and reserved for those to which the government had a specific responsibility to assist, such as veterans, Native Americans, and merchant seamen. Although the national government gave pensions to veterans who had fought for the North during the Civil War, for example, this was an anomaly.

Social reformer Jane Addams founded Hull House, Chicago's first social settlement, in 1899, the programs of which shaped social welfare and labor movements in the early twentieth century.

Why was **Hull House** significant?

Created by Jane Addams in Chicago in 1889, Hull House was the city's first social settlement, and soon became a model for the social welfare and labor movements of the early twentieth century. Serving one of Chicago's poor and diverse immigrant neighborhoods, Addams and other residents of the settlement provided services as far-reaching as kindergarten and daycare facilities for children of working mothers, an employment bureau, an art gallery, and several libraries. By 1900 Hull House activities had expanded to include the Jane Club (a cooperative residence for working women), the first Little Theater in America, a labor museum, and a meeting place for trade union groups. Hull House residents and its neighborhood launched the Immigrants' Protective League, the Juvenile Protective Association—the first juvenile court in the nation—and a Juvenile Psychopathic Clinic. Hull House investigations led to the creation and enactment of the first factory laws in Illinois and the first model tenement code. Through its efforts, the Illinois legislature enacted protective legislation for women and children and in 1903 passed a groundbreaking child labor law and an

The American Red Cross has been serving the United States in times of disaster, emergency, and war since 1881. A 1918 poster appeals for support of the organization's Christmas Roll Call program.

accompanying compulsory education law. Hull House reformers saw their efforts expand to the national level with the creation of the Federal Children's Bureau in 1912 and the passage of a federal child labor law in 1916, thus welcoming the beginnings of federal social and labor law.

What was the **Progressive movement**?

The Progressive movement, or Progressive era, which took place in the United States between 1895 and 1920, was characterized by a campaign for economic, social, and political reform. Ignited by the rapid growth of industrialism, city slums, and immigration rates, the Progressive movement attempted to relieve these social ills by creating laws that would provide more power to the common people and slow the rise of capitalism. Under the leadership of William Jennings Bryan, America's Democratic Party established an income tax rather than the previous property tax, giving less power to those rich who had hidden property in stocks and bonds. Bryan also helped establish increased government regulation of business in order to stop illegal business practices and government monopolies that limited competition. Economic reforms that took place during the Progressive era included the creation of the minimum wage in certain states. Social reforms included improved living conditions for the poor and safety regulations in factories and homes. Political reforms included the passage of the Seventeenth Amendment in 1913, which established the right of citizens to vote directly for U.S. senators.

What is the importance of the **American Red Cross**?

Founded by Clara Barton in 1881 and modeled after the International Red Cross, the American Red Cross is a humanitarian organization led by volunteers that provides relief to victims of disasters and helps people prevent and prepare for emergencies. In the aftermath of an earthquake, flood, tornado, fire, hurricane, or other natural disaster, the Red Cross provides relief services to communities across the nation. While most people know the American Red Cross as the source of half of America's blood supply, the organization also provides health and safety training to the public and provides emergency social services to U.S. military members and their families. The International Red Cross and its American counterpart were born out of a desire to bring assistance to those in need, prevent and alleviate human suffering, and protect life and health without preference to nationality, religious beliefs, class, or political affiliation.

Who was the **first president since the Civil War to make a public statement for civil rights**?

On October 26, 1921, in a speech in Birmingham, Alabama, President Warren G. Harding advocated civil rights for all Americans, including African Americans. Earlier, he reversed President Woodrow Wilson's policy of excluding African Americans from federal positions, supported an antilynching bill, and advocated the establishment of an interracial commission to find ways to improve race relations. While both Republicans and Democrats played a role in derailing these presidential initiatives, Harding remained true to his underlying philosophy of civil rights and equal treatment for all.

What was the **Great Depression** and how did it give way to **Roosevelt's New Deal**?

The Great Depression of the 1930s was a period of great economic crisis for the United States. With national unemployment reaching between 13 and 15 million people, the era pointed to the need for average Americans to have a far-reaching social safety net. The Great Depression wiped out the few existing sources of assistance that were in place for the needy, and ushered in President Franklin D. Roosevelt's New Deal, the largest set of relief policies and federal domestic legislation to be enacted in U.S. history. These policies led to the establishment of a range of administrative agencies between 1933 and 1935, all of which were meant to provide relief for the needy, recovery for the nation at large, and long-range reform of the nation's economic institutions. The phrase "New Deal" was applied to the entire body of reform legislation passed during Roosevelt's first two terms, although the following measures are the most widely referenced: the National Industrial Recovery Act (NIRA), the Agricultural Adjustment Act (AAA), the Public Works Act (PWA), the Tennessee Valley Authority Act (TVA), the Wagner Labor Relations Act, the Securities and Exchange Act, and the Social Security Act.

What was the **New Deal**?

Franklin D. Roosevelt's response to the unprecedented crisis of the Great Depression and its economic aftermath was to initiate the "New Deal," a series of economic measures designed to reinvigorate the economy and restore the confidence of the American people in their banks and other key institutions. Orchestrated by a core group of FDR advisors recruited from academia and industry known as the "Brain Trust," the New Deal enacted

A group of men plant trees on the Nett Lake Reservation in Minnesota in 1933 as part of a Civilian Conservation Corps (CCC) project, one of the New Deal programs implemented by President Franklin D. Roosevelt.

fifteen major laws. One of the most significant of these was the Banking Act of 1933, which brought an end to the panic that arose from the nation's failed banking system.

Other significant New Deal measures included the establishment of the Works Progress Administration (WPA), the Civilian Conservation Corps (CCC), and the Agricultural Adjustment Administration (AAA). The most infamous measure of the New Deal was the 1935 Social Security Act, which led to the establishment of the Social Security Administration and the creation of a national system of old-age pensions and unemployment compensation. Social Security also granted federal financial support to dependent children, the handicapped, and the blind. In addition, the New Deal created number of significant regulatory agencies, known as "alphabet agencies" for their acronyms. These included the Securities and Exchange Commission (SEC), established to apprehend a further crash of the stock market; the Federal Housing Administration (FHA), which ultimately made home ownership affordable for millions of everyday Americans; and the National Labor Relations Board (NLRB), the Civil Aeronautics Authority (CAA) (later known as the Federal Aviation Administration, or FAA), and the Federal Communications Commission (FCC).

What was the significance of the **Works Progress Administration**?

Under Roosevelt's New Deal, some of the very first programs to be created were those that provided direct cash assistance and work relief, such as the Works Progress

Administration (WPA). Established in 1935 and often called the most important relief agency of the New Deal, the WPA built or improved more than 2,500 hospitals, 6,000 school buildings, and nearly 13,000 playgrounds in the eight years it was operative. It provided funds for federal theater, arts, and writers projects that enriched the nation's cultural life. However, most of the WPA's money, a total of $11 billion by 1943, went for short-term work projects to assist the unemployed, helping more than 3 million people reach financial security at peak periods of service.

How did the New Deal change America?

While the New Deal went a long way in alleviating the effects of the Great Depression, its measures were not sweeping enough to restore America to complete and steady employment. Conservatives argue, for example, that the New Deal brought too much government intervention in the economy, while liberals argue that it did not go far enough. Liberals argue that in order to be truly effective, the Roosevelt administration should have enacted a far more comprehensive program of direct federal aid to the poor, disenfranchised, and unemployed. However, most economists and historians agree that the New Deal's greatest achievements transcended economic boundaries—that at a time in history where democracy was under attack overseas, the New Deal restored the faith of the American people in their country and its institutions. Most notably, the New Deal transformed the federal government into an active instrument of social justice and established a network of laws and institutions designed to protect the American economy from the excesses of liberal capitalism.

Besides FDR's New Deal, what are some of the names of **other presidents' domestic programs**?

Before the New Deal, Woodrow Wilson named his domestic policy the "New Freedom." Following in Franklin D. Roosevelt's footsteps, Harry Truman called his program the "Fair Deal"; John F. Kennedy was known for his "New Frontier," and Lyndon Johnson was known for his "Great Society."

When was the **Peace Corps** created?

The brainchild of President John F. Kennedy, the Peace Corps was an international service program authorized by Congress in 1961 to "promote world peace and friendship." Created as a volunteer agency that aids the poor of developing nations, the Peace Corps works in the areas of education, community development, agriculture, health care, and public works on special community projects to meet these nations' needs. Having served 135 nations with over 165,000 volunteers to date, the Peace Corps enjoys a rich history of meeting the needs of a variety of ethnic peoples while sharing the ways of American culture.

What was the **War on Poverty**?

To remedy the social ills of the era—the number of children living on welfare had increased from 1.6 million in 1950 to 2.4 million by 1960 and was still rising—President Lyndon Johnson created his controversial domestic program known as the "War on Poverty." Under this program, Johnson established an agency (known as a "community action agency," or CAA) in each city and county to coordinate all federal and state programs designed to help the poor. The CAAs in turn would supervise agencies providing social services, mental health services, health services, and employment services. In 1964 Congress passed the Economic Opportunity Act, establishing the Office of Economic Opportunity, to run this program. Although Johnson spent approximately $1 billion per year on his "war," the CAA system was never effective and so embroiled in partisan controversy that it was abolished during the Nixon administration.

What is **VISTA**, and why was it created?

The idea of creating a national service program for low-income, needy individuals was birthed soon after the Peace Corps was created. Developed under President John F. Kennedy as the National Service Corps, VISTA (Volunteers in Service to America) was not realized until the Johnson administration under the Economic Opportunity Act of 1964 in his "War on Poverty" legislation. Along with Head Start and other antipoverty programs, VISTA's goal was to eliminate "poverty in the midst of plenty by opening to everyone the opportunity to work and the opportunity to live in decency and dignity." As such, VISTA is a full-time, year-long volunteer program for adult men and women who commit themselves to increasing the capability of low-income people to improve the conditions of their own lives. Volunteers work with community-based nonprofit agencies, where they address issues such as homelessness, illiteracy, economic development, and neighborhood revitalization. VISTA, along with the National Civilian Community Corps, is part of the AmeriCorps program, which offers participants educational vouchers in exchange for a term of service. Since 1965, over 120,000 Americans have performed national service as VISTA volunteers. An offshoot of VISTA is Friends of VISTA, which was founded in 1981 to protect the VISTA program from funding cuts and to promote improvements and expansions in the program.

Why was **Social Security** created?

Social Security was created to provide permanent programs that would address the issue of income instability among Americans. Specifically, the Social Security Act of 1935 created a scope of national programs aimed at protecting people against loss of income due to retirement, disability, or unemployment, and ushered in an era where the national government became a major contributor to the economic security of Americans on an extensive and ongoing basis. The act established old-age insurance, now known as Social Security, assistance for the needy, old, blind, and families with dependent children, and unemployment insurance. Although the programs that were originally created under the Social Security Act of 1935 have been modified, these three initial aspects still form the basis of twenty-first-century income security policies.

Which first lady sponsored the **"Just Say No"** anti-drug campaign?

Nancy Reagan's "Just Say No" antidrug campaign was the one major policy program she heralded during her tenure as first lady to Ronald Reagan from 1981 to 1989. Based on the response Reagan felt a youth should give when confronted with drugs and alcohol ("Just say no!"), this pioneer campaign involved a bevy of public service announcements, speeches, and "Just Say No to Drugs" clubs among children around the nation. In response to Reagan's efforts, Congress funded a "National Crusade for a Drug-Free America," and the first lady traveled to 65 cities in 33 states, the Vatican, and eight foreign countries in the course of eight years. Her mission was to "bring public awareness, particularly parental awareness, to the problems of drug abuse." Reagan also held two international drug conferences in an effort to alert the international community to how drugs and alcohol damage the youth population. While her tenure as first lady commanded both praise and condemnation from the general public, social scientists and drug experts criticized her for not comprehending the full complexity of the drug problem in America. Specifically, many called to her attention the president's initiatives to cut federally financed drug education programs while she simultaneously toured the country in support of a drug-free America.

Which first lady took a special interest in **adult literacy**?

As the first lady to President George Bush from 1989 to 1993, Barbara Bush established an adult literacy campaign in response to the 23 million Americans who were functionally illiterate. Believing that "reading to children early and often is the single most important thing parents can do to prepare them to start school ready to learn," in 1989 she established the Barbara Bush Foundation for Family Literacy to support family literacy programs, break the intergenerational cycle of illiteracy, and establish literacy as a value in every American family. As of 2002, the foundation has funded 309 family literacy programs in 44 states. In support of her campaign, Bush regularly appeared on "Mrs. Bush's Story Time," a national radio program that stresses the importance of reading aloud to children, and authored two books, *C. Fred's Story* and the best-selling *Millie's Book*, the profits of which benefited her literacy cause.

What was George Bush's **"Thousand Points of Light"**?

In his acceptance speech at the 1988 Republican convention, George Bush coined the terms "a kinder and gentler nation" and "a thousand points of light" as the cornerstones of his view of the future. As president, Bush extended his Thousand Points of

Light philosophy, which stressed community service and citizenship as the "lights," or keys, to improving society's ills. He has defined points of light as "caring citizens who volunteer their time and effort to help make the world a better place than they found it—whether through public service, or working through their church or synagogue, or a local club or organization." His philosophy became the cornerstone of his social policy agenda, as Bush called upon commercial businesses to join voluntarily in solving the nation's problems of illiteracy, drug abuse, unwed teen pregnancy, youth delinquency and suicide, AIDS, homelessness, hunger, and unemployment. To foster volunteering, in 1989 Bush created the Office of National Service in the White House and the following year established the Points of Light Foundation. In addition, Bush signed the National and Community Service Act of 1990, which authorizes grants to schools to support service learning (now known as Learn and Serve America) and demonstration grants for national service programs to youth corps, nonprofits, and colleges and universities.

SOCIAL WELFARE PROGRAMS: SOCIAL SECURITY, SSI, TANF, MEDICARE, AND MORE

What is the difference between **"contributory"** and **"noncontributory"** welfare programs?

The Social Security Act of 1935 distinguished between two kinds of welfare policies: "Social Security," a contributory program to which people must pay in order receive benefits; and "public assistance" or "welfare," noncontributory programs for which eligibility is determined according to income. Noncontributory programs, such as Medicaid, Supplemental Security Income (SSI), Temporary Assistance to Needy Families (TANF), and food stamps, are called "means-tested" programs because they are only available to those whose incomes fall below government-specified levels. Non-means-tested, contributory programs include Social Security, unemployment compensation, and Medicare.

What are **in-kind benefits**?

Both Medicaid and food stamps provide for their recipients what are termed "in-kind benefits," because they supply noncash goods and services that would otherwise have to be paid for in cash by the recipient.

How does **Social Security** work?

The Social Security program provides financial protection to more than 152 million workers and their families, and pays monthly Social Security retirement, disability, or survivors benefits to more than 45 million Americans. Whether a person works for someone else or is self-employed, Social Security is funded by taxes. As a person works and pays taxes, he or she earns "credits" that count toward eligibility for future Social Security benefits, including retirement benefits, disability benefits, family benefits, survivors benefits, and Medicare. A person's Social Security benefit is a percentage of earnings averaged over most of an individual's working lifetime. Low-income workers receive a higher rate of return than those in the upper income brackets, but a worker with average earnings can expect a retirement benefit that represents about 40 percent of his or her average lifetime earnings. Workers can retire as early as age 62 and get reduced Social Security benefits, or wait until full retirement at age 65 and receive full benefits. Starting in 2003, the retirement age will increase gradually until it reaches 67 for people born in 1960 or later.

How was Social Security challenged in the early 1980s and what changes were made to the law?

In the early 1980s the Social Security program faced a serious financing crisis. President Ronald Reagan appointed a blue-ribbon panel, known as the Greenspan Commission, to study the financing issues and make recommendations for legislative changes. The final bill, signed into law in 1983, made numerous changes in the Social Security and Medicare programs, including the taxation of Social Security benefits; the first coverage of federal employees; the raising of the retirement age; and an increase in the reserves in the Social Security trust funds.

What is the **Senior Citizens' Freedom to Work Act**?

In April 2000 President Clinton signed into law the Senior Citizens' Freedom to Work Act of 2000, eliminating the retirement earnings test for beneficiaries at or above normal retirement age. This law allowed approximately 900,000 people who were collecting Social Security benefits but also working to not have their benefits reduced because of work.

Is Social Security **bankrupt**?

Unless Americans are willing to pay higher taxes, many social services, including Social Security, will be difficult to sustain, and social scientists project that Social Security will be bankrupted as baby boomers look to collect benefits from a smaller group of people paying into the program. Many people think that their Social Security tax contributions are held in interest-bearing accounts earmarked for their own future retirement needs. However, the Social Security taxes paid by today's workers and their employers go mostly to fund benefit payments for today's retirees. Social Security is now taking in more in taxes than is paid out in benefits, and the excess money is credited to Social Security's trust funds. As of 2000, there was about $900 billion in the trust funds, which are projected to grow to more than $6 trillion in the next 25 years. But benefit payments will begin to exceed taxes paid in 2015, and the trust funds will be exhausted in 2037. At that time, Social Security will be able to pay only about 72 percent of benefits owed if no changes are made to the current system.

What does the **SSI program** do?

Supplemental Security Income (SSI) is a federal income supplement program funded by general tax revenues. It is designed to help aged, blind, and disabled people who have little or no income by providing them with cash to meet basic needs for food, clothing, and shelter. Initially begun under the Social Security Act to help the aged or blind, supplemental income programs were expanded in 1950 to include the permanently and totally disabled. Today the Supplemental Security Income (SSI) program pays monthly benefits to more than 6.6 million Americans.

What are **food stamps**?

Food stamps are tickets that can be exchanged like money at authorized stores to pay for food items. Enacted by the Federal Food Stamp Act of 1964, the food stamp program is the most significant food plan in the United States, providing food stamps for needy individuals at the expense of the federal government while states pay the costs of determining eligibility and distributing the stamps. Food stamps are available to those individuals who work for low wages, are unemployed or work part-time, receive public assistance, are elderly or disabled, or are homeless. The Personal Responsibility and Work Opportunity Reconciliation Act of 1996 (PRWORA) substantially reduced the size of the food stamp program, making adjustments, for example, to the Thrifty Food Plan, a low-cost food budget used to calculate food stamp awards. Under this change, it eliminated the benefits previously available to most legal immigrants and created time limits for benefits to adults without dependents. Subsequently, however, Congress has restored some benefits to selected groups.

What is **TANF**?

The Temporary Assistance for Needy Families (TANF) program was created by the Welfare Reform Law of 1996. TANF became effective July 1, 1997, and replaced what was then commonly referred to as "welfare": Aid to Families with Dependent Children (AFDC) and the Job Opportunities and Basic Skills Training (JOBS) programs. The

Office of Family Assistance in the U.S. Department of Health and Human Services oversees the Temporary Assistance for Needy Families (TANF) program, which provides assistance and work opportunities to needy families by granting states the federal funds and wide flexibility to develop and implement their own welfare programs.

What is **Charitable Choice**?

Charitable Choice is a legislative provision designed to remove unnecessary barriers to the receipt of certain federal funds by faith-based organizations and create a "level playing field" between faith-based and community organizations and other groups that use federal funds in delivering social services. Mandated in January 2001 by an executive order of President George W. Bush, the provision prohibits states from discriminating against religious organizations when choosing providers under certain federal grant programs, as long as the programs are implemented in a manner that is consistent with the First Amendment. While Charitable Choice is designed to improve access to federal funding for faith-based organizations, it does not establish a new funding stream dedicated to these groups.

What does unemployment insurance do?

In general, the federal-state Unemployment Insurance program provides unemployment benefits to eligible workers who are unemployed through no fault of their own, for example, those who experience loss of a job because of an industry- or companywide layoff versus those who voluntarily quit their jobs. Unemployment insurance payments, known as benefits, are intended to provide temporary financial assistance to unemployed workers who meet the requirements of state law, as each state administers its own unemployment insurance program and determines benefit amounts and the length of time benefits are available. Although state unemployment programs vary considerably in levels of benefits, length of benefit payment, and eligibility for benefits, the most generous programs are active in the northern industrial states, where labor unions are the most powerful. In the majority of states, benefit funding is based solely on a tax imposed on employers, with only Alaska and New Jersey requiring minimal employee contributions. In general, about half the people that are unemployed in the United States at any one time receive benefits.

What is **workers' compensation**?

The concept that workers should be compensated for work-related injuries, and that governments should administer programs to ensure compensation, emerged in the United States during the first few decades of the twentieth century. Workers' compensation laws are designed to ensure that employees who are injured or disabled on the job are provided with fixed monetary awards, and to provide benefits for dependents of those workers who are killed because of work-related accidents or illnesses. Some laws also protect employers and fellow workers by limiting the amount an injured employee can recover from an employer and by eliminating the liability of coworkers in most accidents. Each state has its own workers' compensation laws to handle claims from employees who are injured on the job; federal statutes are limited to federal employees or those workers employed in some significant aspect of interstate commerce. In 1911 Wisconsin became the first state to enact a workers' compensation law that stood in court. In 1917 the U.S. Supreme Court ruled that states could legally require employers to provide compensation to injured workers. As a result, many states revised their laws to include mandatory workers' compensation.

What does the **Equal Employment Opportunity Commission** do?

Established by Title VII of the Civil Rights Act of 1964, the U.S. Equal Employment Opportunity Commission (EEOC) coordinates all federal equal employment opportunity regulations, practices, and policies. The commission interprets employment discrimination laws, monitors the federal sector employment discrimination program, provides funding and support to state and local Fair Employment Practices Agencies (FEPAs), and sponsors outreach and technical assistance programs. Any individual who believes he or she has been discriminated against in an employment situation may file an administrative charge with the EEOC. After investigating the charge, the EEOC determines if there is reasonable cause to believe discrimination has occurred. If reasonable cause is found, the EEOC attempts to reach a voluntary resolution between the charging party and the respondent, bringing suit in federal court if no resolution is reached.

What **educational policies** assist the poor and disenfranchised?

Federal aid to education has been a part of the national policy agenda since the mid-twentieth century. However, because education is primarily a state and local responsibility in the United States, the structure of education finance in America reflects this predominant state and local role. Of the roughly $650 billion spent nationwide on education at all levels, 91 percent comes from state, local, and private sources. On January 8, 2002, President George W. Bush signed into law the No Child Left Behind Act of 2001, the most sweeping reform of the Elementary and Secondary Education Act (ESEA) since ESEA was enacted in 1965. The act redefines the federal role in K-12 education with a goal of closing the achievement gap between disadvantaged and minority students and their peers in America's public school system. States enact a variety of programs through federal funds that are meant to meet the act's goals: stronger accountability for results, increased flexibility and local control, expanded options for parents, and an emphasis on proven teaching methods.

In President Bush's fiscal year 2002 budget plan, he unveiled his Reading First reform agenda in response to the statistic that 70 percent of low-income fourth-graders cannot read at grade level. The Reading First program is an investment of $5 billion over five years to ensure that every child in America can read by third grade, with special emphasis on intervention efforts aimed at children in kindergarten through second grade who are at risk of falling behind. As a part of his Reading First reform agenda, Bush called for a reform of America's successful Head Start program, a child development program that has served low-income children and their families since 1965, by making school readiness the program's priority.

What is **Head Start**?

Created in 1965 and administered by the Administration for Children and Families within the U.S. Department of Health and Human Services, Head Start and Early Head Start are comprehensive child development programs that serve children from birth to age five, pregnant women, and their families. While Head Start programs are child-focused with the overall goal of increasing the school readiness of young children in low-income families, they also provide a range of individualized services in the areas of education and early childhood development; medical, dental, and mental health; nutrition; and parent involvement. Because Head Start services low-income families, its programs are meant to be responsive and appropriate to each child's and family's developmental, ethnic, cultural, and linguistic heritage and experience. Under President George W. Bush's Reading First reform agenda, Head Start will move to the Department of Education in order to provide a greater emphasis on school readiness skills, including pre-reading and numeric skills.

When was **Medicare** created?

The decade of the 1960s brought additional changes to the Social Security program, most notably the passage of Medicare. In 1965 Congress enacted the Medicare program, which provides medical benefits for individuals over the age of 65, and an accompanying Medicaid program for the poor, regardless of age. Under Medicare, health coverage is extended to Social Security beneficiaries, those who have permanent kidney failure, and certain people with disabilities. Part A is automatically granted to older Americans when they become eligible for Social Security and includes hospitalization, nursing care, and home health services; an optional Part B may be purchased at a minimal amount for physicians' services, diagnostic services, outpatient services, and X-rays. Nearly 20 million beneficiaries enrolled in Medicare in the first years of the program, and today it is nation's largest health insurance program, covering over 39 million Americans.

What is **Medicaid**?

Enacted by the Social Security Act of 1965, Medicaid is the largest program providing medical and health-related services to America's low-income and needy population.

Medicaid is a jointly funded, federal-state health insurance program for approximately 36 million individuals including children, the aged, the blind and/or the disabled, and people who are eligible to receive federally assisted income maintenance payments.

What **housing policies** exist?

Key federal agencies play the most important role in establishing affordable housing for low-income families. The U.S. Department of Housing and Urban Development (HUD) creates programs that promote affordable housing and community reinvestment, including community development block grant programs, voucher programs, and its HOPE VI (Homeownership and Opportunity for People Everywhere) program, which provides funds to transform the nation's most distressed public housing into functioning communities. HUD has also supported the redevelopment of vacant, abandoned, and underused commercial and industrial sites through its Brownfields Economic Development Initiative. In addition to HUD, the Environmental Protection Agency (EPA) is active in the Smart Growth Network, a national coalition of developers, planners, government officials, and community development organizations who make expanding neighborhoods a priority. The EPA works to promote smart growth through its brownfields and air and water quality programs. However, despite the federal housing policies that exist, only 30 percent of low-income individuals and families eligible for housing assistance actually receive it. According to HUD, in 1993 worst-case housing needs reached an all-time high of 5.3 million households.

What is **HUD**?

The Department of Housing and Urban Development Act of 1965 created HUD as a cabinet-level agency whose mission is to create opportunities for homeownership; provide housing assistance for low-income Americans; work to create, rehabilitate, and maintain the nation's affordable housing; enforce the nation's fair housing laws; and spur economic growth in distressed neighborhoods. Today HUD helps provide decent, safe, and affordable housing to more than 4.3 million low-income families through its public housing, rental subsidy, and voucher programs, and plays a major role in providing shelter for America's most vulnerable populations: the working poor, minorities, Native Americans, people with disabilities, people with AIDS, the elderly, and the homeless.

What have recent presidential administrations done to help **homelessness**?

Approximately 650,000 people are homeless on any given night in America. In 2001, President George W. Bush's administration created a $1 billion grant program to aid the homeless. The government's grants were given to the states to help homeless individuals and families find emergency shelter, transitional housing, and permanent homes. The largest amount of grant money was earmarked for California at $165.4 million, with New

York coming in second at $123 million. State governments were expected to use the funds to create and improve their emergency shelters, as well as to provide job training, health care, child care, and drug and alcohol counseling for the communities they serve.

During the Reagan-Bush era, homelessness became recognized as a significant social problem when the number of homeless increased as the result of a weak economy and cuts in federal aid for housing and income assistance. Partly in response, Congress enacted the Stewart B. McKinney Homeless Assistance Act in 1987, which distributed funds directly to state and local governments so they could decide how best to serve their homeless populations. In the 1990s, HUD began emphasizing the need for permanent shelter, but government efforts to increase programs serving the homeless were met with a corresponding increase in people accessing these services—causing policymakers and service providers to question whether these services really alleviated the homelessness problem in America at all. When Bill Clinton became president, he addressed the issue of homelessness just shortly after assuming office, promising in 1993 to develop a single coordinated federal plan for "breaking the cycle of homelessness and preventing future homelessness." However, the Clinton administration came under attack for its broken promises and overall lack of support to this group. When Clinton announced his fiscal year 1998 budget proposal, he was berated for recommending $295 million less funding than the year prior for all homeless assistance programs, leaving many to doubt his commitment to homelessness and other social welfare programs.

HEALTH CARE REFORM AND WELFARE REFORM

How did the **Clinton administration attempt to address the health care crisis**?

Although the passage of a universal health care bill was an early priority of the Clinton administration (including First Lady Hillary Rodham Clinton), it died in the 103rd Congress when Democrats and Republicans were unable to agree on coverage and cost issues. The Clintons' comprehensive health care plan promised that no American would be denied needed care while simultaneously guaranteeing to restrain costs—a feat most members of Congress thought was impossible. The proposed plan called for forming state-run cooperatives called "health alliances" and drew heavy attack from businesses, who were required under the plan to pay for 80 percent of health care costs, and from the Health Insurance Association of America. When the Republican Congress took office in 1995, Speaker of the House Newt Gingrich created his "Contract with America" in response.

What was Newt Gingrich's **Contract with America**?

Shortly after the Democrats seized control of the White House in 1992 after 12 years of Republican rule, members of Congress and the public at large felt that President Bill Clinton had not done enough to act on his campaign promise of ending welfare "as we know it" or institute a comprehensive health care plan. Conservative Republican Newt Gingrich, then Speaker of the House, developed his Contract with America, which set the Republican legislative agenda for the 104th Congress. The contract maintained that the federal government was too big, spent too much, and had generally become unresponsive to the public. It maintained that the American Dream was out of reach for too many families because of burdensome government regulations and harsh tax laws, and called for greater personal responsibility on the part of the country's citizens. The Congress pledged to cut spending for welfare programs and enact a tough "two-years-and-out provision" with work requirements to promote individual responsibility, and ushered in the beginning discussions of welfare reform that led to the signing of the Personal Responsibility and Work Opportunity Reconciliation Act (PRWORA) of 1996.

What is welfare reform?

In the summer of 1996, President Bill Clinton signed the Personal Responsibility and Work Opportunity Reconciliation Act (PRWORA), which radically transformed the nation's welfare system. When scholars and laypeople alike refer to "welfare reform" they are generally referring to the changes that this recent law brought about, which laid the groundwork for ongoing reconstruction of welfare systems on a state-by-state basis. Specifically, the law made cuts in assistance programs for children and families totaling $54 billion over six years. It abolished Aid to Families with Dependent Children (AFDC), the primary cash aid program for families; JOBS, the work and training program for welfare recipients; and Emergency Assistance to Families with Children, a program that provided emergency help to families with children for a maximum of one month per year, and replaced these programs with a block grant of federal funds given to states. The bill cut $23 billion from the food stamp program over six years, and almost $3 billion over six years from child nutrition programs. The welfare reform legislation terminated SSI eligibility for most noncitizens (this provision was scaled back in 1997 legislation) and tightened the eligibility rules for awarding SSI disability benefits to children.

Why is **welfare reform** the subject of ongoing debate?

The Personal Responsibility and Work Opportunity Reconciliation Act (PRWORA) of 1996—generally referred to as the Welfare Reform Act—was designed to promote self-reliance by making it harder for the public to rely on government assistance, and many policy makers support the overall national climate of dissuading a "culture of dependency." Critics, however, have maintained that the changes outlined in the Welfare Reform Act only further impoverished many poor families. Today the gap between rich and poor is widening, with over 40 percent of American children living in poverty. In addition, unprecedented budget surpluses at both state and federal levels—state surpluses for the 1999 fiscal year totaled $35 billion, according to a January 2000 *New York Times* article—make it appear as if Americans have the economic ability to help society's disenfranchised, but not the willingness to do so. Attempts to continue PRWORA have surfaced in the Bush administration's welfare reauthorization proposal. In May and June 2002 the House and Senate each passed its version of a welfare reform bill, both of which keep the essential shape of the welfare system established in 1996 and provide states with annual welfare grants of $16.5 billion per year.

What is the **Ticket to Work and Work Incentives Improvement Act of 1999**?

In December 1999 President Clinton signed the Ticket to Work and Work Incentives Improvement Act. This law provides disability beneficiaries with a voucher they may use to purchase vocational rehabilitation services, employment services, and other support services. The law provides incentive payments to providers for successful rehabilitation in which the beneficiary returns to work. The new provisions also provide a number of safeguards to the beneficiaries to protect their benefits and health. Taken together, the Ticket to Work initiative seeks to shift the emphasis in the disability program away from mere maintenance of benefits toward rehabilitating the disabled and assisting them in returning to productive work.

What is the **Welfare-to-Work** program?

With the Personal Responsibility and Work Opportunity Reconciliation Act (PRWORA), poverty programs were moved from a federal "safety net" to state-directed efforts focused on actively moving individuals "from welfare to work." In accordance with this federal shift, a number of state and local employment training programs are in place to help low-income individuals or families get off welfare. The Welfare-to-Work program provides a variety of services at the state level to help hard-to-employ welfare recipients and non-custodial parents to get and keep jobs that will lead to self-sufficiency. The U.S. Department of Labor provides Welfare-to-Work grants to states and local communities to create additional job opportunities for recipients of Temporary Assistance for Needy Families (TANF), and provide many welfare recipients with the job placement services, transitional employment, and other support services they need to make the successful progression into long-term unsubsidized employment.

Former welfare recipients gain job skills as part of the Cleveland Works program, one of many "welfare-to-work" programs adopted in the 1990s meant to move individuals off of public assistance and into jobs.

How do Americans **pay for the welfare state**?

Americans pay for the welfare state, or public assistance programs, by paying taxes. For example, the total programs outlined in the Personal Responsibility and Work Opportunity Reconciliation Act (PRWORA) cost the American taxpaying public $700 million over six years. Contributory programs, such as Medicare, unemployment compensation, and Social Security, are financed by taxation as well, as a form of "forced savings" that compel contributors to save for the future. Funds to pay for Social Security and Medicare have mostly come from increases in payroll taxes, which places most of the burden on low- and middle-income families. In addition, charitable giving to nonprofit agencies helping low-income populations make up a substantial amount of these agencies' budgets.

What **major policies** are in place to help the poor break the cycle of poverty?

Policymakers maintain that educational policies are the single most important force in the redistribution of poverty in America, citing programs as varied as the preschool program Head Start and charter schools and school vouchers, which are designed to improve the delivery of quality education to America's children. Further, employment and training programs were created and continue to be modified to give adults the skills they need to successfully compete in the job market, although some states have had more success than others at actually improving employment rates. Housing policies are another area of policy emphasis, since appropriate housing for low-income individuals and families helps keep them off the street and allows for greater health and employment standards overall.

What is the future of social policy in the United States?

Social scientists agree that changes in population demographics will severely challenge Social Security. When the Social Security program was created in 1935, a 65-year-old had an average life expectancy of 77; today, it's 82 years—and rising. In addition, 76 million baby boomers will begin retiring in about 2010, and in about 30 years there will be nearly twice as many older Americans as there are today. At the same time, the number of workers paying into Social Security per beneficiary will drop from 3.4 to 2.1—changes that will undoubtedly strain Social Security as it exists now. As for other social service programs that are covered under the Personal Responsibility and Work Opportunity Reconciliation Act (PRWORA) of 1996, many analysts say it is too early to tell whether these programs, and the reforms instituted by the act, have any long-lasting hold. For all the attention paid to the sharp drop in welfare caseloads over the past five years, there remain thousands of low-income Americans who still must receive cash assistance under TANF in order to survive. The future of social policy depends, in part, on whether PRWORA will be extended by Congress and how the Bush administration chooses to address health and welfare issues.

What does President George W. Bush's **fiscal year 2003 budget** have to do with Social Security?

Under President Bush's proposed fiscal year 2003 $2.1-trillion budget plan, the federal government needed to divert $1.73 trillion in Social Security money to fund other programs through 2012, including the war on terrorism. In addition, Bush's tax cut—approved in 2001 and totaling $1.3 trillion to be phased in over 10 years—severely reduced the anticipated federal budget surpluses and forced the government to dig into Social Security revenue, despite the fact that both the Republican and Democratic parties promised during campaign time not to touch that money. While the president's tax plan calls for two more rounds of tax cuts in 2004 and 2006, it is yet to be seen whether those future cuts will go through at the expense of Social Security funds.

ECONOMIC POLICY

ECONOMIC POLICY 101

What is **economic policy**?

Economic policies are public policies designed to meet the government's economic goals, such as making and maintaining a market economy and promoting economic growth and prosperity. Maintaining and promoting a market economy involves federal subsidies to various markets, including the railroad market of the nineteenth century, the agricultural market of the twentieth century, and the national highway system in the 1930s and 1950s. In the research and development sector of the twenty-first century, subsidies support scientific research and development, computer microchip manufacturing, and high-tech industries. Economic growth is fostered primarily through taxation policies, balancing the federal budget, public lands disposal policies, and public works policies.

How is a **capitalist economy promoted**?

The American free enterprise, or capitalist, economy thrives in part from the abundance of government activity in this arena, including environmental protection, the protection of property rights, the maintenance of law and order, the enforcement of government contracts, the government's adherence to a common monetary system, corporate charters, the issuance of patents and copyrights, and bankruptcy legislation. In recent history, the greatest economic successes have occurred when the U.S. government helped to create an environment in which entrepreneurial business activity could thrive. For example, economists cite the reduction in tax and regulatory burdens in the late 1970s and early 1980s and enhanced trade as two economic factors that helped ignite the 1980s economic boom.

The trading floor of the New York Stock Exchange is a symbol of American economic activity and prosperity.

When did the **government's role in formulating economic policy** first achieve major impact?

The New Deal era of the 1930s marked a major turning point in U.S. economic history. This period, more than other, defined the government as an active and extensive participant in regulating the nation's private economy. President Franklin D. Roosevelt's New Deal program, meant to get the country back on its feet during the Great Depression, marked the first time that government regulated businesses in such a major way, became a provider of social security for the people, and was viewed as being ultimately responsible for maintaining a thriving economy. With its alphabet agencies and numerous work and social programs, the New Deal instituted a number of reforms in almost every are of the economy: finance, agriculture, labor, industry, and consumer protection.

Were there any attempts to **regulate the business market before the 1930s**?

Yes. In response to nineteenth-century million-dollar corporations who controlled the market and set price standards, the government intervened to protect small businesses, laborers, and consumers. The first national regulatory policy was the Interstate Commerce Act of 1887, which created the Interstate Commerce Commission, charged with controlling the railroad's monopolistic business practices. On its heels the Sherman Antitrust Act of 1890 was passed by Congress in an effort to extend the government's regulatory power, which would control all monopolies, including "trusts" and other agreements companies enacted in order to eliminate competition in the marketplace. Additional legislation further solidified the regulation already in place, including the Federal Trade Commission Act of 1914, which established the Federal Trade Commission as an independent agency charged with keeping American business competition free and fair, and the Clayton Antitrust Act of 1914, which strove to eliminate practices that may be detrimental to fair competition, including price discrimination. The creation of the Federal Reserve System in 1913, which was established to regulate the banking industry, was the last major regulatory move of the federal government until comprehensive national regulation began in the 1930s.

What is the difference between **economic regulation and social regulation**?

Economic regulation has to do with the government's involvement in the nation's economic matters, such as the control of business practices, industry rates, and transportation and service routes of businesses. Social regulation, on the other hand, involves the government's oversight of the quality and safety of goods and products, as well as the conditions under which those goods and products are manufactured. An example of social regulation is the U.S. Consumer Product Safety Commission's role as an independent federal regulatory agency, which works to save lives and keep families safe by reducing the risk of injuries and deaths associated with consumer products.

What is meant by the **social regulation era**?

The social regulation era is usually defined as that period of U.S. history between the mid-1960s and the mid-1970s, during which Congress enacted a long list of social regulatory legislation dealing with issues of consumer protection, health and safety, and environmental protection. These included the goal-specific Federal Meat Inspection Act, the Poultry Products Inspection Act, and the Lead-Based Paint Poison Prevention Act, as well as the more far-reaching Clean Air Act of 1970 and Employee Retirement Income Security Act of 1974, which was enacted to protect workers who had worked for substantial periods under pension plans.

In addition, the federal government set up several new regulatory agencies to serve as watchdogs over these new regulations, including the Consumer Product Safety Commission, charged with dealing with consumer product safety; the Occupational Safety and Health Administration (commonly called OSHA), which works to prevent injuries and protect the health of America's workers; the Environmental Protection Agency, founded to protect the nation's environment; the Mining Enforcement and Safety Administration, dedicated to promoting improved safety and health conditions in the nation's mines; and the National Highway Traffic Safety Administration, responsible for reducing deaths, injuries, and economic losses resulting from motor vehicle crashes. As a result of this legislation and these agencies, many industries that operated relatively free of government intervention now discovered that government regulation greatly influenced the way they did business.

What is the concept of **deregulation**?

Arguing that the federal government's economic regulatory programs had their flaws, often resulting in monopoly profits, service discrimination, an overall inefficiency in industry operations, and an atmosphere where new businesses could not compete or enter the market, economists and others began to call for "deregulation." Deregulation involves a less active role in government intervention in the economy. This philosophy was touted in the 1980s by economic-conservative presidents Ronald Reagan and George Bush, both of whom opposed government intervention in promoting commerce, claiming that regulatory techniques stifled the marketplace. And because President Bill Clinton built on the philosophy of his predecessors, the 1990s saw substantial deregulation in the telecommunications and agricultural industries, as well as the environment, where pollution control and endangered species laws were relaxed.

ENVIRONMENTAL POLICY AS A COMPONENT OF ECONOMIC POLICY

What do **public policy** and **the environment** have to do with one another?

The regulation of environmental activity is undertaken by the government to protect the public health and the nation's environment. Areas of concern to the government include detrimental business policies and practices that ultimately harm the public, including those that result in air and water pollution. Since issues like pollution are a "social cost" of doing business and since businesses have no real economic incentive to clean up their pollutants, it is the responsibility of the government to control pollution through its policy process. In addition, public interest groups supporting environmental protection—including the Wilderness Society, the Sierra Club, Greenpeace, and the Environmental Defense Fund—continually lobby Congress to adopt new environmental legislation and strengthen existing laws. The tension arises between these groups and their supporters and the business community, who bear most of the financial costs of implementing pollution controls and argue that the increased cost of doing "clean" business comes at the expense of economic growth and job creation. For example, the George Bush administration estimated that the costs of adhering to the Clean Air Act of 1990 cost businesses more than $20 billion annually. Despite the opposition, since the 1970s Congress has passed many far-reaching pollu-

Government regulations and enforcement by the Environmental Protection Agency (EPA) target industrial polluters (like this coke plant in Pittsburgh, Pennsylvania) and other threats to the environment to ensure the safety of the nation's air, water, and land.

tion control laws in an effort to clean up pollution and dispose of hazardous wastes safely, including the Clean Air and Clean Water Acts of the 1970s (and amendments made to the Clean Air Act in the 1990s); the Resource Conservation and Recovery Act of 1976; the Comprehensive Environmental Response, Compensation, and Liability Act of 1980; and the Pollution Prevention Act of 1990.

What is the role of the **Environmental Protection Agency**?

Established in 1970, the U.S. Environmental Protection Agency (EPA) is the nation's largest regulatory agency, charged with developing and enforcing regulations under existing environmental laws. The agency is responsible for researching and setting national standards for a variety of environmental programs, issuing permits, and monitoring and enforcing compliance. Where national standards are not met, the EPA issues sanctions and takes other steps to assist the states in reaching the desired levels of environmental quality. The agency also works with states, industries, and all levels of government in a wide variety of voluntary pollution prevention programs and energy conservation efforts. Prior to the establishment of the EPA, the national government was not prepared to make a coordinated attack on the nation's pollutants and polluters, and so early EPA efforts focused on repairing the damage already done and establishing new criteria to guide Americans in promoting a cleaner environment.

Is George W. Bush's administration seen as being **supportive of the environment**?

Generally, no. The Bush administration came under attack early on for its non–environmentally friendly decisions, including allowing oil drilling in the red rocks of Utah and Colorado's canyons; permitting an open-pit gold mine on a California desert site that the Quechan Indian tribe considered sacred; and signaling to land developers nationwide that they can build on wetlands without, in many cases, replacing them. However, most controversial was Bush's energy proposal, which included opening part of the Arctic National Wildlife Refuge to oil and natural gas exploration. Also under attack was Bush's proposal to invalidate protection of more than half a million acres of land deemed essential for the survival of endangered species in southern California, which environmentalists feared would be used as a precedent to encroach upon other protected lands across the country. In addition, environmentalists referred to Bush's fiscal year 2003 budget—which proposed cutting approximately $300 million from funds already allocated to the Environmental Protection Agency—as an indication of the president's priorities. Although the EPA said that the agency was cutting funds from projects that didn't align with administration goals, environmentalists continued to push for funding.

ECONOMIC STABILITY: USING MONETARY AND FISCAL POLICY TO ACHIEVE BALANCE

What is the difference between **recession** and **inflation**?

Periods of economic stability, defined by a national climate of economic growth, a rising national income, and high employment, are often followed by periods of economic instability, which, conversely, involve recession and inflation. Recession is a general decline or "slump" in the economy that is characterized by negative business growth. It occurs as a result of declined investments, decreased production, high unemployment rates, and a disproportion between the quantity of goods produced and the consumers' ability to purchase them.

Inflation, on the other hand, means that there is too much consumer demand for the available supply of goods and services, therefore driving the price of goods up. Inflation is the result of an increase in the amount of circulating money beyond the needs of trade; because there is an oversupply of currency, the law of supply and demand dictates that the value of money decreases. The most common cause of inflation is war, since government borrowing, an increase in the money supply, and a decreased supply of consumer goods all increase consumer demand and thereby cause rising prices.

In order to combat these forms of instability and return the nation to a more healthy economic landscape, the national government employs either monetary or fiscal policy. During the late 1970s, for example, U.S. fiscal policy deliberately created a recession to counteract inflation. The resulting recession of the early 1980s was marked by renewed growth, lower interest rates, and a decrease in inflation.

Do inflation and recession happen **at the same time**?

No. Inflation and recession are opposite trends in the business cycle and not simultaneous processes. Recession, or the downward trend of business, is often accompanied by deflation, an economic term that is characterized by declining prices. Because of high unemployment rates that characterize a recession, people have less money to spend on consumer goods, thereby lowering prices.

What is monetary policy?

Monetary policy is a type of government regulation in which the government controls the nation's money supply and interest rates. The nation's "money" involves currency, bank deposits, and financial assets. The ultimate targets of monetary policy are maximum employment, stable prices, and moderate long-term interest rates.

What is the **Federal Reserve System**?

The Federal Reserve System (often called "The Fed") is the central bank of the United States. Founded by Congress in 1913, its primary goal is to provide the nation with a more flexible and more stable monetary and financial system. Since its inception, the Federal Reserve's role in banking and the economy has expanded, and today its main duties include: conducting the nation's monetary policy by influencing the money and credit conditions in the economy with a goal of full employment and stable prices; supervising and regulating banking institutions to ensure the soundness of the nation's banking and financial system and to protect the credit rights of consumers; maintaining the stability of the financial system and containing the systemic risk that may arise in financial markets; and providing select financial services to the U.S. government, the public, financial institutions, and foreign official institutions, including operating the nation's payments system.

Because the Federal Reserve System is an independent central bank, its decisions do not have to be ratified by the president or any part of the executive branch. However, the entire system is subject to oversight by Congress because the Constitution grants Congress the power to coin money and set its value. Under these guidelines, the Federal Reserve must operate within the framework of the government's overall objectives of economic and financial policy.

Federal Reserve Board chairman Alan Greenspan and his colleagues are most commonly associated with influencing interest rates, which is one of the means by which "the Fed" regulates banking and influences monetary policy in an effort to maintain the nation's financial health.

What is the significance of the **Federal Reserve Act**?

Before Congress created the Federal Reserve System, periodic financial panics occurred, contributing to bank failures, business bankruptcies, and general economic slumps. After a severe economic crisis in 1907 prompted Congress to establish the National Monetary Commission, which put forth proposals to create an institution that could address these financial crises, Congress passed the Federal Reserve Act, signed into law by President Woodrow Wilson on December 23, 1913. The act provided for the establishment of Federal Reserve Banks, the creation of more effective supervision of banking in the nation, and the ability to furnish elastic currency, among other things.

What is the purpose of the **Federal Reserve Board**?

The Federal Reserve System is composed of a central government agency, the Board of Governors, or Federal Reserve Board, located in Washington, D.C., as well as 12 regional Federal Reserve Banks, located in major cities across America. The Federal Reserve Board is responsible for the formation and implementation of monetary policy. Specifically, it shares responsibility with the Federal Reserve Banks for supervising and regulating the country's financial institutions and activities; providing banking services to depository institutions and the federal government; and ensuring that consumers receive adequate information and fair treatment in their dealings with the banking system.

How is the **Federal Reserve Board** structured?

The Federal Reserve Board is composed of seven members appointed by the president and confirmed by the Senate. The full term of a board member is 14 years, and the appointments are staggered so that one term expires on January 31 of each even-numbered year. After serving a full term, a board member may not be reappointed.

What tools does the Federal Reserve System use to **conduct monetary policy**?

The Federal Reserve System uses three tools to conduct monetary policy in the United States: (1) open market operations, which involve the buying and selling of U.S. government (mainly Treasury) securities in the open market to influence the level or reserves in the depository system; (2) reserve requirements, or requirements regarding the amount of funds that commercial banks and other depository institutions must hold in reserve against deposits; and (3) the discount rate, the interest rate charged to commercial banks and other depository institutions when they borrow money from a regional Federal Reserve Bank.

Where does the Federal Reserve System get its money?

The income from the Federal Reserve System comes primarily from the interest in U.S. government securities that it has acquired through open market operations. Other major sources of income include the interest on foreign currency investments held by the system; interest on loans to depository institutions (the rate on which is the discount rate); and fees received for services provided to depository institutions, such as check clearing, fund transfers, and automated clearinghouse operations. After it pays its expenses, the Federal Reserve turns the rest of its earnings over to the U.S. Treasury.

How do the functions of the Federal Reserve System **affect consumers**?

Since the late 1960s, the number of federal laws intended to protect consumers in credit and other financial transactions has been growing. Congress has assigned the Federal Reserve the duty of implementing these laws and ensuring that the public receives comprehensive information and fair treatment. The Federal Reserve's responsibilities in this area include: writing and interpreting regulations to carry out many of the consumer-protection laws; reviewing bank compliance with the regulations; investigating complaints from the public; addressing issues of state and federal jurisdiction; testifying before Congress on consumer protection issues; and directing a community affairs program. Along these lines, the Federal Reserve is advised by a Consumer Advisory Council, whose members represent the interest of consumers, community groups, and creditors nationwide, and whose meetings are open to the public.

What is **fiscal policy**?

Fiscal policy is the federal government's policy regarding taxation and spending, as set by Congress and the presidential administration and conducted through the federal budget process. Fiscal policy is used to influence the overall operation of the economy and maintain economic stability. Methods of taxation are both deliberate and discretionary on the part of the government; however, there are also some "automatic" stabilizers that have been built into the economy to automatically reduce taxes and increase government spending during periods of economic sluggishness. For example, mandatory spending for social service programs such as unemployment insurance, Medicaid, and food stamps increases because eligibility for benefits increases in times of high unemployment. In addition, tax payments automatically fall as personal income and corporate profits decline.

What is the **federal budget**?

The budget system of the U.S. federal government, known as the federal budget, provides the means for the president and Congress to decide how much money to spend, what to spend it on, and how to raise the money they have decided to spend. Through the budget system, they determine the allocation of resources among the agencies of the federal government. While the budget system focuses primarily on dollars, it also allocates other resources, such as federal employment. The president's budget is generally viewed as a detailed outline of the administration's policy and funding priorities, as well as a presentation of the economic outlook for the coming fiscal year. The president's budget, which estimates spending, revenue, and borrowing levels, is compiled from input by the various federal agencies, with funding broken down by budget-function categories. The budget document is usually quite detailed, often comprising several thick volumes of text, charts, and graphs. The budget runs for a single fiscal year, or accounting period, beginning on October 1 of one calendar year and running through September 30 of the following calendar year.

Does the **Constitution mandate a federal budget**?

Although the Constitution does not require the president to present an annual budget, in 1921 the Budget and Accounting Act became law and laid the foundation for the modern budget process, which includes the president's budget. More recently, the Congressional Budget and Impoundment Control Act of 1974 established a timetable for the annual budget process, which is kicked off each year by the presidential budget submission. The Budget Act specifies that the president's budget should be presented to Congress on or before the first Monday in February, which generally coincides with the timing of the president's annual State of the Union Address.

What is the **Office of Management and Budget's role** in the federal budget?

The Office of Management and Budget's (OMB) predominant role is to assist the president in overseeing the preparation of the federal budget and to supervise its administration in executive branch agencies. In helping to formulate the president's spending plans, the OMB evaluates the effectiveness of agency programs, policies, and procedures, assesses competing funding demands among agencies, and sets funding priorities. The OMB ensures that agency reports, rules, testimony, and proposed legislation are consistent with the president's budget and with administration policies.

What process does the **federal budget go through in order to be enacted**?

The federal budgeting process has three main components: formulation of the budget by the president and the Office of Management and Budget (OMB); congressional action on the budget; and, finally, implementation. First, the president outlines his financial proposal and recommends priorities for the allocation of government resources. While the budget focuses on the next fiscal year, it also covers at least the four years following the budget year in order to reflect long-term goals. During the budget's formulation, the president, the director of the OMB, and other Executive Office officials continually exchange information, proposals, and evaluations bearing on policy decisions with the secretaries of the departments and the heads of the government agencies. Decisions reflected in previously enacted budgets, including the one for the fiscal year in progress, and reactions to the last proposed budget influence decisions concerning the upcoming budget. In addition, the president considers projections of the nation's economic outlook, prepared jointly by the Council of Economic Advisers, the OMB, and the Treasury Department. The entire formulation process involves the simultaneous consideration of the resource needs of individual programs, the allocation of resources among federal government agencies, total outlays (money spent) and receipts (money taken in) that are appropriate in relation to current and prospective economic conditions, and statutory constraints.

Congress considers the president's budget proposals and approves, modifies, or disapproves them. Congress can—and often does—change funding levels, eliminate programs, or add programs that are not at the president's request. It can add or eliminate taxes and other sources of receipts, or make other changes that the affect the amount of receipts collected. Through the process of adopting a budget resolution, Congress agrees on levels for total spending and receipts, the size of the deficit or surplus, and the debt limit. The budget resolution then provides the framework within which congressional committees prepare appropriations bill and other spending and receipts legislation, such as changes to the tax code. After negotiating back and forth, the president and Congress reach a concensus on a budget they feel is for the best benefit of the American people. During the execution of the budget, government agencies may not spend more than Congress has appropriated.

Does the government ever find that **it needs more money than it budgeted for**?

Yes. While the federal budget is being executed, the government often finds that it needs to spend more money than Congress has appropriated for the fiscal year because of circumstances that were not anticipated when the budget was created. For example, more money might be needed to provide assistance to a particular city struck by a natural or unforeseen disaster, and under these types of circumstances, Congress often grants additional funds. For example, Congress approved $40 billion in emergency funds to aid the city of New York immediately following the September 11, 2001, terrorist attacks.

What is sequestration?

Established in 1985 by the Balanced Budget and Emergency Deficit Reduction Act, also known as the Gramm-Rudman-Hollings Act, sequestration is an across-the-board cut in federal spending according to a presidential order. A sequestration order can only be issued if Congress fails to meet a budgetary requirement, such as a deficit target or a spending limit.

What is the difference between a **budget surplus and a budget deficit** and how are they used in fiscal policy?

Fiscal policy involves deliberate decisions by the president and Congress to either run a budget surplus or a budget deficit. When outlays (funds spent by the government) exceed receipts (funds taken in), the difference is called a deficit. The government finances deficits primarily by borrowing. When receipts exceed outlays, the difference is a surplus, and the government uses the surplus to reduce debt. (The government's debt, or debt held by the public, is approximately the cumulative amount of borrowing to finance deficits, less repayments from surpluses.) Surpluses and deficits are achieved by either increasing or decreasing government spending while keeping taxes constant; by increasing or cutting taxes while keeping spending stable; or by various combinations of changes in taxing and spending. For example, President George W. Bush's proposed fiscal year 2003 $2.1-trillion budget plan relied on deficit spending in order to achieve its objectives.

Why is a **budget surplus** important?

Put simply, a budget surplus occurs when revenues exceed spending in any year—just as a deficit occurs when spending exceeds revenues. With certain exceptions, the national debt is the sum total of our deficits, minus our surpluses, over the years. Budget surpluses are necessary to help repay the national debt; indeed, history shows that when the federal government incurs a surplus, it generally repays debt held by the public. In 1998, the federal budget reported its first surplus ($69 billion) since 1969. In 1999, the surplus nearly doubled to $124 billion. As a result of these surpluses, federal debt held by the public was reduced from $3.8 trillion at the end of 1997 to $3.6 trillion at the end of 1999. With prudent fiscal policies, it is possible for the national budget to remain in surplus for many years; however, as of 2002, the budget surplus has been shrinking—its reduction due to a weaker economy, increased government spending, and tax cuts.

What is the **national debt** exactly?

The national debt is divided into two main categories: debt held by the public and debt the government owes itself. *Debt held by the public* is the total of all federal deficits, minus surpluses, over the years. This is the cumulative amount of money the federal government has borrowed from the public, through the sale of notes and bonds of varying sizes and time periods until maturity. The cumulative amount of borrowing from the public—i.e., the debt held by the public—is the most important measure of federal debt because it is what the government has borrowed in the private markets over the years, and it determines how much the government pays in interest to the public. Debt held by the public was $3.6 trillion at the end of 1999—roughly the net effect of deficits and surpluses over the last 200 years. Individuals and institutions in the United States hold about two-thirds of debt held by the public; the rest is held in foreign countries.

Debt held by the public does not include *debt the government owes itself*—the total of all trust fund surpluses and deficits over the years, like the Social Security surplus, which the law says must be invested in federal securities. Because the large budget deficit was turned into a surplus, the debt held by the public was reduced in the two years prior to fiscal year 2001 for the first time since 1969. The sum of debt held by the public and debt the government owes itself is called *gross federal debt.* At the end of 1999, it totaled $5.6 trillion. Finally, another measure of federal debt is debt subject to legal limit, or the *legal debt,* which is similar to gross federal debt. When the government reaches the limit, it loses its authority to borrow more to finance its spending; at that point, the president and Congress must enact a law to increase the limit.

What is the difference between **the deficit** and **the debt**?

The deficit is the fiscal-year difference between what the government takes in from taxes and other revenues, called receipts, and the amount of money the government spends, called outlays. The items included in the deficit are considered either on-budget or off-budget. (The off-budget items are typically comprised of the two Social Security trust funds—old-age and survivors insurance and disability insurance—and the Postal Service fund.) Generally, on-budget outlays tend to exceed on-budget receipts, while off-budget receipts tend to exceed off-budget outlays.

The national debt can be thought of as accumulated deficits plus accumulated off-budget surpluses. The on-budget deficits require the U.S. Treasury to borrow money to raise the cash needed to keep the government operating. The Treasury borrows the money by selling Treasury securities like T-bills, notes, bonds, and savings bonds to the public. Additionally, the government trust funds are required by law to invest accumulated surpluses in Treasury securities. The Treasury securities issued to the public and to the government trust funds (called intragovernmental holdings) then become part of the total debt.

Often the distinction in terms is likened to a personal budget. Let's suppose you need some extra money this month. Since you are cash short, you have a "budget deficit." Therefore, you borrow the money you need. The amount you borrowed (and now owe) is called your "debt." Of course, you must pay interest on your debt. If next month you don't have enough money to repay what you borrowed you must borrow some more (another budget deficit), and you'll still have to pay the interest on the loan. If you have a deficit every month, you keep borrowing and your debt grows.

How is the government's ability to finance its debt tied to the economy?

The government's ability to finance its debt is tied to the size and strength of the economy, or Gross Domestic Product (GDP). Debt held by the public was less than 40 percent of GDP at the end of 1999. As a percentage of GDP, debt held by the public was highest at the end of World War II, at 109 percent, then fell to 24 percent in 1974 before gradually rising to a peak of over 49 percent in the mid-1990s. That decline, from 109 to 24 percent, occurred because the economy grew faster than the debt accumulated; although debt held by the public rose from $242 billion to $344 billion in those years, the economy grew faster.

Just **how in debt** is the United States?

Early 2002 estimates cite the national debt at almost $6 trillion. The U.S. Treasury Department's Bureau of the Public Debt monitors this figure, so interested parties can simply view the continuously updated "Public Debt to the Penny" chart to gather a precise daily figure. With the estimated population of the United States at more than 286 million, each citizen's share of the debt, if you were to calculate it, would be somewhere in the neighborhood of $20,000.

Was the country **always in debt**?

Although the United States was not always in debt, much of its history has been spent in debt. The total public debt is largely a legacy of war, economic recession, and inflation, and represents the accumulated deficits in the government's budgets over the years. The United States first got into debt in 1790 when it assumed the Revolutionary war debts of the Continental Congress. At the end of 1790, the gross public debt was approximately $75 million. For a brief period in the mid-1830s the public debt was virtually nonexistent. In 1916, at the start of World War I, the public debt was $1 billion, rising to a peak of $26 billion in 1919 to finance the war. The debt declined for the next decade, until the Great Depression of the 1930s, during which the debt increased from $16 billion to $42 billion. During World War II the public debt rose sharply to a peak of $279 billion in 1946. From its postwar low in 1949, the outstanding public debt grew gradually for nearly the next two decades until, beginning at the time of the Vietnam War in the mid-1960s, the rate of the debt's increase accelerated sharply.

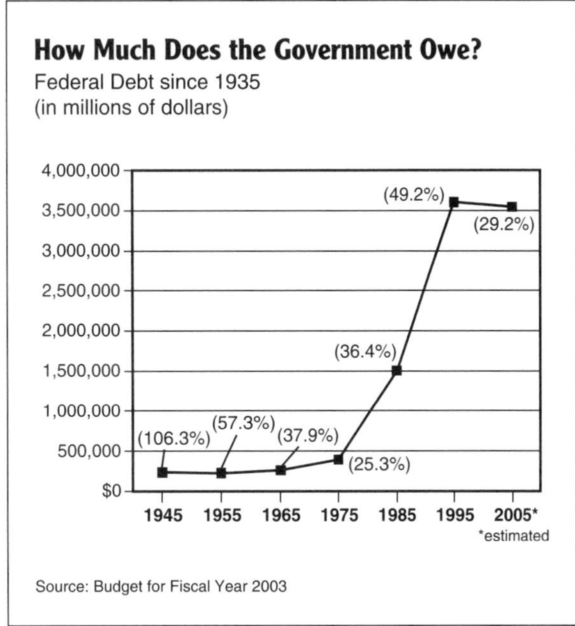

The amout of federal debt has grown significantly since the Vietnam War era, especially during the 1980s. Percentages indicate the amount of debt compared to the gross national product.

How is the **national debt reduced**?

Federal budget surpluses are the primary mechanism for reducing the national debt. The money the federal government uses to pay its bills—its revenues or receipts—comes mostly from taxes. In the two years prior to fiscal year 2001, revenues were greater than spending, and the government was able to reduce the national debt with the difference between revenues and spending—that is, the surplus. In January 2001, the Congressional Budget Office (CBO) projected that the budget surplus would be $5.6 trillion over 10 years; in fiscal year 2002, the projected surplus was reduced by $4 trillion, according to CBO estimates for the same 10-year window—a 71 percent decline.

What are the **positives and negatives to the economy** of paying down the national debt?

Economists and proponents of paying down or paying off the national debt usually cite several favorable benefits to the U.S. economy—namely, lower long-term interest rates, leading to stronger investment and growth; reduced competition for funds loaned to private enterprises; and a greater margin to absorb the budget deficits that will occur when baby boomers start drawing Social Security benefits. In addition, reducing the interest obligations that must be paid on the debt frees the government to spend money on social and economic programs. However, many economists have debunked these reasons as myths, saying that driving down the national debt is not all it's trumped up to be. For one thing, critics such as economist William F. Hummel contend, paying down the debt does not create a surplus of money for the private sector, it simply transfers dollars from taxpayers to bond owners, and erodes assets that are held as savings. Those securities, together with the monetary base created by the federal government, comprise the net financial wealth of the private sector. By taxing that wealth away, the economy is impacted negatively.

In his article, "Zeroing the National Debt," Hummel is quick to point out the value of U.S. Treasury securities, which play a central role in the banking system. Their abundance helps maintain market liquidity—making them particularly valuable for the federal government to buy and sell in executing its monetary policy. On an international scale, because Treasury bills (called T-bills) are traded daily in enormous volume among banks and other financial institutions around the world, a substantial supply of risk-free, interest-bearing Treasury securities is crucial to maintaining the U.S. dollar as the world's primary reserve currency. Paying off the national debt would leave global financial markets with no benchmark risk-free asset in the form of U.S. government securities. If the U.S. government were to dismiss itself from the credit markets, it would handicap its ability to resume borrowing.

What does the **Department of the Treasury** do?

Comprised of the Office of the Secretary and various departmental offices, the Department of the Treasury performs a wide variety of functions. The Bureau of Engraving and Printing makes the nation's paper currency and the United States Mint produces the nation's coins. The Internal Revenue Service collects income taxes and other forms of federal government revenue. Law enforcement functions fall under the jurisdiction of the United States Customs Service, the Bureau of Alcohol, Tobacco, and Firearms, and the United States Secret Service. Maintaining the federal government's accounts is the job of the Financial Management Service, and processing the sale and redemption of Treasury bonds, notes, and bills is the responsibility of the Bureau of the Public Debt. Finally, the Treasury is charged with overseeing and regulating savings institutions and national banks, managed through its Office of the Comptroller of the Currency and Office of Thrift Supervision.

Part of the Treasury Department's mission involves promoting prosperous and stable American and world economies, managing the government's finances, and safeguarding the nation's financial systems. Upholding this mission, the secretary of the Treasury is responsible for formulating and recommending domestic and international-

New quarters flow from a minting machine at the U.S. Mint in Philadelphia, Pennsylvania. The Department of Treasury oversees the production of the nation's paper currency and coins.

al financial, economic, and tax policy; participating in the formulation of broad fiscal policies that have general significance for the economy; and managing the public debt. The secretary oversees the activities of the Treasury Department in carrying out the position's major law enforcement responsibilities, in serving as the financial agent for the U.S. government, and in manufacturing coins and currency.

What is the purpose of **taxation**?

The primary purpose of taxation is to raise revenue for the government. The income tax, or the tax paid on personal or corporate income, is the primary vehicle for collecting this revenue. Besides raising revenue, another important objective of the income tax is to collect revenue in a manner that reduces existing wealth disparities between the lowest and highest income tax brackets, often called the government's redistribution of wealth policy. Finally, taxation is used to encourage a capitalist economy; since tax laws allow deductions for business expenses, they encourage individuals and companies to expand production, invest in advertising, and hire staff, all of which contribute to the economy.

Besides taxation, where does the federal government **get its money**?

The government gets its money, or revenues, from a variety of sources. Primarily, the government is funded by the individual income tax. In 2001, individual income taxes raised an estimated $972 billion for the government, equal to about 9.7 percent of the

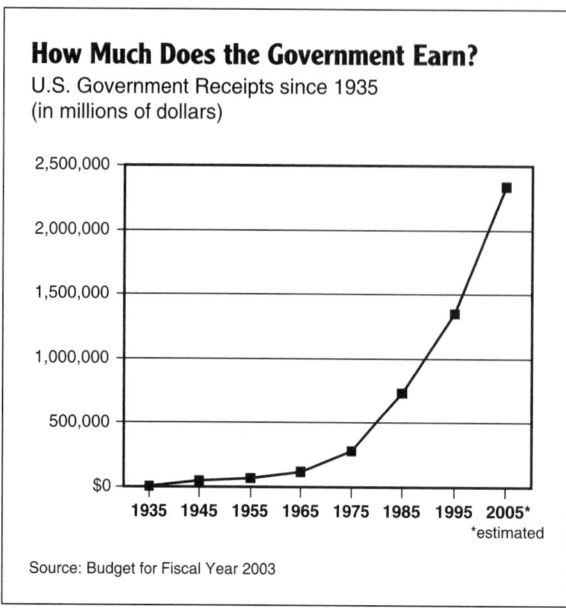

Taxation from a variety of sources makes up the bulk of government receipts, the amount of which has grown significantly since 1975.

Gross Domestic Product (GDP). In addition, the government receives money from social insurance payroll taxes, which include Social Security taxes, Medicare taxes, unemployment insurance taxes, and federal employee retirement payments. This source of revenue has grown from 2 percent of GDP in 1955 to 6.8 percent in 2001. Unlike the personal income tax, corporate income taxes, which raised an estimated $195 billion, have shrunk steadily as a percent of GDP, from 4.5 percent in 1955 to 1.9 percent in 2001. In addition to these three methods of collecting money, the government applies excise taxes to various products, including alcohol, tobacco, transportation fuels, and telephone services. The government earmarks some of these taxes to support certain activities—including the development and maintenance of highways and airports and airways—and deposits others in its general fund. The government also collects estate and gift taxes, customs duties, and miscellaneous revenues—for example, Federal Reserve earnings, fines, penalties, and forfeitures.

What is meant by **progressive** and **regressive taxation**?

In the United States, income tax is said to be "progressive" or "graduated," meaning that the heaviest tax payments are made by those with the highest income levels. Because the rate of taxation increases with each higher income bracket, income tax is progressive. If the burden falls on people in lower income brackets to pay a higher proportion of their income than people in higher income brackets, then the tax is called regressive.

When was the **income tax** enacted?

While tariffs on imported goods were the main funding method the federal government relied on in the early nineteenth century, it often employed the income tax sporadically throughout later years of that century. Congress enacted the first income tax law in 1862 in order to fund the Civil War, and as a progressive tax it was a forerunner of the modern income tax. The Tax Act of 1862 established the office of Commissioner of

Internal Revenue, who was given the power to assess, levy, and collect taxes, and much of the original job description remains in effect today. In 1913, with the passage of the Sixteenth Amendment, the Constitution made the income tax a permanent part of the U.S. tax system by giving Congress legal authority to tax income, and a subsequent revenue law granted Congress the power to tax both individuals and corporations.

Who was the **first president to file an income tax return**?

On March 14, 1923, President Warren G. Harding became the first president to file an income tax return.

What is the role of the **IRS**?

A division of the Treasury Department created by Congress in 1862, the Internal Revenue Service (IRS) is responsible for administering and enforcing the nation's internal revenue laws and related statutes enacted by Congress. As the nation's tax collection agency, its mission is to provide America's taxpayers with quality service by helping them understand and meet their tax responsibilities and by applying the tax law with integrity and fairness to all Americans. The IRS deals directly with more Americans than any other public or private institution. In 2000, for example, the IRS collected more than $2 trillion in revenue and processed 226 million tax returns. This service cost taxpayers 39 cents for each $100 collected by the IRS, the lowest cost/collection ratio since 1954.

What tax law did President George W. Bush sign?

On June 7, 2001, despite opposition from many Democratic leaders, President George Bush signed the Economic Growth and Tax Relief Reconciliation Act, which included a variety of tax cuts totaling $1.3 trillion to be phased in over a 10-year period. The act offers benefits to a broad range of taxpayers through relief provisions. Mainly benefiting married couples, families with children, single mothers, seniors, and those who would receive tax cuts to help pay for education, childcare, and other expenses, the act also completely eliminates the income tax liability for 3.9 million individuals and families.

How many times in recent U.S. history has the federal government **enacted a major tax cut for its citizens in order to stimulate the economy**?

During the twentieth century, there were only three instances of significant tax cuts: in the 1920s under presidents Warren Harding and Calvin Coolidge; in the 1960s under President John F. Kennedy; and in the 1980s under President Ronald Reagan, who initiated a 30-percent across-the-board tax rate reduction plan modeled after John F. Kennedy's successful tax cut 20 years earlier. In all three cases the tax cuts

President George W. Bush signs a $1.35 trillion tax cut into law in June 2001. Bush and his supporters contended that the tax cut would give Americans more money to spend, thus stimulating the economy.

stimulated the economy. In Kennedy's case, the inflation-adjusted Gross Domestic Product grew by more than 50 percent during the 1960s, a postwar record. Reagan's 1981 tax cuts led to what then became the longest peacetime economic expansion in U.S. history, a record that was broken during the 1990s when economic expansion was accompanied by a decrease in government spending.

What was President Clinton's 1992 commitment to a **"middle-class tax cut"** all about and why did it fall by the wayside?

President Bill Clinton's 1992 campaign promise for a "middle-class tax cut," which targeted the middle class and shifted the burden of paying taxes to the upper class, was born out of middle-class America's distaste over predecessor George Bush's tax increases and Bush's refusal to focus on the nation's economic recession. Clinton's tax cut was motivated by the goal of encouraging economic growth through increased public consumption. The theory behind such a tax cut was that if people save money on their taxes they will spend it on day-to-day commodities (thus promoting the economy) rather than saving or investing those monies. After learning that the federal deficit was much greater than he initially thought, Clinton broke his campaign promise, and the middle-class tax cut never came to be. In fact, Clinton increased taxes by $240 billion in 1993, proposed increasing them again in 1994 to pay for government-run health care, and vetoed tax cuts in 1995.

Senate Majority Leader Tom Daschle (D–SD) outlines his opposition to the 2001 tax cut implemented by President George W. Bush.

What are some of the **milestones of President George W. Bush's economic policy**?

Faced with a 5.8 percent nationwide unemployment rate in January 2002, the Bush administration turned its attention from the war on terrorism to address the nation's economic status. Although Bush's so-called "economic security bill"—which focused on large tax breaks for businesses, an accelerated cut in income tax rates, and expanded benefits for the unemployed—met with disapproval in the Democratic-controlled Senate, Bush continued to advocate his 2001 tax cut and further cuts under the premise that if people can keep more of their own money (i.e., pay less taxes), then they will naturally pour this saved money into the economy, which will eventually be strengthened. His fiscal year 2003 budget is a $2.1 trillion plan that forgoes national debt reduction and many domestic programs to finance homeland security, the war on terrorism (including beefing up Defense Department spending), and new tax cuts that are meant to stimulate the economy. Bush outlined $590 billion in tax cuts to take place over 10 years, with many new cuts taking effect in 2003 and 2004.

What was **Reaganomics**?

"Reaganomics" is the term for President Ronald Reagan's economic policy of the 1980s, which relied on the school of economic thought known as "supply-side economics." The theory of supply-side economics says that supply always creates demand.

President Ronald Reagan's brand of economic policy, which resulted in deregulation and tax cuts as well as an increase in the national debt, was termed "Reaganomics."

Proponents maintain that if the government stimulates the production of goods and services, demand will be created, and the economy will be strengthened. Supply-siders believe that high personal and corporate taxes produce damaging economic incentives that lead people to work less and to invest less than they normally would. Therefore, supply-side policy recommendations typically include deregulation of heavily regulated industries, promotion of greater competition through lowering barriers to international trade, and measures to repeal special subsidies and tax loopholes targeting particular industries, as well as the implementation of lower and more uniform tax rates across the board, which are meant to increase investment and economic activity. While the Reagan administration advocated deregulation and cut taxes for the wealthy and for businesses, it failed to apply the other factor of supply-side economics, the decrease of government spending. Instead, Reagan increased the federal government's budget, resulting in deficit spending, so that by the time he left office the national debt had grown from $730 billion to $2.1 trillion.

What is **"trickle-down economics"**?

Closely associated with the President Ronald Reagan's tax cuts for the wealthy is the concept of "trickle down economics," which asserts that the more the wealthy are allowed to grow wealthier and invest their money in the economy, the more wealth will "trickle down" into lower socioeconomic groups. When implementing his tax cut, Reagan upheld that the tax reduction would jump-start America's economy because the investor class would have more money to spend on factory and business expansions, thereby creating jobs and causing money to "trickle down" to the working class. He furthered maintained that his tax cut would release "the dynamics of the free market," spurring growth, increasing federal revenue, and balancing the U.S. budget by 1983. The trickle-down theory, implemented primarily by Republicans and generally upheld to be an invention of politicians rather than a sound economic theory, has been criticized by the recent administrations—then-Vice President George Bush had previously called supply-side economics and its trickle-down cousin "voodoo economics."

What is the role of the Federal Trade Commission?

The Federal Trade Commission (FTC) is a government agency that enforces a variety of federal antitrust and consumer protection laws. The commission seeks to ensure that the nation's markets function competitively, efficiently, and are free of undue restrictions. The commission also works to enhance the smooth operation of the marketplace by eliminating acts or practices that are unfair or deceptive. In general, the commission's efforts are directed toward stopping actions that threaten consumers' opportunities to exercise informed choice. Finally, the commission undertakes economic analysis to support its law enforcement efforts and to contribute to the policy deliberations of Congress, the executive branch, and other independent agencies, as well as state and local governments when requested.

What is the role of the **Department of Commerce**?

The U.S. Department of Commerce promotes job creation, economic growth, sustainable development, and improved living standards for all Americans by working in partnership with businesses, universities, communities, and workers. Specifically, the Department of Commerce works to: (1) build for the future and promote U.S. competitiveness in the global marketplace by strengthening and safeguarding the nation's economic infrastructure; (2) keep America competitive with cutting-edge science and technology and an unrivaled information base; and (3) provide effective management and stewardship of the nation's resources and assets to ensure sustainable economic opportunities.

The Commerce Department touches the lives of Americans daily and in many ways that the public is probably unaware. It makes possible the weather reports broadcast every morning on the morning news and facilitates technology that Americans use in the workplace and home every day, It supports the development, gathering, and transmitting of information essential to competitive business and makes possible the diversity of companies and goods found in America's (and the world's) marketplaces. The Commerce Department also supports environmental and economic health for the communities in which Americans live, and every 10 years, it conducts the constitutionally mandated census.

What is the **Federal Deposit Insurance Corporation**?

In an effort to bring stability to the banking system after the stock market crash of the late 1920s and during the Great Depression of the 1930s, Congress created the Federal Deposit Insurance Corporation (FDIC). The intent was to form an institution that would provide a federal government guarantee of deposits so that customers' funds, within certain limits, would be safe and available to them on demand. Since the start of FDIC insurance on January 1, 1934, not one depositor has lost a cent of insured funds as a result of economic or banking failure. With a mission of maintaining stability in the nation's banking system, today the FDIC performs three primary functions: (1) it insures deposits up to $100,000 in virtually all United States banks and savings and loan associations; (2) it arranges a resolution for each failing institution; and (3) it promotes the soundness of insured depository institutions and the U.S. financial system by identifying, monitoring, and addressing risks to the deposit insurance funds. The FDIC also is the primary federal regulator of about 6,000 state-chartered "nonmember" banks (commercial and savings banks that are not members of the Federal Reserve System).

FOREIGN POLICY

FOREIGN POLICY BASICS

How is **foreign policy** defined?

Foreign policy is a catch-all phrase used to describe a country's position and policies concerning other countries, including diplomatic, military, commercial (trade), and others. In totality, foreign policy can be described as the way that a nation's government behaves in relation to world affairs. American foreign policy, for example, includes decisions that the government makes involving treaties and alliances, international trade, foreign economic and military aid, how it beefs up or cuts its Defense Department and budget, its relationship to the United Nations, nuclear weapons testing, disarmament discussions, and, most recently, its reaction to worldwide terrorist groups. Lesser-realized foreign policy decisions include the presidential administration's position on consumer imports and exports, immigration, and economic sanctions.

Who makes **foreign policy**?

As the nation's chief diplomat and commander in chief of its armed forces, the president of the United States holds the responsibility for making and conducting foreign policy. The president negotiates and signs international treaties, makes international agreements, or pacts, with heads of foreign nations, and uses military force abroad in combat. However, the U.S. Congress also has power in the areas of military and foreign affairs, specifically holding the sole power to declare war, and thus shares the spotlight with the president. Congress's expressed powers include several "war powers"—the power to raise and support armies, to provide and maintain a navy, and to establish rules regarding the functioning of its military forces—and the power to regulate foreign commerce. As the nation's lawmaking entity, Congress has the power to act on matters affecting national security and the Senate has authority to approve treaties.

Defense Secretary Donald Rumsfeld, left, and Secretary of State Colin Powell play key roles in the development and implementation of U.S. foreign policy, as have those who have held those offices before them.

Do the **states** play any role in foreign affairs?

According to Article I of the Constitution, the states are not sovereign, have no standing in international law, and play no role in foreign affairs.

Who **helps the president** shape foreign policy?

The secretary of state, as head of the State Department, and the secretary of defense, as head of the Defense Department, are the two key players in shaping foreign policy and military affairs. As the ranking member of the president's 14-member cabinet and fourth in line of presidential succession, the secretary of state is the president's principal adviser on foreign policy and the person chiefly responsible for U.S. representation abroad. Headquartered at the Pentagon, the Defense Department provides the military forces needed to deter war and to protect the security of the nation. The secretary of defense is the principal defense policy adviser to the president and is responsible for the formulation and execution of general defense policy. In the George W. Bush administration, the secretary of state is Colin Powell and the secretary of defense is Donald Rumsfeld. In addition to these two key players, the secretary of the treasury, the chair of the Joint Chiefs of Staff, and the director of the Central Intelligence Agency (CIA) all play a role in advising the president in their respective areas of authority.

What does the **State Department** do exactly?

As the lead U.S. foreign affairs agency, the Department of State, or State Department, "helps to shape a freer, more secure, and more prosperous world through formulating, representing, and implementing the president's foreign policy." To carry out U.S. foreign policy, the Department of State performs several functions. It leads interagency coordination and manages the allocation of resources in conducting foreign relations. The State Department also represents the United States overseas and conveys U.S. policies to foreign governments and international organizations through U.S. embassies and consulates in foreign countries and diplomatic missions. The department coordinates and supports international activities of other U.S. agencies, hosts official visits, and performs other diplomatic missions. It also conducts negotiations and concludes agreements and treaties on issues ranging from trade to nuclear weapons.

Where did the **Department of State** get its name?

On September 15, 1789, Congress passed "an Act to provide for the safe keeping of the Acts, Records, and Seal of the United States, and for other purposes." This law changed the name of the Department of Foreign Affairs to the Department of State because certain domestic duties were assigned to the agency, including the publication of laws in the United States, the recording of the commissions of presidential appointees, and the preparation and authentication of copies of records under the department's Great Seal. Other domestic duties that the department has been responsible for at various times includes issuance of patents on inventions, publication of the census returns, management of the mint, control of copyrights, and regulation of immigration. While most of these domestic functions have been transferred to other agencies, the Department of State is still responsible for the storage and use of the Great Seal, the performance of protocol functions for the White House, and the drafting of certain presidential proclamations.

What role does the **National Security Council** play?

The National Security Council (NSC) is the president's principal forum for considering national security and foreign policy matters with his senior national security advisors and cabinet officials. Since its inception in 1947 under President Harry Truman, the function of the council has been to advise and assist the president on national security and foreign policies. The council also serves as the president's principal arm for coordinating these policies among various government agencies. Chaired by the president, the NSC is made up of the vice president, the secretary of state, the secretary of the treasury, the secretary of defense, and the assistant to the president for national security affairs. The chairman of the Joint Chiefs of Staff is the statutory military advisor to the council, and the director of the CIA is the intelligence advisor. Besides this core group, several others often attend NSC meetings, including the chief of staff to the president, the counsel to the president, and the assistant to the president for economic policy.

An Amnesty International demonstration against China's policy toward Tibet is an example of that group's efforts to end human rights violations worldwide.

What role do **interests groups** play in foreign policy?

While there are a host of special interest groups that are concerned with domestic policy issues, increasingly groups are organizing to support or oppose American foreign policy decisions. The most far-reaching foreign affairs group is the Council on Foreign Relations, a New York City–based nonpartisan membership organization, research center, and publisher dedicated to increasing America's understanding of the world and contributing ideas to U.S. foreign policy. A host of other groups dedicated to specific agendas formally lobby Congress to enact specific policies; for example, the American Israel Public Affairs Committee and the National Association of Arab-Americans both take a specific position on the Arab-Israeli conflict and work to have their voices heard in the halls of Congress.

Do the **American people** have any power over U.S. foreign policy?

Yes, to the extent that the American people have any power over any policy that the government makes. Individuals are most effective in changing foreign policy when they align themselves with one of the various interest groups that fight for specific foreign policy issues. Ethnic interest groups can often help Americans relate to policy from the perspective of national identity or ethnicity; for example, the American Israel Public Affairs Committee is comprised of people of Jewish faith who take a formal position on America's relationship with Israel. In addition, human rights interest groups like Amnesty International or Human Rights Watch, who work from the global perspective to address the treatment of people who live under harsh conditions and strict political regimes, appeal to many Americans who want to have a voice in the implementation of global human rights.

What is the relationship between **democracy** and **foreign policy**?

The end of the cold war and the fall of communism, which occurred with the collapse of the Soviet Union in 1991, was a major victory for democracy. With the end of the Warsaw Pact and armed confrontation in Europe, many countries that had previously been suppressed for decades rose to form new nation-states under the principles of democracy. In addition, areas of the Middle East, South and Southeast Asia, and South Africa fought for democracy. With more and more democratic nations on the rise, the United States and other nations were forced to choose how they would respond to these new nation-states. The globalization of major economies around the world led the United States to support worldwide capitalism. However, U.S. foreign policy has also tempered its support of capitalization and the sustenance of economic markets with its commitment to democracy, supporting nations who strive toward democratic means and encouraging those without democratic governments to adopt them. The reasoning behind this stance is that democratic nations that find peaceable means to work out their disputes perpetuate a world secure for democracy. Of the 57 nations that successfully made the transition to a democratic government between 1980 and 1995, the United States provided governance assistance to 36 of them.

PROMOTING FOREIGN POLICY

What are the **components** of foreign policy?

There are many components to foreign policy, and many tools a country uses in order to maintain peace and achieve its policy commitments and military goals. In democratic nations like the United States, chief among them is diplomacy, which are peaceful actions, mainly in the form of meetings, visits abroad, and discussions, in order to propel a specific agenda. Another is adherence to the United Nations (UN), the international peacekeeping structure, and its goals and agenda, including its philosophy of "collective security," which states that an attack against any UN member country is considered an attack against all member countries. Military deterrence, such as the mobilization of armed forces during peacetime, the stabilization or expansion of the defense budget, and the development of intelligence forces, are other important aspects of foreign policy. The United States also adheres to the international monetary structure that is upheld by the World Bank and provides economic aid to needy countries.

What is a **treaty**?

A treaty is a formal agreement between two or more sovereign states. Treaties have the same legal standing as acts that are passed by Congress, and the Senate must approve any treaties the president or the secretary of state negotiates by a two-thirds vote before it can become effective. However, although the Constitution requires the Senate's "advise and consent" to a treaty, the Senate does not have the power to ratify treaties. Once the Senate approves the treaty, the president ratifies it by exchanging a formal notification with the other party to the agreement.

What is the difference between a **bilateral** and **multilateral treaty**?

Treaties, also known as conventions, agreements, accords, and protocols, depending upon the form they take, are either bilateral or multilateral. A bilateral treaty is a treaty between two sovereign nations, and a multilateral treaty is a treaty between three or more sovereign nations.

What is an executive agreement?

An executive agreement is a name for an international agreement, or pact, that is made between the president of the United States and the head of another foreign state. While most executive agreements are a natural extension of legislation passed by Congress or out of Senate-approved treaties, an executive agreement differs from a treaty in that it doesn't require the consent of the Senate. In two landmark cases of the 1930s and 1940s, the Supreme Court held that executive agreements are as binding as treaties and are a part of the supreme law of the land.

What is **diplomacy**?

In short, diplomacy is the representation of a government to other foreign governments by peaceful means. The State Department uses diplomacy, which usually takes the form of discussions or "peace talks," to promote and protect American interests and manage constructive relations with other world powers and with international institutions. This form of diplomacy is also used to help prevent local conflicts from becoming wider wars that could threaten its allies, embroil American troops, and create instability in key regions, and to address global challenges, such as terrorism and international crime and narcotics. In addition, America's diplomatic goals include preventing the proliferation of weapons of mass destruction and the spread of communicable diseases, nuclear smuggling, humanitarian crises, trafficking in human trade (such as for the purpose of slavery or prostitution), and environmental degradation. Of the 191 countries in the world, the United States maintains diplomatic relations with some 180 of them and with many international organizations.

What is the **Foreign Service**?

The Foreign Service is the diplomatic branch of the U.S. State Department. Its over 4,200 foreign service officers represent America abroad; analyze and report on political, economic, and social trends in the host country; and respond to the needs of American citizens abroad.

What is an ambassador?

Officially titled Ambassador Extraordinary and Plenipotentiary, an ambassador is the official representative of the United States stationed on foreign soil. Ambassadors are appointed by the president of the United States, with Senate approval, and as the personal representative of the president report to him through the secretary of state. Their primary responsibility is to keep the president abreast of the events in the host country, as well as negotiate certain diplomatic agreements and protect the rights of American citizens abroad.

Who was the **first woman Foreign Service officer** to become an ambassador?

Frances E. Willis was appointed Ambassador to Switzerland on July 20, 1953, and served until May 5, 1957. Willis later served as Ambassador to Norway from 1957 to 1961 and Ambassador to Ceylon (now Sri Lanka) from 1961 to 1964. Willis was also the third woman ever to become a Foreign Service officer when she was appointed to that position on August 29, 1927.

What is **diplomatic immunity**?

Although all people within a sovereign state are subject to its laws and jurisdictions, ambassadors are regularly granted diplomatic immunity, meaning they are not subject to the laws of the state to which they are posted, and cannot be arrested, sued, or taxed by their host government. This philosophy assumes that the ambassador will act within the laws of the land and with the utmost respect for the country he or she serves, which is why the mistreatment of diplomats is considered an extensive breach of international law. Ambassadors' official residences are their embassies, which, like their papers and other personal possessions, cannot be searched or seized without their consent.

What is the difference between an **embassy** and a **consulate**?

An embassy is the official residence and offices of an ambassador. A consulate, on the other hand, is a nation's office of public officers who work in the ports and trade centers of a foreign country to protect its nationals—for example, the American Consulate in Spain aids Americans traveling to and within Spain. A consulate's various duties include promoting and protecting American commercial interests; issuing passports and verifying citizenship; mediating with local officials in cases of legal matters involving American citizens; and approving the conditions of the cargo, crew, and passengers of shipping vessels leaving for U.S. ports.

Is there an American consulate or embassy in **every foreign country**?

No. However, in most countries with which it has diplomatic relations, the United States maintains an embassy, which usually is located in the host country's capital. The United States also may have consulates in other large commercial centers or in dependencies of the country. Several countries have U.S. ambassadors accredited to them who are not resident in the country. In a few special cases—such as when it does not have full diplomatic relations with a country—the United States may be represented by only a U.S. Liaison Office or U.S. Interests Section, which may be headed by an officer rather than an ambassador. In all, the United States maintains nearly 260 diplomatic and consular posts around the world, including embassies, consulates, and missions to international organizations.

What is the **United Nations**?

Created in 1945 by the representatives of 51 countries, the United Nations (UN) is the world's foremost keeper of the peace. It was created as an international organization with the primary goals of maintaining international peace and security, developing friendly relations among nations, and cooperating in solving international economic, social, cultural, and humanitarian problems, including promoting respect for human rights and fundamental freedoms. Among the UN's most substantial achievements has been the development of a body of international law—conventions, treaties, and standards—that plays a key role in promoting international peace. Many of the treaties brought about by the UN form the basis of the law governing relations among nations today. The 189 countries that are members of the UN have agreed to accept the obligations of the UN Charter, which upholds them to maintain international peace and security and to develop friendly relations with one another.

How does the **United States rely on the United Nations** to forward its foreign policy goals?

The United States relies on the United Nations to help propel its foreign policy goals and asks for its support in times of international conflict. Since its inception, the United Nations and its Security Council—the primary arm of the UN that deals with international peace and security—have often been called upon to prevent disputes from escalating into war, to persuade opposing countries to talk things out rather than use force of arms, or to help restore peace when conflict does break out. Examples of the U.S.-UN alliance in wartime include the UN-sponsored intervention of the United

The United Nations Security Council, which considers matters of international peace and security, meets at its headquarters in New York City in March 2002 to approve a resolution outlining United Nations assistance to Afghanistan.

States in Korea in 1950, the UN's condemnation of Iraq's invasion of Kuwait in 1990, and its approval of a blockade of Iraq during the 1991 Gulf War. Also, the UN deployed peacekeeping troops into Bosnia during the mid-1990s, and in 1999 established in Kosovo (Federal Republic of Yugoslavia) an interim international administration following the end of NATO air bombings and the withdrawal of Yugoslav forces from the region. Most recently, the UN has supported the global war on terrorism by calling on all member states to intensify their efforts against terrorism after the September 11, 2001, attacks, including denying "financial and all other forms of support and safe haven to terrorists and those supporting terrorism"; instituting millions of dollars of food aid for Afghanistan; and helping finance the new Afghan Interim Authority after the fall of the militia-run Taliban government.

How does the **international monetary structure** relate to foreign policy?

Fearing the economic repercussions brought about by World War I, the United States and its allies created a new international economic structure that would respond to the needs of the postwar world. It included the creation of two institutions, the International Bank for Reconstruction and Development (commonly referred to as the World Bank) in 1944 and the International Monetary Fund (IMF) in 1946. While the World Bank was instituted to provide long-term loans to countries for capital investment, the International Monetary Fund was created to provide short-term monetary assistance to countries in order to facilitate trade. Today, both institutions serve developing countries with billions of dollars of loans in an effort to improve socioeconomic conditions and eliminate poverty. The United States contributes to both the World Bank and International Monetary Fund, helping to enable these independent entities to support economically challenged countries and strengthen their fiscal health.

What is **economic aid**?

Economic aid is the direct financial aid to a country in dire need of assistance, often as a result of oppression or war. The first major plan of economic assistance in the twentieth century was the Marshall Plan, enacted by the United States in 1947–1948 as a plan to help rebuild war-torn Europe. Since that time, economic aid has been a fundamental, diplomatic part of U.S. foreign policy, implemented through the United States Agency for International Development (USAID), the independent government agency that provides economic development and humanitarian assistance to advance U.S. economic and political interests around the globe. The U.S. economic aid program has the twofold purpose of furthering America's foreign policy interests in expanding democracy and free markets while improving the lives of the citizens of the developing world. Through USAID, the United States provides economic assistance to four regions of the world: sub-Saharan Africa; Asia and the Near East; Latin America and the Caribbean; and Europe. Since October 2001, USAID has provided more than $124 million in humanitarian and reconstruction assistance to Afghanistan.

How do **Americans feel about the government's economic aid policies**?

While the United States has a long history of extending a helping hand to those people overseas struggling to make a better life or striving to live in a free and democratic country, its economic aid program is not without criticism. Policy makers and the general public alike have argued that economic aid rarely benefits the people directly, and instead goes to funding the governments, its military, and its political elites. Despite this criticism, according to a poll conducted by the Program on International Policy Attitudes (a joint program of the Center for the Study of Policy Attitudes and the Center for International and Security Studies of the University of Maryland), "An overwhelming majority of Americans embrace the principle that the United States should give some aid to help people in foreign countries who are in genuine need. Eighty percent of those polled agreed that 'the United States should be willing to share at least a small portion of its wealth with those in the world who are in great need.'"

What is **NAFTA**?

In November 1993, Congress passed the North American Free Trade Agreement (NAFTA), which was subsequently launched the following year by Canada, the United States, and Mexico in an effort to form the world's largest free trade area. Designed to foster increased trade and investment among these three countries, NAFTA effectively removed most barriers to trade and investment, including most tariffs paid on agricultural goods. Although this agreement was a major part of President Bill Clinton's foreign policy agenda, supported by a majority of both Republicans and Democrats in Congress, it came under substantial opposition from organized labor, former presidential candidate and conservative Pat Buchanan, and presidential candidate and multimillionaire Ross Perot. Since its passage, policymakers and public interest groups have debated its effectiveness.

Despite its opposition, the government is quick to note that since NAFTA's implementation U.S. agricultural exports to Mexico have nearly doubled. Mexico imported $6.5 billion of U.S. agricultural products in 2000, making it the nation's third largest agricultural market, and Canada imported record levels of many key U.S. commodities in 2000. The government has argued that import competition has increased under NAFTA for some commodities, an unexpected development when barriers to trade begin to come down and trade is subject to open marketing conditions. As the largest of the NAFTA countries and with a strong economy and currency, it is not surprising that U.S. imports have grown strongly, providing Americans consumers with a broader array of competitively priced products.

What is the **European Union**?

The European Union (EU) is an alliance of 15 European countries. Comprised of Belgium, Germany, France, Italy, Luxembourg, the Netherlands, Denmark, Ireland, the United Kingdom, Greece, Spain, Portugal, Austria, Finland, and Sweden, the EU's mission is to organize and promote relations between these countries. Specifically, it focuses on advancing economic and social goals, through the establishment of the EU single monetary market in 1993 and the launching of a single currency in 1999; building and establishing EU law, including legislation and treaties; and providing a united "international" front with respect to foreign policy, common humanitarian aid to non-EU countries, united action in international crises, and common positions within international organizations. When the United States called upon the EU to support the war on terrorism, for example, the EU responded as one like entity, contributing to emergency preparedness, air transport security, and humanitarian aid.

The United States and the European Union share many like-minded foreign-policy goals, including promoting peace and democracy around the world and contributing to the expansion of world trade and closer economic relations. Like the United States, the EU has promised to promote the Middle East peace process, support United Nations human rights activities, and fight against worldwide organized crime, terrorism, and drug trafficking. Recognizing the importance of American support for European integration, in 1971 the EU Commission opened a U.S. delegation (which in essence functions like an embassy), with full diplomatic privileges and immunities. The Head of Delegation was accorded full ambassadorial status by the United States in

1990, representing the commission in its dealings with the U.S. government for all matters within EU jurisdiction.

FOREIGN POLICY THROUGHOUT AMERICAN HISTORY

What is the difference between **isolationism** and **internationalism** and what do they have to do with U.S. foreign policy?

Throughout much of the United States' early history, America was said to be an isolationist country, that is, one concerned chiefly with its domestic affairs and that held little interest in the affairs of other nations. Because "isolationism" is a term that generally characterizes an intentional refusal to become involved in foreign countries' matters, many historians prefer to use the term "unilateralism," or the spirit of acting independently, to characterize early American foreign policy. Since World War II, however, both terms have not entered U.S. foreign-policy vocabulary. Instead, the United States has adopted a policy of "internationalism," based on a philosophy that no one country can live in isolation, that war and political strife elsewhere in the world affect other countries, and that the countries of the world are better off living in an atmosphere of international respect and concern rather than in the pursuit of self-seeking individual interests.

What is unilateralism?

A term often used when discussing foreign policy in general, and the United States in particular, unilateralism simply means acting alone, often without the consultation or support of other nation-states.

What is **multilateralism**?

In a foreign-policy context, multilateralism is closely related to internationalism, and involves the forging of alliances and coalitions among nation-states in order to achieve common foreign-policy goals. Multilateralism came into political parlance in the wake of the September 11, 2001, terrorist attacks, because it described the reinvigorated foreign-policy stance of the United States.

What **traditional foreign policy roles** has the United States taken in its history?

American foreign policy has adopted different roles at different times, while consistently reflecting a historic preference for unilateral action. Its various roles reflect both the challenges and opportunities confronting the United States as well as America's internal political, economic, and social conditions. Traditionally, those roles include: (1) the "Napoleonic" role, which maintains that in order to ensure democracy for itself a nation must persuade other countries to adopt democracy as well, even if it means taking military action to do so, as when the United States ousted the 1990 Sandinista government of Nicaragua and the military rulers of Haiti in 1994; (2) the "Holy Alliance" role, which strives to prevent any disruption of the world's existing distribution of power, even if this means "not rocking the boat" by supporting an existing dictatorship; (3) the "balance-of-power" role, a common ploy of nineteenth-century government, whereby major world powers volley against one another in an effort to ensure that no one power or government becomes supreme and dominates the others; and (4) the "capitalist" role, which favors expanding trade opportunities with other countries, regardless of their form of government.

Did the **Continental Congress** have anything to do with foreign policy in the pre-constitutional era?

Yes. In 1776, founding father John Adams, under the direction of the Continental Congress, drafted a Plan of Treaties that expressed many early U.S. foreign policy positions. While the Plan of Treaties was designed primarily to enhance the prospects of a treaty with France that would solidify the U.S.-French alliance in the Revolutionary War, it advocated greater freedom of trade between nations without political or military ties. Two key commercial principles of the plan included reciprocity, a stipulation whereby U.S. traders would receive the same treatment as a national of another country; and unconditional most-favored-nation status, which guaranteed that U.S. exports would receive the lowest tariffs offered to any other country. As the first blueprint for U.S. foreign policy, the Plan of Treaties helped shape the Monroe Doctrine and U.S. foreign relations for the next 150 years.

Who was **Robert Livingston**?

The Articles of Confederation, the first constitution of the United States, permitted Congress to select "such committees and civil officers as may be necessary for managing the general affairs of the United States." Shortly after the congressional resolution of January 10, 1781, Congress appointed Robert Livingston, a delegate from New York, as the first Secretary for Foreign Affairs. He took office on October 20, 1781, and served until June 4, 1783. According to one historian, Livingston experienced considerable frustration in office, complaining that his duties were not "clearly defined and he was never given a free hand." Later Livingston served as Minister to France and in 1803 negotiated the Louisiana Purchase.

What was America's **biggest diplomatic success during the Revolutionary War**?

The single most important success of American diplomacy during the Revolutionary War was the critical link America forged with France. The first and only alliance established by America until the twentieth century, this partnership was built by the efforts of the French Foreign Minister, Comte de Vergennes, and Benjamin Franklin. Vergennes saw the American War for Independence as a way to restore the balance of power in Europe and to avenge the humiliation suffered at British hands during the Seven Years War (1754–1763), while Franklin embraced the compatibility of French and American interests in denying the British control of North America east of the Mississippi River. After the signing of treaties of alliance and commerce between America and France on February 6, 1778, the French provided supplies, arms and ammunition, uniforms, and French troops and naval support to the beleaguered Continental Army. The French navy transported reinforcements to the southern American army under the Marquis de Lafayette, fought off a British fleet, and protected Generals Washington and Rochambeau's march to Virginia. With an almost evenly divided American-French army of 16,000, Washington laid siege to 8,000 British forces at Yorktown and forced their surrender on October 19, 1781, for all practical purposes successfully ending the Revolutionary War.

What was the significance of the **Franco-American Treaty of 1778**?

The Franco-American Treaty, also known as the Treaty of Alliance between France and the United States, was the first U.S. treaty to be signed, finalized in Paris on February 6, 1778, and ratified by Congress in May of that year. Negotiated by Benjamin Franklin, Arthur Lee, and Silas Deane, the treaty solidified America's relationship with France in battling Great Britain during the Revolutionary War. The terms of the treaty were that France would recognize and support the sovereignty and independence of the United States of America, and in return the United States and France would unite and function as one military unit should war break out between France and Britain. In addition, the treaty stipulated that neither France nor the United States would make peace with England until the independence of the United States was recognized. Although the treaty was essential to America's victory of the Revolutionary War, the United States abandoned the terms of the Franco-American Treaty only 15 years later when France and Britain went to war and President George Washington issued his Proclamation of Neutrality, essentially adapting a position of impartiality to the war.

What was the **first U.S. treaty with a non-European nation**?

The first U.S. treaty with a non-European nation was a Treaty of Friendship and Amity signed with Morocco on June 23, 1786. Thomas Barclay, the U.S. Consul General in Paris, negotiated it. It was valid for 50 years and was renewed in 1837.

Benjamin Franklin (1706–1790), America's first diplomat, arrives in Paris in 1778, where he is credited with forging a critical alliance with France, resulting in that country's support of American efforts during the Revolutionary War.

When was the **first time the federal government offered foreign aid**?

In an act approved by Congress on March 3, 1812, the federal government appropriated $50,000 for the relief of Venezuelans who had succumbed to a devastating earthquake. As the first federal foreign aid act passed by Congress, some congressmen opposed the act because the Constitution did not expressly authorize the passage of such legislation. While it is true that the act was based on an implied power of the federal government, it nevertheless set the precedent for future acts of foreign aid that today are commonplace among America's foreign-policy priorities.

Who holds the title of the **America's first diplomat**?

Benjamin Franklin (1706–1790), generally considered the most distinguished scientific and literary American of his age, was America's first diplomat. He served from 1776 to 1778 on a three-man commission to France charged with the critical task of gaining French support for American independence. French aristocrats and intellectuals embraced Franklin as the personification of the New World enlightenment, stamping his image on medallions, rings, watches, and snuffboxes. His popularity and diplomatic skill—along with the first American battlefield success at Saratoga—convinced France to recognize American independence and conclude an alliance with America in 1778. Franklin presented his credentials to the French court in 1779, becoming the first American minister (the eighteenth-century equivalent of ambassador) to be received by a foreign government. Franklin's home in Passy, just outside Paris, became the center of American diplomacy in Europe. When Thomas Jefferson succeeded Franklin in 1785, the French Foreign Minister Comte de Vergennes asked, "It is you who replace Dr. Franklin?" to which Jefferson replied, "No one can replace him, Sir; I am only his successor."

Who was the first secretary of state?

On September 29, 1789, President George Washington appointed Thomas Jefferson (1743–1826) of Virginia, then Minister to France, to be the first secretary of state under the new Constitution. The author of the Declaration of Independence, Jefferson was one of the leading statesmen of his day, the most famous American political philosopher, and holder of five years' experience as American Minister in Paris, the epicenter of Europe's diplomacy. When Jefferson assumed his duties on March 22, 1790, the United States had only two diplomatic posts and 10 consular posts. Jefferson drew the distinction between the politically oriented diplomatic service and commercially directed consular service, and he initiated the practice of requiring periodic reports from American diplomats and consuls abroad. Although his sympathies belonged to France, Secretary of State Jefferson favored the policy of neutrality in European conflicts. Although he failed to resolve any of the outstanding issues facing American foreign policy—protection of American territorial integrity from Great Britain and Spain, the right to navigate the Mississippi River, or treaties of commerce with Madrid and London—he laid the groundwork for eventual resolution of these problems.

What was **America's foreign policy during the nineteenth century**?

As an isolationist nation, America was not characterized by any particular foreign policy during the nineteenth century. While Americans coveted trade and contracts that would fulfill trading arrangements with other nations, that was the extent of their intercontinental dealings. Americans strongly believed in federalism and feared that foreign involvement would only cause the national government to grow at the expense of the states, as well as the presidency at the expense of Congress; in addition the necessities of foreign policy—a professional diplomatic corps, a trained armed forces, and military secrets—only alienated the people from their government. Historians cite the 1796 farewell address of President George Washington as the impetus for the nation's lack of foreign involvement, in which he warned, "foreign influence is one of the most baneful foes of republican government" and "the great rule of conduct for us in regard to foreign nations is, in extending our commercial relations to have with them as little *political* connection as possible." While Washington advocated temporary alliances for emergencies, he felt that permanent alliances would only foster dependence on the part of America. That philosophy took root and drove American foreign policy until the early twentieth century.

What events characterized **Thomas Jefferson's foreign policy** once he became president of the United States?

Although Thomas Jefferson entered office determined to limit the scope of the federal government, he was forced to deal with a host of foreign affairs that caused him to rethink the power of a strong centralized government. When Jefferson assumed the presidency he made his first foreign policy move by sending a naval squadron to fight the Barbary pirates, who were harassing American commerce in the Mediterranean. This resulted in a war with Tripoli, in which Jefferson was forced to exercise the power of the U.S. Navy and to reconsider his policy of reducing the military. This military coup was followed by diplomatic negotiation and the acquisition of the Louisiana Territory from Napoleon for $15 million in 1803, which effectively doubled the size of the nation. Although the Constitution made no provision for the acquisition of new land, Jefferson decided to override the legalistic interpretation of the Constitution and forgo the passage of a constitutional amendment to validate the purchase—effectively contributing to the principle of implied powers of the federal government.

During Jefferson's second term, he was increasingly preoccupied with keeping the nation from involvement in the Napoleonic wars, although both England and France interfered with the neutral rights of American merchantmen. Jefferson's attempted solution, an embargo upon American shipping (known as the Embargo Act of 1807) and suspension of trade with both France and England, decreased U.S. exports by 80 percent and devastated the American economy. The Embargo Act of 1807 alienated the hard-hit mercantile Northeast and contributed to America's deteriorating relationship with Great Britain, which eventually led to the War of 1812.

What was the **War of 1812**?

Under the administration of James Madison, who was president from 1809 until 1817, America's relations with Great Britain grew worse, and the two countries moved rapidly toward war. Triggered by British attacks on U.S. ships headed to France and the impressment of American sailors, on June 18, 1812, the United States declared war on Great Britain. After numerous battles and faced with the depletion of the British treasury due to the heavy costs of the Napoleonic Wars, Great Britain finally accepted defeat and signed the Treaty of Ghent in December 1814, ending the war and reinstating borders and treaty obligations between the two nations. The U.S. victory revitalized America and popularized Madison as a leader, the first president to come under attack from a foreign nation. While the war was called the "Second American Revolution," it marked a turning point for U.S.-British policy, as both nations agreed to thereafter test a new form a diplomacy that would rely on consultation and binding arbitration rather than military force.

What was the **Monroe Doctrine**?

Building upon America's entrenched spirit of isolationism, in 1823 President James Monroe reinstated America's intention to distance itself from European affairs and warned that the United States would oppose Europe's attempts to extend political control over the Western Hemisphere, including any attempts to recolonize a revolutionary Latin America or Russia's effort to advance its presence on the western coast of North America. Known as the Monroe Doctrine, Monroe's foreign policy arrangement was more a threat than anything else. Since the U.S. government did not have the military muscle to back up its policy, the British ignored Monroe's declaration that "any attempt on their part to extend their system to any portion of this hemisphere [is] dangerous to our peace and safety," and expanded their colonial presence in Latin America after 1823 without any action on the part of the United States.

Who came up with the term **"benevolent assimilation"**?

President William McKinley, known for his natural kindness and evenhandedness, coined the term "benevolent assimilation" to describe American foreign policy when the U.S. took over the Philippines from Spain in 1898. History cites a December 21, 1898, letter that McKinley penned to General Harrison Gray Otis and sent via Secretary of War Russell Alger. Specifically, he noted: "It should be the earnest and paramount aim of the military administration to win the confidence, respect, and affection of the inhabitants of the Philippines by assuring them in every possible way that full measure of individual rights and liberties which is the heritage of free peoples, and by proving to them that the mission of the United States is one of benevolent assimilation, substituting the mild sway of justice and right for arbitrary rule."

What is **"dollar diplomacy"**?

During the period from 1909 to 1913, President William Howard Taft and Secretary of State Philander C. Knox followed a foreign policy known as "dollar diplomacy." Taft shared the view held by Knox, a corporate lawyer who had founded the giant conglomerate U.S. Steel, that the goal of diplomacy was to create stability and order abroad in order to promote American commercial interests. Knox not only used diplomacy to improve financial opportunities, but believed in investing private capital to further U.S. interests overseas. Dollar diplomacy was evident in extensive U.S. interventions in the Caribbean and Central America, especially in measures undertaken to safeguard American financial interests in the region. In China, Knox secured the entry of an American banking conglomerate, headed by financier J. P. Morgan, into the construction of a railway from Huguang to Canton. In spite of successes, dollar diplomacy failed to counteract economic instability and the tide of revolution in countries like Mexico, the Dominican Republic, Nicaragua, and China.

Which president is identified with the term **"watchful waiting"**?

Although many people think that President Woodrow Wilson coined the phrase "watchful waiting" to refer to his policy of neutrality toward Europe during his first administration, Wilson actually used the phrase to refer to American relations with Mexico, not Europe. In his annual message to Congress on December 2, 1913, Wilson said of this country, "We shall not, I believe, be obliged to alter our policy of watchful waiting."

When did the **traditional system of foreign policy** end—and why?

America's isolationist, or unilateralist, policy came to close with the end of World War I in 1918. With the war, the "balance of power system" that previously played the European nations off of one another and prevented the European powers from engaging in world war had disintegrated, along with much of Europe's political systems. Out of the war, America emerged as one of the world's great powers. Internally, the United States was about to trade its familiar domestic system of federalism with a stronger national government. All of the conditions that had made a traditional system of isolation comfortable for the United States were being stripped away, and the country was challenged to grow in its response to the new states of the world.

What was the **League of Nations**?

Under his philosophy that ruled his terms in office, "No one but the President seems to be expected … to look out for the general interests of the country," President Woodrow Wilson asserted international leadership in building a new world order in the wake of World War I. Faced with international challenges unlike any president before him, in 1917 he proclaimed America's entrance into World War I as a crusade to make the world "safe for democracy." American war goals included Wilson's peace plan—the Fourteen Points—which strove to prevent the secret alliances and treaties that pulled the world into World War I, to open up non-white colonial holdings to eventual self-rule, and to ensure a general disarmament after the war. One of the points would establish a peacekeeping entity, "a general association of nations … affording mutual guarantees of political independence and territorial integrity to great and small states alike," known as the League of Nations. After the Germans signed the armistice in November 1918, Wilson traveled to Paris to try to build enduring peace. He later presented the resulting Versailles Treaty to the Senate, containing the Covenant of the League of Nations, which ultimately failed to pass Senate approval.

Without the participation of the United States, the League of Nations was handicapped from its inception and officially disbanded in 1946. Despite his failure to rally the United States into the peacekeeping league, Wilson is regarded as one of America's most visionary foreign-policy presidents, influencing the foreign policies of such later presidents as Franklin D. Roosevelt, Harry Truman, Richard Nixon, Jimmy Carter, George Bush, and Bill Clinton.

Woodrow Wilson's actions to end World War I and his vision for maintaining peace established him as one of America's most influential presidents in terms of foreign policy.

How has **foreign policy evolved since World War II**?

The aftermath of World War II was the major catalyst in propelling a new era of foreign policy in the United States. A new viewpoint of the role of foreign policy had developed, one that required diplomacy and the sober consideration of antagonistic political world powers. In response, the United States adopted a policy of internationalism, entering into treaties with other nations to forward its foreign policy goals and provide security through alliances. Most notable among these was the 1949 North Atlantic Treaty that formed the North Atlantic Treaty Organization, or NATO, which brought together the United States, Canada, and most of Western Europe. With its NATO allies and a new philosophy of joining with other powers to abate the enemy, the United States fought to contain communism and the threat that the superpower Soviet Union proposed—by building a nuclear weapons arsenal and engaging in the Korean and Vietnam Wars in an effort to "contain" Soviet power. During the cold war period, identified as the post–World War II decades until the collapse of communism in 1991, the United States adopted a foreign policy role that focused on the primary goals of restricting the expansion of communism, limiting the Soviet Union's influence, and maintaining military strength as a method of discouraging attack.

What was the **cold war**?

Rather than a single military conflict, the "cold war" is a term used to describe the shifting struggle for power and military strength between the Western powers, includ-

A U.S. soldier serves as a member of the NATO-led peacekeeping troops in Bosnia in 2002. In addition to its focus on defense, NATO often dispatches peacekeepers to troubled regions in Europe.

ing the United States, and the Communist bloc, primarily the Soviet Union, from the end of World War II until the collapse of communism in the late 1980s and early 1990s. This period of East-West competition and tension fell short of full-scale war, and instead was characterized by mutual perceptions of hostile intention between military-political alliances, or blocs, competition for influence in third world countries, and a major superpower arms race. The cold war period is characterized by the American foreign policy principles of internationalism, as executed in the formation of alliances with other world powers in an effort to ensure the world's collective peace; "containing" the threat of communism as posed by the Soviet Union's increasing reach into Eastern Europe; and military deterrence, building the military strength of America and its allies in an effort to deter an attack from the Soviet Union.

What is the role of **NATO**?

The North Atlantic Treaty Organization, commonly called NATO, was organized in 1949 as a result of the North Atlantic Treaty. Composed of the United States and 18 other European democratic countries, its goal is to ensure these countries' joint security through political and military cooperation. Originally formed by 12 countries to promote the collective defense of Western Europe, particularly against the communist threat posed by the Soviet Union, the United States and each of the member countries agreed to act collectively to meet aggression in any of the world's key regions, maintaining that "an armed attack against one or more of them in Europe or in North America shall be considered an attack against them all." With the collapse of the Soviet Union and communism in the late 1980s and early 1990s, the NATO alliance now covers much of Eastern Europe, with the Czech Republic, Hungary, and Poland being recent additions to the alliance.

While defense remains the basic mission of NATO, the organization has in recent years become a peacekeeper, as seen in its role in the 1999 air bombing of Serbia and the forcing of Serbian troops to withdraw from Kosovo. Indeed, NATO acknowledges its call to address threats to European security from ethnic and regional conflicts; to promote cooperation with Russia, the Ukraine, and other countries outside the NATO alliance; and to provide humanitarian aid. Today, NATO leads two major peacekeeping operations in the Balkans.

What is NATO's relationship with **Russia**?

Although NATO was originally formed in 1949 to defend the West against the Soviet Union, in May 2002 NATO created a limited partnership with Russia. Although the organization does not recognize Russia as full member in the alliance, it organized the NATO-Russia Council to join with Russia to fight the war on terrorism. NATO and Russia will work together to fight the "common enemy" known as global terrorism, control the spread of nuclear weapons around the world, promote arms control, cooperate on search-and-rescue operations at sea and other practical matters, and react to yet-undetermined "new threats and challenges." Because of the new relationship, Russia will have a seat at NATO's decision-making table when issues of terrorism and weapons proliferation are discussed. However, Russia does not have the power to veto NATO policy decisions. The agreement mirrors the changes that have taken place since the fall of communism in Europe and Russia's desire to align itself with nations it once viewed as antagonistic. The historic alliance was forged four days after President George W. Bush and President Vladimir Putin of Russia signed a nuclear arms reduction treaty to deactivate two-thirds of each nation's arsenal within 10 years, signaling a new strategic relationship between the two countries.

What is **containment** and what does it have to do with the **Truman Doctrine**?

Containment refers to "containing" communist influence around the world, and as a philosophy it was a major part of United States' foreign policy after World War II came to close in 1945. The policy of containment began with the Truman administration, specifically the Truman Doctrine of 1947, which provided U.S. military and economic assistance to Greece and Turkey in order to contain the Soviet Union's forceful communist expansion in the postwar years. The policy of containment remained a core part of American foreign policy until the Soviet Union's collapse in the late 1980s and early 1990s.

What was the **Marshall Plan**?

As the war-torn nations of Europe faced famine and economic crisis in the wake of World War II, the United States proposed to rebuild the continent in the interest of political stability and a healthy world economy. On June 5, 1947, in a commencement address at Harvard University, Secretary of State George C. Marshall first called for American assistance in restoring the economic infrastructure of Europe. Western Europe responded favorably, and, fanned by the fear of communist expansion, in March 1948 Congress passed the Economic Cooperation Act and approved funding that would eventually rise to more than $12 billion for the rebuilding of Western Europe.

The Marshall Plan, otherwise known as the European Recovery Program, not only brought extensive investment into Western Europe but stimulated the U.S. economy by establishing markets for American goods. Although Soviet and Eastern European participation initially was invited, due to Soviet concern over potential U.S. economic domination of its satellite nations and opposition by American politicians to funding recovery in communist nations, the Marshall Plan was applied solely to Western Europe. Thus, it exacerbated East-West tensions by effectively excluding the Soviet Union and the Eastern bloc from any hope of cooperation with Western Europe and by reviving an economically strong Germany. The Marshall Plan has been recognized as a great humanitarian effort, and Marshall became the only general ever to receive a Nobel Peace Prize for his efforts.

What did MAD stand for in the cold war era?

During much of the cold war, world superpowers the Soviet Union and the United States promoted the testing of nuclear weapons in an effort to gain military one-upsmanship. After the Soviet Union's explosion of its own atomic bomb in 1949, both countries fervently expanded their nuclear arsenals, leading to the stalemate position commonly referred to as MAD, or mutually assured destruction. MAD guaranteed that a strike by either superpower against the other would result in a devastating counterstrike—thus providing a strong means of deterrence against attack.

What was the **Cuban Missile Crisis**?

Shortly after his inauguration, President John F. Kennedy permitted a band of armed and trained Cuban exiles to invade their homeland and attempt to overthrow the communist regime of Fidel Castro. Although the aborted coup was a failure, it triggered a series of events that led the Soviet Union to turn its communist focus toward Cuba to install nuclear missiles. When news of this came to Kennedy in October 1962, he imposed a quarantine on all offensive weapons bound for Cuba. While the world stood on the brink of nuclear war, the Russians backed down and agreed to remove missiles from Cuba after Kennedy secretly agreed to dismantle American missiles in Turkey. The

President Richard Nixon and Soviet premier Leonid Brezhnev sign the Strategic Arms Limitations Agreement in Moscow in May 1972 to reduce their countries' respective stockpiles of nuclear weapons.

American response to what became known as the Cuban Missile Crisis evidently persuaded Moscow of the futility of nuclear blackmail. After the crisis, both sides recognized the vital interest in stopping the spread of nuclear weapons and slowing the "arms race"—a contention that led to the test ban treaty of 1963 and culminated in the Strategic Arms Reduction Treaties (START I and START II) of the 1990s, in which the United States and Russia agreed to cut their nuclear arsenals by more than 50 percent.

What was the **War Powers Resolution**?

The nation's opposition to the Vietnam War and Congress's frustration over not being able to effect war policy moved Congress to pass the War Powers Resolution of 1973, which was implemented to place limits on the president's war-making powers. The act specifies that the president must make every effort to consult Congress prior to engaging U.S. armed forces into overseas hostilities; the president can only deploy troops into hostile situations for a 60-day period during peacetime unless Congress approves a longer period; and the president is limited to responding to an emergency, such as rescuing American hostages, without congressional approval. Although President Richard Nixon vetoed the bill, Congress overrode the veto and the War Powers Resolution became law. Since its passage, however, the constitutionality of the law has been challenged and tested—primarily by President Ronald Reagan's deployment of U.S. Marines into Lebanon in 1982 and President George Bush's U.S. response to Iraq's invasion of Kuwait in the early 1990s.

In March 1979, Egyptian president Anwar al-Sadat, President Jimmy Carter, and Israeli prime minister Menachem Begin signed the Egypt-Israeli Peace Treaty, the terms of which were facilitated by Carter after a series of meetings held at Camp David.

What is **détente**?

Détente is the policy embraced by Richard Nixon's administration as the United States withdrew its troops from Vietnam. A French term meaning "a relaxing of tensions," détente under Nixon involved a distinct decision on the part of the United States to improve its relations with the Soviet Union and with China. Ushering in a new era of cooperation, in 1972 Nixon and Soviet premier Leonid Brezhnev signed the Strategic Arms Limitations Talks (SALT) agreement, dedicated to reducing each country's nuclear arms arsenals. While relations with mainland China increased steadily since the adaptation of détente, the Soviet Union continued to apply its doctrine of communist expansionism by providing economic aid and military support to revolutionary movements around the world. Détente ended when the Soviets invaded Afghanistan in 1979, and Presidents Jimmy Carter and Ronald Reagan responded by readapting the foreign policy philosophy of containment.

What were the **Camp David Peace Accords**?

The premiere foreign policy achievement of the Carter administration was the signing of the Camp David Peace Accords. The peace process in the Middle East that began with Secretary of State Henry Kissinger during Richard Nixon's administration accelerated after President Anwar al-Sadat of Egypt undertook the unprecedented step of traveling to Jerusalem in November 1977. There, he extended an olive branch to the Israeli government in the form of a peace proposal: the return of occupied lands in exchange for a guarantee of security. In order to facilitate talks, President Jimmy Carter invited Sadat and Israeli Prime Minister Menachem Begin to the United States for a series of meetings in September 1978. Carter, supported by Department of State experts, played a key role during the intensive rounds of bargaining that took place between Egypt and Israel, eventually persuading both sides to compromise short of their maximum demands by offering massive amounts of foreign aid.

What two agreements came from the Camp David Peace Accords?

Two agreements in principle arose from the Camp David meetings. The first included a statement on eventual self-government for the West Bank and Gaza Strip areas as well as the inclusion of Jordanian and Palestinian representatives in future talks. The second agreement consisted of diplomatic recognition of Israel by Egypt in exchange for the return of territories occupied since 1967. As negotiations toward a formal treaty followed, Carter continued his personal involvement in the process. On March 26, 1979, Sadat, Carter, and Begin signed the Egyptian-Israeli Peace Treaty, which formalized the specific details of the arrangements agreed to at Camp David. However, the Camp David Accords and the subsequent treaty did not include a comprehensive settlement of the problems in the Middle East. A substantive peace framework among Israel, its other Arab neighbors, and the Palestinian Liberation Organization would not be birthed until the 1990s.

Who was the **first U.S. president to address a joint session of the British Parliament**?

On June 8, 1982, Ronald Reagan became to the first American president to address a joint session of the British Parliament. In a speech that reinforced his foreign-policy philosophy of communist containment, Reagan chided the Soviet Union for its stifling policies, saying, in part, "In an ironic sense, Karl Marx was right. We are witnessing today a great revolutionary crisis. But the crisis is happening not in the free, non-Marxist West but in the home of Marxism-Leninism, the Soviet Union. It is the Soviet Union that runs against the tide of history by denying freedom and human dignity to its citizens."

How did **President Ronald Reagan** create the possibility for the **end of the cold war**?

With the rise in 1985 of Soviet leader Mikhail Gorbachev, President Ronald Reagan began a working relationship with the world superpower that led to four summit meetings and a treaty banning intermediate nuclear missiles in Europe. During his last three years in office, Reagan met with Gorbachev in Geneva, Switzerland, in 1985; in Reykjavik, Iceland, the following year; in Washington, D.C., in 1987; and in Moscow in 1988. The result of their diplomatic discussions was the INF Treaty, signed by Reagan and General Secretary Gorbachev on December 8, 1987. The INF (intermediate-range nuclear forces) Treaty was the first nuclear arms control agreement to actually reduce nuclear arms, rather than simply establish ceilings on arms production. Altogether it resulted in the elimination by May 1991 of almost 1,000 longer- and shorter-range U.S. INF missile systems (that is, nuclear-armed ground-launched ballistic and cruise missiles with ranges of between 300 to 3,400 miles) and almost 2,000 Soviet INF missile systems. The treaty also established other such pioneering measures as continuous monitoring operations in each country, designed to confirm that production of prohibited missiles had ceased. Amidst an increasing democratic world brought about by the collapse of communism in Eastern Europe in 1989, the Soviet Union finally dismantled in 1991, bringing an official end to the cold war.

What was the **Iran-Contra Affair** all about?

While President Ronald Reagan was touted for his efforts toward negotiating the 1987 INF Treaty banning intermediate nuclear missiles, his administration fell under attack during the Iran-Contra Affair that came to a head in November of that year. In an effort to gain the release of Americans held hostage by pro-Iranian groups in Lebanon, the Reagan administration secretly sold weapons to Iran, the profits from which were used to fund Contra rebels fighting an anti-communist regime in Nicaragua. Not only did Reagan's actions violate the law, but press scrutiny focused on the fact that they violated his personal pledge never to provide arms to terrorist nations. While Reagan avoided prosecution due to a lack of evidence linking him to the transfer of funds to the Contras, a special investigation implicated top members of his administration, including National Security Council staff member Lieutenant Colonel Oliver North. As a result, several top-level officials on Reagan's staff were prosecuted, his top national security advisers resigned, and Reagan himself suffered the embarrassment of having to appoint a commission to oversee the reorganization of his national security.

Why did **President George Bush** send U.S. troops into **Panama** in 1989?

President Bush sent American troops into Panama to overthrow the corrupt regime of General Manuel Noriega, who was threatening the security of the Panama Canal and the Americans living there. Noriega had also cancelled the results of a free election after losing the vote, and was well-known as a drug lord immersed in a drug syndicate that included Cuban leader Fidel Castro and Contra rebels in Nicaragua. While the invasion brought Noriega to the United States for trial as a drug trafficker and reinstated a popularly elected government in Panama, many of Bush's critics noted the shortsightedness of the attack. When the Bush administration failed to supply its promised foreign aid to build Panama's economy, it was criticized for choosing Panama as a vehicle for Bush's "compartmentalized" approach to foreign policy—that is, an action that was made hastily and void of a larger foreign-policy philosophy.

What was **Operation Desert Storm**?

George Bush's greatest test as president came in 1990, when Iraqi President Saddam Hussein accused Kuwait and the United Arab Emirates of flooding the world oil market and invaded Kuwait. Saddam Hussein's rejection of diplomatic efforts to solve the Iraqi-Kuwaiti oil crisis pushed President Bush to use military force in order to restore Kuwait's sovereignty, resulting in the 43-day-long air war (generally known as the 1990–1991 Persian Gulf War) and ensuing 100-hour land battle dubbed "Operation Desert Storm." With the support of the United Nations, who condemned the Iraqi invasion and instituted a trade embargo on Iraq, as well as superpower Soviet Union, it was possible to forge an alliance against Saddam Hussein. But while the war achieved its goal of forcing Hussein out of Kuwait, it allowed him to survive with his power and military strength largely intact, much to the chagrin of the U.S. public, who ultimately judged Bush's actions as ineffectual. This and other domestic- and foreign-policy blunders, including Bush's failure to implement his vision for a "New World Order" after the cold war, ultimately left him with a weakened presidency and gross lack of support from the American public.

What was the **Kyoto Protocol**?

Negotiated by more than 160 nations in December 1997, the Kyoto Protocol aims to reduce emissions of certain greenhouse gases, primarily carbon dioxide. From December 1 through 11, 1997, representatives of these nations—including the United States—met in Kyoto, Japan, to negotiate reducing carbon dioxide output, pursuant to the objectives of the Framework Convention on Climate Change of 1992. The outcome of the meeting was the Kyoto Protocol, in which the developed nations agreed to limit their emissions relative to the levels emitted in 1990. Because approximately 83 percent of the greenhouse gas emissions in 1990 were carbon dioxide released by the use of energy, actions to reduce greenhouse gases have a significant impact on energy markets. The United States agreed to reduce emissions from 1990 levels by 7 percent between 2008 and 2012.

What was the failed **Middle East Peace Agreement** under President Bill Clinton?

By 1998 the peace process between Israel and the Palestinians, which had begun with hope four years earlier with the signing of the Oslo Declaration of Principles, had virtually ceased. In October 1998 President Clinton presided over the signing of the Wye River Memorandum between Israeli prime minister Benjamin Netanyahu and Palestinian leader Yasser Arafat. While Clinton said the agreement was designed "to rebuild trust and renew hope for peace," its unprecedented terms—requiring the Israelis to withdraw from a further 13 percent of the West Bank and to begin the release of Palestinian prisoners and requiring the Palestinians to take action against Palestinian Liberation Organization militants—ultimately wallowed, and the peace process went into deadlock. While part of the agreement was executed, including an Israeli withdrawal from some of the territories, the Palestinians did not implement the arms reduction clause and other parts of the agreement, and the Israelis did not continue with subsequent stages of withdrawal. In September 1999 the Israelis and Palestinians signed a revised deal based on the stalled Wye River accord, and in March 2000 Israel finally handed over West Bank territory to the Palestinians amounting to the last part of the transfer originally agreed to in 1998. However, relations between Israel and Palestine have been violent despite spoken promises and signed accords, leading to a yet a new call for peace by the current Bush administration.

With what **communist Southeast Asian nation** did President Bill Clinton announce an amicable relationship had been established?

Exchanging visits to one another's countries over 1998 and 1999, President Bill Clinton and President Jiang Zemin of China announced they were working together to build a "constructive strategic partnership" between the two countries. However, critics were quick to point out that by early 1999 Beijing had responded to the "strategic partnership" by waging a harsh crackdown on Chinese dissidents, threatening Taiwan with a missile buildup, and engaging in ongoing espionage against the United States. The Clinton administration was chided for advancing large corporate interests in China at the expense of other key interests such as national security and human rights. Indeed, the close of the Clinton administration experienced continued and escalated debate over U.S.-China relations.

What are the **foreign-policy highlights from Bill Clinton's presidency**?

Although President Clinton was mired in personal scandal for much of his administration, political scientists generally give Clinton an A for effort for his foreign-policy decisions. These include successfully dispatching peacekeeping forces to war-torn Bosnia and bombing Iraq when Saddam Hussein stopped United Nations inspections for evidence of nuclear weapons. He also earned kudos for his diplomatic role in agenting peace negotiations in Northern Ireland between Catholics and Protestants, for officiating peace talks between Israel and the Palestine Liberation Organization, and for his determined steps to end Haiti's military dictatorship. In addition, Clinton became a global proponent for an expanded North Atlantic Treaty Organization (NATO), increased open international trade, and a worldwide effort against drug trafficking. Although much of Clinton's successes were ultimately attributed to Secretary of State Madeleine Albright, his administration nevertheless enjoys a solid foreign-policy legacy.

Madeleine Albright, appointed secretary of state by President Bill Clinton in 1997, is credited with leading much of the Clinton administration's foreign policy success.

What was **Madeleine Albright's significance** in American politics and foreign policy?

Madeleine Albright became the first woman to serve as secretary of state when she was selected for this position by President Bill Clinton in 1997. As the highest ranking woman in the United States government during her tenure, Albright was responsible for a host of foreign-policy milestones, including the ratification of the Chemical Weapons Convention, enforcing America's assertiveness in worldwide human rights, and making progress toward stability in Eastern and Central Europe. Building upon her experience as U.S. Ambassador to the United Nations under Clinton and president of the Center for National Policy prior to that, Albright was credited with bringing a tough, outspoken approach to foreign policy in the second Clinton cabinet. Upon her appointment she was immediately faced with many thorny internal State Department issues, including a greatly reduced budget and the U.S. presence in Bosnia. However, with a hardball negotiating stance that earned her praise among her colleagues, Albright navigated the foreign-policy landscape with finesse and in retrospect was credited for much of Clinton's successes in the foreign-policy arena.

What is the **Anti-Ballistic Missile Treaty**, and why did America announce its intent to withdraw from the treaty?

In December 2001, President George W. Bush announced the United States' formal intent to withdraw from the 1972 Anti-Ballistic Missile (ABM) Treaty, giving the United States the option to withdraw from the treaty in June 2002. Under the terms of the treaty, the United States and the former Soviet Union agreed that each country could only have two restricted ABM deployment areas. Exact limits were imposed on the ABM systems that may be deployed, and both countries agreed to limit the improvement of their ABM technology. Considering the cold war "long gone" and the treaty a hindrance to "developing effective defenses" against terrorism, Bush cited the ambitious pursuits of North Korea and Iran in developing weapons of mass destruction as a key reason for developing a missile defense system to combat the terrorist threat. Despite an initial rebuff from Russian president Vladimir Putin over the incident, the U.S. and Russia have increasingly forged a deeper alliance in the post–September 11 era. In May 2002 Putin and President Bush signed a nuclear-arms reduction treaty, in which each nation agreed to destroy its nuclear arsenal by two-thirds by the end of 2012. Bush and Putin also agreed to expand their nations' limited cooperation on the development of missile defense systems. Despite the new alliance, Russia continues to support a nuclear power project in Iran.

What is meant by the **"new arms race"**?

The "new arms race" refers to twenty-first-century efforts by countries to actively develop or acquire nuclear, chemical, and biological weapons. Such factors as Islamic hostility toward democracy, Middle East corruption, widespread poverty in core pockets of the world, and the failures of globalization have lead countries like Libya, Iran, Iraq, and North Korea to actively develop or acquire nuclear arms in an effort to defend themselves against superpowers like the United States or China. According to *Nation* correspondent Jonathan Schell, "The post–cold war era did not end the old U.S-Russian arms race. What it signaled was a new period of proliferation of chemical, biological, and nuclear weapons to states like India, Pakistan, Iran, and Iraq." Indeed, political scientists recognize that Iran is potentially just a few years away from becoming a nuclear power. In addition nuclear wastes are not being properly disposed of in Russia, and U.S. arsenals of biological and chemical weapons have found their way into third world countries. With the disbanding of the Anti-Ballistic Missile Treaty (ABM), the beefing up of military assets, and President George W. Bush's desire to target the "axis of evil" that exists between terrorist countries, the United States itself has seemingly joined this new arms race. Long an adherent of the nuclear balance of power that the ABM Treaty ensured between the U.S. and Russia, the United States is just one of many countries that has entered into a new era—one that insists on unprecedented antiterrorist measures and increased security and defense systems.

What are some of the **major policy issues** the secretary of state has taken on **since the September 11, 2001, terrorist attacks**?

When Colin Powell became secretary of state in 2001, he said at his confirmation hearing that a guiding principle of foreign policy would be that "America stands ready to help any country that wishes to join the democratic world." As such, Secretary Powell stressed the importance of working with the international community and the Afghan people to help them rebuild Afghanistan after the military action and fall of the Taliban. The United Nations has said that the country needs more than $1 billion in support, and part of the responsibility of the secretary of state lay with supporting those efforts. Other issues include monitoring terrorist countries such as Iraq, Iran, and North Korea and deciding how the United States might respond to any terrorist threats that would emanate out of this "axis of evil," as President Bush called them in his 2002 State of the Union Address; working with the U.S.'s coalition of terrorist partners (including Europe, Russia, Saudi Arabia, and Japan) to assemble their anti-terrorist agendas; encouraging the Israelis and Palestinians to resume peace talks that might quelch war in the Middle East; and paying diplomatic visits to India and Pakistan in an effort to avoid an outbreak of nuclear war there.

How has United States foreign policy changed post–September 11?

One of the most significant changes in American foreign policy has been the United States' relationship Russia, its longtime enemy. In opposition throughout the cold war, the two nations teamed up to fight the global war on terrorism. In May 2002 the United States and Russia signed a nuclear-arms reduction treaty, in which each nation agreed to reduce its stockpile of nuclear arms by two-thirds. However, foreign policy experts are quick to hold the September 11, 2001, terrorist attacks on the World Trade Center and the Pentagon responsible for changing many things about U.S. foreign policy—most notably its exchange of unilateralism for multilateralism, where tactical alliances reach to countries previously at odds with the United States, like Pakistan and Uzbekistan. Because the dividing line of global relations is no longer between democracy and communism and the threat of future terrorist attacks is real, the United States has called on the aid of many developed nations to join its fight against terrorist activity.

NATIONAL DEFENSE AND DOMESTIC SECURITY

TERRORISM

What is **terrorism**?

There is no universally accepted definition of terrorism. In fact, it has been said that "One man's terrorist is another man's freedom fighter." Even the United States government has trouble deciding on a precise definition. In 1986, the Vice President's Task Force on Terrorism defined it as "the unlawful use or threat of violence against persons or property to further political or social objectives. It is usually intended to intimidate or coerce a government, individuals or groups, or to modify their behavior or politics." Today, a widely used definition in U.S. political circles is that of the Federal Bureau of Investigation (FBI). The FBI states, "Terrorism is the unlawful use of force or violence against persons or property to intimidate or coerce a government, the civilian population, or any segment thereof, in furtherance of political or social objectives." Both of these definitions, and many others like them, share the common element of politically motivated behavior, while also taking into account that an increasing number of extremist acts are carried out in the name of religious or cultural causes.

What is the difference between **domestic** and **international terrorism**?

The FBI categorizes terrorism in the United States as one of two types—domestic terrorism or international terrorism. Domestic terrorism involves groups or individuals whose terrorist activities are directed at elements of our government or population without foreign direction. International terrorism involves groups or individuals whose terrorist activities are foreign-based and/or directed by countries or groups outside the United States or whose activities transcend national boundaries. Acts of domestic terrorism include the April 1995 Oklahoma City federal building bombing and the July 1996 Olympic Games bombing in Atlanta, Georgia.

In the United States, most terrorist incidents have involved small extremist groups who use terrorism to achieve a designated objective, and should be viewed as distinct from nonviolent civil disobedience or protest. According to the Federal Emergency Management Agency (FEMA), a terrorist attack can take several forms, depending on the technological means available to the terrorist, the nature of the political issue motivating the attack, and the points of weakness of the terrorist's target. Bombings have been the most frequently used terrorist method in the United States. Other possibilities include an attack at transportation facilities, an attack against utilities or other public services, or an incident involving chemical or biological agents. At the World Trade conference in Seattle in 1999, some 300 to 400 international anarchists were able to turn a nonviolent protest against the World Trade Association into a riot, sending the city into chaos. Radical environmental and animal rights groups, such as the Earth Liberation Front and the Animal Liberation Front, remain among the most active domestic terrorist organizations.

Are there any precedents in American history to the **2001 World Trade Center and Pentagon attacks**?

Yes. While the September 11, 2001, terrorist attacks marked a distinct level of unsurpassed terrorist activity against the citizens of the United States, there have been other times in America's recent history that terrorist activity occurred on its soil. According to reports published by the FBI, since the mid-1980s there have been two major international terrorist incidents in the United States—defined by the FBI as an act committed by a group or individual that is foreign-based and/or directed by countries or groups outside the United States. One of the incidents was the notorious 1993 World Trade Center bombing, which led to the trial of 22 Islamic fundamentalists. On February 26, 1993, a bombing in the parking garage of the World Trade Center in New York City resulted in the deaths of five people and thousands of injuries. The bomb left a crater 200 by 100 feet wide and five stories deep. At the time, the World Trade Center was the second largest building in the world, housing 100,000 workers and visitors each day. The other incident involved the April 1992 occupation by five opponents of the Iranian regime of the offices of the Iranian Mission to the United Nations in New York City. Although the five pled guilty and were sentenced to a short jail term, the action was not directed against U.S. citizens, leaving many to really question whether that act should be considered a "terrorist action."

Acts of domestic terrorism include the April 1995 Oklahoma City federal building bombing, which left 168 Americans dead and more than 500 wounded, and the July 1996 Olympic Games bombing, in which a pipe bomb exploded at Centennial Olympic Park in Atlanta, Georgia, killing two people and injuring more than 100 others. The

Smoke pours from the World Trade Center buildings in New York City following the deliberate crash of two jets into the towers on September 11, 2001.

The April 1995 bombing of the Murrah Federal Building in Oklahoma City, Oklahoma, in which 168 people were killed, is considered the worst act of domestic terrorism in U.S. history.

FBI suspected domestic terrorists and some members of local militia groups, who were questioned without any arrests. Terrorist activity in the 1980s includes the 1983 bombing of the United States Capitol Building in Washington, D.C., during which a bomb exploded in the cloak room next to the Senate. More recently, antiabortion terrorists have bombed or torched medical clinics, murdered medical professionals, and delivered hundreds of anthrax threats. In May 2002, a trail of pipe bombs was discovered in rural mailboxes across five midwestern states, leading to the arrest of 21-year-old college student Luke Helder.

What is the **worst act of domestic terrorism** in U.S. history?

The most substantial act of domestic terrorism occured on April 19, 1995, when a truck bomb exploded outside the Alfred P. Murrah Federal Building in Oklahoma City, killing 168 people, including 19 children, and injuring more than 500. Because of the sheer number of casualties and the fact that children were killed, "Oklahoma City" is referred to as the worst act of domestic terrorism in United States history. Timothy McVeigh, the Persian Gulf War army veteran responsible for the bombing, said the act was meant to draw America's attention to a national government he felt infringed upon citizens' right to bear arms. In his biography, *American Terrorist*, McVeigh said the bombing was a statement against the government's actions during the 1993 standoff with the Branch Davidians at Waco, Texas, and the 1992 siege of white separatist

Randy Weaver's cabin at Ruby Ridge, Idaho—both of which were controversial and involved the deaths of citizens at the hands of the government.

In 1997 McVeigh was indicted on charges of using a weapon of mass destruction "to kill and injure innocent persons, and to damage the property of the United States" and sentenced to death. Five days before McVeigh was scheduled to die, U.S. Attorney General John Ashcroft delayed the execution because the FBI admitted to withholding more than 4,000 pages of documents during McVeigh's trial. McVeigh was put to death by lethal injection on June 11, 2001. Terry Nichols, his convicted accomplice, was sentenced to life in prison.

Who is Theodore Kaczynski?

Theodore Kaczynski is known to most people as the "Unabomber," a one-time math professor turned recluse who waged an 17-year "antitechnology" bombing campaign in various American cities. His attacks from 1978 to 1995 killed three people and injured 29. The anonymous culprit who had managed to evade federal investigators for years was dubbed the "Unabomber" because his early targets were university professors and airline executives (hence the acronym UNA). Kaczynski was discovered in 1996 when his older brother, David, tipped off investigators after recognizing Theodore's ramblings—which denounced technology and the ruin of the environment—in the newspaper. Kaczynski was convicted in 1998 for the murder of the three men and sentenced to life in prison without parole.

What acts of organized terrorism around the world have involved **U.S. citizens** directly?

Significant anti-American terrorist activity dates back to the late 1970s, when in November 1979 Islamic students stormed the U.S. Embassy in Tehran, Iran, and held 52 Americans hostage for 444 days. Other reports of terrorist activities overseas that directly involved U.S. citizens during the 1980s include: the April 1983 suicide car-bombing that blew up the U.S. embassy in Beirut, Lebanon, and killed 17 Americans; the October 1983 Shiite suicide bomber who blew up U.S. Marine barracks in Beirut and killed more than 200 American servicemen; and the September 1984 car bombing at the U.S. embassy annex in East Beirut, which killed 16 and injured the American ambassador. In June 1985 Shiite gunmen forced a TWA jet into Beirut and 39 Americans were held hostage for 17 days. In September 1986 the Pan Am hijacking at Karachi Airport in Pakistan resulted in the deaths of 20 people. And in December 1988 a Pan Am Boeing 747 exploded over Lockerbie, Scotland, killing 270 people.

In the 1990s and early 2000s several terrorist attacks against Americans occurred. In June 1996 a truck bomb exploded outside the Khobar Towers housing complex near

U.S. Marines and an Italian soldier search through the rubble of the barracks destroyed by a suicide car bomb attack in Lebanon in October 1983. 241 servicemen died in the bombing.

Dharan, Saudi Arabia, killing 19 U.S. Air Force personnel and injuring more than 500 Americans and Saudis. Two years later, in August 1998, U.S. embassies in Kenya and Tanzania were bombed, resulting in the deaths of more than 200 people, 12 of them Americans. The October 12, 2000, USS *Cole* incident involved a suspected terrorist bomb that exploded during a refueling operation in Aden, Yemen, and left 17 American sailors presumed or confirmed dead.

How were these attacks handled on a **political** level?

Prior to September 11, 2001, terrorist attacks against U.S. interests (except for the Iran hostage crisis, which was an anomaly) were treated as criminal matters with international governments. In order to avoid messy political situations with allied governments, the United States sought to press criminal charges against these terrorists, and asked for retribution from foreign governments. For example, six men were convicted in federal court of conspiracy in the 1993 World Trade Center bombing. In the wake of September 11, however, rather than use the federal court system, the Bush administration advocated secret military tribunals for select terrorists. The use of a secret court has little precedence in American history, and the administration encountered a storm of controversy about the plan. The administration has since modified its position, promising that suspected terrorists will have the right to an appeal and, with major national security exceptions, to have their trials conducted in public.

Navy destroyer USS *Cole* was the target of a bomb attack while refueling at a port in Aden, Yemen, in October 2000. Seventeen crewmembers were killed.

What is counterterrorism?

Counterterrorism involves those efforts a nation uses to combat or counteract terrorist activity. Counterrrorist campaigns take place on many levels, often involving multifaceted military surveillance and attack, diplomatic efforts, economic strategy, and law enforcement and intelligence tactics. In the wake of the September 11, 2001, terrorist attacks, the concept of counterterrorism took on added meaning. A unique, worldwide campaign involving many countries around the world joined together to fight a slippery foe: those terrorist groups that might threaten international stability and the interests of democratic nations.

What is the **war on terrorism**, exactly?

The "war on terrorism" is a phrase that encompasses the philosophy, response, and military action undertaken by the United States in reaction to the September 11, 2001, terrorist attacks. In a meeting on September 12 with his National Security team, President George W. Bush said, "The deliberate and deadly attacks which were carried out yesterday against our country were more than acts of terror. They were acts of war." Although military retaliation was involved—targeting Islamic terrorist Osama bin Laden and Afghanistan, the country that housed him and his Al Qaeda terrorist network—the American response to terrorism is not solely military. Instead, it is being fought at home and abroad through multiple operations, including diplomatic, financial, investigative, humanitarian, and homeland security efforts. Because the enemy is not one particular country, but rather a somewhat elusive entity known as terrorism, political scientists have likened the war on terrorism in some respects to the cold war: just as continuous pressure from many nations caused communism to collapse from within, the idea is that continuous pressure from the world will cause the collapse of terrorism.

From a diplomatic point of view, the United Nations Security Council unanimously enacted a binding resolution requiring all member countries to pursue terrorists and those who support them, financially or otherwise. Nineteen NATO nations invoked Article V declaring an attack on one as an attack on all, and the Organization of American States invoked the Rio Treaty, obligating signatories to consider an attack against any member as an attack against all. Financially, the United States and other nations have frozen millions of dollars in assets belonging to the Taliban, bin Laden, and the Al Qaeda network. More than 150 countries have joined the effort to disrupt terrorist assets. On an investigative front, counterterrorist operations have been intensified with more than 200 intelligence and security services worldwide. The State Department's Rewards for Justice Program offered up to $25 million for information leading to the arrest or conviction of those who have committed or are planning acts of international terrorism. On a humanitarian front, the United States is the leading donor of humanitarian aid to the Afghan people, allocating more than $500 million in assistance in 2001. During military operations, the United States continued air drops of food and other humanitarian relief supplies for the Afghan people. Homeland Security measures include strengthening the nation on multiple levels in an effort to thwart off future terrorist attacks.

To what extent is terrorism—and conversely counterterrorism—a **worldwide phenomenon**?

When infamous terrorist Osama bin Laden singled out the United Nations and various world leaders as potential targets of terrorism in a videotaped message in November 2001, he made clear his conviction that all free nations pose a threat to the Islamic world—thus casting the issue of terrorism into an unprecedented global context. Apart from Al Qaeda–related terrorism, which exists on a sophisticated international level, many other terrorist groups exist around the world. These groups are frequently concerned with domestic issues, acting in opposition to the established government. In his November 10, 2001, speech to the United Nations, President George W. Bush framed the issue of terrorism in its broadest possible context by stating that every UN member country was a potential target of terrorism. Indeed, the Bush administration often stated in the aftermath of the World Trade Center and Pentagon attacks that every democracy in the world is a target for extremist groups. "This enemy attacked not just our people, but all freedom-loving people everywhere in the world. The United States of America will use all our resources to conquer this enemy. We will rally the world," Bush said.

Because every UN member nation is a potential victim, every UN member nation has a responsibility to crack down on terrorist financing within its borders, to share intelligence information with one another, and to coordinate law enforcement activities. To that end, the Bush administration called on countries as diverse at Pakistan, France, and the United Kingdom to send troops in support of the U.S. counterterrorism war against Afghanistan and bin Laden. Not stopping with Afghanistan as a counterterrorist target, Bush made it clear that any nations who harbored terrorists were potential targets of the U.S. war on terrorism, and cited North Korea, Iran, and Iraq as an "axis of evil, aiming to threaten the peace of the world" in his January 2002 State of the Union address.

Al Qaeda leader Osama bin Laden appears on Al Jazeera television in October 2001, praising the success of the September 11 attacks.

Has the United States ever teamed up with **Russia and China** to fight a common enemy prior to September 11, 2001?

No. In the days following the September 11, 2001, terrorist attacks both President Jiang Zemin of China and President Vladimir Putin of Russia vowed to support the United States' effort in the fight against their common enemy, terrorism. Although both countries have not been traditional supporters of U.S. foreign policy, both China and Russia supported the U.S.-led war on terrorism primarily because of their concerns over Muslim separatists in their own countries. The UN Security Council, whose permanent members include Russia and China, issued a resolution condemning the attack and soliciting the aid of all member countries in the war on terrorism.

Despite China's historic opposition to any kind of "interference in other countries' internal affairs"—a philosophy it has undertaken in part because of fears of igniting tension in its own troubled regions of Taiwan, Tibet, and Xinjiang—President Jiang willingly supported the antiterrorist cause. In China's border region of northwestern Xinjiang, China is fighting Muslim separatists who are waging a war for independence against Chinese rule. Because the separatists obtain weapons and military training from Muslim rebel groups in Afghanistan, China is willing to become a world antiterrorist ally. China also participates in the Shanghai Cooperation Organization, which unites China, Russia, Kazakhstan, Kyrgyzstan, Tajikistan, and Uzbekistan to fight "terrorism, separatism and extremism" in that region of the world. Founded in 1996 with a goal of brokering border disputes, the Shanghai Cooperation Organization has evolved into a dynamic alliance focused on stabilizing common borders, limiting the growth of separatist groups, and partnering in world antiterrorist efforts.

Similarly, Islamic fundamentalists helped fuel a rebellion in Chechnya that Russia had great difficulty containing. Russia's ongoing border war with Afghanistan and concerns about incursions from Afghanistan-based Taliban forces into the former Soviet Muslim republics, and therefore into Russia, have troubled the state. Russia positioned 25,000 troops on the border between Tajikistan and Afghanistan, sealing those borders as well as the critical ones with Iran and Pakistan, in an effort to cut off the Taliban from much-needed fuel and ammunition.

In what ways is a president's administration defined by the manner in which it **responds to crises** and the **public's perception of those responses**?

President George W. Bush received high public ratings in the months following the World Trade Center and Pentagon attacks, and kudos from both the public and government officials for his handling of the war in Afghanistan. However, a consensus for his handling of foreign affairs has not been reached yet, and may not be for some time. Often a president's legacy is either applauded or tainted by the way that the president and his administration respond to a domestic or international crisis, as well as the way both the media and the public interpret that response. Jimmy Carter's presidency, for example, was derailed by Carter's inability to resolve the Iranian hostage crisis. Ronald Reagan's reputation was enhanced due to his handling of the space shuttle *Challenger* explosion. Likewise, Bill Clinton's administration was applauded for its handling of the Oklahoma City bombing, but ultimately the accomplishments of Clinton's presidency were overshadowed by the Monica Lewinsky affair. Presidential crisis response and the spin that the media and others put on these affairs are ultimately tallied to provide an overall impression of an administration's effectiveness.

How is the **responsibility to react to terrorism** spread across the U.S. government?

America's homeland defense system, charged with protecting the country against terrorist attacks, is run by the Office of Homeland Security. However, the office must coordinate at least 45 federal agencies and obtain their cooperation in order to meet its own goals. In addition, the U.S. Department of Justice coordinates the efforts of multiple agencies, each with strong international ties, in an effort to combat terrorism. Departments and agencies across the spectrum of the federal government that are solicited for support include: the State Department; the Federal Bureau of Investigation; the National Security Council; the Council of Economic Advisors; the Central Intelligence Agency; the Customs Service; the Immigration and Naturalization Service (INS); the Department of Defense; the Treasury Department; the Federal Aviation Administration; the Federal Emergency Management Agency (FEMA); the Environmental Protection Agency; the Department of Transportation; the Coast Guard; and the Drug Enforcement Administration.

In order to unite the government's system against terrorism and instill more accountability, in June 2002 President George W. Bush proposed organizing a cabinet-level Department of Homeland Security. If approved by Congress, the department would oversee all aspects of homeland security, uniting agencies from eight existing Cabinet departments, including the INS, FEMA, the Border Patrol, the Coast Guard, the Customs Service, the Secret Service, and the newly created Transportation Security Administration, which is responsible for airport security.

What does the **Office of Homeland Security** do?

In response to the September 11, 2001, terrorist attacks, President George W. Bush established the Office of Homeland Security to develop and coordinate a comprehensive national strategy to strengthen protections against terrorist threats or attacks in the United States. Led by Tom Ridge, former governor of Pennsylvania, the new team coordinates federal, state, and local counterterrorism efforts. The office is charged with detecting, preparing for, preventing, protecting against, responding to, and recovering from terrorist attacks within the United States, coordinating with various government agencies as necessary to meet its goals.

Reflecting the priority the president has attached to the homeland security agenda, the fiscal year 2003 budget directs $37.7 billion to homeland security, up from $19.5 billion in 2002. The department's initial goals include building an emergency management system, supporting America's "first responder" community, creating a medical system that can better cope with bioterrorism, and establishing a more effective border management system. Despite its ambitious beginnings, President Bush recognized the Office of Homeland Security wasn't enough to defend the country against attack or respond to national emergencies, such as the anthrax outbreak—in part because Ridge has a small staff and no authority over any of the other federal agencies' budgets. Developed inside the White House staff by executive order, the Office of Homeland Security lies outside of congressional oversight, which has been a source of contention between the president and Congress since its inception. These reasons prompted Bush in June 2002 to propose the creation of the cabinet-level Department of Homeland Security. If approved by Congress, the new department will effectively replace the Office of Homeland Security. Ridge is the top contender for the position of department secretary.

Director of Homeland Security Tom Ridge announces a five-level color-coded terrorism warning system in March 2002 in order to help citizens gauge the seriousness of terror alerts issued by the government after the September 11 attacks.

What are the chief functions of the **Homeland Security Council**?

The Homeland Security Council is responsible for advising and assisting the president with respect to all aspects of homeland security. Established by executive order in response to the September 11, 2001, terrorist attacks, the council serves as the mechanism for ensuring coordination of homeland security-related activities of executive departments and agencies as well as effective development and implementation of homeland security policies. Members include the president and the vice president, the secretary of the treasury, the secretary of defense, the attorney general, the secretary of health and human services; the secretary of transportation; the director of the Federal Emergency Management Agency; the director of the Federal Bureau of Investigation; the director of the Central Intelligence Agency; the assistant to the president for homeland security; and other cabinet members and federal officials the president may choose to include in key discussions.

What national security agency was the **predecessor to the Office of Homeland Security**?

The U.S. Commission on National Security was the predecessor to the Office of Homeland Security. Created by Congress in 1998 based on a conversation between President Bill Clinton and Speaker of the House Newt Gingrich, the commission was chartered by the secretary of defense and charged with security of the American homeland. The co-chairs were former senators Warren B. Rudman, a Republican from New Hampshire, and Gary Hart, a Democrat from Colorado. Other members included former U.S. representative to the United Nations Andrew Young, former secretary of defense James R. Schlesinger, and Newt Gingrich.

Renamed the U.S. Commission on National Security/21st Century, the commission now operates as a federal advisory committee. In its new role it has tackled a broad range of issues, from securing the national homeland to redesigning government institutions and examining human requirements for national security, including the role of Congress. While most analyses of national security have focused on U.S. military capabilities and on America's diplomatic efforts, the commission has focused on more broader issues in relation to America's security, including technological advances, the education of America's youth, and commercial relationships.

What is the role of the **State Department** in counterterrorist activity?

The State Department is the primary federal agency dealing with international terrorism. It takes the lead role on the diplomatic front abroad to advance the cause of the coalition against terrorism—working closely with other agencies and organizations to shut down terrorist financial networks, provide humanitarian aid, investigate terrorist organizations and activities, and bring terrorists to justice. Its Office of Counterterrorism coordinates all U.S. government efforts to improve counterterrorism cooperation with foreign governments. Along with the State Department's terrorism task forces, the office coordinates responses to major international terrorist incidents that are in progress. Another primary responsibility of the office is to develop, coordinate, and implement American counterterrorism policy. In general, this policy is defined by a "strike no deal" attitude when responding to terrorist groups. In addition, the policy involves bringing all terrorists to justice for their crimes, isolating and applying pressure to states that sponsor terrorists, and bolstering counterterrorism capabilities in those countries that have an amicable relationship with the United States.

What is the role of the **attorney general**?

The attorney general is head of the Department of Justice and chief law enforcement officer of the federal government. As such, the attorney general is in charge of a variety of agencies that play a role in the war on terrorism, including the Federal Bureau of Investigation, the Immigration and Naturalization Service, the Drug Enforcement Administration, and the Bureau of Prisons. Often dubbed America's "top cop," he or she represents the United States in all legal matters, and advises the president and heads of the executive departments on a variety of issues, including national security. In addition, the attorney general represents the national government before the U.S. Supreme Court in important cases.

Playing a prominent role in the thwarting of terrorist activity, Attorney General John Ashcroft said, "My job is to prevent terrorism, and I'm going to do everything I can think of that's within the limits of our Constitution." Ashcroft responded to the September 11, 2001, terrorist attacks with a series of measures that have left many to question how far Ashcroft is willing to go to push the constitutional envelope. He has supported secret military tribunals to try suspected Al Qaeda terrorists, detained for an extended period of time hundreds of people on immigration violations, and gathered more than 8,000 Muslim men in America for questioning. He has also granted the Justice Department the authority to overrule immigration judges and allowed federal officials to eavesdrop on conversations between certain prisoners and their attorneys. While Ashcroft and many of his supporters maintain that these measures are necessary to fight the war on terrorism, others fear that these actions infringe upon civil liberties and threaten to concentrate too much power in the executive branch.

What is the purpose of the **U.S. Senate Committee on Intelligence**?

Chaired by Bob Graham, a Democratic senator from Florida, the U.S. Senate Committee on Intelligence is charged with overseeing and making continuing studies of the intelligence activities and programs of the United States government. The committee submits to the Senate appropriate proposals for legislation and reports to the Senate concerning such intelligence activities and programs. In doing so, the Select Committee on Intelligence makes sure that the appropriate departments and agencies of the United States provide informed and timely intelligence necessary for the executive and legislative branches to make sound decisions affecting the security and vital interests of the nation. In addition, the committee provides legislative oversight to the intelligence activities of the country to assure that such activities are in conformity with the Constitution and laws of the United States.

What is the content of the most recent **antiterrorism law**?

On October 26, 2001, President George W. Bush signed into law the USA Patriot Act of 2001. Commonly known as the Antiterrorism Act, the law was initiated to "help law enforcement to identify, to dismantle, to disrupt, and to punish terrorists before they strike," according to President Bush. Under the new law, criminal sentences for committing acts of terrorism or aiding terrorists are increased, and it is a federal crime to commit an act of terrorism against a mass transit system. Until this law was in effect, law enforcement agencies were required to get a new warrant for each new district they investigated, even when they were investigating the same suspect. Under this new law, warrants are valid across all districts and across all states, making them "federal" warrants. The government gained wider latitude in detaining and deporting known terrorists and their supporters, and the statute of limitations on terrorist acts was lengthened, as were prison sentences for terrorists.

The legislation gives law enforcement officials better tools to put an end to financial counterfeiting, smuggling, and money laundering, allowing the Treasury Department to require banks to make much greater efforts to determine the sources of large overseas private banking accounts. The law authorizes intelligence operations and criminal operations to share vital information, and allows for the government surveillance of all communications used by terrorists, including e-mails, the Internet, and cell phones. The intelligence community's wiretapping authority has also been greatly expanded—for instance, the law allows for "roving wiretaps" on a terrorist suspect, so that any telephone used by that person may be monitored. A bioterrorism provision was also added to the law, making it illegal for any person or group to possess substances that can be used as biological or chemical weapons for any purpose other than a "peaceful" one.

What significant **counterterrorism legislation** passed in the wake of the Oklahoma City bombing?

In April 1996—after much shuffling between both houses of Congress and just a day shy of the first anniversary of the Oklahoma City bombing—Congress passed an antiterrorism bill to fight domestic terrorism. Signed into law by President Bill Clinton on April 24, 1996, the Antiterrorism and Effective Death Penalty Act of 1996 imposes limits on federal appeals by death row inmates and other prisoners and makes the death penalty available in some international terrorism cases and in cases where a federal employee is killed on duty. The bill also makes it a federal crime to use the United States as a base of organization for acts of overseas terrorism. The law prohibits fundraising in the United States by groups that the U.S. government deems terrorist and gives the federal government greater power to deport anyone suspected of terrorist activity. The bill also authorized hundreds of millions of dollars in taxpayer funding for federal law enforcement agencies, including the Federal Bureau of Investigation, the Drug Enforcement Administration, the Immigration and Naturalization Service, and the Customs Service.

What is the **1978 Foreign Intelligence Surveillance Act**?

The Federal Wiretap Act, which allows federal wiretapping with a court order, was enacted in 1968, and has undergone major revisions since that time as Congress has tried to keep up with changing technology. The Foreign Intelligence Surveillance Act (FISA) of 1978 established legal guidelines for foreign intelligence surveillance separate from domestic law enforcement surveillance. Aimed at furthering U.S. counterintelligence efforts, the law allows for a special U.S. court to consider requests for searches or wiretaps, generally requiring a lower standard of proof for approval than in traditional criminal cases. FISA allows wiretapping of aliens and citizens in the United States based on a finding of probable cause to believe that the target is a member of a foreign terrorist group or an agent of a foreign power. For U.S. citizens and permanent resident aliens, there must also be probable cause to believe that the person is engaged in activities that "may" involve a criminal violation.

Whom do I **contact** if I suspect terrorism?

The FBI encourages the public to report any suspected violations of U.S. federal law, including any events related to the September 11, 2001, terrorist attacks and any other suspected terrorist activity. The FBI can be contacted 24 hours a day, every day. Citizens contact the FBI by calling their local FBI office or by submitting a tip online via the FBI Tips and Public Leads form. The FBI's Field Office Contact Information page (available at http://www.fbi.gov/contact/fo/info.htm) lists the addresses and phone numbers of FBI offices across the country, as well as links to their web sites. The Tips and Public Leads form is available at https://www.ifccfbi.gov/complaint/terrorist.asp. To reach the FBI's headquarters in Washington, D.C., call 202-324-3000 or write to: Federal Bureau of Investigation, J. Edgar Hoover Building, 935 Pennsylvania Ave. NW, Washington, DC 20535-0001.

SELECT AGENCIES AND MILITARY UNITS THAT DEAL WITH TERRORISM AND DISASTER RELIEF

What is the role of the **CIA**?

The Central Intelligence Agency, or CIA, is an independent government agency charged with providing comprehensive and timely foreign intelligence on national security topics—from international drug rings to terrorism. The agency conducts counterintelligence activities, covert operations, special activities, and other functions related to foreign intelligence and national security. Created in 1947 with the signing of the National Security Act by President Harry Truman, the CIA's mission is to support the president, the National Security Council, and all officials who make and execute the U.S. national security policy.

The Central Intelligence Agency feeds into the overall U.S. government effort to combat international terrorism by collecting, analyzing, and disseminating intelligence on foreign terrorist groups and individuals. Under CIA director George Tenet, the CIA is responsible for coordinating America's intelligence community, which includes 13 different agencies, including the FBI, the Defense Intelligence Agency, and the National Security Agency. The CIA was given added authority by the Bush administration in the wake of the September 11, 2001, terrorist attacks. The CIA's paramilitary unit, the Special Activities Division, played a prominent role in the war in Afghanistan, sending its specialized teams and unmanned aerial vehicles into the region to infiltrate Al Qaeda and Taliban troops.

What does the **FBI** do?

The Federal Bureau of Investigation (FBI) is the principal investigative arm of the United States Department of Justice. One of 32 federal agencies with law enforcement responsibilities, the FBI has the authority to investigate specific violations of federal criminal law, as well as provide other law enforcement agencies with cooperative services, such as fingerprint identification, laboratory examinations, and police training. The FBI's mandate—which is the broadest of all federal investigative agencies—authorizes it to investigate all federal criminal violations that have not been specifically assigned by Congress to another federal agency. The FBI's investigative functions fall into the categories of civil rights, counterterrorism, foreign counterintelligence, organized crime and drug trafficking, violent crimes and major offenders, and financial crime.

What is the FBI's role in domestic counterterrorism?

The FBI plays a role in domestic counterterrorism primarily through the exchange of information and close, daily coordination among U.S. law enforcement and intelligence entities. Examples of this cooperation include the National Infrastructure Protection Center and the National Domestic Preparedness Office. The FBI investigates bombings or attempted bombings that appear to have been initiated by terrorist or revolutionary groups. It collects evidence, interviews witnesses, develops leads, and identifies and apprehends those responsible. The FBI assists U.S. attorneys in preparing evidence or exhibits for trial as well. The FBI also investigates domestic hate crimes and "monitors" any potential terrorist groups in the United States as dictated by the guidelines of the attorney general.

Does the FBI ever get involved with **foreign counterintelligence**?

Yes. As the country's lead counterintelligence agency, the FBI is responsible for detecting and lawfully countering actions of foreign intelligence services and organizations that gather sensitive information about the United States. The FBI will investigate wherever a foreign entity conducts intelligence activities in the United States that adversely affect national interests. The espionage or "spying" activities may involve the acquisition of classified, sensitive, or proprietary information from the U.S. government or U.S. companies.

The FBI came under attack in the months following September 11, 2001, for disregarding warnings from field agents about several Middle Eastern flight students and suspicious terrorist activities. FBI Director Robert S. Mueller III then proposed an FBI restructuring plan that involved shifting hundreds of agents from various positions to counterterrorism positions. The reorganization proposed a permanent staff of more than 3,700 agents dedicated to counterterrorism, an increase of 70 percent from pre–September 11 levels. Mueller identified the FBI's top priorities as "protect[ing] the United States from terrorist attack" and "protect[ing] the United States against foreign intelligence operations and espionage." The FBI's focus on intelligence gathering and thwarting terrorist attacks represents a shift from its traditional crime-solving duties.

How does the FBI differ from the **Central Intelligence Agency, the Drug Enforcement Adminstration, and the Bureau of Alcohol, Tobacco and Firearms**?

The primary difference between the FBI and the CIA is that the CIA has no law enforcement function. Rather, it collects and analyzes information that is vital to the formation of U.S. policy, particularly in areas that impact national security. In addition, the CIA collects information only on foreign countries and their citizens, and is prohibited from collecting information regarding "U.S. persons," a term that includes U.S. citizens, resident aliens, legal immigrants, and U.S. corporations—regardless of where they are located. To the contrary, the FBI is the primary law enforcement agency for the U.S. government, charged with enforcement of more than 200 federal laws. The FBI also differs from the Drug Enforcement Administration, which is a single-mission agency charged with enforcement of drug laws, as well as the Bureau of Alcohol, Tobacco, and Firearms, the government agency whose primary investigative responsibility is enforcement of federal firearms statutes and the investigation of arsons and bombings that are not related to terrorism.

Other than war, when is the **U.S. military** called on?

The U.S. military—U.S. Army, U.S. Navy, U.S. Air Force, U.S. Marines, the Coast Guard, and, when called into active duty, the National Guard—is often required to protect and further U.S. national interests at home and abroad in a variety of ways other than war. Generally, they involve supporting overall military strategy and foreign affairs policy. The military is often sent to foreign countries to promote regional stability, maintain or achieve democratic states, retain U.S. influence and access abroad, provide humane assistance to distressed or war-torn areas, and combat terrorism.

Peacekeeping operations support diplomatic efforts to maintain peace in areas of potential conflict. The United States may participate in peacekeeping operations when requested by the United Nations or regional affiliations of nations, or on its own initiative. The peacekeeping force deters violent acts by its physical presence in violence-prone locations. *Nation assistance* involves promoting long-term stability, developing sound and responsive democratic institutions, promoting strong free-market economics, and providing an environment that allows for orderly political change and economic progress. *Humanitarian assistance* operations provide emergency relief to victims of natural or manmade disasters. Their activities include refugee assistance, the distribution of food programs and medical treatment and care, the restoration of law

National Guard troops were assigned to patrol airports and bridges and assist at border crossings and other locations in the wake of the September 11, 2001, terrorist attacks, in the hopes that the increased security presence would deter or prevent additional incidents.

and order, and damage control, including environmental cleanup or fire fighting. When *combating terrorism*, the Department of Defense fulfills a supporting role to the Department of State and Department of Justice. This may involve military action or more defensive measures to minimize U.S. vulnerability to terrorism.

In addition, the U.S. military supports efforts domestically—providing disaster relief, offering humanitarian assistance, and forging counterdrug and antiterrorism efforts within the United States.

What are **special operations units** and under what circumstances are they deployed?

Special operations units are small units within the U.S. Army that are called upon during times of war or special military operations. They include the U.S. Army Rangers, the Special Forces (otherwise known as "Green Berets"), and Special Operations Aviation Regiments (such as the "Night Stalkers"). The units are made up of combinations of trained specialized personnel, equipment, and tactics that exceed the standard capabilities of conventional military forces. They dispatched into foreign nations as part of politically sensitive missions—where only the best equipped and most proficient forces can be sent in order to avoid detection and possible mission failure. Special operations units are often used in counterterrorism missions, unconventional warfare, special reconnaissance missions, psychological operations, and operations that focus on eliminating weapons of mass destruction.

What role does the National Guard play in disaster control and relief?

The National Guard is a member part of the United States Reserve Forces, provided for in the Second Amendment to the Constitution: "A well regulated militia, being necessary to the security of a free state, the right of the people to keep and bear arms shall not be infringed." As such, the National Guard serves both the state and federal governments in times of need—during natural disasters, state emergencies, and civil unrest. Because each state's National Guard units are equipped and trained by the U.S. Army and Air Force, they often step in to help keep order during natural disasters and state emergencies, providing emergency relief such as humanitarian assistance and aeromedical evacuation. Following the terrorist attacks of September 11, 2001, for example, more than 50,000 guardsmen were called on to direct first aid efforts toward rescue and salvage workers in New York City.

What is the **Centers for Disease Control and Prevention**?

The Centers for Disease Control and Prevention (CDC) is recognized as the lead federal agency for protecting the health and safety of American people. As an agency within the Department of Health and Human Services, the CDC serves as the national focus for developing and applying disease prevention and control, environmental health, and health promotion and education activities designed to improve the health of the people of the United States. The agency stepped into the limelight after the 2001 anthrax scare, providing information about the infectious bacterial disease as well as methods of prevention and treatment. In addition, the agency took a lead role in disseminating information about bioterrorism, emergency preparedness, and emergency response to both everyday citizens and health care personnel. The CDC continues to fight against infectious diseases of all kinds, with particular emphasis on emerging and epidemic infectious diseases. A large part of its effort involves equipping and strengthening local, state, and national public health departments to respond to growing threats from biological and chemical terrorism.

How does the **Red Cross** operate?

While the American Red Cross has long been associated with running blood banks and distributing blood to those involved in natural disasters across the United States (indeed, the organization is responsible for half of the nation's blood supply), the organization is much broader. In the aftermath of a natural disaster, the Red Cross provides relief services to communities across the country, including blood, emergency medical treatment, first-aid supplies, food, shelter, and other basic necessities. It plays

Red Cross volunteers assist residents of Jarrell, Texas, after a twister hit that town in 1997. The Red Cross responds with help and support after natural disasters and other emergencies.

a large part in helping families return to self-sufficiency after a natural disaster, by providing groceries, new clothes, rent, emergency home repairs, transportation, household items, medicine, and occupational tools. In addition, its volunteers assist and feed emergency workers, handle inquiries from immediate family members outside the disaster site, and link disaster victims to other available resources.

The Red Cross is not part of the U.S. government, but rather a humanitarian organization led by volunteers. It works closely with a number of government agencies—for example, the Federal Emergency Management Agency (FEMA)—in times of crisis. In addition, the Red Cross is responsible for giving aid to members of the U.S. Armed Forces through its various services.

What was the **controversy surrounding the Red Cross** in the wake of the September 11, 2001, attacks?

Shortly after the September 11, 2001, terrorist attacks, the Red Cross established the Liberty Disaster Fund, set up to provide victims' families with additional funding to cover a full year of basic living expenses, including housing, food, utilities, tuition, child care, and health care. More than $800 million was contributed to the fund in the immediate aftermath of September 11. In October 2001, Red Cross president Dr. Bernadine Healy resigned after public controversy on the Red Cross's decision to spend a significant portion of the fund on administrative needs and withhold some of the monies for future disasters. She also disagreed with the board's refusal to recognize an Israeli agency, Magen David Adom, as the official emblem of the Israeli Red Cross. By December 2001, the Red Cross had officially apologized to America's citizens and disbursed $275 million to those affected by the terrorist attacks.

What does the **National Domestic Preparedness Office** do?

The Department of Justice, through the FBI, coordinates the domestic preparedness programs and activities of the United States to ensure that a coordinated crisis and consequence management infrastructure is in place to address the threat posed by terrorist use of weapons of mass destruction. Established in 1988, the National Domestic Preparedness Office (NDPO) serves as a single point of contact and clearinghouse for this information. Staffed by officials from a variety of federal agencies, the office assumes overall responsibility for coordinating the government's efforts to prepare America's communities for terrorist incidents involving weapons of mass destruction.

Primarily, this means working with the men and women on the front lines—the state and local emergency response community. This community is made up of members of the medical profession, emergency management, public officials, fire fighters, law enforcement, and (if necessary) military personnel. The NDPO's goal is to coordinate their many efforts, providing emergency responders access to information and federal government resources while reducing confusion and duplication of effort. Because the NDPO is the contact point of a diverse team of personnel (including the Department of Defense, FBI, Federal Emergency Management Agency, Department of Health and Human Services, Department of Energy, and Environmental Protection Agency), it eliminates confusion at the local level and provides a way for services to be distributed effectively to those citizens affected by a terrorist attack.

What does **FEMA** do?

Founded in 1979, the Federal Emergency Management Agency, known simply as FEMA, is an independent agency of the federal government that has multifaceted responsibilities during a time of national disaster. Its responsibilities cover the whole range of a disaster cycle, and include advising on building codes and flood plain management, teaching people how to get through a disaster and assisting them when disasters strike, helping equip local and state emergency preparedness, making disaster assistance available to states and local communities, supporting the nation's fire service, and administering the national flood and crime insurance programs. As part of America's emergency management system, FEMA works in partnership with other organizations, including state and local emergency management agencies, more than 20 federal agencies, and the American Red Cross.

Up until the early 1970s, more than 100 federal agencies were involved in some aspect of disasters, hazards, and emergencies. FEMA brought many of the separate disaster-related responsibilities under one roof. It has dealt with disasters and emergencies as far-reaching as the contamination of Love Canal in the mid-1970s, the 1979 accident at the Three Mile Island nuclear power plant, the 1989 Loma Prieta Earthquake, and 1992's Hurricane Andrew. The terrorist attacks of September 11, 2001, focused the agency on issues of national preparedness and homeland security, and tested the agency in unprecedented ways. The agency coordinated its activities with the newly formed Office of Homeland Security, and FEMA's Office of National Preparedness was given responsibility for helping to ensure that the nation's first responders were trained and equipped to deal with weapons of mass destruction.

How do certain government agencies—such as the National Transportation Safety Board—play a role in **disaster relief**?

Many federal agencies don't always make the front-page news, but they play a major behind-the-scenes role in disaster relief. One such agency is the National Transportation Safety Board (NTSB), an independent federal agency that investigates every civil aviation accident in the United States and significant accidents in the other modes of transportation (railroad, highway, marine, and pipeline). It conducts special investigations and safety studies, and issues safety recommendations to prevent future accidents. Since its creation in 1967, the NTSB has investigated more than 110,000 aviation accidents and thousands of surface transportation accidents—playing a key role in determining what when wrong and why. In so doing, it has become one of the world's premier accident investigation agencies. NTSB investigators investigate significant accidents around the world, and are often the first ones on site when an airline or other transportation disaster affects a local community. Although it has no regulatory or enforcement powers, its reputation for thoroughness has enabled the NTSB to achieve success in shaping transportation safety improvements.

How do **local agencies**—such as fire and police departments—contribute to disaster control?

State and local government agencies—such as law-enforcement agencies, fire departments, police departments, and paramedics—play a key role in the safety of communities and provide invaluable services in times of local disaster. The men and women who make up these groups are often called "first responders" and "first response teams" because they are the first to arrive at the scene of a disaster, be it a fire, flood, or bombing. As such, they are responsible for everything that is immediately needed at the scene of an emergency, including extinguishing fires, rescuing survivors, applying first aid, rerouting traffic, and setting up roadblocks. In the hours that followed the September 11, 2001, terrorist attacks, for example, New York City firefighters and police were the first responders to the attacks on the World Trade Center. At the Pentagon, police, fire, and search and rescue workers from Arlington County, Virginia, were the first at the scene. Many cities and counties have a domestic preparedness program in place to assist emergency personnel in the event of a terrorist incident or mass-casualty event. Devised by teams of professionals in areas such as hazardous materials, environmental issues, and weapons of mass destruction, these programs help disburse fire and police teams to the sites of disaster and provide them with adequate support once they arrive and begin work.

What is a **Citizen Corps**, and what role does it play in times of natural disasters?

A Citizen Corps is a network of volunteer programs that helps citizens take a more active role in crime prevention and emergency management preparedness in their communities, including providing critical support to first responders during times of emergency. The Citizens Corps program was created as a part of President George W. Bush's USA Freedom Corps program, which asks all Americans to commit at least two years of their lives—the equivalent of 4,000 hours—to the service of others.

Citizens Corps works at the local level. Its programs include an expanded Neighborhood Watch, which has a new emphasis on keeping an eye out for terrorist activity within one's community; Volunteers in Police Service, through which everyday Americans help with police department administrative duties so that law enforcement professionals can spend more time on front-line duty; and Medical Reserve Corps, through which volunteer health professionals assist physicians during large-scale emergencies. Citizens Corps has also developed a Community Emergency Response Team, made up of men and women who are trained in emergency preparedness and in basic disaster techniques. By going through this training, citizens are able to take a more active part in emergency management planning in their communities and to give critical support to first responders during an emergency. Many communities also offer Operation TIPS, a nationwide program for the millions of workers whose jobs position them to witness unusual events, such as truckers, letter carriers, and train conductors. These workers receive training and materials to recognize suspicious activity and a formalized way to report such activity to their nearest FBI field office.

These volunteer programs are run by locally organized groups of citizens and headed by leaders from all sectors of a community, including local elected officials, emergency managers, safety officials such as the local fire chief and police chief, leaders of volunteer organizations, representatives from local health care agencies, and transportation and communications providers. These leaders work with state and federal agencies, such as the Federal Emergency Management Agency, the Department of Justice, and the Department of Health and Human Services, to bring training and information to local communities.

Air traffic controllers play a key role in ensuring the safety and security of air passengers.

What role has the **FAA** played in recent history?

As part of the Department of Transportation, the Federal Aviation Administration (FAA) is charged with regulating civil aviation and promoting safety in the skies. As such, the agency operates a network of airport towers, air route traffic control centers, and flight service stations. It develops air traffic rules, allocates the use of airspace, and provides for the security control of air traffic to meet national defense requirements.

The FAA came to the forefront of national news during the terrorist attacks on September 11, 2001. Just minutes after American Airlines Flights 11 and 175 from Boston crashed into the World Trade Center, the FAA shut down all New York City area airports. It quickly halted all flight operations at U.S. airports, marking the first time in U.S. history that air traffic nationwide was stopped. In the days that followed, Americans awaited announcements from the FAA that would update them on their ability to travel. As part of a key disseminator of information, the FAA adopted a critical role in disaster control. In the weeks and months that followed, the FAA played a key part in the changes instituted within the airline industry, including enacting stricter security at airports, increasing security measures on aircraft, and implementing new procedures for crews in the event of a hijacking. In addition, the Airport Security Federalization Act passed by Congress in November 2001 federalized airport security and charged the FAA with training airline security workers and calling them to higher standards. The bill also requires all checked baggage to be screened for bombs and explosives, cockpit doors to be reinforced and locked while aircrafts are in flight, federal security directors at every airport, and a significant increase in the number of sky marshals.

Why was the White House Commission on Aviation Safety and Security created?

The White House Commission on Aviation Safety and Security was established by President Bill Clinton on August 22, 1996, with a charter to study and implement strategies to improve aviation safety and security, including air traffic control, both domestically and internationally. In the wake of concerns over the crash of Trans World Airlines Flight 800, President Clinton asked the commission to focus its attention on the issue of security in the skies. Also known as the Gore Commission because it was chaired by Vice President Al Gore, the commission conducted an intensive inquiry into civil aviation safety, aviation security, and air traffic control modernization. After gathering information from a broad range of aviation specialists, federal agencies, consumer groups, and industry leaders, it finalized its recommendations to the president in February 1997. The majority of the recommendations involved increasing security measures, to which Congress responded by appropriating more than $400 million for the acquisition of new explosives detection technology and other security enhancements on commercial airlines.

FORMS OF ATTACK: BIOLOGICAL AND CHEMICAL WEAPONS

What are **biological and chemical weapons**?

The Federal Emergency Management Agency defines biological agents as infectious microbes or toxins used to produce illness or death in people, animals, or plants. Biological agents can be dispersed as aerosols or airborne particles. Terrorists may use biological agents to contaminate food or water. Chemical agents are poisonous gases, liquids, or solids that have toxic effects on people, animals, or plants. Chemical agents kill or incapacitate people, destroy livestock, or ravage crops. The severity of injuries depends on the type and amount of the chemical agent used and the duration of exposure. Some chemical agents are odorless, tasteless, and difficult to detect. They can have an immediate effect (a few seconds to a few minutes) or a delayed effect (several hours to several days).

Biological and chemical weapons have been used primarily to terrorize an unprotected civilian population, and not as a weapon of war—primarily because of fear of retaliation and the likelihood that the agent would contaminate the battlefield for a long period of time. Nevertheless, because they are used with the intent to kill, biological and chemical agents are described as "weapons." The Persian Gulf War in 1991 and other recent confrontations in the Middle East have been feared as opportunities for chemical or biological warfare to be used. Biochemical agents (namely anthrax) sent by mail in the United States were used by terrorists in the wake of the September 11, 2001, attacks. The Department of Defense estimates that as many as 26 nations possess biological and chemical agents and an additional 12 may be seeking to develop them.

09-11-01
THIS IS NEXT
TAKE PENACILIN NOW
DEATH TO AMERICA
DEATH TO ISRAEL
ALLAH IS GREAT

Letters contaminated with anthrax were mailed to several politicians and media organizations in September 2001, resulting in five deaths and a review of safe mail handling procedures by organizations, citizens, and the U.S. Postal Service.

What is **"bioterrorism"**?

"Bioterrorism" is a term assigned to biological warfare at the hands of terrorists. It emerged in the popular media shortly after incidents involving the biological agent anthrax occurred in the United States. Because biological agents cannot necessarily be detected and may take time to grow and cause a disease, it is almost impossible to know immediately that a biological attack has occurred—making it especially life-threatening to a population. Among the 26 nations that may possess biological or chemical weapons, the Bush administration has suggested that Iraq and Iran are actively engaged in the production of chemical or biological warfare and the acquisition of ballistic missile technology to deliver it. The administration has maintained that those countries may pass them along to terrorist organizations, and thus precautionary measures against these forms of warfare have become a priority for the United States government.

What are the **most likely agents** that will be used in a biological attack?

Scientists estimate that at least 70 different types of biological agents could be produced and used for biological warfare. While no one knows exactly what agents will be used by terrorists, scientists and government officials have identified anthrax, smallpox, plague, botulism, brucellosis, tularemia, Q fever, and viral hemorrhagic fever as the most likely possibilities. These agents are all easily transmitted and have the potential of causing high mortality rates and a high level of social disruption. Specifically, smallpox, eradicated from the world as an epidemic in 1977, is considered a likely candidate for biological attack. Because vials of the smallpox virus were stockpiled by the United States and Russia, the virus could have been accessed by terrorist groups. The disease is caused by a virus that is transmitted via the air and is fatal in approximately 30 percent of cases. The possibility that smallpox may reemerge as a biological weapon caused U.S. health officials to take inventory of existing vaccine supplies—concluding that that nation only has little more than 15 million doses.

Are there any **systems in place to deal with an outbreak** of biological and chemical warfare?

If government officials were to become aware of a biological attack through an informant or warning by terrorists, or if a chemical agent attack were to occur, citizens would most likely be instructed to either seek shelter where they are and seal the premises or evacuate immediately. Since exposure to chemical agents can be fatal, strict precautionary measures need to be undertaken should an incidence of chemical warfare occur. Since the September 11, 2001, terrorist attacks, emergency service personnel have been trained to deal with such outbreaks, and gas masks, vaccines, and antibiotics are being stockpiled by local health agencies so that they can be made available should an outbreak occur. Communication networks and early-warning signals have also been established, helping to prepare public health workers for an attack.

Even the relatively few outbreaks of anthrax that occurred in late 2001 severely taxed state public health systems. In response, Congress approved legislation to spend about $3 billion over 2002 to prepare the country for future bioterrorist attacks. The money is allocated for developing and producing anthrax and smallpox vaccines, as well as antibiotics and other medicine; to increase public health networks around the country and expand the scope of the U.S. Centers for Disease Control and Prevention (CDC) so that can more readily respond to an attack; and improve U.S. food safety measures overall. Other specific precautions are being undertaken. For example, the Strategic National Pharmaceutical Stockpile, which holds an emergency reserve of medical supplies, is being expanded. The federal government has provided grants to states for bioterrorism planning and emergency coordination. And the CDC has focused on expanding its laboratory capacity and training of public health personnel, specifically in the area of disease surveillance. Restricting the access to biological agents in the United States—including anthrax, smallpox, and more than 30 others that are known to exist in laboratories all over the country—has been another point of government focus.

Who responds to a **bioterrorist attack**?

Initially, the response is on the local front—through public health investigation personnel, laboratory technicians, police and fire departments, and other emergency service personnel. Generally, the first 24 to 48 hours of an emergency outbreak are confined to local public health officials, who in turn communicate to their state authorities, such as the state public health department, disaster management teams, and the National Guard. The federal agencies that are geared up to respond to a bioterrorist attack include the Centers for Disease Control and Prevention, the Federal Emergency Management Association, the Federal Bureau of Investigation, and the Department of Defense.

With the anthrax scare that shook the nation in 2001, what should make me suspicious of a piece of mail?

In the wake of the anthrax outbreaks in the United States, the United States Postal Service issued seven warning signs that should make a person suspicious of a piece of mail: (1) it is unexpected or from someone you don't know; (2) it is addressed to someone no longer at your address; (3) it is handwritten and has no return address or bears one that you can't confirm is legitimate; (4) it is lopsided or lumpy in appearance; (5) it is sealed with excessive amounts of tape; (6) it is marked with restrictive endorsements such as "personal" or "confidential"; and/or (7) it is stamped with excessive postage.

The Postal Service suggests that anyone who receives a package with the above warning signs lay the package aside. A suspicious piece of mail should not be handled—which includes shaking, bumping, or sniffing it. Those who come in contact with suspect mail should wash their hands thoroughly with soap and water, and then notify local law enforcement authorities.

What do I do if I believe I've been **exposed to a biological or chemical agent**?

The Centers for Disease Control and Prevention (CDC) recommends that citizens who believe they have been exposed to a biological or chemical agent contact their local health department and/or local police or other law enforcement agency. The CDC web site provides a list of state and local health departments at http://www.cdc.gov/ other.htm#states.

Where can I find more information on **bioterrorism**?

Information on bioterrorism preparedness and response can be found online from the U.S. Department of Health and Human Services Centers for Disease Control and Prevention (CDC), as well as its newly created Office of Health Preparedness. Additional resources include the Food and Drug Administration (FDA), the National Institutes of Health (NIH), and the Federal Emergency Management Agency (FEMA). In addition, information on bioterrorism can be obtained from state and local public health departments, which have the advantage of being more specifically applicable to a particular location.

What are some other **historical examples** where biological and chemical warfare have been used?

History is filled with examples of the deliberate use of biological and chemical agents as weapons. In Europe during the Middles Ages, infected cadavers were hurled over walls into cities that were under siege. During the French and Indian War, the British supplied the Indians with blankets infected with smallpox in a deliberate attempt to reduce the number of Native American tribes. During World War I, Germany used anthrax to infect livestock that was exported to the Allied forces, and used mustard gas to cause almost one million casualties. During World War II, Germany used Zykon-B gas against the Jews, Roma, and Soviet prisoners of war. The Japanese conducted biological weapons research on prisoners of war, resulting in thousands of deaths. The Japanese also conducted biological warfare "experiments" on 11 Chinese cities by contaminating their water and food supplies with anthrax and other biological agents. They also released fleas that had fed on plague-infected rats to initiate the plague among the Chinese. While these tactics ended in 1942, many Japanese scientists disclosed their results to the United States. In that same year, the United States began an offensive biological program at Camp Detrick, Maryland, and 5,000 bombs filled with anthrax spores were produced there. During the Korean War, North Korea and China made allegations that the United States had engaged in biological warfare using anthrax. (Biological agents that were stockpiled by the U.S. military were destroyed in the early 1970s.)

One of the most recent examples of biological terrorism involves the 1991 Persian Gulf War, during which Iraq sponsored a biological weapons program. Although no biological weapons were used during the war, Iraqi officials admitted to developing such a program that included research on and the production of anthrax. In the early 1990s it was discovered that Iraq had produced 8,000 liters of anthrax spores—enough to kill every human being on earth. In another part of the world, 1995 witnessed the terrorist group Aum Shinrikyo's release of sarin nerve gas in a Tokyo subway station, killing 12 people and sickening more than 5,000. Further investigation revealed that the doomsday cult had made unsuccessful attacks in Japan using aerosols of anthrax and had spent an estimated $30 million on chemical weapons research.

Have **terrorists within the U.S. not affiliated with groups connected to the Middle East** ever threatened to use chemical or biological weapons?

Yes. Antiabortion extremists continually send abortion clinics threatening mail boasting anthrax contamination. In December 2001, for example, "God's warrior," the antiabortionist and federal fugitive Clayton Lee Wagner, was arrested after sending more than 500 letters and packages containing fake anthrax samples to clinics. Several years earlier, in 1998, Larry Wayne Harris and an accomplice were arrested in Las Vegas because they claimed to have deadly military-grade anthrax in their possession. Although the charges were later dropped because the materials turned out to be a harmless anthrax vaccine, at the time of Harris' arrest he was already on probation from a 1995 conviction for illegally ordering bubonic plague bacteria by mail.

Is **nuclear warfare** a viable method of attack by terrorist groups?

Yes. Although terrorist Osama bin Laden told journalists in November 2001 that he and his Al Qaeda network possessed chemical and nuclear weapons and "reserve the right to use them," Western security experts believe it is highly unlikely that bin Laden actually possesses nuclear weapons. However, both Al Qaeda and other terrorist groups have pursued the acquisition of nuclear materials. The Japanese doomsday cult Aum Shinrikyo, for example, recruited nuclear physicists from Moscow and attempted to buy Russian nuclear warheads. In addition, antiterrorism experts acknowledge that there is increasing evidence of illegal trafficking in nuclear materials, and that a number of countries hostile to the United States are developing nuclear weapon capabilities, some of whom harbor or are known to support terrorist groups. On the watch list of these states are Iran and Iraq.

Since the end of the cold war, a nuclear black market has emerged in and around the former Soviet Union. While both the United States and Russia have agreed to cut their nuclear arsenals, facilities in the new republics where weapons-grade nuclear materials are stored are poorly guarded, and there have been many reported cases of theft and smuggling—leading many foreign policy and antiterrorist experts to believe that enough radioactive material exists in the hands of terrorists to cause substantial damage. The U.S. Department of Energy estimates that there are 603 metric tons of weapons-grade material stored in the former Soviet Union—enough to make about 41,000 nuclear weapons. Given these statistics, members of Congress have asked the federal government to dedicate up to $30 billion over the next decade to prevent the acquisition and use of nuclear weapons by terrorists.

Which countries are known to have **nuclear weapons**?

Eight countries are known to possess nuclear weapons: the United States, Russia, China, Great Britain, France, India, Pakistan, and Israel. Pakistan's program was built almost entirely through black markets and industrial espionage. Russia maintains some 15,000 nuclear warheads, and security is a continual concern, though there is no confirmed case of a warhead being lost.

CHRONOLOGY OF ANTI-AMERICAN TERRORIST ATTACKS

Terrorist attacks against American interests are hardly a recent phenomenon. Individuals and groups who take issue with U.S. political or business activity have demonstrated their opposition through terrorist means since the 1960s, both in the states and abroad.

Date	Details
May 1, 1961	In the first hijacking of a U.S. aircraft, Puerto Rican-born Antuilo Ramierez Ortiz forces at gunpoint a National Airlines plane to fly to Havana, Cuba, where he is given asylum.
August 28, 1968	U.S. Ambassador to Guatemala John Gordon Mein is murdered by a rebel faction when gunmen force his official car off the road in Guatemala City and rake the vehicle with gunfire.
July 30, 1969	U.S. Ambassador to Japan A.H. Meyer is attacked by a knife-wielding Japanese citizen.
September 3, 1969	U.S. Ambassador to Brazil Charles Burke Elbrick is kidnapped by the Marxist revolutionary group MR-8.
July 31, 1970	In Montevideo, Uruguay, the Tupamaros terrorist group kidnap U.S. Agency for International Development adviser Dan Mitrione; his body is found on August 10.
March 2, 1973	U.S. Ambassador to Sudan Cleo A. Noel and other diplomats are assassinated at the Saudi Arabian Embassy in Khartoum by members of the Black September organization.
May 4, 1973	U.S. Consul General in Guadalajara, Mexico, Terrence Leonhardy is kidnapped by members of the People's Revolutionary Armed Forces.
January 27-29, 1975	Puerto Rican nationalists bomb a Wall Street bar, killing four and injuring 60; two days later, the Weather Underground claims responsibility for an explosion in a bathroom at the U.S. Department of State in Washington.
May 26, 1978	A suspicious package explodes at Northwestern University in Evanston, IL, injuring a security guard. Over the next two decades, the "Unabomber" sends a string of similar bombs are sent to university professors and corporate leaders, killing three and injuring 29, as part of his antitechnology campaign. In April 1996, recluse Theodore Kaczynski is arrested after the *New York Times* and *Washington Post* publish his "manifesto," prompting Kaczynski's brother to alert the FBI after recognizing the writing.
November 4, 1979	After President Jimmy Carter agrees to admit the Shah of Iran into the U.S., Iranian radicals seize the U.S. embassy in Tehran and take more than 60 hostages. Several are soon released, but the remaining 52 continue to be held. Carter orders complete embargo of Iranian oil; other economic embargoes followed. On April 8, 1980, Carter severs diplomatic relations following failure of negotiations. In April, Carter authorizes a top-secret mission, Operation Eagle Claw, to rescue hostages, but the operation is aborted on April 25 following the crash of three of the eight helicopters involved in the mission. Eight servicemen are killed when a helicopter collides with refueling plane. After 444 days in captivity, hostages are released on January 20, 1981, just hours after President Ronald Reagan takes the oath of office.
August 31, 1981	The Red Army explodes a bomb at the U.S. Air Force Base at Ramstein, West Germany.
December 4, 1981	Three American nuns and one lay missionary are found murdered outside San Salvador, El Salvador. They are believed to have been assassinated by a right-wing death squad.
April 8, 1983	A U.S. citizen is seized by the Revolutionary Armed Forces of Colombia (FARC) and held for ransom.

Date	Details
April 18, 1983	Sixty-three people, including CIA station chief Kenneth Haas and CIA chief Middle East Analyst Robert C. Ames, are killed and 120 others are injured in a 400-pound suicide truck-bomb attack on the U.S. Embassy in Beirut, Lebanon.The Islamic Jihad claims responsibility.
May 25, 1983	A U.S. Navy officer in El Salvador is assassinated by the Farabundo Marti National Liberation Front.
October 23, 1983	Simultaneous suicide truck-bomb attacks are made on American and French compounds in Beirut, Lebanon. A 12,000-pound bomb destroys the U.S. compound, killing 242 Americans, while 58 French troops are killed when a 400-pound device destroys a French base. Islamic Jihad claims responsibility.
November 15, 1983	A U.S. Navy officer is shot by the 17 November terrorist group in Athens, Greece, while his car is stopped at a traffic light.
December 12, 1983	The U.S. embassy in Kuwait is bombed in a series of attacks that also include the French embassy, the control tower at the airport, the country's main oil refinery, and a residential area for employees of Raytheon, an American company. Six are killed and more than 80 injured. Suspects are believed to be members of Al Dawa, an Iranian-backed group. Seventeen people are tried in Kuwait for the bombings; they become known as the Kuwait 17 or the Al Dawa 17, and their release becomes a demand in future kidnappings and hijackings.
March 16, 1984	The Islamic Jihad kidnaps and later murders Political Officer William Buckley in Beirut, Lebanon. Other U.S. citizens not connected to the U.S. government are seized over a succeeding two-year period.The Reagan administration devises a plan to secretly sell military supplies to Iran—an activity that has been banned by Congress—in exchange for return of the hostages.Three hostages are eventually released as a result of the deal. Funds from the sales are secretly and illegally funneled to the Contras fighting to overthrow the Sandanista government in Nicaragua.When the deal becomes public, it is known as the Iran-Contra Affair.
April 12, 1984	Eighteen U.S. servicemen are killed and 83 people are injured in a bomb attack on a restaurant near a U.S. Air Force Base in Torrejon, Spain. Responsibility is claimed by Hizbollah.
September 20, 1984	About 20 people, including two U.S. military personnel, are killed when a truck bomb explodes outside the U.S. embassy annex in East Beirut.The U.S. suspects elements of the Hizbollah group in the bombing.
December 3, 1984	Kuwait Airways Flight 221, en route from Kuwait to Pakistan, is hijacked and diverted to Tehran, Iran. Hijackers demand the release of the Kuwait 17.When their demands aren't met, the hijackers kill two American officials from the U.S. Agency for International Development. On the sixth day of the standoff, Kuwait forces storm the plane and release the remaining hostages. Iran arrests the hijackers, but never brings them to trial, and they are allowed to leave the country.
February 7, 1985	Under the orders of narcotics trafficker Rafael Cero Quintero, Drug Enforcement Administration agent Enrique Camarena Salazar and his pilot are kidnapped, tortured, and executed in Mexico.
June 14, 1985	TWA Flight 847 is hijacked en route to Rome from Athens by two Lebanese Hizbollah terrorists and forced to fly to Beirut. Hijackers demand the release of the Kuwait 17 as well as 700 Shiite Muslim prisoners held in Israel and southern Lebanon. Eight crew members and 145 passengers, including 39 Americans, are held for 17 days, during which one American hostage, U.S. Navy diver Robert Dean Stethem, is murdered and his body dumped on the tarmac. After being flown twice to Algiers, the aircraft is returned to Beirut after Israel releases 435 Lebanese and Palestinian prisoners.

Date	Details
June 19, 1985	Four U.S. Marines and two American businessmen are gunned down at an outdoor cafe in San Salvador, El Salvador. A total of 13 people are murdered.
June 23, 1985	An Air-India flight explodes over the Atlantic Ocean, killing everyone aboard, including four Americans.
August 8, 1985	Car bomb explodes at the U.S. Rhein-Main air base in Frankfurt, West Germany, killing two and injuring 20. The next day, the body of a U.S. soldier murdered for his ID papers is found.
October 7, 1985	Four Palestinian Liberation Front terrorists seize the Italian cruise liner *Achille Lauro* in the eastern Mediterranean Sea, taking more than 700 hostages. Hijackers demand release of Palestinian prisoners held in Egypt, Italy, and other countries. One U.S. passenger, disabled 69-year old tourist Leon Klinghoffer, is murdered before the Egyptian government offers the terrorists safe haven in return for the hostages' freedom. U.S. Navy fighters intercept the plane the escaped hijackers are on and force it to land in Italy. The hijackers are arrested and tried in an Italian court, where they are found guilty in 1986.
November 23, 1985	An EgyptAir airplane en route from Athens to Malta and carrying several U.S. citizens is hijacked by the Abu Nidal Group. One American is killed. Egyptian commandos later storm the aircraft on Malta; 60 are killed.
December 27, 1985	In simultaneous suicide attacks, the U.S. and Israeli check-in desks at the international airports in Rome and Vienna are bombed. Twenty are killed, including five Americans. The U.S. blames Libya and sends navy ships and warplanes to patrol the Gulf of Sidra, in waters Libya claims as it own but not recognized as such by other nations.
March 30, 1986	A Palestinian splinter group detonates a bomb as TWA Flight 840 approaches Athens International Airport, killing four U.S. citizens.
April 5, 1986	Two U.S. soldiers are killed and 79 American servicemen are injured in a Libyan bomb attack on the La Belle Disco in West Berlin, West Germany, a popular nightspot for off-duty servicemen. The U.S. blames Libya for the bombing, and on April 15, the U.S. launches retaliatory attacks on Tripoli and Benghazi as part of Operation El Dorado Canyon.
April 24, 1987	Sixteen U.S. servicemen riding in a Greek Air Force bus near Athens are injured in an apparent bomb attack, carried out by the revolutionary organization known as 17 November.
December 26, 1987	Catalan separatists bomb a Barcelona bar frequented by U.S. servicemen, killing one U.S. citizen.
February 17, 1988	U.S. Marine Corps Lt. Col. Williams Higgins is kidnapped and murdered by the Iranian-backed Hizbollah group while serving with the United Nations Truce Supervisory Organization (UNTSO) in southern Lebanon.
April 14, 1988	The Organization of Jihad Brigades explodes a car bomb outside a USO Club in Naples, Italy, killing one U.S. sailor.
June 28, 1988	The defense attache of the U.S. embassy in Greece is killed when a car bomb is detonated outside his home in Athens.
December 21, 1988	Pan American Airlines Flight 103, en route from London to New York, is blown up over Lockerbie, Scotland, by a bomb believed to have been placed on the aircraft in Frankfurt, West Germany, by Libyan terrorists. 270 people on board are killed, including 189 Americans and 11 people on the ground in Lockerbie. No group takes credit for the bombing.
April 21, 1989	The New People's Army (NPA) assassinates Col. James Rowe in Manila. The NPA also assassinates two U.S. government defense contractors in September.
January 15, 1990	The Tupac Amaru Revolutionary Movement bombs the U.S. embassy in Lima, Peru.
May 13, 1990	The New People's Army (NPA) kills two U.S. Air Force personnel near Clark Air Force Base in the Philippines.

Date	Details
January 18-19, 1991	Iraqi agents plant bombs at the U.S. ambassador to Indonesia's home residence and at the USIS library in Manila.
January 17-21, 1992	A senior official of the corporation Philippine Geothermal is kidnapped in Manila by the Red Scorpion Group, and two U.S. businessmen are seized independently by the National Liberation Army and by Revolutionary Armed Forces of Colombia (FARC).
January 25, 1993	Gunman opens fire at CIA headquarters in Langley, VA, killing two CIA employees and wounding three others. Suspected Pakistani gunman Mir Amal Kansi is turned over to U.S. authorities by Afghan individuals to face trial in the U.S. On November 10, 1997, he is found guilty of capital murder and nine other charges.
January 31, 1993	Revolutionary Armed Forces of Colombia (FARC) terrorists kidnap three U.S. missionaries.
February 26, 1993	The World Trade Center in New York City is badly damaged when a 1000-pound car bomb planted by Islamic terrorists explodes in an underground garage. The bomb kills six people and injures more than 1,000. Four followers of Umar Abd al-Rahman, an Egyptian cleric who preached in the New York area, are tried for the attack; all are convicted March 4, 1994, in federal court on all 38 charges against them. On June 6, 1998, Ramzi Yousef, an associate of Osama bin Laden, is sentenced to life in prison without parole for orchestrating the attack.
April 14, 1993	The Iraqi intelligence service attempts to assassinate former U.S. president George Bush during a visit to Kuwait. In retaliation, the U.S. launches a cruise missile attack two months later on Baghdad, Iraq.
February 25, 1994	Jewish right-wing extremist and U.S. citizen Baruch Goldstein machine-guns worshippers at a mosque in West Bank town of Hebron, killing 29 and wounding about 150.
September 23, 1994	FARC rebels kidnap U.S. citizen Thomas Hargrove in Colombia.
December 24, 1994	Members of the Armed Islamic Group seize an Air France Flight to Algeria. The four terrorists are killed during a rescue effort.
March 8, 1995	Two unidentified gunmen kill two U.S. diplomats and wound a third in Karachi, Pakistan.
April 19, 1995	Right-wing extremists Timothy McVeigh and Terry Nichols destroy the Alfred P. Murrah Federal Building in Oklahoma City with a massive truck bomb that kills 168 and injures hundreds more in what is at the time the largest terrorist attack on American soil. McVeigh is convicted and given the death sentence; he is executed June 11, 2001. Nichols is sentenced to life in prison.
July 4, 1995	In India, six foreigners, including two U.S. citizens, are taken hostage by Al-Faran, a Kashmiri separatist group. One non-U.S. hostage is later found beheaded.
August 21, 1995	Hamas claims responsibility for the detonation of a bomb on a bus in Jerusalem that kills six and injures more than 100 persons, including several U.S. citizens.
September 13, 1995	A rocket-propelled grenade is fired through the window of the U.S. embassy in Moscow, ostensibly in retaliation for U.S. strikes on Serb positions in Bosnia.
November 13, 1995	The Islamic Movement of Change plants a bomb in a Riyadh, Saudi Arabia, military compound that kills one U.S. citizen, several foreign national employees of the U.S. government, and more than 40 others.
January 19, 1996	Revolutionary Armed Forces of Colombia (FARC) guerrillas kidnap a U.S. citizen and demand a $1 million ransom. The hostage is released on May 22.
January 31, 1996	Members of the Liberation Tigers of Tamil Eelam (LTTE) ram an explosives-laden truck into the Central Bank in the heart of downtown Colombo, Sri Lanka, killing 90 civilians and injuring more than 1,400 others, including two U.S. citizens.

Date	Details
February 9, 1996	An Irish Republican Army (IRA) bomb detonates in London, killing two persons and wounding more than 100 others, including two U.S. citizens.
February 15, 1996	Unidentified assailants fire a rocket at the U.S. embassy compound in Athens, causing minor damage to three diplomatic vehicles and some surrounding buildings. Circumstances of the attack suggest it was an operation carried out by the 17 November group.
February 16, 1996	Six alleged National Liberation Army (ELN) guerrillas kidnap a U.S. citizen in Colombia. The hostage is released nine months later.
February 26, 1996	In Jerusalem, a suicide bomber blows up a bus, killing 26 persons, including three U.S. citizens, and injuring some 80 persons, including three U.S. citizens.
March 4, 1996	Hamas and the Palestine Islamic Jihad (PIJ) both claim responsibility for a bombing outside of Tel Aviv's largest shopping mall that kills 20 persons and injures 75 others, including two U.S. citizens.
May 13, 1996	Arab gunmen open fire on a bus and a group of Yeshiva students near the Bet El settlement, killing a dual U.S.-Israeli citizen and wounding three Israelis. No one claims responsibility for the attack, but Hamas is suspected.
May 31, 1996	A gang of former Contra guerrillas kidnaps a U.S. employee of the Agency for International Development (USAID) who was assisting with election preparations in rural northern Nicaragua. She is released unharmed the next day after members of the international commission overseeing the preparations intervene.
June 9, 1996	Unidentified gunmen open fire on a car near Zekharya, killing a dual U.S./Israeli citizen and an Israeli. The Popular Front for the Liberation of Palestine (PFLP) is suspected.
July 27, 1996	A pipe bomb explodes during the Olympic games in Atlanta, GA, killing two people and wounding more than 100.
June 25, 1996	A fuel truck carrying a bomb explodes outside the U.S. military's Khobar Towers housing facility in Dhahran, Saudi Arabia, killing 19 U.S. military personnel and wounding 515 persons, including 240 U.S. personnel. Several groups claim responsibility for the attack.
August 17, 1996	Sudan People's Liberation Army (SPLA) rebels kidnap six missionaries in Mapourdit, including a U.S. citizen, an Italian, three Australians, and a Sudanese. The SPLA releases the hostages 11 days later.
November 1, 1996	In Sudan, a breakaway group from the Sudanese People's Liberation Army (SPLA) kidnaps three International Committee of the Red Cross (ICRC) workers, including a U.S. citizen, an Australian, and a Kenyan. On December 9, the rebels release the hostages in exchange for ICRC supplies and a health survey for their camp.
December 3, 1996	A bomb explodes aboard a Paris subway train as it arrives at the Port Royal station, killing two French nationals, a Moroccan, and a Canadian, and injuring 86 persons, including one U.S. citizen. No one claims responsibility for the attack, but Algerian extremists are suspected.
December 11, 1996	Five armed men claiming to be members of the Revolutionary Armed Forces of Colombia (FARC) kidnap and later kill a U.S. geologist at a methane gas exploration site in La Guajira Department.
December 17, 1996	Twenty-three members of the Tupac Amaru Revolutionary Movement (MRTA) take several hundred people hostage at a party given at the Japanese ambassador's residence in Lima, Peru. Among the hostages are several U.S. officials, foreign ambassadors and other diplomats, Peruvian Government officials, and Japanese businessmen. The group demands the release of all MRTA members in prison and safe passage for them and the hostage takers. The terrorists release most of the hostages in December but hold 81 Peruvians and Japanese citizens for several months.

Date	Details
January 2-13, 1997	A series of letter bombs with Alexandria, Egypt, postmarks are discovered at Al-Hayat newspaper bureaus in Washington, New York City, London, and Riyadh, Saudi Arabia. Three similar devices, also postmarked in Egypt, are found at a prison facility in Leavenworth, KS. Bomb disposal experts defuse all the devices, but one detonates at the Al-Hayat office in London, injuring two security guards and causing minor damage.
February 14, 1997	Six armed Colombian guerrillas kidnap a U.S. oil engineer and his Venezuelan pilot in Apure, Venezuela. The kidnappers release the Venezuelan pilot on February 22. According to authorities, the FARC is responsible for the kidnapping.
February 23, 1997	A Palestinian gunman opens fire on tourists at an observation deck atop the Empire State Building in New York City, killing a Danish national and wounding visitors from the U.S., Argentina, Switzerland, and France before turning the gun on himself. A handwritten note carried by the gunman claims this was a punishment attack against the "enemies of Palestine."
February 24, 1997	National Liberation Army (ELN) guerrillas kidnap a U.S. citizen employed by a Las Vegas gold corporation who was scouting a gold mining operation in Colombia. The ELN demands a ransom of $2.5 million.
March 7, 1997	FARC guerrillas kidnap a U.S. mining employee and his Colombian colleague who were searching for gold in Colombia. On November 16, the rebels release the two hostages after receiving a $50,000 ransom.
July 31, 1997	Three Middle Eastern men are arrested after a tip to New York City police. Police find explosives and evidence the three planned to attack a New York subway station.
September 4, 1997	Three suicide bombers from Hamas detonate bombs in the Ben Yehuda shopping mall in Jerusalem, killing eight persons, including the bombers, and wounding nearly 200 others. A dual U.S./Israeli citizen is among the dead, and seven U.S. citizens are wounded.
October 23, 1997	In Colombia, National Liberation Army (ELN) rebels kidnap two foreign members of the Organization of American States (OAS) and a Colombian human rights official at a roadblock. The ELN claims that the kidnapping is intended "to show the international community that the elections in Colombia are a farce."
October 30, 1997	Al-Sha'if tribesmen kidnap a U.S. businessman near Sanaa, Yemen. The tribesmen seek the release of two fellow tribesmen arrested on smuggling charges and several public works projects they claim the government promised them. They release the hostage on November 27.
November 12, 1997	Two unidentified gunmen shoot to death four U.S. auditors from Union Texas Petroleum Corporation and their Pakistani driver after they drive away from the Sheraton Hotel in Karachi. The Islami Inqilabi Council, or Islamic Revolutionary Council, claims responsibility in a call to the U.S. Consulate in Karachi. In a letter to Pakistani newspapers, the Aimal Khufia Action Committee also claims responsibility.
March 21-23, 1998	FARC rebels kidnap a U.S. citizen in Sabaneta, Colombia. FARC members also kill three persons, wound 14, and kidnap at least 27 others at a roadblock near Bogota. Four U.S. citizens and one Italian are among those kidnapped, as well as the acting president of the National Electoral Council (CNE) and his wife.
April 15, 1998	Somali militiamen abduct nine Red Cross and Red Crescent workers at an airstrip north of Mogadishu. The hostages include a U.S. citizen, a German, a Belgian, a French, a Norwegian, two Swiss, and one Somali. The gunmen are members of a subclan loyal to Ali Mahdi Mohammed, who controls the northern section of the capital.
June 21, 1998	Rocket-propelled grenades explode near U.S. embassy in Beirut.

Date	Details
August 7, 1998	A bomb explodes at the rear entrance of the U.S. embassy in Nairobi, Kenya, killing 12 U.S. citizens, 32 Foreign Service Nationals (FSNs), and 247 Kenyan citizens. About 5,000 Kenyans, six U.S. citizens, and 13 FSNs are injured. The U.S. embassy building sustains extensive structural damage. Almost simultaneously, a bomb detonates outside the U.S. embassy in Dar es Salaam, Tanzania, killing seven FSNs and three Tanzanian citizens, and injuring one U.S. citizen and 76 Tanzanians. The explosion causes major structural damage to the U.S. embassy facility. The U.S. government holds Osama bin Laden responsible. On August 20, the U.S. launches cruise missile strikes against suspected terrorist installations in Afghanistan and the Sudan. Bin Laden is later indicted by U.S. grand jury for the bombings. On May 5, 2001, a U.S. district court finds four of bin Laden's followers guilty of conspiring to kill Americans, including those in the African embassy bombings.
October 18, 1998	A National Liberation Army (ELN) bomb explodes on the Ocensa pipeline in Columbia, killing approximately 71 persons and injuring at least 100 others. The pipeline is jointly owned by the Colombia State Oil Company Ecopetrol and a consortium including U.S., French, British, and Canadian companies.
November 15, 1998	Armed assailants follow a U.S. businessman and his family home in Cundinamarca Department and kidnap his 11-year-old son after stealing money, jewelry, one automobile, and two cell phones. The kidnappers demand $1 million in ransom. On January 21, 1999, the kidnappers release the boy.
January 2, 1999	A UN plane carrying one U.S. citizen, four Angolans, two Philippine nationals, and one Namibian is shot down, according to a UN official. No deaths or injuries are reported. Angolan authorities blame the attack on National Union for the Total Independence of Angola (UNITA) rebels. UNITA officials deny shooting down the plane.
February 14, 1999	A pipe bomb explodes inside a bar in Uganda, killing five persons and injuring 35 others. One Ethiopian and four Ugandan nationals die in the blast, and one U.S. citizen working for USAID, two Swiss nationals, one Pakistani, one Ethiopian, and 27 Ugandans are injured. Ugandan authorities blame the attack on the Allied Democratic Forces (ADF).
February 25, 1999	Revolutionary Armed Forces of Colombia (FARC) kidnaps three U.S. citizens working for the Hawaii-based Pacific Cultural Conservancy International. On March 4, the bodies of the three victims are found in Venezuela.
March 1, 1999	One hundred-fifty armed Hutu rebels attack three tourist camps in Uganda, kill four Ugandans, and abduct three U.S. citizens, six Britons, three New Zealanders, two Danish citizens, one Australian, and one Canadian national. Two of the U.S. citizens and six of the other hostages are subsequently killed by their abductors.
March 23, 1999	Armed guerrillas kidnap a U.S. citizen in Boyaca, Colombia. The National Liberation Army (ELN) claims responsibility and demands $400,000 ransom. On July 20, ELN rebels release the hostage unharmed following a ransom payment of $48,000.
May 30, 1999	In Cali, Colombia, armed ELN militants attack a church in the neighborhood of Ciudad Jardin, kidnapping 160 persons, including six U.S. citizens and one French national. The rebels release approximately 80 persons, including three U.S. citizens, later that day.
June 27, 1999	In Port Harcourt, Nigeria, armed youths storm a Shell oil platform, kidnapping one U.S. citizen, one Nigerian national, and one Australian citizen, and causing undetermined damage. A group calling itself "Enough is Enough in the Niger River" claims responsibility. Further seizures of oil facilities follow.

Date	Details
August 4, 1999	An Armed Forces Revolutionary Council (AFRC) faction kidnaps 33 UN representatives near Occra Hills, Sierra Leone. The hostages include one U.S. citizen, five British soldiers, one Canadian citizen, one representative from Ghana, one military officer from Russia, one officer from Kyrgyzstan, one officer from Zambia, one officer from Malaysia, a local bishop, two UN officials, two local journalists, and 16 Sierra Leonean nationals.
October 1, 1999	Burmese dissidents seize the Burmese embassy in Bangkok, Thailand, taking 89 persons hostage, including one U.S. citizen.
December 23, 1999	Colombian People's Liberation Army (PLA) forces kidnap a U.S. citizen in an unsuccessful ransoming effort.
May 1, 2000	In Makeni, Sierra Leone, Revolutionary United Front (RUF) militants kidnap at least 20 members of the United Nations Assistance Mission in Sierra Leone (UNAMSIL) and surround and open fire on a UNAMSIL facility, according to press reports. The militants kill five UN soldiers in the attack. RUF militants kidnap 300 UNAMSIL peacekeepers throughout the country, according to press reports. On May 15 in Foya, Liberia, the kidnappers release 139 hostages. On May 28, on the Liberia and Sierra Leone border, armed militants release unharmed the last of the UN peacekeepers. In Freetown, according to press reports, armed militants ambush two military vehicles carrying four journalists. A Spaniard and one U.S. citizen are killed in a May 25 car bombing in Freetown for which the RUF is probably responsible. Suspected RUF rebels also kidnap 21 Indian UN peacekeepers in Freetown on June 6. Additional attacks by RUF on foreign personnel follow.
June 27, 2000	In Bogota, Colombia, ELN militants kidnap a five-year-old U.S. citizen and his Colombian mother, demanding an undisclosed ransom.
August 12, 2000	In the Kara-Su Valley in Kyrgyzstan, the Islamic Movement of Uzbekistan takes four U.S. citizens hostage. The Americans escape on August 12.
October 1, 2000	Unidentified militants detonate two bombs in a Christian church in Dushanbe, Tajikistan, killing seven persons and injuring 70 others. The church was founded by a Korean-born U.S. citizen, and most of those killed and wounded are Korean. No one claims responsibility.
October 12, 2000	In Sucumbios Province, Ecuador, a group of armed kidnappers led by former members of defunct Colombian terrorist organization the Popular Liberation Army (EPL) take ten employees of Spanish energy consortium REPSOL hostage. Those kidnapped include five U.S. citizens, one Argentine, one Chilean, one New Zealander, and two French pilots who escaped four days later. On January 30, 2001, the kidnappers murder American hostage Ronald Sander. The remaining hostages are released on February 23 following the payment of $13 million in ransom by the oil companies.
October 12, 2000	In Aden, Yemen, a small dingy carrying explosives rams the destroyer USS *Cole*, killing 17 sailors and injuring 39 others. Supporters of Osama bin Laden are suspected.
December 30, 2000	A bomb explodes in a plaza across the street from the U.S. embassy in Manila, injuring nine persons. The Moro Islamic Liberation Front is likely responsible.
September 11, 2001	Two hijacked airliners crash into the twin towers of the World Trade Center in New York City. Soon thereafter, the Pentagon is struck by a third hijacked plane. A fourth hijacked plane, suspected to be bound for a high-profile target in Washington, crashes into a field in southern Pennsylvania. More than 3,000 U.S. citizens and other nationals are killed as a result of these acts. President Bush and Cabinet officials indicate that Osama bin Laden is the prime suspect and that they considered the U.S. to be in a state of war with international terrorism. In the aftermath of the attacks, the U.S. forms the Global Coalition Against Terrorism.

Date	Details
September–November 2001	About a week after the attacks on the World Trade Center and the Pentagon, letters containing anthrax spores begin arriving at the offices of news agencies and political figures, including Senator Tom Daschle. As of November, five people die as a result of exposure to anthrax, including two postal workers.
December 22, 2001	On American Airlines Flight 63, en route from Paris, France, to Miami, FL, Richard Reid, a British national with suspected ties to Islamic extremists, attempts to use a match to detonate plastic explosives hidden in his shoes. Reid is subdued by flight attendants and passengers. The flight is diverted to Boston's Logan International Airport, where Reid is arrested and charged with interfering with a flight crew. After this incident, the Federal Aviation Administration issues a new directive to randomly inspect the shoes of airline passengers.
January 23, 2002	Daniel Pearl, reporter for the *Wall Street Journal,* is kidnapped while on his way to interview a Muslim fundamentalist leader in Pakistan. His kidnappers initially demand release of Pakistani detainees at the U.S. naval base at Guantanamo Bay, Cuba. Pearl's death is confirmed on February 22, when a videotape of his murder is received by FBI and Pakistani officials. Four Islamic militants are convicted of Pearl's murder; three are given life sentences, and one is sentenced to death.
March 17, 2002	During services at the Protestant International Church in Islamasbad, Pakistan, an unknown number of men enter the church and throw up to six grenades, of which two explode. The attack kills five, including two Americans, and injures 40, including 10 Americans. The church is located in the diplomatic quarter of Islamasbad, about 300 yards from the U.S. embassy.
May 3-7, 2002	Over the course of several days, 18 pipe bombs are planted in rural mailboxes in Illinois, Iowa, Nebraska, Colorado, and Texas. Anti-government letters accompany the bombs. Six people are injured when some of the bombs detonate. College student Lucas Helder is arrested May 7 in Nevada. He was on his way to California with six unexploded pipe bombs in his car.

GOVERNMENT INSTITUTIONS

THE EXECUTIVE BRANCH

THE PRESIDENT'S ROLES AND RESPONSIBILITIES

What is the **executive branch**?

The executive branch of the federal government is the unit headed by the president of the United States that consists of various entities and organizations of administrative, regulatory, or policy-implementing character. The 14 departments are the most visible of these entities, the heads of which comprise the cabinet. These departments include the Department of Defense, the Department of State, the Department of Energy, and the Department of the Interior. In addition, the executive branch includes a number of agencies, such as the Central Intelligence Agency (CIA) and the Environmental Protection Agency (EPA), as well as distinct smaller boards, committees, commissions, and offices created either by law or presidential directive. Immediately assisting the president are the agencies and entities of the Executive Office of the President, including, for example, the Council of Economic Advisors and the National Security Council.

What is the president's **job description**?

The president's chief duty is to protect the Constitution and enforce the laws made by Congress. However, he also has a host of other responsibilities tied to his "job description": recommending legislation to Congress; calling special sessions of Congress; delivering messages to Congress; signing or vetoing legislation; appointing federal judges; appointing heads of federal departments and agencies and other principal federal officials; appointing representatives to foreign countries; carrying on official business with foreign nations; acting as commander in chief of the armed forces; and granting pardons for offenses against the United States.

What are the **enumerated constitutional powers** of the president?

Article II of the Constitution vests the "executive power" in the president. Although there is some dispute among scholars as to whether such executive power consists only of the authorities enumerated for the president or whether it also includes powers that are implied in Article II, most scholars lean toward the latter interpretation. These powers are those expressly granted to the president within the text of the Constitution, as found in Article II, Sections 2 and 3.

The president is commander in chief of the U.S. Army, Navy, Air Force, and, when called into action, the National Guard. The president may require the written opinion of military executive officers, and is empowered to grant reprieves and pardons, except in the case of impeachment. The president receives ambassadors and other public ministers, ensures that the laws are faithfully executed, and commissions all officers of the United States. The president has power—by and with the advice and consent of the Senate—to make treaties, provided that two-thirds of the senators present concur. The president also nominates and appoints ambassadors, other public ministers and consuls, justices of the Supreme Court, federal judges, and other federal officers, by and with the advice and consent of the Senate. The president has the power to temporarily fill all vacancies that occur during the recess of the Senate. In addition, the president may, under extraordinary circumstances, convene "emergency" sessions of Congress. Further, if the two houses disagree as to the time of adjournment, the president may adjourn the bodies. In addition to these powers, the president also has enumerated powers that allow him to directly influence legislation. The Constitution directs the president to periodically inform Congress on the State of the Union, and to recommend legislation that is considered necessary and expedient. Also, Article I, Section 7 of the Constitution grants the president the authority to veto acts of Congress.

What are the **implied constitutional powers** of the president?

The president possesses certain powers that are not enumerated in the Constitution. The implied powers are the subject of continued debate among scholars for three primary reasons: the degree of importance of the presidency in the political strategy of the Constitution is not cut and dry; the president's authority in international relations is extensive and vaguely defined in the Constitution; and the president is often said to have "inherent" or residual powers of authority. For example, although the Constitution does not grant the president the express power to remove administrators from their offices, as the chief executive the president holds power over executive branch officers, unless such removal power is limited by public law. Note, however, that the president does not have such implied authority over officers in independent establishments: When Franklin D. Roosevelt removed a member of the Federal Trade Commission, an independent regulatory agency, the Supreme Court ruled the act invalid in 1935.

Another implied constitutional power is derived from the president's authority as commander in chief. Although Congress has the explicit power to declare war, the president holds the responsibility to protect the nation from sudden attack and has the ability to initiate military activities overseas without a formal declaration of war. Through the War Powers Resolution of 1973, Congress sought to define more clearly the conditions under which presidents unilaterally can authorize military action abroad.

What are the president's various **roles**?

Although the Constitution only clearly assigns to the president the roles of chief executive and commander of the country's armed forces, today the president of the United States assumes six basic roles: chief executive; chief of state/foreign relations; commander in chief; chief legislator; chief of party; and chief citizen, or popular leader.

What are the president's duties and roles as **chief executive**?

When wearing the hat of chief executive, sometimes called chief administrator, the president has four main duties: (1) enforcing federal laws and court rulings; (2) developing various federal policies; (3) appointing federal officials; and (4) preparing the national budget. Within the executive branch, the president has broad powers to manage national affairs and the workings of the federal government. The president can issue rules, regulations, and instructions called executive orders, which have the binding force of law upon federal agencies but do not require congressional approval. The president may also negotiate "executive agreements" with foreign countries that are not subject to Senate confirmation. The president nominates—and the Senate confirms—the heads of all executive departments and agencies, together with hundreds of other high-ranking federal officials. In addition, the president solely appoints other important public officials, including aides, advisors, and hundreds of other positions. Presidential nomination of federal judges, including members of the Supreme Court, is subject to confirmation by the Senate. Another significant executive power involves granting a full or conditional pardon to anyone convicted of breaking a federal law—except in a case of impeachment. In addition, as the nation's chief executive the president prepares the national budget.

What are the president's duties and roles as **chief of state**?

As the chief of state, the president is the ceremonial head of the United States. Under the Constitution, the president is the federal official primarily responsible for the relations of the United States with foreign nations. As chief of state, the president appoints ambassadors, ministers, and consuls, subject to confirmation by the Senate, and receives foreign ambassadors and other public officials. With the secretary of state, the president manages all official contacts with foreign governments. On occasion, the president may personally participate in summit conferences where chiefs of state meet for direct consultation. For example, President Woodrow Wilson headed the American delegation to the Paris conference at the end of World War I; President Franklin D. Roosevelt met with Allied leaders during World War II; and every president since Roosevelt has convened with world leaders to discuss economic and political issues and to reach foreign policy agreements.

Through the Department of State, the president is responsible for the protection of Americans abroad and of foreign nationals in the United States. The president decides whether to recognize new nations and new governments, and negotiate treaties with other nations, which become binding on the United States when approved by two-thirds of the Senate.

How is the president commander in chief?

Article II, Section 2 of the Constitution states that the president is the commander in chief of the U.S. Army, Navy, and, when it is called into federal service, state militias (now called the National Guard). Historically, presidents have used this authority to commit U.S. troops without a formal declaration of war. However, Article I, Section 8 of the Constitution reserves to Congress the power to raise and support the armed forces as well as the sole authority to declare war. These competing powers have been the source of controversy between the legislative and executive branches over war making, so much so that in 1973 Congress enacted the War Powers Resolution, which limits the president's authority to use the armed forces without specific congressional authorization, in an attempt to increase and clarify Congress's control over the use of the military. In addition, the armed forces operate under the doctrine of civilian control, which means that only the president or statutory deputies—such as the secretary and deputy secretary of defense—can order the use of force. The chain of command is structured to insure that the military cannot undertake actions without civilian approval or knowledge.

How is the president the **chief legislator**?

Despite the constitutional provision that "all legislative powers" shall be vested in the Congress, the president, as the chief formulator of public policy, plays a major legislative role. The president can veto any bill passed by Congress and, unless two-thirds of the members of each house vote to override the veto, the bill does not become law. Much of the legislation dealt with by Congress is drafted at the initiative of the executive branch. In his annual and special messages to Congress, the president may propose legislation he believes is necessary. If Congress should adjourn without acting on those proposals, the president has the power to call it into special session. But beyond this official role, the president, as head of a political party and as principal executive officer of the U.S. government, is in a position to influence public opinion and thereby the course of legislation in Congress.

To improve their working relationships with Congress, in recent years presidents have set up a Congressional Liaison Office in the White House. Presidential aides keep abreast of all important legislative activities and try to persuade senators and representatives of both parties to support administration policies.

How does the president exercise **veto power**?

There are two types of vetoes available to the president. The regular veto, called a "qualified negative veto," is limited by the ability of Congress to gather the necessary two-thirds vote of each house for constitutional override. The other type of veto is not explicitly outlined in the Constitution, but is traditionally called a "pocket veto." As an "absolute veto" that cannot be overridden, it becomes effective when the president fails to sign a bill after Congress has adjourned and is unable to override the veto. The president's veto authority is one of his significant tools in legislative dealings with Congress. It is not only effective in directly preventing the passage of legislation undesirable to the president, but serves as a threat, thereby bringing about changes in the content of legislation long before the bill is ever presented to the president.

What was the **line item veto**?

The Line Item Veto Act of 1996 gave the president the authority to cancel certain new spending and entitlement projects, as well as the authority to cancel certain types of limited, targeted tax breaks. The president could make these cancellations within five days of the enactment of a money bill providing such funds. These line item vetoes could then be subject to a two-thirds veto override by the House and Senate. President Bill Clinton used the line item veto to make 82 cancellations, and Congress overrode 38 of the cancellations, all within a single military construction bill. In 1998, the U.S. Supreme Court ruled the line item veto unconstitutional, in violation of the Presentment Clause in Article I, Section 7 of the Constitution, which requires that every bill that passes the House and Senate must be presented to the president for either approval or disapproval.

Does the president have any control over the sessions of **Congress**?

Under the Constitution the president may convene Congress, or either house, "on extraordinary occasions." It is usual for the president when calling an extra session to indicate the exact matter that needs the attention of Congress. However, once convened, Congress cannot be limited in the subject matter that it will consider. The president is also empowered by the Constitution to adjourn Congress "at such time as he may think proper" when the House and Senate disagree with respect to the time for

Former presidents Ronald Reagan, Jimmy Carter, Gerald Ford, and Richard Nixon accompany President George Bush at the dedication of the Ronald Reagan Presidential Library in Simi Valley, California, in 1991.

adjournment; however, to date no president has exercised this power. Many constitutional experts believe the provision applies only in the case of extraordinary sessions.

How is the president the **chief of party**?

As chief of party, or party leader, the president is the acknowledged leader of the political party that controls the executive branch. He helps form the party's position on policy issues and strives to elect party members to Congress so that his party dominates in both the House and the Senate. While most presidencies are divided governments—that is, one party controlling the executive office and another party controlling the Congress—a unified party in both the executive and legislative departments makes it much easier for the president to propel his legislative agenda.

In what ways is the president the **chief citizen**?

President Franklin D. Roosevelt probably summed up the duties of this role best when he said, "[The presidency] is preeminently a place of moral leadership." As a representative of the nation's people, the president automatically assumes the role of its chief citizen, or popular leader. The nature of this role mandates a certain trust between the president and the people, since it is the president's duty to work for the public interest amidst competing private interests, and to place the nation's best interests above the interests of any one group or citizen. In turn, the president relies on public support to help pass his legislative agenda through Congress—gaining the trust of the public with regard to these issues through exposure, straightforwardness, and strong leadership.

Because of these multiple powers and roles, has the presidency ever been criticized as being **too powerful**?

Yes. Because of the vast array of presidential roles and responsibilities, coupled with a prominent national and international presence, political analysts have tended to place great emphasis on the president's powers. Some have even spoken of the "the imperial presidency," referring to Franklin D. Roosevelt's terms in office.

However, seldom does the public hear about the sobering realities a new president discovers when assuming office: an inherited bureaucratic structure that can be difficult to manage and slow to change direction; the power to appoint officials that extends only to some 3,000 people out of a government work force of about three million; and a "machine-like" system that often operates independently of presidential intervention. Rather than becoming "all powerful," analysts have often pointed to the president feeling "all bureaucratic": new presidents are immediately confronted with a backlog of decisions from the outgoing administration; they inherit a budget formulated and enacted into law long before they came to office; and they must conform with treaties and informal agreements negotiated by their predecessors. After only a short time in office, a new president often discovers that Congress has become less cooperative of his agenda and the media more critical—even of his personal life. The president is forced to build at least temporary alliances among diverse, often conflicting interests, and the president must strike compromises with Congress in order to adopt legislation.

Despite these constraints, every president achieves at least some of his legislative goals and prevents by veto the enactment of other laws he believes *not* to be in the nation's best interests. Moreover, the president uses his unique position to articulate ideas and advocate policies that relate to national issues, which then have a better chance of entering the public consciousness than those held by his political rivals—thus adding to his political power. The president's authority in the area of foreign relations and his careful execution of multilateral policy add to his clout as a world leader. So while a president's power and influence are limited in some areas, they are still greater than those of any other American, in or out of political office.

What is the difference between and **executive power** and **executive privilege**?

These two similar terms have vastly different meanings. *Executive powers* are those powers granted to the president by the Article II of the Constitution, and include: the power to execute, or enforce, federal law; the power to issue and implement executive orders, or directives that have the effect of law; the power to nominate ambassadors,

Whitewater prosecutor Kenneth Starr's investigation of President Bill Clinton's suspicious business dealings led to the revelation of Clinton's affair with White House intern Monica Lewinsky and Clinton's attempts at a cover-up, which led to his impeachment in 1998.

top-ranking government officials, officers, and judges of the Supreme Court; and the power to remove government officials from office. *Executive privilege*, on the other hand, is a presidential practice that generally refers to the president's right to withhold information. Executive privilege is a claim that presidents generally make to support the fact that, as the nation's chief executive, they have the discretion to decide that certain information be withheld from the public, Congress, or the courts for national security reasons. Although the Supreme Court has ruled that presidents are entitled to this privilege, it has maintained that the privilege is not unlimited and its scope is subject to judicial determination.

When have recent presidents tried to invoke **executive privilege**?

Generally maintaining that it is in "the public's best interest" not to disclose certain information, presidents of late have attempted to invoke executive privilege at various times—most notably Richard Nixon's refusal to turn over White House tapes during the Watergate investigation. Arguing that executive privilege may not be invoked to deny the courts access to evidence needed in a criminal proceeding, the prosecutor asked the U.S. Supreme Court to compel Nixon to release all of his taped conversations with his advisors. Bill Clinton tried to evoke executive privilege twice. First, claiming "client-lawyer confidentiality," he initially refused to turn over his notes with his lawyer to a Senate committee during the Whitewater investigation. Later, he tried to prevent the testimony of two of his advisors before the grand jury during independent counsel Kenneth Starr's investigation of his sexual relations with White House intern Monica Lewinsky. Ultimately, the grand jury denied his request.

What is an **independent counsel**?

In 1988 the Supreme Court upheld the constitutionality of the independent counsel law. These independent counsels investigate and prosecute alleged criminal conduct of high-ranking officials. They can only be removed by the attorney general of the United States, not the president, and then only for "good cause, physical disability, mental incapacity, or other impairing conditions."

Can **anyone** run for president?

No. According to Article II, Section 1 of the Constitution, any person seeking the presidency must be a natural-born citizen, at least 35 years old, and a resident of the United States for at least 14 years. Constitutional scholars have debated whether a child born abroad of an American parent constitutes "a natural-born citizen." While most maintain that such a person should qualify as a natural-born citizen, no definitive consensus has been reached.

How many **terms** can a president serve?

Article II, Section 1 of the Constitution mandates that the president serve a four-year term. This time period was chosen because the framers agreed that four years was enough time for a president to have learned the ropes, demonstrated his leadership abilities, and established sound policies. The Constitution placed no limit on the number of terms that a president might serve until 1951, with the adoption of the Twenty-second Amendment, which states that "no person shall be elected to the office of the President more than twice, and no person who has held the office of President, or acted as President, for more than two years of a term to which some other person was elected President shall be elected to the office of the President more than once. " As a result, each president can serve a maximum of eight years in office; however, a president who has succeeded to the office beyond the midpoint in a term to which another person was originally elected could potentially serve for more than eight years. In these exceptional cases, the president would finish out his predecessor's term and then seek two full terms on his own. Under these conditions, the maximum amount of time that he could serve would be 10 years.

Has any president served **more than two terms**?

Yes. While early presidents, beginning with George Washington, refused to seek more than two terms of office and established the unwritten rule of not pursuing a third term, Franklin D. Roosevelt broke tradition by winning a third term in 1940 and a fourth term in 1944. He was the only president to ever serve more than two terms, since shortly thereafter the Twenty-second Amendment was passed, placing term limits on the executive office.

Have other **term limits** been suggested?

Since the Twenty-second Amendment was passed in 1951, several presidents—including Harry Truman, Dwight Eisenhower, and Ronald Reagan—have called for its repeal. Their main argument has centered around the fact that the amendment places an arbitrary time limit on the office, and that the ultimate will of the people should be regarded when electing their chief officer, despite the amount of time that he has already served. Critics of the amendment concur, saying the time limit undercuts the authority of a two-term president, especially in the latter half of his second term. Still other presidents, most recently Jimmy Carter, have lobbied for a single, nonrenewable six-year term, arguing that this time period would allow the president to more feasibly focus on implementing long-term policies that would benefit the nation and release him from the pressure of campaigning for a second term—a cumbersome task that automatically distracts him from the day-to-day responsibilities of the office.

When does the president actually begin his term?

When the Constitution was ratified, Congress was given power to determine the date for beginning the operations of the new presidential administration, and it set the date of March 4, 1789. Although George Washington did not take the oath of office until April 30 of that year, his term officially began on March 4. Later, the Twentieth (or so-called "lame duck)" Amendment, which was ratified in 1933, established January 20 as the date on which presidents would be inaugurated. In 1937, Franklin D. Roosevelt became the first president to take the oath on January 20.

What is the **presidential oath**?

The oath of the office for the president is outlined in Article II, Section 1 of the Constitution, as reads as follows: "I do solemnly swear (or affirm) that I will faithfully execute the office of President of the United States, and will, to the best of my ability, preserve, protect, and defend the Constitution of the United States." Usually, the chief justice of the Supreme Court administers the oath, although there is no provision made for this within the Constitution. In fact, throughout American history other judges have administered the oath at times of unexpected presidential succession.

What are the president's **salary and benefits**?

As of January 20, 2001, the president's salary is $400,000 per year. Congress sets the president's salary, which cannot be increased or decreased during a presidential term.

In addition, the president is allocated a $50,000-a-year taxable expense allowance to be spent however the president chooses. During his term in office, the president also enjoys many perks, including living in the White House, orchestrating office suites and a large staff, sailing on the presidential yacht, flying in his private jet (*Air Force One*), holding meetings at the Camp David resort, and enjoying abundant travel and entertainment funds, among other benefits. In addition, since 1959 each former president has received a lifetime pension.

In 1868, Andrew Johnson (1808–1875) was the first president to be impeached on charges of usurpation of the law, corrupt use of veto power, interference at elections, and various misdemeanors. The Senate ultimately acquitted Johnson by one vote.

What is **impeachment**?

Impeachment is the process by which the president, vice president, federal judges and justices, and all civil officials of the United States may be removed from office. Officials may be impeached for treason, bribery, and other high crimes and misdemeanors. The House of Representatives has sole authority to bring charges of impeachment, by a simple majority vote, and the Senate has sole authority to try impeachment charges. An official may be removed from office only upon conviction, which requires a two-thirds vote of the Senate. The Constitution provides that the chief justice shall preside when the president is tried for impeachment.

How many presidents have been **impeached**?

Throughout America's history, only two presidents have been impeached: Andrew Johnson and Bill Clinton. In 1868, impeachment proceedings were initiated against

Following accusations of abuse of power and obstruction of justice during the Watergate scandal, on August 8, 1974, President Richard Nixon announces his resignation from office on national television.

Johnson by the House of Representatives, who charged Johnson with usurpation of the law, corrupt use of veto power, interference at elections, and various misdemeanors. However, the 54-member Senate proceedings acquitted Johnson by one vote. In December 1998 the House of Representatives brought two articles of impeachment against President Clinton: perjury—lying under before a federal grand jury—about the precise nature of his sexual relations with White House intern Monica Lewinsky, and obstruction of justice by withholding evidence about, and influencing others to conceal, his affair with Lewinsky. Ultimately, the Senate rejected both charges, and Clinton remained in office.

Many also cite Richard Nixon in the list of impeached presidents, but that is a misnomer. Amidst the Watergate scandal, in July 1974 the House Committee on the Judiciary approved three articles of impeachment against Nixon, including the obstruction of justice and the abuse of presidential power. However, the charges never went to trial. On August 8, 1974, President Nixon publicly announced his resignation, making him the first president in American history to resign from office.

How many presidents have **resigned from office**?

Just one president has ever resigned from office: Richard Nixon. Under the threat of impeachment, Nixon resigned as the 37th president of the United States on August 9, 1974. Nixon, who had completed a little over a year and a half of his second term, was succeeded by Vice President Gerald Ford.

If something incapacitates the president, **who is in charge**?

The vice president serves concurrently with the president, and holds the right of succession. The Twenty-fifth Amendment to the Constitution, adopted in 1967, details the process of presidential succession. It describes the specific conditions under which the vice president is empowered to take over the office of president if the president should become incapacitated. It also provides for resumption of the office by the president in the event of his recovery. In addition, the amendment enables the president to name a vice president, with congressional approval, when the second office is vacated.

If a president **dies, resigns, or is removed from office**, what happens?

According to the Twenty-fifth Amendment, adopted in 1967, the vice president succeeds to the office if the president dies, resigns, or is removed from office by impeachment.

Who would succeed to the presidency if the office becomes vacant and **there is no vice president**?

According to Article II, Section I of the Constitution, Congress fixes the order of succession following the vice president. According to the effective law on succession, the Presidential Succession Act of 1947, should both the president and vice president vacate their offices, the Speaker of the House of Representatives would assume the presidency. Next in line is the president pro tempore of the Senate (a senator elected by that body to preside in the absence of the vice president), and then cabinet officers in designated order: secretary of state, secretary of the treasury, secretary of defense, attorney general, secretary of the interior, secretary of agriculture, secretary of commerce, secretary of labor, secretary of health and human services, secretary of housing and urban development, secretary of transportation, secretary of energy, secretary of education, and secretary of veterans affairs.

What role does the **vice president** serve?

The limited role of the vice president is introduced in Article II, Section 1 of the Constitution, which provides that the president "shall hold his Office during the Term of four Years ... together with the Vice President...." In addition to his role as president of the Senate, the vice president is empowered to succeed to the presidency, according to Article II and the Twentieth and Twenty-fifth Amendments to the Constitution. His right of succession has often been mentioned as his most coveted privilege. The executive functions of the vice president include participation in cabinet meetings and, by statute, membership on the National Security Council and the Board of Regents of the Smithsonian Institution.

However, although the Constitution spends little time assigning any roles to the office of vice president and traditionally the office has not been highly regarded, more recent presidents have assigned larger roles to their vice presidents. These include advising the president in domestic and foreign policy matters and carrying out a host of political and diplomatic duties in the name of the executive office. Unlike other members of the president's staff, the vice president is not subject to removal from office at the hand of the president. Under no circumstances may the president formally remove his vice president.

What are the **qualifications** for vice president?

The qualifications for vice president are the same as the president. According to Article II, Section 4 of the Constitution, the vice president must be a natural-born citizen, at least 35 years old, and have been a resident of the United States for at least 14 years.

What happens if there is a **vacancy** in the office of the vice president?

According to the Twenty-fifth Amendment, ratified in 1967, whenever there is a vacancy in the office of the vice president, the president has the authority to nominate a vice president, who can then take office upon confirmation by a majority vote of both houses of Congress.

Has a vice president ever **resigned**?

Yes, two vice presidents have resigned. John C. Calhoun resigned on December 28, 1932, three months before his term expired, to become senator from South Carolina. Spiro T. Agnew resigned on October 10, 1973, after pleading no contest to a charge of federal income tax evasion. Following Agnew's resignation, President Richard Nixon nominated Gerald Ford, the minority leader of the House, to fill the vice presidential vacancy. In accordance with the provisions of the Twenty-fifth Amendment under which Ford had been nominated, the Senate and House approved the nomination and Ford was sworn into office on December 6, 1973. On August 9, 1974, less than a year later, Ford became president following Nixon's resignation. Shortly thereafter, Ford nominated Nelson A. Rockefeller to be vice president, who was confirmed and sworn into office on December 19, 1974. In a span of just over one year, two situations arose for using the provisions of the Twenty-fifth Amendment to fill a vacancy in the vice presidency.

Which vice presidents **succeeded to the presidency** upon the death or resignation of the presidents under whom they served?

A total of nine vice presidents had this honor: John Tyler, Millard Fillmore, Andrew Johnson, Chester A. Arthur, Theodore Roosevelt, Calvin Coolidge, Harry Truman, Lyndon Johnson, and Gerald Ford. Four of these nine who succeeded to the presidency were elected for additional four-year terms: Theodore Roosevelt, Calvin Coolidge, Harry Truman, and Lyndon Johnson.

How many vice presidents were **elected to the presidency** at the conclusion of their terms?

Only four vice presidents were elected to the presidency at the conclusion of their vice presidential terms: John Adams, Thomas Jefferson, Martin Van Buren, and George Bush. Many people also incorrectly add Richard Nixon to this list; however, Nixon was the first vice president elected president several years *after* his vice presidential term. Nixon was vice president under President Dwight Eisenhower from January 1953 to January 1961 and did not return to government service again until January 1969, when he was inaugurated president of the United States.

When was the first—and only—time that a president/vice president team was **not elected** by the people?

The Gerald Ford/Nelson Rockefeller team ran the United States federal government without being elected to their posts as president and vice president. Both reached office under the provisions of the Twenty-fifth Amendment.

Under the Richard Nixon presidency, Vice President Spiro Agnew resigned on October 10, 1973, leaving the position vacant. In accordance with the Twenty-fifth Amendment, President Nixon nominated Gerald Ford, House Republican leader from Michigan, as his vice president. Upon Senate confirmation, Ford assumed that role on December 6, 1973. When President Nixon resigned the presidency on August 9, 1974, Ford succeeded to the presidency, becoming the 38th president of the United States. He was then left to nominate a vice president, choosing former New York governor Nelson Rockefeller on August 20, 1974. After protracted hearings, Rockefeller was sworn in on December 19, 1974, as the new vice president of the United States.

What is the role of the **first lady**?

Although this position is unpaid, unelected, and unappointed, the first lady—that is, the wife of the president—is a dynamic force unto her own. Today the first lady role is in itself a "powerful political institution, complete with office, staff, and budgetary resources rivaling those of key presidential advisors," according to political science professor Robert Watson, author of *The Presidents' Wives: Reassessing the Office of First Lady*. Although the Constitution is silent on the first lady's role, and by law immediate members of the president's family cannot be appointed to a position in the federal government, many first ladies have assumed informal powers that exceed even cabinet secretaries. The first lady acts as the social host of the White House, and performs at least a minimum level of campaigning, hosting, social activism, advocacy of pet projects, and public appearances. In addition, many recent first ladies—including Barbara Bush in her family literacy promotion and Hillary Clinton in her roll as task force leader in President Bill Clinton's effort to reform health care—have embraced key responsibilities, necessitating the management of large staffs and budgets.

Including roles the public generally expects of first ladies and responsibilities commonly undertaken by twentieth-century first ladies since Eleanor Roosevelt (who was first lady from 1933 to 1945), Watson has identified 11 fundamental duties of the modern office: wife and mother; public figure and celebrity; nation's social hostess; symbol of the American woman; White House manager and preservationist; campaigner; social advocate and champion of social causes; presidential spokesperson; presidential and political party booster; diplomat; and political and presidential partner.

Margaret Chase Smith of Maine, who served as a senator from 1948 to 1972, was nominated for president at the 1964 Republican National Convention, making her the first woman presidential candidate selected at a major party convention.

Do the **White House staff** and the first lady ever work together?

Absolutely. Rosalyn Carter, first lady from 1977 to 1981, was one of the late-twentieth-century first ladies who followed the suit of early first ladies by utilizing the services of various executive agencies' staff. In effect, Carter reorganized the modern office of the first lady, so that today's first lady offices include roughly 20 to 28 full-time paid employees. In addition, today's first ladies use staff from the president's office, including speechwriters, schedulers, and policy experts. Nancy Reagan's office, for example, had 18 to 22 employees, in addition to the use of clerical White House staffers. Hillary Clinton drew on 15 staff positions to aid in her role as first lady, including assistant to the president/chief of staff to the first lady; press secretary to the first lady; special assistant to the first lady; and deputy social secretary.

When was the term **"first lady"** first used?

The term "first lady," when used as a synonym for the wife of the president, is generally attributed to Mary Clemmer Ames, a journalist for the *Independent* who first used this term in an 1877 article she wrote describing the inauguration of President Rutherford B. Hayes on March 5, 1877. The term didn't become popular until 1911, when a comedy about Dolley Madison entitled *The First Lady in the Land* made its debut at the Gaiety Theater in New York City.

Have any **women** ever run for president?

Beginning with Victoria Claflin Woodhull, the presidential nominee of the People's Party (Equal Rights Party) in 1872, women have consistently appeared on the presidential ballots of a variety of parties. The first woman presidential candidate selected at a major political party convention was Margaret Chase Smith of Maine. Smith was nominated on July 15, 1964, at the Republican National Convention in San Francisco, California. The most notable woman presidential candidate of late is Elizabeth Hanford Dole. Married to former Senator Bob Dole (himself a Republican presidential nominee in 1996), Dole served as president of the Red Cross from 1990 to 1999 before deciding to run for president of the United States in 1999. She ultimately withdrew prior to the Republican National Convention due to a lack of funding.

Is it reasonable to expect a **woman president** anytime soon?

With more women serving in Congress, in state elected offices, and as governors than any time in America's history, the answer would have to be yes. A record number of women are jockeying for governorships in 2002, which is traditionally a strong post for upward mobility into the executive office. Front-runners for governorships include Kathleen Kennedy Townsend (D–MD), Maryland's first woman lieutenant governor; (D–MI) Jennifer Granholm, the first woman to serve as attorney general in Michigan; and Linda Lingle (R–HI), mayor of Maui County, Hawaii, and former Republican chairman. Political analysts say that both the 2002 elections and the presidential race in 2004 will focus on issues of national security. Women such as National Security Advisor Condoleezza Rice and Environmental Protection Agency head Christine Todd Whitman have paved the way for women to be taken seriously when they discuss matters of national security. In addition, Representative Nancy Pelosi (D–CA) became the highest-ranking woman in Congress when she was elected House Minority Whip in January 2002. If the Democrats gain control of the House of Representatives in November 2002, then Pelosi could become Speaker of the House—second in line to succeed the president.

In what way is **President George W. Bush** a "first"?

George W. Bush, the 43rd president of the United States, is a "first" in several ways. He is the first president to hold an MBA degree from Harvard, the first president to have been a business manager of a professional baseball team (the Texas Rangers), the first president to send his father on a diplomatic mission (to attend a November 2001 memorial for British victims of the Word Trade Center attack), and the first president to appoint an Asian American woman, Elaine Chao, to his cabinet. While he was the fourth man to assume the presidency without winning the popular vote, he enjoyed the highest job rating of any president before him in the weeks following the September 11, 2001, terrorist attacks.

In what ways is former **President Bill Clinton** a "first"?

There are several traits that make former President Bill Clinton a presidential "first." He is the first Rhodes scholar and Arkansas native to become president in American history.

Presidents of the United States

Name	Vice President	Term	Party
George Washington b. 1732 Westmoreland County, VA; d. 1799	John Adams	1789-1797	Federalist
John Adams b. 1735, Braintree (now Quincy), MA; d. 1826	Thomas Jefferson	1797-1801	Federalist
Thomas Jefferson b. 1743, Albemarle County, VA; d. 1826	Aaron Burr, George Clinton	1801-1809	Democratic/ Republican
James Madison b. 1751, Port Conway, VA; d. 1826	Aaron Burr, George Clinton	1809-1817	Democratic/ Republican
James Monroe b. 1758, Westmoreland, VA; d. 1831	Daniel D. Tompkins	1817-1825	Democratic/ Republican
John Quincy Adams b. 1767, Braintree (now Quincy), MA; d. 1848	John C. Calhoun	1825-1829	Democratic/ Republican
Andrew Jackson b. 1767, Waxhaw, SC; d. 1845	John C. Calhoun, Martin Van Buren	1829-1837	Democratic
Martin Van Buren b. 1782, Kinderhook, NY; d. 1862	Richard M. Johnson	1837-1841	Democratic
William Henry Harrison b. 1773, Charles City County VA; d. 1841	John Tyler	1841-1841	Whig
John Tyler b. 1790, Charles City County, VA; d. 1862	None	1841-1845	Whig
James Knox Polk b.1795, Mecklenburg County, NC; d. 1849	George Mifflin Dallas	1845-1849	Democratic
Zachary Taylor b. 1784, Orange County, VA; d. 1850	Millard Fillmore	1849-1850	Whig
Millard Fillmore b. 1800, Cayuga County, NY; d. 1874	None	1850-1853	Whig
Franklin Pierce b. 1804, Hillsboro, NH; d. 1869	William R. King	1853-1857	Democratic
James Buchanan b. 1791, near Mercersburg, PA; d. 1868	John C. Breckinridge	1857-1861	Democratic
Abraham Lincoln b. 1809, Hardin County, KY; d. 1865	Hannibal Hamlin, Andrew Johnson	1861-1865	Republican
Andrew Johnson b. 1808, Raleigh, NC; d. 1875	None	1865-1869	Democratic
Ulysses Simpson Grant b. 1822, Point Pleasant, OH; d. 1885	Schuyler Colfax, Henry Wilson	1869-1877	Republican
Rutherford Birchard Hayes b. 1822, Delaware, OH; d. 1893	William Wheeler	1877-1881	Republican
James Abram Garfield b. 1831, Cuyahoga County, OH; d. 1881	Chester A. Arthur	1881-1881	Republican
Chester A. Arthur b. 1829, Fairfield, VT; d. 1886	None	1881-1885	Republican
Steven Grover Cleveland b. 1837, Caldwell, NJ; d. 1908	Thomas Hendricks	1885-1889	Democratic

Presidents of the United States (cont.)

Name	Vice President	Term	Party
Benjamin Harrison b. 1833, North Blend, OH; d. 1901	Levi P. Morton	1889-1893	Republican
Steven Grover Cleveland b. 1837, Caldwell, NJ; d. 1908	Thomas Hendricks	1893-1897	Democratic
William McKinley b. 1843, Niles, OH; d.1901	Garret Hobart, Theodore Roosevelt	1897-1901	Republican
Theodore Roosevelt b. 1858, New York, NY; d. 1919	Charles Fairbanks	1901-1909	Republican
William Howard Taft b. 1857, Cincinnati, OH; d. 1930	James Sherman	1909-1913	Republican
Thomas Woodrow Wilson b. 1856, Staunton, VA; d. 1924	Thomas Marshall	1913-1921	Democratic
Warren Gamaliel Harding b. 1865, Morrow County, OH; d. 1923	Calvin Coolidge	1921-1923	Republican
John Calvin Coolidge b. 1872, Plymouth, VT; d. 1933	Charles Gates Dawes	1923-1929	Republican
Herbert Clark Hoover b. 1874, West Branch, IA; d. 1964	Charles Curtis	1929-1933	Republican
Franklin Delano Roosevelt b. 1882, Hyde Park, NY; d. 1945	John Nance Garner, Henry Agard Wallace, Harry S Truman	1933-1945	Democratic
Harry S Truman b. 1884, Lamar, MO; d.1972	Alben William Barkley	1945-1953	Democratic
Dwight David Eisenhower b. 1890, Denison, TX; d. 1969	Richard M. Nixon	1953-1961	Republican
John Fitzgerald Kennedy b. 1917, Brookline, MA; d. 1963	Lyndon B. Johnson	1961-1963	Democratic
Lyndon Baines Johnson b. 1908, near Stonewall, TX; d. 1973	Hubert H. Humphrey	1963-1969	Democratic
Richard Milhous Nixon b. 1913, Yorba Linda, CA; d. 1994	Spiro T. Agnew, Gerald R. Ford	1969-1974	Republican
Gerald Rudolph Ford b. 1913, Omaha, NE	Nelson Rockerfeller	1974-1977	Republican
James Earl Carter, Jr. b. 1924, Plains, GA	Walter Mondale	1977-1981	Democratic
Ronald Wilson Reagan b. 1911, Tampico, IL	George H. W. Bush	1981-1989	Republican
George Herbert Walker Bush b. 1924, Milton, MA	Dan Quayle	1989-1993	Republican
William Jefferson Clinton b. 1946, Hope, AR	Albert Gore	1993-2001	Democratic
George Walker Bush b. 1946, New Haven, CT	Richard Cheney	2001-	Republican

Although he is not the youngest man to become president, he (b. 1946) and Vice President Al Gore (b. 1948) hold the title for the youngest winning ticket in history. (At 42, Theodore Roosevelt was the youngest man to become president, when he succeeded William McKinley after McKinley's death; John F. Kennedy, at 43, was the youngest elected president.) In 1992, the team became the only all-Baptist ticket and the first all-southern ticket to win the presidential race since 1828—when Democrats Andrew Jackson and John C. Calhoun were elected president and vice president, respectively. Beyond these presidential firsts, Clinton is also the youngest ex-governor in U.S. history. Other less-glamorous firsts include: the first elected president to be impeached, the first to be sanctioned for lying in court, the first sitting president to be subpoenaed, and the first sitting president served with formal legal ethics complaints. He is also the only president to have used the line item veto.

THE EXECUTIVE OFFICE, EXECUTIVE DEPARTMENTS AND INDEPENDENT AGENCIES AND COMMISSIONS

What is the **Executive Office of the President**?

The Executive Office is more like an umbrella agency than an individual office. As the president's right hand, the Executive Office embodies the White House Office (which contains more than 400 staff members), as well as about a dozen separate agencies, or offices, staffed by the president's most trusted advisers and assistants.

Which **offices** are included in the Executive Office of the President?

The Executive Office includes various offices that directly assist the president. These include the Council of Economic Advisers, the Council on Environmental Quality, the Domestic Policy Council, the National Economic Council, the National Security Council, the Office of Administration, the Office of Faith-Based and Community Initiatives; the Office of Homeland Security; the Office of Management and Budget; the Office of National AIDS Policy; the Office of National Drug Control Policy; the President's Foreign Intelligence Advisory Board; the Office of the United States Trade Representative; and the White House Military Office.

What is the role of the **White House staff**?

The White House office is the workplace of the White House staff—key personnel and political staff whose offices are located in the East and West Wings of the White House.

The White House staff exists to help the president carry out the role of chief executive officer. The president's more than 400 staff are directed by the chief of staff. The staff includes the president's most trusted aides, the counselor to the president, a number of senior advisors, and top officials who work with the president in the areas of foreign policy, the economy, national health care, the media, and defense. It also includes the president's press secretary, the president's physician, and the staff of the first lady.

What is the **president's cabinet**?

The president's cabinet has been commonly regarded as an institution whose existence has relied more upon custom than law. Article II, Section 2 of the Constitution states that the president "may require the Opinion, in writing, of the principal Officer in each of the executive Departments, upon any subject relating to the Duties of their respective Offices." The historical origins of the cabinet can be traced to the first president, George Washington. After the First Congress created the State, Treasury, and War Departments and established the Office of the Attorney General, Washington made appropriate appointments and, subsequently, found it useful to meet with the heads, also known as secretaries, of the executive departments. The cabinet could act as the president's primary advisory group; in practice, however, presidents have used it, along with other advisors and ad hoc arrangements, as they deemed necessary.

Who are the **cabinet members**?

Traditionally, the membership of the cabinet has consisted of the heads of the executive departments, such as the Department of Defense and the Department of Energy. All departments are headed by a secretary, except the Department of Justice, which is headed by the attorney general. From the earliest days, presidents have also included others in cabinet meetings. In recent years, the president's chief of staff, the director of the Central Intelligence Agency, and the director of the Office of Management and Budget, among others, have been accorded cabinet rank.

How are cabinet members **chosen**?

The president appoints each head of the 14 executive departments. While each of these appointments is subject to confirmation by the Senate, rejections are rare. Many factors influence whom the president chooses: appointees are generally members of the president's party, those who played a role in the president's recent campaign, or those who have outstanding professional qualifications and personal experience related to the appointed position. In broad terms, the president also takes into account geographic location—thus, the secretary of the interior is often from the western United States, where most of the department's work is executed—as well as personal characteristics, such as gender and race.

How many **women and minorities** have served in the president's cabinet to date?

Including President George W. Bush's current administration, 18 women, 12 African Americans, 5 Hispanics, and 2 Asian Americans have held cabinet posts. While President Bill Clinton chose more women, more African Americans, and more Hispanics than any of his predecessors, Bush's administration followed suit with a broad mix of women and people of color. Bush's cabinet includes three women: Secretary of Agriculture Ann M. Veneman, Secretary of Interior Gale Norton, and Secretary of Labor Elaine Chao; two African Americans, Secretary of State Colin Powell and Secretary of Education Rod Paige; and two Asian Americans, Secretary of Labor Elaine Chao and Secretary of Transportation Norman Mineta. In addition, Mineta served as secretary of commerce under President Clinton, becoming the first Asian American to ever serve in a president's cabinet.

How are **executive departments and agencies** created?

Executive departments, like the Department of Defense or the Department of Justice, must be created by statute. Today there are 14 executive departments. On the other hand, agencies in the executive branch may be created by a variety of means: statute, internal departmental reorganizations, or, in some cases, presidential directive. In his constitutional capacity as chief executive or commander in chief, or by delegation of authority by Congress, the president can create various agencies or units by executive order. All agencies, however, must ultimately be given a statutory authority if they are to receive appropriations or their decisions are to have legal force.

What is the **new cabinet-level department** President Bush introduced during his presidency?

In an effort to defend the United States from terrorist attacks, eliminate security gaps, and unite Washington in its defense of the country, in June 2002 President George W. Bush proposed creating a cabinet-level department to oversee homeland defense. Dubbed the Department of Homeland Security, Bush's new agency would be charged with overseeing all aspects of homeland defense: protecting the nation's borders, ensuring airline security, responding to emergencies, and analyzing potential terrorist threats to the United States. If approved by Congress, the Department of Homeland Security would encompass agencies from eight existing cabinet departments, including the Immigration and Naturalization Service, the Border Patrol, the Coast Guard, and the Transportation Security Administration. At a cost of $37 billion, the new department would be the largest overhaul to the national government since 1947, when the Department of Defense was created. Bush's new agency would become the third-largest cabinet department, and the first new one since 1989, when the Department of Veterans Affairs was formed. Tom Ridge, Bush's chief advisor on homeland defense, is the top contender for the position of department secretary.

What are the **14 cabinet departments** currently in place?

As of June 2002, the following departments make up the president's cabinet: Department of Agriculture, Department of Commerce, Department of Defense, Department of Education, Department of Energy, Department of Health and Human Services, Department of Housing and Urban Development, Department of the Interior, Department of Justice, Department of Labor, Department of State, Department of Transportation, Department of the Treasury, and Department of Veterans Affairs. The descriptions of these departments and their individual agencies, as written in the following questions, reflect pre-restructuring attempts.

What is the Department of Agriculture?

Created in 1862, the U.S. Department of Agriculture (USDA) is one of the country's oldest federal departments. The USDA supports agricultural production to ensure fair prices and stable markets for producers and consumers, works to improve and maintain farm income, and helps to develop and expand markets abroad for agricultural products. The department attempts to curb poverty, hunger, and malnutrition by issuing food stamps to low-income individuals and families; by sponsoring educational programs on nutrition; and by administering other food assistance programs, primarily for children, expectant mothers, and the elderly. It maintains production capacity by helping landowners protect the soil, water, forests, and other natural resources. The USDA administers rural development, credit, and conservation programs that are designed to implement national growth policies, and it conducts scientific and technological research in all areas of agriculture. Through its inspection and grading services, the USDA ensures standards of quality in food for sale.

What is the **Department of Commerce**?

Created in 1903 as the Department of Commerce and Labor, which split into two separate departments in 1913, the Department of Commerce serves to promote the nation's international trade, economic growth, and technological advancement. It offers assistance and information to increase U.S. competitiveness in the global marketplace; administers programs to create new jobs and to foster the growth of minority-owned businesses; and provides statistical, economic, and demographic information for business and government planners.

The department is made up of a variety of agencies. The National Institute of Standards and Technology, for example, promotes economic growth by working with industry to develop and apply technology, measurements, and standards. The National Oceanic and Atmospheric Administration, which includes the National Weather Service, works to improve understanding of the earth's environment and to conserve the nation's coastal and marine resources. The Patent and Trademark Office promotes the progress of science and the useful arts by securing for authors and inventors the exclusive right to their creations and discoveries. The National Telecommunications and Information Administration advises the president on telecommunications policy and works to foster innovation, encourage competition, create jobs, and provide consumers with better quality telecommunications at lower prices.

What does the **Department of Defense** do?

The Department of Defense was created in 1947 with the merger of the Department of War (established in 1789), the Department of the Navy (established in 1798), and the Department of the Air Force (established in 1947). Headquartered in the Pentagon, the Department of Defense is responsible for all matters relating to the nation's military security. It provides the military forces of the United States, which consist of more than one million men and women on active duty. They are backed, in case of emergency, by 1.5 million members of state reserve components, known as the National Guard. The National Security Agency, which coordinates, directs, and performs highly specialized intelligence activities in support of U.S. government activities, also comes under the direction of the Department of Defense.

The department directs the separately organized military departments of the U.S. Army, U.S. Navy, U.S. Marine Corps, and U.S. Air Force, as well as the four military service academies and the National War College, the Joint Chiefs of Staff, and several specialized combat commands. The Defense Department maintains forces overseas to meet treaty commitments, to protect the nation's outlying territories and commerce, and to provide air combat and support forces. Nonmilitary responsibilities include flood control, development of oceanographic resources, and management of oil reserves. Although the secretary of defense is a member of the cabinet, the secretaries of the army, navy, and air force are not.

Why is the **Department of Education** necessary?

While schools are primarily a state responsibility in the U.S. system of education, the Department of Education provides national leadership to address critical issues in American education and serves as a clearinghouse of information to help state and local decision makers improve their schools. Created in 1979, and formerly part of the Department of Health, Education, and Welfare, the department establishes policy for and administers federal aid-to-education programs, including student loan programs, programs for disadvantaged and disabled students, and vocational programs. In the 1990s, the Department of Education focused on raising standards of education for all students; improving teaching; involving parents and families in children's education; making schools safe, disciplined, and drug-free; increasing access to financial aid for students to attend college; and helping all students become technologically literate.

What does the **Department of Energy** do?

Created in 1977 as the result of growing concern over the nation's energy problems of the 1970s, the Department of Energy assumed the functions of several government agencies already engaged in the energy field. Staff offices within the Energy Department are responsible for the research, development, and demonstration of energy technology; energy conservation; civilian and military use of nuclear energy; regulation of energy production and use; pricing and allocation of oil; and a central energy data collection and analysis program. The Department of Energy protects the nation's environment by setting standards to minimize the harmful effects of energy production and by conducting environmental and health-related research, such as studies of energy-related pollutants and their effects on biological systems.

What is the role of the **Department of Health and Human Services**?

Established in 1979, when the Department of Health, Education, and Welfare (created in 1953) was split into separate entities, the Department of Health and Human Services (HHS) directly touches the lives of millions of Americans. The department oversees 300-plus programs. Its largest component, the Health Care Financing Administration, administers the Medicare and Medicaid programs, which jointly provide health care coverage to more than 60 million elderly, disabled, and low-income individuals, including 15 million children. HHS also administers the National Institutes of Health (NIH), the world's premier medical research organization, supporting some 30,000 research projects on diseases like cancer, Alzheimer's, diabetes, arthritis, heart ailments, and AIDS. Other HHS agencies ensure the safety and effectiveness of the nation's food supply and drugs; work to prevent outbreaks of communicable diseases; provide health services to the nation's American Indian and Alaska Native populations; and help to improve the quality and availability of substance abuse prevention, addiction treatment, and mental health services.

What does the **Department of Housing and Urban Development** do?

Created in 1965, the Department of Housing and Urban Development (HUD) manages programs that assist community development and help provide affordable housing for low-income families. Fair housing laws, administered by HUD, are designed to ensure that individuals and families can buy a home without being subjected to discrimination. HUD directs mortgage insurance programs that help families become homeowners and a rent-subsidy program for low-income families that otherwise could not afford appropriate housing. In addition, it operates programs that aid neighborhood rehabilitation, preserve urban centers, and encourage the development of new communities. HUD also protects the home buyer in the marketplace and fosters programs to stimulate the housing industry.

The Drug Enforcement Administration (DEA), an agency of the Department of Justice, is charged with enforcing laws involving narcotics and controlled substances and stopping drug-trafficking operations.

What is the **Department of the Interior**?

Created in 1849 as the nation's principal conservation agency, the Department of the Interior is responsible for most of the federally owned public lands and natural resources in the United States. The U.S. Fish and Wildlife Service administers 500 wildlife refuges, dozens of wetland management districts, dozens of national fish hatcheries, and a network of wildlife law enforcement agents. The National Park Service administers more than 370 national parks and monuments, scenic parkways, riverways, seashores, recreation areas, and historic sites, through which it preserves America's natural and cultural heritage. Through the Bureau of Land Management, the department oversees the land and resources—from rangeland vegetation and recreation areas to timber and oil production—of millions of hectares of public land located primarily in the West. The Bureau of Reclamation manages scarce water resources in the semiarid western United States. The department regulates mining in the United States, assesses mineral resources, and has major responsibility for protecting and conserving the trust resources of American Indian and Alaska Native tribes.

What is the function of the **Department of Justice**?

Formed in 1870, the Department of Justice represents the U.S. government in legal matters and courts of law, and renders legal advice and opinions upon request to the president and to the heads of the executive departments. The Justice Department is headed by the attorney general of the United States, the chief law enforcement officer of the federal government. Its Federal Bureau of Investigation (FBI) is the principle law enforcement body for federal crimes, and its Immigration and Naturalization Service (INS) administers immigration laws. A major agency within the department is the Drug Enforcement Administration (DEA), which enforces narcotics and controlled substances laws, and tracks down major drug trafficking organizations.

In addition to giving aid to local police forces, the department directs U.S. district attorneys and marshals throughout the country, supervises federal prisons and other penal institutions, and investigates and reports to the president on petitions for paroles and pardons. The Justice Department is also linked to INTERPOL, the International Criminal Police Organization, charged with promoting mutual assistance between law enforcement agencies in almost 200 member countries.

What is the job of the **Department of Labor**?

Established in 1913, the Department of Labor promotes the welfare of wage earners in the United States, helps improve working conditions, and fosters good relations between labor and management. It administers federal labor laws through such agencies as the Occupational Safety and Health Administration (OSHA), the Employment Standards Administration, and the Mine Safety and Health Administration. These laws guarantee workers' rights to safe and healthy working conditions, hourly wages and overtime pay, freedom from employment discrimination, unemployment insurance, and workers' compensation for on-the-job injury. The department also protects workers' pension rights, sponsors job training programs, and helps workers find jobs. Its Bureau of Labor Statistics monitors and reports changes in employment, prices, and other national economic measurements.

What are the functions of the **State Department**?

Created in 1789, the Department of State advises the president, who has overall responsibility for formulating and executing the foreign policy of the United States. The department assesses American overseas interests, makes recommendations on policy and future action, and takes necessary steps to carry out established policy. It maintains contacts and relations between the United States and foreign countries, advises the president on recognition of new foreign countries and governments, negotiates treaties and agreements with foreign nations, and speaks for the United States in the United Nations and in other major international organizations. The department maintains more than 250 diplomatic and consular posts around the world. In 1999, the Department of State integrated the U.S. Arms Control and Disarmament Agency and the U.S. Information Agency into its structure.

What is the **Department of Transportation**?

Formed in 1966, the Department of Transportation establishes the nation's overall transportation policy through almost a dozen operating units that manage highway planning, development, and construction; urban mass transit; railroads; civilian aviation; and the safety of waterways, ports, highways, and oil and gas pipelines. For example, the Federal Aviation Administration operates a network of airport towers, air traffic control centers, and flight service stations across the country. The Federal Highway Administration provides financial assistance to the states to improve the interstate highway system, urban and rural roads, and bridges. The National Highway Traffic Safety Administration establishes safety performance standards for motor vehicles and motor vehicle equipment. The Maritime Administration operates the U.S. merchant marine fleet. The U.S. Coast Guard, the nation's primary maritime law enforcement and licensing agency, conducts search and rescue missions at sea, combats drug smuggling, and works to prevent oil spills and ocean pollution.

What does the **Department of the Treasury** do?

Created in 1789, the Department of the Treasury is responsible for serving the fiscal and monetary needs of the nation. The department performs four basic functions: it formulates financial, tax, and fiscal policies; serves as financial agent for the U.S. government; provides specialized law enforcement services; and manufactures coins and currency. The Treasury Department reports to Congress and the president on the financial condition of the government and the national economy. It regulates the sale of alcohol, tobacco, and firearms in interstate and foreign commerce; supervises the printing of stamps for the U.S. Postal Service; operates the Secret Service, which protects the president, the vice president, their families, and visiting dignitaries and heads of state; suppresses counterfeiting of U.S. currency and securities; and administers the Customs Service, which regulates and taxes the flow of goods into the country. The department includes the Office of the Comptroller of the Currency, the Treasury official who executes the laws governing the operation of approximately 2,900 national banks. The Internal Revenue Service (IRS) is responsible for the determination, assessment, and collection of taxes—the source of most of the federal government's revenue.

Why is the **Secret Service** part of the Department of the Treasury?

Although it may seem strange today that the Secret Service falls under the jurisdiction of the Department of the Treasury, the hierarchy is based in historical logic. During the Civil War, approximately one-third of all the currency in circulation was counterfeit, there were then about 1,600 state banks designing and printing their own notes, and there were approximately 4,000 varieties of counterfeit notes—making it difficult to detect a counterfeit note from a genuine note. While officials believed that the adoption of a national currency in 1863 would solve the counterfeiting problem, soon the nation-

Secret Service agents accompany President Gerald Ford's motorcade in Milwaukee, Wisconsin, in 1976.

al currency was counterfeited. Because it became necessary for the government to take enforcement measures, the Secret Service became a bureau of the Treasury Department on July 5, 1865, with its major responsibility being the elimination of counterfeiting.

Soon after that point the Secret Service began to evolve into the entity we are familiar with today. Public sentiment after the assassination of President William McKinley in 1901 demanded better protection of the nation's chief executive. Because the Secret Service was the only law enforcement agency of the federal government at the time, it was logical to place the protection of the president under its jurisdiction. This unique mission officially became a permanent responsibility of the Secret Service in 1906. Today the Secret Service also protects various other important government officials.

What does the **Department of Veterans Affairs** do?

Originally established as an independent agency in 1930 and elevated to cabinet level in 1989, the Department of Veterans Affairs dispenses benefits and services to eligible veterans of U.S. military service and their dependents. The Veterans Health Administration provides hospital and nursing-home care and outpatient medical and dental services through a range of medical centers, retirement homes, clinics, nursing homes, and Vietnam Veteran Outreach Centers across the United States. The Department of Veteran Affairs also conducts medical research in such areas as aging, women's health issues, AIDS, and post-traumatic stress disorder. The Veterans Benefits Administration (VBA) oversees claims for disability payments, pensions, specially adapted housing, and other services, while the VA's National Cemetery System provides burial services, headstones, and markers for veterans and eligible family members at more than 100 cemeteries throughout the United States.

Who are the current **cabinet secretaries**?

The cabinet includes the vice president of the United States and, by law, the heads, or secretaries, of 14 executive departments. Under the Bush administration, the following people make up the cabinet: Agriculture Secretary Ann Veneman; Commerce Secretary Don Evans; Defense Secretary Donald Rumsfeld; Education Secretary Rod Paige; Energy Secretary Spencer Abraham; Health and Human Services Secretary Tommy Thompson; Housing and Urban Development Secretary Mel Martinez; Interior Secretary Gale Norton; Attorney General John Ashcroft; Labor Secretary Elaine Chao; Secretary of State Colin Powell; Transportation Secretary Norman Mineta; Treasury Secretary Paul O'Neill; and Veterans Affairs Secretary Anthony Principi.

In addition, cabinet-level rank also has been accorded to Andrew H. Card, Jr., the president's chief of staff; Christine Todd Whitman, administrator of the Environmental Protection Agency; Tom Ridge, director of the Office of Homeland Security; Mitchell E. Daniels, Jr., director of the Office of Management and Budget; John Walters, director of the Office of National Drug Control Policy; and Robert B. Zoellick, the United States Trade Representative.

What are **independent agencies** and **regulatory commissions**?

In general, the independent agencies comprise all federal administrative agencies not included under the executive departments or under the direct, immediate authority of the president. These many and diverse organizations range from regulatory commissions to government corporations, such as the U.S. Postal Service, to a wide variety of boards and foundations. Some of these, such as the Smithsonian Institution, are long standing, while others have been created over the years as the federal government has increased its responsibilities. Independent regulatory commissions have been established by Congress—beginning in the 1880s with the now-defunct Interstate Commerce Commission—to regulate some aspect of the U.S. economy. Among these are the Securities and Exchange Commission, the Federal Communications Commission, the Federal Trade Commission, and the Nuclear Regulatory Commission. Such agencies are not independent of the U.S. government and are subject to the laws that are approved by Congress and executed by the president.

What are the various **independent agencies** in operation today?

Called independent because they are not part of the executive departments, the more than 100 independent agencies of the federal government vary widely in scope and purpose. While some are regulatory groups with powers to supervise certain sectors of the economy, others provide special services either to the government or to the people. In most cases, the agencies have been created by Congress to deal with matters that have become too complex for the scope of ordinary legislation. Among the most important independent agencies: the Central Intelligence Agency (CIA); the Environmental Protection Agency (EPA); the Federal Communications Commission (FCC); the Federal Emergency Management Agency (FEMA); the Federal Reserve Board; the Federal Trade Commission (FTC); the General Services Administration (GSA); the Immigration and Naturalization Service (INS); the National Aeronautics and Space Administration (NASA); the National Archives and Records Administration (NARA); the National Labor Relations Board (NLRB); the National Science Foundation (NSF); the Office of Personnel Management (OPM); the Peace Corps; the Securities and Exchange Commission (SEC); the Small Business Administration (SBA); the Social Security Administration (SSA); the United States Agency for International Development (USAID); and the United States Postal Service (USPS).

How has the **United States Postal Service** changed from a federal department to a quasi-public corporation?

The United States Postal Service (USPS) is operated by an autonomous public corporation that replaced the Post Office Department in 1971. In response to years of financial neglect and fragmented control that had impaired the Post Office Department's ability to function, in May 1969 Postmaster General Winton M. Blount proposed a basic reorganization of the Post Office Department, then one of the federal government's many departments. President Richard Nixon asked Congress to pass the Postal Service Act of 1969, calling for removal of the Postmaster General from the Cabinet and creation of a self-supporting postal corporation wholly owned by the federal government. As a result, the Post Office Department was transformed into the United States Postal Service, an independent establishment of the executive branch of the government of the United States.

The U.S. Postal Service is responsible for the collection, transportation, and delivery of the mail, and for the operation of thousands of local post offices across the country. It delivers hundreds of millions of messages and billions of dollars in financial transactions each day to eight million businesses and 250 million Americans. It also provides international mail service through the Universal Postal Union and other agreements with foreign countries. An independent Postal Rate Commission, also created in 1971, sets the rates for different classes of mail.

What is the **Presidential Transition Act**?

One of the key responsibilities of a new administration is staffing the executive branch. A number of activities were underway during the Clinton administration to ease the burden of presidential appointees and better prepare them for leading the federal government. The Presidential Transition Act of 2000, signed into law by President Bill Clinton on October 12, 2000, provides for an efficient transfer of authority from one administration to the next and outlines specific roles for a number of federal agencies, including the General Services Administration (GSA), the Office of Personnel Management, the Office of Presidential Personnel, and the U.S. Archivist. As a result of the law, a transition-coordinating council was specifically created to provide the president-elect's team with orderly transition to the new administration.

Why has the government been likened to a **bureaucracy**?

When referencing the structure of the Federal Bureau of Investigation (FBI) before the Senate Judiciary Committee in June 2002, FBI agent Coleen Rowley used the concept of an "ever-growing bureaucracy" of "endless, needless paperwork" to describe the agency. The word "bureaucracy," in the sense that it is any large and complexly organized administrative body, has often been used to describe the federal government. In fact, many Americans simply use the word "bureaucracy" as a synonym for big government. The sense of the word, however, implies more than that. A bureaucracy is hierarchical in structure, meaning that the people and the top dictate work to the people at the bottom, and every person follows a chain of command. Each person in the bureaucracy has a specialized job to do, and there are definitive rules and regulations that mandate how the organization is run. In these ways, the federal bureaucracy encompasses all of the agencies, people, and procedures through which the government operates—from the way that it makes and execute public policy to the way that it deals with the public and the media.

What is the discussion in recent years to **"downsize" government**?

With nearly three million employees with a combined payroll of over $190 billion, it's easy to see why Americans have argued to "downsize" the federal government—that is, to decrease the number of personnel and simplify the machinery through which the executive branch operates in an effort to expedite decision-making processes and implement policy more effectively. However, when one considers the size and scope of the executive branch, as well as the many duties it carries out for the American public, it's hard to imagine how this task might be accomplished. Many argue that it is the nearly 150 independent agencies within the executive branch that make Americans' lives manageable: by delivering the mail, collecting taxes, regulating business procedures, and administering Social Security programs. Although there has been a concerted effort among most recent administrations to cap "big government," the daily workings of the federal government don't appear to be downsizing anytime soon.

THE LEGISLATIVE BRANCH

THE U.S. CONGRESS: ITS POWERS AND FUNCTIONS

What is **Congress**?

The Congress of the United States is the legislative (lawmaking) and oversight (government policy review) body of the country's national government. The U.S. Congress consists of two houses—the Senate and the House of Representatives. A member of the Senate is referred to as a senator, and a member of the House of Representatives is called a representative or congressman or congresswoman. The term "member of Congress" is also used to refer to a representative.

How is Congress **divided** and why?

As part of the government's overall system of checks and balances, Article I of the Constitution grants all legislative powers of the federal government to a Congress divided into two chambers: a Senate and a House of Representatives. In the early republic, senators were not elected by direct vote of the people but chosen by state legislatures and viewed as representatives of their home states. Their primary duty was to ensure that their states were treated equally in all legislation. The delegates to the Constitutional Convention reasoned that if two separate groups—one representing state governments and one representing the people—must both approve every proposed law, there would be little danger of Congress passing legislation hurriedly or aimlessly. One house could always check the other, just like in the British Parliament. The passage of the Seventeenth Amendment allowed for direct election of the Senate by the people, although did not substantially alter this balance of power between the two houses.

The Capitol Building in Washington, DC, considered to be a premier symbol of democracy, houses the U.S. Congress.

What is meant by the term **"bicameralism"**?

Bicameralism is the name given to a legislative system made up of two separate chambers, usually called the upper house and the lower house, each serving as a check on the other's power. In most cases, the members of each chamber are elected on a different basis. For example, in the U.S. Congress, two senators are elected from each of the 50 states, whereas the number of House members assigned to each state varies according to the state's population. Examples of bicameral legislatures include the Australian Parliament, the Parliament of Great Britain, the Russian Federal Assembly, the South African Parliament, and the National Congress of Chile.

Are the terms **"Congress"** and **"legislative branch"** interchangeable?

No. Although people often use these two words interchangeably, Congress is actually a part of the larger legislative branch of the federal government. In addition to Congress—the House of Representatives and the Senate—the legislative branch includes the architect of the Capitol, the Government Printing Office (GPO), the Library of Congress, and the legislative support agencies. The architect's main duties involve the construction, maintenance, and renovation of the Capitol Building as well as the congressional office buildings and other structures in the Capitol complex, such as the Library of Congress buildings. The GPO publishes the Congressional Record, congressional committee hearings and reports, and other congressional documents, as well as many executive branch publications. In addition to providing library services, research, and analysis to Congress, the Library of Congress is also the national library. It houses premier national book, map, and manuscript collections, serves a major role assisting local libraries in book cataloging and other services, and supervises the implementation of U.S. copyright laws. In addition, three support agencies—the Congressional Budget Office, the Congressional Research Service in the Library of Congress, and the General Accounting Office—directly assist Congress in the performance of its duties.

What are the **characteristics** of Congress?

The U.S. Congress is known primarily as the nation's lawmaking body. However, in order to make laws and carry out its other responsibilities as the "first branch of government" in a democracy like the United States, several inherent features are necessary. Norman J. Ornstein, author of *The Role of the Legislature in Western Democracies*, outlines several of these characteristics. The first and foremost characteristic of Congress is its intrinsic link to the citizens of the nation, otherwise known as *representation*. As John Stuart Mill wrote in 1862, in a representative democracy the legislature acts as the eyes, ears, and voice of the people: "[T]he proper office of a representative assembly is to watch and control the government: to throw the light of publicity on its acts, to compel a full exposition and justification of all of them which any one considers questionable; to censure them if found condemnable…." The U.S. Congress represents a permanent and independent link between the public and the government. Through elections, petitions, lobbying, and participation in political parties and interest groups, citizens can express their will and affect the outcomes of the legislative process.

In addition to representing the public will, Congress has other distinguishing features. For instance, it operates under a system of *collective decision making*. A large group of individuals come together, at least in theory, as equals. While some members may assume leadership positions or special responsibilities, each member's vote is weighed equally. In addition, Congress adopts policies and makes laws through the process of *deliberation*, and its decisions do not need to proceed from the rule of law or specific legal precedents, making Congress very different from the courts. In addition to the above, Congress performs a unique *educational* role. Individual legislators simplify complicated issues and define policy choices. They use their resources and expertise to filter information from many sources and to resolve conflicting ideological positions, ultimately presenting their constituents with clear-cut options. This educational function has become increasingly important as society has become more complex, the scope of government activity has become more extensive, and the public has gained increased access to legislative proceedings, particularly via television and the Internet. Another defining characteristic of Congress is its *dual role of the legislators*. On the one hand, Congress makes laws that affect the entire nation and are presumably intended to be for the entire nation's well-being. On the other hand, its indi-

Senators and representatives assemble on the floor of the House to officially open the session of the 105th Congress in January 1997.

vidual members, the legislators, have a duty to represent the interests of their individual constituencies—a tension unique to a representative government, like the United States, that has districts.

How do the House of Representatives and the Senate **represent the people**?

Of the two chambers of Congress, the House of Representatives is the one considered closest to the electorate. Because members run for reelection every two years, representatives come to know their constituents well. They are more likely to reflect accurately the views of the local citizenry, advocate the needs of their districts, and be alert to changes in popular opinion. However, the Constitution's framers believed that these same characteristics might lead to a short-term view of what constitutes good public policy. For that reason, the Senate was constructed to protect against the popular sentiment of the day. Senators hold longer terms than representatives, running for election every six years. Moreover, the Senate is a continuing body, meaning that only one-third of its membership runs for reelection at any one time. This continuity and the longer term are meant to enable senators to resist the pressure of popular opinion and to serve as a restraining influence for House action. The framers expected senators to be older, wiser, and more deliberative than representatives and thus able to offer a long-term perspective on what makes beneficial and substantial public policy.

What are the **enumerated powers** of Congress?

Article I, Section 1 of the Constitution grants "all legislative powers" to Congress. The authority to make laws is regarded as Congress's most important power. Article I, Section 8 of the Constitution empowers Congress to perform a host of specific duties, known as Congress's enumerated, or express, powers. These are the power to levy taxes, collect revenue, pay debts, and provide for the general welfare; the power to borrow money; the power to regulate interstate and foreign commerce; the power to establish uniform rules of naturalization and bankruptcy; the power to coin money and regulate its value; the power to punish counterfeiters; the power to establish a postal system; the power to enact patent and copyright laws; the power to establish federal courts inferior to the Supreme Court; the power to declare war; the power to provide for the armed forces; the power to impeach and try federal officers; and the exclusive legislative power over the District of Columbia. Congress is also given the power to enact such laws as may be "necessary and proper" to implement its mandate in Article I. The power to enact laws is also contained in certain amendments to the Constitution. In addition, Article II, Section 2 grants the Senate the power to consent to the ratification of treaties and confirm the nomination of public officials. While a few of the powers outlined in Article I are outdated (such as the power to punish piracy), they nevertheless remain in effect.

What is the **"necessary and proper"** clause?

Article I, Section 8 of the Constitution grants Congress the authority to "make all Laws which shall be necessary and proper for carrying into Execution the foregoing powers, and all other powers vested by this Constitution in the government of the United States." This clause, when coupled with one or more of the specific enumerated powers outlined in Article I, Section 8, allows Congress to increase the scope of its authority and undertake responsibilities that are known as its *implied powers*. For example, the explicit power to tax and provide (spend) for the general welfare is implied to mean that Congress has the power to spend tax money for highways, public school aid, and Social Security—none of which are explicitly mentioned in the Constitution. Congress is also expressly given the power to raise an army; this express power assumes the implied power of specifying regulations concerning who can join the army. The "necessary and proper" clause is also known as the "elastic" clause because it has been expansively stretched and interpreted by the Supreme Court to fit almost any circumstance.

What are Congress's **implied powers**?

Congress's implied powers are justified by the "necessary and proper" clause of the Constitution, which grants Congress far-reaching powers to do its job. When discussing the scope of Congress's implied powers, scholars note several landmark Supreme Court cases. In *McCulloch v. Maryland* (1819) the Supreme Court ruled that the necessary and proper clause gave Congress the power to create a national bank (an implied power) as an aid to carrying out its enumerated borrowing and taxing powers. *U.S. v. Gettysburg Electric Railway Co.* (1896) considered whether Congress had the power to condemn a railroad's land in what was to be Gettysburg National Military Park, and found that the power to condemn the railroad's land was implied by the enumerated powers of Congress to declare war and equip armies because creation of the park strengthens the motives of the citizen to defend "the institutions of his country." A highly guarded implied power that is almost always mentioned when discussing Congress is its oversight function.

What are the limits to congressional authority?

The Tenth Amendment to the Constitution sets definite limits on congressional authority, by providing that powers not delegated to the national government are reserved to the states or to the people. In addition, the Constitution specifically forbids certain acts by Congress. It may not suspend the writ of habeas corpus—a requirement that those accused of crimes be brought before a judge or court to review the charges against them before being imprisoned—unless necessary in time of rebellion or invasion. In addition, Congress may not pass laws that condemn people for crimes or unlawful acts without a trial; pass any law that retroactively makes a specific act a crime; levy direct taxes on citizens, except on the basis of a census already taken; tax exports from any one state; provide specially favorable treatment in commerce or taxation to the seaports of any state or to the vessels using them; or authorize any titles of nobility.

What are the two **executive powers** the Constitution gives to the Senate?

While the Constitution assigns the House and Senate equal responsibility for such tasks as declaring war, assessing taxes, and making all laws necessary for the operation of the government, the Senate holds *exclusive* authority to advise and consent on treaties and review and approve or reject presidential appointees to executive and judicial branch posts. These two areas of authority are called the Senate's executive powers, or executive business, because these categories of business come from the president. From its earliest years, the Senate has wholeheartedly guarded these powers. In its history, the Senate has rejected 27 of 148 Supreme Court appointments but only 9 of more than 700 cabinet appointees. The Senate has rejected relatively few of the hundreds of treaties it has considered in its history.

What is **"advice and consent"**?

Under the Constitution, presidential nominations for executive and judicial posts take effect only when confirmed by the Senate, and international treaties become effective only when the Senate approves them by a two-thirds vote. The requirement for a two-thirds vote ensures that a treaty will need bipartisan support to be approved. These two functions of the Senate are said to be performed with the Senate's "advice and consent."

Does the House have any **exclusive powers**?

Yes. Article I, Section 7 gives special, exclusive powers to the House of Representatives. The constitutional provision that "all Bills for raising Revenue shall originate in the House of Representatives" is an adaptation of an earlier English practice. It was based on the principle that the national purse strings should be controlled by a body directly responsible to the people. Therefore, when the Constitution was written, the authority for initiation of revenue legislation was vested in the House of Representatives, where the members are subject to direct election every two years. However, the Constitution also guarantees the Senate's power to "propose or concur with Amendments as on other Bills." In addition to this exclusive power, only the House holds the power of impeachment; that is, the authority to charge the president, vice president, or other civil officers with "Treason, Bribery, or other high Crimes and Misdemeanors." Besides initiating the impeachment process, only the House can pass articles of impeachment.

What are **Congress's war powers**?

Although the Constitution states that the president is the commander in chief of the U.S. Army, Navy, and, when it is called into federal service, the National Guard, historically presidents have used this authority to commit U.S. troops without a formal declaration of war. However, Article I, Section 8 of the Constitution reserves to Congress the power to raise and support the armed forces as well as the sole authority to declare war. These competing powers have been the source of controversy between the legislative and executive branches over war making. In 1973, Congress enacted the controversial War Powers Resolution, which limits the president's authority to use the armed forces without specific congressional authorization, in an attempt to increase and clarify Congress's control over the use of the military. In addition, the armed forces operate under the doctrine of civilian control, which means that only the president or statutory deputies (the secretary and deputy secretary of defense) can order the use of force. The chain of command is structured to insure that the military cannot undertake actions without the approval or knowledge of the people of the United States.

What is the procedure to **commit America's military force to war**?

The Constitution provides Congress with the authority to declare war. This has occurred on only five occasions since 1789, the most recent being World War II. However, the president, as commander in chief, has implied powers to commit the nation's military forces, which has occurred on more than 200 occasions in U.S. history. Moreover, Congress may authorize the use of the military in specific cases through public law. The 1973 War Powers Resolution tried to clarify these respective roles of the president and Congress in cases involving the use of armed forces without a declaration of war. The president is expected to consult with Congress before using the armed forces "in every possible instance," and is required to report to Congress within 48 hours of introducing troops. According to the resolution, the use of the armed forces is to be terminated within 60 days, with a possible 30-day extension by the president, unless Congress acts during that time to declare war, enacts a specific authorization for use of the armed forces, extends the 60-to-90-day period, or is physically unable to meet as a result of an attack on the United States.

What is Congress's **oversight function**?

Congressional "oversight," or Congress's "watchful care" role, is one of the most effective jobs that Congress has adopted to influence the executive branch. It applies to cabinet departments, executive agencies, regulatory commissions, and the presidency. Congressional oversight of policy implementation and administration takes a variety of forms and utilizes various techniques. These range from specialized investigations by select committees to the use of extra-congressional mechanisms, such as offices of inspector general and study commissions. Because of its "watchdog" nature, the oversight power of Congress has helped to force officials out of office, change policies, and provide new statutory controls over the executive. Oversight is an integral part of the system of checks and balances between the legislative and executive branches, and as such is supported by a variety of authorities—the U.S. Constitution, public law, and chamber and committee rules.

Although Congress's oversight function takes many forms, it is primarily exercised through the following means: committee inquiries and hearings; formal consultations with and reports from the president; Senate advice and consent for presidential nominations and for treaties; House impeachment proceedings and subsequent Senate trials; and House and Senate proceedings under the Twenty-fifth Amendment in the event that the president becomes disabled or the office of the vice president becomes vacant. In addition, the oversight function covers informal meetings between legislators and executive officials; congressional membership on governmental commissions; and studies by congressional committees and support agencies such as the Congressional Budget Office, the General Accounting Office, and the Office of Technology Assessment.

What are Congress's **powers of investigation**?

One of the most important nonlegislative functions of Congress is the power to investigate. This power is usually delegated to committees—either to the standing committees, to special committees set up for a specific purpose, or to joint committees composed of members of both houses. Investigations are conducted to gather information on the need for future legislation, to test the effectiveness of laws already passed, to inquire into the qualifications and performance of members and officials of the other branches, and, on rare occasions, to lay the groundwork for impeachment proceedings. Frequently, committees call on outside experts to assist in conducting investigative hearings and to make detailed studies of issues.

The investigative power has certain associated powers. One is the power to publicize investigations and their results. Most committee hearings are open to the public and are widely reported in the mass media. Congressional investigations thus represent one important tool available to lawmakers to inform the citizenry and pique public interest in national issues. Congressional committees also have the power to compel testimony from unwilling witnesses and to cite for contempt of Congress witnesses who refuse to testify and for perjury those who give false testimony.

What role does Congress play in the **impeachment process**?

The president, vice president, and all civil officers of the United States are subject to impeachment, and their conviction results in an automatic removal from office. Under the Constitution, the House of Representatives has the power to impeach a government official, in effect serving as prosecutor. The Senate then holds the impeachment trial, serving as jury and judge, except in the impeachment of a president when the chief justice presides. Once the Senate votes for impeachment, there is no appeal. Congress's impeachment power is often considered the most serious power of Congress. Congress is so conscious of this power that impeachment proceedings have been initiated in the House only 62 times since 1789. Only 17 federal officers have been impeached: 2 presidents, 1 cabinet officer, 1 senator, and 13 federal judges. Sixteen cases have reached the Senate. Of these, two were dismissed before trial because the individuals had left office, seven ended in acquittal, and seven in conviction. Each of the seven Senate convictions involved a federal judge.

What role does Congress play in a **contested presidential election**?

In the case of a contested presidential election, the Constitution grants Congress two roles: to officially count the ballots and announce the results of the electoral college votes for president and vice president, and to elect the president and vice president if the electoral college fails to do so. The electoral college ballots for the November 2000 election were counted officially in a joint session of the U.S. Congress, held on January 6, 2001. Had no majority materialized behind one candidate, the House and Senate would have then, pursuant to the Constitution, proceeded immediately to an election for president and vice president, known formally as a "contingent election."

According to the Twelfth Amendment, in a contingent election the House is instructed to vote state by state, with each state receiving one vote. A majority of the

50 states is needed to win the presidency, or 26 votes. The Constitution is silent on how each state is to determine its one vote. Most likely, the representatives of each state would meet first to take a straw poll within their delegation. In the seven states that have only one representative, that member would make the decision for his or her state. In the Senate, the Constitution authorizes the vote to be taken member by member, with a majority of 51 votes from among the 100 senators needed to win the vice presidency. In the case of a tie, the president of the Senate (the current vice president of the United States) would break the tie.

What is Congress's scope of authority over the **independent agencies**?

Independent agencies—that is, all federal administrative agencies not included under the executive departments or under the direct, immediate authority of the president—include regulatory commissions, government corporations such as the U.S. Postal Service, and a wide variety of boards and foundations. Their commissioners, directors, and governors are appointed by the president and confirmed by the Senate. In addition to confirming the president's selections, independent regulatory commissions have long been established by Congress—beginning in the 1880s with the now defunct Interstate Commerce Commission—to regulate some aspect of the U.S. economy. These include the Securities and Exchange Commission, the Federal Communications Commission, the Federal Trade Commission, and the Nuclear Regulatory Commission. Such agencies are subject to the laws Congress generates and the president signs. In addition, almost all the independent regulatory commissions rely on government funding as determined by Congress. Finally, they are subject to periodic authorization and appropriations hearings in Congress, where their activities and operations are reviewed.

What was the makeup of the **107th Congress**?

The 107th Congress, which officially began on January 3, 2001, was made up of the following: In the House of Representatives, there were 221 Republicans, 211 Democrats, and two Independents, one aligned with each party. In the Senate, there were 49 Republicans, 50 Democrats, and one Independent. The average age of representatives was 53.4; of senators, 59. A substantial majority of members in both houses had a college education, and the dominant profession of members was law, followed by business. Protestants made up the majority religious affiliation. A record number of women—61 in the House and 13 in the Senate—served in this Congress, as well as substantial number of people of color: 21 Hispanics, 38 African Americans, 2 Native Americans, and 8 members of Asian or Native Hawaiian/Pacific Islander descent.

Who are some **"first" women** of Congress?

The first woman to serve in the Senate was 88-year-old Rebecca Latimer Felton of Georgia. Appointed to fill a vacancy in a symbolic concession to the women's suffrage movement, Felton served for just twenty-four hours, from noon on November 21 to noon on November 22, 1922. Because of her short term, she is very rarely mentioned as the first woman senator. Credit usually goes to Hattie Caraway, who was the first woman *elected* to the Senate. Although Caraway was first appointed to fill the vacancy caused by the death of her husband, Senator Thaddeus Caraway, she later won a special election in 1932. She ran for reelection, and won several times, ending her term in January 1945. As the first woman to chair a Senate standing committee, Caraway also takes credit as the first woman to preside over the Senate.

In 1916, social reformer Jeannette Rankin (R–MT) was the first woman elected to the House of Representatives—at a time when most states had yet to allow women the right to vote.

The first female member of the House of Representatives was Jeanette Rankin, a representative from Montana who served from 1917 to 1919. The first black woman elected to the House of Representatives was Shirley Chisholm, in 1968. In 1972 she ran for president of the United States on the Democratic ticket. Although Chisholm entered a substantial number of primaries, she only received 7 percent of the vote. She continued to serve as a representative until January 1983. Carol Moseley-Braun of Illinois was the first African American senator, a post she held for one term, from 1993 to 1999, before becoming the U.S. ambassador to New Zealand.

Who was the **first African American** to serve in Congress?

Hiram R. Revels, an African American born to free parents in 1827, was elected as a Republican to the Senate in 1870, after the Senate resolved a challenge to his credentials. A few members attempted to block his seat, arguing that Revels had not been a U.S. citizen for the nine years required of all senators. Although they maintained that black Americans had only become citizens with the passage of the 1866 Civil Rights Act—just four years earlier—Revels' supporters argued that he had been a voter many years earlier in Ohio and was therefore a citizen. He served as a senator for his state, Mississippi, until March 1871.

Who was the first Native American to serve in Congress?

In 1907, Charles Curtis of Kansas became the first American Indian to become a U.S. senator. He was also the first to serve as U.S. Republican Senate majority leader. In addition to being a "first," Curtis holds the record for the senator who served on the most subcommittees at one time. He resigned from the Senate in March 1929 to become President Herbert Hoover's vice president, thus becoming the first—and only—Native American vice president.

HOW CONGRESS OPERATES

What are the **duties** of members of Congress?

While Article I of the Constitution outlines the powers of Congress and the qualifications necessary for election, there is no guidance on the specific duties that each individual member must perform on a daily basis. However, the following represents typical member duties. First, each member is responsible for *local representation*, meaning that members advocate on behalf of the economic needs and political interests of their local district or state in Washington. Members analyze proposed legislation, keep in touch with local opinion leaders, and read and answer their mail and phone calls. Related to this are their *office management* duties, which involve managing a staff of up to 22 people for House members and an average of 38 people for senators. Each member is also responsible for *constituency service*, meaning that members alert their constituents to federal government actions and programs, and respond to requests for information about federal activities. Members provide their constituents with help in obtaining federal benefits and grants, and seek federal funds for local projects and programs. Members are also involved in *national policy making*, negotiating with their colleagues to reconcile various regional interests in order to create one national policy. Members meet to exchange views and information with officials from the executive branch, lobbyists, representatives from the business community, professionals, and academics. They analyze proposed legislation for its national implications. In addition, all members must stay involved in their *committee work*, which means developing expertise in the subject matter of their respective committee assignments. On average, a House member serves on two committees, and a senator serves on four. Members attend committee meetings and take testimony or mark-up legislations, prepare amendments to bills under committee consideration, and vote on motions, amendments, and decisions on whether or not to report a bill out from committee to the floor.

Members must stay on top of their *oversight and investigation* responsibilities, supervising the activities of government agencies and reviewing the expenditures and implementation of government programs. Members respond to scandals and crises through their work on investigatory panels. Their *work on the floor* involves participating in floor debate, offering amendments to bills in debate, casting floor votes on legislation, and preparing and delivering floor statements during legislative debates. *Congressional leadership responsibilities* include persuading fellow members to vote with their party, heading discussions with their party caucus to arrive at a common position on various issues, and negotiating agreements with the other party on when and how to consider specific bills on the floor. In addition, leaders negotiate with the president of the United States on legislation. Members play a *public role*, speaking on behalf of their party to the press, educating the public via meetings and public appearances, and serving as a role model for public service, civic responsibility, and voter participation. While all of this is happening, members of Congress must keep an eye toward the future, organizing and maintaining a *campaign for reelection* to office.

How many people does it take to do the work of Congress?

The U.S. Congress is comprised of the House of Representatives and the Senate, all told some 540 people. The Congress unites 435 representatives of the people, 100 Senators from 50 states, and 5 delegates from the territories of the United States—an assembly of 540 to make the laws that govern the nation and carry out their other powers and duties. In addition to this core group, more than 17,000 staff members serve individual members and committees.

What are the **terms and sessions** of Congress?

A given Congress begins at noon, January 3, of each odd-numbered year following a general election, unless by law a different day is designated. A Congress lasts for two years, with each year normally constituting a separate session. The Legislative Reorganization Act of 1970 requires Congress to adjourn *sine die* ("without a specified day") no later than July 31 of each year unless there is a declared war, or unless Congress otherwise provides. In odd-numbered years, Congress must take an August recess if it doesn't adjourn by July 31. Neither the House nor the Senate may adjourn for more than three days (excluding Saturdays, Sundays, and holidays) without the agreement of the other chamber. It has also become a common practice for Congress to adjourn after making provision for the House and Senate leaders to summon Congress back into session in emergency circumstances. Similarly, the president has constitutional authority to summon the Congress for a special session when necessary.

What are **joint sessions** and **joint meetings**?

Joint sessions and joint meetings are the two primary ways that a Congress convenes. Congress holds joint sessions to receive addresses from the president, such as State of the Union and other addresses, and to count electoral ballots for president and vice president. Congress also holds joint meetings to receive addresses from such dignitaries as foreign heads of state or heads of governments or from distinguished American citizens. Of the two types of gatherings, the joint session is the more formal and typically occurs upon adoption of a concurrent resolution passed by both Houses of Congress. The joint meeting, however, typically occurs when each of the two Houses adopts a unanimous agreement to recess in order to meet with the other legislative body. Since 1809, the practice has been to hold joint sessions and joint meetings in the Hall of the House of Representatives, the larger of the two chambers. Except for the first inauguration in 1789, in which Congress convened in joint session to inaugurate President George Washington, these special occasions have occurred outside of the regular legislative calendars. Occasionally one chamber will convene a legislative session prior to attending the ceremony, but unless both do so and subsequently adjourn to attend the ceremony, the inauguration is not a joint session.

What are **party leaders**?

The political parties in the House and Senate, namely Republicans and Democrats, elect leaders to represent them on the floor, to advocate their policies and viewpoints, to coordinate their legislative efforts, and to help determine the schedule of legislative business. The leaders serve as spokespersons for their parties and for the House and Senate as a whole. Since the framers of the Constitution did not anticipate political parties, these leadership posts are not defined in the Constitution, but have evolved over time. The House, with its larger membership, required majority and minority leaders in the nineteenth century to expedite legislative business and to keep their parties united. The Senate did not formally designate party floor leaders until the 1920s, although several caucus chairs and committee chairs had previously performed similar duties.

In both Houses, the parties also elect assistant leaders, or "whips." The majority leader is elected by the majority-party conference (or caucus); the minority leader by the minority-party conference. Third parties rarely have enough members to warrant the need to elect their own leadership, and independents generally join one of the larger party organizations to receive committee assignments.

Are the majority leaders **elected** by their respective houses of Congress?

No. Rather, members of the majority party in the House, meeting in caucus or conference, select the majority leader. In a similar meeting, the minority-party members select their minority leader. In the Senate, the majority and minority parties also hold separate meetings to elect their leaders.

What is a **party caucus** or **party conference**?

A party caucus or conference is the name given to a meeting of all party members in the House or Senate, whether regular or specially called. The term "caucus" or "conference" can also mean the organization of all party members in the House or Senate. House Democrats refer to their organization as a "caucus." House and Senate Republicans and Senate Democrats call their three organizations "conferences." The caucus or conference officially elects party floor leaders, the party whips, and nominates each party's candidates for the Speakership or president pro tempore and other officers in the House or Senate.

The chairs of the party conferences and other subordinate party leaders are elected by vote of the conference or caucus at the beginning of each Congress. Regular caucus or conference meetings provide a forum in which party leaders and members can discuss party policy, pending legislative issues, and other matters of mutual concern. The party caucus or conference also traditionally establishes party committees with specialized functions. The caucus or conference may also decide to appoint "task forces" to perform research on a new policy proposal, or to assist the formal leadership in developing a party position on important legislation. Traditionally these task forces are disbanded once their work is complete.

How much are members of Congress **paid**?

As of January 2002, each senator and representative receives an annual salary of $150,000. The House and Senate majority and minority leaders earn more, $166,700. The Speaker of the House earns $192,600. Members of Congress are paid from the U.S. Treasury.

These figures would have seemed astronomical to the framers of the Constitution, who met in Philadelphia on June 26, 1787, to decide, among other things, the operations of the Congress of the United States. At that meeting they established the term of office and the source of compensation. Benjamin Franklin was very vocal about his view on Senate salaries. Since he believed the Senate should represent the nation's wealthy classes, if no salary were provided then only wealthy persons would serve. He warned that if the convention authorized salaries, the public might suspect it of having "carved out places" for the younger delegates who would be natural senators. When put to a vote, Franklin's proposal nearly won, but then the question arose as to who might pay the salaries if they were offered. Several delegates suggested the individual states. James Madison reminded them that this would destroy the principle that senators were to be "impartial umpires and Guardians of justice and General good," reflecting national as well as state interests. It would also ruin the plan for a six-year term, as states could in effect recall senators by withholding their salaries. This motion also failed. The framers subsequently decided that members of Congress should be paid out of the national treasury, but—in their wisdom—left it to the new Congress to decide how and how much.

Do members of Congress ever **change their party affiliation**?

During the nineteenth century, as political parties evolved, senators often changed parties or helped create new parties. However, twentieth- and twenty-first-century members of Congress—Republicans, Democrats, and independents alike—rarely changed their party affiliation. The most publicized recent example is James Jeffords, a senator from Vermont. Jeffords, who had served 26 years in Congress before making a switch, left the Republican Party in June 2001 to become an Independent. At the beginning of 2001, the Senate was equally divided between Democrats and Republicans. Jeffords' switch threw the Senate—however marginally—to the control the Democrats, thus changing the balance of the entire legislative body. Jeffords cited his desire to bring balance to the Senate's deliberative process (indeed the legislative agenda overall) as his primary reason for switching parties.

Along with Jeffords, Republican senator Strom Thurmond from South Carolina is cited in this category. A member of the Republican Party since 1964, Thurmond began his career as a Democrat. However, when the Democratic Party adopted a strong civil rights policy for its 1948 campaign, Thurmond ran for president on the States Right ("Dixiecrat") ticket, receiving 39 electoral votes, the third largest independent electoral vote in U.S. history. He then switched to the Democratic Party again in 1956, where he stayed until 1964. Other notables include Richard Shelby of Alabama, who made the switch from Democrat to Republican in 1994; Ben Nighthorse Campbell of Colorado, who made the switch from Democrat to Republican in 1995; and Bob Smith of New Hampshire, who went from Republican to Independent to Republican again, in 1999.

Are members of Congress **privileged from arrest**?

To some extent, yes. Article I, Section 6 of the Constitution states that senators and representatives "shall in all Cases, except Treason, Felony, and Breach of the Peace, be privileged from Arrest during their Attendance at the Session of their respective Houses, and in going to and returning from the same." The phrase "Treason, Felony, and Breach of the Peace" has been interpreted to mean all indictable crimes, and the Supreme Court has held that the privilege against arrest does not apply in any criminal cases.

Can members of Congress be **removed from office or disciplined for misconduct**?

Yes. The Constitution states that "Each House shall be the Judge of the ... Qualifications of its own Members ... [and may] punish its Members for disorderly Behaviour, and with the Concurrence of two thirds, expel a Member." Thus, disciplinary actions taken against a member are a matter of concern for that house alone. Each chamber has established a committee charged with reviewing allegations of misconduct against its members: the House Committee on Standards of Official Conduct and the Senate Ethics Committee. The Rules of the House and Senate also contain a Code of Official Conduct. The ethics committees review charges against a member filed by another member or by a private citizen.

What generally happens when members of Congress act inappropriately?

The expulsion of a member is the most severe form of discipline the House or Senate can impose. According to the Constitution, this action requires an affirmative vote of two-thirds of the members of the chamber voting, a quorum being present. Alternatively, the House may vote to "censure" a member for misconduct. Censuring requires only a majority vote, and, under party rules in the House, a censured member automatically loses any committee or party leadership positions held during that Congress. In the Senate, the terms "censure" and "denunciation" are used almost interchangeably for violations of this magnitude. A less severe form of disciplinary action is a "reprimand," again imposed by either chamber by a simple majority vote. Typically, reprimands are reserved for ethical violations that are minor, or appear to be unintentional on the part of the member. Additionally, members of Congress are subject to prosecution for treason, felony, or breach of the peace. Generally, when a member has been indicted for a felony, a "leave of absence" from any party or committee leadership position must be taken for as long as the charges are pending. Usually, the House or Senate will not initiate internal disciplinary action until the criminal proceedings against the member have been completed. In July 2002, Representative James Traficant (D–OH) became only the fifth member in history to be expelled from the House after his conviction on charges of racketeering, bribery, and tax evasion.

How do members of Congress differ from **delegates and resident commissioners**?

The post of delegate was established by ordinance from the Continental Congress and confirmed by a law of Congress. From the time of the early republic, the House of Representatives has admitted delegates from territories or districts organized by law. Delegates and resident commissioners may participate in House debate but they are not permitted to vote on the floor. All serve on committees of the House and have powers and privileges equal to other members in committee, including the right to vote in committee. The House profile of the 107th Congress has four delegates and one resident commissioner.

THE U.S. SENATE

Can anyone run for **Senate**?

Article I, Section 3 of the Constitution outlines the qualifications for members of the Senate. A senator must meet a higher level of qualifications than a representative. In order to run for office, a senator must be at least 30 years old, must have been a citizen of the United States for at least nine years, and must be an inhabitant of the state from which he or she is elected. Although most senator-elects are residents of their states and often longtime participants in their communities, under the inhabitant qualification it is not mandatory that the senator have lived in the state for any set length of time.

How many **senators** are there?

Article I of the Constitution states that the Senate "shall be composed of two senators from each State," making the Senate smaller than the House of Representatives. By the end of the 1st Congress in 1790, the Senate had only 26 members. The size of the Senate has grown with the growth of the country, and today 100 senators represent the 50 states.

What is **"equal representation"**?

Unlike members of the House of Representatives, U.S. senators do not have congressional districts. Rather, senators represent an entire state. Each state has two senators, thus giving each state "equal representation" in Congress.

How are **senators** elected?

Originally, the Constitution provided that state legislatures would elect senators, but in 1913 the Seventeenth Amendment established direct election of senators by "the people." Since that time, voters in each state cast their ballots for their senator of choice at the regularly scheduled November elections.

How long is a senator's **term of office**?

Under the Constitution, each state is entitled to two senators, each serving a six-year term. Senate terms are staggered and the Senate is a continuous body, which means that approximately one-third of the total membership of the Senate is elected every two years. This prohibits every senator from being up for reelection at the same time. The continuity of the office and the longer term (as compared to a representative) was established by the Founding Fathers to ensure that senators would be better able to resist the pressures of the popular culture and restrain the House, a body often subject to public whim. However, because of the Constitution's fundamental principle of representative democracy—that the people should choose who governs them—there are no term limits for members of Congress. According to statistics of the 107th Congress, the average length of service in the Senate is 11 and a half years.

Has Congress ever considered **term limits** for its members?

Yes. Overall, the general public supports limiting the terms of senators and representatives. A 1996 poll by the Tarrance Group showed that 77 percent of Americans favor term limits, and these limits are supported in all regions of the United States and by both sexes and by blacks and Hispanics. Proponents of term limits say that "careerism" is the dominant motive of most legislators. By removing that motive, they argue, term limits would make Congress less swayed by public opinion and more deliberative. In addition, long-term congressional incumbency tends to distort representation. By becoming overly comfortable with the federal government and insulated from the public, members are more likely to develop interests in conflict with those of their constituents. Term limits therefore would work to keep elected officials more in touch with voters. Frequent rotation of elected officials would help assure continuous energy and innovative thinking. Despite public support, in May 1995 the Supreme Court ruled in *U.S. Term Limits v. Thornton* that state-imposed term limits on federal lawmakers are unconstitutional. Imposing a limit on the amount of times a member of Congress can run for reelection requires constitutional amendment. When the Senate debated in April 1996 on such an amendment, it fell far short of the two-thirds support needed to send it to the states for ratification. The amendment, if passed, would have provided for a uniform term limit of 12 years for both representatives and senators.

How did former first lady **Hillary Rodham Clinton** run for the Senate in New York, a state in which she had never lived?

The Constitution requires that a prospective senator be a resident of the state when elected. Clinton only needed to establish a residence in New York State at any time prior to election day to meet the constitutional requirement, and she did so when she purchased a home in Chappaqua. However, this issue of residency did not pass under the radar of the voting public, who questioned the length of Clinton's residency in the state, whether the residency was real or merely technical, and her overall familiarity with the Big Apple and its environs. Nevertheless, the voters of New York ultimately elected her. This wasn't the first time New York elected a "new" senator, having voted Daniel P. Moynihan (in 1977) and Robert F. Kennedy (in 1965) to the Senate, both of whom moved to New York only a short time before running for office.

How are **vacancies due to death, resignation, or expulsion** filled?

When a vacancy occurs in the Senate for any reason, the Seventeenth Amendment directs the governor of the state to call an election to fill such vacancy, and authorizes the legislature to make provision for an immediate appointment pending such election. Among the states, only Arizona does not allow the governor to make interim appointments, and instead requires a special election to fill any Senate vacancy. Prevailing practice in the states is that a special election to fill the vacancy is held at the time of the next statewide general election.

How did the **drafters of the Constitution** originally envision the role of the Senate?

Those who wrote the Constitution created the Senate as a safeguard for the rights of states and minority opinion in a system of government designed to allocate greater power at the national level. They modeled the Senate on colonial governors' councils and on the state senates that had evolved from them. The framers intended the Senate to be an independent body of responsible citizens who would share power with the president and the House of Representatives. In defining the position, James Madison explained that the Senate's role was "first to protect the people against their rulers [and] secondly to protect the people against the transient impressions into which they themselves might be led."

To balance power between the large and small states, the Constitution's drafters agreed that states would be represented equally in the Senate and in proportion to their populations in the House. Further preserving the authority of individual states, they provided that state legislatures would elect senators. To guarantee senators' independence from short-term political pressures, the framers assigned them a six-year term, three times as long as that of popularly elected House members. Responding to fears that a six-year Senate term would produce an aristocracy far from the will of the people, the framers specified that one-third of the terms would expire every two years, thus combining the principles of continuity and rotation in office. In the early weeks of the Constitutional Convention, the participants had tentatively decided to give the Senate sole power to make treaties and to appoint federal judges and ambassadors. As the convention drew to a close, however, they agreed to divide these powers between the Senate and the president. The framers determined that the ratification of a treaty would require a two-thirds vote, so that certain states could not unite against others, by a simple majority vote, for commercial or economic gain. In dealing with nominations, senators as statewide officials would be uniquely qualified to identify suitable candidates for federal judicial posts and would confirm them, along with cabinet secretaries and other key federal officials, by a simple majority vote.

What **two major changes** were made to the Senate in the twentieth century?

The first major change occurred in 1913 when, due to a Republican party split, the Democrats took control of the Senate and established the position of majority floor leader. They established this position to push through the party's legislative agenda.

Within a decade the post of party floor leader had begun to achieve the influence in conducting the Senate's business that it has today. A second major change in the Senate's structure occurred in 1913 with the ratification of the Constitution's Seventeenth Amendment, which provides for the direct popular election of senators. While the selection of senators by state legislatures had worked reasonably well for the Senate's first half-century, eventually deadlocks began to occur between the upper and lower houses of those bodies. This problem delayed state legislative business and deprived states of their full Senate representation. By the start of the twentieth century, direct popular election of senators had become a major objective for reformers who sought to remove control of government from the influence of special interests and corrupt state legislators. The amendment marked the only structural modification of the framers' original design of the Senate.

Who is the **president of the Senate** and what is his or her role?

Article I, Section 3 of the Constitution provides that "the Vice President of the United States shall be the President of the Senate." In this role, the vice president presides over the Senate, makes parliamentary rulings (which may be overturned by a majority vote of the Senate), and may cast tie-breaking votes. In the early republic, vice presidents presided on a regular basis, but in recent years they are present in the chair only when a close vote is anticipated, during major debates, or on important ceremonial occasions—such as the swearing in of newly elected senators or during joint sessions of Congress. In the absence of the vice president, the Senate elects a president pro tempore (meaning president "for the time being") to preside. In recent decades it has become traditional for this post to go to the senior senator from the majority party. The president pro tempore assigns other members of the majority party to preside by rotation during each day's proceedings. These senators and the president pro tempore retain their rights to vote on all issues before the body and to debate when they are not presiding.

Do senators have **individual seats** assigned to them?

Yes. The individual seats in the Senate are numbered and assigned on request of senators in order of their seniority. Democrats occupy the west side of the chamber on the vice president's right; Republicans sit across the main aisle to the vice president's left. There is no set rule for the seating of Independents. By custom, the majority and minority leaders occupy the front row seats on either side of the aisle, and the majority and minority whips occupy the seats immediately next to their party's leader.

Do the terms **"senior senator"** and **"junior senator"** apply to age or service?

The words "senior" or "junior" as applied to the two senators from a state refer to their length of continuous service in the Senate, and not to their ages. Thus, a senior senator may be younger in age than the junior senator from the same state.

NOTABLE SENATORS

Almost 1,900 men and women have served in the U.S. Senate since the formation of the national government. Many are considered notable based upon their influence on policy and history, others for breaking barriers or achieving "firsts." The following is a selective list of senators who fit that description.

John C. Calhoun (1782–1850) Early in his career, John C. Calhoun was a supporter of the American System, a program that provided federal government aid for internal improvements and tariff protection for American industries. In contrast, while serving as senator, the South Carolinian was an avid defender of slavery and states' rights, often engaging in dramatic debates with Daniel Webster on these issues. As a prominent spokesman for issues affecting the South, Calhoun led the adoption of the doctrine of nullification, which held that the states have the right to reject legislation that goes against their interests, ultimately leading to the Civil War.

Daniel Webster (1782–1852) A Federalist Party leader, Daniel Webster was one of his era's most prominent advocates of American nationalism. In 1827, as the Federalist Party was dissolving, Webster aligned himself with the Republican Party and was elected senator from Massachusetts. Webster's stance that the preservation of the Union was critical made him a key figure in the states' rights debates that led up to the Civil War, as evidenced by his famous speech in opposition to South Carolina senator Robert Hayne's support of the doctrine of nullification. A stirring speech Webster delivered on the terms of the Compromise of 1850, which in an effort to preserve the Union allowed for new territories joining the Union to determine themselves whether to allow slavery, is said to have played a critical role in its acceptance, although it ultimately cost Webster the support of antislavery forces from the North and members of his own party.

Henry Clay (1777–1852) After serving as Speaker of the House of Representatives from 1811–1814, 1815–1820, and 1823–1824, Henry Clay was elected to the Senate in 1831 as a leader of the National Republicans (precursor to the Whig Party). Clay has been called the Great Pacificator for his efforts toward unifying the nation during pre–Civil War turmoil, especially his work in achieving a compromise between President Andrew Jackson and legislators from the South who, based on the doctrine of nullification, opposed tariffs that they thought were detrimental to their interests.

Jefferson Davis (1808–1889) Future Confederate leader Jefferson Davis was senator from Mississippi from 1847–1851 and again from 1857–1861. As senator he often stated his support of slavery and states' rights, but he initially opposed the idea of secession from the Union as a means of maintaining the principles of the South. Even after steps were being taken toward secession, he attempted to keep the Southern states in the Union. When Mississippi seceded, he followed and withdrew from the Senate. In 1861, Davis was elected president of the Confederate States and was inaugurated in February 1862.

Hiram R. Revels (1827–1901) In 1870, Hiram Revels, a Republican from Mississippi, became the first African American to serve as senator when he was elected to fill the position vacated by Jefferson Davis when Mississippi seceded from the Union. A Civil War veteran with a varied career in state politics, Revels served until 1871.

Rebecca Latimer Felton (1835–1930) In 1922, Rebecca Felton became the first woman to serve in the Senate. She was appointed by Georgia Governor Thomas Hardwick to replace Thomas Watson, who died in office. Felton's appointment came one day after Congress adjourned for the fall elections, leaving her no opportunity to serve. When the new session started, Senator-elect Walter George agreed to claim his seat a day late. This allowed the 87-year-old Felton the opportunity to serve one day as senator. She delivered a short speech before promptly resigning.

Robert LaFollette (1855–1925) Although a member of the Republican Party almost his entire career, Robert LaFollette remained independent in his views about corruption and support for Progressive reforms. As governor of Wisconsin, he instituted direct primary elections and campaign spending limits in order to weaken the influence of party machines and corporations. LaFollette's three terms in the Senate were notable for his opposition to President Woodrow Wilson's decision to support the Allies when war broke out in Europe in 1914. When LaFollette voted against declaring war in 1917 and openly criticized the war effort and the Treaty of Versailles, an attempt was made to have him removed from the Senate. In 1924, as a Progressive Party candidate, LaFollette ran for president and garnered one sixth of the popular vote.

Robert F. Wagner (1877–1953) Born in Hesse-Nassau, Germany, Robert Wagner immigrated to the United States as a child and completed a law degree from New York Law School. As senator from New York from 1927–1949, Wagner was a prominent in directing New Deal legislation, especially those involving labor issues. Specifically, Wagner was instrumental in drafting legislation such as the National Industrial Recovery Act, the National Labor Relations Act, the Social Security Act, and the Home Loan Act.

Robert Taft (1889–1953) Son of President William Howard Taft, Robert Taft served as a Republican senator from Ohio from 1939 to his death in 1953. A conservative leader in the Senate who favored isolationism, he was a staunch opponent of President Franklin D. Roosevelt's New Deal programs and opposed the nation's involvement in NATO and the United Nations. Taft was instrumental in drafting the Taft-Hartley Act of 1947 (also known as the Labor-Management Relations Act), which was designed to create equity in the collective bargaining process between management and labor. During the Eisenhower administration, Taft was Senate majority leader and a trusted advisor to the president.

Arthur H. Vandenberg (1884–1951) An influential Republican senator from Michigan, Arthur Vandenberg is noted for his important role in establishing foreign policy after World War II, gaining the support of both parties for President Harry Truman's foreign policy plan while serving as chairman of the Senate Committee on Foreign Affairs. A former isolationist who announced his conversion to a more internationalist viewpoint in what was called the "speech heard round the world," Vandenberg succeeded in securing Senate support and approval of the Truman Doctrine, the Marshall Plan, and NATO, as well as establishing the overall bipartisan approach to the cold war.

Joseph McCarthy (1909–1957) In 1950, Joseph McCarthy, a Republican senator from Wisconsin, gained national attention by claiming that Communists had "infested" the State Department. As a result, a special Senate committee was mobilized to investigate the charges and found them to be groundless. Undeterred, McCarthy continued to wage a relentless and hysterical anti-communist crusade that played upon the public's fears of Communism and attempted to implicate numerous public figures in highly controversial public hearings.

Strom Thurmond (1902–) The longest serving senator in U.S. history, Strom Thurmond was a write-in candidate for the Senate in 1954 after a prominent career in South Carolina as a judge, state senator, and governor. In 1957, Thurmond staged the longest filibuster in Senate history, speaking for over 24 hours against a civil rights bill. Originally a Democrat, Thurmond switched to the Republican Party in 1964. In 1996, at age 94, he was elected to serve his eighth term in the Senate, although he has announced he will not seek reelection in 2002, at age 100.

Edward Kennedy (1932–) Although he is a noted member of what is arguably America's most prominent political family, Ted Kennedy's distinction as a 40-plus-year senator from Massachusetts is related to his overall body of work. Widely recognized as a civil rights champion and health care advocate, Kennedy currently serves as chairman of the Senate Committee on Health, Education, and Labor. Kennedy was a critical figure in the opposition of the Supreme Court nominations of both G. Harrold Carswell and Robert Bork, and he was also a faithful defender of President Bill Clinton during his 1998–1999 impeachment crisis.

John McCain (1936–) Son and grandson of prominent navy admirals, John McCain served as a naval aviator in Vietnam and was shot down and held as a prisoner of war in Hanoi for over five years. McCain was elected as a Republican senator from Arizona in 1985. A significant foreign policy figure and a leading defender of Native American rights, McCain has been an outspoken advocate for campaign finance reform.

Carol Moseley-Braun (1947–) In 1992, Illinois Democrat Carol Mosely-Braun became only the fourth African American and first African American woman to serve in the Senate. She served one term, and is currently the American ambassador to New Zealand and Samoa.

Ben Nighthorse Campbell (1933–) Elected in 1992, Ben Nighthorse Campbell, a chief in the Northern Cheyenne tribe, is the only American Indian presently serving in the Senate. A Republican senator from Colorado and son of a Northern Cheyenne Indian father, Campbell was the first American Indian to chair the Indian Affairs Committee. He is known for his support of issues regarding public lands and natural resources.

Hillary Rodham Clinton (1947–) In 2000, Hillary Rodham Clinton became the first first lady, former or current, to be elected to the Senate (or to any public office, for that matter) and the first woman selected statewide in New York.

THE HOUSE OF REPRESENTATIVES

Can **anyone** run for the House?

Article I, Section 2 of the Constitution outlines the qualifications for members of the House of Representatives. A member of the House must be at least 25 years of age when entering office, must have been a U.S. citizen for at least seven years, and must be a resident of the state in which the election occurred.

How are House members **nominated and elected**?

In most states, House candidates of major political parties are nominated by primary election. Some states also provide for a party convention or committee recommendation in conjunction with a primary. In many states, no primary election is held for a particular office if the candidate is unopposed for nomination. In most states, minor party candidates are nominated according to individual party rules and procedures. Independent candidates are nominated by self-declaration.

Major party candidates are given automatic ballot access in all states, while minor party and independent candidates must meet various state requirements, such as a certain number of petition signatures of registered voters, in order to be placed on the general election ballot. Representatives are elected by plurality vote in the congressional district in which they are candidates. The only major exception to this rule in federal general elections is found in the District of Columbia, which requires that a candidate receive a majority of popular votes in order to be elected as its delegate to the House. In the event that no candidate receives the requisite majority, a runoff election is scheduled. In addition, Louisiana requires that all candidates compete in an all-party primary election. Under this arrangement, a candidate who receives a majority of votes is declared the winner, and the general election is canceled for that office.

How long is a representative's **term of office**?

The Constitution entitles each state to at least one representative, who serves a two-year term. According to the statistics of the 107th Congress, the average length of service in the House is nine years.

How are **vacancies due to death, resignation, or expulsion** filled?

Article II, Section 2 of the Constitution requires that all vacancies in the House of Representatives be filled by election. All states require special elections to fill any House seat that becomes vacant during the first session of a Congress. Procedures governing vacancies occurring during the second session of a Congress differ from state to state, and are largely dependent on the amount of time intervening between the vacancy and the next general election.

What is the size of the House of Representatives?

The membership of the House of Representatives is fixed by law at 435 members representing the 50 states. In addition to the 435 representatives, there is one delegate for each of the following: the District of Columbia, the Virgin Islands, Guam, and American Samoa. Each delegate is elected for a two-year term. In addition, there is a resident commissioner from Puerto Rico who is elected for a four-year term. The delegates and the resident commissioner can sponsor legislation and vote in committees, but not in the House chamber.

How is the **size** of the House determined?

According to the Constitution, each state is entitled to at least one representative. Additional House seats are apportioned (distributed) on the basis of state population. Population figures used for apportionment are determined on the basis of each 10-year census. Following the 2000 census, the average district size was 650,000 people. In order to minimize the differences in district populations among the states, since 1941 Congress has used the method of "equal proportions" to calculate actual apportionment.

What is meant by the term **"member-at-large"**?

A member-at-large is a representative of the House of Representatives who has been elected by the voters of an entire state rather than by those in a specific congressional district. States with small populations have a member-at-large. Consequently, there are only seven such states: Alaska, Delaware, Montana, North Dakota, South Dakota, Vermont, and Wyoming.

Which states have the **most representatives** in Congress?

Because the number of representatives per state is based on the state's population, those states with the largest populations have the most representatives. The 10 biggest states with the most representatives are: California (52 members), New York (31), Texas (30), Florida (23), Pennsylvania (21), Illinois (20), Ohio (19), Michigan (16), New Jersey (13), and North Carolina (12).

What is **redistricting**?

Every 10 years, following the U.S. Census, political district boundaries are adjusted to take into account population changes that have occurred over the preceding decade, a process known as redistricting. Districts are redrawn so that they are as equal in population as possible. Redistricting committees at the state and county level develop proposed plans and changes in district boundaries. These new district plans are passed by both houses of the legislature at the state level, and the board of supervisors at the county level. The governor then signs legislation for the new district lines to become effective.

Do the federal government or the states **define the congressional districts**?

Congress fixes the size of the House of Representatives as well as the procedure for apportioning the number of representatives among the states, and the states proceed from there. State legislatures pass laws defining the physical boundaries of congressional districts, within certain constraints established by Congress and the Supreme Court (through its reapportionment and redistricting rulings). Each state is apportioned its number of representatives by means of the Department of Commerce's decennial census.

In the early years of the republic, most states elected their representatives at large. The practice of dividing a state into districts, however, was soon instituted. Congress later required that representatives be elected from "districts composed of a contiguous and compact territory," but this requirement is no longer in federal law. The redistricting process has always been provided for by state law, but Congress can choose to exercise greater authority over redistricting. In 1967, for example, by law Congress prohibited at-large elections of representatives in all states entitled to more than one representative. Today, all states with more than one representative must elect their representatives from single-member districts.

What is **"gerrymandering"**?

The term "gerrymandering" means the drawing of district lines in order to maximize the electoral advantage of a political party or faction. The term was first used in 1812, when Elbridge Gerry was the governor of Massachusetts, to characterize the state's redistricting plan. Gerry persuaded the state legislature to create a district in order to favor the election of a fellow Republican. Because of the district's unique shape, one critic reportedly observed, "That looks like a salamander!" to which another observer quipped, "That's not a salamander, that's a gerrymander." Since that incident, gerrymandering has become a common term in popular political discussions.

What do the **House majority and minority leaders** do?

Since the nineteenth century, the House of Representatives has chosen majority and minority leaders to expedite legislative business and to keep their parties united. These leaders are elected every two years in secret balloting of the party caucus or conference. The role of the majority leader has been defined by history and tradition. This officer is charged with scheduling legislation for floor consideration; planning the daily, weekly, and annual legislative agendas; consulting with members to gauge party sentiment;

Congressman Newt Gingrich (R–GA) served as Speaker of the House from 1995 to 1999.

and, in general, working to advance the goals of the majority party. The minority leader serves as floor leader of the "loyal opposition," and is the minority counterpart to the Speaker of the House. Although many of the basic leadership responsibilities of the minority and majority leaders are similar, the minority leader speaks for the minority party and its policies and works to protect the minority's rights.

What does the **Speaker of the House** do?

Article I, Section 2 of the Constitution states: "The House of Representatives shall chuse [sic] their Speaker and other Officers." The Speaker acts as leader of the House and combines several roles: the institutional role of presiding officer and administrative head of the House, the partisan role of leader of the majority party in the House, and the representative role of an elected member of the House. The Speaker appoints chairs to preside over the Committee of the Whole, appoints all special or select committees, appoints conference committees, has the power of recognition of members to speak, and makes many important rulings and decisions in the House. The Speaker may vote, but usually does not, except in case of a tie. The Speaker and the majority leader determine the legislative agenda for the House and often confer with the president of the United States and with the Senate leadership. In addition to these roles, the Speaker of the House is second in line to succeed the president.

Who held the position of the **Speaker of the House** for the longest period of time?

Sam Rayburn of Texas, who was a member of the House for more than 48 years, served as Speaker for 17 years and 2 months. However, the record for longest continuous service as Speaker is held by Thomas P. "Tip" O'Neill of Massachusetts, who served consecutively for 10 years, surpassing other long-running contenders, such as John McCormack (8 years, 11 months), Champ Clark (7 years, 10 months), and Joseph G. Cannon (7 years, 3 months).

Who are the **officers of the House** and how are they chosen?

Elected officers include the Speaker of the House, clerk (the chief legislative officer of the House), sergeant at arms (who is responsible for maintaining order on the floor and in the galleries when the House is in session), chief administrative officer (CAO, the principal House officer responsible for the financial management of House of Representatives accounts), and chaplain (who opens each daily House session with a prayer and provides pastoral services to House members, their families, and staff). Together, these officers comprise the principal managers for the House of essential legislative, financial, administrative, and security functions. Their duties are outlined in House rules and in statutes. Because the Constitution says that the House "shall chuse [sic] their Speaker and other officers," the members vote on who shall be officer as they do on any other question, except that in most cases it is strictly a party vote. Republicans and Democrats both meet before the House organizes for a new Congress, and choose a slate of officers. These two slates are presented at the first session of the House, and the majority-party slate can be expected to be selected. Traditionally, the majority party's nominee for chaplain is not contested.

Another officer, the inspector general, is appointed jointly by the Speaker, majority leader, and minority leader. The inspector general is the chief investigative officer of the House, whose office conducts periodic audits of House financial and administrative offices and operations. In addition, there is a general counsel, the chief legal advisor to the House, who is appointed by the Speaker in consultation with a bipartisan legal advisory group, which includes the majority and minority leaders. Finally, the historian preserves the historical records of the House and its members, encourages historical research on the House, and conducts original research and writing on the history of the House. The historian is appointed by the Speaker.

Do members of the House have **individual seats** on the chamber floor?

Representatives had individual seats until the 63rd Congress (1913), but now members may sit where they choose. Democrats occupy the east side of the chamber, on the Speaker's right; Republicans sit across the main aisle, on the Speaker's left. Two tables each on the Democratic and Republican sides of the aisle are reserved for committee leaders during debate on a bill reported from their committee and for party leaders.

CONGRESSIONAL COMMITTEES

What is a **committee**?

A committee is a panel of members elected or appointed to perform some service or function for its parent body. Committees are essential to the effective operation of legislative bodies. As "little legislatures," committees monitor ongoing governmental operations, identify issues suitable for legislative review, gather and evaluate information, and recommend courses of action to their house or to Congress. Congress has four types of committees: standing, special or select, joint, and, in the House, a Committee of the Whole. Except for the Committee of the Whole, committees conduct investigations, make studies, issue reports and recommendations, and, in the case of standing committees, review and prepare measures on their assigned subjects for action by their respective houses. Most committees divide their work among several subcommittees or, in some cases, task forces, but only the full committee may submit reports or measures to its house or to Congress. With rare exceptions, the majority party in a house holds a majority of the seats on its committees, and their chairs are also from that party.

What is a **subcommittee**?

Most committees form subcommittees with legislative authority to consider and report bills on particular issues within the range of authority of the full committee. Committees may assign their subcommittees such specific tasks as the initial consideration of measures and oversight of laws and programs in their areas. Subcommittees are responsible to and work with guidelines established by their parent committees. Consequently, their number, independence, and autonomy vary among committees.

What are **party committees**?

The party caucus or conference traditionally establishes party committees with specialized functions. Party committees generally nominate party members to serve on the various committees of the House or Senate, subject to approval by the caucus or conference. Policy committees generally discuss party positions on pending legislation. Steering committees generally plan the schedule of chamber action on pending legislation. Research committees conduct studies on broad policy questions, generally before committees of the House or Senate begin action on legislation. Campaign committees provide research and strategy assistance to party candidates for election to the House or Senate. The chairs of party committees are generally elected by their respective party caucus or conference; the exception is the House Democratic Steering Committee, which is chaired by the Speaker of the House when the Democrats are in the majority or by the Democratic floor leader when the Democrats are in the minority.

What are **congressional standing committees** and why are they necessary?

Standing committees are permanent panels made up of members of a chamber. Each panel has authority over measures and laws in certain areas of public policy, such as health, education, energy, the environment, foreign affairs, and agriculture. Each chamber has its own standing committees, which allows it to consider many issues at the same time. Each committee selects, from the measures it receives each Congress, a relatively small number (approximately 10 percent) that merit committee review and subsequent consideration by the full chamber. Because of the small size of committees—and the often lengthy service of members on the same panel—committees provide an effective means of managing Congress's enormous workload and gaining expertise over the range and complexity of subjects with which the federal government deals.

Were **standing committees** always in existence?

Yes. Although Congress has used standing committees since its earliest days, it did not predominantly rely on them during its first quarter century. In these early years, legislative proposals were considered initially by all members of one chamber in plenary session; afterward, each proposal was referred to a temporary, ad hoc committee responsible for working out a proposal's details and making any technical changes. As the amount of legislative proposals increased, especially in certain subject areas, permanent committees replaced temporary ones for more expeditious screening and processing of legislation before its consideration by an entire chamber.

What are the **standing committees** of the House?

In the 107th Congress, the following 19 standing committees were named: Agriculture; Appropriations; Armed Services; Budget; Education and the Workforce; Energy and Commerce; Financial Services; Government Reform; House Administration; International Relations; Judiciary; Resources; Rules; Science; Small Business; Standards of Official Conduct; Transportation and Infrastructure; Veterans' Affairs; and Ways and Means.

What are the **standing committees** of the Senate?

In the 107th Congress, the following 16 standing committees were named: Agriculture, Nutrition, and Forestry; Appropriations; Armed Services; Banking, Housing, and Urban Affairs; Budget; Commerce, Science, and Transportation; Energy and Natural Resources; Environment and Public Works; Finance; Foreign Relations; Governmental Affairs; Health, Education, Labor, and Pensions; Judiciary; Rules and Administration; Small Business; and Veterans' Affairs.

Who **sits on standing committees** and how are they selected?

Before members are assigned to committees, each committee's size and the proportion of Democrats to Republicans must be decided by each chamber's party leaders. The total number of committee slots allotted to each party is approximately the same as the ratio between majority-party and minority-party members in the full chamber. Members are then assigned to committees in a three-step process, in which the first step is the most critical and decisive. Each of the two principal parties in the House and Senate is responsible for assigning its members to committees, and, at the first stage, each party uses a committee on committees to make the initial recommendations for assignments. At the beginning of a new Congress, members express preferences for assignment to the appropriate committee on committees; most incumbents prefer to remain on the same committees in order to retain their committee seniority and build upon their expertise. These committees on committees then match preferences with committee slots, following certain guidelines designed in part to distribute assignments fairly. They then prepare and approve an assignment slate for each committee, and submit all slates to the appropriate full-party conference for approval. Approval at this second stage often is granted easily, but the conferences have procedures for disapproving recommended members and nominating others instead. Finally, at the third stage, each committee submits its slate to the pertinent full chamber for approval, which is generally granted.

Who is the **committee chair**, and what does his or her selection have to do with **"seniority rule"**?

Generally, it has been the custom for a member who served longest on the majority side of a committee to become its chair or, if on the minority side, its ranking member. Members are ranked from the chair or ranking member down, according to length of service on the committee. Modifications—including party practices, term limits on chairmanships, and limits on the number of committees and subcommittees chaired—have caused the seniority rule to be less rigidly followed in recent Congresses. Nevertheless, length of service on a committee remains the predominant criterion for choosing its chair and ranking member.

In both chambers, nominees for committee chair are subject to public votes, first in meetings of their party colleagues (in conference or caucus), then in the full chamber. Members who interrupt their service in a chamber but subsequently return to the Congress start again at the bottom of a committee list. Returning members outrank other new members who have no prior service. New members also earn seniority over other newly elected members by having prior service in the other legislative chamber. In some cases, in which two members have equal time in service in a chamber, prior service as a state governor or state legislator also may contribute to the determination of seniority.

What is a **select committee**?

The House and Senate select committees usually for limited time periods and for limited purposes. Although there are exceptions, most have not been given legislative power—that is, the authority to consider and report legislation to the full chamber. After completing its purpose, such as an investigation of a government activity and making a related report, the select committee disbands. Recently, however, the chambers have allowed select committees to continue to exist over extended periods of time. Some, such as the House and Senate Select Committees on Intelligence, have been granted legislative authority.

What are **joint committees** and how are they established?

Joint committees are those committees that have members chosen from both the House and Senate, generally with the chairmanship rotating between the most senior majority-party senator and representative. In general, select committees do not have legislative power to consider and report legislation to the full chambers. These committees can be created by statute, or by joint or concurrent resolution, although all existing ones have been established by statute. Congress now has four permanent or long-term joint committees, the oldest being the Joint Committee on the Library, which dates from 1800. The other three are the Joint Economic Committee, the Joint Committee on Printing, and the Joint Committee on Taxation. In addition, Congress sometimes establishes temporary joint committees for particular purposes, such as the Joint Congressional Committee on Inaugural Ceremonies, which is formed every four years to handle the organizational and financial responsibilities for the inauguration of the president and vice president of the United States.

What is the **House Committee of the Whole**?

The Committee of the Whole House on the State of the Union (or Committee of the Whole) is a hybrid form of the House itself. Technically, it is a committee of the House on which all representatives serve and that meets in the House chamber. However, it is governed by different procedural rules than other House meetings. This concept of the "grand committee" has been carefully developed from the early days of the House and in modern practice gives the House a more expeditious means for considering the complex and often controversial legislation referred to it.

Historically, it was devised by the English House of Commons to give them the ability to debate privately and not have their votes committed to record. The Committee of the Whole in the U.S. House permitted recorded votes beginning in January 1971. The House resolves itself into a new Committee of the Whole for the consideration of each bill. A specific Committee of the Whole is dissolved when it "rises and reports with a recommendation" to the House. When the Committee rises after not having resolved the matter committed to it, that bill is carried on the calendar as "unfinished business of the Committee of the Whole" until consideration has been finally completed. When a bill or resolution is considered in the Committee of the Whole, there first is a period of time, usually one hour, for general debate on the merits of the bill or resolution. If enforced, a quorum (a group considered complete enough to conduct business) in the Committee of the Whole is 100 members (whereas 218 are required in the House to conduct business). After general debate, members may offer amendments, with each speech for or against an amendment being limited to five minutes. If a recorded vote is desired on any amendment, the call for the vote must be seconded by 25 members (whereas 44 or more are required in the House). When the amending process is completed, the Committee of the Whole "rises," and reports its actions to the House through the Speaker. The House then votes on whether or not to adopt the amendments recommended by the Committee of the Whole, and then votes on final passage of the measure, as amended. The Senate stopped using the Committee of the Whole as a parliamentary forum for debate in 1986.

What is the role of the **House Rules Committee**?

The House Rules Committee makes recommendations to the House on possible changes to the standing rules of the House, as well as the order of business on the House floor. The committee affects the order of business by reporting resolutions that make it possible for the House to begin acting on a bill that is on the House or union calendar. These resolutions are known as special rules or simply as "rules." Each special rule may also propose a set of ground rules for debating and amending a particular bill that is different from the normal rules for considering legislation. For example, a special rule may impose limitations on the amendments that members can propose to a bill, or it may allow an amendment to be offered, even though it violates a standing rule of the House. The House as a whole decides by majority vote whether to accept, reject, or modify each special rule that the Rules Committee proposes. The Senate Committee on Rules and Administration also considers possible changes to the standing rules of the Senate, but it doesn't determine the order of business on the Senate floor. In addition, the Senate committee reports on resolutions to fund the work of all the Senate committees. In the House, this responsibility belongs to the Committee on House Administration.

CONGRESS AND LAWMAKING

How does the **legislative perspective** differ in the Senate and in the House?

The power to legislate is vested in a Congress with two distinct bodies, the Senate and the House of Representatives. While the concurrence of both houses is required to enact a law, each chamber has a distinct mission, different rules of procedure, and unique traditions. The Congress does not act as one homogenous unit; rather, conflict is inherent in this bicameral legislature. Conflict primarily arises in the passage of a bill into law, where it easier to block a bill's passage than enact its passage. In recent Congresses, not even 6 percent of all bills became law.

In the lawmaking process, the House is meant to reflect the wishes of the majority of Americans. The Senate, on the other hand, is meant to force the debate necessary to thoroughly examine popular opinion. In short, the House is more centralized and organized than the Senate, and the Senate is more deliberative. Because deliberation involves delaying the passage of proposals until adequate discussion has taken place, the Senate's rules and traditions give advantages to the minority—such as limited debate—in an effort to stop the majority from acting too swiftly. The opposite is true of the House: Its rules and traditions favor the majority to ensure that the people's views prevail and that no minority obstructs them. Further, the rules give House leaders more control over the legislative process and allow House members to specialize in legislative areas; the rules of the Senate, on the other hand, limit their power and discourage specialization. Finally, due to factors such as their length of terms and the constituencies they serve, members of the House serve local interests with specific legislative agendas, while senators serve larger, more diverse constituencies. Senators have the added benefit of considering new ideas and ways of uniting various interests, and thus serve as the agents for interests organized on a statewide or national basis.

What are the **four forms of legislation** introduced in Congress?

Congressional legislation takes one of the following four forms: the bill, the joint resolution, the concurrent resolution, and the simple resolution. A *bill* is the form used for most legislation, whether permanent or temporary, general or special, public or private. Bills are presented to the president of the United States for action when approved in identical form by both the House of Representatives and the Senate. Like a bill, *joint resolutions* may originate either in the House of Representatives or in the Senate. There is little practical difference between a bill and a joint resolution. Both are subject to the same procedure, and joint resolutions become law in the same manner as bills. The only exception to this is a joint resolution proposing an amendment to the Constitution. On approval of such a resolution by two-thirds of both the House and Senate, it is not presented to the president for approval. Rather, it is sent directly to the administrator of general services for submission to the individual states for ratification. Matters affecting the operations of both the House of Representatives and Senate are usually initiated by means of *concurrent resolutions*. Instead of being presented to the president for signature, on approval by both the House of Representatives and Senate, they are signed by the clerk of the House and the secretary of the Senate. A matter concerning the operation of either the House of Representatives or Senate alone is initiated by a *simple resolution*. Like concurrent resolutions, they are not presented to the president for action.

What role does Congress play in the process of **amending the Constitution**?

To protect the Constitution from hasty alteration, Article V stipulates that amendments to the Constitution be proposed either by two-thirds of both houses of Congress (290 out of 435 members of the House and 67 out of 100 senators) or by two-thirds of the states, meeting in convention. The proposals must be ratified by one of two methods: either by the legislatures of three-fourths (or 38) of the states, or by convention in three-fourths of the states, with the Congress proposing the method to be used. Only the Twenty-first Amendment (which repealed Prohibition and thus the Eighteenth Amendment) was ratified using the convention method.

Because the terms for amending the Constitution are so stringent, it is not often done. Since 1789, over 10,000 amendments have been proposed in Congress. Of those, only 33 were sent to the states for ratification, and only 27 were ultimately ratified. Examples of recent amendments that received much congressional attention but failed to survive the process include the Flag Desecration Amendment, the Balanced Budget Amendment, the Equal Rights Amendment, a Term Limits Amendment, and a School Prayer Amendment.

What is a **quorum**?

A quorum is the number of senators or representatives that must be present to do business. The Constitution requires a simple majority of senators (51) for a quorum. Often, fewer senators are actually present on the floor, but the Senate presumes that a quorum is present unless the contrary is shown by a roll call vote or quorum call. Likewise, in the House of Representatives, a quorum is a simple majority of the members. When there are no vacancies in the membership, a quorum is 218. When one or more seats are vacant, because of deaths or resignations, the quorum is reduced accordingly. Because of members' other duties, a quorum often is not actually present on the House floor. But any member may insist that a quorum be present. If the Speaker agrees, a series of bells ring on the House side of the Capitol and in the House office buildings to alert members to come to the chamber and record their presence.

What is a **whip**?

The Democratic and Republican whips assist the Democratic and Republican leadership, respectively, in managing the party's legislative program on the House and Senate floor. The whip keeps track of all legislation and ensures that all party members are present when important measures are to be voted upon. When a vote appears to be close, the whips contact absent members of their party, and advise them of the vote. The authority of the whips over party members is informal; in Congress, a member may vote against the position supported by a majority of the member's party colleagues because of personal opposition or because of opposition evident within his or her constituency. In most cases, parties take no disciplinary action against colleagues who vote against the party position. The majority and minority whips in the House and Senate are elected by party members in their respective chambers. Because of its large number of members, the House majority and minority whips appoint deputy whips to assist them in their activities.

How is a **bill** introduced?

In both the House and Senate, any number of members may join in introducing a single bill or resolution. The first member listed is the sponsor of the bill, and all members' names following the sponsor's are the bill's co-sponsors. When introduced, a bill is referred to the committee or committees that have authority over the subject with which the bill is concerned. Under the standing rules of the House and Senate, bills are referred by the Speaker of the House and by the presiding officer in the Senate. In practice, the House and Senate parliamentarians act for these officials and refer the vast majority of bills.

How does a **bill become a law**?

Every year Congress considers hundreds of legislative proposals. In the year 2000 alone, more than 100 House bills became law, and more than 70 Senate bills became law. For every bill that is proposed, there is a series of steps it must go through before it becomes law. To begin with, a bill must pass both bodies of Congress in the same form before it can be presented to the president of the United States for signature into law. The process begins when a representative has an idea for a new law. He or she becomes the sponsor of that bill and introduces it by giving it to the clerk of the House or by placing it in a box, called the "hopper." The clerk assigns a legislative number to the bill, with the initials "H.R." for bills introduced in the House and "S." for bills introduced in the Senate. The Government Printing Office (GPO) then prints the bill and distributes copies to each representative for his or her review.

The bill is then referred by the Speaker to one or more of the 22 standing committees of the House. The standing committee, or often a subcommittee, studies the bill and hears testimony from experts and people interested in the bill, including lobbyists, interest groups, and those of the academic and business community. After hearing an array of opinions, the committee may decide to release the bill with a recommendation to pass it, revise the bill and release it, or lay it aside so that the House cannot vote on it. Releasing the bill is called "reporting it out," while laying it aside is called "tabling." If the bill is released, it then goes on a calendar, or a list of bills awaiting action. At this point, the House Rules Committee may call for the bill to be voted on quickly, limit the debate, or limit or prohibit amendments. Undisputed bills may be passed by unanimous consent, or by a two-thirds vote if members agree to suspend the rules.

The bill now goes to the floor of the House for consideration and begins with a complete reading of the bill. There is a time allotted for general debate on the bill, and there is a time allotted for amending the bill, one part at a time, under a rule that limits speeches on amendments to five minutes each. A third reading (of the title only) occurs after any amendments have been added. If the bill passes by simple majority (218 of 435), the bill moves to the Senate.

In order to be introduced in the Senate, a senator must be recognized as the presiding officer and announce the introduction of the bill. Just as in the House, the bill is assigned to one of the Senate's 16 standing committees by the presiding officer; the Senate committee studies and either releases or tables the bill. Once released, the bill goes to the Senate floor for consideration. When the Senate considers the bill, members can debate it indefinitely. When there is no more debate, the bill is voted on. A simple majority (51 of 100) passes the bill.

The bill now moves onto a conference committee, which is made up of members from each House. The committee's primary role is to work out any differences between the House and Senate versions of the bill. The revised bill is sent back to both houses for their final approval. Once approved, the bill is printed by the GPO in a process called enrolling. The clerk from the introducing house certifies the final version. The Speaker of the House and then the vice president sign the enrolled bill. Finally, the bill is sent to the president for his signature and enactment into law.

What options does the **president of the United States** have once both houses have passed a bill?

Once both houses of Congress have passed a bill, the president has three choices: First, he can sign the bill within 10 days (Sundays excepted), whereupon it becomes a law. Second, the president may veto the bill—that is, return it to Congress, stating his objections, without a signature of approval. In this case, Congress may override the veto with a two-thirds vote in each House. The bill would then become a law despite the president's veto. Third, the president may hold the bill without taking any action. Two different developments may occur in this situation depending upon whether Congress is in session. If Congress is in session, the bill becomes law after the expiration of 10 days (excluding Sundays), even without the president's signature. If Congress has adjourned, the bill does not become law, and this procedure is called a "pocket veto."

What is the difference between a **veto** and a **pocket veto**?

According the Constitution, a veto is the procedure by which the president of the United States refuses to approve a bill or joint resolution and thus prevents its enactment into law. A regular veto occurs when the president returns the legislation to the house in which it originated. The president usually returns a vetoed bill with a message indicating his reasons for rejecting the measure. The veto can be overridden only by a two-thirds vote in both the Senate and the House. The Constitution grants the

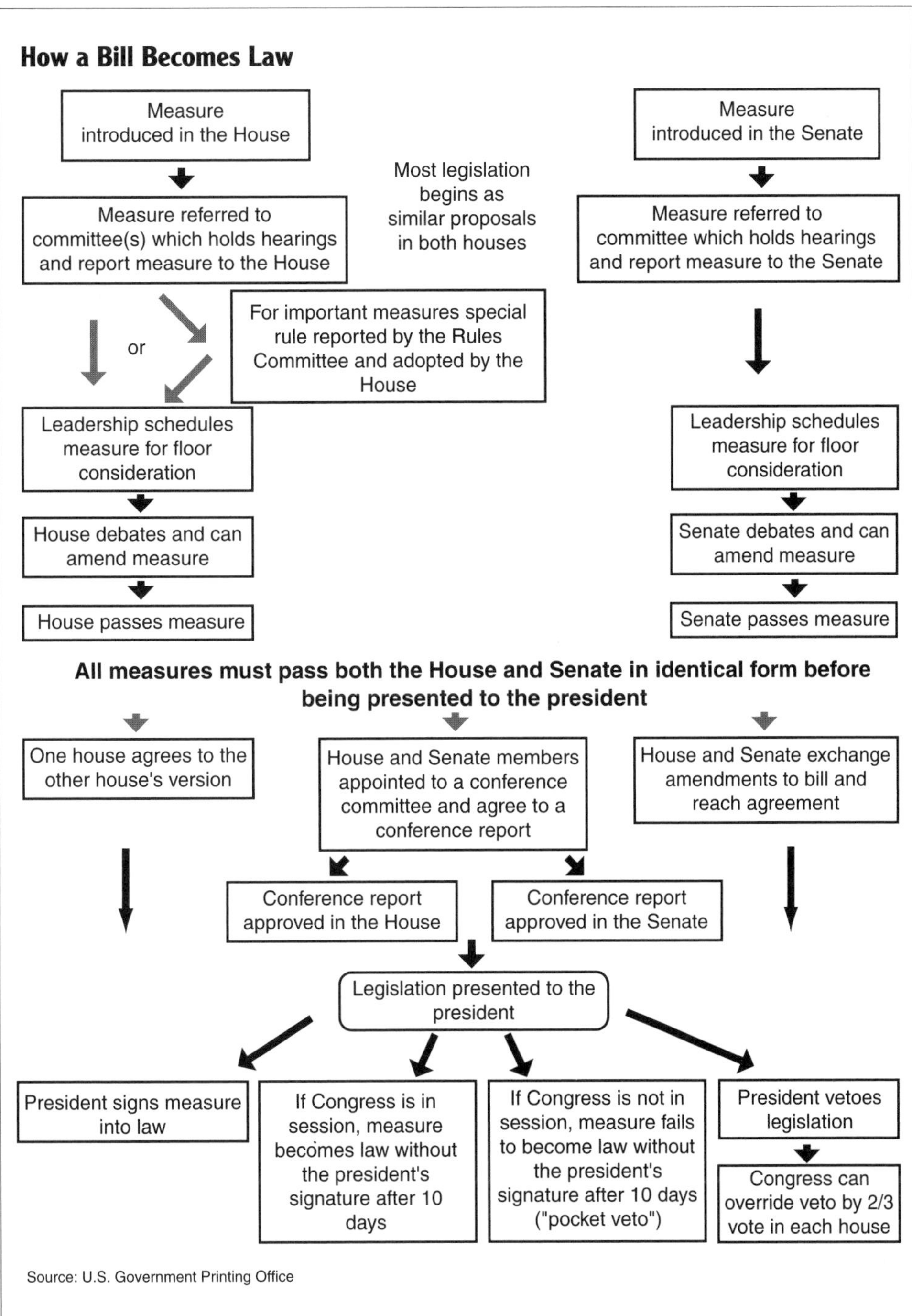
How a Bill Becomes Law
Measure introduced in the House
Measure referred to committee(s) which holds hearings and report measure to the House
or
For important measures special rule reported by the Rules Committee and adopted by the House
Leadership schedules measure for floor consideration
House debates and can amend measure
House passes measure
Most legislation begins as similar proposals in both houses
Measure introduced in the Senate
Measure referred to committee which holds hearings and report measure to the Senate
Leadership schedules measure for floor consideration
Senate debates and can amend measure
Senate passes measure
All measures must pass both the House and Senate in identical form before being presented to the president
One house agrees to the other house's version
House and Senate members appointed to a conference committee and agree to a conference report
House and Senate exchange amendments to bill and reach agreement
Conference report approved in the House
Conference report approved in the Senate
Legislation presented to the president
President signs measure into law
If Congress is in session, measure becomes law without the president's signature after 10 days
If Congress is not in session, measure fails to become law without the president's signature after 10 days ("pocket veto")
President vetoes legislation
Congress can override veto by 2/3 vote in each house
Source: U.S. Government Printing Office

president 10 days to review a measure passed by the Congress. If the president has not signed the bill after this time period, it becomes law without his signature. However, if Congress adjourns during the 10-day period, the bill does not become law, and this is known as a "pocket veto."

How often does the president **use his veto power**?

Although the first presidents used their veto power sparingly (George Washington used it just twice during his two terms in office), use of both kinds of veto power has become more common over the course of American presidential history. Presidents Franklin D. Roosevelt, Grover Cleveland, and Harry Truman hold the record for most legislation vetoed. Of the recent presidents, Ronald Reagan exercised 78 vetoes, George Bush 44 vetoes, and Bill Clinton 38 vetoes. Congress has overridden only a handful of regular vetoes from Washington to Clinton, overriding about 7.1 percent of the regular vetoes during this period. The presidents with the highest percentage of vetoes overridden are Franklin Pierce, Andrew Johnson, Gerald Ford, Richard Nixon, and Woodrow Wilson.

What role does **debate** play in the legislative process?

The standing rules of the Senate and House promote deliberation by permitting senators and representatives to debate at length and by precluding a simple majority from ending a debate when they are prepared to vote to approve a bill. Although the right to debate is considered one of the most pivotal for shaping what occurs on the House and Senate floors, it has its limitations. In the House, no matter is subject to more than one hour of debate, usually equally divided between the majority and the minority, without unanimous consent. Moreover, the majority can call for the "previous question," and bring the pending matter to an immediate vote. In the Committee of the Whole, the period of time spent in general debate is determined in advance. Amendments are subject to the five-minute-per-side rule, but can extend beyond 10 minutes of debate per amendment when unanimous consent is granted or when "pro forma" amendments are offered. A nondebatable motion to close debate is necessary to end debate on any specific amendment and bring it to a vote.

In the Senate, debate is normally without restriction, unless time limits are agreed to by unanimous consent. The ability to extend debate at will—to "filibuster"—enables a senator to delay the final vote on a measure, or even to prevent it altogether. Filibusters can be broken only by negotiation or through the use of a formal procedure known as "cloture." A successful cloture motion requires at least a three-fifths vote, or 60 senators. If they vote for cloture, the filibuster comes to a gradual end. Thirty hours of further debate are permitted in the post-cloture period prior to the vote on final passage. However, senators do not usually extend debate after they have voted for cloture.

What is a filibuster?

The word "filibuster" is an informal term for any attempt to block or delay Senate action on a bill or other matter by debating it at length, by offering numerous procedural motions, or by any other delaying or obstructive actions. The lack of debate limitations in Senate rules creates the possibility of filibusters. Individual senators or minority groups of senators who adamantly oppose a bill or amendment may speak against it at great length, in the hope of changing their colleagues' minds, winning support for amendments that meet their objectives, or convincing the Senate to withdraw the bill or amendment from further consideration on the floor. Opposing senators also can delay final floor action by offering numerous amendments and motions, insisting that amendments be read in full, demanding roll call votes on amendments and motions, and a using a variety of other devices. The only formal procedure that can break a filibuster is cloture.

What is **cloture**?

Cloture is only procedure by which the Senate can vote to place a time limit on consideration of a bill or other matter, and thereby overcome a filibuster. Under the cloture rule, the Senate may limit consideration of a pending matter to 30 additional hours, but only by vote of three-fifths of the full Senate, normally 60 votes.

How are **conference committees** used to resolve differences in legislation?

From the days of the early republic, differences on legislation between the House and Senate have been committed to conference committees to work out a settlement. The most usual case is that in which a bill passes one chamber with amendments unacceptable to the other. In such a case, the chamber that disagrees with the amendments generally asks for a conference, and the Speaker of the House and the presiding officer of the Senate appoint the "managers," as the conferees are called. Generally, they are selected from the committee or committees having charge of the bill. After attempting to resolve the points in disagreement, the conference committee issues a report to each chamber. If the report is accepted by both chambers, the bill is then enrolled and sent to the president of the United States for signature. If the report is rejected by either chamber, the matter in disagreement comes up as again for debate, as if there had been no conference. Unless all differences between the two Houses are resolved, the bill fails.

How does a member of Congress **decide how to vote**?

Members of Congress are asked hundreds of times a year to cast their "yea" or "nay" votes on a variety of bills, motions, and amendments that cover every conceivable issue of the day, from gun control and abortion rights to trade with China. The overall rate of participation—tallied at 95 percent of all votes held in the last few Congresses—suggests that members take this responsibility seriously. Amid conflicting opinions regarding any piece of legislature, a member must make a decision, often in very little time. Because members are accountable to their constituents for the way they voted on a particular issue, members almost always do some form of research into any public policy issue. They review statistics, legal analyses, newspaper editorials, and arguments from special interest groups. Members consider the cost to the taxpayer and spend time trying to gain an accurate idea of how their constituents feel about any given legislative proposal. In addition, party caucuses and senior members exert their own influence over members, supplying research and analysis to members in an effort to promote a specific argument or position. In 1998, for example, 56 percent of all the votes cast in both the House and Senate reflected strong party unity. In addition to these influences, the president of the United States voices his opinion, and a member must assess whether the president's threatened veto might block passage of a measure.

When does a **bill become "dead"**?

A bill may be introduced at any point during a two-year Congress. It remains eligible for consideration throughout the duration of that Congress until the Congress ends or adjourns *sine die* ("without a specified day"). If it is not considered within that time frame, the bill fails, or "dies."

What happens to a bill **after** it becomes a law?

The provisions of a law take effect immediately unless the law itself specifies another date. The law may also outline which executive departments, agencies, or officers are empowered to carry out or enforce the law. The written document is sent to the National Archives and Records Administration, where it is assigned a number. It is then published in individual form as a "slip law." At the end of each session of Congress, these new laws are consolidated in a bound volume called U.S. Statutes at Large. In addition, all permanent, general laws currently in force are included in the Code of Laws of the United States of America, commonly called the U.S. Code. The Office of Law Revision Counsel, part of the institutional structure of the House of Representatives, is responsible for preparing and issuing annual supplements to keep the U.S. Code current.

What is **logrolling**?

The term "logrolling" derives from the early American practice of neighbors gathering together to help clear land by rolling off and burning felled timber. In the political arena, it has to do with exchanging political favors, specifically the trading of votes among legislators to achieve passage of projects that are of interest to one another.

Logrolling mainly occurs when members of Congress must vote on bills about which they are not experts, or in fact know very little, and turn to a more knowledgeable congressional colleague for advice. If the issue is of little interest to the uniformed member of Congress, he will often pledge his "yea" vote for that bill, in exchange for a similar favor: the promise of a future "yea" vote from his more knowledgeable colleague on a future piece of legislation. Logrolling often takes place on specialized legislation that targets money or projects to selected congressional districts.

What is meant by the term **"pork barrel"** legislation?

The term "pork barrel" came into political parlance in the post–Civil War era, when plantation owners would hand out rations of salt pork to their former slaves, distributing them from wooden barrels. When the term is used in reference to a particular bill, it implies legislation loaded with benefits from members of Congress to their constituents back home, courtesy of the federal taxpayer. However, there is wide disagreement about what makes a bill "pork." Those critical of the practice feel it is unfair that a member with political skill can obtain federal funds for his district or state when the same benefits are not received by other parts of the nation with similar needs. Proponents argue that the nature of America's diverse geographic and cultural regions warrants projects that may only benefit one area. For example, areas that regularly suffer from severe flooding or other destructive acts of nature consider federal funds to build dams essential to their recovery, and would never call that project "pork." Further, proponents argue that projects such as water reclamation, environmental clean-up, and highway improvements generate local jobs and bring political kudos to the member of Congress who worked to get the project funded—making it a part of the member's obligation to his constituency rather than simply an indiscriminate benefit to his or her region.

THE JUDICIAL BRANCH

THE JUDICIAL SYSTEM

What is the **"supreme law of the land"**?

The term "supreme law of the land" refers to all laws of the United States made according to the Constitution and treaties made under the authority of the United States. All judges throughout the country must uphold them, regardless of any statutes that exist in individual state constitutions or laws.

What does the term **"equal justice under law"** mean?

"Equal justice under law" is the main principle of the judicial system in the United States. Engraved above the entrance of the Supreme Court building, it means that every person in the United States is entitled to receive equal and fair treatment from the law. These words express the ultimate responsibility of the Supreme Court, which, as the nation's highest tribunal, hears all cases and controversies arising under the Constitution or the laws of the United States. As the final reviewer and judge of the law, the Court is charged with ensuring the American people the promise of equal justice under law, and thereby, also functions as guardian and interpreter of the Constitution.

What are the **two types of court systems** in the United States?

There are two types of court systems, or judiciaries, in the United States: federal and state. The federal judiciary is made up of more than 100 courts. Each state has its own number of courts, which can reach into the thousands, and which are responsible for trying the majority of cases in the country.

Juries are made up of randomly selected citizens who are charged with carefully considering the facts presented in court in order to make a decision on a case.

How is the U.S. court system **organized**?

The U.S. judicial system is not one single system, but rather a collection of multiple, independently functioning courts. The federal court system is an integrated system divided into many geographic units and levels of hierarchy. In addition to this system, each state has a system of local courts. Under this dual federal/state court structure, the U.S. Supreme Court is the final judge of federal law, while the highest court of each state (usually called state supreme courts) has the ultimate authority to interpret matters of the law of its state. When federal constitutional or statutory matters are involved, the federal courts have the power to decide whether the state law violates federal law. The functioning of these systems is complicated by the fact that there are multiple sources of law, and courts of one system are often called upon to interpret and apply the laws of another jurisdiction. In addition, more than one court may have the authority to hear a particular case.

The federal judiciary and the individual state judicial systems are each constructed like a pyramid. Entry-level courts at both the state and federal levels are called *trial courts,* in which witnesses are called, evidence is presented, and a jury or sometimes a judge reaches a conclusion based on the law. At the top of each pyramid structure is the *court of last resort,* which has the authority to interpret the law of that jurisdiction. At the federal level, this court is the U.S. Supreme Court; at the state level, it is the state supreme court. In most states and in the federal system there is also a mid-level *court of appeals*. The vast majority of courts at both the state and federal level are "courts of general jurisdiction," meaning that they have authority to decide many different types of cases. There are no special constitutional courts in the United States: Any court has the power to declare a law or action of a government executive to be unconstitutional, subject to review by a higher-level court.

What is **"due process of law"**?

The Fifth Amendment's words that no person shall "be deprived of life, liberty, or property without due process of law" expresses one of the most important principles of the Constitution. The Founding Fathers shaped this constitutional guarantee because they believed that a person's life, liberty, and property should not be threatened by or taken away because of the arbitrary or unreasonable action of the government, but rather could only be limited if the government followed a proper course of legal action. The Fourth, Fifth, Sixth, and Eighth Amendments provide a number of procedural guarantees for those accused of crimes and, taken together, those guarantees are often called due process rights. The Fifth Amendment's same words are in the Fourteenth Amendment, which holds the states to the same restrictions.

What are the **two types of jury systems** in the United States?

There are two types of juries serving distinct functions in the federal trial courts: trial juries (also known as petit juries) and grand juries. A civil trial jury is typically made up of six to 12 members. In a civil case, the role of the jury is to listen to the evidence presented at a trial, to decide whether the defendant injured the plaintiff or otherwise failed to fulfill a legal duty to the plaintiff, and to determine what the compensation or penalty should be. A criminal trial jury is usually made up of 12 members. Criminal juries decide whether the defendant committed the crime as charged. A judge usually sets the sentence. Verdicts in both civil and criminal cases must be unanimous. A jury's deliberations are conducted in private, out of sight and hearing of the judge, litigants, witnesses, and others in the courtroom.

A grand jury, which normally consists of 16 to 23 members, has a more specialized function. The prosecutor in federal criminal cases, the United States attorney, presents evidence to the grand jury for them to determine whether there is "probable cause" to believe that an individual has committed a crime and should be put on trial. If the grand jury decides there is enough evidence, it will issue an indictment against the defendant. Grand jury proceedings are not open to the public.

Do we as citizens have an **obligation to the judicial process**?

Absolutely. A fundamental right of citizens is to have their judicial case heard and decided by a "jury of their peers." Since "peers" means you and me, then every U.S.

citizen, in his or her role as a juror, performs a vital role in America's judicial system. As a juror, citizens support this fundamental right of their fellow neighbor and perform a basic civic function essential to the concept of democracy.

How are jurors selected?

Before potential jurors are summoned for service, their names are randomly drawn from voter lists (or sometimes licensed driver lists). Random selection allows for accessing a fair cross-section of the community and prohibits discrimination in the selection process. Because the Jury Act calls for a random selection of names, individuals cannot volunteer for service. The people whose names are selected are then mailed a questionnaire to determine whether they meet the legal qualifications of jury service. In order to be eligible, a potential juror must be at least 18 years old, be a citizen of the United States, and have resided within the judicial district that the court serves for one year. In addition, a potential juror must be able to read, write, understand, and speak the English language; be mentally and physically sound; and not have been convicted of a felony or have felony charges pending. Individuals who receive questionnaires are legally required to complete and return them to the clerk's office, which then screens the completed questionnaires to determine who is eligible. In some courts, however, qualification questionnaires and summonses—documents that legally require a citizen to report for jury duty—are mailed together. Members of the armed forces on active duty, professional fire and police department personnel, and active public officers of federal, state, or local governments are exempt from serving on juries.

THE FEDERAL COURT SYSTEM

How and when was the **federal court system** established?

During the period of the Articles of Confederation, from 1781 to 1789, the laws of the United States were not subject to a national court system or judiciary. Rather, they were interpreted haphazardly by the individual states, which often ignored interstate disputes or settled them unfairly. When the Founding Fathers shaped the Constitution, they followed the words of Alexander Hamilton, who maintained that "laws are dead letters without courts to expound and define their true meaning and operation." The articles and clauses they wrote were developed to meet the need of an arbiter (reviewer) of law with a national jurisdiction. Thus, Article III provides for one Supreme Court and such inferior courts as Congress may "ordain and establish." Additionally, Article I, Section 8 states that Congress has the power "to constitute tribunals inferior to the Supreme Court." The Judiciary Act of 1789 formally established the Supreme Court and federal court system.

What role does **Congress** play with respect to the federal courts?

The Constitution gives Congress the power to create federal courts other than the Supreme Court and to determine their jurisdiction, or area of authority and control. In addition, Congress controls the type of cases that are addressed in the federal courts. As part of the checks and balances system, Congress has three other basic responsibilities that determine how the courts operate. First, it decides how many judges there should be and where they will work. Second, through the confirmation process, Congress determines which of the president's judicial nominees ultimately become federal judges. Third, Congress approves the federal courts' budget and grants money for the judiciary to operate—an amount that constitutes less than 1 percent of the federal budget.

How is the **federal court system** structured?

The Supreme Court is the highest court in the federal judiciary. Congress has established two levels of federal courts under the Supreme Court: the trial courts (also known as district courts) and the appellate courts (also known as circuit courts). Together, the courts comprise a three-tiered system of justice.

There are 94 major trial courts, or district courts, in the United States. Each state has at least one, and no district court's jurisdiction includes more than one state. District court cases are usually heard by a single judge, who must be a resident of the district in which he or she presides. In addition to the district courts, Congress has created several special courts that have original jurisdiction over certain types of cases—for example, tax courts, customs courts, and military tribunals. Decisions of the district courts, special courts, administrative agencies, and state supreme courts may be appealed to the 13 U.S. courts of appeals. Often referred to as "circuit courts," these appellate courts also respect state boundaries, with several states making up one federal judicial circuit. There is a separate court of appeals for the District of Columbia and another called the Federal Circuit, both of which handle appeals generated by agencies of the federal government. Judges on circuit courts usually sit in panels of three; for especially controversial cases, all the judges on the circuit will hear the case together *en banc* (together), although this situation rarely occurs. At the peak of the federal judicial system is the U.S. Supreme Court, which is the final arbiter of the law—that is, the ultimate authority in deciding legal matters. It is the court of last resort for all legal cases in the United States, including matters of administrative law and constitutional questions.

What are the **district courts** and how are they organized?

The United States' 94 district courts are the trial courts in the federal judicial system. Over 600 judges handle 80 percent of the federal caseload—more than 300,000 cases per year. The 94 districts include at least one district in each state, the District of Columbia, and Puerto Rico. Each district includes a United States bankruptcy court as a unit of the district court. In addition, three territories of the United States—the Virgin Islands, Guam, and the Northern Mariana Islands—have district courts that hear federal cases, including bankruptcy cases. In district courts most federal cases are first tried and decided, and are generally heard by a single judge. Within limits set by Congress and the Constitution, the district courts have jurisdiction to hear nearly all categories of federal cases, including both civil and criminal matters. These cases include everything from personal injury to tax fraud.

There are two special trial courts that have nationwide jurisdiction over certain types of cases. The Court of International Trade addresses cases involving international trade and customs issues. The United States Court of Federal Claims has jurisdiction over most claims for money damages against the United States, disputes over federal contracts, unlawful "takings" of private property by the federal government, and a variety of other claims against the United States.

What are the **courts of appeal** and how are they organized?

The 94 judicial districts are organized into 12 regional circuits, each of which has a United States court of appeals, often called "circuit courts." Each court has from six to 28 judges. A court of appeals hears appeals from the district courts located within its circuit, as well as appeals from decisions of federal administrative agencies. Cases are generally presented to the courts sitting in panels consisting of three judges. There also is a Court of Appeals for the Federal Circuit with a nationwide jurisdiction to hear appeals in specialized cases, such as those involving patent, trademark, and copyright laws and cases decided by the Court of International Trade and the Court of Federal Claims.

What are the **"special courts"**?

Within the federal court system, Congress created certain "special courts" to hear a narrow range of cases pertaining to specific matters. These include the Court of Appeals for the Armed Forces, which reviews court-martial convictions of all of the armed services, and the Court of Veterans Appeals, which reviews decisions of the Board of Veterans Appeals. Grouped in this category are the United States Court of Federal Claims, which hears various claims against the United States, and the Tax Court, which hears controversies involving the payment of taxes. Various territorial courts and the courts of the District of Columbia are also special courts. In addition, there are a few other courts composed of regular U.S. district and appellate judges who provide their services in addition to their regular duties.

How is the **power of the federal courts** limited?

First and foremost, the power of the federal judiciary is limited by the system of checks and balances that exists in the federal government, which divides power among the executive, legislative, and judicial branches. The Constitution allows Congress to change the Supreme Court's jurisdiction; propose Constitutional amendments that, if ratified, can reverse judicial decisions; and impeach and remove federal judges. Only the president of the United States, with the advice and consent of the Senate, can appoint federal judges.

According to the Constitution, the federal courts can only exercise judicial powers and perform judicial work. They cannot make laws, which is the job of Congress, or enforce and execute laws, which is the job of the executive branch. Within their power to perform judicial work, the federal courts can only hear certain types of cases, those that fall both within the scope defined by Article III, Section 2 of the Constitution and congressional statutes. Selected types of cases that may be heard in the federal courts include cases in which the United States government or one of its officers is either suing someone or being sued. In addition, the federal courts may decide cases for which state courts are inappropriate or might be suspected of partiality.

What kind of **cases** do the federal courts hear?

In general, federal courts decide cases that involve the United States government, the United States Constitution or federal laws, or controversies between states or between the United States and foreign governments. A case that raises such a "federal question" may be filed in federal court, including, for example, a claim by an individual who may be entitled to money under a federal government program such as Social Security, a claim by the government that someone has violated federal laws, or a challenge to actions taken by a federal agency.

A case also may be filed in federal court based on the "diversity of citizenship" of the litigants (those involved in the case), such as between citizens of different states, or between United States citizens and those of another country. To ensure fairness to the out-of-state litigant, the Constitution provides that such cases may be heard in a federal court—but only if such cases involve more than $75,000 in potential damages. Claims below that amount may only be pursued in state court. Federal courts also have jurisdiction over all bankruptcy matters, which Congress has determined should be addressed in federal courts rather than the state courts. Through the bankruptcy process, individuals or businesses that can no longer pay their creditors may either seek a court-supervised liquidation (selling off for cash) of their assets, or they may reorganize their financial affairs and work out a plan to pay off their debts.

How are **federal judges** chosen?

According to the Constitution, Supreme Court justices, court of appeals judges, and district court judges are nominated by the president of the United States and confirmed by the Senate. The Senate Judiciary Committee typically conducts confirmation hearings for each nominee. Often, senators and members of the House who are of the president's political party recommend the names of potential nominees. However, the nomination process is often at odds with the confirmation process. The Senate is often leery of the nomination of judges whom they view as either too "liberal" or too "conservative." For example, the Democratic-controlled Senate played a major role in shaping the federal judiciary in President George W. Bush's administration. Democrats objected to Bush's judicial nominees on many grounds, including their contention that Bush's candidates tend to be conservative. As of May 2002, of the 100 candidates Bush nominated to the federal bench, the Senate confirmed half. Also as of May 2002, nine of Bush's 30 nominees to federal appeals courts were confirmed.

How long are the **terms** of federal judges and how are they **compensated**?

The Founding Fathers believed that an independent federal judiciary was essential to ensure fairness and equal justice for all citizens of the United States. Therefore, the Constitution makes specific allowances for federal judges' terms and salaries. According to Article III, federal judges—those of the Supreme Court, courts of appeals, and most federal district courts—have "good behavior" tenure as specified in the Constitution, which is generally considered to be a lifetime appointment. They can be removed from office only through impeachment and conviction by Congress. A few exceptions to the life term exist. Judges of the Court of Federal Claims, Tax Court, Court of Appeals for the Armed Forces, and Court of Veterans Appeals have 15-year terms, and judges of the territorial district courts in Guam, the Virgin Islands, and the Northern Mariana Islands have 10-year terms.

Congress sets the salaries and benefits that all federal judges receive. Judicial salaries are roughly equal to salaries of members of Congress. The Constitution states that the compensation of federal judges "shall not be diminished during their Continuance in Office," which means that neither the president nor Congress can reduce the salary of a federal judge. These two protections help an independent judiciary to decide cases free from popular opinion and political influence.

What are federal judges' **qualifications**?

The Constitution does not specify any requirements for federal judgeships. However, members of Congress, who typically recommend potential nominees, and the Department of Justice, which reviews nominees' qualifications, have developed their own informal criteria for selecting judges. In addition, the president, who appoints all federal judges, typically has a variety of individuals in mind for nomination, especially if he is considering appointments to the Supreme Court. Critics agree that the criteria for nomination include competency (including judicial or government experience), ideology or policy leanings (including justices with the president's party affiliation), religion, race, and gender. Historically, nominees have often been close friends of the president or those within his administration. However, presidents of late have looked beyond their immediate circle, typically nominating very accomplished private or government attorneys, judges in state courts, magistrate judges or bankruptcy judges, or law professors.

Has a federal judge ever been **impeached**?

Yes. In United States history, only 13 federal judges have been impeached—that is, accused and tried of certain wrongdoings. Of them, seven were convicted and removed from their positions by the Senate. Three late-twentieth-century examples include Harry E. Claiborne of the U.S. District Court in Nevada in 1986, on charges of income tax evasion and remaining on the bench following criminal conviction; Alcee Hastings of the U.S. District Court in Florida in 1989, on charges of perjury and conspiring to solicit a bribe; and Walter Nixon of the U.S. District Court in Mississippi in 1989, on charges of perjury before a federal grand jury.

Can anyone **observe a federal case** in process?

Yes. With certain very limited exceptions, each step of the federal judicial process is open to the public. A person who wishes to observe a court in session may go to the federal courthouse, check the court calendar, and watch a proceeding. Anyone may review the pleadings and other papers in a case by going to the clerk of court's office and asking for the appropriate case file. By conducting their judicial work in public view, judges enhance public confidence in the courts, and they allow citizens to learn firsthand how America's judicial system works. In a few situations the public may not have full access to court records and court proceedings, and these restrictions usually relate to high-profile trials. In these cases, there is often not enough space in the courtroom to accommodate all observers, and courtroom access may be restricted for security or privacy reasons. In addition, the judge may choose to place certain documents "under seal," meaning that they are not available to the public. Examples of sealed information include confidential business records, certain law enforcement reports, and juvenile records. Unlike most of the state courts, the federal courts generally do not permit television or radio coverage of trial court proceedings.

THE SUPREME COURT

What is the **Supreme Court** and how is it organized?

As mandated by the Constitution, the Supreme Court of the United States is the highest court in America. The Supreme Court was created as outlined in the Constitution

The Supreme Court building in Washington, DC, has housed the activities of the nation's highest court since 1935.

and by authority of the Judiciary Act of September 24, 1789. It was organized on February 2, 1790. The Court is composed of the chief justice of the United States and, since 1869, eight associate justices. Congress, which governs the Court's organization by legislation, varied the number of justices between five and 10 in the period prior to 1869. Congress requires six justices for a quorum—that is, a minimum number present—to do Court business.

What is the **jurisdiction** of the Supreme Court?

The Constitution limits the Supreme Court to dealing with "cases" and "controversies." The first chief justice of America, John Jay, clarified this restriction early in the Court's history by declining to advise President George Washington on the constitutional implications of a proposed policy decision. The Court does not advise the government or heads of state; rather, its function is limited only to deciding specific cases.

The Constitution states that the Supreme Court has original jurisdiction in all cases that affect ambassadors to the United States, other public ministers and consuls, and those in which a state is a party. The Constitution provides Congress with the authority to regulate the appellate jurisdiction of the Court—that is, Congress has authorized the Supreme Court to review judgments of lower federal courts and the highest courts of the states. The Supreme Court also has original jurisdiction in a select number of cases arising out of disputes between states or between a state and the federal government. In addition, the Supreme Court has the power of "judicial review," granted in 1803 when it was invoked by Chief Justice John Marshall in *Marbury v. Madison*. In that decision, Chief Justice Marshall ruled that the Supreme Court had a responsibility to overturn unconstitutional legislation, and that this power was a necessary consequence of its sworn duty to uphold the Constitution.

What is the importance of **judicial review**?

The Supreme Court's authority to overturn legislation or executive actions that, in the Court's judgment, conflict with the Constitution is based in America's democratic system of checks and balances. This power of "judicial review"—the authority to review acts of the other branches of government and the states and determine their constitutionality—has given the Court a crucial responsibility. Through the power of judicial review, the Court is charged with assuring citizens' individual rights as guaranteed by the Constitution, as well as in maintaining a "living Constitution" whose broad provisions are continually applied to complicated new situations.

While the function of judicial review is not explicitly described in the Constitution, it had been considered before the Constitution's adoption. Before 1789, state courts had already overturned legislative acts that conflicted with state constitutions. Moreover, many of the Founding Fathers expected the Supreme Court to assume this role in regard to the Constitution; Alexander Hamilton and James Madison, for example, underlined the importance of judicial review in the Federalist Papers. Since the first time judicial review was enacted, in *Marbury v. Madison* (1803), the Court has sparingly used this power: Between 1803 and 1999 the Court found a federal law unconstitutional in only 143 cases. While most of these decisions affected outdated laws no longer supported by either the president or Congress, some of the Court's ruling in this area were extremely controversial, including *Dred Scott v. Sandford* (1857), which declared the Missouri Compromise unconstitutional; *Lochner v. New York* (1905), which ruled that New York State could not regulate bankers' working conditions; and *Schechter Poultry Corp. v. United States* (1935), which declared the National Industrial Recovery Act unconstitutional.

What is the significance of ***Marbury v. Madison***?

Marbury v. Madison (1803) was the first Supreme Court case in which the Court exercised the power of judicial review. In that case, William Marbury, a last-minute judicial appointment by President John Adams at the end of Adams' term, sued James Madison, the secretary of the state under the new administration, for not upholding the appointment. The basis for Marbury's lawsuit was the Judiciary Act of 1789, which said that anyone not properly appointed could request a court order to obtain a due appointment, and that the Supreme Court had original jurisdiction in this type of case. Chief Justice John Marshall ruled the Supreme Court was not the place to address Marbury's case because the Constitution did not grant the Supreme Court "original jurisdiction" in this area. Thus, the terms of the Judiciary Act of 1789 violated the Constitution and therefore the act was void. Chief Justice Marshall's logic was that because the Constitution is the highest law in the land, established by the people, no entity expected to follow the laws of that document (i.e., Congress) should be able to make other laws that are in conflict with it.

With the *Marbury* decision, the Court took on the authority to declare acts of Congress unconstitutional if those acts exceeded the powers granted by the Constitution. Perhaps more importantly, however, the Court established itself as the arbiter of the Constitution, a role it has taken on ever since. It is because of this role that the Court was able to greatly expand people's civil liberties throughout the twentieth century.

How do Supreme Court justices **interpret the Constitution**?

Rarely is interpreting the Constitution a straightforward task. Because Supreme Court cases are complex, the Supreme Court has adopted various perspectives of constitutional interpretation, or doctrines, when exercising judicial review. The first is the doctrine of *original intent*. Original intent involves determining the constitutionality of a law on the basis of the original intent of the Founding Fathers. Justices who follow the doctrine of original intent often review key documents in order to "get inside the founders heads," including the Federalist Papers, James Madison's notes at the Constitutional Convention, and speeches made during the ratifying campaign. Those who criticize this theory claim that the issues before the Court today are more complex than 200 years ago and were probably never considered by the Constitution's authors. Instead, they view the Constitution as a *living document*, adaptable in light of the changing times, and maintain and that a law's constitutionality should be judged in the context of the entire history of the United States as a nation. In short, whether or not a given law is constitutional should reflect current societal conditions and values. Critics say this doctrine is highly subjective, since it reduces constitutional interpretation to an individual justice's perception of history.

From these two viewpoints emerged a third type of interpretation, often called the *plain meaning of text* doctrine. Under this doctrine, a law's constitutionality is measured against what the words of the Constitution obviously seem to say. Adherents to this perspective say that, unlike original intent, this measuring stick does not require debates about the intentions of a small group of men hundreds of years ago; unlike the living constitution theory, it does not invite a personal perspective of the country's history. However, reviewing the Constitution in terms of what it "seems to say" is not without controversy, since the framers purposely included ambiguous language in order to win ratification.

What is meant by the terms **"judicial restraint"** and **"judicial activism"**?

The various theories of Constitutional interpretation govern how any given justice will vote on a particular case. "Judicial restraint" maintains that the Court should use restraint when deciding whether or not to overturn a prior Court decision. "Judicial activism," on the other hand, says that sometimes precedents need to be overturned in light of today's societal conditions. Of the sitting justices, only two moderates—Sandra Day O'Connor and Anthony M. Kennedy—favor judicial restraint, since they believe that the people's elected representatives, not the Court, should change the laws. These two justices believe so strongly in judicial restraint that they are willing to uphold past decisions even if they do not personally agree with them. The more liberal justices—David H. Souter, Stephen Breyer, and Ruth Bader Ginsburg—favor judicial activism, because they believe that it may not always be appropriate to apply Court decisions of the past to complex twenty-first-century issues. The three conservative justices—William H. Rehnquist, Clarence Thomas, and Antonin Scalia—believe in judicial activism to a degree; they favor reversing only liberal decisions so that the original meaning of the Constitution can be restored. Only Justice John Paul Stevens cannot be neatly packaged into any one of these categories because he does not vote predictably.

What is the role of the solicitor general?

The solicitor general is a key officer in the Department of Justice. Often called the federal government's "chief lawyer," the solicitor general's job is to represent the United States in all Supreme Court cases in which the United States is a party. In addition, the solicitor general decides which cases the federal government should ask the Supreme Court to review, and what position the United States should take in cases before the Supreme Court. When the government wants to present its point of view in a certain case, it is the solicitor general who files the *amicus curiae* brief (a brief filed by a person or group that is not directly involved in a case but who has a vested interest in how it is decided).

How does a case **reach** the Supreme Court?

Most cases that reach the Supreme Court come from either the highest state courts or the federal courts of appeal. Most reach the Court by writ of certiorari, which in Latin means "to be made more certain." In essence, this writ is an order that the Court makes to a lower court to send up the record in a given case for the Court's review. Either party in a legal case can petition the Supreme Court to issue a writ of certiorari, although the Court only considers a limited number of petitions. If the Court denies a certiorari, then the decision of the lower case stands. A handful of cases also reach the Supreme Court by certificate, whereby a lower court asks the Supreme Court to clarify the rule of law that should apply in a particular case.

In order to have access to the courts, cases must meet certain criteria: the case before the court must be an actual controversy, rather than just a hypothetical one, and there must be two opposing parties involved; the parties to the case must prove a substantial stake in the case's outcome; and the case must be heard in a time period during which the case is still relevant. Cases that reach the Supreme Court are also dependent upon the justice's priorities, and often the Court's criteria for hearing a case are subjective. Justices consider a blend of information, such as whether a lower court decision conflicts with an existing Supreme Court ruling, whether the issue at hand was decided differently by two lower courts and needs the Court to resolve it, and whether the issue has potentially greater social significance beyond the interests of the parties directly involved.

How does the Supreme Court **reach a decision** and who sets this procedure?

The internal review process of the Court has largely developed over time by custom, while the procedures to be followed by petitioners to the Court are established in rules set forth by the Court. Each year the Court receives more than 7,000 petitions from state and lower federal courts. While examining all of the cases submitted, the Court agrees to hear oral arguments on about 90 each term. Also, the justices, without hearing oral arguments, decide a limited number of other cases—usually fewer than 75. The rest of the petitions are denied.

After initially examining each case submitted, the justices hold a private conference to decide which cases to schedule for oral argument, which to decide without argument, and which to deny. If at least four justices agree, a case will be taken by the Court for a decision, with or without oral argument, and the other petitions for review will be denied. If oral argument is heard, the parties are generally allowed a total of one hour to argue the issues and respond to questions from the justices. Later, in conference, the justices reach their decision by simple majority or plurality vote. A tie vote means that the decision of the lower court is allowed to stand. It is possible for such a vote to occur when one or three justices do not participate in a decision.

What are **briefs** and ***amicus curiae* briefs**?

Briefs are detailed documents filed with the Court before the oral argument is presented. Often running hundreds of pages, these critical documents are carefully crafted statements that support a particular side of the case. *Amicus curiae* ("friend of the court" in Latin) briefs are filed by individuals or public interest groups who are not parties in the case but who have a vested interest in its outcome. They are often a regular part of highly charged cases that involve issues such as abortion, the death penalty, or the separation of church and state. However, no matter how much a third party wants to express its opinion to the Supreme Court, *amicus curiae* briefs can only be filed with the Court's permission and by its specific request.

What is **opinion writing**?

In short, opinion writing is the way Supreme Court decisions are explained. The Court's opinion outlines the decision of the Court with regard to a particular case, and the Court's logic, or justification, for having reached the conclusion it did. The Court's opinion is often called the *majority opinion*. In addition, one or more of the justices who agree with the Court's decision will write a *concurring opinion*, which, in essence, makes or emphasizes a point to the argument that was not expressed in the majority opinion. Similarly, justices also write *dissenting opinions*, which voice a justice's reasons for disagreeing with the Court's majority opinion.

Who writes the opinions of the Supreme Court?

When the justices have decided a case, the chief justice, if voting with the majority, may write the opinion himself or assign an associate justice to write the opinion of the Court. If the chief justice is in the minority, the senior associate justice in the majority may write the opinion him- or herself or assign another associate justice in the majority to write the opinion. The individual justices may write their own concurring or dissenting opinions in any decision, and these statements often become references for discussing the implications of the case.

What is a ***per curiam*** **opinion**?

Almost all opinions, whether majority opinions or concurring or dissenting arguments, are dozens of pages long. However, some opinions the Court issues are very brief, often just a paragraph or two in length. These opinions, called *per curiam* opinions after their Latin meaning "for the court," are reserved for the less complicated cases.

What happens once a **decision** has been reached?

Once the Supreme Court rules on a particular case, it does not implement its decision. Rather, it sends the case back to the lower court from which it came, with instructions for that court to act in accordance with the Supreme Court's opinion. The lower court often has quite a bit of leeway in interpreting the Court's decision. In cases where the Supreme Court's decision affects only one central government agency, the decision usually becomes effective immediately. However, in the majority of rulings in which the Court's decisions affect many administrative and elected officials, the Court's decisions often take years to put into place. For example, many school districts remained segregated years after the Court declared the unconstitutionality of public school segregation in *Brown v. Board of Education of Topeka* (1954). A decision on the ways that warrantless searches are conducted would affect more than just police officers and chiefs of police, but also state attorneys general, local prosecutors, and trial court judges—all of whom must follow a new code of conduct in order for the Court's decision to be truly meaningful at an everyday level.

Why is so much **importance** placed on a Supreme Court decision?

The finality of the Court's decisions and the implications those decisions have on America's civil liberties is sobering. Article VI of the Constitution states that the Constitution and the laws of the United States made "in Pursuance thereof " shall be the supreme law of the land. When the Supreme Court rules on a constitutional issue, that judgment is virtually final; its decisions can only be altered by the procedure of constitutional amendment or by a new ruling of the Court. When the Supreme Court decides a case, particularly on constitutional grounds, it becomes the standard for lower courts and legislators when a similar question arises, thus setting a precedent for how future laws are made. Under its power of judicial review, the Court can declare laws unconstitutional, thus making them null and void.

How has the **Supreme Court's power** gradually expanded?

In the early years of the nation's existence, the judiciary was the weakest of the three branches of government. Chief Justice John Marshall greatly strengthened the judiciary when he established the principle of judicial review by declaring an act of Congress unconstitutional in *Marbury v. Madison* (1803). Although the Supreme Court only exercised this power one time prior to the Civil War (in *Dred Scott v. Sandford*, 1857), the establishment of judicial review made the judiciary more of an equal player with the executive and legislative branches. In fact, some scholars contend that the power of judicial review makes the Supreme Court in many ways a "lawmaking body" unto itself.

Since that time of equal footing, the Supreme Court has slowly expanded its power, particularly in the last 50 years. The Court has made substantive changes in policy areas, including school desegregation, legislative apportionment, obscenity, abortion, and voting rights. Without a doubt, the framers never imagined that the authority of the Supreme Court would encompass decisions regarding everything from gay rights to euthanasia, let alone the federal judiciary's hand in educational policy, hiring decisions, or affirmative action. In addition, since the 1960s the Court has broadened the way it does business—by allowing class action suits and aligning itself with various constituencies, such as civil rights, consumer, and feminist groups.

What kinds of cases does the Supreme Court hear today?

Few people are unaware that the Supreme Court has issued dozens of landmark decisions throughout the twentieth century, including *Brown v. Board of Education of Topeka* (1954), *Baker v. Carr* (1962), *Engel v. Vitale* (1962), *Miranda v. Arizona* (1966), *Roe v. Wade* (1973), and *United States v. Nixon* (1974), to name a few. Both the cases themselves and the Supreme Court's rulings—as far-reaching as segregation in public schools and the president's executive privilege—reflected the climate of the Court and the conflicts facing America at critical points in the nation's history. With

Pro-life and pro-choice advocates demonstrate in front of the Supreme Court building in response to the Court's decision in the case of *Webster v. Reproductive Services,* which increased the state's power to limit abortion, in July 1989.

the appointment of four new justices in the 1990s—David H. Souter, Clarence Thomas, Ruth Bader Ginsburg, and Stephen G. Breyer—and an overall conservative Court, recent rulings have placed limits on affirmative action, voting rights, the separation of church and state, and the power of the federal government in relation to the states. However, the Court has expanded several rights, including free speech, women's rights, and gay rights.

No time is perhaps more contentious that the early twenty-first century, when the Court ruled on a variety of issues, including the 2000 presidential election, the Fifth Amendment, hospital drug testing, religious activities for schools, heat-sensing police surveillance, freelance copyright protection, and Internet pornography. In the 2001–2002 term alone, the Supreme Court heard cases that dealt with issues as varied as tax exemption for Indian tribes, warrantless searches, due process guarantees, student grading and privacy rights, competition among rival phone companies, and the rights of mentally retarded convicted murderers.

How is the Court subject to **public opinion**?

Although the framers of the Constitution intended the Supreme Court to rule on cases solely on the basis of facts and law, and to be above the pressures of the general public, today's Supreme Court is indeed pressured by the citizenry. Virtually every public interest group—from pro-lifers to environmentalists—seek out good test cases

Supreme Court nominee Robert Bork, center, begins his 1987 confirmation hearings with the support of former president Gerald Ford, left, and Senator Bob Dole. The Senate ultimately voted to reject Bork's nomination, based largely on his ultraconservative views.

to present to the Court in hopes of advancing their policy positions. In fact, in most cases heard by the Supreme Court, either the government or a public interest group acts as the sponsoring party or an *amicus curiae* (third party). Groups as varied as the American Civil Liberties Union, the NAACP Legal Defense Fund, Concerned Women for America, and Americans United for Life Legal Defense Fund routinely act in this way, highlighting lower court decisions and ideological conflict for the judges in their *amicus* briefs. In addition, because of its controversial decisions on everything from gun control, abortion, affirmative action, and gay rights, the Supreme Court has routinely been the target of interest group protests outside the courtroom. The press-heavy 1989 pro-choice rally in Washington, D.C., was part of an intense and well-orchestrated lobbying effort to influence the outcome of *Webster v. Reproductive Services*. On another front, interest groups have recently begun lobbying against prospective Supreme Court justice nominees, as they did successfully in 1987 when President Ronald Reagan nominated former U.S. solicitor general Robert Bork to the bench. The Senate rejected Bork's nomination largely because of the influence of those who opposed Bork's extremely conservative opinions and points of view.

NOTABLE SUPREME COURT DECISIONS

Among the thousands of cases that have gone before the U.S. Supreme Court, a handful are considered landmark because of the implications of the Court's decision. The list below provides details on select cases that illustrate the power and range of Supreme Court decisions.

Year	Case	Summary of Decision
1803	*Marbury v. Madison*	In the first instance in which a law passed by Congress was declared unconstitutional, the Court established its right to overturn acts of Congress, a power not explicitly granted by the Constitution. Initially the case involved Secretary of State James Madison, who refused to seat four judicial appointees although they had been confirmed by the Senate.
1819	*McCulloch v. Maryland*	The Court's decision upheld the right of Congress to create a Bank of the United States, ruling that it was a power implied but not enumerated by the Constitution. In doing so, the Court advanced the doctrine of implied powers, or a loose construction of the Constitution; Chief Justice John Marshall maintained that the Court would sanction laws reflecting "the letter and spirit" of the Constitution.
1824	*Gibbons v. Ogden*	In a case that defined broadly Congress's right to regulate commerce, the Court held that the New York law regulating the operation of steamboats in that state was unconstitutional, since the power to regulate interstate commerce, which extended to the regulation of navigation, belonged exclusively to Congress. In the twentieth century, Chief Justice John Marshall's broad definition of commerce was used to uphold legislation protecting civil rights.
1857	*Dred Scott v. Sandford*	This controversial case that intensified the national debate over slavery involved Dred Scott, a slave who was taken from a slave state to a free territory. Scott filed a lawsuit claiming that because he had lived on free soil he was entitled to his freedom. Chief Justice Roger B. Taney disagreed, ruling that blacks were not citizens and therefore could not sue in federal court. Taney further inflamed antislavery forces by declaring that Congress had no right to ban slavery from U.S. territories, thus narrowing the scope of national power while increasing that of the states.
1896	*Plessy v. Ferguson*	This infamous decision asserted that "equal but separate accommodations" for blacks on railroad cars did not violate the "equal protection under the laws" clause of the Fourteenth Amendment. By defending the constitutionality of racial segregation, the Court paved the way for the repressive Jim Crow laws of the South.
1914	*Weeks v. United States*	In a unanimous decision, the Court maintained that, according to the Fourth Amendment, private possessions obtained in a search conducted without a search warrant cannot be used against a defendant and in fact must be returned to the defendant.
1919	*Schenck v. United States*	The Court upheld the Espionage Act, which allowed for the arrest of individuals attempting to cause insubordination in the military or to obstruct military recruitment. In determining this action to be beyond the scope of free speech, Justice Oliver W. Holmes said that a person who encourages draft resistance during a war is a "clear and present danger."

Year	Case	Summary of Decision
1935	*Schechter Poultry Corp. v. United States*	In a decision that invalidated the National Industrial Recovery Act, which gave the president the power to implement industrial codes, regulate workers' hours and wages, and determine the minimum age of employees, the Court declared that Congress could not delegate its power to the president.
1943	*West Virginia Board of Education v. Barnette*	The Court ruled that the West Virginia Board of Education's requirement that all students and teachers in public schools must salute the flag is unconstitutional under the First Amendment, reversing its prior decision in *Minersville School District v. Gobitis* (1940).
1944	*Korematsu v. United States*	The Court determined that the rights of an individual Japanese American who lived in an area that was deemed off-limits to those of Japanese ancestry (under Executive Order 9066) were secondary to the government's need to protect itself against espionage during wartime, thereby upholding the unconstitutional internment of Japanese American citizens during World War II.
1954	*Brown v. Board of Education of Topeka*	This case invalidated racial segregation in schools and led to the unraveling of de jure segregation in all areas of public life. In the unanimous decision spearheaded by Chief Justice Earl Warren, the Court invalidated the *Plessy* ruling, declaring "in the field of public education, the doctrine of 'separate but equal' has no place" and contending that "separate educational facilities are inherently unequal." Future Supreme Court justice Thurgood Marshall was one of the NAACP lawyers who successfully argued the case.
1957	*Roth v. United States*	The Court's ruling determined that obscene materials are not protected by the First Amendment, and defined obscene materials as those that appeal to "prurient interests" and lack any "redeeming social importance."
1961	*Mapp v. Ohio*	In maintaining the Fourth Amendment protection against illegal search and seizure, the Court extended the federal exclusionary rule to the states, preventing state prosecutors from using illegally obtained evidence in a criminal trial.
1962	*Engel v. Vitale*	In a case that has defined the bounds of the separation of church and state, the Court ruled that official prayer in public schools is a violation of the Constitution's establishment clause (which prohibits the establishment of a national religion) after a group of 10 parents sued the board of education in Hyde Park, New York, over the expectation that students would recite a specific prayer each school day.
1963	*Gideon v. Wainwright*	The Court overturned the Florida felony conviction of Clarence Earl Gideon, who had defended himself after having been denied a request for free counsel. The Court held that the state's failure to provide counsel for a defendant charged with a felony violated the Fourteenth Amendment's due process clause. Gideon was given another trial, and with a court-appointed lawyer defending him, he was acquitted.
1964	*New York Times v. Sullivan*	L.B. Sullivan, a police commissioner in Montgomery, Alabama, had filed a libel suit against the *New York Times* for publishing inaccurate information about certain actions taken by the Montgomery Police Department. In overturning a lower court's decision, the Supreme Court held that debate on public issues would be inhibited if public officials could sue for inaccuracies that were made by mistake, and thus extended the First Amendment rights of the press. The ruling made it more difficult for public officials to bring libel charges against the press, since the official had to prove that a harmful untruth was told maliciously and with reckless disregard for truth.

Year	Case	Summary of Decision
1966	*Miranda v. Arizona*	The Court overturned the conviction of Ernesto Miranda, who had confessed to a crime during police questioning without knowing he had a right to have an attorney present, ruling that criminal suspects must be warned of their rights before they are questioned by police. These rights are: the right to remain silent, to have an attorney present, and, if the suspect cannot afford an attorney, to have one appointed by the state. The police must also warn suspects that any statements they make can be used against them in court. Miranda was retried without the confession and convicted.
1971	*Lemon v. Kurtzman*	In a decision that actually involved three separate but similar cases, the Court maintained that the use of public funds to supplement or reimburse the salaries of teachers of secular subjects in nonpublic schools—and indeed, any government assistance to religious schools—violated the establishment clause, the section of the Constitution that explicitly states that the government may not establish a national religion. Chief Justice Berger's majority opinion outlined what has become known as the "Lemon test" for determining whether a law violates the establishment clause.
1971	*New York Times v. United States*	The Court ruled that the Nixon administration's attempts to exercise prior restraint to block the *New York Times*' publication of a classified Defense Department study of American activities during the Vietnam War known as "The Pentagon Papers" were in violation of the First Amendment's guarantee of freedom of the press. Justice Brennan determined that since publishing the information would not jeopardize the immediate safety of American troops, prior restraint was unjustified.
1972	*Furman v. Georgia*	This Court decision found all death penalty statues then in force in the states to be in violation of the Eighth and Fourteenth Amendments, but held out the possibility that if they were rewritten so as to be less subjective and randomly imposed, they might be constitutional (as the Court has subsequently held in many instances).
1973	*Roe v. Wade*	In the decision that legalized abortion and is at the center of the current controversy between "pro-life" and "pro-choice" advocates, the Court ruled that a woman has the right to an abortion without interference from the government in the first trimester of pregnancy, contending that it is part of her "right to privacy." The Court maintained that right to privacy is not absolute, however, and granted states the right to intervene in the second and third trimesters of pregnancy.
1974	*United States v. Nixon*	When President Richard Nixon refused to turn over audio tapes subpoenaed in the course of the Watergate investigation, citing "executive privilege," or the right of the president to withhold information from the other branches of government in cases involving confidentiality or national security, the Court determined that executive privilege was not absolute nor above subpoena, especially in the face of due process of law. Nixon turned over the tapes and resigned shortly thereafter.
1978	*Regents of the University of California v. Bakke*	In the case that imposed limitations on affirmative action to ensure that providing greater opportunities for minorities did not come at the expense of the rights of the majority, the Court ruled that while race was a legitimate factor in school admission, the use of rigid quotas was not permissible. In

Year	Case	Summary of Decision
		other words, affirmative action was unfair if it lead to reverse discrimination. The case involved the University of California, Davis, Medical School and Allan Bakke, a white applicant who was rejected from the school twice even though there were minority applicants admitted with significantly lower entrance qualifications than his.
1985	*New Jersey v. T.L.O.*	In considering a case in which a school principal's search of a high-school student's purse resulted in the discovery of evidence of drug use and trafficking, the Court maintained that the Fourth Amendment applies to public school officials, who must observe "reasonableness" standards when—but are not required to obtain search warrants before—searching students suspected of breaking the law or school rules.
1986	*Bowers v. Hardwick*	In a case involving enforcement of Georgia's law against sodomy, the Court ruled that states have the power to regulate sexual relations in private between consenting adults of the same sex.
1988	*Hazelwood v. Kuhlmeier*	The Court ruled that schools are free to set guidelines and standards for the content that appears in a student newspaper without violating the First Amendment, because it is reasonable to allow schools to determine the appropriateness of content issued under their authority.
1989	*Texas v. Johnson*	The Court ruled that flag burning is a constitutionally protected form of expression, asserting that "if there is a bedrock principle underlying the First Amendment, it is that the Government may not prohibit the expression of an idea simply because society finds the idea itself offensive or disagreeable."
1989	*Webster v. Reproductive Health Services*	The Court upheld a Missouri law forbidding public employees to perform most abortions, prohibiting the use of public buildings for abortions, and requiring a fetal viability test prior to abortions after the twentieth week of pregnancy. This case set a precedent allowing other states to restrict access to abortions.
1990	*Cruzan v. Missouri Department of Health*	The Court's decision maintained that due process of law cannot be denied even to those incapable of pursuing due process themselves—in this case, an incapacitated patient whose family is pursuing the right of that patient to refuse life-support treatment. A victory for the right-to-die movement, the decision in effect validated a person's right to refuse medical treatment.
1995	*Vernonia School District v. Acton*	The Court determined that random drug testing of high school athletes is not a violation of the Fourth Amendment right against unreasonable search and seizure, and that the government's (school's) right to ensure the safety of minors under its supervision overrides the privacy rights of those students.
1996	*United States v. Virginia*	In a case that affected attitudes toward woman serving in the military, the Court ruled that the Virginia Military Institute's policy of admitting only male students was in violation of the Fourteenth Amendment, and that the establishment of a parallel program for women failed to meet the requirements of the equal protection clause.
2002	*Board of Education of Independent School District 92 v. Earls*	Extending the *Vernonia* decision, the Court upheld that random drug testing for students involved in any extracurricular activities is not a violation of the Fourth Amendment, citing the need to detect and prevent drug use as outweighing the right to privacy.

The nine current justices of the Supreme Court—who are appointed for life—comprise the highest court in America.

THE JUSTICES

What is the role of the **chief justice**?

In addition to hearing cases and writing opinions, as presiding officer of the Court the chief justice is responsible for the Court's administration. The federal law outlines these administrative duties, which range from assigning associate justices and himself to the circuit courts to approving regulations for the protection of the Court building and grounds. In practice, the chief justice oversees all matters affecting the justices and procedures of the Court. The statutory duties of the chief justice—which reach beyond the Court itself—include the administrative leadership of the entire federal judicial system. The chief justice is chair of the Judicial Conference of the United States (a "board of trustees" for the federal court), chair of the Federal Judicial Center, and overseer of the Administrative Office of the United States Courts, unofficially dubbed the "housekeeper" and statistician for the federal court system. By statute, the chief justice sits on the boards of the National Gallery of Art, the Smithsonian Institution, and the Hirshorn Museum.

Who were the **Supreme Court chief justices** over history?

Sixteen Supreme Court chief justices have served the United Sates since the Court's inception. They are: John Jay (1789–1795); John Rutledge (1795); Oliver Ellsworth

(1796–1800); John Marshall (1801–1835); Roger B. Taney (1836–1864); Salmon P. Chase (1864–1873); Morrison R. Waite (1874–1888); Melville W. White (1888–1910); Edward D. White (1910–1921); William Howard Taft (1921–1930); Charles Evans Hughes (1930–1941); Harlan Fiske Stone (1941–1946); Fred M. Vinson (1946–1953); Earl Warren (1953–1969); Warren E. Burger (1969–1986); and William H. Rehnquist (1986–present).

Who are the Supreme Court justices?

Although Congress has periodically altered the size of the Court (the lowest number of justices serving being six, and the most 10), since 1869 the number of justices has held steady at nine. Today the Supreme Court is comprised of the chief justice of the United States, William H. Rehnquist, and eight associate justices. The eight associate justices are John Paul Stevens, Sandra Day O 'Connor, Antonin Scalia, Anthony M. Kennedy, David H. Souter, Clarence Thomas, Ruth Bader Ginsburg, and Stephen G. Breyer. Besides serving on the Court, each justice is assigned to one of the Court of Appeals for emergency response purposes.

Which **chief justices** also served as associate justices?

Only five men in Supreme Court history have fulfilled both positions: John Rutledge, Edward D. White, Charles Evans Hughes, Harlan Fiske Stone, and William H. Rehnquist.

Which justice served the **shortest term**? Which justice served the **longest**?

The justice who served the least amount of time is John Rutledge, who served one year as associate justice and four months as chief justice, although he never received confirmation by the Senate. William O. Douglas served the longest, for more than 36 years. Other contenders came close to Douglas by just two years: Stephen J. Field, John Marshall, Joseph Story, Hugo Black, and William J. Brennan all served for 34 years or slightly more. Marshall's 34-plus-year tenure was the longest for a chief justice.

Who became the **first woman member of the Supreme Court**?

Appointed by President Ronald Reagan in 1981, Justice Sandra Day O'Connor is the first woman justice on the Supreme Court bench. O'Connor is known for her moderate leanings and is regarded as one of the Court's most influential members. Prior to her Court appointment, O'Connor held several posts in Arizona: assistant attorney general, state senator, and superior court judge. Governor Bruce Babbitt appointed her to the Arizona Court of Appeals in 1979. Ruth Bader Ginsburg, the only other female Supreme Court justice, was appointed by President Bill Clinton in 1993.

On the Bench: The Supreme Court Today

Name	Year Appointed	Appointing President	General Voting Record	Prior Judicial Post
William H. Rehnquist b. 1924	1972	Richard Nixon; elevated to Chief Justice by Ronald Reagan	Conservative	Assistant Attorney General, Office of Legal Counsel
John Paul Stevens b. 1920	1975	Gerald Ford	Liberal	U.S. Court of Appeals for the Seventh Circuit
Sandra Day O'Connor b. 1930	1981	Ronald Reagan	Moderate	Arizona Court of Appeals
Antonin Scalia b. 1936	1986	Ronald Reagan	Moderate	U.S. Court of Appeals for the District of Columbia Circuit
Anthony M. Kennedy b. 1936	1988	Ronald Reagan	Moderate	U.S. Court of Appeals for the Ninth Circuit
David H. Souter b. 1939	1990	George Bush	Liberal	U.S. Court of Appeals for the First Circuit
Clarence Thomas b. 1948	1991	George Bush	Conservative	U.S. Court of Appeals for the District of Columbia Circuit
Ruth Bader Ginsburg b. 1933	1993	Bill Clinton	Liberal	U.S. Court of Appeals for the District of Columbia Circuit
Steven Breyer b. 1938	1994	Bill Clinton	Liberal	U.S. Court of Appeals for the First Circuit

Who was the **first African American justice**?

Thurgood Marshall—Howard University Law School valedictorian, civil rights activist, and great-grandson of a slave—was nominated to the Supreme Court by President Lyndon Johnson in 1967. As chief counsel for the National Association for the Advancement of Colored People (NAACP) for two decades prior to his Supreme Court tenure, the liberal Marshall argued many precedent-setting cases. He is best known for his representation in *Brown v. Board of Education of Topeka* (1954), in which racial segregation of American public schools was declared unconstitutional. President John F. Kennedy appointed Marshall to the United States Court of Appeals for the Second Circuit in 1961, and from 1965 to 1967 Marshall served as solicitor general under Presi-

Sandra Day O'Connor, the first woman to serve on the U.S. Supreme Court, was appointed by President Ronald Reagan in 1981.

dent Lyndon Johnson. Marshall retired from the Court bench in 1991, after which the conservative African American justice Clarence Thomas took his seat.

What were some of the more interesting highlights of **Ruth Bader Ginsburg's appointment**?

Ruth Bader Ginsburg, the second woman in history to sit on the Court, was appointed in 1993 by President Bill Clinton. When Justice Byron White announced in March 1993 that he would retire from the Supreme Court, the Clinton administration put together its list of potential nominees. However, Ginsburg's name was not on the list, until her husband, Martin Ginsburg, began lobbying for his wife's seat on the Court through an intensive letter-writing campaign. Mr. Ginsburg called on such notables as legal scholars, academics, the presidents of Stanford and Columbia Universities, and Texas governor Ann W. Richards, who called or wrote the White House rallying for Ginsburg's nomination. Clinton was commended by many for nominating Ginsburg, a woman of Jewish faith, to fill the traditionally "Jewish seat" on the Court, which had been vacant for over 20 years.

Which **Supreme Court justice nomination** came under Senate scrutiny and a highly publicized Senate confirmation trial?

President George Bush's 1991 nomination of Clarence Thomas, the second African American to sit on the Court, was extremely controversial. Thomas, a past chair of the Equal Employment Opportunity Commission (EEOC), was opposed to affirmative actions programs that he felt gave preferential treatment to minorities. As a conservative, Thomas stood in stark contrast to the man he was replacing, African American civil rights activist Thurgood Marshall, raising eyebrows among the Democratic-controlled Senate Judiciary Committee. Generally supported by the black population and civil rights groups, Thomas initially escaped a certain degree of media criticism. However, Anita Hill, a former EEOC lawyer and past employee of Thomas', soon came forward with charges of sexual harassment, igniting fiery confirmation hearings before the Senate Judiciary Committee. After a sensational examination, the Senate finally confirmed Thomas by a narrow margin. However, many commentators note that Thomas' nomination was perhaps most costly to George Bush, who as a result of his choice lost the support of women voters in the 1992 presidential election.

Thurgood Marshall, the first African American Supreme Court justice, served on the Court from 1967 until his retirement in 1991.

Which **president** appointed the most justices?

President George Washington appointed the most justices—a total of 11—but only 10 actually served. In the twentieth century, President Franklin D. Roosevelt appointed a total of nine justices during his terms in office, including such notables as Hugo Black, Felix Frankfurter, and William O. Douglas.

What was **Franklin D. Roosevelt's Court-packing plan**?

After President Roosevelt's New Deal programs were put in place, the Supreme Court ruled several of those measures unconstitutional, including the National Recovery Act and the Guffey Coal Act of 1935. The Court invalidated FDR's Agricultural Adjustment Act, ruling that the processing tax that funded federal subsidies to farmers was unconstitutional, and that the states, not the federal government, held the power to regulate agriculture. Fearful that the Court would apply their states-rights reasoning to multiple New Deal measures and that his carefully crafted domestic policy would falter, in February 1937 Roosevelt sent Congress a bill to reorganize the federal judiciary.

Dubbed the "Court-packing" plan by its critics, the bill cited the inability of the federal courts to handle their overwhelming caseload and proposed multiple judicial reforms, including the president's appointment of one justice to the Supreme Court for every one who refused to retire by age 70. It also called for a maximum of six new Supreme Court justices. Roosevelt's argument lost credibility when the Supreme Court began ruling in Roosevelt's favor, upholding both a Washington State minimum wage law and the Social Security Act. The bill died in July 1937, amidst an angry citizenry who voiced its outrage over what it branded Roosevelt's plan to rig the American judiciary. Despite this upheaval, due to deaths and retirements in the Court, Roosevelt was able to appoint seven new associate judges over the next four years.

Who was the only full-term president who did not appoint a Supreme Court justice?

In the twentieth century, only President Jimmy Carter failed to appoint any Supreme Court justices to the bench. In addition, three other presidents in U.S. history made no appointments: William Harrison, Zachary Taylor, and Andrew Johnson.

STATE COURTS

What is the role of **state courts**?

The primary function of the state courts is to hear disputes between private parties and between private parties and the government. Because almost every state court has the power to exercise judicial review, they fulfill the role of "watchdog" on the conduct of other state and local government agencies.

What kind of **law** applies to state courts?

Four basic forms of law are applied in the states courts: constitutional law, statutory law, administrative law, and common law. *Constitutional law* deals with those laws based on the articles of the Constitution. Laws affecting a citizen's civil liberties fall under constitutional law. *Statutory law* embodies those laws or statues that are adopted by legislative bodies (such as the U.S. Congress and the state legislatures), the people (through the powers of initiative or referendum), and civil councils. (Initiative is the petition process by which voters put a proposed constitutional amendment or statute on the ballot; referendum is the process whereby a measure passed by a legislature is submitted to voters for either their approval or rejection.) *Administrative law* is the term used to describe law that embodies the rules and regulations of federal, state, or local executive officers. *Common law* refers to unwritten law that has formulated over centuries and is based upon the generally accepted ideas of the court. Common law applies to those situations where a violation has already occurred; *equity*, on the other hand, is a code of law that seeks to prevent wrongdoings before they occur, and is often carried out in the form of an injunction.

What kind of **cases** do the state courts hear?

Most cases are handled in the state court system. In fact, 99 percent of legal disputes in American courts are decided in the separate state court systems. State courts have jurisdiction over virtually all divorce and child custody matters, probate and inheritance issues, real estate questions, and juvenile matters. In addition, they handle most criminal cases, contract disputes, traffic violations, small claims, and personal injury cases.

How are **state courts** structured?

Because states are free to structure their judicial systems as they choose, each state system varies somewhat. However, most states have chosen a four-level model. At the lowest level are courts of limited jurisdiction, which hear minor civil and criminal cases—for example, traffic, juvenile, and small claims courts that settle disputes involving small sums of money. These are the "workhorses" of the state judicial system because they process the majority of the state's legal cases. The next level consists of state courts of general jurisdiction. These are the major trial courts of the state, empowered to hear more serious criminal cases and civil cases in which large sums of money are involved. Most states have a third tier, the intermediate court of appeals, where a party can appeal a case. Finally, there is the top level, called the state supreme court. Legal custom allows each losing litigant one appeal (with the notable exception of the prosecution in a criminal case). In states without an intermediate appellate court, the state supreme court must hear these appeals.

What is the **state supreme court's role** and how is it organized?

As the highest court in the state judicial system, the state supreme court primarily reviews the decisions of lower courts that are appealed to it. The size of the state supreme court is determined by each state's constitution, although in most states somewhere between five and seven justices sit on the bench. Like the U.S. Supreme Court in the federal system, the state supreme court is the "court of last resort" at the state level, having the final say in all state law. State supreme court cases that raise questions of federal law may be appealed to the U.S. Supreme Court, although few seldom are. An appeal from a state supreme court will only be heard in the U.S. Supreme Court if a matter of federal law is involved in the case and the Supreme Court agrees to hear the appeal.

How are **state judges** selected?

Another detail left to the states' discretion is the method of selecting judges. While all federal judges are appointed for life terms by the president of the United States with the approval of the Senate, four primary methods are currently used to select state judges: partisan elections, nonpartisan elections, election by the state legislature, and appointment by the governor, which includes a merit system for selecting candidates. Sometimes called the "Missouri Plan" after the first state to adopt it, within the merit system judicial nomination boards screen applicants of judicial posts and send a list of the best-qualified candidates to the governor of the state, who makes the final selection. In 23 states, the governor appoints the justices; in four states, the legislature selects the judges; and in 23 states, voters choose.

ORIGINS OF AMERICAN GOVERNMENT

THE COLONIAL ERA

EARLY EXPLORATION OF THE AMERICAS

What is the significance of the **European Age of Exploration on the founding of America**?

The European countries' decision to seek a water route to Asia at the end of the fourteenth century resulted in one of the most significant eras in the history of the world. By the mid–eighteenth century, virtually the entire world, including the continents of the Americas, became known to them, and their attempts to conquer and colonize these new lands were the beginning of what we now call a global economy. Unfortunately, European possession of the new lands also ushered in some of the most unethical behaviors in the history of western civilization—most notably the African slave trade and the aggressive invasion of lands settled by peaceful natives. To this day, the world's political and economic structures still show the powerful influences of the European Age of Exploration.

Did **Christopher Columbus** discover America?

Italian mariner Christopher Columbus (1451–1506) sailed in the service of King Ferdinand and Queen Isabella of Spain and made four voyages to the Caribbean and South America between 1492 and 1504. Columbus' claim to fame rests on the fact that in 1492 he led in the first successful discovery of the Americas, or "New World," when, believing he had reached the outskirts of the India, he touched foot on the islands off Cuba and Hispaniola. However, archaeological evidence from the northern Atlantic coast of North America suggests that the Vikings visited and for a time inhabited the area several hundred years before Columbus embarked on his voyages. Perhaps it is more accurate to say that the native peoples living in the Americas before the arrival of Columbus were the true discoverers of these lands.

Italian explorer Christopher Columbus (center, kneeling) is credited with discovering America and known for his 1492 landing on the islands off Cuba and Hispaniola.

How did **America** get its name?

The New World that Christopher Columbus encountered was not named for Columbus but rather for a relatively obscure Florentine seaman named Amerigo Vespucci (1454–1512). In 1508, two years after the death of Columbus, a geographer and mapmaker named Martin Waldseemuller (?–1521), who was an admirer of Vespucci, announced that Amerigo had discovered this part of the world and therefore it should be named America. The suggestion took hold and appeared on the new maps, and thus historians still refer to the lands that Columbus encountered as the Americas.

What exploration attempts were involved in **establishing North America**?

In the period following the fifteenth-century discoveries and conquests of the Spanish and Portuguese, geographic expansion was entirely the work of the English, French, and Dutch. During the next 200 years, nearly every considerable remaining land mass in the world, with the exception of Antarctica, was explored and mapped by explorers from these countries. Since the English, French, and Dutch were latecomers to world exploration and conquest, most of the prime lands were already occupied and defended by Spanish and Portuguese forces, and so their efforts concentrated on lands unclaimed by either country, in North America. At the time, it was believed by many that a "Northwest Passage" existed, a water route to India either around or through the North American continent. It was primarily this search for the Northwest Passage that revealed the wonders of the North American interior to Europeans.

ENGLAND CLAIMS TERRITORY IN THE NEW WORLD

How did **England venture into the New World**?

The English colonization of North America was the result of the patrimonial philosophy that the king of England, on the basis of discovery and exploration by Englishmen, was the rightful owner of any unclaimed territory and he could do with it as he saw fit. With the support of strong monarchs and capital from investment companies, England began to plant settlements in North America.

What is **imperialism**?

Imperialism is the policy and practice of extending a nation's power over new territories and their economies. Hence, many historians term England "imperialistic England" for its supremacy over the North American colonies.

What is a **colony**?

A colony is a territory ruled over by a foreign country without becoming a part of that country, especially in the case where natives of that country move to the territory in large numbers to become permanent residents.

What was a **charter**?

A charter was a written grant of authority from the king. Charters were issued to trading companies, groups of colonists, and individuals, giving them the legal right to venture to the New World and establish a colony. All of the 13 English colonies were established on the basis of the king's charter, with the exception of Georgia, whose charter was granted by Parliament. Additionally, the charters authorized several types of colonial governments.

What was a **trading company**?

The first permanent English settlement—Jamestown, Virginia—was founded by a trading company chartered by the king. Joint-stock trading companies were run by wealthy businessmen and had emerged during the sixteenth century for the express purpose of conducting commerce with various parts of the world. They were chartered by the government and given certain benefits, such as monopoly of trade in a particular region. In return, these companies were expected to protect the political interests of England and to assume the expense of governing the colonies. The joint-stock system allowed risks and costs, and also profits, to be shared between the company and the king.

What was the role of **the London Company and the Plymouth Company**?

In 1606, King James I (1566–1625) chartered two trading companies, the London Company and the Plymouth Company, to establish settlers in the New Land. The London Company was granted the right to colonize the southern part of "Virginia," and the Plymouth Company was granted the right to colonize the northern part. The next year three ships landed settlers at Jamestown, Virginia. The first colonists, then, were actually employees of the London Company. These chartered companies became the feudal lords of their promised lands, with the purpose of establishing a presence on the land and making a profit for the shareholders.

What were **indentured servants**?

During colonization, there were two kinds of indentured servants: voluntary and involuntary. Voluntary servants were people, often trained in a craft or skill, who could not afford passage to the colonies. In exchange for their passage, they agreed to work for a period of four to seven years for a colonial master. At the end of this period, the servant became a freeman and was usually granted land, tools, or money by the former master. Involuntary indentured servants were either criminals whose sentence was a period of servitude, or the impoverished, or those in debt. Most cases of indentured servitude were involuntary. The period of obligation to a colonial master was longer than that of a voluntary servant, usually seven to 14 years. But, like their counterparts, the involuntary servants also received land, tools, or money at the end of their contract, and they, too, became freemen. Approximately 60 percent the colonial immigrants were indentured servants.

Many indentured servants were drawn from England, Ireland, Scotland, and Germany. In European ports, people contracted themselves or became involuntarily contracted to ship captains, who transported them to the colonies where their contracts were sold to the highest bidder. Colonial laws ensured servants would fulfill the term of their obligation; any servant who ran away was severely punished. Laws also protected the servants, whose masters were obligated to provide them with housing, food, medical care, and even religious training. The system was prevalent in the mid-Atlantic colonies, but it was also used in the South. When the economies of the Caribbean islands failed at the end of the 1600s, plantation owners sold their slaves to the mainland, where they worked primarily on southern plantations, replacing indentured servants by about 1700. In other colonies, the system ended with the American Revolution (1775–1783).

What was the **headright system**?

The arrival of indentured servants in the American colonies addressed a labor shortage that emerged in the early 1600s. In 1618, the Virginia Company, a joint-stock enterprise that encouraged the development of Virginia, adopted a new charter based on the "head-right system": Englishmen who could pay their own Atlantic crossing were granted 50 acres of land; each of their sons and servants were also granted an additional 50 acres. Other colonies were also developed under the headright system, with the land amounts varying by colony. Soon there were more farms than there was labor to work the fields. The colonists solved this problem through the system of indentured servitude.

THE PILGRIMS JOURNEY TO THE NEW WORLD

Who were the original **Pilgrims**?

The Pilgrims were not explorers, but rather early settlers who sought religious freedom from the Anglican church in England and self-government in the New World. Since their journey to the New World was a religious journey, they described themselves as pilgrims.

Why did the **Pilgrims leave their home** for the unknown?

A group of people originally from England, the Pilgrims were known as Separatists—Protestants who separated from the Anglican Church of England to set up their own church. In 1609 they fled their home in Scrooby, England, and settled in Holland. Fearing their children would lose contact with their own culture and become assimilated into the Dutch culture, the group decided to voyage to America to establish their own community.

Under what **conditions did the Pilgrims travel**?

The Pilgrims were in all likelihood familiar with stories of the explorations in the New World and with the settlement in Virginia. Although they possessed neither adequate resources, nor patrons, nor a patent (a document granting the privilege to assume lands), they decided to travel to America. At this time, the Virginia Company was attempting to cure its financial ills by offering privileges and lands to "undertakers" who would set up private plantations. With the help of Sir Edwin Sandys, they secured a patent on June 19, 1619, and an unofficial assurance that the king would not harm them. Although the patent provided that they should settle within Anglican Virginia, they were to be allowed to live as a distinct body with their own government, subject only to the laws of the colony as a whole. They expected to obtain a grant of religious toleration. During the delay that ensued while the Pilgrims awaited royal approval of their grant, Thomas Weston, the leader of a group of London merchant adventurers, obtained a patent from the Virginia Company in the name of John Pierce, one of his associates. Approaching the Pilgrims in Leyden, he persuaded them to abandon their patent and join his group with the promise that the adventurers would supply the funds and handle the business end of the undertaking.

According to the agreement reached by the two parties, those persons going to the colony were to stand as equal partners with the London adventurers in the company. Three groups shared in the investment: 70 London adventurers who paid 10 pounds sterling per share; planters who received one share each for their labor; and adventurer planters who were reckoned as having two shares each, one by purchase and a second by going to America. The adventurers in London were to exercise no civil authority over the planters. In addition to these passengers and the crew, 101 passengers departed from Plymouth, England, on September 16, 1620. The Pilgrims comprised less than half the group. There were approximately 35 Pilgrims from Leyden, but of the 66 passengers recruited by the adventurers from London and Southampton, most were "strangers." Because the *Speedwell*, the ship in which the Pilgrims had come from Leyden, proved unseaworthy, all had to crowd aboard the *Mayflower* at Plymouth.

When did the ***Mayflower*** reach Cape Cod?

In 1620 the Pilgrims arrived on the rocky western shore of Cape Cod Bay, Massachusetts. Their transatlantic crossing had taken 66 days aboard the *Mayflower*. Two babies were born during the passage, bringing the number of settlers to 103, only approximately 35 of whom were Pilgrims.

What was the **Mayflower Compact**?

Because the *Mayflower* passengers had traveled beyond the jurisdiction of the Virginia Company's patent, they needed to establish some form of legitimate government. On November 11, 1620, the Pilgrims drafted an agreement by which the adult male passengers aboard the *Mayflower* formed a body politic that was authorized to enact and enforce laws for the community. The men on the *Mayflower* signed the Mayflower Compact as a basis for their new civil government. The infamous quote from this brief document, "We solemnly and mutually, in the presence of God, and one of another, covenant and combine ourselves together in a civil body," bound the settlers to create a representative government and abide by its laws.

Why was the Mayflower Compact not a **constitution**?

When the Pilgrims drafted the Mayflower Compact, it was in the form of a Separatist Church covenant. By its terms, the 41 signatories (the adult male passengers aboard the *Mayflower*) formed a "civill body politick," giving them the power to enact laws for the common good and obligating all to obey such laws. It provided the group of colonists with a basic form of government, but it was not a constitution, since it did not outline the rules by which the government would operate, nor discuss the limitations of its powers, as a true constitution does. Further, constitutions declare the liberties of individuals and government restraints in relation to these liberties. However, the Mayflower Compact was a landmark document in its own right, since it provided a precedent for later voluntary democratic compacts that would establish a contractual relationship between the government and the governed.

What **conditions met the Pilgrims**?

The first year was difficult for the handful of Pilgrims that arrived on the *Mayflower*, and they met many hardships. Thirty-five more colonists arrived aboard the *Fortune*, putting a strain on already limited resources. Sicknesses such as pneumonia, tuberculosis, and scurvy claimed many lives, including that of Plymouth's first governor John Carver (1576–1621). Furthermore, the merchants in the group challenged the purity of the settlement. Having secured a new patent from the Council of New England in June 1621, the lands of New Plymouth Colony were held in common by both the Pilgrims and the merchants. But this communal system of agriculture proved unsuccessful, and in 1624 William Bradford (1590–1657), who had succeeded Carver as governor, granted each family its own parcel of land. The Wampanoag Indians, who had previously occupied the land settled by the Pilgrims, proved friendly and were helpful advisers in agricultural matters. In 1626 the Pilgrims bought out the merchants' shares, and claimed the colony for themselves. Though they were inexperienced at government before arriving in America and had not been formally educated, the Pilgrims successfully governed themselves according to the Scriptures, and Plymouth Colony remained independent until 1691, when it became part of Massachusetts Bay Colony, founded by the Puritans.

ENGLISH PHILOSOPHY THAT SHAPED EARLY COLONIAL THOUGHT

What was the concept of **sovereignty** that the colonists had been ruled under?

British kings under whom the colonists were ruled in England believed that the government was all-powerful and held supreme authority, or sovereignty, over the people.

King John signs the Magna Carta, the landmark document that in 1215 established the concept of limited government by recognizing personal liberties and placing bounds on the power of the monarchy.

This ideology would hold the colonists until pre–Revolutionary War tensions ultimately forced them to challenge the rules of their mother country. The colonists would adopt a concept of *popular sovereignty* for their new government, giving the people the right to rule, or govern themselves.

What is the **Magna Carta**?

The Magna Carta is a landmark English document that established that the power of the English monarchy was not absolute. In 1215, King John (1167–1216) was forced to sign the document, known as "the Great Charter," by his barons, who were angered by the king's encroachment on their rights. The document, which includes such basic rights as trial by jury and due process of law, protected the people from an authoritarian government and helped set the stage for the concept of a limited government that would be created in the New Land.

The charter has been credited with insuring personal liberty and putting forth the rights of the individual. It stipulated that the king, like the people he ruled, was subject to the laws of the land. In that the Magna Carta made a provision for a Great Council, to be comprised of nobles and clergy who would approve the actions of the king in relation to his subjects and ensure the tenets set forth in the charter were upheld, it is credited with laying the foundation for a parliamentary government in England. It is still considered by many to be the cornerstone of constitutional government.

What is the **Petition of Right**?

The Petition of Right, which English King Charles I (1600–1649) was forced to sign in 1628 before Parliament would give him additional tax money, challenged the idea of the divine right of kings, and established that even a monarch must obey the laws of the land. This document limited the king's power by ensuring political rebels trial by jury before imprisonment; forbidding the king to declare martial law, or military rule, during peacetime; and forbidding the king to tax the people without the consent of the parliament.

What does **"divine right"** mean?

Divine right is the concept of government that dominated the sixteenth- and early-seventeenth-century Europe and maintains that a monarch receives the right to rule directly from God (hence the term "divine") and not from the people.

What is the English Bill of Rights?

In order to limit the powers of King William III (1650–1702) and Mary of Orange (1662–1694), who ascended to the throne in 1689, and to prevent abuse of powers in future monarchs, Parliament issued a declaration, later enacted as the Bill of Rights. The English Bill of Rights severely limited royal power: It prohibited a standing army during peacetime without the consent of Parliament; required that all parliamentary elections be free; and prevented lawmaking without the consent of parliament. It also provided for the right to a fair and speedy trial, and freedom from cruel and unusual punishment. Since the Bill of Rights served to assert the role of Parliament in the government of England, it is considered one of the seminal documents of British constitutional law.

Who was **John Locke** and why was he important?

English philosopher John Locke (1632–1704) challenged the concept of a king's divine right to rule, and instead introduced the concept of the "social contract" of government. Locke's idea about government—mainly that it can only exist with the consent of the people—had an enormous effect on the politics of the next century and sowed the seeds for the American Revolution. The American Declaration of Independence and the Constitution are based on principles set forth in Locke's essay, *Two Treatises of Civil Government*, wherein Locke proposes a theory for the origins and purpose of government based on natural law.

What is the concept of **natural law**?

Philosopher John Locke maintained that because God had given each person his or her life, it was part of God's "natural law" that the individual was the only rightful owner of his life, that each had this right equally, and that the right was therefore inalienable. Locke argued that before government existed, each person had sole responsibility for the defense of his or her own rights. For convenience and the better protection of their rights, people established societies with governments by consenting to a social contract. For Locke, it followed that the only legitimate reason a government had for existing was to preserve and protect rights. If the government violated individual rights, it destroyed the social contract, and this violation released the individual from any obligation and justified rebellion in order to establish a new social contract.

What **ideas did the English colonists bring** with them that would help shape the government of the United States?

Three cornerstones of English thought helped establish the government of the New Land: government is ordered—that is, there is an inherent order, or hierarchy, in government; government is limited, and not all-powerful; and government is representative, serving the will of the people and representing their voice.

What is an **ordered government**?

An ordered government is one of the fundamental ideals upon which the European settlers thought a government should be based. Quite simply, it is one that has an orderly regulation of units of government and governmental offices. The units of townships and counties and the offices of sheriff and justice of the peace are just a few of the creations that were established in response to the colonists' desire for an ordered hierarchy.

What is a **limited government**?

A limited government is just that: limited in its scope and power. Coming from under the authoritarian rule of the king, colonists saw a need for a new government that was not all-powerful. Closely tied to this concept is the ideal that each individual has certain rights that the government cannot take away or infringe upon, and the government is thus limited in the way that it relates to its people. The signing of the Magna Carta in 1215 established the concept of limited government in England.

What is a **representative government**?

A representative government represents it people. The concept that government should serve the will of the people had been growing in England for a number of centuries, so when the colonists developed a new government it was essential that the means for representing the voice of the people be integrated into their new system.

What was the **Iroquois League**?

Although the European settlers came to the Americas with their own views of government and established a new government in a New Land, they did not bring government itself to the Americas. Native Americans had their own kind of government in place—in the form of political institutions that worked to accomplish the goals of the state and political leaders who enacted these goals. The most complex of these was called the Iroquois League, a confederation formed by five Native American groups: the Seneca, Cayuga, Oneida, Onondaga, and Mohawk (they were later joined by the

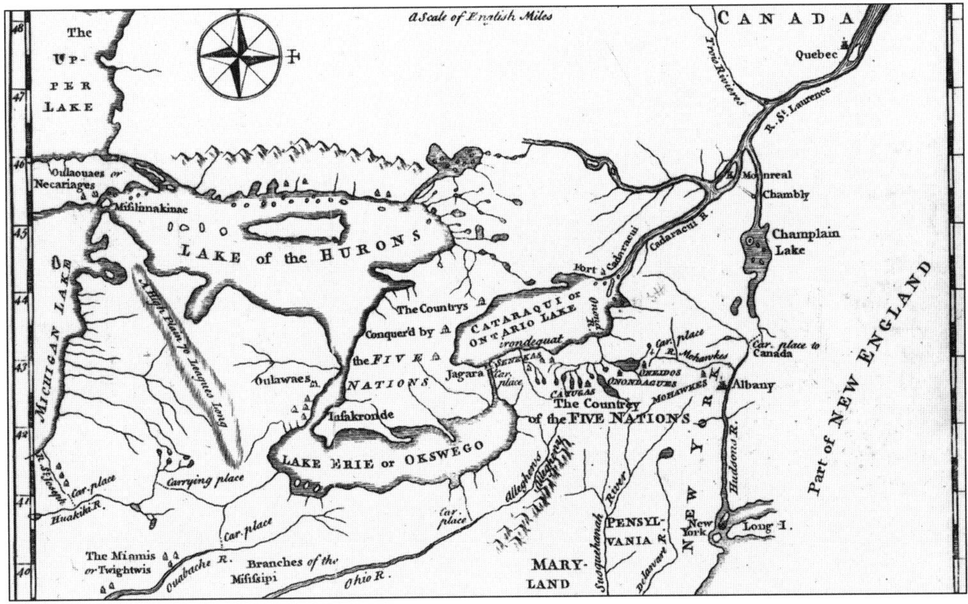

Parts of what are now New York, Canada, and the Great Lakes region made up the country of the Iroquois League, a confederation of Native American tribes that governed the area for more than 200 years until overcome by the increased European presence in America.

Tuscarora tribe). The league was established to end conflicts among the groups, but it turned into a successful form of government that lasted for more than 200 years.

THE PLANTING OF THE COLONIES AND BRITISH COLONIAL GOVERNMENT

Where was the **first successful English settlement**?

The first permanent English settlement was founded at Jamestown, Virginia, in 1607. Virginia was the first of 13 colonies established in North America.

What was the **Lost Colony**?

While many people consider Virginia to be the first colony, it is more appropriate to say that it was the first *successful* colony. Few people have heard about the so-called Lost Colony, a failed attempt by the English to establish a colony in the Americas. Originally established in 1587 on Roanoke Island, off the coast of North Carolina, by 1590 it had dis-

English explorer Sir Walter Raleigh (1552–1618) is credited with commissioning one of the first settlements in America, the so-called "Lost Colony" on Roanoke Island, in 1587. By 1590, the colony had disappeared without a trace.

appeared without a trace. Navigator Sir Walter Raleigh (1554–1618) sent a group of colonists to America, but these ships were headed for areas near Chesapeake Bay, farther north (in present-day Virginia). Reaching the outer banks, the ships' commander refused to take the colonists to their destination and instead left them at Roanoke Island, the site of earlier failed attempts at colonization. The colonists' leader, John White, returned to England for supplies in August 1587. However, the ongoing war between England and Spain prevented him from returning to the colony until three years later. Arriving back at Roanoke in August 1590, he expected to be met by family members and the 100 or so settlers. Instead he discovered an abandoned area.

Two theories explain what might have become of the lost colonists: Since the shore of Chesapeake Bay was their original destination, the colonists might have moved there but, encountering resistance, perished at the hands of the Indians. Other evidence suggests that the colonists became integrated with several Indian tribes living in North Carolina. Either way, they were never seen again by Europeans.

What was the **Plymouth Settlement**?

Though their colonial charter from the London Company specified the Pilgrims were to settle in Virginia, they decided to establish their colony at what is now known as Cape Cod, well outside the company's jurisdiction. By December 1620, just several months after landing in the New World and a month after drafting the Mayflower Compact, the Pilgrims had chosen the site for their settlement and began building at New Plymouth. The Plymouth Settlement was the second colony established in North America.

What was the difference between how the two early colonies of **Virginia and Massachusetts** were founded?

Virginia, the first colony, was organized as a commercial venture under the king's charter. Its first colonists were the employees of the private trading corporation, the

Early settlers work to build the fort at Jamestown, Virginia, the first permanent English settlement established in 1607.

Virginia Company. Massachusetts, on the other hand, was claimed by the Pilgrims, people who traveled from England to North America in search of greater religious freedom. Both sets of people, however, were shaped by their English heritage, and the formation of the colonies reflects that fact.

Who founded **Massachusetts Bay Colony**?

The Puritans who founded Massachusetts Bay Colony were, like the Pilgrims, religious Protestants (both sects "protested" the Anglican Church). But while the Pilgrims separated from the church, the Puritans wished to purify it. Their religious movement began in England during the 1500s and they were influenced by the teachings of reformer John Calvin (1509–1564). They also had strong feelings about government, maintaining that people can only be governed by contract (such as a constitution), which limits the power of a ruler. When King James I ascended the throne of England in 1603, he was the first ruler of the royal family of Stuart. The Stuart monarchs, particularly James' successor, King Charles I, tried to enforce absolute adherence to the High Church of Anglicanism and viewed the Puritan agitators as a threat to the authority of the Crown.

Persecuted by the throne, groups of Puritans fled England for the New World. One group was granted a corporate charter for the Massachusetts Bay Company (1629). Unlike other such contracts, which provided the framework for establishing colonies in America, this one did not require the stockholders to hold their meetings in England. Stockholders who made the voyage across the Atlantic would become voting citizens in their own settlement; the board of directors would form the legislative assembly; and the company president, Puritan leader John Winthrop (1588–1694), would become the governor. In 1630 they settled in what is today Boston and Salem, Massachusetts, establishing a Puritan Commonwealth. By 1643, more than 20,000 Puritans had arrived in Massachusetts, in what is called the Great Migration. Puritans also settled Rhode Island, Connecticut, and Virginia during the colonial period.

What were the **Dutch colonial holdings**?

New Netherlands was the only Dutch colony on the North American mainland. It consisted of lands surrounding the Hudson River (in present-day New York) and, later, the lower Delaware River (in New Jersey and Delaware). Explorers from the Netherlands (Holland) first settled the area in about 1610. In 1624 the colony of New Netherlands was officially founded by the Dutch West India Company. On behalf of the company, in 1626 Dutch colonial official Peter Minuit (1580–1638) purchased the island of Manhattan from the American Indians for an estimated $24 in trinkets. The colonial capital of New Amsterdam (present-day New York City) was established there. The Dutch held the colony until 1664 when it was conquered by the English under the direction of the Duke of York (James II, 1633–1701), the king's brother. The English sought the territory since New Netherlands separated its American holdings. Under British control the area was divided into two colonies—New Jersey and New York.

What were the **Swedish colonial holdings**?

The Swedish possessions consisted of a small colony called New Sweden, established in 1638 at Fort Christina (present-day Wilmington), Delaware. The Swedes gradually extended the settlement from the mouth of the Delaware Bay (south of Wilmington) northward along the Delaware River as far as present-day Trenton, New Jersey. The settlers were mostly fur traders, though there was farming in the colony as well. In 1655 the territory was taken by the Dutch in a military expedition led by director general of New Netherlands Peter Stuyvesant (c. 1610–1672). For nine years the territory was part of the Dutch colonial claims called New Netherlands. In 1664 the English claimed it and the rest of New Netherlands. Delaware was established as a British proprietary colony, which it remained until the outbreak of the American Revolution. New Sweden was the only Swedish colony in the Americas.

What were the **13 colonies** and how long did it take them to be established?

Each of 13 colonies were established separately, and for different reasons, over the course of 125 years. Just prior to the outbreak of the Revolutionary War, the 13 colonies were: Virginia, founded in 1607 by the London Company; Massachusetts Bay

Colony, founded in 1628 by the Puritans; New Hampshire, founded in 1629 by John Mason; Maryland, founded in 1634 by Lord Baltimore; Rhode Island, founded in 1636 by Roger Williams; Connecticut, founded in 1636 by emigrants from Massachusetts; Delaware, founded in 1638 by William Penn; North Carolina and South Carolina, founded in 1663 by eight nobles; New York, founded in 1664 by the Duke of York; New Jersey, founded in 1664 by Lord John Berkeley and Sir George Carteret; Pennsylvania, founded in 1681 by William Penn; and Georgia, founded in 1732 by James Oglethorpe.

What did the charters have to do with classifying the colonies and establishing forms of government?

Charters not only granted the right to colonize, they determined the rules for establishing government in the colonies. For the government of the London Company, which established the colony of Virginia at Jamestown, there was a superior council in England with general powers that directed a subordinate council in the colony that was required to govern according to the laws of England. The colonists had no share in their own government; rather they were granted the liberties guaranteed to all Englishmen at the time, such as trial by jury and free speech. The company had the power to make and enforce laws for the colony, as long as they were in concurrence with English law. Three types of colonial government were outlined in the charters: royal (or crown), charter (also known as corporate), and proprietary (a form of chartered government). Regardless of their beginnings, at the start of the American Revolution, colonial government was either royal or chartered.

What was a **royal colony**?

A royal colony was subject to the direct control of the king of England. The king named a governor to serve as the colony's chief executive, and a council, also appointed by the king, served as an advisory body to the royal governor. Over time, the governor's council came to be defined as the upper house of the colonial legislature and the highest court in the colony. The lower house of a bicameral, or two-house, legislature was elected by those property holders who met voting qualifications. It shared with the governor and his council the right to tax and the right to spend. The governor appointed the judges for the colony's courts. Under this royal colony system, the laws passed by the legislature had to be approved by the king. On the eve of the American Revolution, the royal colonies were New York, New Hampshire, Massachusetts, New Jersey, Virginia, North Carolina, South Carolina, and Georgia.

What was a **charter colony**?

A charter colony was founded based on a charter, or written grant of authority, from the king of England. Because the two charter colonies (at the time of the American

Revolution) of Connecticut and Rhode Island were established based on charters granted to the colonists themselves, they were self-governing. These colonists drew up their own charters and presented them to the king, an act that set a precedent in America for written contracts that defined governmental power. According to these charters, the governors were elected by the male property-holders in each colony. The legislatures of the charter colonies were bicameral, or of two parts, but not subject to the governor's veto or the Crown's approval. Colonial judges were appointed by the legislature, but appeals could be taken to the king. The charters that established these two colonies were the most liberal of all charters.

What was a **proprietary colony**?

Proprietary colonies were a form of a chartered colony. They were those colonies established by a proprietor; that is, a person to whom the king of England had made a grant of land. According to the king's charter, the land could be governed according to the laws of the owner, but the owner had to acknowledge the sovereignty of the king. The governments of these colonies were similar to those of the royal colonies, with one notable exception: the governor was appointed by the proprietor. The legislatures were bicameral, with the exception of Pennsylvania; the upper house was appointed by the proprietor, and the lower house was elected by male property holders. The governor's council did not act as one house of legislature as with the royal colonies. The laws, except those of Maryland, were subject to the approval of and veto by the king. Just before the Revolutionary War, there were three propriety colonies: Delaware, Maryland, and Pennsylvania. Lord Baltimore was granted Maryland in 1632, and William Penn was granted Pennsylvania in 1681. Penn also acquired Delaware from the Swedes, who first settled the colony. The colonies of New York, New Jersey, North Carolina, and South Carolina also began as proprietary colonies, but later became royal colonies.

What were the principle differences between **royal** and **chartered** governments?

Governments in the American colonies were of two principle types: royal and chartered. The Crown owned and governed a *royal* colony and appointed the chief executive officer, called a governor. A *chartered* colony was privately owned. It was a gift, by charter, of royal lands and powers to a trading company or a private person, by the king. This first type of chartered colony included Virginia and Plymouth. Both were founded by selling stock to the public. The second type of chartered colony was known as a *proprietary* colony and was administered by a governor who was either appointed by the colony owners or chosen by the people of the colony. Examples are William Penn's grant of Pennsylvania and Lord Baltimore's grant of Maryland. The proprietary colonies were self-governing, as long as the proprietors did not try to establish laws and institutions that were contrary to English precedents. The trend, however, during the colonial period was for the colonies that were discovered by explorers and supported financially by the king to be taken over by the Crown as royal colonies. By the middle of the eighteenth century all the American colonies were under the direct rule of the Crown and were governed by a chief executive appointed by the king. Exceptions were the proprietary colonies of Deleware, Maryland, and Pennsylvania and the incorporated colonies of Connecticut and Rhode Island, which maintained independent status until the American Revolution.

What does **bicameral** mean?

Bicameral means a legislative body consisting of two chambers. The following colonies had bicameral legislatures: Connecticut, Rhode Island, Maryland, Delaware, Virginia, Massachusetts, New Hampshire, North Carolina, South Carolina, New York, and New Jersey. Today, the U.S. Congress is bicameral, consisting of a Senate and House of Representatives.

What does **unicameral** mean?

Unicameral means a legislative body consisting of one chamber. Only two colonies had unicameral legislatures: Pennsylvania and Georgia.

How did **Virginia** become a royal colony?

King James I, for whom the colonial capital Jamestown was named, was at first content with colonization under the London Company's direction. But in 1624, he charged the company with mismanagement and revoked its charter, and Virginia became the first royal colony. Virginia remained a royal colony until 1776, although royal governors such as Sir Francis Wyatt and Sir George Yeardley continued to call meetings of the general assembly without the Crown's approval. A serious challenge to self-government came during 1629 to 1635 with Governor John Harvey's "executive offenses," including the knocking out of a councilor's teeth and the detaining of a petition of protest to the king.

What was the **Charter Oak Affair**?

The Charter Oak Affair of 1685 to 1688 began when King James II revoked the Connecticut charter. In 1687, Sir Edmund Andros (1637–1714) went to Hartford, dissolved the colonial government, and demanded that the colonists return the charter. In response, Captain John Wadsworth hid it in an oak tree. After the Glorious Revolution in England in 1688, which established a constitutional balance between the Crown and Parliament, the charter was taken out and used as the law of the colony. Subsequent British monarchs allowed for the restoration of rights, and the event solidified the concept of loyalty to a constitution, rather than loyalty to a king.

What was the role of the **governor**?

The royal governor of an American colony was appointed to serve the interests of the king and Great Britain, as well as the interests of the colony. Because these were not always compatible, his responsibilities were often in conflict, and sometimes impossible to reconcile. Governors of proprietary companies were responsible for serving the owners.

The appointed royal governor arrived with a commission and a set of instructions from the king. (It was the Board of Trade that issued these—the king only approved them.) The commission authorized the form of government in the colony. It was to consist of a legislature made up of a Crown-appointed council of important local citizens and an elected assembly. This body had the power to pass legislation for governing of the colony, provided the laws passed did not run counter to the laws of England. The legal basis of the governor's instructions was never clarified. The colonists saw them merely as guidelines for the governor that could be dispensed with in new situations. In Britain, however, they were seen as royal commands that carried with them the force of law.

The governor's primary function was to run the colony's political affairs. If he was to be an effective leader, he first studied local politics, learning about the various factions and their leaders. He had the power of patronage, thus appointing judges, justices of the peace, and many secondary posts. This power gave him a strong hold over local affairs, because he only appointed those who would support his policies. As the eighteenth century progressed, the government in Britain cut back on his authority to make local appointments and forced on him more and more appointees from England. These people (known as spoilsmen) felt little responsibility to the governor and often refused to obey his orders. Consequently the governor's control over local affairs diminished significantly. In 1774, Lord Dunmore, governor of Virginia, said that if he had the power of appointments he could have put down the revolution. This is unlikely, but it indicates the extent to which the governor's power had diminished.

The governor was also the commander in chief of the colony. His power in this area was held in tight check by the legislature, which was seldom willing to appropriate money for military ventures unless the colony was certain to benefit from them. After 1755 the governor's military power was limited even further by placement of a stateside British commander in chief who controlled all royal troops. In naval matters the governor had even less power. After 1689 he had no jurisdiction over the personnel of British warships stationed in his colony. After 1702 he had no control at all over the activities of royal ships. As a result, naval commanders tended to flaunt their powers and ignore colonial courts, creating a real threat to civil authority.

Did **governors rule independently**?

Colonial governors did not rule their colonies as independent authorities. They had to work with two local bodies, the council and the assembly. The council, usually about 12 in number, was an advisory board to the governor. Its members were chosen by the governor with the consent of the Board of Trade; in proprietary colonies, they were appointed by the owners or elected. Often, councilmen were colonials, men of standing in the colony, and usually served for life. Some of the governor's functions could only be carried out with the consent of the council, such as summoning the assembly, issuing paper money, establishing martial law, and appointing judges and other officers. But in other matters, such as suspending officers and dissolving the legislature, the governor could act alone. The governor sat with the council in its judicial function and was president of the court, but his vote counted no more than any other. The council can be seen as a parallel to the House of Lords and as a predecessor to the Senate of the United States Congress.

What was the role of the **assembly**?

The assembly was an elected body with franchise requirements varying from colony to colony. Generally, however, an assemblyman had to be white, at least 21 years of age, Christian (in most colonies Protestant), and a person of property. The assembly made the laws of the colony, though these had to be approved by the royal government in England. Governors frequently were in conflict with their assembly, especially if they tended to take a highly authoritarian stance with them. The governor's main control over the assembly was his right to veto legislation, even before it was sent to England for approval. The assembly, on the other hand, because of its right to initiate all money bills, had control over the governor. In many instances, when the assembly was displeased with the governor's actions, it would simply refuse to raise the money to pay the governor's salary until he consented to meet its wishes. In addition, the assembly could delay any appropriations bills favored by the governor.

When did the **Virginia legislature** first meet?

In a Jamestown church on July 30, 1619, the convening of the first representative assembly in the New World took place. The Virginia legislature consisted of a council chosen by the London Company and a house of burgesses (or representatives) from each settlement in the colony elected by the colonists. This event marked the reality of self-government through locally elected representatives and became an important precedent for the English colonies.

What **types of local government** did the colonies establish?

The colonies developed two leading types of local government, the New England town and the southern county. Towns were shaped in New England as the first colonists came as groups—either as congregations or those seeking religious freedom—wanting to live in close proximity. The rugged soil and harsh climate and the presence of Indians encouraged small-scale farming and residence in tightly knit, compact communities. The southern colonies were settled under different circumstances, by individual entrepreneurs who were met with land and climate conducive to large-scale agriculture. The plantation system active in that region necessitated a unit of local government larger than that of the North, and hence the county was born.

A hybrid, called a county-town, emerged in the middle colonies. In all three types, the units of local government had only as much power as the central government delegated to them. The New England town fostered a spirit of democracy, while the county tended to lean toward aristocratic government.

What were the characteristics of a **town**?

The town was the leading unit of local self-government in New England. Towns were incorporated, and their boundaries and powers were defined by the colonial legislatures. The town was governed by town meetings, where discussions about political issues took place, and voters exercised the town's powers. In this sense, the town was a direct democracy. In between town meetings, a board of between three and 13 selectmen, including a town clerk and constable, managed the affairs of the town. Other town officers included the treasurer, assessors, collectors, and clerks. The town was also an electoral unit, with direct representatives to the colonial legislature chosen at its meetings.

What were the characteristics of a **county**?

Unlike towns, counties had no popular assembly, and so by nature were less democratic than the town. The principle officers were the lieutenant, sheriff, justices of the peace, and coroners, who were appointed by the governor at the recommendations of the justices of the peace. The justices dominated county government, and thus the county became the unit of representation in the colonial assembly and that of military, judicial, and fiscal administration.

What were the **qualifications for voting**?

Each colony had its own qualifications for voting, however every colony limited the act to white, male property owners. Eight colonies required that voters own real estate; five required that voters own private property; and certain colonies included religious qualifications. Only a small percentage of those who entitled to vote actually did. Election districts were large, transportation and communication were not well developed, and party organization was just beginning. As in England, there were two political parties: the Tories, who supported royal power; and the Whigs, who opposed it.

Why couldn't women vote at this time?

The American colonies, and later the United States, based their legal system on English common law. Under common law, a married woman could not own property (even property she brought into the marriage) and had no legal identity separate from her husband's. During the colonial period, voting and office holding usually were restricted to property owners and hence closed to married women. There were a few instances of unmarried women (spinsters or widows) as property owners voting in the colonial period, and at least one woman tried to serve in a colonial legislature. On January 21, 1648, Margaret Brent, a landowner who would have been entitled to a vote in the assembly if she had been a man, tried unsuccessfully to be seated in the Maryland House of Burgesses. She demanded two votes in the assembly, one as the executrix for the estate of the deceased governor and one for herself as a freeholder.

COLONIAL PEOPLE AND PERSONALITIES

Who was **Captain John Smith**?

It was the energy, resourcefulness, and military skill of Captain John Smith (1580–1631) that historians say saved the Plymouth Colony from both starvation and destruction by the Indians. Smith met with Indian chief Powhatan (c. 1550–1618) to negotiate the purchase of foodstuffs and furs from the Indians. His understanding of many European languages was evidence of a natural talent, and he soon became fairly proficient at the local Indian tongues, enhancing his ability to negotiate with the tribes and establishing himself, in the minds of the local Indians, as the leader of the white settlement. As the leader of the Jamestown settlement, he charted the coast and wrote the first American book, *A True Relation*, which effectively publicized English colonization of the New World.

What was the **relationship between the colonists and the Indians** like?

Early encounters between European colonists and Native Americans were often warm and cooperative in spirit, though there were exceptions to this. As time passed, however, and English settlements expanded up and down the coast and further inland, tentative economic and social bonds that had been established began to fray. Many tribal leaders became increasingly alarmed at white encroachment. These fears spurred Opechancanough, leader of an alliance of Indian tribes known as the Powhatan Confederacy, to lead a murderous attack on the Jamestown, Virginia, settlement in 1622 that killed 350 colonists. In the aftermath of the massacre, the Virginia colonists suspended their modest efforts to incorporate willing Indians into their society. Violence between Indian and colonial groups became increasingly commonplace.

The Indians proved unable to present a united front against the English, who established their preeminent position throughout New England and the coastal

European settlers established trade relationships with the Native Americans, exchanging items such as metal objects and weaponry for animal pelts and agricultural goods.

colonies with advantageous treaties and victories in a series of bloody conflicts. As the seventeenth century unfolded, colonists resorted to increasingly ruthless measures to neutralize the Indians. Various Indian tribes struck back on occasion (such as in King Philip's War of 1675), but by the end of the 1670s the English dominated all of the areas where they had settled. During the first half of the eighteenth century, the power and standing of various Indian tribes in eastern North America continued to diminish. Even the Iroquois League (comprised of the Cayuga, Mohawk, Oneida, Onondaga, Seneca, and Tuscarora tribes), which had proven to be both resilient and cunning in its dealings with the English and the French in previous decades, found that its long-time strength was eroding under the increasing European presence.

What role did **Chief Powhatan and his Algonkian Indian Confederacy** play?

In the late 1500s and early 1600s, the Indian chief Wahunsonacock presided over the Powhatan Confederacy, an alliance of Indian tribes and villages stretching from the Potomac River to the Tidewater region of present-day Virginia (comprising 128 to 200 villages consisting of eight to nine thousand inhabitants and encompassing up to 30 different tribes). The English called Wahunsonacock "Powhatan" (Falls of the River), after the village where the Indian leader dwelled. (Today this village is Richmond, Virginia.) As ruler of this region, Powhatan played a pivotal role in relations with early

English colonists in Virginia. Powhatan's daughter, Pocahontas (c. 1595–1617), married John Rolfe (1585–1622), the English colonist who developed tobacco farming in Virginia. Powhatan's brother, Opechancanough, led the Powhatan uprisings against English settlers in 1622 and 1644.

Powhatan was an important figure in the opening stages of English efforts to settle in the Tidewater region, in particular the Jamestown expedition of 1607. Setting foot on the shores of Powhatan's domain, the English were unaware that they were trespassing on a land ruled by a shrewd and well-organized head of state. Powhatan, approximately 60 years old at the time, could easily have demolished the faltering community, but instead chose to tolerate the English for a time—one reason being his desire to develop trade with them. Metal tools and weaponry were of special interest to Powhatan. Despite a mutual desire for trade, relations between Powhatan and the Virginia settlers were rocky, and attacks and counterattacks were common. In 1614, a degree of harmony was eventually achieved after the marriage of Pocahontas (who, in 1613, was kidnapped by the Virginia settlers) to John Rolfe. After the marriage of his daughter, Powhatan negotiated a peace settlement that produced generally friendly relations with the English until a few years after Powhatan's death.

What happened to the **American Indians** who were living on the land the English were trying to settle?

Although American Indians lived in the Western hemisphere for thousands of years before the European settlers came, they lacked the unity required to resist the new explorers. Although they initially welcomed the Europeans, the Native Americans were soon conquered, exploited, and often enslaved. While they retained the legal right of occupancy in their land, they legally forfeited the right of dominion. This meant that the British could colonize while the Indians retained ownership of their lands with authority over their tribal issues. The pressure on the Indians to convert to Christianity and become farmers, and the cultivation of increased portions of land by the colonists to support tobacco export added to tensions between the two groups. Tensions mounted and warfare broke out, formally ending in a treaty that the Indians signed recognizing English authority.

Who was **William Bradford**?

William Bradford (1590–1657) was one of the signers of the Mayflower Compact, the second governor of Plymouth, and the Pilgrims' principal leader during his lifetime. First elected governor in 1621, he was reelected 30 times in the next 35 years, primarily for his honesty, diligence, and leadership that fostered colonial survival despite deadly winters, hostile Indians, and bloodthirsty pirates. He is famous for his *History of Plymouth Plantation, 1620–1647,* which chronicled the moral resolve of the early Pilgrims and sealed their place in American history and folklore.

Who was **John Winthrop**?

John Winthrop (1587–1649) was an English lawyer whose Puritan convictions led him to settle in Massachusetts Bay, where he was elected governor. He remained the preeminent leader of the colony, intent on building a godly, Puritan commonwealth, and served as governor during four periods (1629–1634, 1637–1640, 1642–1644, and 1646–1649). He came into conflict with the "freemen" of the colony who resented his belief that governors and magistrates should rule as they best saw fit (he was a theocrat, not a democrat). He was elected president of the New England Confederation in 1643.

When did the first Africans arrive in the British colonies of North America?

In 1619, a Dutch ship carrying 20 Africans landed at Jamestown, Virginia. They were put to work as servants—not as slaves. Though they had fewer rights than their white counterparts, they were able to gain their freedom and acquire property, which prompted the development of a small class of "free Negroes" in colonial Virginia. For example, there is record of an Anthony Johnson arriving in Virginia in 1621 as a servant. He was freed one year later, and about 30 years after that he imported five servants himself, receiving from Virginia 250 acres of land for so doing. Another former servant, a carpenter named Richard Johnson, obtained one hundred acres for importing two white servants in 1654. These two men were part of the small class of free Negroes that existed in Virginia throughout the colonial period.

COLONIAL GOVERNMENT ALLIANCES, PLANS, AND CONSTITUTIONS

What was the **New England Confederation**?

In 1643 the Massachusetts Bay, Plymouth, New Haven, and Connecticut settlements formed the New England Federation, an early attempt at unity against the Native Americans. Meeting in Boston on May 29, 1643, the representatives "readily yielded each to the other, in such things as tended to the common good," and drew up articles of confederation. When the last of the four General Courts ratified them on September 8, 1643, the articles became binding. The United Colonies of New England, thereby established, encompassed all of the settlements along the coast and rivers from Long Island to New Hampshire. Rhode Island, which the Puritans considered anarchical, and Maine were not included. The United Colonies of New England did not consider themselves a nation, but rather individual governments allied by a treaty.

As stated in the preamble to the articles, the purposes of the confederation were to preserve the purity of the Puritans' religion and to worship free of interference, to promote cooperation, and to provide for defense. The articles themselves specified the duties and powers of the confederation's commissioners, the structure of the confederation, and the rules of procedure. Because there was no judicial authority over all the members, each colony could interpret the articles to meet its own needs.

The governing body of the confederation was to consist of two commissioners chosen annually from each colony. Approval of a matter required the votes of six commissioners, although only four could declare war in a state of emergency. Thus the Massachusetts Bay colony could not veto the wishes of the other three colonies. Each commissioner actually served as one of his colony's ambassadors. In matters of military preparation, declaration of war, and arbitration, the four colonies did surrender to the commissioners their individual power to act. Yet, while the confederation in theory possessed vague executive and judicial powers, in actuality it had only advisory powers in most areas. The articles specified that each colony's military obligation should be in proportion to its means and population. Each must send aid if one of the other three colonies should be invaded and must participate in all "just" wars. The commissioners were empowered to decide if the confederation should wage an offensive war, and no colony could do so without their approval. Apart from military affairs, actual power rested with the general courts of the member colonies. The commissioners could not pass legislation binding on the general courts, nor were they directly responsible to the people. They could neither levy taxes nor requisition supplies. Because the commissioners had no powers of enforcement, a colony that disagreed with a particular decision could simply nullify it by refusing to comply. To avoid conflict, the remaining colonies usually compromised.

Although the Articles of Confederation eventually died in 1684 when the danger of the native tribes passed and tension among the settlements increased, the Board of Commissioners did perform numerous important services for the four participating colonies. It established various civil agreements of interest to all four colonies and arbitrated intercolonial disputes. Policies concerning the Indians and regulations governing runaway slaves and the extradition of criminals were also within its domain. In the judicial realm, the commissioners established uniform standards for probating wills and served as an admiralty court. Although serious flaws were inherent in the Confederation of the United Colonies of New England, it was to be the longest-lived interstate confederation in American history. The leadership that the confederation provided was essential to the existence of the colonies in their early years. It concentrated the colonies' resources in military emergencies and protected the three weaker colonies from encroachment by the Massachusetts Bay colony. Most important of all, it preserved the peace in New England.

What was the purpose of the **Albany Plan of 1754**?

In 1754, the British Board of Trade called a meeting of seven of the northern colonies: Connecticut, Massachusetts, Maryland, New York, New Hampshire, Pennsylvania, and Rhode Island. The purpose of the meeting was to discuss the issues surrounding colonial trade and danger of attacks by the French and their Indian allies. At this meeting in Albany, New York, Benjamin Franklin proposed his Albany Plan of Union (later to be known as the Albany Plan of 1754), which called for the formation of an annual congress of delegates from each of the 13 states. The purpose of the plan was to create a union that would be empowered to raise military forces, wage war and declare peace with the American Indians, regulate trade with them, levy taxes, and collect customs duties. Although the plan was not adopted by the colonists or the king, it contained many elements later incorporated into various state constitutions and the two national constitutions of the Revolutionary period.

What is **Benjamin Franklin** most known for?

While most people know Benjamin Franklin (1706–1790) as an inventor and scientist, few realize the American statesman was active in a wide array of American colonial and pre-Revolutionary affairs, and even helped draft the Declaration of Independence. At the outbreak of the French and Indian War in 1754, Franklin was chosen a delegate to the Albany Congress, where he presented his Albany Plan for the 13 disunited English mainland colonies. In 1757, he was appointed colonial agent for the Pennsylvania Assembly and sent to England to lobby for the overthrow of the Penn family proprietorship. With the passage in 1765 of the hated Stamp Act, Franklin became actively involved in the colonial protest movement and came to be recognized as a leading spokesman for American rights.

What was the **Fundamental Orders of Connecticut**?

When they first came to America, the Puritans established settlements at Windsor (1633), Wethersfield (1634), and Hartford (1636). In 1639, these three communities joined together to form the Connecticut Colony, choosing to be governed by the Fundamental Orders, a relatively democratic framework for which the Reverend Thomas Hooker (c. 1586–1647) was largely responsible. According to some historians, the Fundamental Orders comprised the world's first written constitution. The document, issued on January 14, 1639, included a preamble declaring a covenant among the inhabitants and enacted 11 laws that provided for a government consisting of a general court, or legislature, meeting biannually, and a governor. The franchise, following English practice, was restricted to qualified householders. Office holding, however, was limited to "freemen" or those who could demonstrate to the general court that they possessed substantial property. As a result, the ensuing years witnessed the growing prestige of the magistrates, and the "democratic principle," so cherished in earlier times, was lost.

What early constitutions did **William Penn** make?

As proprietor of the colony of Pennsylvania, William Penn (1644–1718) was given enormous power to make laws and wars (subject to approval by the king and the freeman of Pennsylvania), levy taxes, coin money, regulate commerce, sell land, appoint officials, administer justice, and construct a government. From the beginning, Penn virtually gave up his lawmaking power and granted suffrage to property holders of 50 acres or 50 British pounds. Even before coming to Pennsylvania, he forged his "first frame of government" to serve as a constitution for the new colony. Under it, a 72-member council, presided over by a governor, monopolized executive, legislative, and judicial power, although a 200-member assembly could veto or amend the council's legislation. Both the council and the assembly were elective bodies, with a property qualification for voting.

When the two houses proved to be unwieldy, Penn issued a "second frame," or Charter of Liberties, in 1683, reducing the number of councilors to 18 and assemblymen to 36, and modifying the suffrage requirement. During the two years that Penn governed the colony, more than 150 laws were passed by the legislature. In 1696, Governor William Markham issued a "third frame" which further modified suffrage requirements, reduced the council to 12 members and the assembly to 24, and granted the latter body the right to initiate legislation. A "fourth frame," known as the Charter of Privileges, was drawn up by Penn in 1701. This document created a one-house legislature by vesting legislative power in the assembly, subject to the governor's veto, and limiting the council to executive and judicial powers. The council was appointed by the governor instead of being elected by the freemen. The Charter of Privileges remained in force until 1776.

Why was the **Charter of Privileges** significant?

Pennsylvania's proprietor, William Penn, issued the Charter of Privileges in order to end almost 20 years of quarreling between council and assembly, the council asserting its superior status against the assembly's demands for a greater share in the government of the colony. The assembly had considerably enlarged its power from 1692 to 1694 when the colony was under royal rule. The "third frame," issued after the Crown returned Pennsylvania to Penn, also extended the prerogatives of the assembly, and the Charter of Privileges establishing a unicameral legislature represented a further triumph for that body.

GROWING ECONOMIC AND DEMOCRATIC INDEPENDENCE

How did the **Glorious Revolution of England** affect colonists?

The Glorious Revolution of 1688, which established a constitutional balance between the Crown of England and Parliament, established a limited, constitutional monarchy in England, and ushered in an era of religious toleration, freedom of the press, and a broader role for England's citizens. This change overseas affected the colonies in various ways: full religious freedom was adopted into colonial practices; ideals such as free speech and free press spread more rapidly through the colonies; and, recognizing that England was not an all-powerful, everyday presence in America, the colonies developed a broader sense of independence and American citizenship.

What is meant by the **period of salutary neglect**?

The period of salutary neglect is generally defined as the period between 1714 and 1739, during which the then-American colonists had grown accustomed to running their own affairs. During this period, the colonies dealt more with the monarchy than with Parliament, colonial assemblies had the right of taxation (known as "power of the purse"), and colonial contributions to the French and Indian War (fought by France against England and its American allies from 1754 to 1763) were virtually nonexistent.

What was the **spirit of the colonies** as they grew?

As the colonies started to flourish and grow, a growing spirit of independence emerged. Although each colony was separately controlled by the King of England by English law, the colonies developed a large measure of self-government. Over the century and a half that followed the first settlement at Jamestown, Virginia, each colonial legislature assumed its own broad lawmaking powers. By the mid-1700s, the relationship between England and the colonies had become federal; that is, a central government in London was responsible for the colony's defense and foreign affairs. The mother country also provided the colonies with a uniform monetary and credit system, as well as a common market for colonial trade. Outside of these governances, however, the colonies could rule independently, and little money was taken from them in direct taxes to pay for the central government overseas. The few trade regulations that Parliament set were disregarded by the colonies.

What is **mercantilism**?

An economic system that developed as feudalism was dissolving, mercantilism advocates strict government control of the national economy. Its adherents believe a healthy economy can only be achieved through state regulation. The goals of mercantilism are to accumulate bullion (gold or silver bars), establish a favorable balance of trade with other countries, develop the nation's agricultural concerns as well as its manufacturing concerns, and establish foreign trading policies. In the mid-1700s, the system was established to benefit England: the colonies could benefit the mother country by providing inexpensive raw materials and a guaranteed market for manufactured goods; the system would result in a steady flow of gold to the mother country; and the concept required government regulation in order to be effective.

Despite obstacles, how did the **economy thrive** in the colonies?

From the founding of Jamestown to the outbreak of the American Revolution more than 150 years later, the British government administered its American colonies within the context of mercantilism: the colonies existed primarily for the economic benefit of the empire. Great Britain valued its American colonies especially for their tobacco, lumber, indigo, rice, furs, fish, grain, and naval stores, relying particularly in the southern colonies on black slave labor.

The economy of colonial America was based on farming—especially of tobacco—and trade of raw materials with Europe. In order to develop their economies, the colonies were forced to recognize the limitations under which they operated, many of them imposed by England. The scarcity of goods-producing tools and machines, lack of business capital, questions regarding appropriate mediums of financial exchange (paper money versus coinage), unskilled workers, poor transportation options, high freight rates, and limited disposable income all worked against the development of colonial industries. Additionally, England prohibited the emigration of skilled workers and the export of machinery to the colonies. English manufacturers also opposed any arrangements that might challenge their interests. Colonial acts that might prompt industries to compete with English industries, such as tariffs on English goods, were vetoed by colonial governors or disallowed by the Privy Council, a legislative body in England that supervised the colonies.

However, despite these obstacles, the sheer grit and determination of the colonists, the abundance of natural resources, and slave labor allowed the colonists to flourish. The colonies were able to tap into the European demand for potash (a potassium compound used in glassmaking), fish, and furs, and they became a major shipbuilding center: By the end of the colonial period, one-third of all British ships were constructed in America. Industries designed to address common household needs also proliferated: Businesses devoted to textiles, leather-making, brewing, iron mining, and millwork all proved successful for the colonists.

How did **England react to America's growing economic independence**?

England was determined to reap the benefits of the colonies' burgeoning economy. Parliament passed increasingly restrictive commercial trade laws that were designed to regulate colonial trade for Britain's benefit while also ensuring that America remained under English control. While the first of these laws, collectively known as the Navigation Acts, were passed in the mid-seventeenth century, it was not until the 1760s, when enforcement was tightened, that the laws emerged as a serious source of friction between Britain and its colonies. Some rules placed stipulations on the markets with which America could trade, while other laws required that such products as tobacco, sugar, and indigo go to England before moving on to their ultimate destinations overseas—thus allowing English businessmen to gain a cut of the profits. England also introduced laws that required the colonies to ship their goods on vessels owned and operated by Englishmen. Despite such measures, however, America's commerce with the rest of the world accounted for about one-seventh of England's trade total in the 1770s.

How were the **economies divided** between the colonies?

On the North American coast, three distinct areas developed into economic regions. Commerce was key in defining the economy of New England, including the manufacturing industries of ship building and rum. Plantation agriculture that employed slave labor characterized the southern colonies, where cotton, tobacco, indigo, and other items were harvested. And the middle colonies adapted an economy that was a rich blend of the other two regions, specializing in manufacturing iron and exporting fur to England.

How did **slave labor** contribute to the growing economies of the colonies?

The slave trade was an integral part of the trade patterns that evolved in the American colonies. British and Dutch ships took rum and other products to West Africa and traded them for slaves. European agents, who had set up trading along the coast, managed this exchange. The slave vessels, known as slavers, anchored off the coast until they had a full cargo and then set a course west to the Americas, a trade route termed "triangular trade."

The slaves from the west coast of Africa who were first imported to the American colonies in the seventeenth century came mainly by way of the West Indies. It was not until the eighteenth century that they came directly to North America, mainly through the Carolinas. There were not very many slaves before the expansion of the plantations in the eighteenth century. It is estimated that in 1640, Virginia had about 300 slaves and in 1670, about 2,000 (out of a total population of 40,000). Though estimates vary widely, it seems that British North America received about 425,000 slaves out of the 10 million or more who were carried to the New World during the three centuries of the slave trade.

In the seventeenth century slaves were found mainly in Virginia and the northern colonies. Normally they worked on farms, alongside their masters. They cleared land, planted and harvested crops, repaired buildings and fences, and generally participated in all the tasks required to keep a farm going, and in that respect were largely responsible for the success rate of the settling of land. By the late seventeenth and early eighteenth centuries, tobacco growing increased and, more importantly, rice, indigo, and, later, cotton were introduced as southern crops. From these crops evolved the plantation economy of the South, which required slave labor to keep it evolving and thriving. By the eighteenth century, slavery in the southern colonies was an integral part of the plantation economy—so much that it could not exist without slave labor.

The slave trade was an integral part of the economies of the early colonies, as European traders established a triangular route trafficking goods and humans between Europe, Africa, and the New World. Slave labor was also key to the growth and prosperity of southern plantations.

How were the **southern plantation system** and the **slave trade** linked?

The economy of the southern British colonies on the American mainland was based primarily on agriculture. Beginning in the late seventeenth century, the plantation system was widely used to exploit the land. Plantations in the low country of South Carolina and Georgia concentrated mostly on growing rice and indigo. Because these crops required large amounts of land and were labor intensive, the plantations in these areas were huge and held large slave populations. The second type of plantations included the earliest tobacco plantations located in the coastal regions of North Carolina, Virginia, and Maryland. Tobacco required less land and fewer slaves. But the cultivation of tobacco quickly used up nutrients in the soil, and the owners spread their holdings into the Piedmont regions of the Carolinas and Virginia. The plantation system spread westward with the crop. The plantation system made the African slave an integral part of the colonial agricultural economy in the eighteenth and nineteenth centuries and created a social crisis that would eventually lead to the Civil War in 1861.

What **monetary system** was in place in the colonies?

Since the settlements in the New World were all possessions of their mother countries (England, Spain, France, Portugal, and the Netherlands), they did not have monetary systems of their own. England forbade its American colonies to issue money. Colonists used whatever foreign currency they could get their hands on. Pieces of eight (from Spain), *reals* (from Spain and Portugal), and shillings (from England) were in circulation; the pieces of eight were most common.

There were frequent money shortages in the colonies, which usually ran a trade deficit with Europe. The colonies supplied raw goods to Europe, but finished goods, including manufactured items, were mostly imported, resulting in an imbalance of trade. With coinage scarce, most colonists conducted trade as barter, exchanging goods and services for the same. In 1652 Massachusetts became the first colony to mint its own coins; that year there was no monarch on the throne of England. Although the issue of coinage by colonists was strictly prohibited by England, the Puritans of Massachusetts continued to make their own coins for some 30 years thereafter, stamping the year 1652 on them as a way to circumvent the law.

What were **writs of assistance**?

Writs of assistance were general search warrants that England used to enforce mercantilist laws with the colonists. During the French and Indian War, the French and Spanish islands in the West Indies, cut off from Europe by the British navy, continually opened their ports to American ships for importing and exporting goods. This trade was very profitable to the New England merchants, but the British ministry considered in abominable because it supported the French. Strict enforcement of the trade laws were then made by Britain, who prohibited this trading. In order to prevent the smuggling of goods into the New England colonies, customs officials used writs of assistance issued by the Superior Court of Massachusetts.

When King George II died in 1760, the writs expired, and in 1761, colonial lawyer James Otis (1725–1783) argued in a Boston courtroom against these the writs of assistance, claiming that the use of these general warrants, which did not list a specific object, violated the colonists' right of privacy and were "against the fundamental principles of law." He argued they were unconstitutional in principle because they contradicted the English principle that a man's home (and by extension a merchant's warehouse) was his castle, and no officer of the law could invade it without a special warrant duly sworn, showing evidence of a law being broken. Although Otis lost the case and the writs were reissued, a more meaningful victory had taken place: The powers of Parliament were challenged. Otis argued that the rights of the colonists were protected by the constitution of the British empire, and acts of Parliament contrary to those fundamental principles were null and void.

How did the **French and Indian War** impact colonists?

While the vast North American continent had seen bloodshed earlier in the eighteenth century as a result of conflicts between representatives of France and England, the

French and Indian War, which was fought between 1754 and 1763, had a dramatically greater impact on the lives of the colonists. In fact, this war between the two European giants was sparked by a clash over ownership of America's lands. The tense truce that existed between France and England after the 1748 Treaty of Aix-la-Chappelle, which ended King George's War, began to fray within months of the treaty signing as events in America spurred renewed animosity. French and English expeditions, determined to secure America's fertile Ohio Valley for themselves, grappled for control of the region. The French forces quickly constructed a chain of forts in the area. They then defeated largely Virginian colonial contingents in a number of skirmishes over other fort sites. These developments prompted the British government to order the colonies to enlist the support of the Iroquois League, a band of Indian tribes that had grown increasingly unhappy with English trade and land policies. The members of the 1754 Albany Congress, convened to address Iroquois concerns in order to win their support, also heard Benjamin Franklin propose a plan of colonial union known as the Albany Plan. Franklin's idea was tabled, but it marked the first serious discussion of such an arrangement in the colonies.

Although first years of the war were dominated by the French, during the early 1760s, the English forces gradually cut French supply lines both on land and at sea, as the British navy assumed dominion over the waters of the Atlantic Ocean. In 1763 France handed over its North American holdings to England in the Treaty of Paris. However, the English victory in the French and Indian War further frayed relations between Britain and its colonies: With France vanquished from North America,the colonists along the eastern seaboard saw little need for the protective presence of English troops. Conversely, the settlers of the western territories had barely been able to put down an Indian rebellion led by the Ottawa chief Pontiac in 1763; the ill-conceived British plan of western settlement that was unveiled in its aftermath did little to endear England to American colonists.

The colonies enjoyed a large measure of internal self-government until the end of the French and Indian War, which resulted in the loss of French Canada to the British. To prevent further troubles with the Indians, the British government in 1763 prohibited the American colonists from settling beyond the Appalachian Mountains. Heavy debts forced London to decree that the colonists should assume the costs of their own defense, and the British government enacted a series of revenue measures to provide funds for that purpose. But soon, the colonists began to insist that they could be taxed "only with their consent," and the struggle grew to become one of local versus imperial authority.

Why was the **"Parson's Cause"** significant?

It was the so-called "Parson's Cause" of 1763 which suggested that the rights of citizens were superior to acts of Parliament and propelled newly established Virginia lawyer Patrick Henry (1736–1799) to legal and political prominence. This legal case resulted from a Virginia statute that regulated the salaries of Anglican ministers. By law, Anglican clerics were to be paid in tobacco. As a result of crop-destroying droughts, tobacco farmers petitioned the Privy Council, a legislative body in England that supervised the colonies, for relief. They established the Two Penny Act of 1758, which provided that all debt or salaries be paid with money instead of tobacco, although the rate of currency was depreciated and the clergy only received in value one-third of their salary. Although the Two Penny Act was subsequently disallowed in 1759 by England, the clergy sued the farmers for back pay, and it was the county courts who had to determine its validity, since it was passed without the usual consent by the Privy Council. In court Henry argued that although the Two Penny Act was a necessary and good law, by annulling it the king, in effect, destroyed the original compact between a king and his people. Unless a king rules justly, he argued, the people are not obligated to obey him. Although the Parson's Cause was a small isolated incident that established Henry's reputation, it symbolizes the willingness of Americans to fight against infringement upon their rights.

REVOLUTION AND INDEPENDENCE

AN EMERGING SPIRIT OF INDEPENDENCE

How did the **relationship between the colonies and Great Britain** change during the pre-Revolutionary period?

In the years preceding the American Revolution, English ministers and members of Parliament often treated the colonists with disrespect. England regarded the Americans as its citizens under their traditional imperialistic system, yet refused to grant them rights enjoyed by their countrymen in Britain. In some cases, England passed legislation that had significant impact on millions of colonists without making even the mildest inquiry into its reception in America. In other instances, England's lawmakers simply ignored the complaints of Americans, disregarding cries for compromise or reconciliation and expressing outrage when the colonies subsequently balked.

Meanwhile, in America the English colonists had become both confident in their own abilities and disillusioned with the motivations of their mother country. By the mid-1700s the pioneers of the New World felt that they had carved a viable and vibrant society out of a dangerous wilderness. America, the colonists declared, was a place where one's destiny was shaped by talent and perseverance rather than bloodlines. Life on the edge of the civilized world had brought about changes in the colonists' attitudes and outlook, primarily those of self-sufficiency and autonomy. A tough brand of independence took root in American soil, and as the years passed, the colonists felt less and less inclined to heed the words of their foreign domineering empire. The tenuous relationship of royal authority and colonial autonomy became stretched over the period between 1763 and 1776, final resulting in the Revolutionary War.

How did the **end of the French and Indian War** set the stage for the American Revolution?

At the close of the French and Indian War in 1763, which resulted in the defeat of the French in America and established Great Britain as the major force in Europe, the colonies in North America saw the years ahead as an age of opportunity and possibility. The removal of France allowed colonists to turn their attention to matters of livelihood rather than war, and they were largely united in their enthusiasm for the future. However, the English victory in the war further frayed relations between Britain and its colonies. With France vanquished from North America, the colonists along the eastern seaboard saw little need for the protective presence of English troops. Conversely, the settlers of the western territories had barely been able to put down an Indian rebellion led by the Ottawa chief Pontiac in 1763. The ill-conceived British plan of western settlement that was unveiled in its aftermath did little to endear England to American colonists, and began to sew the seeds for even greater independence on the part of the colonists.

The debt of this war would lead England to pass legislation to raise money, which would be refuted by the colonists who did not want to pay taxes. The revenue acts that were passed—including the Sugar Act of 1764 and the Stamp Act of 1765—caused the colonists to protest, and tension between the colonists and England quickly increased. England's ineffective efforts to continue the interdependence of trade between the colonists and the mother country upset the already delicate balance between royal authority and local autonomy. A climate of mutual suspicion developed, and it was not long before London's leaders truly believed that the colonists were rebellious in nature. Similarly, the colonists intimately believed that Parliament wanted to destroy their government and stop their popular assemblies. It was such fears, tension, and distrust that ultimately lead the colonists into outright rebellion against England.

What were the **main conflicts** that lead up to the **American Revolution**?

The American colonies' relationship with England, which had grown increasingly strained during the first half of the eighteenth century, continued to deteriorate during the 1750s and 1760s. American resentment of English trade restrictions and taxation was exacerbated by Parliament's refusal to grant the colonies a representative voice in the British empire. By the early 1770s, the anger of the independent-minded colonists, who had forged productive lives for themselves out of the American wilderness, was beginning to crest.

The Townshend Acts (a new set of levies passed in 1767), the Boston Massacre of colonists by British troops (1770), the destruction of the British revenue cutter HMS *Gaspee* by American smugglers (1772), the Boston Tea Party protest (1773), and the Intolerable Acts (a set of 1774 laws which included the closing of Boston harbor and severely limited self-governance in Massachusetts) were major events that contributed to the animosity between the two sides, and in September 1774 the First Continental Congress convened to discuss the colonies' options. Observers on both sides of the Atlantic warned that revolution could well result if the complaints of the colonies were not addressed. But England proved unwilling to change its methods of governance, and America subsequently declared its independence. From 1775 to 1783 British troops and the colonists' Continental Army battled for control of the American colonies in the Revolutionary War.

King George III of England, to whom the Declaration of Independence was specifically addressed, saw the colonies establish their independence during his reign.

What **change in leadership** in England affected England's relationships with its colonists?

It was shortly after King George III (1738–1820) came to the throne as king of England in 1760 that Britain's laws and attitudes became more stringent with the colonies. His reign from 1760 to 1820 characterized the ongoing struggle between the Crown and Parliament, the major objective of the king being to maintain the power of the monarchy as an independent and active factor in the British political process. Under Parliament's new prime minister, George Grenville, restrictive trading acts already in place were elaborated and strictly enforced by Parliament—not the king—and a new set of taxes was imposed upon the colonies, mostly to pay to for the British troops left in American as a result of the French and Indian War. Although during pre-Revolutionary events and the Revolutionary War the American colonists insisted that their objections were with Parliament and the king's ministers, the Declaration of Independence (1776) was directed against King George III himself, thus making it clear that the Americans were determined to break all ties with England and be free from the supreme royal authority of the king.

Who were the **Whigs**?

Whigs were members of political parties in Scotland, England, and the United States. The name is derived from *whiggamor* (meaning "cattle driver"), which was a derogatory term used in the seventeenth century to refer to Scottish Presbyterians who opposed King Charles I of England (1600–1649). (Charles, who ruled from 1625 to 1649, was deposed in a civil war and was subsequently tried in court, convicted of treason, and beheaded.) The British Whigs, who were mostly merchants and landed gentry, supported a strong Parliament. They were opposed by the aristocratic Tories who upheld the power of the king. During the pre-Revolutionary period, the Whigs dominated political life in England.

THE REVENUE ACTS AND THEIR PROTESTS (1764–1766)

Who was **George Grenville**?

George Grenville (1712–1770) was Britain's new minister of finance, who in 1763 sought to raise money to help pay for the cost of the 10,000 British troops left in the colonies for the colonists' protection as a result of the French and Indian War. Under his direction, existing laws were more strictly enforced, including the 1733 Molasses Act tax, which colonists evaded through smuggling molasses, and new legislation was enacted, known collectively as the Revenue Acts. These acts included the Sugar Act of 1764, the Currency Act of 1764, the Stamp Act of 1765, and the Quartering Act of 1765. This intervention of Parliament outright destroyed the delicate balance between England and the colonists, and as these laws were passed and the threat to colonists increased, a philosophy of revolution resulted.

What does **"taxation without representation"** mean?

In the early 1760s England decided to levy taxes on the colonies to help pay off the cost of the French and Indian War (which had doubled the British national debt), and to defray costs associated with maintaining an English army in America. Many colonists resisted such taxes, however, pointing out that the colonies were not represented in Parliament and so should not be liable for paying taxes. England argued that its government offered virtual representation (each member of Parliament represented the interests of Great Britain at large); "taxation without [actual] representation" was not acceptable to the colonists and declared a "travesty" by Boston attorney James Otis. Soon the colonists began to insist that they could be taxed "only with their consent," and the struggle over England's power to tax the colonists began.

What was the **Sugar Act of 1764**?

Also called the Revenue Act of 1764, this act was the first passed by Parliament in its effort to tax the colonists. It increased the duties on a variety of goods imported by the colonists, such as indigo, sugar, coffee, and wine, and reduced the duty on foreign molasses. By reducing the duty on molasses, Parliament hoped to cut the motivation for smuggling that was rampant in the colonies as a result of the Molasses Act of 1732 (which imposed a high duty on non-British molasses), and hence increase the Crown's revenue.

How was the **Sugar Act enforced**?

The Sugar Act of 1764 established a Vice-Admiralty court for Americans located in Nova Scotia. This court was meant to provide a solution to the lackadaisical enforcement of trade laws that was found in common-law juries, which were lenient on colonial smugglers since they were made up of their friends and business associates. By contrast, the Vice-Admiralty courts did not have juries, and under their procedural rules the burden of proof fell on the accused. Therefore, merchants whose vessels were seized on even the slightest evidence often lost them. Americans such as the activist and lawyer John Adams (1735–1826) vehemently opposed these courts, since it made Americans secondary citizens subject to procedures less than those of their British counterparts, who were allowed jury trials in England when they were accused of violating trade laws. This type of discrimination was at the heart of the colonists' concerns, and the existence of these courts continued to be a colonial point of contention throughout the pre-Revolutionary period.

What was the **Currency Act of 1764**?

As a result of the unfavorable trade balance that resulted at the end of the French and Indian War, there was a shortage of hard currency and deflation ensued. In response, Parliament passed the Currency Act of 1764, which banned paper currency as legal tender. Although restrictions were placed on paper money in New England in 1751, the Currency Act applied to the remaining colonies in America. The act did not specifically prevent the issue of paper money, only the use of it as payment for debts or taxes. Additionally, money that was currently in circulation could not be reissued. Partly because the act was passed just two weeks after the Sugar Act, and partly because the local economy was aggravated by its passage, the Currency Act fueled the colonist's frustration with the current economic climate and significantly affected their acceptance of the Stamp Act the following year.

Why was the Stamp Act of 1765 so critical to the pre-Revolutionary landscape?

A series of events—starting with the writs of assistance controversy in 1761 and continuing with the passage of the Sugar Act in 1764—angered the colonists, but it was the proposal of the Stamp Act of 1765 that proved most crucial in eroding relations between England and its temperamental colonies. According to the new law, which intended to raise 60,000 British pounds per year, colonists would have to buy stamps that would be required for use on all manner of documents, licenses, newspapers, and other publications. The money from the purchased stamps would go to the English government to help pay off the French and Indian War debt. Offenders were to be tried in Vice-Admiralty courts (without trial by jury), which formerly had jurisdiction only over affairs relating to the sea and commerce. New taxes meant payments in cash, but money, scarce in the agriculturally oriented colonies, became tighter than ever because Britain's finance minister George Grenville had persuaded Parliament the previous year to adopt the Currency Act, which forbade the provincials to continue making their own paper money as legal tender. Colonial reaction to the Stamp Act was swift and harsh. Previously, one colony would often raise issue with a tax, while another would not oppose it. This time, however, all of the colonial legislatures unified in protest, recognizing that if Britain were able to take away the colonies' right to tax themselves, other rights might more easily be lost in the future. The colonial assemblies prepared petitions against the proposed tax, as well as any other taxation dictated by parliament. Men like John Adams wrote articles for the Boston Gazette, arguing against Europe's tyrannical system of government. In February 1765 the act was passed, and in May of that year Patrick Henry, as a newly elected representative to the Virginia House of Burgesses, introduced seven resolutions in opposition to the act. Although five of the resolutions were relatively moderate (and accepted by the House), two of the resolves claimed virtual legislative independence for the colony. In October, 27 delegates from nine colonies assembled in New York to protest the act in a meeting known as the Stamp Act Congress.

What were the **Stamp Act Resolves**?

The Stamp Act Resolves were a list of reasons for refusing to cooperate with Parliament's recently proposed Stamp Act taxes of 1765. Orator Patrick Henry, who delivered them in a stirring speech in May 1765 to the Virginia House of Burgesses, persuaded the burgesses to pass five out of seven of his resolves—putting Virginia in the forefront of colonial resistance to Britain.

The first four resolves laid out the colony's reasons for claiming the right to tax themselves. That right rested on both the royal charter (the original agreement between the king and the colonists) and on history (the colony had always set its own taxes in the past). The fifth resolve claimed that only the elected assembly can tax the colony, and that any attempt to take that power away has a manifest tendency to destroy British as well as American freedom. The sixth and seventh resolves went even further, stating that the colonists had no obligation to obey laws that their own legislature had not approved, and that anyone who said that the colony did not have the right to decide its own taxes shall be deemed an enemy to the colony. Though not endorsed by the burgesses, these last three resolves were included with the others when the list was published throughout the colonies. With their publication Henry took his place with other radicals, such as Samuel Adams, at the forefront of American resistance to Britain.

Why did the **Stamp Act Congress** meet?

Soon after the Stamp Act Resolves were passed by the House of Burgesses, the Massachusetts legislature issued a call for a congress from all the colonies to meet to consider ways of securing relief. The Stamp Act Congress, comprised of legislators from nine colonies, met in October 1765 and declared that it would not recognize parliamentary efforts to tax the colonists, since such action was "taxation without representation." It is here they prepared their Declaration of Rights and Grievances against the new British policies, which was sent to the king. They acknowledged Parliament's authority to regulate trade (to legislate) for the welfare of the whole empire, but objected to taxation. Additionally, the delegates resolved to import no goods that required payment of a duty. Most importantly, their action marked the first time a large number of colonies joined together to oppose the British government.

By November 1, the date the stamps were to go on sale, none were available. The Sons of Liberty, a militant group of supporters of independence, had "persuaded" almost every designated stamp distributor to resign. Colonial merchants also aided the cause by curtailing imports from Britain until the oppressive Stamp Act was repealed.

Was the **Stamp Act of 1765** repealed?

Yes. In March 1766, after a year of sometimes violent protests and widespread disregard for the legislation, the Stamp Act was repealed by Parliament. At that time, finance minister George Grenville was out of office (for reasons unrelated to America), and the ministry was under the Marquis of Rockingham (1730–1782). He had opposed the Stamp Act and now listened to the protest of British merchants suffering from the colonial economic boycott. By stressing the disruption of trade and ignoring American rioting, and by employing Benjamin Franklin's erroneous testimony that the colonists opposed only internal taxes (the Stamp Act), Rockingham secured repeal of the Stamp Act after Parliament passed the vaguely worded Declaratory Act, which affirmed Parliament's power to pass laws affecting the colonies.

How was **Benjamin Franklin** tied to the Stamp Act protests?

With the passage of the Stamp Act in 1765, Benjamin Franklin (1706–1790) became actively involved in the colonial protest movement. Initially opposed to the measure, he suggested instead the "usual constitutional method" (e.g., requisitions among the various colonies) of raising needed revenue. After the bill was enacted, Franklin urged compliance. Misreading completely that the measure would be universally and successfully opposed in America, he recommended his friend John Hughes be appointed as stamp distributor for Pennsylvania. In February 1766 during the parliamentary debates over repeal of the Stamp Act, Franklin was summoned to appear before the committee of the whole of the House of Commons. In his answers to the many questions asked of him, Franklin was articulate in pointing out that the stamp duties were contrary to custom and uncollectible. The account of this parliamental encounter was published, establishing Franklin as a leading spokesperson for American rights.

What was the **Quartering Act of 1765**?

Passed by Parliament in May 1765, the Quartering Act ordered colonists to provide housing and supplies for British troops that remained in the colonies as result of the French and Indian War. The act, passed at the request of General Thomas Gage (1721–1787), who was based in New York, required colonists to liberally provide soldiers with bedding, fuel, pots and pans, candles, vinegar, salt, and a ration of beer, cider, or rum. An addition made in 1766 allowed commanders to request rooms in inns and unoccupied houses. Colonial agents, including Benjamin Franklin, had been consulted in drafting the act in order to ensure that it contained appropriate provision for preventing and correcting abuses. Most of the colonies accepted the law, except for New York and Boston.

What was the **Declaratory Act**?

Although the Stamp Act was repealed by Parliament in 1766, new laws were passed and new policies enforced in order to tie the colonists more closely to their mother country. One of these was the Declaratory Act, which affirmed Parliament's power to pass laws affecting the colonies "in all cases whatsoever." The law did not specifically mention taxes. Since the establishment of this act was tied to the repeal of the Stamp Act, Americans rejoiced without knowing the Declaratory Act's precise meaning.

Who were the **Sons of Liberty**?

In the late 1760s growing numbers of Americans began to question their obligations to England, and some began to speak of independence. Many colonists remained loyal to England throughout the Revolution, but others denounced British tyranny and supported calls for self-government. The Sons of Liberty, a group formed in reaction to the Stamp Act of 1765, was a particularly visible and militant supporter of independence. Founded by Samuel Adams, this underground organization was largely responsible for many pre-Revolutionary resistance acts, including the Boston Tea Party.

Who was **James Otis**?

The Boston lawyer James Otis (1725–1783) led the resistance to the revival of the Sugar Act in 1761 and opposed the British use of writs of assistance (general search warrants). As the main political thinker in Massachusetts at the time, he wrote several political pamphlets, including *The Rights of the British Colonies Asserted and Proved* (1764). Although Otis was a strong defender of colonial rights, he abhorred violence and did not anticipate the soon-coming American Revolution.

How did **Patrick Henry** establish himself as one of the great orators of the pre-Revolutionary era?

In defending his resolutions for the Stamp Act of 1765 before the House of Burgesses, Patrick Henry (1736–1799) is reported to have said, "Tarquin and Caesar had each his Brutus, Charles the First his Cromwell, and George the Third...." Henry was then supposedly interrupted by the Speaker of the House John Robinson with cries of "Treason! Treason!" Myth now mixes with reality. At this point, Henry allegedly stared at the speaker and completed his sentence with "... may profit by their example! If this be treason, make the most of it!" Since contemporary accounts of this oration, including a famous one written by Thomas Jefferson in 1814, differ significantly, it is not known for sure just what was said. However, what is known is that Henry's speech acted as a catalyst for colonial opposition to the Stamp Act and thrust him into a leadership role in the anti-English agitation of the late 1760s and early 1770s. In the following decade, Henry continued to lead, primarily by oration, the struggle in Virginia against English tyranny.

TIGHTENING CONTROL ON THE COLONIES (1766–1774)

What were the **Townshend Revenue Acts**?

The Townshend Acts, named after the British colonial minister Charles Townshend who enacted them, were a series of revenue laws imposed on the colonies by Parliament. Seizing upon Benjamin Franklin's testimony preceding the Stamp Act's repeal, to the effect that Americans opposed on principle only *internal taxes,* Townshend declared that if the colonists adhered to such a distinction they should be saddled with *external* duties on tea, lead, paper, paints, and glass. The danger to Americans in the subsequent Revenue Act of 1767 containing these proposals was not in the sums of money colonists would pay. The danger rather was that Parliament persisted in its efforts to destroy the colonists' constitutional rights, not only by taxing them without their consent but also by a provision in the act stating that part of the amount collected was to be used of necessity to pay the salaries of judges and governors in America, thus making them independent of the financial jurisdiction of the colonial assemblies.

The assemblies believed themselves threatened on still another front by the Quartering Act of 1765. When barracks were unavailable British troops in the colonies were to be lodged in taverns and other public houses at the expense of provincial authorities. The colonists felt that Parliament was taxing Americans indirectly by ordering their assemblies to levy monies for the upkeep of royal regiments. Although the American legislatures after 1765 usually provided for the army's needs, they were careful to maintain their constitutional integrity by avoiding a precise compliance with the letter of the law. But when New York (because of its location, it was the colony most frequently called upon for support) enacted a measure providing for the housing of troops that was deemed inadequate by the military, Parliament suspended the colony's legislature until it bowed to the letter of the British Quartering Act. New York did not back down, nor did the other assemblies, and when a compromise on military appropriations for New York was reached with local leaders, the ministry secured a lifting of the ban, but not before Americans realized that a dangerous precedent had been set in temporarily depriving citizens of the British empire of their political representation.

Additionally, Townshend brought about a reorganization of the customs service in America to guarantee collections of the new taxes as well as to achieve greater compliance with the older Navigation Acts of the mid–seventeenth century. Previously controlled from Great Britain, customs officers in the colonies were now under a special board sitting in Boston; they would predictably be zealous in the handling of their assignment, for a third of all fines received in the Vice-Admiralty courts went to the customs men. For that matter, additional courts were established the following year, in which many merchants faced charges of violating the exceedingly complicated provisions of the Sugar Act of 1764.

Although these various British measures prompted a less violent reaction in the colonies than the Stamp Act of 1765, they collectively represented an even larger threat to American rights. The point was brought home when, in response to the customs collectors' appeal for protection, the secretary of state for the colonies, the Earl of Hillsborough (Wills Hill), ordered General Thomas Gage, the British commander in chief in North America, to station regular troops in Boston. In 1770, the ministry of Lord North convinced Parliament to repeal all the Townshend duties except the one on tea, a symbol of Parliament's authority to tax.

In March 1770, British soldiers fire upon demonstrators angry over the Townshend Acts—taxes imposed upon the colonists—killing five people in what became known as the Boston Massacre and further fueling the colonists' resentment of England's control.

What was the **Boston Massacre**?

As new laws were passed by Great Britian in order to keep the colonists under their royal thumb, colonists began to show their resentment and opposition by disregarding the laws altogether. Mob violence was commonplace at several colonial ports, and colonists supported a boycott on English goods. Finally, on March 5, 1770, British troops in Boston fired on a crowd that had assembled, killing five men, in an event history will forever call the Boston Massacre. The "Boston Massacre" may have been a misnomer, the result of extreme harassment of the British "redcoats," and triggered, according to defender John Adams, by Crispus Attucks, an escaped slave who was the first to die and "to whose mad behavior, in all probability, the dreadful carnage of that night is chiefly to be ascribed." The result of the attack caused Americans to wonder if their respective colonies would be the next to have a standing army in their midst—one seemingly intent on destroying their liberties not only by its presence but through violent means.

In the wake of the Boston Massacre, it was not the townspeople who had provoked the riot who had to stand trial but the British soldiers who had fired their weapons in self-defense. Though the particular soldiers were acquitted, lawyer Samuel Adams made so much of the event that he was able to force Governor William Hutchinson (1711–1780) to withdraw all 600 British troops from the city of Boston and keep them in barracks at Castle William. The event and subsequent removal of soldiers quieted the city, and the repeal of the Townshend Acts, along with the reinstatement of the dissolved assemblies, brought a period of relative peace in the colonies from 1770 to 1772.

Who were the **Committees of Correspondence**?

Organized resistance to the Boston Massacre and to overall encroachment by Great Britain on the colonies was formed through the Committees of Correspondence, a small group of revolutionaries that had branched out of a group the revolutionist Samuel Adams created in 1772. In March 1773, the Virginia House of Burgesses proposed an intercolonial committee, and within a year committees were organized throughout the 13 colonies, allowing for a network of cooperation and the exchange of information among revolutionaries.

What was the burning of the *Gaspee*?

On June 9, 1772, the HMS *Gaspee*, a British warship, was docked at Providence, Rhode Island, while pursuing a merchant ship suspected of smuggling. The next night, eight boatloads of men, led by the wealthy Providence merchant John Brown, boarded the ship, wounded its lieutenant William Dudingston, and burned the ship in retaliation to Dudingston's harassment of local farmers and fishermen in his mission to put an end to smuggling in Rhode Island. When England threatened to revoke Rhode Island's charter if they couldn't provide a reasonable explanation for the event, Rhode Island half-heartedly apologized, ending the sensationalism of the incident.

What was the **Tea Act of 1773**?

On May 10, 1773, Parliament passed the Tea Act, which lightened duties on tea imported into Britain to give relief to the East India Company, which had seven years' supply in warehouses on the Thames River and was being strained by storage charges. However, the act permitted tea to be shipped at full duty to the American colonies and to be sold directly to retailers, eliminating colonial middlemen and undercutting their prices. The passage of the Tea Act coincided with the Parliament's passage of a Regulating Act, which was an effort to bring the East India Company under government control.

Was the **Boston Tea Party** really a party?

Slightly disguised as Mohawk Indians, members of the Sons of Liberty boarded ships in the Boston Harbor in December 1773 in reaction to the tax Britain had imposed on tea. In protest, they dumped a shipload of tea (23,000 pounds) belonging to the East India Company into the Boston harbor. The origins of the famous Tea Party—which was really an outright defiance toward taxation and not at all celebratory—are found in Parliament's repeal, in 1770, of all the external taxes embodied in the controversial Townshend Revenue Act, except the tax on tea, which was to remain principally as a symbol of the mother country's right to tax the colonists.

How did **England react** to the Boston Tea Party?

Ironically, British politicians acted not with the purpose of disciplining the Americans but with the intention of boosting the sagging fortunes of the giant East India Company. After unsuccessful attempts to help the ailing corporation with huge investments in India, the prime minister of Great Britain, Frederick North, Earl of Guilford (1732–1792), secured passage of the Tea Act, which for the first time allowed the East India Company to sell tea directly to America and to do so through its own agents; previously it had sold its product to English wholesale merchants, the tea then passing into the hands of American wholesalers and retailers. By removing the profits formerly obtained by English and American middlemen, and by the adding a provision eliminating English duties on tea exported to the New World possessions, the company hoped to undersell Dutch-smuggled leaves in America, even though the provincials would still have to pay the remaining Townshend tax of three pence on each pound.

Everywhere in North America, North's move met stiff resistance. Merchants accused the ministry of giving the East India Company and its agents a monopoly of the local tea market that would be followed in time by other monopolies in the American trade. More frightening to Americans was the constitutional threat; they were vulnerable already since the taxed herb had been purchased in America after 1770. Now, if they consumed even more of the dutied drink, they would implicitly admit the authority of Parliament to tax them. In fact, they saw in Lord North's efforts a cynical attempt to get them to "barter liberty for luxury." Consignees charged with collecting the tax in New York, Philadelphia, and Charleston, like the stamp tax collectors before them, were persuaded to resign their commissions. The outcome was different in Boston, where Governor Hutchinson supported the consignees and refused to let the tea ships return to England without first unloading their cargo.

When the colonists performed the task of unloading, Parliament's response was one of unparalleled severity. It passed the Coercive Acts—otherwise known as the Intolerable Acts—in order to bring rebellious Massachusetts under control by closing the port of Boston, altering the structure of government in the colony, allowing British officials and soldiers accused of capital offenses to be tried in England or, to avoid a hostile local jury, in a colony other than the one where the offense had occurred, and providing for the quartering of troops once more in the town of Boston. Massachusetts and the other 12 colonies did not accept this verdict, as it struck at the foundations of self-government more than any other of Parliament's actions.

Colonists disguised as Native Americans dump crates of tea into Boston harbor in December 1773 to protest the tea tax imposed by England. In response to this defiance, Parliament passed the harsh Intolerable Acts, the terms of which led directly to the Revolutionary War.

What were the **Intolerable Acts of 1774**?

The Intolerable Acts, also known as the Coercive Acts, were five laws passed by the British Parliament early in 1774. Intended to assert British authority in the Massachusetts colony, the measures were seen as punishment for the Boston Tea Party that had taken place in December 1773. In brief, the laws enacted the following: closure of the port of Boston until the tea was paid for (the Port Bill); an English trial for any British officer or soldier who was charged with murder in the colonies; the change of the charter of Massachusetts such that the council had to be appointed by the British and that town meetings could not be held without the (British-appointed) governor's permission; the requirement that the colonists house and feed British soldiers; and the extension of the province of Quebec southward to the Ohio River. A separate Quebec Act set up an undemocratic government in that expanded colony.

Closing the Boston port and quartering troops in private households were unprecedented, and colonial charters had never been outrightly revoked—only annulled through *quo warranto* judicial proceedings. While the British intention was to bring the Massachusetts colony under control (and actually the fifth act was not intended to have any punitive effect on the colony), the result was instead to unite all the colonies in opposition to British rule. In this regard, the acts are seen as the major precursor to the American Revolution.

What is **sedition**?

Sedition is defined as laws, deeds, or words that disrupt the authority of a government. In early common law, the scope of the offense was broad enough that it included prosecution for uttering a derogatory remark against the king. The Sedition Act of 1798—which stated that any treasonable activity, including the publication of "any false, scandalous and malicious writing," was punishable by fine and imprisonment—generated so much controversy that no similar laws were enacted in the United States until the twentieth century. Although there have been several statutes since the 1700s that forbid seditious statements and writing, the protection of speech and press that the First Amendment to the Constitution guarantees all individuals has made them difficult to enforce except during times of national strife.

What is **treason**?

The term treason embodies various acts of disloyalty. It has its roots in English law, specifically the Statute of Treasons (1350), which was designed to keep civil disorder to a minimum. The statute distinguished high treason from petty treason: Petty treason was an offense committed against a person, while high treason constituted an offense either against the king's majesty (i.e., sovereign power) or against the safety of the commonwealth. These acts included attempts to kill or dethrone the king or queen; to counterfeit coinage or replicate the royal seal; and to declare war against the kingdom. Because the framers did not want to repeat the cruel methods that were used to execute traitors in England, they were clear in defining treason in Article III of the Constitution: "Treason against the United States shall consist only in levying war against them, or in adhering to their enemies, giving them aid and comfort. No person shall be convicted of treason unless on the testimony of two witnesses to the same overt act, or on confession in open court."

What is **tarring and feathering**?

A popular form of mob violence in Great Britain, particularly against tax collectors, tarring and feathering began to appear in New England seaports in the 1760s and was most often used by patriot mobs against loyalists. Burning-hot tar—readily available in shipyards—was applied to the victim, who was then covered in feathers, often causing serious burns. Once the mixture dried, it was extremely difficult to remove. In colonial America before the Townshend Acts, Whig merchants threatened the punishment of tarring and feathering in an effort to enforce their series of nonimportation agreements. The practice of tarring and feathering evolved, and Boston mobs began to tar and feather an individual's property and possessions rather than his body.

What was the **"Hutchinson Letters" affair**?

Appointed as colonial agent for Massachusetts in 1770, Benjamin Franklin had become convinced of the "duplicity" of Governor Thomas Hutchinson and his relatives. In 1772 he became wittingly involved in the so-called "Hutchinson Letters" affair. He came into the possession of six letters supposedly written by the Massachusetts governor in the late 1760s to William Whately (formerly secretary to the chancellor of the Exchequor George Grenville) advocating in strong terms that "there must be an abridgment of what are called English Liberties" in the colonies. The letters mysteriously surfaced in Boston, where they were published and widely circulated in both England and America.

To prevent a duel between Thomas Whately, executor of the estate of William Whately, and John Temple, whom Whately accused of turning over the letters, Franklin was forced to admit that it was he who had transmitted the letters to America. The English government dismissed Franklin from his office as deputy postmaster general for North America and summoned him on January 29, 1774, to a public humiliation before the Privy Council in the Cockpit. Solicitor General Alexander Wedderburn, convinced that Franklin had stolen the Hutchinson letters, denounced him publicly and unmercifully as a man without honor. Up to this time, Franklin had been convinced that reconciliation between England and America was possible and would be mutually beneficial. With the loss of his postal position and his subsequent public humiliation, Franklin became a leading proponent of quasi-autonomy or complete independence for the American colonies.

Which colorful **political personalities** emerged during this period?

Although there were a number of independent spirits during the pre-Revolutionary era, three troublemakers—Samuel Adams, Patrick Henry, and Thomas Paine (1737–1809)—stand out as key forces in their own right. As the founder of the Sons of Liberty, Samuel Adams is often called the "Father of the American Revolution" because he did more than any other person to entice a break between Britain and the American colonies. A leading figure in the colonial legislature, Adams organized resistance to the Stamp Act (which demanded all papers carry a stamp as proof of paid tax), opposed the Townshend Acts (which imposed taxes on glass, lead, tea, and paper imported into the colony), and instigated the Boston Tea Party, at which a shipload of tea was dumped into Boston Harbor. The renegade lawyer Patrick Henry opposed Britain's policy of taxation and joined in Adams' view that the Stamp Act was a threat to liberty.

Although Henry is known for his leadership in the Virginia House of Burgesses (the legislative assembly) and as the orator of the Stamp Act Resolves, he is mostly remembered for his famous statement, "Give me liberty, or give me death," which roused the likes of Virginia patriots Thomas Jefferson, George Washington, and Richard Henry Lee as he announced Virginia's approval to the Continental Congress. Fellow revolutionary Thomas Paine used the power of the written word to speak out in favor of independence, and his pamphlet, *Common Sense*, was the main vehicle in which he outlined the reasons why the colonies should break from England. Twenty-five editions of *Common Sense* were printed in 1776, spreading the argument for revolution to all classes of free people throughout the colonies.

Why was **Samuel Adams** called the "Father of the American Revolution"?

The radicals' most effective leader was Samuel Adams (1722–1803) of Massachusetts, who earned the title "Father of the American Revolution" (or "Father of Independence") for his spirit, determination, and leadership qualities. Although he is known primarily for his active role in opposing the Stamp Act and the Townshend Acts and for orchestrating the Boston Tea Party, Adams' influence extended far beyond his role in aggravating the loyalists. From the time he graduated from Harvard College in 1740 Adams toiled tirelessly for a single cause: independence. Adams was always a public servant in some capacity—inspector of chimneys, tax collector, and moderator of town meetings. A shrewd politician, he had a primary goal of freeing people from their awe of social and political superiors, making them aware of their own power as individuals, and rallying them to action. As a motivator of the people toward independence, he published dozens of articles in newspapers and made speeches in town meetings, instigating resolutions that appealed to the colonists' democratic impulses.

Samuel Adams, founder of the Sons of Liberty and leader of the Boston Tea Party, was a key personality in establishing America's independence from British rule.

By the time of the battles of Lexington and Concord in 1775, Adams' career as a propagandist and agitator had peaked. However, Adams continued to stay active in politics, and at the First and Second Continental Congresses, he represented Massachusetts by signing the Declaration of Independence, espousing immediate political separation from Britain, and recommending the formation of state governments and a confederation among the new states. He supported George Washington for commander in chief of the Continental Army, and helped draft the Articles of Confederation, America's first attempt at government.

What types of **political writing** preceded the Revolution?

In 1767, the Philadelphia lawyer John Dickinson published *Letters from a Farmer in Pennsylvania* in their first installments. Dickinson drafted the resolutions and grievances of the Stamp Act Congress two years prior as a member of that body, and his *Letters* on the nonimportation and nonexportation agreements continued to appear through much of 1768, winning him wide popularity in the colonies. Other writers joined the battle, most notably Thomas Jefferson, who expressed the thinking of many of his countrymen in 1774. His pamphlet, *Summary View*, referred to the king as the "chief magistrate" of the empire and denied the authority of Parliament to legislate for the colonies in any case whatsoever. In addition, Samuel Adams published his famous "circular letters," arguing that Parliament did not have unlimited power to supersede the will of popular assemblies in the colonies.

Most students of the pre-Revolutionary era are familiar with Thomas Paine, whose *Common Sense* is heralded as the most popular pre-Revolutionary pamphlet. Published anonymously by Paine in January 1776, *Common Sense* was an instant best-seller, with 120,000 copies sold within three months of its distribution. Often called "the book that started the American Revolution," Paine's political pamphlet rallied the hearts of revolutionaries by placing blame for the suffering of the colonies on the reigning British monarch, George III. It called for an immediate declaration of independence, noting that it was the moral obligation of America break free from its mother country. Not long after publication, the spirit of Paine's argument found resonance in the Declaration of Independence. Although the pamphlet made Paine internationally famous, he continued to inspire the patriots during the Revolutionary War with a series of pamphlets titled *The American Crisis*.

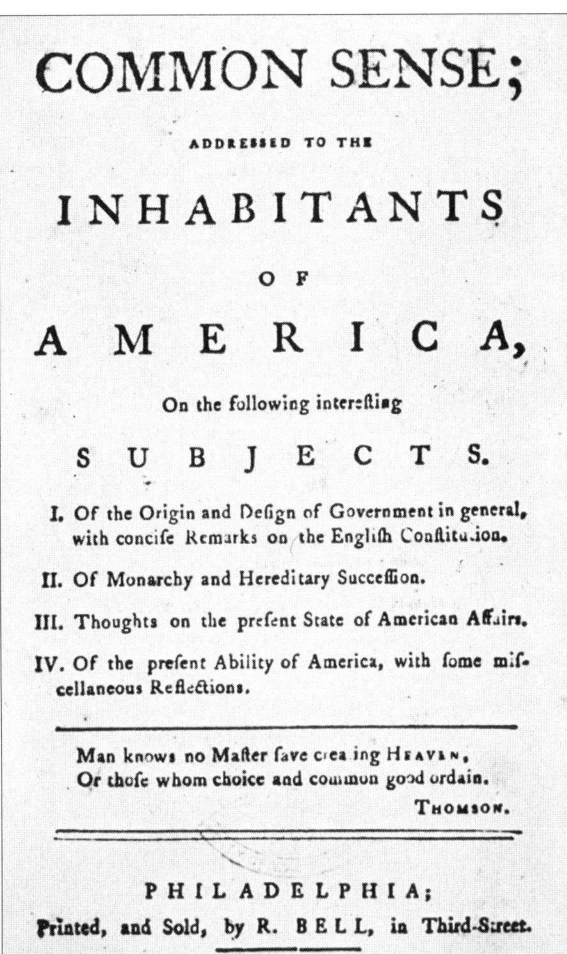

COMMON SENSE;

ADDRESSED TO THE

INHABITANTS

OF

AMERICA,

On the following interesting

SUBJECTS.

I. Of the Origin and Design of Government in general, with concise Remarks on the English Constitution.

II. Of Monarchy and Hereditary Succession.

III. Thoughts on the present State of American Affairs.

IV. Of the present Ability of America, with some miscellaneous Reflections.

Man knows no Master save creating HEAVEN,
Or those whom choice and common good ordain.
THOMSON.

PHILADELPHIA;
Printed, and Sold, by R. BELL, in Third-Street.
MDCCLXXVI.

Thomas Paine's pamphlet *Common Sense*, which outlined reasons why the colonies should break from England, sold over 120,000 copies in three months.

THE CONTINENTAL CONGRESSES CONVENE (1774–1776)

When was the **First Continental Congress** convened?

In response to the Intolerable Acts, the Massachusetts and Virginia assemblies called together a meeting of the colonies. The First Continental Congress, composed of 56 delegates from 12 of the 13 colonies (Georgia was not represented), met in Philadelphia on September 5, 1774. For almost two months, the Congress met to discuss the current situation with Great Britian and set a course of action. It was in this meeting that two major proposals were made—a general boycott of English goods and the organizing of a militia.

Before adjourning on October 26, Congress dispatched the Declaration of Rights—a series of declarations and addresses to the king, to the people of Great Britain, and to the citizens of America. The delegates called for a return to the relationship the colonies had enjoyed with the mother country in the years prior to 1763 and asked for a repeal or withdrawal of policies and laws, beginning with the decision to keep an army in America and concluding with the Coercive Acts. In Great Britain the appeals of Congress fell largely on deaf ears. As early as November 18, 1774, King George III informed his prime minister, Lord Frederick North (Earl of Guilford), that "the New England governments are in a state of rebellion, blows must decide whether they are to be subject to this country or independent." The meeting provided for another intercolonial meeting the following spring, and over the course of the next few months all the colonial legislatures (including Georgia's) supported the actions of the First Continental Congress.

Is it true that the **First Continental Congress** was made up of **conservatives and radicals**?

Yes. From the outset of the Congress the delegates' main objective was to review their relationship with Great Britain. Since Parliament had refused to recognize the colonists' repeated attempts to distinguish between taxation and legislation regulating trade for the benefit of the empire but not for revenue, many Americans felt they had no choice but to conclude that Parliament had no control over them at all. Men like Thomas Jefferson, who referred to the king as the "chief magistrate" of the empire and denied the authority of Parliament to legislate for the colonies in any case whatsoever, were called radicals. Also known as Patriots, or Whigs, they urged a united resistance to the unconstitutional acts of Parliament. Some of the congressmen, however, were reluctant to reject the word of Parliament completely, and instead urged for compromise and reconciliation with the mother country. They were generally termed conservatives, or Tories. Extreme conservatives would later become active supporters of England during the Revolutionary War and be known as Loyalists because they retained their allegiance to England. Although the result was a compromise resolution of both viewpoints, stating that by consent, not by right, Parliament might regulate commerce in the interest of all, these two groups became increasingly at odds with one another.

Who were the **Patriots**?

Patriots were those revolutionists who supported an independent America, free from control of British rule. They would go to war for their convictions, and called themselves Patriots after their love for their country. With two million people who hailed freedom as their cause, they were the party in the majority, although little military training, lack of a navy, and minimum canons and gunpowder contributed to their weaknesses as an army. Patriots that fill history books include such notables as: General George Washington, commander of the Continental Army; James Madison, a member of the Virginia legislature and Continental Congress; John Adams, a delegate to Continental Congress; Samuel Adams, a Boston tax collector, member of the Massachusetts legislature, and delegate to the First and Second Continental Congresses;

Patriot Mary McCauley (1754–1832), known as "Molly Pitcher" because she carried water to wounded soldiers during the Revolutionary War, mans a cannon at the Battle of Monmouth in Freehold, New Jersey.

Benjamin Franklin, a publisher, printer, inventor, and deputy postmaster general for the colonies; Patrick Henry, a Virginia lawyer and orator; John Paul Jones, an American naval officer; Thomas Paine, a political philosopher and author of *Common Sense*; and Paul Revere, a silversmith and engraver who took part in the Boston Tea Party.

Lesser-known Patriots include Mary McCauley, otherwise known as "Molly Pitcher" for carrying water to wounded soldiers during the Revolutionary War; James Lafayette, an African American "double agent" and Revolutionary War hero; and Abigail Adams, a writer and the wife of John Adams, who would become the second president of the United States.

Who were the **Loyalists**?

Loyalists, or "Tories" as their adversaries called them, were those American men and women who supported Great Britain and their colonial rule of America. Loyalists believed that independence would give rise to mob rule and result in the loss of economic benefits derived from membership in the British mercantile system. The majority of Loyalists were small farmers, artisans, and shopkeepers. In addition, British officials, wealthy merchants, and Anglican ministers, especially in Puritan New England, tended to remain loyal to the Crown. By mid-1775, Loyalists who openly opposed the Patriots and who supported Britain were no longer tolerated in the colonies and exiled.

Approximately 19,000 Loyalists, armed and supplied by the British, fought in the American Revolution. They included African American slaves, who were promised freedom if they fought for the British; Native Americans, who believed the British would not infringe upon their land; and other men and women, generally located in the southern colonies, who felt the colonists were reactionary and wild. Some well-known loyalists include: King George III of England, key supporter of the policy that lead to the Revolutionary War; William Howe, commander of the British Army during the Revolution, whose victories included the Battle of Bunker Hill (1775), the capture of New York City (1776), and the Battle of Brandywine (1777); General Thomas Gage, an English general and the last royal governor of Massachusetts; and Lord Charles Cornwallis, a major general responsible for driving General Washington out of New Jersey but eventually defeated at Yorktown by French and American armies. Other loyalists, who eventually left America after the American Revolution, include William Franklin, the son of Benjamin, and John Singleton Copley, the greatest American painter of the period.

What were the **Suffolk Resolves**?

Endorsed by the delegates early in the proceedings of the First Continental Congress, the Suffolk Resolves were adopted earlier by Massachusetts' Suffolk County (hence the name). These resolutions denounced the Coercive Acts as unconstitutional, urged the people to prepare militarily, and called for an immediate end of trade with the British empire.

When did the Second Continental Congress convene?

After fighting broke out at Lexington and Concord in April 1775, the colonies again sent representatives to Philadelphia, convening the Second Continental Congress on May 10, 1775. Delegates—including George Washington, Thomas Jefferson, Benjamin Franklin, and John Hancock as its president—organized and prepared for the fight, creating the Continental Army and naming Washington as its commander in chief. With armed conflict already underway, the Congress nevertheless moved slowly toward proclaiming independence from Britain: On July 10, two days after issuing a declaration to take up arms, the Congress made another appeal to King George III, hoping to settle the matter without further conflict. The Congress adjourned on August 2, 1775, with the legislators agreeing to reconvene six weeks later.

What was the role of the Second Continental Congress **once the Revolution began**?

When the Second Continental Congress convened in May 1775, its goals included establishing a national army and halting the colonies from attempting to make separate reconciliation agreements with England. With the small battles continuing and news of the

Members of the Second Continental Congress sign the Declaration of Independence in Philadelphia, Pennsylvania, on July 4, 1776, officially breaking ties with England to form a new nation.

battle at Bunker Hill, the Congress encouraged the separate colonies to organize their own militias. The Congress also designated a patriot army to be headed by George Washington, and ordered American troops to march north into Canada by autumn. The Congress voted to print paper money to help pay for this army, to establish a post office, and to send commissioners to negotiate with Indians. In July 1775, the Congress sent the Olive Branch Petition to Britain in an attempt to mend the divide between the colonies and the British government. The Congress was no longer a temporary council of Americans articulating constitutional doctrines; it was the central government of a people at war. The attempt at reconciliation with the king failed, and the following summer the Second Continental Congress achieved its most famous act when it approved the Declaration of Independence, breaking off all ties with Great Britain.

Why was the **Second Continental Congress** so important to the foundations of government?

In essence, the Second Continental Congress became America's first government. Although it had no constitutional base, and was denounced by Great Britain, it was supported by the people and fueled by public opinion. It functioned as the first government for five years—from the adoption of the Declaration of Independence in July 1776 until the Articles of Confederation went into effect on March 1, 1781. In that time period, it fought the Revolutionary War, raised armies and a navy, made treaties with foreign countries, and in general performed all the functions of a government.

Prominent lawyer, patriot, and orator Patrick Henry delivers his famous "Give me liberty, or give me death" speech to the Virginia Assembly in 1775.

During this time, the unicameral Congress exercised both legislative and executive powers. Each colony—and later state—had one vote in legislative issues, and executive duties were allocated to a committee of delegates.

THE AMERICAN REVOLUTION (1775–1781)

What are the significance of the words, **"Give me liberty, or give me death!"**?

On March 23, 1775, the leaders of Virginia argued whether or not Virginia should become involved in the Revolutionary War. In response, the great orator Patrick Henry delivered a speech before the Virginia Assembly in which he concluded with the words, "Give me liberty, or give me death!" This historical phrase signaled Henry's desire for Virginia to fight at all costs, and acted as a motto for every American soldier who wanted to see America freed from the British.

Why **independence**, and why now?

In the opening months of 1776 the colonists faced a momentous and fundamental decision. Should they content themselves with a return of British authority as it exist-

American and British soldiers engage in hand-to-hand combat in the Battle of Lexington and Concord in 1775, the first battle of the Revolutionary War.

ed prior to 1763, or should they irrevocably sever all political ties with, and dependence upon, the mother country? Since Great Britain was unwilling to give them that choice, offering instead only total surrender to parliamentary sovereignty, Americans in increasing numbers concluded that complete independence, not merely autonomy within the empire, must be their goal. Many of the undecided were won over to defiance of the Crown as a result of Parliament's Prohibitory Act, which called for a naval blockade of the colonies, the seizure of American goods on the high seas, and the dragooning of captured provincial seamen into the Royal Navy. For many colonists news of the British Ministry's decision to employ German mercenaries for use in America was the last straw. The requirements of the struggle itself lent weight to the idea of complete separation. Men would not do battle wholeheartedly for vaguely defined purposes, nor would the French or Spanish aid deemed essential to military success be forthcoming if the colonies fought merely for a greater freedom within the empire.

How did the **American Revolution** begin?

Determined that the British empire be preserved at all costs and unwilling to lose control in America, the king responded to the Declaration of Rights with even more repressive actions, and in April 1775 fighting broke out between the redcoats (as British soldiers were known) and patriots (colonial soldiers). On April 19, at the command of the British governor of Massachusetts, General Thomas Gage, 700 British soldiers marched to Concord, Massachusetts, and destroyed the supplies and weapons that colonists had gathered there. Seventy American minutemen assembled on the nearby Lexington green and readied themselves for battle. After killing eight colonists and injuring less than a dozen others in this brief encounter, the British soldiers withdrew and fought their way back to Boston. The minutes-long battle was called the Battle of Lexington and Concord, the first exchange of rifle and bayonet fire that heralded the beginning of the American Revolution.

How long did the American Revolution last?

Officially, the war lasted from April 19, 1775, until October 19, 1781, with the defeat of General Charles Cornwallis and his British troops at Yorktown, Virginia. Although Cornwallis' defeat did not immediately end the war—it would drag on inconclusively for almost two more years—this event marked the final battle between the British and Americans, and it prompted the British government to pursue peace negotiations with America.

What does the phrase **"the shot heard 'round the world"** signify?

At the Battle of Lexington and Concord, the first shot of the American Revolution was fired. Dubbed "the shot heard 'round the world," if officially triggered the fighting between the British and the Americans, although no knows for sure which side fired the first shot that morning.

Who was **Paul Revere**?

Although Paul Revere (1735–1818) made many contributions to the United States of America, he is best known for his "midnight ride" of April 18, 1775, when, as an express rider for Boston's Sons of Liberty, he rode his horse from Boston to Lexington, Massachusetts, to warn patriots that the British troops were coming. Historians have pointed out that many legends depicting Revere as a lone rider delivering the message "The British are coming!" are simply not accurate. Nonetheless, Revere's actions triggered an elaborate "alarm system" in the countryside that grew exponentially as hundreds were enlisted in the cause of spreading the word. These warnings enabled the colonists to mount a resistance against the British in the first battle of the Revolution.

Who were the **minutemen**?

Minutemen were the American men who went to war against the British. They were called minutemen because they had to be ready at a minute's notice. These members of the militia were first organized in Massachusetts by Committees of Safety but their numbers soon grew by the thousands to include other militiamen from other colonies.

Members of the colonial militia of New England were known as minutemen, because of the need for them to be ready to fight at a moment's notice.

Who were the **redcoats**?

Redcoats were the British soldiers who waged war with the Americans, so called because of the bright red waistcoats they wore. Also called "lobsterbacks" by the Loyalists for their red backs, these 500,000 men were well trained, disciplined, and organized. They were supported by the English navy (then heralded the best navy in the world), an ample supply of weaponry, and the backing of their mother country. Although they outnumbered the patriots, they lacked the strong motive to fight that the freedom fighters were famous for.

What was the **Battle of Bunker Hill**?

In June 1775 American troops were driven from Bunker (Breed's) Hill near Boston, Massachusetts, at great British cost in the first major battle of the war. While American troops were dug in along the high ground of Breed's Hill they were attacked by a frontal assault from more than 2,000 British soldiers who stormed up the hill. Acting upon orders not to fire until they could see "the whites of their eyes"—an expression that survived the Revolution and made its way into popular vernacular—the Americans ran out of ammunition and were left with only bayonets and stones to defend themselves. The British succeeded in taking the hill, but at a loss of more than 1,000 men. Americans lost about 400 men, including the colonial leader General Joseph Warren.

General George Washington (1732–1799), elected commander of the Continental Army at the Second Constitutional Convention, leads troops at the Battle of Monmouth in 1778.

What was the **Continental Army**, and what role did **George Washington** play in it?

The Battle of Lexington and Concord led the New England colonies to lay siege to Boston and prompted the Second Continental Congress to organize a colonial army, called the Continental Army, under the command of General George Washington, one of the Virginia delegates. The Continental Army, which eventually came to include regiments from all 13 colonies as well as Canada, was supported by local militias in many regions of the country. On July 3, 1775, at Cambridge, Massachusetts, Washington took command of his poorly trained troops and embarked upon leading a war that would last six years. Ensuing battles resulted in both victories and defeats for Washington and his men, until finally in 1781 he forced the surrender of General Charles Cornwallis at Yorktown.

What was **George Washington's role in early American politics** and what was his overall effect on the Revolutionary era?

Although George Washington (1732–1799) goes down in history books as the first president of the United States, he is remembered as a determined military leader and voice of independence long before he ever took his oath of office on April 30, 1789. From 1759 to the outbreak of the American Revolution, Washington served in the Virginia House of

Burgesses. As tensions with England grew, Washington firmly voiced his opposition to Britain's restrictions upon America. When the Second Continental Congress assembled in Philadelphia in May 1775, Washington was elected commander in chief of the Continental Army—an appointment that would challenge his resolve as a leader, administrator, and military strategist. Washington's wartime experience gave him a continental perspective, and his Circular Letter to the States in June 1783 emphasized his favor of a strong central government—an entity he would later help build. After the Revolution Washington realized that the nation under its Articles of Confederation was not functioning well, and so became a key instrument in the steps leading to the Constitutional Convention at Philadelphia in 1787, where he supported ratification of the Constitution in order to "establish good order and government and to render the nation happy at home and respected abroad." When the new Constitution was ratified, the electoral college unanimously elected Washington president of the United States.

Besides these early revolutionary acts, Washington is remembered for helping translate the Constitution into a workable instrument of government. Under his direction, the Bill of Rights was added; an executive branch was established, with the executive departments—State, Treasury, and War—evolving into an American cabinet; the federal judiciary was inaugurated; and the congressional taxing power was activated to pay the Revolutionary War debt and to establish American credit at home and abroad.

What was the significance of the **Newburgh Address**?

Historians generally cite George Washington's handling of the Newburgh Address, in which he defused the mutinous feelings of some troops who were discouraged by the Continental Congress's refusal to pay pensions, as a renowned episode in his career. At a meeting on March 15, 1783, to discuss the issue, Washington encouraged the officers to maintain their loyalty to the Congress. He began to respond to a letter he had received from a congressman by opening with the remarks, "Gentlemen, you will permit me to put on my spectacles, for I have not only grown gray but blind in the service of my country." These words signified Washington's empathy with his men, who were brought to tears and quickly disregarded the animosity they felt toward the Congress. The Newburgh affair shocked the Congress, and the following week it promised the officers five years of pay in lieu of the half-pay pensions already approved but not provided.

What was the **Olive Branch Petition**?

Despite the outbreak of armed conflict, the idea of complete separation from England was still inconceivable to some members of the Continental Congress. In July 1775, John Dickinson drafted a resolution, known as the Olive Branch Petition, asking the king to prevent further hostile action until a mutual agreement could be worked out. The petition fell on deaf ears, however, and King George III issued a proclamation on August 23, 1775, declaring the colonies to be in a state of rebellion.

As he faced execution at the hands of British soldiers, American patriot and spy Nathan Hale (1755–1776) declared, "I only regret that I have but one life to lose for my country."

Who earns the title of **America's first spy**?

Twenty-one-year-old Nathan Hale (1755–1776) volunteered to spy on the British for General George Washington. While dressed as a Dutch schoolteacher he managed to sneak behind enemy lines and record everything he saw in his "schoolbook" in Latin. Although he was captured by the British and sentenced to death by hanging, his final words live on in history books to this day: "I only regret that I have but one life to lose for my country."

Why did **France** get involved in the war?

The American victory at Saratoga, New York, in October 1777—coupled with other triumphs at Trenton and Princeton, New Jersey, in previous months—convinced France, a long-time enemy of England, to support the colonies' efforts to free themselves. After Britain's defeat at Saratoga, France saw an opportunity to weaken its longtime foe and restore the balance of power that had been upset by the French and Indian War (1754–1763).

France began providing aid to the colonies in May 1776, when it sent 14 ships with war supplies to America. In fact, most of the gunpowder used by the American armies came from France. On February 6, 1778, America and France signed a Treaty of Amity and Commerce, in which France recognized America and offered trade concessions. They also signed a Treaty of Alliance, which stipulated that if France entered the war, neither country would lay down its arms until America won its independence, that neither would conclude peace with Britain without the consent of the other, and that each guaranteed the other's possessions in America. This was the only bilateral defense treaty signed by the United States until 1949.

How did **France's alliance with America** fuel the revolutionary fire?

The Franco-American alliance soon broadened the conflict between America and the British. In June 1778 British ships fired on French vessels, and England and France went to war. In 1779 Spain, hoping to reacquire territories taken by Britain in the French and Indian War, entered the conflict on the side of France, but not as an ally of the Americans. In 1780 Britain declared war on the Dutch, who had continued to trade with the Americans. With France in the lead, the combination of these European powers was a far greater threat to Britain than the American colonies standing alone.

What was the **Native Americans' reaction** to the American Revolution?

During the American Revolution many Indians sided and fought with the Patriots. But most ended up siding with the British, primarily because King George III of England promised to protect their lands from encroaching American settlers. Previously united, the six tribes of the Iroquois League—a peacekeeping organization that dealt with concerns of peace and war and unified a confederacy of 50 clan leaders from the Seneca, Cayuga, Onandaga, Oneida, Mohawk, and Tuscarora tribes—were split irrevocably by the Revolution.

At first, the league declared its neutrality, but soon the British persuaded the Mohawk, Seneca, Cayuga, and Onondaga to join them. The Oneida and Tuscarora sided with the Americans, making it the first time that the league planned to fight on opposite sides. A leading figure among the British troops was the Mohawk chief Thayendenaga, or Joseph Brant. He conducted many raids throughout the course of the war, notably those in Cherry Valley, New York (November 1778) and Wyoming Valley (July 1778). In the summer of 1779, a Continental Army regimen led by General John Sullivan swept through upstate New York and devastated the league's lands, effectively putting an end to the organization and forcing the tribes to relocate into Canada on a tract that became known as the Six Nations Reserve.

Who was **Benedict Arnold** and why is he considered a traitor?

As an American Patriot in the Revolutionary War, Benedict Arnold's (1741–1801) heroics began in September 1775 when he led an expedition of riflemen against Quebec, the capital of British Canada. For the next five years Arnold served the Patriot side in multiple battles. However, in an act that has made his name synonymous with trea-

A map of the United States as settled by the Treaty of Paris, which ended the Revolutionary War.

son in American history, General Arnold, as commander of the American fort at West Point, New York, in 1780 conspired to hand it over to the British. In return, he was to receive the modern-day equivalent of about $1 million and become a general in the British army. His treason was discovered when his British contact, Major John André, was captured with key documents in Arnold's handwriting. After standing trial and being convicted of espionage, André was hung. The British appointed Arnold brigadier general, and he retired to England although he was never given a military command.

Who was **Betsy Ross**?

Betsy Ross (1752–1836) was a businesswoman often called the "patriot of Philadelphia." The owner of a small upholstery shop, at George Washington's request she agreed to sew a flag that would unite the 13 colonies in their fight for independence from Great Britain. Because this story was first told by one of her grandsons in the 1870s, historians say there is no real evidence that she designed or made the first flag of the United States in 1776, only that she was the official flag maker for the Pennsylvania navy.

What was the significance of the **Peace Treaty of Paris**?

With the defeat of General Charles Cornwallis at Yorktown, Virginia, a new British government decided to pursue peace negotiations with the Americans in Paris in early

1782, with the American side represented by Benjamin Franklin, John Adams, and John Jay. On April 15, 1783, Congress approved the final treaty, and England and its former colonies signed it on September 3. Known as the Treaty of Paris, the peace settlement acknowledged the independence, freedom, and sovereignty of the 13 former colonies, now states, to which England granted the territory west to the Mississippi River, north to Canada, and south to Florida, which was returned to Spain. The fledgling colonies had finally become independent states.

How did the **American Revolution end**?

The conflict raged on through the end of the 1770s and into the 1780s, but in October 1781 the war for independence finally came to a close. The defeat of General Charles Cornwallis and his British troops at Yorktown, Virginia, ended the majority of the fighting, although small skirmishes continued for two more years. Weary of its war with the rebellious colonies and aware of threats from other European nations at home, England decided to make peace with America, even at the price of conceding its independence. In 1783, after months of negotiation with English, French, and Spanish representatives, an agreement was reached, and the Treaty of Paris formally recognized America as an independent nation.

How did the American Revolution constitute the birth of a new nation?

By spring 1776 a spirit of independence was mounting in America. Various military successes and the acts of the Continental Congress inspired leaders, and after the Virginia delegate Richard Henry Lee's proposal for the states to be independent triggered the appointment of a committee to write a formal declaration of independence, it wasn't long before the Declaration of Independence was signed on July 4, 1776. This document broke all ties with England, and officially declared the 13 colonies as 13 united states, birthing a new nation.

What significance does the American Revolution have **today**?

Twenty-first-century Americans living under a free government owe a lot to the American Revolution, which was fought for many of the freedoms people sometimes take for granted today. These include the right to elect a head of government who can only act by the consent of the people; the right to elect public officials who must obey the law just like other Americans; and the civil rights of free speech, free religion, a fair trial, and justice for all men and women, regardless of position in life.

CHRONOLOGY OF THE AMERICAN REVOLUTION

Date	Event
1773	Parliament passes the Molasses Act, which imposes a high duty on non-British molasses.
1760	King George III ascends to the throne of England, beginning what will be a 60-year reign.
December 2, 1761	A writ of assistance is issued in Boston. The writs were general warrants allowing officials to search for smuggled materials within any suspected premises. Citing rights guaranteed in English common law, Boston attorney James Otis denounces the writs.
February 10, 1763	England and France sign the Treaty of Paris, ending the French and Indian War. Canada and the continent east of the Mississippi become part of the British empire.
October 7, 1763	King George III signs the Proclamation of 1763, prohibiting English settlement west of the Appalachians.
1764	James Otis publishes *The Rights of the British Colonies Asserted and Proved.*
April 5, 1764	Parliament passes the American Revenue Act. Popularly known as the Sugar Act, it increases duties on items imported to the colonies, including sugar, textiles, wines, and indigo dye.
May 24, 1764	James Otis denounces "taxation without representation" and encourages the colonists to oppose British tax laws.
September 1, 1764	The Currency Act is passed, prohibiting the colonists from issuing paper money.
March 22, 1765	Parliament passes the Stamp Act, which imposes the first taxes on the American colonies to be paid directly to the British Crown. Designed to pay for British troops on the American frontier, the act requires revenue stamps on newspapers, pamphlets, playing cards, dice, almanacs, and legal documents purchased by the colonists. In addition, violators would be tried in Vice-Admiralty courts without juries. In response, Samuel Adams forms Sons of Liberty groups, which are secret organizations led by prominent citizens. The groups use coercion to force stamp agents to resign their posts. The name is taken from a speech given by Colonel Issac Barré, a member of the British House of Commons, against the Stamp Act.
March 24, 1765	Parliament passes the Quartering Act, which orders colonists to provide housing and supplies for British troops remaining in the colonies after the French and Indian War.
May 29, 1765	During a speech in the Virginia Convention, Patrick Henry delivers the now-famous line: "If this be treason, make the most of it."
October 7, 1765	The colonies respond to the Stamp Act by convening the Stamp Act Congress in New York City. The congress passes a resolution on October 17 calling on King George III to repeal the Stamp Act as well as other acts passed in 1764.
March 18, 1766	Parliament repeals the Stamp Act, but the same day it passes the Declaratory Act, asserting the British government's absolute authority over the American colonies.
1767	Philadelphia lawyer John Dickinson publishes *Letters from a Farmer in Pennsylvania.*
June 29, 1767	Parliament passes the Townshend Revenue Acts, which impose taxes on lead, paint, paper, glass, and tea imported by the colonists. In addition, the New York legislature is suspended until it agrees to quarter British soldiers. The colonists respond by boycotting British goods.
October 1, 1768	Lord Hillsborough, secretary of state for the colonies, sends British troops to Boston to enforce customs laws.

Date	Event
May 1769	The Royal Governor of Virginia dissolves the Virginia House of Burgesses in response to the burgesses' official condemnation of "taxation without representation."
March 5, 1770	Parliament repeals the Townshend Acts. Import duties are removed from all items but tea. The Boston Massacre occurs when British soldiers guarding a customs house open fire on a crowd of 60 townspeople who had been harassing them. Five colonists are killed and six wounded.
June 9, 1772	The British revenue cutter *Gaspee* runs aground south of Providence, Rhode Island. Eight boatloads of men led by merchant John Brown storm the ship that night and burn it. The British government announces that the perpetrators would be tried in England and not in the colonies. The perpetrators are never caught.
March 1773	Dabney Carr, member of Virginia's House of Burgesses, suggests the formation of a standing committee of Correspondence and Inquiry to contact the other legislatures in an effort to gain united support against the British.
May 10, 1773	Parliament passes the Tea Act, which maintains the long-standing tax on imported tea. The act also gives the East India Company a monopoly on tea trade in the Americas.
December 16, 1773	Protesting the Stamp Act, colonists stage the Boston Tea Party. Disguised as Mohawk Indians, a group of colonists from the Sons of Liberty board British ships docked in the harbor and dump 23,000 pounds of tea belonging to the East India Company overboard.
March 1774	Parliament passes the Coercive Acts, known in the colonies as the "Intolerable Acts." The acts include: 1) the Boston Port Bill (effective June 1, 1774), which closes the port of Boston until the East India Company is compensated for its tea destroyed during the Boston Tea Party; 2) the Massachusetts Government Act (effective May 20, 1774), which virtually annuls the charter of the colonies and gives the royal governor control over town meetings; 3) the Quartering Act (updated June 2, 1774), which requires colonists to provide living quarters and supplies to British soldiers anywhere in the colonies, including in private households; and 4) the Administration of Justice Act (effective May 20, 1774), which states that British officials accused of capital crimes in the colonies would be removed from colonial jurisdiction and returned to Britain for trial. A fifth act, the Quebec Act, which changed the borders of Canada, was considered by the colonists to be part of the Intolerable Acts because of its date (effective May 20, 1774).
September 5–October 26, 1774	The First Continental Congress meets in Philadelphia, with George Washington, Patrick Henry, and John Hancock in attendance. Congress passes the Declaration of Rights, which asserts the rights of colonists and rejects the absolute British authority over the colonies.
September 9, 1774	Meeting in the home of Daniel Vose, Suffolk County delegates issue the Suffolk Resolves, which denounce the British closing of the Port of Boston and demand the end of military occupation.
November 18, 1774	King George III informs Prime Minister George Grenville that the colonies are in a state of rebellion.
March 23, 1775	Patrick Henry gives a speech that includes the now-famous phrase, "Give me liberty or give me death."
March 30, 1775	England declares Massachusetts to be in a state of rebellion and passes the New England Restraining Act, which requires the colonies to trade only with Britain.
April 18, 1775	Paul Revere, an express rider for Boston's Sons of Liberty, rides his horse at night to warn the colonists of the planned British attack on Lexington.

Date	Event
April 18-19, 1775	British soliders are confronted by Massachusetts militiamen, or "minutemen," at Lexington on April 18, and Concord on April 19. The "shot heard 'round the world' begins the American War of Independence.
April 23, 1775	King George III declares the colonies to be in open rebellion.
May 10, 1775–August 2, 1775	The Second Continental Congress convenes in Philadelphia; attendees include Thomas Jefferson, Benjamin Franklin, John Hancock, and George Washington.
June 15, 1775	The Continental Congress appoints George Washington commander of the Continental Army.
June 16-17, 1775	On June 16, colonists occupy Bunker Hill overlooking Boston. Colonists are told not to fire on the British until they see "the whites of their eyes." The next afternoon, British troops attack and force the colonists to withdraw.
July 1775	The Second Continental Congress sends the Olive Branch Petition to Britain to try to mend relations between the colonists and Britain.
July 3, 1775	George Washington takes command of colonial troops at Cambridge, MA.
August 23, 1775	King George III issues proclamation declaring the colonies to be in a state of rebellion.
November 28, 1775	The Continental Congress authorizes the establishment of the American navy.
December 2, 1775	Parliament passes the Prohibitory Act, which includes a naval blockade of the colonies, seizure of American goods on the high seas, and dragooning of captured provincial seamen into the Royal Navy.
December 31, 1775	British forces defeat colonial forces at the Battle of Quebec in Canada.
January 9, 1776	Thomas Paine publishes *Common Sense,* outlining the reasons why the colonies should break from England.
February 27, 1776	Colonial forces defeat British forces at the Battle of Moore's Creek Bridge in NC.
May 15, 1776	Virginia becomes the first colony to call for independence when it sends delegate Richard Henry to the Continental Congress to introduce a resolution that severs ties to Great Britain.
June 28, 1776	Final draft of the Declaration of Independence presented to the Continental Congress. Colonial forces defeat British forces at the Battle of Fort Sullivan in Charleston, SC.
July 4, 1776	The Declaration of Independence is signed in Philadelphia. It breaks all ties with Britain and unites the 13 colonies as 13 states. It uses the phrase "United States of America" for the first time.
August 1776	British forces land on Long Island.
September 5, 1776	British forces occupy New York City.
September 22, 1776	America's first spy, Nathan Hale, is hanged by the British. His famous quote lives on: "I only regret that I have but one life to lose for my country."
December 1776	Congress sends Benjamin Franklin to France to urge the French to ally with America.
December 26, 1776	George Washington crosses the Delaware River and captures the Hessian force at Battle of Trenton in NJ.
January 3, 1777	Colonial forces, under George Washington, defeat British forces at the Battle of Princeton in NJ.
July 2, 1777	British forces recapture Fort Ticonderoga.
July 31, 1777	The Continental Congress votes to use the volunteer services of 19-year-old French aristocrat Marquis de Lafayette.
September 19, 1777	British forces defeat colonial forces at Freeman's Farm outside Saratoga, NY.
October 7, 1777	British and colonial forces meet again at Saratoga, this time at Bemis Heights. The Americans force the British army to retreat to fortifications in Saratoga.

Date	Event
November 15, 1777	Continental Congress votes approval of the Articles of Confederation, which are then submitted to the states.
February 6, 1778	France enters the war following the signing of the Treaty of Amity and the Commerce Treaty of Alliance.
July 17, 1778	France declares war on Britain.
June 23, 1779	Spain declares war on Britain.
April 14, 1780	British forces defeat colonial forces at the Battle of Monck's Corner in SC.
May 12, 1780	Charleston, SC, falls to the British.
May 29, 1780	British forces defeat colonial forces at the Battle of Waxhaws in SC.
August 16, 1780	British forces defeat colonial forces at the Battle of Camden in SC.
October 7, 1780	Colonial forces defeat British forces at the Battle of King's Mountain in NC.
January 17, 1781	Colonial forces defeat British forces at the Battle of Cowpens in SC.
March 1, 1781	Articles of Confederation go into effect.
March 15, 1781	British forces defeat colonial forces at the Battle of Guilford Courthouse in NC.
September 8, 1781	British forces defeat colonial forces at the Battle of Eutaw Springs in SC.
October 19, 1781	General Cornwallis surrenders at Yorktown, VA, ending the war.
March 15, 1783	George Washington convinces Revolutionary War officers, in his Newburgh Address, not to rebel against the new government because of its failure to keep promises made to the Continental Army. Congress approves the Treaty of Paris.
June 1783	George Washington's Circular Letter to the States emphasizes his support of a strong central government.
September 3, 1783	The Treaty of Paris is signed to end the war.

THE DECLARATION OF INDEPENDENCE

Which was the **first colony to call for independence**?

On May 15, 1776, Virginia became the first colony to call for independence, when it sent one of its delegates, Richard Henry Lee, to the Continental Congress to introduce a resolution that severed ties with Great Britain.

What was **Richard Henry Lee's Resolution**?

On June 7, 1776, Richard Henry Lee of Virginia presented Congress with a resolution from Virginia's convention "that these United colonies are and of right ought to be free and independent states, that they are absolved from all allegiance to the British Crown, and that all political connection between them and state of Great Britain is & ought to be totally dissolved...." Lee's resolution not only called for independence, it called on Congress to take measures to secure foreign assistance and to form a confederation, or league of independent states, to bind the colonies more closely together.

How did the **delegates respond** to Lee's Resolution?

Lee's Resolution initiated heated debate among the delegates. On the one side, James Wilson of Pennsylvania, John Dickinson of Delaware, Robert Livingston of New York, and John and Edward Rutledge of South Carolina argued that the time was not right for independence. While New England and Virginia were united in support, the middle colonies—New York, New Jersey, Pennsylvania, Maryland, and Delaware— were not ready to cut ties with the mother country and instead insisted that the Congress wait until all the colonies were unanimously of one mind. On the other side, Lee was joined by John Adams, George Wythe of Virginia, and others in arguing that a declaration of independence was the only logical solution to its conflict with Great Britian. Congress decided to postpone action on Lee's Resolution until July 1, 1776, but in the meantime set up committees to consider each point of Lee's proposal. In addition, a committee of five men was set up to work on a formal declaration of independence, chaired by Thomas Jefferson, and the next day, 12 of the 13 colonies (and on July 9, New York, totaling 13) voted for independence.

What is the **function of the Declaration of Independence**?

The Declaration of Independence, formally adopted on July 4, 1776, by the Continental Congress, announced the birth of a new nation and set forth a philosophy of human freedom that would become a dynamic force throughout the entire world. The preamble borrows from English Enlightenment political philosophy, specifically John Locke's *Second Treatise on Government*, when it justifies the people's right to overthrow a government that denies them their natural rights: "We hold these truths to be self-evident, that all men are created equal, that they are endowed by their Creator with certain unalienable Rights, that among these are Life, Liberty and the pursuit of Happiness. That to secure these rights, Governments are instituted among Men, deriving their just powers from the consent of the governed, that whenever any Form of Government becomes destructive of these ends, it is the Right of the People to alter or to abolish it, and to institute a new Government, laying its foundation on such principles, and organizing its powers in such form, as to them shall seem most likely to effect their Safety and Happiness."

Here, Thomas Jefferson linked Locke's principles directly to the situation in the colonies. To fight for American independence was to fight for a government based on popular consent in place of a government rule by an authoritarian king—a government that could secure natural rights to life, liberty, and the pursuit of happiness. The body of the Declaration lists the colonists' grievances against the king of England and, for the first time, officially employs the phrase "United States of America," uniting the 13 colonies into 13 united states that from this point in history would function under one nation.

Was **Thomas Jefferson** supposed to write the Declaration of Independence?

Actually, no. Despite Jefferson's reputation as a writer, he expected John Adams, the foremost public leader for independence, to draw up the document. But Adams, who was busy on the committees for foreign treaties and the Board of War, refused Jefferson's request to draft the declaration. Meanwhile, the Second Continental Congress had formed a committee composed of Thomas Jefferson of Virginia, John Adams of Massachusetts, Benjamin Franklin of Pennsylvania, Robert Livingston of New York, and Roger Sherman of Connecticut to prepare a statement concerning independence. The now-famous document was drafted by Jefferson as its principal author, with some assistance from Adams and Franklin. A total of 47 alterations, including the insertion of three complete paragraphs, was made to the text before it was presented to Congress on June 28, 1776.

Who **signed** the Declaration of Independence?

On July 5, 1776, a copy of the Declaration of Independence was published in Philadelphia, signed by the president of Congress, John Hancock, and the secretary of Congress, Charles Thomson. The next day it was printed for the first time in a newspaper, and on July 9 was publicly read in Philadelphia. Although the document was not signed by all delegates to Congress, by August 2 the Declaration of Independence was formally signed by 56 delegates, including two future presidents, three future vice presidents, and 10 future members of the U.S. Congress.

Does the Declaration of Independence have any **legal significance**?

No. The purpose of the Declaration of Independence was not to change the legal status of America; on July 2, 1776, Congress had voted to sever the colonies from the British

Empire. The intent of Thomas Jefferson and his colleagues was to explain and justify the action of Congress in terms meaningful to Americans and Europeans alike.

Who holds the title **"Father of the Declaration of Independence"**?

As the Declaration's primary author, historians agree that Thomas Jefferson (1743–1826) holds that title.

Why was the Declaration of Independence considered a **revolutionary document**?

The Declaration of Independence not only hails a historical milestone for America as an independent nation, it is regarded as the document that, more than any other, single-handedly expresses the democratic spirit that embodies American politics, both then and now. By the time the Declaration of Independence was signed in 1776, Americans had completely transformed their political ideology and, instead of complacently accepting the belief that kings had a God-given right to rule, created a new political mindset that put people at the heart of government. The Declaration of Independence is the first united colonial document that expresses these ideas, calling forth both the right and obligation of the colonists to create a new nation and a new government.

Is the **slave trade** mentioned in any of the country's primary documents?

No. In the original draft of the Declaration of Independence, Thomas Jefferson denounced the slave trade. However, slave traders in New England, along with Georgia and South Carolina planters, forced Jefferson to remove the clause. Although the slave trade is not referred to in the Articles of Confederation, before 1808 the Constitution forbade Congress to use its power to interfere with and possibly terminate the slave trade. South Carolina lifted its constraints on slave importation in 1804, and until 1808, when Congress was given the power to intervene and passed a law banning the slave trade, 40,000 slaves were transported into that state. Again, as they had during the drafting of the Declaration of Independence, New England slave traders and southern planters resisted the law imposed by Congress, and smuggling slaves into the country became a lucrative practice. Although slave trading was defined as piracy by Congress in 1820, no one was executed for committing this crime until the onset of the Civil War.

BIRTH OF A NEW NATION

THE FIRST STATE GOVERNMENTS

Why did the **states develop their own constitutions**?

After the outbreak of the Revolutionary War when the New Hampshire and South Carolina provincial congresses asked Congress for advice on how to govern, Congress responded by urging each colony to establish its own government, stating that each should have "full and free representation of the people" and to "establish such a form of Government, as in their judgment will best produce the happiness of the people." In each colony the provincial congress declared itself to be the House of Representatives, claimed the office of governor vacant, and continued governing. By the end of 1775 royal authority had collapsed in most of the American colonies. In response, each state except Connecticut and Rhode Island, who simply eliminated the references to the monarch in their colonial charters, drew up new plans of government.

What were the **main features of the first state constitutions**?

Most of the new constitutions of 1776 and 1777 created systems that looked a lot like the old charter governments, although the governor was almost completely under the assembly's control. He would be chosen by the assembly or by the people and would not have power to veto the assembly's actions. Virginia, which drew up the first constitution in June 1776, began its constitution with a declaration of rights, a model other states followed. Beginning with a declaration of rights displayed the states' belief that the purpose of government was to secure rights to its citizens. Pennsylvania created a unique government, with a single-house legislature chosen every year by all adult male taxpayers, making the legislature the most representative body in the world. Although the first state constitutions differed from one another, several common features permeated the documents: each was based upon *popular sovereignty*, meaning that the government could only rule with the consent of the governed; each upheld a *limited government*, with many restrictions; seven constitutions contained a *bill of rights*, outlining "inalienable rights" for the people; and there was a *separation of powers* among the state governments, whereby their authority was divided among the executive, legislative, and judicial branches.

Which seven state constitutions contained a **bill of rights**?

The constitutions of Delaware, Maryland, Massachusetts, New Hampshire, North Carolina, Pennsylvania, and Virginia all contained a bill of rights.

How were the state constitutional conventions formed?

When the Massachusetts legislature submitted a constitution to the people of the state in 1778, the people rejected it because the legislature did not have the power to write a constitution. The idea emerged that a constitution could not be written by a legislature but had to originate from a special convention that the people had chosen specifically to write a constitution. This convention would represent the sovereign power of the people and could create a fundamental law, delegating power to the legislature that the constitution created. New Hampshire held the first constitutional convention in June 1778, although the constitution this convention submitted to the people was rejected. After 1778, states used conventions, rather than the legislature, to draw up their fundamental laws.

THE FORMATION OF A NATIONAL GOVERNMENT (1781–1789)

What were the **Articles of Confederation**?

Although each state created a new government, the states were also members of a union, the United States of America. As the United States they formed treaties with other nations, maintained General George Washington's army, issued paper money, and borrowed money to pay for the war. In the weeks after independence was declared, John Dickinson (1732–1808) began drafting a plan of union, and in autumn 1777 Congress submitted this plan to the states. This early agreement was not a constitution, but rather an "agreement to cooperate," that attempted to unite the 13 original states.

In November 1777, Congress voted its approval of a constitution for the United States—the Articles of Confederation—and submitted it to the states to accept or reject. Under the Articles, the Congress continued as the only branch of the central government. Each state could choose no fewer than two and no more than seven delegates to Congress. In addition, each state could have only one vote in Congress. A simple majority of states assembled decided issues, except for specified matters that required the consent of nine (out of 13). Each state alone could tax itself or regulate its commerce, although each had to contribute its share of money (based upon improved lands) to the upkeep of the Confederation. Each state claiming territory in the Trans-Appalachian region was allowed to keep its possessions instead of turning them over to the United States. Individually, the states were to retain their "sovereignty, freedom and independence" not specifically granted by Congress. In turn, Congress's authority covered making war and peace, making military and naval appointments, requisitioning men and money from the states, sending out and receiving ambassadors, negotiating treaties and alliances, settling Indian relations, managing postal affairs, coining money, deciding weights and measures, and settling disputes between states. Although Congress approved the Articles in 1777, they were not ratified by all of the states until 1781. The Articles served as the nation's basic charter of government until the first government under the Constitution of the United States was formed in 1789.

What were the shortcomings of the Articles of Confederation?

There were many shortcomings in the Articles of Confederation, which according to its own words granted the Continental Congress limited powers and allowed each state to retain its sovereignty. First, Congress had no direct authority over citizens of the United States, but rather had to work through the states; as such it could not pass laws or levy taxes that would allow it to carry out its responsibilities of defending the nation. Second, Congress could not regulate trade between the states or with other nations. Third, Congress could not stop the states from issuing their own currency, and as a result the country was inundated with various currencies. Fourth, because there was no executive branch, Congress had to complete all administrative duties, weighing itself down. And finally, because there was no judiciary system in place, the national government had to trust the state courts to enforce national laws and settle interstate disputes. The Articles' greatest weakness, however, was its lack of creation of a strong central government. Although briefly during the war the states submitted to the national government's authority, once the war was over each state resumed its sovereignty and was unwilling to give up its rights—including the power to tax—to a fledgling national government.

What **type of government** did the Articles of Confederation create?

This first government was known as a confederation or confedecracy, because the national government derived all of its powers directly from the states. Congress was denied power to raise taxes or regulate commerce, and many of the powers it was authorized to exercise required the approval of a minimum of nine states (out of 13), thereby handicapping its ability to do business.

How did the **states attempt to remedy these weaknesses**?

With a central government unable to enforce any regulations on the states, the states argued among themselves and became increasingly suspicious of one another's activities, taxing each other's goods, banning one another's trade, and printing their own money. Economic instability spread throughout the states, prices of goods soared, and the concept of sound credit disappeared. The states refused to support the central government, and several of them made agreements with foreign countries, even though the Articles forbade it. Most of the states organized their own militias. In 1785 and 1786, some states began to discuss ways to strengthen the national government, with Maryland and Virginia leading the way in a meeting held at Alexandria, Virginia to address their trade issues.

How did the Articles of Confederation compare with past attempts at creating a union?

All delegates to the Continental Congress understood the importance of unity, and thus many attempts at creating a union preceded the formation of the Articles of Confederation. In 1754, when France threatened the colonies, Benjamin Franklin proposed a plan of union that called the colonies to unite under a general council, with a governor appointed by the king. In 1774 Joseph Galloway proposed a similar plan of union, but by this time delegates from Massachusetts were not willing to support any concessions to British power. Galloway's plan was struck from the record, and he would remain loyal to the king while his colleagues in Congress drifted toward independence. In the summer of 1775 Franklin proposed another plan of union, with Congress serving as a governing body for the colonies. Silas Deane of Connecticut proposed a similar plan, but Congress was consumed with other problems and did not seriously consider either.

How did the Articles of Confederation **lay the groundwork for the U.S. Constitution**?

Dissatisfaction with the Articles of Confederation was aggravated by the hardships of a postwar depression, and in 1787—the same year that Congress passed the Northwest Ordinance, providing for the organization of new territories and states on the frontier—a convention assembled in Philadelphia to revise the Articles. The convention adopted an altogether new constitution, the present Constitution of the United States, which greatly increased the powers of the central government at the expense of the states. This document was ratified by the states with the understanding that it would be amended to include a bill of rights guaranteeing certain fundamental freedoms. These freedoms—including the rights of free speech, press, and assembly, freedom from unreasonable search and seizure, and the right to a speedy and public trial by an impartial jury—are assured by the first 10 amendments to the constitution, adopted on December 5, 1791, and officially known as the Bill of Rights.

What was **Maryland's influence** over the formation of the union?

By March 1779, all states except Maryland had approved the Articles of Confederation. Maryland, which lacked claims to lands northwest of the Ohio River, withheld support of the Articles until states with extensive land claims, notably New York and Virginia, surrendered their western lands to the Confederation. Feeling pressure to do so, the states agreed, and Maryland approved the Articles on March 1, 1781, the date the Articles went into effect.

What happened at the **Annapolis Convention**?

The early negotiations between Maryland and Virginia were so successful that Virginia proposed that all states send delegates to a meeting at Annapolis, Maryland, to discuss trade regulation. However, only five states—Delaware, New Jersey, New York, Pennsylvania, and Virginia—sent delegates to Annapolis on September 11, 1786, which rendered the talks ineffective because any amendment to the Articles of Confederation required the agreement of all 13 states. Congressman James Madison called for a national convention to continue the talks, and in February 1787 Congress agreed to call the states to a new convention, the Philadelphia Convention, "for the sole and express purpose of revising the Articles of Confederation." However, the meeting in Philadelphia became the Constitutional Convention.

What was **Shays' Rebellion**?

Like the rest of the nation, Massachusetts suffered a severe postwar depression characterized by an almost complete collapse of currency. Farmers from 50 western Massachusetts towns met in Hampshire County in August 1786 and petitioned the Massachusetts legislature to issue paper money for the payment of their debts and to revise the state constitution to correct inequities in taxation, representation, and the legal system. The legislature ignored their petition and on August, 29, 1786, an angry mob of 1,500 farmers, led by the Revolutionary War veteran Daniel Shays, marched to Springfield, Massachusetts, where it shut down civil courts and attempted to prevent the Supreme Judicial Court from trying criminal prosecutions for debt and foreclosing on their farms. Shays' Rebellion ended on January 25, 1787, when the Massachusetts militia suppressed a threatened attack on the Springfield Arsenal. Many leaders felt that Shays' rebellion, as the embodiment of mob rule, was the evidence of an unchecked democracy. Thus the event helped accelerate the movement away from the Articles of Confederation—which allowed states to maintain sovereignty over the federal government—toward a stronger central government as proposed by the Constitutional Convention and adopted by the states in 1789.

Why are the 1780s known as the **Critical Period**?

The 1780s witnessed a string of economic, political, and foreign policy problems, earning it the name of the Critical Period—when the United States would either make it or break it—in most U.S. history books. The American Revolution was followed by a severe economic depression in 1784 and 1785, forcing many states to impose charges on goods from other states to raise revenue. In addition, the national government was on the verge of bankruptcy, and a shortage of hard currency made it difficult to do business. Many of the nation's fledgling industries were flooded by British imports. Economic problems were especially pronounced in the South, where planters lost about 60,000 slaves during the Revolution and suffered under the new British trade regulations that prohibited the southern states from selling many of their agricultural products in the British West Indies, previously one of the South's leading markets. In addition, Britain violated the Peace Treaty of Paris by refusing to evacuate its military posts because the states wouldn't restore loyalist property that had been confiscated during the Revolution. At the same time, Spain failed to recognize American claims to territory between the Ohio River and Florida and in 1784 closed the Mississippi River to American trade.

Having not yet implemented the Constitution, the United States of America was operating under an inadequate framework of government that many leaders felt threatened its independence. By 1787 many of the nation's leaders were especially concerned that the tyrannical majorities in state legislatures threatened fundamental freedoms, including freedom of religion and the rights of property holders.

THE CONSTITUTION OF THE UNITED STATES

What was the **Constitutional Convention** and when did it convene?

Beginning on May 25, 1785, and running approximately five months, the Constitutional Convention consisted of an assembly of delegates who convened in Philadelphia at Independence Hall. They initially met to discuss revisions to the Articles of Confederation, but soon abandoned the revision in order to create a new constitution that would allow for a strong federal government.

Who **attended** the Constitutional Convention?

Every state except Rhode Island sent delegates, although the delegates were in attendance at varying times. In all, 74 men were appointed as delegates, 55 attended at one time or another, and approximately 40 were responsible for the hands-on work of developing a constitution. The delegates were the elite of the American republic: lawyers, merchants, physicians, planters, and at least 19 slave owners. Twenty-six were college-educated, 34 were lawyers or had studied law, 3 were physicians, approximately 40 had served as legislators, 13 had held state offices, and as many as 20 had helped write state constitutions. Because of the unique gifts of this assembly, Thomas Jefferson referred to them as an "assembly of demigods."

The most active delegates in favor of establishing a stronger federal government were James Madison and George Mason from Virginia; James Wilson and Gouverneur Morris from Pennsylvania; John Dickinson from Delaware; John Rutledge and Charles Pinckney from South Carolina; and Oliver Ellsworth from Connecticut. The more active and important leaders who preferred to amend the Articles of Confederation were Roger Sherman from Connecticut, William Paterson from New Jersey, Elbridge Gerry from Massachusetts, and Luther Martin from Maryland. George Washington was appointed president of the Convention. Those who did not attend include Richard Henry Lee, Patrick Henry, Thomas Jefferson, John Adams, Samuel Adams, and John Hancock.

Who were the **oldest and youngest members** of the Constitutional Convention?

Benjamin Franklin of Pennsylvania was 81 years old at the time, and Jonathan Dayton of New Jersey was 26.

Were there any **specials rules** that governed the Convention?

On the second session, held on May 28, the delegates adopted several rules regarding how they were to conduct business. They agreed that a majority of the states would be necessary in order to move forward on any issue, and each state would have one vote, a majority of which would carry any given proposal. To protect the interests of each state and avoid public pressure, the Constitutional Convention also adopted a pact of secrecy.

What was the **Virginia Plan**?

Edmund Randolph submitted the Virginia Plan, representing the ideas of James Madison and the interests of the large states, to the Constitutional Convention on May 29, 1787. The plan called for a new government with greatly expanded powers to be executed among three separate branches: legislative, executive, and judicial. It called for a bicameral, or two-house, national legislature, with representation based on population or financial contribution to the central government. The people would elect the members of the lower house, or House of Representatives, who would then elect the members of the upper house, or Senate. The national legislature would, in turn, choose a national executive. The Virginia Plan also provided for a national judiciary and granted the national legislature the power to veto any law passed by the states that was in conflict with national law. Since the states varied in size and wealth, a number of delegates thought the Virginia Plan was biased toward the large states and quickly developed a counterproposal.

What was the **New Jersey Plan**?

William Paterson of New Jersey, representing the small states, presented his alternative plan on June 15, 1787. The New Jersey Plan suggested giving Congress more power over commerce and revenue but keeping equal state representation in the legislature—regardless of population. It also called for a federal executive branch of more than one person, chosen by Congress but dispensable at the motion of a majority of state governors. As the various plans were discussed, central to the debate was how the states would be represented in Congress.

What **agreements** were reached at the Constitutional Convention?

The delegates believed in the concept of the balance of power in politics, which was supported by colonial experience and strengthened by the familiar writings of John Locke. These influences led to the conviction that three equal and coordinating branches of government should be established—legislative, executive, and judicial—so that no one entity could ever gain complete control. The delegates agreed that, like the colonial legislatures and the British Parliament, the legislative branch should consist of two houses. However, amongst this initial agreement, much debate and compromise took place, and generally three main compromises are known to define the Constitutional Convention: the compromise between large and small states over their representation in Congress, known as the Connecticut Compromise; the compromise between the North and the South over how slaves would be counted for taxation and representation, determined by the Three-Fifths Compromise; and the compromise between the North and the South over the regulation and taxation of commerce, known as the Commerce and Slave Trade Compromise.

What was the **Connecticut Compromise**?

The outcome of the debate between the Virginia and New Jersey plans was the Connecticut Compromise, also known as the "Great Compromise." It called for the formation of a bicameral legislature, or two houses of Congress, in order to satisfy both the big and small states. It called for the representatives in the first branch of Congress, or the House of Representatives, to be apportioned according to the state's population. However, in the second branch, or Senate, each state would have an equal vote regardless of the size of its population. Although the plan was not immediately accepted, the delegates preferred the arrangement to the breakup of the union, and finally agreed to the Connecticut Compromise.

What was the **Three-Fifths Compromise**?

Once the Connecticut Compromise settled that the seats in the House would be based on state population, the delegates argued over whether slaves should be counted in the populations of the southern states. Because their numbers were significant—with 90 percent of all slaves residing in Georgia, North Carolina, South Carolina, Maryland, and Virginia—most delegates from the slave-holding states argued that their numbers be factored. The North, however, disagreed. The result ended with the Three-Fifths Compromise, which determined that "three-fifths of all other persons" would be counted; in other words, five slaves would instead be counted as three. This formula was also used to calculate the amount of money raised in each state by any direct tax levied by Congress.

What was the **Commerce and Slave Trade Compromise**?

Although convention delegates agreed that Congress had the power to regulate interstate and foreign trade, many southerners feared that Congress would side with the commercial interests of the northern states, interfere with its slave trade, and try to pay for government out of the export duties of the South's biggest crop, tobacco. The Commerce and Slave Trade Compromise addressed the South's concerns and denied Congress the power to tax the export goods of any states, and initiated a "hands-off" policy whereby it was denied the power to act on the slave trade for at least 20 years.

How did the **framers of the Constitution reconcile their interests and principles**?

The men who met at the Constitutional Convention were willing to make many compromises in order to reach their goal of a strong national government. Although there were arguments, and even shouting matches, over some of the most heated issues, the men pressed on, and when the issue of how the states should be represented in Congress arose Benjamin Franklin suggested forming a separate committee—consisting of one member from each state—to debate the issue. "Compromise" is the word that arises repeatedly in historians' summaries of the Constitutional Convention. In *The Morning of America*, historian Darrett Rutman wrote, "The extraordinary feature of the Philadelphia convention was that the delegates could surmount their fears and prejudices, hammering out one practical compromise after another in the interest of a 'more perfect union.' "

Who earns the title **"Father of the Constitution"**?

James Madison (1751–1836) of Virginia earns the title of "Father of the Constitution" for his contributions as a political theorist and practical politician. In the month before the Constitutional Convention opened Madison poured over historical texts and drew on his legislative experience to analyze the pitfalls of the U.S. government under the Articles of Confederation. In Madison's view the state constitutions, which existed to protect the people from their rulers, actually contributed to a breakdown of social order, because those in power used majority rule to pass laws to protect their private interests. For example, Rhode Island passed paper money laws that helped farmers and hurt their creditors, and Maryland and New York passed navigation laws that favored their commercial interests over the interests of other states or the United States as a whole. To end this self-interest, Madison advocated the establishment of a large national republic whose legislators would act in the best interests of all the people, thus instigating the formation of the new government as established by the Constitution.

Who actually **wrote the Constitution**?

In none of the records of the Constitutional Convention is the literary authorship of any part of the Constitution definitely established. The framers of the Constitution debated proposed plans until July 24, 1787, when a Committee of Detail was appointed, consisting of John Rutledge of South Carolina, Edmund Randolph of Virginia, Nathaniel Gorham of Massachusetts, Oliver Ellsworth of Connecticut, and James Wilson of Pennsylvania. On August 6 these men submitted a draft that included a preamble and 23 articles, totaling 57 sections. Debate continued until September 8, when a new Committee of Style was named to revise the draft, including William Samuel Johnson of Connecticut, Alexander Hamilton of New York, Gouverneur Morris of Pennsylvania, James Madison of Virginia, and Rufus King of Massachusetts, who submitted the final draft on September 12. Historians generally attribute the literary form of the Constitution to Morris, based on Morris' own claim and the papers of Madison.

Who **signed the Constitution**?

On September 17, 1787, after 16 weeks of deliberation, the finished Constitution was signed by 39 of the 42 delegates present, including such historical notables as George Washington, James Madison, Alexander Hamilton, and Benjamin Franklin. Famous dissenters include Edmund Randolph, George Mason, and Luther Martin.

What is meant by the term **"constitution"**?

A constitution embodies the fundamental principles of a government. The U.S. Constitution, adopted by the sovereign power, is amendable by that power only. All laws, executive actions, and judicial decisions must conform to the Constitution, as it is the creator of the powers exercised by the departments of government. Because no law may be passed that contradicts its principles, and no person or government is exempt from following it, it has earned its title as the "supreme law of the land."

What are the **basic principles of the Constitution**?

The final version of the Constitution, approved on September 17, 1787, established a *federal democratic republic* form of government, with an indivisible union of sovereign states. It is a democracy because people govern themselves, representative because people choose elected officials by free and secret ballot, and a republic because the government derives its power from the people. This model of government is based upon the idea of *popular sovereignty,* which upholds that the people are the only source of government's power. Further, the government's power is *limited* because it can only do the things that people have authorized the government to do. The Constitution established a federal government with broad powers that were equally divided among the three branches, firmly establishing the principle of *balanced government,* with a separation of powers and a checks and balances system. Although powerful, the federal republic was created to uphold liberty, guaranteed because a division of power between the federal and state governments, known as *federalism,* would prevent one governmental entity from assuming too much power.

Specifically, Article I, Section 8 gives Congress far-reaching control over domestic, economic, and foreign affairs, in addition to the power to make all laws necessary for executing its powers. The Constitution also contains a long list of powers that are forbidden to the states. The president has widespread authority over the military, foreign policy, and appointments to office. The courts have the power of *judicial review;* that is, the authority to decide whether the government's actions are constitutional. After the Constitution was written, in time the Supreme Court began to assume the power of reviewing the constitutionality of state laws that had been denied to Congress.

Why was a **democracy** chosen?

Although the word "democracy" does not exist in the Declaration of Independence or the Constitution nor was it uttered by our Founding Fathers (who preferred the word "republic"), the framers of the Constitution chose democracy as both a way and form of government and a political mindset because they wanted a government "ruled by the people." The characteristics of the nation's constitutional democracy are everything the Founding Fathers felt would allow for the most effective and successful nation—a recognition of every person's fundamental worth (the widest degree of individual freedom), equality of opportunity, a belief in majority rule, and an upholding of minority rights—all functioning under a banner of popular consent and within a system of interdependent political structures.

Did the framers of the Constitution place equal weight on the concepts of liberty, equality, and democracy?

No. The preamble of the Constitution states that the purpose of the federal government is to "establish Justice, insure domestic Tranquility, provide for the common defense, promote the general Welfare, and secure the Blessings of Liberty to ourselves and our posterity." Although the concept of freedom of each individual and the "Blessings of Liberty" as a nation were highly regarded by the framers, they failed to include clauses that protected the *liberties* of the people. These would not be included until the Bill of Rights, the first 10 amendments to the Constitution that guarantee civil liberties, was added. And although respect for the individual—as a unique entity to be valued—underlies the basis of popular rule in a democracy, not all men and women (or rich or poor, or black or white, for that matter) were treated *equally* in the early republic. The Constitution itself discounted slaves as citizens and counted five slaves for every three free white men in each state's representation in Congress. The principles of *democracy* probably hold the greatest weight in the Constitution, since the word itself embodies a breadth of values, political processes, and political structures that this key document guarantees.

Why was a **three-branch model** chosen?

Although the framers of the Constitution intended to create a stronger central government for the fledgling United States, they also wanted to limit the powers of the government. A three-branch model—the legislative branch (Congress), the executive branch (the president), and the judicial branch (the courts)—distributes the power of the national government among these three authorities, ensuring that not all power is consolidated in one place.

What did the Founding Fathers mean by a **"separation of powers"**?

In 1787, Founding Father Thomas Jefferson wrote to John Adams: "The first principle of a good government is certainly a distribution of its powers into executive, judiciary, and legislative, and a subdivision of the latter into two or three branches." Jefferson's words embody one of the core truths of American government: its separate but shared power structure. Three separate and independent branches—the executive, the legislative, and the judicial—function together as the national government. Each branch has its own set of powers and responsibilities, although there is an intentional overlap of some of the powers. The framers of the Constitution believed that this separation of powers would protect individuals' liberties and prevent the government from abusing its power. The separation of powers is enforced by a system of checks and balances.

What does **"checks and balances"** mean?

Although each branch has its own authority, they are not completely separate or independent of one another. Instead, they are threaded together by a system of "checks and balances" that subjects each branch to a number of constitutional checks, or restraints, by the other branches. The checks and balances system was designed by the Founding Fathers to prevent a concentration of power in any one branch and to protect the rights and liberties of citizens. For example, the president can veto bills approved by Congress and the president nominates individuals to serve in the federal judiciary; the Supreme Court can declare a law enacted by Congress or an action by the president unconstitutional; and Congress can impeach the president and federal court justices and judges.

Did **the states or the people** ratify the Constitution?

The states. Before the Constitution could take effect, it had to be ratified by specially elected conventions in at least nine of the 13 states. Although the Constitution was debated, by June 21, 1788, more than the required nine states had ratified the document in the following order: Delaware, Pennsylvania, New Jersey, Georgia, Connecticut, Massachusetts, Maryland, South Carolina, New Hampshire, Virginia, and New York. After George Washington had been inaugurated president of the United States, North Carolina and Rhode Island ratified.

What is the most widely quoted phrase from the **preamble of the Constitution**?

The opening lines of the preamble of the Constitution, beginning with "We the People," constitute the most oft-quoted phrase of students and scholars alike. Unlike the Articles of Confederation, which spoke to the states and had their best interests in mind, these words of the preamble directly link the Constitution to the people of the United States of America.

What is an **expressed power**?

In order to further guarantee the limits of the new national government, the Constitution grants *expressed* powers; those powers expressly stated in the Constitution. Also called *enumerated* powers, most expressed powers are found in Article I, Section 8, whereby the Constitution expressly gives 27 powers to Congress, including the power of taxation, coining money, regulating foreign and interstate commerce, and declaring war.

What is an **implied power**?

Implied powers, on the other hand, are those powers *not* expressly stated in the Constitution but reasonably implied by the expressed powers. Implied powers are granted by the necessary and proper clause, found in Article I, Section 8. Examples of implied powers include Congress's regulation of labor-management agreements, the prohibition of racial discrimination in public palaces, and the building of an interstate highway system. Although these powers are very diverse, Congress acted on its authority under one expressed power—the power to regulate foreign and interstate commerce—to initiate these acts.

What is an **inherent power**?

An *inherent* power is any power that belongs to the national government simply because it is the national government of a sovereign state, the United States of America. The Constitution does not expressly provide for inherent powers, but they include the powers that national governments have historically held, including the power to regulate immigration, the power to acquire land, and the power to protect its land against rebellion or war.

What is the **"elastic clause"**?

Because the framers wanted to create a dynamic government, they included the necessary and proper clause, also known as the "elastic clause," in Article I, Section 8 of the Constitution. Meant to empower rather than limit government, it gives Congress the authority to pass all laws "necessary and proper" to carry out the enumerated powers outlined in the Constitution.

Is the Constitution a **rigid or flexible document**?

Both. Many historians use the term "rigid" to describe the Constitution because the provisions are in a written document that cannot be legally changed with the same ease and in the same manner as ordinary laws. The British Constitution, on the other hand, has been called "flexible" because it is an unwritten document that can be changed overnight by an act of Parliament. However, many scholars have pointed out that the Constitution is rigid—in that as "the supreme law of the land" it cannot be denied and must be followed—yet flexible enough to allow for changes through a formal amendment and ratification process. Indeed, the Founding Fathers included a provision in the Constitution for amending the document when social, economic, or political conditions demanded it. Twenty-seven amendments have been added since the original Constitution was ratified, and this flexibility has proven to be one of the Constitution's greatest strengths. Without such flexibility, it is inconceivable that a document drafted more than 200 years ago could effectively serve the needs of 260 million people and the thousands of multilevel governmental units in the United States today.

AMENDING THE CONSTITUTION

What is an **amendment**?

The process of constitutional change and growth comes through the Constitution's own amendment—literally, a change or addition in its written words that then become part of the Constitution itself.

How is the Constitution **amended**?

Under Article V of the Constitution, there are two ways to propose amendments to the Constitution. To propose amendments, two-thirds of both houses of Congress vote to propose an amendment *or* two-thirds of the state legislatures ask Congress to call a national convention to propose amendments. The latter method has not yet been used.

What does the term **"ratification"** mean?

The ratification of a document is the formal approval of it. It is the final consent to the effectiveness of a constitution, constitutional amendment, or treaty. The Constitution was ratified by nine of 13 states before it was legally adopted, and likewise each amendment must be ratified by three-fourths of the states before it can be added to the Constitution as law.

How is an amendment **ratified**?

Article V of the Constitution outlines the two ways for amendments to be ratified by the states. To ratify an amendment, three-fourths of the state legislatures must approve it or ratifying conventions in three-fourths of the states must approve it. The latter method was used only once: to ratify the Twenty-first Amendment, which repealed Prohibition.

How many amendments have been made to the Constitution?

Since 1789, Congress has proposed more than 10,000 joint resolutions calling for amendments to the Constitution. Of these thousands, only 33 of them have been sent to the states, and of those only 27 have been ratified.

Is there a **specified time limit** on the ratification process?

Legally, no. In 1917 when Congress proposed the Eighteenth Amendment to the Constitution, it set a seven-year deadline for the ratification process. Since that time it has set a similar deadline for the ratification of every amendment proposed, with the exception of the Nineteenth Amendment. In the case of *Dillon v. Gloss* (1921) the Supreme Court upheld that Congress can place "a reasonable time limit" on the ratification process, but there has been no legal determination of just how long a "reasonable time limit" is. Indeed, a handful of would-be amendments were never added to the Constitution because they fell short of meeting their deadlines; some notable twentieth-century amendments include a 1924 amendment that would have authorized Congress to regulate child labor, the 1972 Equal Rights Amendment that fell three states short of ratification when it finally died in 1982, and a 1978 amendment to give the District of Columbia seats in Congress, which lost steam in 1985.

What are the amendments and **what changes did they make**?

The most famous are the first 10 amendments to the Constitution, known as the Bill of Rights. Added in 1791, the Bill of Rights guarantees people's basic freedom of expression and belief. Other amendments include the Thirteenth Amendment, which prohibits slavery, added in 1865; the Fourteenth Amendment, which guarantees citizenship, due process, and equal protection under law, added in 1868; the Nineteenth Amendment, which gives women the right to vote, added in 1920; and the Twenty-second Amendment, which limits presidential tenure, added in 1951.

What has been the **longest period** during which no amendment has been added to the Constitution?

Sixty-one years, from 1804 to 1865, is the longest stretch of years between constitutional amendments (in this case, the Twelfth and Thirteenth Amendments).

FEDERALISM

Who were the **Federalists and the Anti-Federalists**, and how did they differ?

Proponents of the Constitution adopted the name "Federalists," taking the name away from their opponents, known as "Anti-Federalists," who claimed that the confederation of states under the Articles of Confederation was a true federal government. Federalist leaders included men like James Madison, Alexander Hamilton, and John Jay, who together wrote a series of 85 newspaper essays collected in a book called *The Federalist* (1788), as well as George Washington and Benjamin Franklin. As nationally known figures they used their prestige and political finesse to organize support for the Constitution. They attracted merchants, lawyers, planters, and other elites, but also artisans, shopkeepers, farmers, and others of the middle classes whose livelihoods would benefit from stronger national economic control.

On the other hand, most Anti-Federalists were not prominent national leaders; however, they vehemently opposed the Constitution for various reasons. Some were opposed to Congress's taxation power, others disliked the president's sweeping authority, and still others objected to the omission of a Bill of Rights to protect individual liberties. In general, however, the Anti-Federalists, many of whom were small farmers, feared that the Constitution created a national government that would be dominated by aristocrats whose nearly limitless power would deprive ordinary people of their independence. Prominent Anti-Federalists included Patrick Henry, Richard Henry Lee, George Mason, and Samuel Adams.

What are the Federalist Papers?

The Federalist Papers are a series of 85 essays published anonymously by Alexander Hamilton, John Jay, and James Madison between October 1787 and May 1788, urging ratification of the Constitution. Because the Constitution sought to increase the power of the national government at the expense of the state governments, the national debate over ratification began almost immediately after the Philadelphia Convention sent the proposed constitution to Congress on September 10, 1787, and its contents became known. Late in September, the New York Independent Journal began printing a series of Anti-Federalist essays by "Cato" (who may have been New York's powerful governor, George Clinton). In order to refute these and other Anti-Federalist tracts, Alexander Hamilton and John Jay, two of New York's most prominent Federalists, agreed to write a series of newspaper essays under the name "Publius." The first (*The Federalist* No. 1), written by Hamilton, appeared in the New York Independent Journal on October 27, and in it Hamilton outlined the purpose of the entire series. The essays would explain the necessity of the union for "political prosperity," the "insufficiency of the present Confederation to preserve that Union," and the need for a more "energetic" government than that which existed under the Articles of Confederation. John Jay wrote the next four installments before ill health forced him to quit. In November, James Madison, who was in New York representing Virginia in Congress, took Jay's place, and between them Madison and Hamilton produced all but one of the remaining eighty essays; Jay wrote No. 64.

Which is the **most famous** of all *The Federalist* essays?

Scholars generally agree that James Madison's first contribution to the series, *The Federalist* No. 10, is the most famous of all the essays. In it Madison discussed the origins of parties, or "factions" as he called them, and he argued that they sprang inevitably from "the unequal distribution of property." Some Anti-Federalists argued that the nation was much too large and too diverse to be governed effectively by a powerful central government without sacrificing people's liberties and freedoms in the process, but in *The Federalist* No. 10 Madison used his ideas about factions to reverse their argument. The nation's size, he wrote, and the great variety of its people and their interests were sources of strength, not weakness. There were so many different groups, so many different interests that would be represented in the new government, that no one faction, no one group, could ever capture control of the national government. Far from inviting tyranny, he argued, the nation's size and diversity, when coupled with the federal republican form of government proposed by the Constitution, would provide a strong check against tyranny.

What is the **significance of the Federalist Papers today**?

Although the effectiveness of the Federalist Papers as political tracts in 1788 has been debated, historians consider the essays important keys to understanding the intentions of the members of the Philadelphia Convention. Historians, scholars, students, and Supreme Court justices alike have studied the papers as a guide to the framers' mindset, in spite of the fact that one author (John Jay) did not attend the Philadelphia Convention, another (Alexander Hamilton) played a very small role there and was himself dissatisfied with the Constitution, and the third (James Madison) came to have serious doubts about the meaning of the Constitution and the kind of government it created within a few years after he wrote his essays for *The Federalist.*

Famous in their own right, the essays have been brought into many public political debates since they were written, particularly during times of constitutional crisis, such as the states' rights debates that preceded the Civil War, the discussion over the constitutionality of President Franklin D. Roosevelt's New Deal policies, and the debate over states' rights and civil liberties in the 1950s. Apart from its partisan political value, many historians and political scientists consider *The Federalist* to be the best existing defense of federal republicanism in general and of the American Constitution in particular. Few would disagree it is among the foremost works of political science ever produced in the United States.

What is **federalism**?

In its simplest definition, federalism is a form of government in which a written constitution divides governmental powers between a central government and several regional governments. In the United States, federalism is the constitutional arrangement to divide sovereignty, or governmental authority, between the national and state governments, each of which enforces its own laws directly on its citizens, and neither of which can change this division of power or amend the Constitution without the consent of the other party. Nearly 40 percent of the world's people live in federalist nations, including Canada, Switzerland, Australia, and Mexico.

Under the Constitution, both the nation and the 50 states pass laws, impose taxes, have their own budgets, and run their own courts. Neither entity gets its power from the other—both get their power directly from the people—and both are subject to the Constitution as the only legal source of authority for both the states and the nation. The Tenth Amendment outlines this division of powers, which in essence produces a dual system of government. By providing for two basic levels of government, federalism allows both the states and the national government to operate over the same people and the same territory simultaneously.

What is a **unitary system**?

The opposite of federalism is a unitary system of government, which favors a centralized government that maintains all the power. Rather than a division of powers among entities, the central government retains all authority, and as such determines by its sole discretion which powers it will delegate or take away. Examples of unitary governments include Great Britain, France, Israel, and the Philippines.

How does the concept of federalism **limit the national government's power**?

Because the concept of federalism allows for a division of powers between the national government and the states, it prohibits the national government from becoming all-powerful. The concept of federalism creates a dual system of government, whereby two sovereigns, each with its own sphere of authority, operate over a nation of people simultaneously. The Tenth Amendment gives a large sphere of power to the states, in which they can exercise all the powers reserved to them as well as those things that the Constitution does not expressly forbid them to do. The national government does not enjoy that same luxury: as a government of delegated powers, it can only carry out the powers that the Constitution specifically grants.

What powers are delegated to the **national government**, and which are reserved by the **states**?

The powers delegated to the national government include: printing money; regulating interstate and international trade; making treaties and conducting foreign policy; declaring war; providing an army and navy; establishing post offices; and making any laws necessary and proper to carry out the these powers. The states enjoy certain reserved powers, or those reserved to them within the federal system, including: issuing licenses; regulating intrastate businesses; conducting elections; establishing local governments; ratifying amendments to the Constitution; taking measures for public health and safety; and exerting powers the Constitution does not delegate to the national government or prohibit the states from using.

Political scientists have noted that sharing power between the national government and state governments allows citizens to enjoy the benefits of both diversity and unity. For example, the national government has the authority to set up a uniform currency system—which benefits interstate travelers and alleviates the states from having to regulate their own currency. However, issues like the death penalty have been left up to the individual states, allowing each state to exercise its own philosophy according to its individual needs.

What powers are **shared by both the national government and the states**?

The national government and the state governments share many powers. For example, both can collect taxes, build roads, borrow money, establish courts, make and enforce laws, charter banks and corporations, spend money for the general welfare, and possess private property for public purposes, with just compensation.

What powers are **denied** to national and state government?

Under the Constitution, the national government may not violate the Bill of Rights; impose export taxes among states; use money from the Treasury without the passage and approval of an appropriations bill; or change state boundaries. State governments may not enter into treaties with other countries; print money; tax imports or exports; impair obligations of contracts; or suspend a person's rights without due process. In addition, neither the national government nor state governments may grant titles of nobility; permit slavery (as established by the Thirteenth Amendment); deny citizens the right to vote due to race, color, or previous servitude (as established by the Fifteenth Amendment); or deny citizens the right to vote because of gender (as established by the Nineteenth Amendment).

What is meant by **"dual federalism"** and what was its role in the nation's early history?

Although state governments have their own constitutions, the laws made in individual states cannot conflict with the Constitution. During the first 100 years of United States history, the states did most of the governing that directly affected the people, while the national government mainly concentrated on foreign affairs. This concept of a two-layer system of government, where each level of government controls its own sphere, is known as "dual federalism." Under this system, sometimes called the traditional system because it reigned from 1789 to 1937, the national government retained less power than the state governments, having little effect on state economics other than promoting interstate commerce. The emphasis of the national government's programs was on internal improvements, public lands disposal, tariffs, and maintaining a national currency, while the state legislatures controlled all property laws (including slavery), commerce laws, insurance laws, education laws, and local government and civil service laws, to name a few.

During this time a divide began to form between the two entities over the issue of who had sovereignty, culminating in the Civil War. After the war, a series of constitutional amendments were passed that outlined the federal government's control over social and economic policy and the protection of the civil rights of citizens. Known as "the Civil War Amendments," these included the Thirteenth Amendment, which prohibited slavery; the Fourteenth Amendment, which defined citizenship and guaranteed due process under the law; and the Fifteenth Amendment, which maintained that a person could not be denied the right to vote based on race. Since 1860, dual federalism continued, but the power of the federal government began to strengthen. However, full national expansions into local and intrastate matters would not come about until the 1930s.

What role did ***McCulloch v. Maryland*** play in the concept of dual federalism?

Dual federalism reigned in America despite landmark Supreme Court cases that ruled for a pro-national interpretation of the Constitution. *McCulloch v. Maryland* (1819) was the premiere case favoring national authority of the economy. In it the Supreme Court ruled that the national government held authority over the states, as implied from the powers delegated to the Congress by the Constitution, specifically Article I, Section 8, which gives Congress the power to "regulate commerce with foreign nations, and among the several States and with the Indian tribes." While the case specifically involved the question of whether Congress had the right to charter a national bank (an explicit power not written in Article I, Section 8), the Supreme Court ruled that such power could be *implied* from those others that were expressly delegated to Congress, specifically the "powers to lay and collect taxes; to borrow money; to regulate commerce; and to declare and conduct war."

Why did the **balance of responsibility transfer to national government** in the 1930s?

During the first 150 years of the nation's history, the concept of dual federalism specifically limited the power of the national government over the economy. The Supreme Court's definition of interstate commerce was so restrictive that the federal government could only pass legislation that applied to the transfer of goods over state lines; the concept of intrastate (within state) commerce was designated to the states. This type of federalism, with strong state control and a weak national government, succeeded until 1937, when the Supreme Court redefined the concept of interstate commerce to allow the national government to regulate the state's economic conditions. In addition, the Great Depression of the 1930s brought an end to dual federalism as states were unable to cope with the nation's economic upheaval. Instead, President

Franklin D. Roosevelt's New Deal brought about a system of "cooperative federalism." Instead of assigning specific functions to each level of government, Roosevelt encouraged the national, state, and local governments to work together on specific programs. Since this time, the United States has moved further and further away from state individualism and toward a greater national uniformity in state laws and citizens' rights.

What is meant by **"cooperative federalism"**?

The concept of dual federalism evolved into "cooperative federalism," whereby intergovernmental cooperation has blurred the lines between the responsibilities of state and national governments. A result of the New Deal era, cooperative federalism encourages states and local governments to comply with national goals. This encouragement is fostered primarily through grants-in-aid, in which Congress gives grant money to local and state governments with the condition that the money is used for a particular congressional goal. In recent years the federal government has assumed increasing responsibility in matters such as health, education, welfare, transportation, and housing and urban development. However, federal programs are usually adopted on the basis of cooperation between state and federal entities, rather than as an imposition from one or more federal bureaucracies.

What is the concept of **"new federalism"**?

Since the mid-1970s, cooperative federalism has turned into a type of "regulated federalism," in which the national government regulates, or controls, the states by withholding monetary aid unless the states meet specifically obligations as outlined by Congress. In rebuttal, the states have fought for more authority, calling their concept "new federalism." Presidents Richard Nixon, Ronald Reagan, and George Bush supported new federalism because they advocated a reversal of the trend toward nationalization, instead calling for a return of fiscal resources and management responsibilities to the states in the form of large block grants and revenue sharing programs.

How do changes in federalism over the years reflect **different interpretations of democracy**?

Advocates of a strong centralized government maintain that playing a strong federal role of setting standards for the nation is the most democratic. Lessening national standards only increases state-to-state discrepancies, present during the first 150 years of America. A true constitutional government maintains the framework of a division of powers as mandated by federalism, which was specified by Americans as a condition of their consent to be government. Additionally, advocates maintain that the expansion of the national government's power was not made at the state's expense, nor has it left the states powerless, as the states continue to make most of the fundamental laws pertinent to their domain, and ultimately have the responsibility of implementing federal programs, such as welfare and public assistance.

Advocates for more state power argue that increased state power is more democratic because it puts the power into the hands of the people at a local level, ensuring the Founding Fathers' intent that no single branch of government—be it executive, legislative, or judicial—gain a tyrannical use of power. They argue that the federal government's excessive involvement in state matters takes the decision-making ability out of domain of the elected officials who are closest to the people they govern and instead puts it into the domain of Washington bureaucrats. The Founding Fathers established constitutional guarantees to safeguard against the abuse of centralized power, and advocates of state power maintain that regulated federalism—which more or less "bribes" states into following congressional agendas by threatening to withhold aid—is an embodiment of that abuse.

STATE GOVERNMENT TODAY

How is **state government** organized?

Like the national government, state governments have three branches: the executive, legislative, and judicial. Each branch functions and works a lot like its national counterpart. The chief executive of a state is the governor, who is elected by popular vote, typically for a four-year term (although New Hampshire and Vermont have two-year terms). Except for Nebraska, which has a single legislative body, all states have a bicameral (two-house) legislature, with the upper house usually called the Senate and the lower house called the House of Representatives, the House of Delegates, or the General Assembly. In most states, senators are elected to four-year terms, and members of the lower house serve two-year terms. The sizes of these two legislatures vary. Typically, the upper house consists of between 30 and 50 members; the lower house is made up of between 100 and 150 members. Minnesota has the largest upper house, with 67 members, and New Hampshire has the largest lower house, with almost 400 members—at least quadruple the number of most states.

Does every state have a **constitution**?

Yes. The constitutions of the various states differ from one another, but they generally follow a structure similar to that of the federal Constitution. Each includes a statement of the rights of the people, often called the Bill of Rights, and a plan for organizing the government. Each state constitution grants the final authority to the people of the state; sets standards, principles, and limitations for governing the state; and details the operation of businesses, banks, public utilities, and charitable institutions within the state. Although a state's constitution is above all other state and local laws within that state, it is subordinate to the U.S. Constitution. In addition, no state can make any law that conflicts in any way with federal law or the state's constitution.

What does **state government** do?

The U.S. Constitution reserves to the states all those powers not expressly delegated to the national government and not specifically denied to the states. They include the power to maintain state militias (the National Guard), regulate intrastate commerce, establish and operate state court systems, levy taxes, and borrow money. In everyday practice, the duties of state government vary from state to state, and they are innumerable. One of the state's primary roles includes the education of its residents, through the establishment of primary and secondary public school systems and colleges and universities. State government is also responsible for promoting people's health and welfare, which it achieves by establishing hospitals, immunization programs, outreaches to the needy and homeless, low-income housing, and antipollution laws. State government plays a role in public safety, by creating and maintaining a police force and a corrections system. Conservation efforts, recreational use of public lands, building and maintaining roads and highway systems, regulating business and commerce, and instituting consumer protection laws are just a handful of the services a state government provides to ensure the overall well-being of its territory and residents. In order to carry out this business, state governments establish local governments and administrative bodies at various levels.

What is the role of the **governor**?

As the main executive officer of a state, the governor is responsible for the well-being of his or state. The details of this job include numerous hands-on administrative tasks and leadership duties. The governor's executive powers include the appointment and removal of state officials, the supervision of thousands of executive branch staff, the formulation of the state budget, and the leadership of the state militia as its commander in chief. Legislative powers include the power to recommend legislation, to call special sessions of the legislature, and to veto measures passed by the legislature. In 43 states, governors have the power of an *item veto*, meaning that he or she can veto several components of a bill without rejecting it altogether. The governor's judicial powers are relegated to the realm of clemency. They include the power to pardon a criminal; the power to reduce a criminal's sentence; the power to reprieve, or postpone, the execution of a sentence; and the power to parole a prisoner.

What are the **qualifications** for governorship?

Each state dictates its own qualifications for governor. However, they generally include being an American citizen, reaching a certain age (usually 25 or 30), and being a resident of the state in which the candidate is running for office. Informal qualifications that come into play include a person's race, sex, name familiarity, party membership, government experience, media personality, political savvy, and perspective on state issues. All states elect their governors to four-year terms, with the exception of New Hampshire and Vermont, which allow for two-year terms. Most states have a term limit of two terms.

Who are the **women governors** currently serving?

Of the more than 2,400 people who have served as governor, only 19 have been women. As of early 2002, women run five states: Jane Swift of Massachusetts, a Republican; Jeanne Shaheen of New Hampshire, a Democrat; Judy Martz of Montana, a Republican; Ruth Ann Minner of Delaware, a Democrat; and Jane Dee Hull of Arizona, a Republican. Of the five states listed, Delaware and Montana don't have a governor's race in 2002. Political analysts and Washington think tanks are predicting that more women will step up to the plate during this election year. Rutgers University's Center for American Women and Politics cites that in 21 of the 36 states where the people are electing new governors in November 2002, a woman could be elected governor.

How is **city government** organized?

According to the U.S. Bureau of the Census, there are almost 88,000 local governmental units in the United States, including cities, counties, municipalities, townships, school districts, and special districts. Because at least 80 percent of America's citizens live in towns or cities, city governments play an important role in the overall context of American life and government. The city directly serves the needs of the people, providing everything from police and fire protection to sanitary codes, health regulations, education, public transportation, and housing. Although city governments are chartered by states, and their charters detail the objectives and powers of the municipal government, in many ways they operate independently from the states. For most big cities, however, cooperation with both state and federal organizations is essential to meeting the needs of their residents. Almost all cities have some kind of central council, elected by the voters, and an executive officer, assisted by various department heads, to manage the city's affairs. Typically, there are three general types of city government: the mayor-council, the commission, and the council-manager, although many cities have developed hybrids of these offices.

What is the role of the **mayor**?

The mayor-council is the oldest form of city government in the United States. Its structure is similar to that of the state and national governments, with an elected mayor as chief of the executive branch and an elected council that represents the various neighborhoods forming the legislative branch. The mayor appoints heads of city departments and other officials, sometimes with the approval of the council. He or she has the power of veto the laws of the city, called ordinances, and often is responsible for preparing the city's budget. The council passes city ordinances, sets the tax rate on property, and apportions money among the various city departments.

How is county government set up?

The county is a subdivision of the state and is usually made up of two or more townships and several villages. New York City is so large that it is divided into five separate boroughs, each a county in its own right: the Bronx, Manhattan, Brooklyn, Queens, and Staten Island. However, most counties serve populations of fewer than 50,000 residents. In most counties across America, one town or city is designated as the county seat, and this is where the government offices are located and where the board of commissioners or supervisors meets. In small counties, the county as a whole chooses boards; in the larger ones, supervisors represent separate districts or townships. The board levies taxes, borrows and appropriates money, sets the salaries of county employees, supervises elections, builds and maintains highways and bridges, and administers national, state, and county welfare programs.

How is the **government of a town** set up?

Thousands of municipal jurisdictions are too small to qualify as city governments, and so these governments are chartered as towns and villages. They deal with strictly local needs, including paving and lighting the streets, ensuring a water supply, providing police and fire protection, establishing local health regulations, arranging for garbage, sewage, and other waste disposal, collecting local taxes to support governmental operations, and, in cooperation with the state and county, directly administering the local school system. The government is usually run by an elected board or council, which might be called the town or village council, board of selectmen, board of supervisors, or board of commissioners. The board may have a chairperson or president who functions as chief executive officer, or there may be an elected mayor. Governmental employees often include a clerk, treasurer, police and fire officers, and health and welfare workers.

What is a **town meeting**?

The town meeting is one aspect of local government that still exists today, although it was created in the early years of the republic. At east once a year the registered voters of the town meet in open session to elect officers, debate local issues, and pass laws for operating the government. As a body, they decide on road construction and repair, construction of public buildings and facilities, tax rates, and the town budget. Having existed for more than two centuries, the town meeting is often called the purest form of direct democracy because governmental power is not delegated, but rather exercised directly by the people. However, town meetings cannot be found in every area of the country; they are mostly conducted in the small towns of New England, where the first colonies were established.

APPENDICES AND INDEX

APPENDIX I

The Constitution of the United States

We the People of the United States, in Order to form a more perfect Union, establish Justice, insure domestic Tranquility, provide for the common defence, promote the general Welfare, and secure the Blessings of Liberty to ourselves and our Posterity, do ordain and establish this Constitution for the United States of America.

ARTICLE I.

SECTION 1. All legislative Powers herein granted shall be vested in a Congress of the United States, which shall consist of a Senate and House of Representatives.

SECTION 2. The House of Representatives shall be composed of Members chosen every second Year by the People of the several States, and the Electors in each State shall have the Qualifications requisite for Electors of the most numerous Branch of the State Legislature.

No Person shall be a Representative who shall not have attained to the Age of twenty five Years, and been seven Years a Citizen of the United States, and who shall not, when elected, be an Inhabitant of that State in which he shall be chosen.

Representatives and direct Taxes shall be apportioned among the several States which may be included within this Union, according to their respective Numbers, which shall be determined by adding to the whole Number of free Persons, including those bound to Service for a Term of Years, and excluding Indians not taxed, three fifths of all other Persons.

The actual Enumeration shall be made within three Years after the first Meeting of the Congress of the United States, and within every subsequent Term of ten Years, in such Manner as they shall by Law direct. The Number of Representatives shall not exceed one for every thirty Thousand, but each State shall have at Least one Representative; and until such enumeration shall be made, the State of New Hampshire shall be entitled to chuse three, Massachusetts eight, Rhode Island and Providence Plantations one, Connecticut five, New York six, New Jersey four, Pennsylvania eight, Delaware one, Maryland six, Virginia ten, North Carolina five, South Carolina five and Georgia three.

When vacancies happen in the Representation from any State, the Executive Authority thereof shall issue Writs of Election to fill such Vacancies.

The House of Representatives shall chuse their Speaker and other Officers; and shall have the sole Power of Impeachment.

SECTION 3. The Senate of the United States shall be composed of two Senators from each State, chosen by the Legislature thereof, for six Years; and each Senator shall have one Vote.

Immediately after they shall be assembled in Consequence of the first Election, they shall be divided as equally as may be into three Classes. The Seats of the Senators of the first Class shall be vacated at the Expiration of the second Year, of the second Class at the Expiration of the fourth Year, and of the third Class at the Expiration of the sixth Year, so that one third may be chosen every second Year; and if Vacancies happen by Resignation, or otherwise, during the Recess of the Legislature of any State, the Executive thereof may make temporary Appointments until the next Meeting of the Legislature, which shall then fill such Vacancies.

No person shall be a Senator who shall not have attained to the Age of thirty Years, and been nine Years a Citizen of the United States, and who shall not, when elected, be an Inhabitant of that State for which he shall be chosen.

The Vice President of the United States shall be President of the Senate, but shall have no Vote, unless they be equally divided.

The Senate shall chuse their other Officers, and also a President pro tempore, in the absence of the Vice President, or when he shall exercise the Office of President of the United States.

The Senate shall have the sole Power to try all Impeachments. When sitting for that Purpose, they shall be on Oath or Affirmation. When the President of the United States is tried, the Chief Justice shall preside: And no Person shall be convicted without the Concurrence of two thirds of the Members present.

Judgment in Cases of Impeachment shall not extend further than to removal from Office, and disqualification to hold and enjoy any Office of honor, Trust or Profit under the United States: but the Party convicted shall nevertheless be liable and subject to Indictment, Trial, Judgment and Punishment, according to Law.

SECTION 4. The Times, Places and Manner of holding Elections for Senators and Representatives, shall be prescribed in each State by the Legislature thereof; but the Congress may at any time by Law make or alter such Regulations, except as to the Place of Chusing Senators.

The Congress shall assemble at least once in every Year, and such Meeting shall be on the first Monday in December, unless they shall by Law appoint a different Day.

SECTION 5. Each House shall be the Judge of the Elections, Returns and Qualifications of its own Members, and a Majority of each shall constitute a Quorum to do Business; but a smaller number may adjourn from day to day, and may be authorized to compel the Attendance of absent Members, in such Manner, and under such Penalties as each House may provide.

Each House may determine the Rules of its Proceedings, punish its Members for disorderly Behavior, and, with the Concurrence of two-thirds, expel a Member.

Each House shall keep a Journal of its Proceedings, and from time to time publish the same, excepting such Parts as may in their Judgment require Secrecy; and the Yeas and Nays of the Members of either House on any question shall, at the Desire of one fifth of those Present, be entered on the Journal.

Neither House, during the Session of Congress, shall, without the Consent of the other, adjourn for more than three days, nor to any other Place than that in which the two Houses shall be sitting.

SECTION 6. The Senators and Representatives shall receive a Compensation for their Services, to be ascertained by Law, and paid out of the Treasury of the United States. They shall in all Cases, except Treason, Felony and Breach of the Peace, be privileged from Arrest during their Attendance at the Session of their respective Houses, and in going to and returning from the same; and for any Speech or Debate in either House, they shall not be questioned in any other Place.

No Senator or Representative shall, during the Time for which he was elected, be appointed to any civil Office under the Authority of the United States which shall have been created, or the Emoluments whereof shall have been increased during such time; and no Person holding any Office under the United States, shall be a Member of either House during his Continuance in Office.

SECTION 7. All bills for raising Revenue shall originate in the House of Representatives; but the Senate may propose or concur with Amendments as on other bills.

Every Bill which shall have passed the House of Representatives and the Senate, shall, before it become a Law, be presented to the President of the United States; If he approve he shall sign it, but if not he shall return it, with his Objections to that House in which it shall have originated, who shall enter the Objections at large on their Journal, and proceed to reconsider it. If after such Reconsideration two thirds of that House shall agree to pass the Bill, it shall be sent, together with the Objections, to the other House, by which it shall likewise be reconsidered, and if approved by two thirds of that House, it shall become a Law. But in all such Cases the Votes of both Houses shall be determined by Yeas and Nays, and the Names of the Persons voting for and against the Bill shall be entered on the Journal of each House respectively. If any Bill shall not be returned by the President within ten Days (Sundays excepted) after it shall have been presented to him, the Same shall be a Law, in like Manner as if he had signed it, unless the Congress by their Adjournment prevent its Return, in which Case it shall not be a Law.

Every Order, Resolution, or Vote to which the Concurrence of the Senate and House of Representatives may be necessary (except on a question of Adjournment) shall be presented to the President of the United States; and before the Same shall take Effect, shall be approved by him, or being disapproved by him, shall be repassed by two thirds of the Senate and House of Representatives, according to the Rules and Limitations prescribed in the Case of a Bill.

SECTION 8. The Congress shall have Power To lay and collect Taxes, Duties, Imposts and Excises, to pay the Debts and provide for the common Defence and general Welfare of the United States; but all Duties, Imposts and Excises shall be uniform throughout the United States;

To borrow money on the credit of the United States;

To regulate Commerce with foreign Nations, and among the several States, and with the Indian Tribes;

To establish an uniform Rule of Naturalization, and uniform Laws on the subject of Bankruptcies throughout the United States;

To coin Money, regulate the Value thereof, and of foreign Coin, and fix the Standard of Weights and Measures;

To provide for the Punishment of counterfeiting the Securities and current Coin of the United States;

To establish Post Offices and Post Roads;

To promote the Progress of Science and useful Arts, by securing for limited Times to Authors and Inventors the exclusive Right to their respective Writings and Discoveries;

To constitute Tribunals inferior to the supreme Court;

To define and punish Piracies and Felonies committed on the high Seas, and Offenses against the Law of Nations;

To declare War, grant Letters of Marque and Reprisal, and make Rules concerning Captures on Land and Water;

To raise and support Armies, but no Appropriation of Money to that Use shall be for a longer Term than two Years;

To provide and maintain a Navy;

To make Rules for the Government and Regulation of the land and naval Forces;

To provide for calling forth the Militia to execute the Laws of the Union, suppress Insurrections and repel Invasions;

To provide for organizing, arming, and disciplining the Militia, and for governing such Part of them as may be employed in the Service of the United States, reserving to the States respectively, the Appointment of the Officers, and the Authority of training the Militia according to the discipline prescribed by Congress;

To exercise exclusive Legislation in all Cases whatsoever, over such District (not exceeding ten Miles square) as may, by Cession of particular States, and the acceptance of Congress, become the Seat of the Government of the United States, and to exercise like Authority over all Places purchased by the Consent of the Legislature of the State in which the same shall be, for the Erection of Forts, Magazines, Arsenals, dock-Yards, and other needful Buildings; And

To make all Laws which shall be necessary and proper for carrying into Execution the foregoing Powers, and all other Powers vested by this Constitution in the Government of the United States, or in any Department or Officer thereof.

SECTION 9. The Migration or Importation of such Persons as any of the States now existing shall think proper to admit, shall not be prohibited by the Congress prior to the Year one thousand eight hundred and eight, but a tax or duty may be imposed on such Importation, not exceeding ten dollars for each Person.

The privilege of the Writ of Habeas Corpus shall not be suspended, unless when in Cases of Rebellion or Invasion the public Safety may require it.

No Bill of Attainder or ex post facto Law shall be passed. No capitation, or other direct, Tax shall be laid, unless in Proportion to the Census or Enumeration herein before directed to be taken.

No Tax or Duty shall be laid on Articles exported from any State.

No Preference shall be given by any Regulation of Commerce or Revenue to the Ports of one State over those of another: nor shall Vessels bound to, or from, one State, be obliged to enter, clear, or pay Duties in another.

No Money shall be drawn from the Treasury, but in Consequence of Appropriations made by Law; and a regular Statement and Account of the Receipts and Expenditures of all public Money shall be published from time to time.

No Title of Nobility shall be granted by the United States: And no Person holding any Office of Profit or Trust under them, shall, without the Consent of the Congress, accept of any present, Emolument, Office, or Title, of any kind whatever, from any King, Prince or foreign State.

SECTION 10. No State shall enter into any Treaty, Alliance, or Confederation; grant Letters of Marque and Reprisal; coin Money; emit Bills of Credit; make any Thing but gold and silver Coin a Tender in Payment of Debts; pass any Bill of Attainder, ex post facto Law, or Law impairing the Obligation of Contracts, or grant any Title of Nobility.

No State shall, without the Consent of the Congress, lay any Imposts or Duties on Imports or Exports, except what may be absolutely necessary for executing its inspection Laws: and the net Produce of all Duties and Imposts, laid by any State on Imports or Exports, shall be for the Use of the Treasury of the United States; and all such Laws shall be subject to the Revision and Controul of the Congress.

No State shall, without the Consent of Congress, lay any duty of Tonnage, keep Troops, or Ships of War in time of Peace, enter into any Agreement or Compact with another State, or with a foreign Power, or engage in War, unless actually invaded, or in such imminent Danger as will not admit of delay.

ARTICLE II.

SECTION 1. The executive Power shall be vested in a President of the United States of America. He shall hold his Office during the Term of four Years, and, together with the Vice-President chosen for the same Term, be elected, as follows:

Each State shall appoint, in such Manner as the Legislature thereof may direct, a Number of Electors, equal to the whole Number of Senators and Representatives to which the State may be entitled in the Congress: but no Senator or Representative, or Person holding an Office of Trust or Profit under the United States, shall be appointed an Elector.

The Electors shall meet in their respective States, and vote by Ballot for two persons, of whom one at least shall not lie an Inhabitant of the same State with themselves. And they shall make a List of all the Persons voted for, and of the Number of Votes for each; which List they shall sign and certify, and transmit sealed to the Seat of the Government of the United States, directed to the President of the Senate. The President of the Senate shall, in the Presence of the Senate and House of Representatives, open all the Certificates, and the Votes shall then be counted. The Person having the greatest Number of Votes shall be the President, if such Number be a Majority of the whole Number of Electors appointed; and if there be more than one who have such Majority, and have an equal Number of Votes, then the House of Representatives shall immediately chuse by Ballot one of them for President; and if no Person have a Majority, then from the five highest on the List the said House shall in like Manner chuse the President. But in chusing the President, the Votes shall be taken by States, the Representation from each State having one Vote; a quorum for this Purpose shall consist of a Member or Members from two-thirds of the States, and a Majority of all the States shall be necessary to a Choice. In every Case, after the Choice of the President, the Person having the greatest Number of Votes of the Electors shall be the Vice President. But if there should remain two or more who have equal Votes, the Senate shall chuse from them by Ballot the Vice President.

The Congress may determine the Time of chusing the Electors, and the Day on which they shall give their Votes; which Day shall be the same throughout the United States.

No person except a natural born Citizen, or a Citizen of the United States, at the time of the Adoption of this Constitution, shall be eligible to the Office of President; neither shall any Person be eligible to that Office who shall not have attained to the Age of thirty-five Years, and been fourteen Years a Resident within the United States.

In Case of the Removal of the President from Office, or of his Death, Resignation, or Inability to discharge the Powers and Duties of the said Office, the same shall devolve on the Vice President, and the Congress may by Law provide for the Case of Removal, Death, Resignation or Inability, both of the President and Vice President, declaring what Officer shall then act as President, and such Officer shall act accordingly, until the Disability be removed, or a President shall be elected.

The President shall, at stated Times, receive for his Services, a Compensation, which shall neither be increased nor diminished during the Period for which he shall have been elected, and he shall not receive within that Period any other Emolument from the United States, or any of them.

Before he enter on the Execution of his Office, he shall take the following Oath or Affirmation: "I do solemnly swear (or affirm) that I will faithfully execute the Office of President of the United States, and will to the best of my Ability, preserve, protect and defend the Constitution of the United States."

SECTION 2. The President shall be Commander in Chief of the Army and Navy of the United States, and of the Militia of the several States, when called into the actual Service of the United States; he may require the Opinion, in writing, of the principal Officer in each of the executive Departments, upon any subject relating to the Duties of their respective Offices, and he shall have Power to Grant Reprieves and Pardons for Offenses against the United States, except in Cases of Impeachment.

He shall have Power, by and with the Advice and Consent of the Senate, to make Treaties, provided two thirds of the Senators present concur; and he shall nominate, and by and with the Advice and Consent of the Senate, shall appoint Ambassadors, other public Ministers and Consuls, Judges of the supreme Court, and all other Officers of the United States, whose Appointments are not herein otherwise provided for, and which shall be established by Law: but the Congress may by Law vest the Appointment of such inferior Officers, as they think proper, in the President alone, in the Courts of Law, or in the Heads of Departments.

The President shall have Power to fill up all Vacancies that may happen during the Recess of the Senate, by granting Commissions which shall expire at the End of their next Session.

SECTION 3. He shall from time to time give to the Congress Information of the State of the Union, and recommend to their Consideration such Measures as he shall judge necessary and expedient; he may, on extraordinary Occasions, convene both Houses, or either of them, and in Case of Disagreement between them, with Respect to the Time of Adjournment, he may adjourn them to such Time as he shall think proper; he shall receive Ambassadors and other public Ministers; he shall take Care that the Laws be faithfully executed, and shall Commission all the Officers of the United States.

SECTION 4. The President, Vice President and all civil Officers of the United States, shall be removed from Office on Impeachment for, and Conviction of, Treason, Bribery, or other high Crimes and Misdemeanors.

ARTICLE III.

SECTION 1. The judicial Power of the United States, shall be vested in one supreme Court, and in such inferior Courts as the Congress may from time to time ordain and establish. The Judges, both of the supreme and inferior Courts, shall hold their Offices during good Behavior, and shall, at stated Times, receive for their Services a Compensation which shall not be diminished during their Continuance in Office.

SECTION 2. The judicial Power shall extend to all Cases, in Law and Equity, arising under this Constitution, the Laws of the United States, and Treaties made, or which shall be made, under their Authority; to all Cases affecting Ambassadors, other public Ministers and Consuls; to all Cases of admiralty and maritime Jurisdiction; to Controversies to which the United States shall be a Party; to Controversies between two or more States; between a State and Citizens of another State; between Citizens of different States; between Citizens of the same State claiming Lands under Grants of different States, and between a State, or the Citizens thereof, and foreign States, Citizens or Subjects.

In all Cases affecting Ambassadors, other public Ministers and Consuls, and those in which a State shall be Party, the supreme Court shall have original Jurisdiction. In all the other Cases before mentioned, the supreme Court shall have appellate Jurisdiction, both as to Law and Fact, with such Exceptions, and under such Regulations as the Congress shall make.

Trial of all Crimes, except in Cases of Impeachment, shall be by Jury; and such Trial shall be held in the State where the said Crimes shall have been committed; but when not committed within any State, the Trial shall be at such Place or Places as the Congress may by Law have directed.

SECTION 3. Treason against the United States, shall consist only in levying War against them, or in adhering to their Enemies, giving them Aid and Comfort. No Person shall be convicted of Treason unless on the Testimony of two Witnesses to the same overt Act, or on Confession in open Court.

The Congress shall have power to declare the Punishment of Treason, but no Attainder of Treason shall work Corruption of Blood, or Forfeiture except during the Life of the Person attainted.

ARTICLE IV.

SECTION 1. Full Faith and Credit shall be given in each State to the public Acts, Records, and judicial Proceedings of every other State. And the Congress may by general Laws prescribe the Manner in which such Acts, Records and Proceedings shall be proved, and the Effect thereof.

SECTION 2. The Citizens of each State shall be entitled to all Privileges and Immunities of Citizens in the several States.

A Person charged in any State with Treason, Felony, or other Crime, who shall flee from Justice, and be found in another State, shall on demand of the executive Authority of the State from which he fled, be delivered up, to be removed to the State having Jurisdiction of the Crime.

No Person held to Service or Labour in one State, under the Laws thereof, escaping into another, shall, in Consequence of any Law or Regulation therein, be discharged from such Service or Labour, But shall be delivered up on Claim of the Party to whom such Service or Labour may be due.

SECTION 3. New States may be admitted by the Congress into this Union; but no new States shall be formed or erected within the Jurisdiction of any other State; nor any State be formed by the Junction of two or more States, or parts of States, without the Consent of the Legislatures of the States concerned as well as of the Congress.

The Congress shall have Power to dispose of and make all needful Rules and Regulations respecting the Territory or other Property belonging to the United States; and nothing in this Constitution shall be so construed as to Prejudice any Claims of the United States, or of any particular State.

SECTION 4. The United States shall guarantee to every State in this Union a Republican Form of Government, and shall protect each of them against Invasion; and on Application of the Legislature, or of the Executive (when the Legislature cannot be convened) against domestic Violence.

ARTICLE V.

The Congress, whenever two thirds of both Houses shall deem it necessary, shall propose

Amendments to this Constitution, or, on the Application of the Legislatures of two thirds of the several States, shall call a Convention for proposing Amendments, which, in either Case, shall be valid to all Intents and Purposes, as part of this Constitution, when ratified by the Legislatures of three fourths of the several States, or by Conventions in three fourths thereof, as the one or the other Mode of Ratification may be proposed by the Congress; Provided that no Amendment which may be made prior to the Year One thousand eight hundred and eight shall in any Manner affect the first and fourth Clauses in the Ninth Section of the first Article; and that no State, without its Consent, shall be deprived of its equal Suffrage in the Senate.

ARTICLE VI.

All Debts contracted and Engagements entered into, before the Adoption of this Constitution, shall be as valid against the United States under this Constitution, as under the Confederation.

This Constitution, and the Laws of the United States which shall be made in Pursuance thereof; and all Treaties made, or which shall be made, under the Authority of the United States, shall be the supreme Law of the Land; and the Judges in every State shall be bound thereby, any Thing in the Constitution or Laws of any State to the Contrary notwithstanding.

The Senators and Representatives before mentioned, and the Members of the several State Legislatures, and all executive and judicial Officers, both of the United States and of the several States, shall be bound by Oath or Affirmation, to support this Constitution; but no religious Test shall ever be required as a Qualification to any Office or public Trust under the United States.

ARTICLE VII.

The Ratification of the Conventions of nine States, shall be sufficient for the Establishment of this Constitution between the States so ratifying the Same.

DONE in Convention by the Unanimous Consent of the States present the Seventeenth Day of September in the Year of our Lord one thousand seven hundred and Eighty seven and of the Independence of the United States of America the Twelfth. In Witness whereof We have hereunto subscribed our Names.

Go. Washington
President and deputy from Virginia

New Hampshire
John Langdon
Nicholas Gilman

Massachusetts
Nathaniel Gorham
Rufus King

Connecticut
Wm Saml Johnson
Roger Sherman

New York
Alexander Hamilton

New Jersey
Wil Livingston
David Brearley
Wm Paterson
Jona. Dayton

Pennsylvania
B Franklin
Thomas Mifflin
Robt Morris
Geo. Clymer
Thos FitzSimons
Jared Ingersoll
James Wilson
Gouv Morris

Delaware
Geo. Read
Gunning Bedford jun
John Dickinson
Richard Bassett
Jaco. Broom

Maryland
James McHenry
Dan of St Tho Jenifer
Danl Carroll

Virginia
John Blair
James Madison Jr.

North Carolina
Wm Blount
Richd Dobbs Spaight
Hu Williamson

South Carolina
J. Rutledge
Charles Cotesworth Pinckney
Charles Pinckney
Pierce Butler

Georgia
William Few
Abr Baldwin

Attest: William Jackson, Secretary

AMENDMENT I.

Congress shall make no law respecting an establishment of religion, or prohibiting the free exercise thereof; or abridging the freedom of speech, or of the press; or the right of the people peaceably to assemble, and to petition the Government for a redress of grievances.

AMENDMENT II.

A well regulated Militia, being necessary to the security of a free State, the right of the people to keep and bear Arms, shall not be infringed.

AMENDMENT III.

No Soldier shall, in time of peace be quartered in any house, without the consent of the Owner, nor in time of war, but in a manner to be prescribed by law.

AMENDMENT IV.

The right of the people to be secure in their persons, houses, papers, and effects, against unreasonable searches and seizures, shall not be violated, and no Warrants shall issue, but upon probable cause, supported by Oath or affirmation, and particularly describing the place to be searched, and the persons or things to be seized.

AMENDMENT V.

No person shall be held to answer for a capital, or otherwise infamous crime, unless on a presentment or indictment of a Grand Jury, except in cases arising in the land or naval forces, or in the Militia, when in actual service in time of War or public danger; nor shall any person be subject for the same offense to be twice put in jeopardy of life or limb; nor shall be compelled in any criminal case to be a witness against himself, nor be deprived of life, liberty, or property, without due process of law; nor shall private property be taken for public use, without just compensation.

AMENDMENT VI.

In all criminal prosecutions, the accused shall enjoy the right to a speedy and public trial, by an impartial jury of the State and district wherein the crime shall have been committed, which district shall have been previously ascertained by law, and to be informed of the nature and cause of the accusation; to be confronted with the witnesses against him; to have compulsory process for obtaining witnesses in his favor, and to have the Assistance of Counsel for his defence.

AMENDMENT VII.

In Suits at common law, where the value in controversy shall exceed twenty dollars, the right of trial by jury shall be preserved, and no fact tried by a jury, shall be otherwise re-examined in any Court of the United States, than according to the rules of the common law.

AMENDMENT VIII.

Excessive bail shall not be required, nor excessive fines imposed, nor cruel and unusual punishments inflicted.

AMENDMENT IX.

The enumeration in the Constitution, of certain rights, shall not be construed to deny or disparage others retained by the people.

AMENDMENT X.

The powers not delegated to the United States by the Constitution, nor prohibited by it to the States, are reserved to the States espectively, or to the people.

AMENDMENT XI.

The Judicial power of the United States shall not be construed to extend to any suit in law or equity, commenced or prosecuted against one of the United States by Citizens of another State, or by Citizens or Subjects of any Foreign State.

AMENDMENT XII.

The Electors shall meet in their respective states, and vote by ballot for President and Vice-President, one of whom, at least, shall not be an inhabitant of the same state with themselves; they shall name in their ballots the person voted for as President, and in distinct ballots the person voted for as Vice-President, and they shall make distinct lists of all persons voted for as President, and of all persons voted for as Vice-President and of the number of votes for each, which lists they shall sign and certify, and transmit sealed to the seat of the government of the United States, directed to the President of the Senate;

The President of the Senate shall, in the presence of the Senate and House of Representatives, open all the certificates and the votes shall then be counted;

The person having the greatest Number of votes for President, shall be the President, if such number be a majority of the whole number of Electors appointed; and if no person have such majority, then from the persons having the highest numbers not exceeding three on the list of those voted for as President, the House of Representatives shall choose immediately, by ballot, the President. But in choosing the President, the votes shall be taken by states, the representation from each state having one vote; a quorum for this purpose shall consist of a member or members from two-thirds of the states, and a majority of all the states shall be necessary to a choice. And if the House of Representatives shall not choose a President whenever the right of choice shall devolve upon them, before the fourth day of March next following, then the Vice-President shall act as President, as in the case of the death or other constitutional disability of the President.

The person having the greatest number of votes as Vice-President, shall be the Vice-President, if such number be a majority of the whole number of Electors appointed, and if no person have a majority, then from the two highest numbers on the list, the Senate shall choose the Vice-President; a quorum for the purpose shall consist of two-thirds of the whole number of Senators, and a majority of the whole number shall be necessary to a choice. But no person constitutionally ineligible to the office of President shall be eligible to that of Vice-President of the United States.

AMENDMENT XIII.

1. Neither slavery nor involuntary servitude, except as a punishment for crime whereof the party shall have been duly convicted, shall exist within the United States, or any place subject to their jurisdiction.

2. Congress shall have power to enforce this article by appropriate legislation.

AMENDMENT XIV.

1. All persons born or naturalized in the United States, and subject to the jurisdiction thereof, are citizens of the United States and of the State wherein they reside. No State shall make or enforce any law which shall abridge the privileges or immunities of citizens of the United States; nor shall any State deprive any person of life, liberty, or property, without due process of law; nor deny to any person within its jurisdiction the equal protection of the laws.

2. Representatives shall be apportioned among the several States according to their respective numbers, counting the whole number of persons in each State, excluding Indians not taxed. But when the right to vote at any election for the choice of electors for President and Vice-President of the United States, Representatives in Congress, the Executive and Judicial officers of a State, or the members of the Legislature thereof, is

denied to any of the male inhabitants of such State, being twenty-one years of age, and citizens of the United States, or in any way abridged, except for participation in rebellion, or other crime, the basis of representation therein shall be reduced in the proportion which the number of such male citizens shall bear to the whole number of male citizens twenty-one years of age in such State.

3. No person shall be a Senator or Representative in Congress, or elector of President and Vice-President, or hold any office, civil or military, under the United States, or under any State, who, having previously taken an oath, as a member of Congress, or as an officer of the United States, or as a member of any State legislature, or as an executive or judicial officer of any State, to support the Constitution of the United States, shall have engaged in insurrection or rebellion against the same, or given aid or comfort to the enemies thereof. But Congress may by a vote of two-thirds of each House, remove such disability.

4. The validity of the public debt of the United States, authorized by law, including debts incurred for payment of pensions and bounties for services in suppressing insurrection or rebellion, shall not be questioned. But neither the United States nor any State shall assume or pay any debt or obligation incurred in aid of insurrection or rebellion against the United States, or any claim for the loss or emancipation of any slave; but all such debts, obligations and claims shall be held illegal and void.

5. The Congress shall have power to enforce, by appropriate legislation, the provisions of this article.

AMENDMENT XV.

1. The right of citizens of the United States to vote shall not be denied or abridged by the United States or by any State on account of race, color, or previous condition of servitude.

2. The Congress shall have power to enforce this article by appropriate legislation.

AMENDMENT XVI.

The Congress shall have power to lay and collect taxes on incomes, from whatever source derived, without apportionment among the several States, and without regard to any census or enumeration.

AMENDMENT XVII.

The Senate of the United States shall be composed of two Senators from each State, elected by the people thereof, for six years; and each Senator shall have one vote. The electors in each State shall have the qualifications requisite for electors of the most numerous branch of the State legislatures.

When vacancies happen in the representation of any State in the Senate, the executive authority of such State shall issue writs of election to fill such vacancies: Provided, That the legislature of any State may empower the executive thereof to make temporary appointments until the people fill the vacancies by election as the legislature may direct.

This Amendment shall not be so construed as to affect the election or term of any Senator chosen before it becomes valid as part of the Constitution.

AMENDMENT XVIII.

1. After one year from the ratification of this article the manufacture, sale, or transportation of intoxicating liquors within, the importation thereof into, or the exportation thereof from the United States and all territory subject to the jurisdiction thereof for beverage purposes is hereby prohibited.

2. The Congress and the several States shall have concurrent power to enforce this article by appropriate legislation.

3. This article shall be inoperative unless it shall have been ratified as an Amendment to the Constitution by the legislatures of the several States, as provided in the Constitution, within seven years from the date of the submission hereof to the States by the Congress.

AMENDMENT XIX.

The right of citizens of the United States to vote shall not be denied or abridged by the United States or by any State on account of sex.

Congress shall have power to enforce this article by appropriate legislation.

AMENDMENT XX.

1. The terms of the President and Vice President shall end at noon on the 20th day of January, and the terms of Senators and Representatives at noon on the 3d day of January, of the years in which such terms would have ended if this article had not been ratified; and the terms of their successors shall then begin.

2. The Congress shall assemble at least once in every year, and such meeting shall begin at noon on the 3d day of January, unless they shall by law appoint a different day.

3. If, at the time fixed for the beginning of the term of the President, the President elect shall have died, the Vice President elect shall become President. If a President shall not have been chosen before the time fixed for the beginning of his term, or if the President elect shall have failed to qualify, then the Vice President elect shall act as President until a President shall have qualified; and the Congress may by law provide

for the case wherein neither a President elect nor a Vice President elect shall have qualified, declaring who shall then act as President, or the manner in which one who is to act shall be selected, and such person shall act accordingly until a President or Vice President shall have qualified.

4. The Congress may by law provide for the case of the death of any of the persons from whom the House of Representatives may choose a President whenever the right of choice shall have devolved upon them, and for the case of the death of any of the persons from whom the Senate may choose a Vice President whenever the right of choice shall have devolved upon them.

5. Sections 1 and 2 shall take effect on the 15th day of October following the ratification of this article.

6. This article shall be inoperative unless it shall have been ratified as an Amendment to the Constitution by the legislatures of three-fourths of the several States within seven years from the date of its submission.

AMENDMENT XXI.

1. The eighteenth article of Amendment to the Constitution of the United States is hereby repealed.

2. The transportation or importation into any State, Territory, or possession of the United States for delivery or use therein of intoxicating liquors, in violation of the laws thereof, is hereby prohibited.

3. The article shall be inoperative unless it shall have been ratified as an Amendment to the Constitution by conventions in the several States, as provided in the Constitution, within seven years from the date of the submission hereof to the States by the Congress.

AMENDMENT XXII.

1. No person shall be elected to the office of the President more than twice, and no person who has held the office of President, or acted as President, for more than two years of a term to which some other person was elected President shall be elected to the office of the President more than once. But this Article shall not apply to any person holding the office of President, when this Article was proposed by the Congress, and shall not prevent any person who may be holding the office of President, or acting as President, during the term within which this Article becomes operative from holding the office of

President or acting as President during the remainder of such term.

2. This article shall be inoperative unless it shall have been ratified as an Amendment to the Constitution by the legislatures of three-fourths of the several States within seven years from the date of its submission to the States by the Congress.

AMENDMENT XXIII.

1. The District constituting the seat of Government of the United States shall appoint in such manner as the Congress may direct: A number of electors of President and Vice President equal to the whole number of Senators and Representatives in Congress to which the District would be entitled if it were a State, but in no event more than the least populous State; they shall be in addition to those appointed by the States, but they shall be considered, for the purposes of the election of President and Vice President, to be electors

appointed by a State; and they shall meet in the District and perform such duties as provided by the twelfth article of Amendment.

2. The Congress shall have power to enforce this article by appropriate legislation.

AMENDMENT XXIV.

1. The right of citizens of the United States to vote in any primary or other election for President or Vice President, for electors for President or Vice President, or for Senator or Representative in Congress, shall not be denied or abridged by the United States or any State by reason of failure to pay any poll tax or other tax.

2. The Congress shall have power to enforce this article by appropriate legislation.

AMENDMENT XXV.

1. In case of the removal of the President from office or of his death or resignation, the Vice President shall become President.

2. Whenever there is a vacancy in the office of the Vice President, the President shall nominate a Vice President who shall take office upon confirmation by a majority vote of both Houses of Congress.

3. Whenever the President transmits to the President pro tempore of the Senate and the Speaker of the House of Representatives his written declaration that he is unable to discharge the powers and duties of his office, and until he transmits to them a writ-

ten declaration to the contrary, such powers and duties shall be discharged by the Vice President as Acting President.

4. Whenever the Vice President and a majority of either the principal officers of the executive departments or of such other body as Congress may by law provide, transmit to the President pro tempore of the Senate and the Speaker of the House of Representatives their written declaration that the President is unable to discharge the powers and duties of his office, the Vice President shall immediately assume the powers and duties of the office as Acting President.

Thereafter, when the President transmits to the President pro tempore of the Senate and the Speaker of the House of Representatives his written declaration that no inability exists, he shall resume the powers and duties of his office unless the Vice President and a majority of either the principal officers of the executive department or of such other body as Congress may by law provide, transmit within four days to the President pro tempore of the Senate and the Speaker of the House of Representatives their written declaration that the President is unable to discharge the powers and duties of his office. Thereupon Congress shall decide the issue, assembling within forty eight hours for that purpose if not in session. If the Congress, within twenty one days after receipt of the latter written declaration, or, if Congress is not in session, within twenty one days after Congress is required to assemble, determines by two thirds vote of both Houses that the President is unable to discharge the powers and duties of his office, the Vice President shall continue to discharge the same as Acting President; otherwise, the President shall resume the powers and duties of his office.

AMENDMENT XXVI.

1. The right of citizens of the United States, who are eighteen years of age or older, to vote shall not be denied or abridged by the United States or by any State on account of age.

2. The Congress shall have power to enforce this article by appropriate legislation.

AMENDMENT XXVII.

No law, varying the compensation for the services of the Senators and Representatives, shall take effect, until an election of Representatives shall have intervened.

APPENDIX 2

The Declaration of Independence

IN CONGRESS, July 4, 1776.

The unanimous Declaration of the thirteen united States of America,

When in the Course of human events, it becomes necessary for one people to dissolve the political bands which have connected them with another, and to assume among the powers of the earth, the separate and equal station to which the Laws of Nature and of Nature's God entitle them, a decent respect to the opinions of mankind requires that they should declare the causes which impel them to the separation.

We hold these truths to be self-evident, that all men are created equal, that they are endowed by their Creator with certain unalienable Rights, that among these are Life, Liberty and the pursuit of Happiness.—That to secure these rights, Governments are instituted among Men, deriving their just powers from the consent of the governed, —That whenever any Form of Government becomes destructive of these ends, it is the Right of the People to alter or to abolish it, and to institute new Government, laying its foundation on such principles and organizing its powers in such form, as to them shall seem most likely to effect their Safety and Happiness. Prudence, indeed, will dictate that Governments long established should not be changed for light and transient causes; and accordingly all experience hath shewn, that mankind are more disposed to suffer, while evils are sufferable, than to right themselves by abolishing the forms to which they are accustomed. But when a long train of abuses and usurpations, pursuing invariably the same Object evinces a design to reduce them under absolute Despotism, it is their right, it is their duty, to throw off such Government, and to provide new Guards for their future security.—Such has been the patient sufferance of these Colonies; and such is now the necessity which constrains them to alter their former Systems of Government. The history of the present King of Great Britain is a history of repeated injuries and usurpations, all having in direct object the establishment of an absolute Tyranny over these States. To prove this, let Facts be submitted to a candid world.

He has refused his Assent to Laws, the most wholesome and necessary for the public good.

He has forbidden his Governors to pass Laws of immediate and pressing importance, unless suspended in their operation till his Assent should be obtained; and when so suspended, he has utterly neglected to attend to them.

He has refused to pass other Laws for the accommodation of large districts of people, unless those people would relinquish the right of Representation in the Legislature, a right inestimable to them and formidable to tyrants only.

He has called together legislative bodies at places unusual, uncomfortable, and distant from the depository of their public Records, for the sole purpose of fatiguing them into compliance with his measures.

He has dissolved Representative Houses repeatedly, for opposing with manly firmness his invasions on the rights of the people.

He has refused for a long time, after such dissolutions, to cause others to be elected; whereby the Legislative powers, incapable of Annihilation, have returned to the People at large for their exercise; the State remaining in the mean time exposed to all the dangers of invasion from without, and convulsions within.

He has endeavoured to prevent the population of these States; for that purpose obstructing the Laws for Naturalization of Foreigners; refusing to pass others to encourage their migrations hither, and raising the conditions of new Appropriations of Lands.

He has obstructed the Administration of Justice, by refusing his Assent to Laws for establishing Judiciary powers.

He has made Judges dependent on his Will alone, for the tenure of their offices, and the amount and payment of their salaries.

He has erected a multitude of New Offices, and sent hither swarms of Officers to harrass our people, and eat out their substance.

He has kept among us, in times of peace, Standing Armies without the Consent of our legislatures.

He has affected to render the Military independent of and superior to the Civil power.

He has combined with others to subject us to a jurisdiction foreign to our constitution, and unacknowledged by our laws; giving his Assent to their Acts of pretended Legislation:

For Quartering large bodies of armed troops among us:

For protecting them, by a mock Trial, from punishment for any Murders which they should commit on the Inhabitants of these States:

For cutting off our Trade with all parts of the world:

For imposing Taxes on us without our Consent:

For depriving us in many cases, of the benefits of Trial by Jury:

For transporting us beyond Seas to be tried for pretended offences

For abolishing the free System of English Laws in a neighbouring Province, establishing therein an Arbitrary government, and enlarging its Boundaries so as to render it at once an example and fit instrument for introducing the same absolute rule into these Colonies:

For taking away our Charters, abolishing our most valuable Laws, and altering fundamentally the Forms of our Governments:

For suspending our own Legislatures, and declaring themselves invested with power to legislate for us in all cases whatsoever.

He has abdicated Government here, by declaring us out of his Protection and waging War against us.

He has plundered our seas, ravaged our Coasts, burnt our towns, and destroyed the lives of our people.

He is at this time transporting large Armies of foreign Mercenaries to compleat the works of death, desolation and tyranny, already begun with circumstances of Cruelty & perfidy scarcely paralleled in the most barbarous ages, and totally unworthy the Head of a civilized nation.

He has constrained our fellow Citizens taken Captive on the high Seas to bear Arms against their Country, to become the executioners of their friends and Brethren, or to fall themselves by their Hands.

He has excited domestic insurrections amongst us, and has endeavoured to bring on the inhabitants of our frontiers, the merciless Indian Savages, whose known rule of warfare, is an undistinguished destruction of all ages, sexes and conditions.

In every stage of these Oppressions We have Petitioned for Redress in the most humble terms: Our repeated Petitions have been answered only by repeated injury. A Prince whose character is thus marked by every act which may define a Tyrant, is unfit to be the ruler of a free people.

Nor have We been wanting in attentions to our Brittish brethren. We have warned them from time to time of attempts by their legislature to extend an unwarrantable jurisdiction over us. We have reminded them of the circumstances of our emigration and settlement here. We have appealed to their native justice and magnanimity, and we have conjured them by the ties of our common kindred to disavow these usurpations, which, would inevitably interrupt our connections and correspondence. They too have been deaf to the voice of justice and of consanguinity. We must, therefore, acquiesce in the necessity, which denounces our Separation, and hold them, as we hold the rest of mankind, Enemies in War, in Peace Friends.

We, therefore, the Representatives of the united States of America, in General Congress, Assembled, appealing to the Supreme Judge of the world for the rectitude of our intentions, do, in the Name, and by Authority of the good People of these Colonies, solemnly publish and declare, That these United Colonies are, and of Right ought to be Free and Independent States; that they are Absolved from all Allegiance to the British Crown, and that all political connection between them and the State of Great Britain, is and ought to be totally dissolved; and that as Free and Independent States, they have full Power to levy War, conclude Peace, contract Alliances, establish Commerce, and to do all other Acts and Things which Independent States may of right do. And for the support of this Declaration, with a firm reliance on the protection of divine Providence, we mutually pledge to each other our Lives, our Fortunes and our sacred Honor.

Georgia
Button Gwinnett
Lyman Hall
George Walton

North Carolina
William Hooper
Joseph Hewes
John Penn

South Carolina
Edward Rutledge
Thomas Heyward, Jr.
Thomas Lynch, Jr.
Arthur Middleton

Massachusetts
John Hancock
Maryland:
Samuel Chase
William Paca
Thomas Stone
Charles Carroll of Carrollton

Virginia
George Wythe
Richard Henry Lee
Thomas Jefferson
Benjamin Harrison
Thomas Nelson, Jr.
Francis Lightfoot Lee
Carter Braxton

Pennsylvania
Robert Morris
Benjamin Rush
Benjamin Franklin
John Morton
George Clymer
James Smith
George Taylor
James Wilson
George Ross

Delaware
Caesar Rodney
George Read
Thomas McKean

New York
William Floyd
Philip Livingston
Francis Lewis
Lewis Morris

New Jersey
Richard Stockton
John Witherspoon
Francis Hopkinson
John Hart
Abraham Clark

New Hampshire
Josiah Bartlett
William Whipple

Massachusetts
Samuel Adams
John Adams
Robert Treat Paine
Elbridge Gerry

Rhode Island
Stephen Hopkins
William Ellery

Connecticut
Roger Sherman
Samuel Huntington
William Williams
Oliver Wolcott

New Hampshire
Matthew Thornton

Further Reading

General Government and Politics

Austin, Eric W. *Political Facts of the United States since 1789.* New York: Columbia University Press, 1986.

Carpini Delli, Michael X., and Scott Keeter. *What Americans Know About Politics and Why It Matters.* New Haven, CT: Yale University Press, 1996.

Corwin, Edward S. *The "Higher Law": Background of American Constitutional Law.* Ithaca, NY: Cornell University Press, 1990.

Corwin, Edward, and J. W. Peltason. *Corwin and Peltason's Understanding the Constitution,* 13th edition. Fort Worth, TX: Harcourt Brace, 1994.

Diamond, Larry. *Developing Democracy, Toward Consolidation.* Baltimore, MD: Johns Hopkins Press, 1999.

Eskin, Blake, ed. *The Book of Political Lists*. New York: Villard, 1998.

Hamilton, Alexander, James Madison, and John Jay. *The Federalist Papers, 1787–1788.* Reprint, New York: Mentor Books, 1961.

Huntington, Samuel. *The Third Wave: Democratization in the Late Twentieth Century.* Norman: University of Oklahoma Press, 1991.

Kelly, Alfred, Winfred A. Harbison, and Herman Beltz. *The American Constitution: Its Origins and Development,* 7th edition. New York: W. W. Norton, 1991.

Mladenka, Kenneth R. *The Unfinished Republic: American Government in the Twenty-First Century.* Upper Saddle River, NJ: Prentice-Hall, Inc, 1997.

Page, Benjamin I., and James R. Simmons. *What Government Can Do: Dealing with Poverty and Inequality.* Chicago: The University of Chicago Press, 2000.

Rosenstone, Steven, and John Mark Hansen. *Mobilization, Participation, and Democracy in America.* New York: Macmillan, 1993.

Sandoz, Ellis. *A Government of Laws: Political Theory, Religion, and the American Founding.* Baton Rouge: Louisiana State University Press, 1990.

Skocpol, Theda, and Morris P. Fiorina, eds. *Civic Engagement in American Democracy.* Washington, DC: Brookings Institution Press, 1999.

Tocqueville, Alexis de. *Democracy in America.* 1835. Reprint, edited by J. P. Mayer and translated by Phillips Bradley. Garden City, NY: Anchor Books, 1969.

Civil Liberties

Abraham, Henry. *Freedom and the Court: Civil Rights and Liberties in the United States,* 5th edition. New York: Oxford University Press, 1994.

Alderman, Ellen, and Caroline Kennedy. *In Our Defense: The Bill of Rights in Action.* New York: William Morrow, 1991.

_______. *The Right to Privacy.* New York: Alfred A. Knopf, 1995.

Alley, Robert S., ed. *The Constitution and Religion: Leading Supreme Court Cases on Church and State.* Amherst, NY: Prometheus Books, 1999.

Brigham, John. *Civil Liberties and American Democracy.* Washington, DC: Congressional Quarterly Press, 1984.

Burns, James MacGregor, and Stewart Burns. *A People's Charter: The Pursuit of Rights in America.* New York: Alfred A. Knopf, 1991.

Constitutional Rights Foundation. "Is a Fair Trial Possible in the Age of Mass Media?" *Bill of Rights in Action* 11, no. 1 (Winter 1994).

Dershowitz, Alan M. *Taking Liberties.* Chicago: Contemporary Books, 1988.

Evans, J. Edward. *Freedom of Religion.* Minneapolis, MN: Lerner, 1990.

Fiss, Owen M. *The Irony of Free Speech.* Cambridge, MA: Harvard University Press, 1996.

Forer, Lois G. *A Chilling Effect: The Mounting Threat of Libel and Invasion of Privacy Actions to the First Amendment.* New York: W. W. Norton, 1987.

Hentoff, Nat. *The First Freedom: The Tumultuous History of Free Speech in America.* New York: Delacorte, 1980.

McCann, Michael W. *Rights at Work.* Chicago: University of Chicago Press, 1994.

Roleff, Tamara R., ed. *Civil Liberties.* From the Opposing Viewpoint series. San Diego, CA: Greenhaven Press, 1999.

Political Parties

Aldrich, John H. *Why Parties?: The Origin and Transformation of Party Politics in America.* Chicago: University of Chicago Press, 1995.

Coleman, John J. *Party Decline in America: Policy, Politics, and the Fiscal State.* Princeton, NJ: Princeton University Press, 1996.

Kurian, George Thomas, ed. *The Encyclopedia of the Democratic Party.* 2 vols. Armonk, NY: M. E. Sharpe, 1997. See also Kurian's supplement to this work, *Supplement to the Encyclopedia of the Democratic Party.* Armonk, NY: M. E. Sharpe, 2002.

__________. *The Encyclopedia to the Republican Party.* 2 vols. Armonk, NY: M. E. Sharpe, 1997. See also Kurian's supplement to this work, *Supplement to the Encyclopedia of the Republican Party.* Armonk, NY: M. E. Sharpe, 2002.

Maisel, L. Sandy, ed. *The Parties Respond: Changes in American Parties and Campaigns,* 3rd edition. Boulder, CO: Westview Press, 1998.

Milkis, Sidney. *The President and the Parties: The Transformation of the American Party System since the New Deal.* New York: Oxford University Press, 1993.

Rockwood, Stephen. *American Third Parties since the Civil War.* New York: Garland Publishing, 1985.

Wattenberg, Martin P. *The Decline of American Political Parties, 1952-1996.* Cambridge, MA: Harvard University Press, 1998.

Elections, Campaigns, and Voting

Boller, Paul F., Jr. *Presidential Campaigns.* New York: Oxford University Press, 1984.

Congressional Research Service and the Library of Congress. *Presidential Elections in the United States: A Primer.* Washington, DC: Government Printing Office, 2000.

Davis, James W. *U.S. Presidential Primaries and the Caucus-Convention System: A Sourcebook.* Westport, CT: Greenwood Press, 1997.

Flanigan, William H., and Nancy H. Zingale. *Political Behavior of the American Electorate,* 9th edition. Washington, DC: Congressional Quarterly Press, 1998.

Fowler, Linda. *Candidates, Congress, and the American Democracy.* Ann Arbor: University of Michigan Press, 1994.

Ginsberg, Benjamin, and Martin Shefter. *Politics by Other Means: Institutional Conflict and the Declining Significance of Elections in America.* New York: Basic Books, 1990.

Niemi, Richard, and Herbert Weisberg. *Controversies in American Voting Behavior.* Washington, DC: Congressional Quarterly Press, 1984.

Polsby, Nelson, and Aaron Wildavsky. *Presidential Elections,* 8th edition. New York: Free Press, 1991.

Shields-West, Eileen. *The World Almanac of Presidential Campaigns.* New York: World Almanac, 1992.

Sorauf, Frank. *Inside Campaign Finance: Myths and Realities.* New Haven, CT: Yale University Press, 1992.

Thernstorm, Abigail M. *Whose Votes Count? Affirmative Action and Minority Voting Rights.* Cambridge, MA: Harvard University Press, 1987.

Thomas, Sue, and Clyde Wilcox, eds. *Women and the Elective Office: Past, Present, and Future.* New York: Oxford University Press, 1998.

Wattenberg, Martin P. *The Rise of Candidate-Centered Politics: Presidential Elections of the 1980s.* Cambridge, MA: Harvard University Press, 1991.

Interest Groups and PACs

Cigler, Allan J., and Burdett A. Loomis. *Interest Group Politics,* 3rd edition. Washington, DC: Congressional Quarterly Press, 1991.

Clawson, Dan, Alan Neustadt, and Denise Scott. *Money Talks: Corporate PACs and Political Influence.* New York: Basic Books, 1992.

Day, Christine. *What Older Americans Think: Interest Groups and Aging Policy.* Princeton, NJ: Princeton University Press, 1990.

Lewis, Charles, and the Center for Public Integrity. *The Buying of Congress: How Special Interest Groups Have Stolen Your Right to Life, Liberty, and the Pursuit of Happiness.* New York: Avon Books, 1998.

Moe, Terry M. *The Organization of Interests.* Chicago: University of Chicago Press, 1980.

Morris, Dick. *Vote.com: How Big-Money Lobbyists and the Media are Losing Their Influence, and the Internet Is Giving Power Back to the People.* Los Angeles: Renaissance Books, 1999.

Petracca, Mark, ed. *The Politics of Interests: Interest Groups Transformed.* Boulder, CO: Westview, 1992.

Sabato, Larry. *PAC Power.* New York: W. W. Norton, 1984.

Sisung, Kelle S., ed. *Special Interest Groups for Students.* Farmington Hills, MI: Gale Group, 1999.

Walter, Jack L. Jr. *Mobilizing Interest Groups in America.* Ann Arbor: University of Michigan Press, 1991.

Public Opinion and the Media

Erikson, Robert S., Norman Luttbeg, and Kent Tedin. *American Public Opinion: Its Origins, Content, and Impact.* New York: Wiley, 1980.

Fallows, James. *Breaking the News: How the Media Undermine American Democracy.* New York: Pantheon Books, 1996.

Graber, Doris. *Mass Media and American Politics.* Washington, DC: Congressional Quarterly Press, 1989.

Nacos, Brigitte L. *The Press, Presidents, and Crises.* New York: Columbia University Press, 1990.

Owen, Diana. *Media Messages in American Presidential Elections.* Westport, CT: Greenwood, 1991.

Selnow, Gary W. *Electronic Whistle-Stops: The Impact of the Internet on American Politics.* Westport, CT: Praeger Press, 1998.

Spero, Robert. *The Duping of the American Voter: Dishonesty and Deception in Presidential Television Advertising.* New York: Lippincott & Crowell Publishers, 1980.

Public Policy (Social, Economic, and Foreign)

Addams, Jane. *Twenty Years at Hull House.* New York: Macmillan, 1910.

Derthick, Martha. *Agency under Stress: The Social Security Administration in American Government.* Washington, DC: Brookings Institution, 1990.

Eckes, Alfred E., Jr. *Opening America's Market: U.S. Foreign Trade Policy since 1776.* Chapel Hill: University of North Carolina Press, 1995.

Gilpin, Robert. *The Political Economy of International Relations.* Princeton, NJ: Princeton University Press, 1987.

Guttmann, Amy. *Democracy and the Welfare State.* Princeton, NJ: Princeton University Press, 1988.

Katz, Michael B. *In the Shadow of the Poorhouse: A Social History of Welfare in America,* 10th edition. New York: Basic Books, 1996.

Kissinger, Henry. *Diplomacy.* New York: Simon & Schuster, 1994.

Klare, Michael. *Rogue States and Nuclear Outlaws: America's Search for a New Foreign Policy.* New York: Hill and Wang, 1995.

Lindbloom, Charles E., and Edward J. Woodhouse. *The Policy-Making Process,* 3rd edition. Englewood Cliffs, NJ: Prentice Hall, 1993.

LaFeber, Walter. *The American Age: United States Foreign Policy at Home and Abroad* since 1750. New York: W. W. Norton, 1989.

Marmor, Theodore R., Jerry L. Mashaw, and Phillip L. Harvey. *America's Misunderstood Welfare State.* New York: Basic Books, 1990.

Ripley, Randall B., and Grace A. Franklin. *Congress, the Bureaucracy, and Public Policy,* 5th edition. Pacific Grove, CA: Brooks/Cole, 1991.

Rubin, Irene S. *The Politics of Public Budgeting: Getting and Spending, Borrowing and Balancing.* Chatham, NJ: Chatham House, 1990.

Skocpol, Theda. *The Missing Middle: Working Families and the Future of Social Policy.* New York: W. W. Norton and Co., 2000.

Van Horn, Carl E., Donald C. Baumer, and William T. Gormley Jr. *Politics and Public Policy,* 2nd edition. Washington, DC: Congressional Quarterly Press, 1992.

Woodward, Bob. *The Commanders.* New York: Simon & Schuster, 1991.

Presidents and Their Administrations

Congressional Quarterly. *The Presidency A to Z: A Ready Reference Encyclopedia.* 3 vols. Washington, DC: Author, 1993.

Crovits, L. Gordon, and Jeremy A. Rabkin, eds. With a foreword by Robert H. Bork. *The Fettered Presidency: Legal Constraints on the Executive Branch.* Washington, DC: American Enterprise Institute for Public Policy Research, 1989.

Faber, Charles F., and Richard B. Faber. *The American Presidents Ranked by Performance.* Jefferson, NC: McFarland & Company, Inc., 2000.

Hill, Larry B., ed. *The State of Public Bureaucracy.* Armonk, NY: M. E. Sharpe, 1992.

Kane, Joseph Nathan. *Presidential Fact Book: The Facts on all the Presidents from George Washington to Bill Clinton.* New York: Random House, 1999.

Milkis, Sidney M. *The President and the Parties: The Transformation of the American Party System since the New Deal.* New York: Oxford University Press, 1993.

Nelson, Michael, ed. *The Presidency A to Z,* 2nd edition. Washington, DC: Congressional Quarterly, 1998.

Patella, Lu Ann, and Fred L. Worth. *World Almanac of Presidential Facts.* New York: Pharos Books, 1993.

Pfiffner, James P. *The Modern Presidency.* New York: St. Martin's Press, 1994.

Sisung, Kelle S. *Federal Agency Profiles for Students.* Farmington Hills, MI: Gale Group, 1999.

Sisung, Kelle S., and Gerda-Ann Raffaelle, eds. *Presidential Administration Profiles for Students.* Farmington Hills, MI: Gale Group, 2000.

Spitzer, Robert. *President and Congress: Executive Hegemony at the Crossroads of American Government.* New York: McGraw-Hill, 1993.

Watson, Robert. *The Presidents' Wives: Reassessing the Office of the First Lady.* Boulder, CO: Lynne Rienner Publishers, 2000.

Wilson, James Q. *Bureaucracy: What Government Agencies Do and Why They Do It.* New York: Basic Books, 1989.

Woodward, Bob. *The Agenda: Inside the Clinton White House.* New York: Simon & Schuster, 1994.

The Legislative Branch

Arnold, R. Douglas. *The Logic of Congressional Action.* New Haven: Yale University Press, 1990.

Baker, Ross K. *House and Senate,* 2nd edition. New York: W. W. Norton, 1995.

Congressional Quarterly. *Guide to the Congress,* 4th edition. Washington, DC: Author, 1991.

Davidson, Roger, and Walter Oleszek. *Congress and Its Members,* 5th edition. Washington, DC: Congressional Quarterly Press, 1996.

Deering, Christopher, and Steven Smith. *Committees in Congress.* Washington, DC: Congressional Quarterly Press, 1997.

Dodd, Larry, and Bruce Oppenheimer, eds. *Congress Reconsidered,* 7th edition. Washington, DC: Congressional Quarterly Press, 2000.

Fisher, Louis. *The Politics of Shared Power: Congress and the Executive,* 3rd edition. Washington, DC: Congressional Quarterly Press, 1993.

Hutson, James H. *To Make All Laws: The Congress of the United States, 1789-1989.* New York: Houghton Mifflin, 1990.

Oleszek, Walter J. *Congressional Procedures and the Policy Process,* 3rd edition. Washington, DC: Congressional Quarterly Press, 1989.

Smith, Steven. *The American Congress,* 2nd edition. Boston: Houghton Mifflin, 1999.

The Judicial Branch

Abraham, Henry. *The Judicial Process,* 6th edition. New York: Oxford University Press, 1993.

Ackerman, Bruce. *The Future of Liberal Revolution.* New Haven, CT: Yale University Press, 1992.

Agresto, John. *The Supreme Court and Constitutional Democracy.* Ithaca, NY: Cornell University Press, 1984.

Carp, Robert, and Ronald Stidham. *The Federal Courts.* Washington, DC: Congressional Quarterly Press, 1985.

Congressional Quarterly. *Guide to the U.S. Supreme Court,* 2nd edition. Washington, DC: 1990.

Goldman, Sheldon, and Thomas P. Jahnige. *The Federal Courts as a Political System.* New York: Harper & Row, 1985.

Hall, Kermitt, L., ed. *The Oxford Companion to the Supreme Court of the United States. New York: Oxford University Press, 1992.*

O'Brien, David M. *Storm Center: The Supreme Court in American Politics,* 5th edition. New York: W. W. Norton, 1999.

Posner, Richard A. *The Federal Courts: Crisis and Reform.* Cambridge, MA: Harvard University Press, 1985.

Rosenberg, Gerald. *The Hollow Hope: Can Courts Bring about Social Change?* Chicago: University of Chicago Press, 1991.

Shapiro, Martin. *Courts: A Comparative Political Analysis.* Chicago: University of Chicago Press, 1981.

Waltman, Jerold L., and Kenneth M. Holland, eds. *The Political Role of Law Courts in Modern Societies.* New York: Macmillan, 1988.

Colonial America and the Revolutionary War

Bailyn, Bernard. *The Ideological Origins of the American Revolution.* Cambridge, MA: Harvard University Press, 1967.

Bober, Natalie S. *Countdown to Independence: A Revolution of Ideas in England and Her American Colonies, 1760-1776.* New York: Atheneum Books, 2001.

Boyd, Julian P. *The Declaration of Independence.* Princeton, NJ: Princeton University Press, 1945.

Carman, Harry J., Harold C. Syrett, and Bernard W. Wishy. *A History of the American People: Volume I to 1877.* New York: Alfred A. Knopf, 1960.

Catton, Bruce, and William B. Catton. *The Bold and Magnificent Dream: America's Founding Years, 1492-1815.* Garden City, NY: Doubleday, 1978.

Cogliano, Francis D. *Revolutionary America, 1763-1815: A Political History.* London and New York, Routledge, 2000.

Dinnerstein, Leonard, and Kenneth T. Jackson. *American Vistas.* New York: Oxford University Press, 1991.

Dumbauld, Edward. *The Declaration of Independence and What It Means Today.* Tulsa: University of Oklahoma Press, 1950.

Findling, John E., and Frank W. Thackery, eds. *Events That Changed America in the Eighteenth Century.* Westport, CT: The Greenwood Press, 1998.

Hazelton, John H. *The Declaration of Independence: Its History.* 1906. Reprint, New York: Da Capo Press, 1970.

Hoffer, Peter Charles. *Law and People in Colonial America,* revised edition. Baltimore and London: The Johns Hopkins University Press, 1998.

Kammen, Michael G., ed. *Politics and Society in Colonial America: Democracy or Deference?,* 2nd edition. Huntington, NY: Robert E. Krieger Publishing Co., 1978.

Lancaster, Bruce. *The American Heritage Book of the Revolution.* New York: American Heritage Publishing Co., 1971.

Maier, Pauline. *From Resistance to Revolution: Colonial Radicals and the Development of American Opposition to Britain, 1765-1776.* New York: Alfred A. Knopf, 1972.

McCusker, John J., and Russell Menard. *The Economy of British America, 1607-1789.* Chapel Hill, NC: University of North Carolina Press, 1985.

Middlekauff, Robert. *The Glorious Cause: The American Revolution, 1763-1789.* Vol. 2 of *The Oxford History of the United States.* New York: Oxford University Press, 1982.

Morris, Richard B. *The American Revolution, 1763-1783.* Columbia: The University of South Carolina Press, 1970.

Reich, Jerome R. *Colonial America,* 3rd edition. Englewood Cliffs, NJ: Prentice Hall, 1994.

Rutman, Darrett B. *The Morning of America, 1603-1789.* Boston: Houghton Mifflin, 1971.

Tate, Thad W. and David L Ammerman, eds. *The Chesapeake in the Seventeenth Century: Essays on Anglo-American Society.* Chapel Hill, NC: University of North Carolina Press, 1979.

Vaughan, Alden T. *America Before the Revolution, 1725-1775.* Englewood Cliffs, NJ: Prentice-Hall, 1967.

Federalism and State and Local Government

Anton, Thomas. *American Federalism and Public Policy.* Philadelphia, PA: Temple University Press, 1989.

Beer, Samuel H. *To Make a Nation: The Rediscovery of American Federalism.* Cambridge, MA: The Belknap Press of Harvard University Press, 1993.

Burns, Nancy E. *The Formation of American Local Governments: Private Values in Public Institutions.* New York: Oxford University Press, 1994.

Dye, Thomas R. *American Federalism: Competition among Governments.* Lexington, MA: Lexington Books, 1990.

Elazar, Daniel. *American Federalism: A View from the States.* New York: Harper & Row, 1984.

Erikson, Robert S., Gerald C. Wright, and John P. McIver. *Statehouse Democracy: Public Opinion and Policy in the American States.* Cambridge, UK: Cambridge University Press, 1993.

Fiorina, Morris. *Divided Government.* New York: Macmillan, 1992.

Peterson, Paul, Barry Rabe, and Kenneth K. Wong. *When Federalism Works.* Washington, DC: Brookings Institute, 1986.

Rivlin, Alice M. "Rethinking Federalism." In *Readings in State and Local Government,* edited by David C. Saffell and Harry Basehart. New York: McGraw-Hill, 1994.

Other Resources

Periodicals

American Spectator

Magazine covering what it terms "the New Economy and the New Political Reality."

Gilder Publishing
291A Main St.
Great Barrington, MA 01230
413-644-2100
800-524-3469
http://www.spectator.org/amspec/index.html
spectatoreditorial@gilder.com
Published monthly. $39 annual subscription.

Brookings Review

Journal containing the scholarly work of the Brookings Institution on public policy.

The Brookings Institution Press
Dept. 029
Washington, DC 20042-0029
202-797-6258
800-275-1447
http://www.brook.edu/dybdocroot/press/review/rev_des.htm
Published 4x/yr. $6/issue; $19.95 annual subscription.

CQ Weekly

Publication providing nonpartisan coverage of Congress.

Congressional Quarterly Inc.
1414 22nd St. NW
Washington, DC 20037
202-887-6279
800-432-2250 ext. 279

http://www.cq.com/products/products.jsp#weekly
customerservice@cq.com
Published 50x/yr.

The Federalist

Email journal providing a survey and analysis of the week's most significant news, policy, and opinion from a conservative perspective.

http://www.federalist.com/
subscriptions@federalist.com
Free by email in three parts: The Monday Brief, the Wednesday Chronicle, and the Friday Digest.

Mother Jones

Magazine committed to social justice through investigative reporting.

Foundation for National Progress
731 Market St., Ste. 600
San Francisco, CA 94103
415-665-6637
800-438-6656
http://www.motherjones.com/magazine/JA02/index.html
subscribe@motherjones.com
Published 6x/yr. $20 annual subscription.

The Nation

Magazine providing a critical discussion of political and social questions.

The Nation Company
33 Irving Pl.
New York, NY 10003
212-209-5400
212-982-9000 (fax)
http://www.thenation.com/
info@thenation.com
Published 47x/yr. $2.95 single issue; $35.97 annual subscription.

National Review

Magazine providing coverage and analysis of politics without what it terms a "liberal bias."

National Review Inc.
215 Lexington Ave.
New York, NY 10016
212-679-7330
815-734 1232
http://www.nationalreview.com/
Published 25x/yr. $59 annual subscription.

The New York Times
General interest newspaper with extensive political coverage.

The New York Times Company
229 W. 43rd St.
New York, NY 10036-3959
800-NYTIMES
http://www.nytimes.com/
Published daily. $572 annual subscription.

Slate
Online magazine providing summaries of top news stories, with particular political coverage.

Microsoft Corporation
1 Microsoft Way
Redmond, WA 98052
URL: http://slate.msn.com//
letters@slate.com
Free online or via email.

The Wall Street Journal
Newspaper providing coverage of U.S. and international business, finance, and politics.

Dow Jones & Company
1155 Avenue of the Americas
New York, NY 10036
800-568-7625
http://online.wsj.com/public/us
wsj.service@dowjones.com
Published 260x/yr. $175 annual subscription.

The Washington Post
General interest newspaper with extensive political coverage.

The Washington Post Company
1150 15th St. NW
Washington, DC 20071
202-334-6100
800-477-4679
http://www.washingtonpost.com/
Published daily.

The Washington Times
General interest newspaper providing coverage of politics and policy.

3600 New York Ave. NE
Washington, DC 20002
202-636-3333
800-277-8500
http://www.washingtontimes.com/

general@washingtontimes.com
Published daily. $91 annual subscription.

Web Sites

About Government
Provides links to sites covering government, politics, political parties, elections and voting, citizenship, news, icons, landmarks, and traditions.
http://www.aboutgovernment.org/govoverview.htm

The American Center for Law and Justice
Engages in litigation, provides legal services, renders advice, counsels clients, and supports attorneys involved in defending Judeo-Christian values.
http://www.aclj.org/

American Civil Liberties Union
Nonpartisan organization. Works in the courts, legislatures, and communities to defend and preserve individual rights and liberties. Uses staff and volunteer lawyers to handle cases concerning civil rights violations.
http://www.aclu.org/

Campaigns and Elections
Provides products and services for people in politics, including articles, publications, software, videos, seminars, a jobline, and a speakers bureau. Published by Votenet Solutions, Inc.
http://www.campaignline.com

Center for American Women and Politics
Research, education, and public service center promoting women's participation in politics, government, and public life. From the Eagleton Institute of Politics of Rutgers, the State University of New Jersey.
http://www.rci.rutgers.edu/~cawp/index.html

Columbia Journalism Review
Lists major media companies and what they own. Also includes a selected list of articles in *CJR* about media ownership.
http://www.cjr.org/owners/

Committee for the Study of the American Electorate
Nonpartisan research institution focusing on issues surrounding citizen engagement in politics. Issues publications on election night projects, media and politics, campaign finance, voter participation, and other topics.
http://www.gspm.org/csae/

Common Cause

Nonpartisan citizens' lobbying organization. Promotes open, honest, and accountable government. Publishes investigative studies on the effects of money in politics and reports on issues of ethics and integrity in government.

www.commoncause.org

Democratic National Committee

Provides Democratic Party news and information. Includes voter outreach and registration services, links to other sites, a store, and a job board.

http://www.democrats.org

Elections Central

Provides the history of each U.S. presidential election since 1789, including popular and electoral votes, states won, issues, and turnout.

www.multied.com/elections

FEC Watch

Monitors the enforcement activities of the Federal Election Commission and other government entities. A project of the Center for Responsive Politics.

http://www.fecwatch.org/

FedWorld

Gateway to information disseminated by the federal government. Managed by the National Technical Information Service of the U.S. Department of Commerce.

http://www.fedworld.gov/

FirstGov

Official U.S. government web portal. Provides a centralized source for locating information from U.S. local, state, and federal government agency web sites.

www.firstgov.gov

Freedom Forum

Nonpartisan foundation dedicated to free press, speech, and "spirit for all." Focuses efforts on an interactive museum of news, First Amendment freedoms, and newsroom diversity.

http://www.freedomforum.org/

Freedom House

Nonpartisan group. Supports democratic values and opposes dictatorships of the far left and far right. Conducts U.S. and overseas research, advocacy, education, and training initiatives that promote human rights, democracy, free-market economies, the rule of law, independent media, and U.S. engagement in international affairs. Original founders include Eleanor Roosevelt and Wendell Willkie.

http://www.freedomhouse.org/

GPOAccess

Provides free electronic access to federal government information, including the *Catalog of U.S. Government Publications*, the *Code of Federal Regulations*, the *Congressional Record*, the federal budget, the *Federal Register*, public presidential papers, the U.S. code, and the U.S. government online bookstore. A service of the U.S. Government Printing Office.

http://www.access.gpo.gov/su_docs/

insidepolitics

Political news and reports. A service of Cable News Network.

http://www.cnn.com/ALLPOLITICS/

League of Women Voters

Nonpartisan political organization. Supports the informed and active participation of citizens in government, works to increase understanding of major public policy issues, and influences public policy thorough education and advocacy.

http://www.lwv.org

The Library of Congress

Serves as the research arm of the U.S. Congress. Is the largest library in the world, with collections of books, recordings, photographs, maps, and manuscripts. Makes its resources available to Congress and the American people and works to sustain and preserve a universal collection of knowledge and creativity for future generations.

http://www.loc.gov

National Center for Policy Analysis

Nonpartisan public policy research organization. Develops and promotes private alternatives to government regulation and control.

http://www.ncpa.org/

opensecrets.org

Tracks money spent in U.S. elections. Web site of the Center for Responsive Politics.

http://www.opensecrets.org/

Political Advocacy Groups

Provides subject and alphabetical directory listings of lobbyists in the United States.

http://www.csuchico.edu/~kcfount/index.html

PollingReport.com

Independent, nonpartisan resource on trends in American public opinion. Features highlights from national polls. State-by-state presidential, congressional, and gubernatorial polls, analyses by pollsters, and other data are available to subscribers.

http://pollingreport.com/

Project Vote Smart

Offers a library of factual information on 40,000 candidates for public office, including federal, state, and local officials. Covers candidates' backgrounds, issue positions, voting records, campaign finances, and performance evaluations from more than 100 liberal and conservative special interest groups.

http://www.vote-smart.org

Reporters Committee for Freedom of the Press

Provides free legal assistance to journalists. Serves as a resource on free speech issues. Issues publications and operates a 24-hour hotline.

www.rcfp.org

Republican National Committee

Provides Republican Party news and information. Includes voter registration services, a store, video clips, and links to other sites.

http://www.rnc.org/

Supreme Court of the United States

Provides news and information on the Supreme Court. Includes court history, information on current and past justices, case tracking system, oral arguments, bar admissions form and instructions, court rules, case handling guidelines, opinions, orders and journals, public information, details on visiting the court, and links to related sites.

http://www.supremecourtus.gov/

THOMAS, Legislative Information on the Internet

Provides access to federal legislative information, including bill summary and status, bill text, and public laws by law number; the *Congressional Record*; roll call votes; and committee information, including House and Senate committee information. Also includes links to other government information and sites. A service of the U.S. Library of Congress.

http://thomas.loc.gov/

U.S. Electoral College

Maintains a variety of information and statistics on presidential elections.

http://www.archives.gov/federal_register/electoral_college/electoral_college.html

U.S. Federal Election Commission

Discloses campaign finance information, enforces the provisions of the Federal Election Campaign Act, and oversees the public funding of presidential elections.

http://www.fec.gov

U.S. Government Documents Ready Reference Collection

Provides a subject arrangement of the most frequently used U.S. government depository document titles at Columbia University Libraries.

http://www.columbia.edu/cu/libraries/indiv/dsc/readyref.html

U.S. House of Representatives

Provides information on House operations, members, committees, leadership, and other organizations, commissions, and task forces.

http://www.house.gov/

U.S. National Archives & Records Administration

Independent federal agency charged with overseeing the management of all federal records, including such historical documents as the Constitution and Declaration of Independence.

http://www.archives.gov/index.html

U.S. Senate

Provides information on Senate members, leadership, committees, roll call tallies, legislative activities, and nominations.

http://www.senate.gov/

USCourts.gov

Functions as a clearinghouse for information from and about the judicial branch of the U.S. government, including the Supreme Court, courts of appeals, district courts, and bankruptcy courts.

www.uscourts.gov

The White House

Official site of the White House. Provides information on the president, vice president, and their wives; news and policies; speeches; appointments; and history and tours. Also provides general information on the federal government.

http://www.whitehouse.gov/

Politically Active Organizations

Professional associations, public interest groups, think tanks, political action committees, and other organizations play a critical role in influencing policy and public opinion on political issues. Following is a list of organizations known for their political activity and impact that represent the range of causes.

Aircraft Owners and Pilots Association (AOPA)

421 Aviation Way
Frederick, MD 21701
301-695-2000
301-695-2375 (fax)
http://www.aopa.org/
aopahq@aopa.org

Founded in 1939. Not-for-profit organization dedicated to general aviation. Describes itself as "the most influential aviation association in the world." Represents its members at the federal, state, and local level. Has more than 375,000 members.

The Alliance of Automobile Manufacturers

1401 H St. NW, Ste. 900
Washington, DC 20005
202-326-5500
202-326-5567 (fax)
http://www.autoalliance.org/

Founded in 1999. Trade association of 13 car and light truck manufacturers that account for more than 90 percent of U.S. vehicle sales. Serves as an advocacy group for the automobile industry on public policy issues.

American Bankers Association (ABA)

1120 Connecticut Ave. NW
Washington, DC 20036
800-BANKERS
http://www.aba.com/default.htm
custserv@aba.com

Founded in 1875. Serves its member banks through federal legislative and regulatory activities and other programs.

American Enterprise Institute for Public Policy Research (AEI)

1150 17th St. NW
Washington, DC 20036
202-862-5800
202-862-7178 (fax)
http://www.aei.org/
info@aei.org

Founded in 1943. Self-described as "one of America's largest and most respected think tanks." Dedicated to preserving and strengthening the foundations of freedom, including limited government, private enterprise, vital cultural and political institutions, and a strong foreign policy and national defense.

American Association for Retired Persons (AARP)

601 E St. NW
Washington, DC 20049
202-434-2277
800-424-3410
202-434-2320 (fax)
http://www.aarp.org/
member@aarp.org

Founded in 1958. Nonprofit membership organization that addresses the needs and interests of persons 50 years of age and older. Seeks to enhance the quality of life for all by promoting independence, dignity, and purpose. Has more than 35 million members.

American Cancer Society (ACS)

1599 Clifton Rd. NE
Atlanta, GA 30329
404-320-3333
800-ACS-2345
404-329-7530 (fax)
http://www.cancer.org/

Founded in 1913. Fights cancer through research, education, patient service, advocacy, and rehabilitation. Maintains more than 3400 local offices.

American Civil Liberties Union (ACLU)

125 Broad St., 18th Fl.
New York, NY 10004-2400
212-549-2500
800-775-2258
212-549-2646 (fax)
http://www.aclu.org/
infoaclu@aclu.org

Founded in 1920. Nonprofit, nonpartisan group that describes itself as "the nation's guardian of liberty, working to defend and preserve the individual rights and liberties guaranteed in the Constitution and laws of the United States." Has nearly 300,000 members and supporters, and maintains offices in almost every state.

American Economic Association (AEA)

2014 Broadway, Ste. 305
Nashville, TN 37203
615-322-2595
615-343-7590 (fax)
http://www.vanderbilt.edu/AEA/
aeainfo@vanderbilt.edu

Founded in 1885. Organization that encourages economic research and freedom of economic discussion, and issues publications on economic subjects. Takes no partisan attitude and does not commit its members to any position on practical economic questions. Has approximately 22,000 economists as members and 5500 institutional subscribers.

American Farm Bureau Federation (AFBF)

225 Touhy Ave.
Park Ridge, IL 60068
847-685-8600
847-685-8896 (fax)
http://www.fb.com/

Founded in 1919. Self-described as "a nonpartisan but politically active organization that represents America's farmers and ranchers at the local, state, national, and international levels." Seeks to improve the financial well being and quality of life of farmers and ranchers. Has more than 5 million members across all 50 states and Puerto Rico.

American Federation of Labor–Congress of Industrial Organizations (AFL–CIO)

815 16th St. NW
Washington, DC 20006
202-637-5000
202-637-5058 (fax)
http://www.aflcio.org/home2.htm
feedback@aflcio.org

Founded in 1955. A voluntary federation of American labor unions that seeks to improve the lives of working families. Represents more than 13 million workers.

Amnesty International of USA (AI)

322 8th Ave.
New York, NY 10001
212-807-8400
800-AMNESTY
212-627-1451 (fax)
http://www.amnesty.org/
admin-us@aiusa.org

Founded in 1961. Impartial, independent worldwide organization that works to promote all the human rights contained in the United Nations' Universal Declaration of Human Rights and other international standards. Has members and supporters in 162 countries and territories. Headquartered in England.

American Israel Public Affairs Committee (AIPCA)

440 1st St. NW, Ste. 600
Washington, DC 20001 USA
202-639-5200
202-347-4918 (fax)
http://www.aipac.org/
update@aipac.org

Founded in 1954. A pro-Israel lobby group. Seeks to affect America's relationship with Israel by working to pass pro-Israel legislative initiatives. Has 65,000 members across all 50 states.

The Brookings Institution (BI)

1775 Massachusetts Ave. NW
Washington, DC 20036
202-797-6000
202-797-6004 (fax)
http://www.brook.edu/dybdocroot/
brookinfo@brookings.edu

Founded in 1916. Independent organization that attempts to improve the performance of American institutions by analyzing emerging public policy issues and offering remedies for them. Issues the *Brookings Review*.

Cato Institute

1000 Massachusetts Ave. NW
Washington, DC 20001-5403
202-842-0200
202-842-3490 (fax)

http://www.cato.org/
cato@cato.org

Founded in 1977. Nonprofit public policy research foundation. Self-described as "seeking to broaden the parameters of public policy debate to allow consideration of the traditional American principles of limited government, individual liberty, free markets, and peace."

Center for Policy Alternatives (CFPA)

1875 Connecticut Ave. NW, Ste. 710
Washington, DC 20009
202-387-6030
800-935-0699
202-387-8529 (fax)
http://www.cfpa.org/
info@cfpa.org

Founded in 1976. Self-described as "the nation's leading nonpartisan progressive public policy and leadership development center serving state legislators, state policy organizations, and state grassroots leaders." Has approximately 10,000 members.

Center for International and Security Studies at Maryland (CISSM)

School of Public Affairs
University of Maryland
College Park, MD 20742-1811
301-405-7601
301-403-8107 (fax)
http://www.puaf.umd.edu/CISSM/default.htm
se64@umail.umd.edu

Founded in 1987. Conducts research on American attitudes toward a variety of international and foreign policy issues facing the United States in the global arena.

Center for National Policy (CNP)

1 Massachusetts Ave. NW, Ste. 333
Washington, DC 20001
202-682-1800
202-682-1818 (fax)
http://www.cnponline.org/

Founded in 1981. Nonprofit, nonpartisan public policy organization dedicated to promoting the public interest.

Christian Coalition of America (CCA)

499 S. Capitol St. SW, Ste. 615
Washington, DC 20003
202-479-6900
202-479-4260 (fax)

http://www.cc.org/
coalition@cc.org

Founded in 1989 by Pat Robertson. Self-described as "American's largest and most active conservative grassroots political organization." Supports a pro-family agenda. Represents nearly 2 million people.

Common Cause (CC)

1250 Connecticut Ave. NW., #600
Washington, DC 20036
202-833-1200
800-926-1064
202-659-3716 (fax)
http://www.commoncause.org/
grassroots@commoncause.org

Founded in 1970. Nonprofit, nonpartisan organization self-described as "representing the unified voice of the people against corruption in government and big money special interests." Promotes open, honest, and accountable government. Has more than 200,000 members.

The Conference Board (TCB)

845 3rd Ave.
New York, NY 10022-6679
212-759-0900
212-980-7014 (fax)
http://www.conference-board.org/
info@conference-board.org

Founded in 1916. Not-for-profit, nonpartisan organization that creates and disseminates knowledge about management and the marketplace to help business strengthen their performance and better serve society.

Consumer Federation of America (CFA)

1424 16th St. NW, Ste. 604
Washington, DC 20036
202-387-6121
202-265-7989 (fax)
http://www.consumerfed.org/
cfa@essential.org

Founded in 1968. Advocacy organization working to advance pro-consumer policy on a variety of issues before Congress, the White House, federal and state regulatory agencies, and the courts. Memberships consists of more than 285 organizations with a combined membership of more than 50 million.

Council on Foreign Relations, Inc. (CFR)

The Harold Pratt House
58 E. 68th St.
New York, NY 10021
212-434-9400
212-434-9800 (fax)
http://www.cfr.org/
communications@cfr.org

Founded in 1921. Nonpartisan think tank dedicated to increasing America's understanding of the world and contributing ideas to U.S. foreign policy. Has 3800 members.

Democratic National Committee (DNC)

430 S. Capitol St. SE
Washington, DC 20003
202-863-8000
202-863-8081 (fax)
http://www.democrats.org/index.html

Founded in 1848. National party organization for the Democratic Party of the United States. Plans the party's presidential nominating convention, provides technical and financial support to party candidates, and works with party organizations, elected officials, candidates, and constituencies to respond to the needs and views of the Democratic electorate and the nation.

Family Research Council

700 13th St. NW
Washington, DC 20005
202-393-2100
800-225-4008
http://www.frc.org

Founded in 1983. Conservative group focusing on issues promoting marriage, family, and a Judeo-Christian worldview.

The Federalist Society for Law and Public Policy Studies (FSLPPS)

1015 18th St. NW, Ste. 425
Washington, DC 20036
202-822-8138
202-296-8061 (fax)
http://www.federalistsociety.org/
fedsoc@radix.net

Founded in 1982. Group of conservatives and libertarians self-described as "dedicated to reforming the current legal order through its commitment to the principles that the state exists to preserve freedom, that separation of governmental powers is central to the Constitution, and that the duty of the judiciary is to say what the law is not what is should be." Has 25,000 members.

Greenpeace USA (GPUSA)

702 H St. NW, Ste. 300
Washington, DC 20001
202-462-1177
800-326-0959
202-462-4507 (fax)
http://www.greenpeace.org/homepage/
greenpeace.usa@wdc.greenpeace.org

Founded in 1971. An independent, campaigning organization that "uses nonviolent, creative confrontation to achieve its goal of ensuring the ability of the Earth to nurture life in all its diversity." Maintains national and regional office in more than 40 countries. Headquartered in Amsterdam, The Netherlands.

Grocery Manufacturers of America (GMA)

1010 Wisconsin Ave. NW, 9th Fl.
Washington, DC 20007
202-337-9400
202-337-4508 (fax)
http://www.gmabrands.com/
info@gmabrands.com

Founded in 1908. Self-described as "the world's largest association of food, beverage, and consumer product companies." Represents its members at the state, federal, and international levels on legislative and regulatory issues. Its members employ more than 2.5 million workers in all 50 states.

Health Insurance Association of America (HIAA)

1201 F St. NW, Ste. 500
Washington, DC 20004-1204 | 202.824.1600
http://www.hiaa.org/

Founded in 1956. Trade association of health insurers that seeks to influence state and federal public policy through advocacy, research, and the accumulation, analysis, and dissemination of critical information to its members.

The Heritage Foundation (THF)

214 Massachusetts Ave. NE
Washington, DC 20002-4999
202-546-4400
202-546-8328 (fax)
http://heritage.org/
info@heritage.org

Founded in 1973. Think tank that formulates and promotes conservative public policies based on the principles of free enterprise, limited government, individual freedom, traditional American values, and a strong national defense.

Hoover Institution on War, Revolution and Peace (HIWRP)

Stanford University
Stanford, CA 94305-6010
650-723-1754
877-466-8374
650-723-1687 (fax)
http://www-hoover.stanford.edu/
horaney@hoover.stanford.edu

Founded in 1919 by Herbert Hoover. Public policy research center devoted to the advanced study of domestic and foreign politics, economics, and political economy, as well as international affairs.

Human Rights Watch (HRW)

350 5th Ave., 34th Fl.
New York, NY 10118-3299
212-290-4700
212-736-1300 (fax)
http://www.hrw.org/
hrwnyc@hrw.org

Founded in 1978. Self-described as "the largest human rights organization based in the United States." Works to protect the human rights of people around the world. Has approximately 8000 members.

Judicial Watch, Inc. (JW)

PO Box 44444
Washington, DC 20026
888-JW-ETHIC
202-646-5199 (fax)
http://www.judicialwatch.org/
info@judicialwatch.org

Founded in 1994. Nonpartisan, nonprofit foundation self-described as "a national people's attorney general." Dedicated to rooting out corruption in government and the legal and judicial systems to promote a return to ethics and morality in American public life.

National Association for the Advancement of Colored People (NAACP)

4805 Mt. Hope Dr.
Baltimore, MD 21215
410-521-4939
877-NAACP-98
410-358-3818 (fax)

http://www.naacp.org/
leadership@naacp.org

Founded in 1909. Focuses on the protection and enhancement of the civil rights of African Americans and other minorities. Has more than 500,000 members.

National Association of Arab Americans (NAAA)

1212 New York Ave. NW, Ste. 230
Washington, DC 20005
202-842-1840
202-842-1614 (fax)
naaainc@erols.com

Founded in 1972. Foreign policy lobbying group self-described as "the premier Arab-American political organization." Dedicated to formulating and implementing an objective and nonpartisan U.S. foreign policy agenda in the Middle East.

National Cable Television Association (NCTA)

1724 Massachusetts Ave. NW
Washington, DC 20036
202-775-3550
http://www.ncta.com/

Founded in 1952. Self-described as "the principal trade association of the cable television industry in the United States." Represents its members on issues affecting the cable and telecommunications industry.

National Organization for Women (NOW)

733 15th St. NW, 2nd Fl.
Washington, DC 20005
202-628-8NOW
202-785-8576 (fax)
http://www.now.org/
now@now.org

Founded in 1966. Self-described as "the largest feminist organization in the nation. Works to eliminate sexism and end all oppression through legal, political, social, and economic change." Has more than 500,000 members.

National Rifle Association (NRA)

11250 Waples Mill Rd.
Fairfax, VA 22030
703-267-1000
800-672-3888
703-267-3989 (fax)
http://www.nra.org/
membership@nrahq.org

Founded in 1871. Self-described as "a major political force and America's foremost defender of Second Amendment rights." Has nearly 3 million members.

National Right to Life Committee

419 7th St. NW, Ste. 500
Washington, DC 20004
202-626-8800
http://www.nrlc.org
nrlc@nrlc.org

Founded in 1973. Concerned with legal issues regarding abortion and euthanasia, as well as medical ethics, with an ultimate goal of protecting human life. Consists of over 3000 chapters in all 50 states and the District of Columbia.

National Women's Political Caucus (NWPC)

1630 Connecticut Ave. NW, Ste. 201
Washington, DC 20009
202-785-1100
202-785-3605 (fax)
www.nwpc.org
info@nwpc.org

Founded in 1971. Self-described as "the only national, multi-partisan, multi-racial grassroots membership organization dedicated to increasing the number of pro-choice women in elected and appointed office regardless of party affiliation." Has members in 38 states.

The Nature Conservancy (TNC)

4245 N. Fairfax Dr., Ste. 100
Arlington, VA 22203-1606
703-841-5300
800-628-6860
703-841-1283 (fax)
http://nature.org/
comment@tnc.org

Founded in 1951. Works with communities, businesses, and individuals to "protect the lands and waters needed for survival by the plants, animals, and natural communities that represent the diversity of life on Earth." Has approximately 1 million members.

People for the Ethical Treatment of Animals (PETA)

501 Front St.
Norfolk, VA 23510
(757)622-PETA
(757)622-0457 (fax)
http://www.peta-online.org/
info@ peta-online.org

Founded in 1980. Nonprofit group that describes itself as the largest animal rights organization it the world. Dedicated to establishing and protecting the rights of all animals. Has more than 700,000 members.

People For the American Way (PFAW)

2000 M St. NW, Ste. 400
Washington, DC 20036
202-467-4999
800-326-7329
202-293-2672 (fax)
http://www.pfaw.org/
pfaw@pfaw.org

Founded in 1980. Self-described as "organizing and mobilizing Americans to fight for fairness, justice, civil rights, and freedoms guaranteed by the Constitution." Has more than 290,000 members.

Pharmaceutical Research and Manufacturers of America (PhRMA)

1100 15th St. NW
Washington, DC 20005
202-835-3400
202-835-3429 (fax)
http://www.phrma.org/

Founded in 1958. Self-described as "representing the country's leading research-based pharmaceutical and biotechnology companies." Has more than 60 member companies.

Planned Parenthood Federation of America, Inc. (PPFA)

810 7th Ave.
New York, NY 10019
212-541-7800
212-245-1845 (fax)
http://www.plannedparenthood.org/
communications@ppfa.org

Founded in 1916 by Margaret Sanger. Self-described as "the world's largest and most trusted voluntary reproductive heath care organization."

The Progress and Freedom Foundation

1301 K St. NW, Ste. 550 E.
Washington, DC 20005-3317
202-289-8928
202-289-6079 (fax)
http://www.pff.org/
mail@pff.org

Founded in 1993. A nonpartisan market-oriented think tank promoting innovative policy solutions for the digital age. Focuses on communications, computing, and telecommunications.

Public Citizen (PC)

1600 20th St. NW
Washington, DC 20009
202-588-1000
800-289-3787
202-588-7798 (fax)
http://www.citizen.org/
pcmail@citizen.org

Founded in 1971 by Ralph Nader. Nonprofit consumer advocacy organization that represents consumer interests in Congress, the executive branch, and the courts.

Republican National Committee (RNC)

310 1st St. SE
Washington, DC 20003
202-863-8500
202-863-8820 (fax)
http://www.rnc.org/
info@rnc.org

Founded in 1856. Provides support to federal, state, and local Republican office holders and campaigns.

Sierra Club

85 2nd St., 2nd Fl.
San Francisco, CA 94105-3441
(415)977-5500
(415)977-5799 (fax)
http://www.sierraclub.org/
information@sierraclub.org

Founded in 1892. Self-described as "America's most influential environmental organization." Uses all lawful means to carry out its grassroots advocacy efforts. Has more than 700,000 members.

Political Commentators

Critics and commentators have long been a part of the political climate; in the twenty-first century, however, the range of available media outlets—network and cable television, radio, print, and the Internet—provide unprecedented means for political commentators to shape public opinion and influence policy as well as achieve celebrity. But who *are* these people? Following are brief biographies of 50 "talking heads" who hold a prominent place in the political landscape.

PAUL BEGALA: Liberal political consultant and commentator. Gained national attention for his work on the successful 1992 presidential campaign of then-governor Bill Clinton. Served in the Clinton White House as counselor to the president. Author of *Is Our Children Learning?: The Case Against George W. Bush*. Wrote the "Capital Hillbilly" column in, and served as contributing editor of, *George* magazine. Cohost of the political discussion program *Crossfire*. Born in 1961 in New Jersey.

DAVID BRODER: Longtime political columnist for the *Washington Post* who won the Pulitzer Prize for commentary in 1973. Regular commentator on the political discussion program *Inside Politics* and participant on other programs, including *Meet the Press* and *Washington Week in Review*. Has authored or coauthored several books on the American political system, including *Behind the Front Page: A Candid Look at How the News Is Made*, *The Man Who Would Be President: Dan Quayle*, and *The Party's Over: The Failure of Politics in America*. Born in 1929 in Chicago Heights, IL.

PAT BUCHANAN: Conservative journalist, commentator, and politician. Served as press spokesman to presidential candidate Richard Nixon in 1968 and, following the election, joined the White House as a speechwriter for Nixon and Vice President Spiro Agnew. Served briefly in the Ford White House and then as director of communications in the Reagan White House. Ran unsuccessfully for the Republican presidential nomination in 1992 and 1996; switched to the Reform Party in 2000. Some of his writings and speeches have been met with charges of racism and anti-Semitism. Has appeared on a number of political discussion programs, including *Crossfire*, *The McLaughlin Group*, and *The Capital Gang*. Born in 1938 in Washington, DC.

WILLIAM F. BUCKLEY: Conservative journalist, writer, and commentator. Founded *National Review* in 1955 as a forum for promoting conservative ideas and causes; continues to serve as the journal's editor-at-large. Has hosted the weekly political discussion program *Firing Line* since 1966, and has written the syndicated column "On the Right" since 1962. Has published several collections of his columns and essays, and contributes to a number of publications, including *Esquire*, *Harper's*, *New York Times Magazine*, *The New Yorker*, *Playboy*, and *Saturday Review*. He has also written a series of successful spy novels. Born in 1925 in New York, NY.

JAMES CARVILLE: Democratic political consultant and commentator. Gained national attention for his work as chief strategist in the successful 1992 presidential campaign of then-governor Bill Clinton. Dubbed the Ragin' Cajun for his aggressive style, Carville also garnered attention for his "opposites attract" romance with Mary Matalin, who served as George Bush's reelection campaign director in his unsuccessful race against Clinton. Carville and Matalin, who married in 1993, wrote about the campaign and their relationship in *All's Fair: Love, War, and Running for President*. Cohost of the political discussion show *Crossfire*. Born in 1944 in Fort Benning, GA.

MONA CHAREN: Conservative columnist and political analyst. Worked as an editorial assistant at *National Review*. Joined the Reagan White House in 1984, first as Nancy Reagan's speechwriter and later in the office of public liaison. Became speechwriter for Republican presidential candidate Jack Kemp in 1986. Has been a commentator on *The Capital Gang* and *Capital Gang Sunday*. Writes a nationally syndicated column. Born in 1957 in New York, NY.

LINDA CHAVEZ: Conservative writer, commentator, and government official. Served in the Reagan White House and as director of the U.S. Commission on Civil Rights. Her stand against quotas, bilingual education, and other social programs has often put her at odds with liberals and Hispanic American groups. Ran unsuccessfully for a seat in the Senate from Maryland in 1990. Writes a syndicated weekly column and has contributed to *New Republic*, the *Wall Street Journal*, the *Washington Post*, and other publications. Has appeared on political discussion programs, including *Equal Time*, *The McLaughlin Group*, and *Nightline*. Born in 1947 in Albuquerque, NM.

ALEXANDER COCKBURN: Liberal journalist, editor, and author. Writes "Beat the Devil," a column for *The Nation*, and a nationally syndicated column. Contributes to a number of periodicals, including *House and Garden*, *Village Voice*, and the *Wall Street Journal*. Coedits, with Jeffrey St. Clair, *CounterPunch*, a newsletter. Author or coauthor of books covering a range of subject matter, including the environment, chess, and politics. Born in 1941 in Scotland.

ANN COULTER: Conservative writer, commentator, and attorney. Author of *High Crimes and Misdemeanors: The Case Against Bill Clinton* and *Slander: Liberal Lies About the American Right*. Has appeared on a number of news and political discussion programs, including

Equal Time, *Politically Incorrect*, and *This Week*. Writes a weekly legal column. Born in 1962 in New Canaan, CT.

STANLEY CROUCH: African American jazz musician and composer, writer, poet, and social critic. Published his first collection of poems, *Ain't No Ambulances for No Nigguhs Tonight*, in 1972, and has continued to publish collections of his poems and essays, as well as a novel. Has been critical of popular black figures, including Toni Morrison, Spike Lee, and Malcolm X. Served as a columnist for *Cricket*, the *Los Angeles Free Press*, the *New York Daily News*, and the *SoHo Weekly News*, and has contributed to various periodicals, including *Esquire*, the *New York Times*, and *The New Yorker*. Serves as contributing editor for *New Republic*. Born in 1945 in Los Angeles, CA.

E. J. DIONNE JR.: Writer, journalist, and historian. Author of *Why Americans Hate Politics: The Death of the Democratic Process*, published in 1991, which examined why Americans have become increasingly alienated from the political process and its focus on a left or right—rather than centrist—position. Worked as a reporter for the *New York Times* and contributes to various periodicals, including *Commonweal*, the *New York Times Book Review*, and *Utne Reader*. Is currently a reporter for the *Washington Post*. Born in 1952 in Boston, MA.

MAUREEN DOWD: Journalist and columnist. Became a reporter for the *New York Times* in 1983 and in 1995 became a columnist on the paper's op-ed page, only the third woman to hold that position. Although some have criticized her columns for focusing on style over substance and for failing to take a stand on difficult issues, she won the 1999 Pulitzer Prize for commentary for her columns covering the impact of President Bill Clinton's affair with Monica Lewinsky. Born in 1952 in Washington, DC.

MATT DRUDGE: Internet journalist and author. Founded the Drudge Report website in 1995 to disseminate rumors and gossip about politics and the entertainment industry. Claims to be the first to report presidential candidate Bob Dole's choice of Jack Kemp as his running mate in 1996. Played a role in breaking the Monica Lewinsky scandal in 1998. Has received criticism for failing to verify information before posting it. Faced a libel suit in 1997 from Clinton aide Sidney Blumenthal following the posting of an item alleging Blumenthal was guilty of domestic violence. Author of the *Drudge Manifesto*. Born in 1967 in Takoma Park, MD.

LARRY ELDER: African American talk show host. Elder, whose fans are called "Elderados," hosts a popular afternoon radio talk show on KABC in Los Angeles. Known for espousing views that frequently put him in opposition with other black figures. Publishes *The Elder Statement*, a monthly newsletter. Born in 1952 in Los Angeles, CA.

MAGGIE GALLAGHER: Conservative columnist and writer. Author of several books on marriage and family, including *Enemies of Eros: How the Sexual Revolution is Killing Family, Marriage and Sex*, *The Abolition of Marriage*, and *The Case for Marriage: Why Married People Are Happier, Healthier and Better Off Financially*. Has contributed to various publications, including *Cosmopolitan*, *National Review*, *New Republic*, the *New York Times*, and the *Wall Street Journal*. Writes a column for *New York Newsday*. Serves as an affiliate scholar at the Institute for American Values.

ELLEN GOODMAN: Longtime columnist for the *Boston Globe*. Her syndicated column, "At Large," covers a wide range of subjects, including abortion, divorce, and parenting. Has published several collections of her columns, including *Close to Home*, *At Large*, *Keeping in Touch*, *Making Sense*, and *Value Judgments*. Won the Pulitzer Prize for commentary in 1980. Also wrote *Turning Points*, which explored how the feminist movement changed the lives of individuals. Born in 1941 in Newton, MA.

NAT HENTOFF: Columnist, writer, and social critic. Began his writing career in 1953 as a jazz critic for *Down Beat* magazine; was fired a few years later for lobbying management to hire African Americans. Turned to writing social criticism for the then fledgling *Village Voice*; continues to write a column for *Village Voice* and has been a columnist for the *Washington Post* since 1984. Has written novels for young adults and works of nonfiction on social issues. Born in 1925 in Boston, MA.

CHRISTOPHER HITCHENS: Liberal columnist and author. Columnist for *The Nation*, *Spectator*, the *Times Literary Supplement*, and *Vanity Fair*. Published collections of his writing in *Prepared for the Worst: Selected Essays and Minority Reports* and *For the Sake of Argument: Essays and Minority Reports*. Has written a number of other books, including *No One Left to Lie To: The Triangulations of William Jefferson Clinton*, about the Monica Lewinsky scandal. Born in 1949 in Portsmouth, England.

DAVID HOROWITZ: Author and civil rights activist. One of the founders of the New Left in the 1960s and former editor of *Ramparts*, a left-wing magazine. Has authored or coauthored numerous books covering a range of topics from prominent American families to economics to the radicalism of the 1960s. His autobiography, *Radical Son*, was published in 1997. Founded the Center for the Study of Popular Culture in 1988. Born in 1939 in New York, NY.

ARIANNA HUFFINGTON: Conservative writer and television personality. Her first book, *The Female Woman*, was published in 1973, shortly after her graduation from Cambridge University. Wrote controversial biographies of Maria Callas and Pablo Picasso. Came to national attention in 1994 during her then-husband's unsuccessful campaign for the Senate seat from California held by Democrat Dianne Feinstein. Has appeared on political discussion programs, including *Crossfire* and *Politically Incorrect*. Helped found the Center for Effective Compassion, which advocates private charity instead of government aid. Is currently a senior fellow at the Progress and Freedom Foundation, a conservative think tank. Born in 1950 in Athens, Greece.

MOLLY IVINS: Liberal columnist for the *Dallas Times Herald* known for her sharp wit in writing about politics and politicians. Made her name covering the Texas legislature and gained national popularity following the 1991 publication of *Molly Ivins Can't Say That, Can She?*, a best-selling collection of her columns. Born in 1942 in River Oaks, TX.

BILL KELLER: Journalist. Longtime reporter and editor for the *New York Times*. Received the Pulitzer Prize for international reporting in 1989 for his coverage of events in the Soviet Union. Became an op-ed columnist and senior writer for the *New York Times Magazine* and other areas of the paper in 2001. Born in 1949.

MICHAEL KINSLEY: Journalist and writer. Former cohost of the political discussion program *Crossfire*. Founded *Slate*, an online magazine published by Microsoft Corporation, in 1996. Contributing writer for *Time*. Has contributed to other publications, including *The New Yorker*, *Vanity Fair*, and *Conde Nast Traveler*. Author of *Big Babies: On Presidents, Politics and National Crazes*. Born in 1951 in Detroit, MI.

CHARLES KRAUTHAMMER: Columnist. Began his career as a psychiatrist, but in 1980 changed directions to become a speechwriter for Vice President Walter Mondale. Served as senior editor for *New Republic*, has been an essayist for *Time* since 1983 and a weekly syndicated columnist for the *Washington Post* since 1985. Published a collection of his essays, *Cutting Edges: Making Sense of the Eighties*, in 1985. Won the Pulitzer Prize for commentary in 1987 for his columns on national issues. Born in 1950 in New York, NY.

NICHOLAS KRISTOF: Journalist. Longtime reporter for the *New York Times*. Along with his wife and fellow *Times* reporter, Sheryl Wu Dunn, won the 1990 Pulitzer Prize for international reporting for their coverage of the Tiananmen Square massacre and its aftermath. The two have written several books about Asia, including *China Wakes: The Struggle for the Soul of a Rising Power*, *The Japanese Economy at the Millennium: Correspondents' Insightful Views*, and *Thunder from the East: Portrait of a Rising Asia*. Born in 1959 in Chicago, IL.

HOWARD KURTZ: Journalist, author, and television show host. Reporter for the *Washington Post* since 1981; writes the "Media Notes" column for the *Post*. Hosts *Reliable Sources*, a weekly television program focusing on the media's coverage of news. Author of several books on the media, including *Media Circus: The Trouble with America's Newspapers*, *Spin-Cycle: Inside the Clinton Propaganda Machine*, *Hot Air: All Talk All the Time*, and *The Fortune Tellers*. Has contributed to various publications, including *American Journalism Review*, *Columbia Journalism Review*, *The New Republic*, *New York Magazine*, *Vanity Fair*, and *Washington Monthly*. Born in 1953 in Brooklyn, NY.

RUSH LIMBAUGH: Conservative radio host, author, and syndicated columnist. Achieved unprecedented popularity and influence in early 1990s, with near-cult following of loyal "dittoeheads" tuning in to hear his self-labeled "daily, relentless, unstoppable pursuit of the truth." Remains a leading personality in the promotion of the conservative agenda. Born in 1951 in Cape Girardeau, MO.

CHRIS MATTHEWS: Journalist, writer, television show host. Served as speechwriter to President Jimmy Carter and as senior aide to House Speaker Tip O'Neill. Became a journalist and worked as Washington bureau chief for the *San Francisco Chronicle* for 13 years; continues to write a nationally syndicated column for the *Chronicle*. Host of the television political discussion program *Hardball with Chris Matthews*. Author of *Now Let Me Tell You What I Really Think*, *Hardball*, and *Kennedy & Nixon*.

DICK MORRIS: Political consultant and campaign strategist who helped Bill Clinton win the Arkansas governor's race twice and the presidential election once. Also worked for Republicans, including Jesse Helms and Trent Lott. He was immediately dumped from Clinton's reelection campaign. He published his memoirs, *Behind the Oval Office: Winning the Presidency in the 1990s*, in 1997. Born 1948 in New York, NY.

LYN NOFZIGER: Conservative political consultant and writer. Ran or participated in a number of political campaigns, including five presidential campaigns. Served in Ronald Reagan's governor's office and in the Reagan White House as press secretary and then assistant for political affairs. Wrote about his time at the White House in his 1992 political memoir *Nofziger* and has also written several western novels. Born in 1924 in Bakersfield, CA.

PEGGY NOONAN: Conservative writer who served as a special assistant to President Ronald Reagan and then as speechwriter for presidential candidate and President-elect George Bush. Generated some controversy by publicly acknowledging which speeches she wrote. Chronicled her Reagan White House years in *What I Saw at the Revolution: A Political Life in the Reagan Era*. Later took on then-first lady Hillary Clinton in *The Case against Hillary Clinton*. Born in 1950 in Brooklyn, NY.

OLIVER NORTH: Conservative writer, lecturer, and radio show host. A lieutenant colonel in the U.S. Marine Corps, North was catapulted into the national spotlight in 1987 because of his testimony before Congress during the Iran-Contra hearings. North was convicted for his part in the scandal, but the convictions were later overturned. Now hosts "Common Sense Radio," a nationally syndicated program. Born in 1943 in San Antonio, TX.

ROBERT NOVAK: Conservative columnist, writer, and commentator. Along with Rowland Evans, cohosts the political discussion program *Evans and Novak*; appears on other political television shows, including *Crossfire* and *Meet the Press*. Along with Evans has written several books on politics and government, including 1981's *The Reagan Revolution: An Inside Look at the Transformation of the U.S. Government*, a flattering look at the Reagan administration and its policies. Writes the nationally syndicated column "Inside Report." Born in 1931 in Joliet, IL.

KATE O'BEIRNE: Journalist and political analyst. Worked for the Heritage Foundation as deputy director of domestic policy studies and then as vice president of government relations. Served as deputy assistant secretary for legislation at the Department of Health and Human Services from 1986–1988. Is currently the Washington editor of *National Review*, a panelist on the political discussion program *The Capital Gang*, and a political analyst on the program *Inside Politics*.

BILL O'REILLY: Television show host and producer, and writer. Worked as a network news reporter before becoming host of the nationally syndicated program *Inside Edition*. In 1996 became host and producer of his own talk show, *The O'Reilly Factor*. Is known for his confrontational style and his pledge to take the "spin" out of news. Author of *The O'Reilly Factor: The Good, the Bad, & the Completely Ridiculous in American Life*, which is part memoir and part commentary. Writes a syndicated weekly column and has contributed articles to several publications, including the *New York Times*, *Newsweek*, and *Parade*. Born in 1949 in Long Island, NY.

CAMILLE PAGLIA: Writer and educator. Generated controversy following the 1990 publication of her first book, *Sexual Personae: Art and Decadence from Nefertiti to Emily Dickinson*, for her unorthodox views on human sexuality and modern feminism. Also wrote *Sex, Art and American Culture: Essays* and *Vamps and Tramps: New Essays*, and has contributed to many journals. Currently teaches at Philadelphia University of the Arts. Born in 1947 in Endicott, NY.

JOHN PODHORETZ: Conservative journalist, author, and speechwriter. Served as speechwriter for presidents Ronald Reagan and George Bush, and later as a special assistant to William Bennett, head of the Office of National Drug Control Policy. Author of *Hell of a Ride*, a behind-the-scenes look at the White House staff during Bush's unsuccessful 1992 reelection campaign. Writes a column for the *New York Post* and contributes to a number of publications, including *American Spectator*, the *New York Post*, *U.S. News and World Report*, and the *Washington Times*. Born in 1961 in New York, NY.

RICHARD REEVES: Writer and historian. Author of a number of books on politics and history. His works on political figures include *A Ford, Not a Lincoln*, which took a critical look at Gerald Ford's first 100 days as president. Has written for a number of magazines, including *Harper's*, *New Leader*, the *New York Times Magazine*, *The New Yorker*, *Playboy*, *Reader's Digest*, and *Saturday Review*. Born in 1936 in New York, NY.

FRANK RICH: Columnist and author. Became chief drama critic at the *New York Times* in 1980; has been writing a column on the op-ed page since 1994 and is senior writer for the *New York Times Magazine*. Author of *Ghost Light: A Memoir* and *Hot Seat: Theater Criticism for The New York Times, 1980-1993*. Born in 1949 in Washington, DC.

WILLIAM SAFIRE: Conservative journalist and author. Served as speechwriter for Spiro Agnew in his unsuccessful 1968 bid for the Republican presidential nomination; later served as senior speechwriter for President Richard Nixon. Wrote about his time in the Nixon White House in *Before the Fall*. Longtime columnist for the *New York Times*; won the Pulitzer Prize for commentary in 1978 for his columns on the financial dealings of Bert Lance, President Jimmy Carter's budget director. Also writes about language and word usage in the "On Language" column in the *New York Times Magazine*. Has written numerous books on politics and language, as well as works of fiction. Born in 1929 in New York, NY.

DEBRA SAUNDERS: Conservative columnist. Has written for the *National Review*, *Reader's Digest*, *Reason*, the *Wall Street Journal*, and *The Weekly Standard*. Has appeared on political discussion programs, including *Politically Incorrect*. Writes a nationally syndicated column. Born in 1954 in Newton, MA.

PHYLLIS SCHLAFLY: Conservative writer and activist. A longtime champion of conservative causes, Schlafly became well known in the 1970s for her opposition to the proposed Equal Rights Amendment. Has authored or coauthored a number of books, including *The Positive Woman*, a comparison of the traditional wife and homemaker to modern feminists. Writes a nationally syndicated column, hosts a weekly talk show, and publishes *The Phyllis Schlafly Report*, a monthly newsletter. Born in 1924 in St. Louis, MO.

TONY SNOW: Conservative columnist and political commentator. Served as deputy assistant to the president for communications and as director of speech writing in the George Bush White House. Is a commentator on National Public Radio and appears regularly on political discussion programs, including *Crossfire*, *Face the Nation*, *The McLaughlin Group*, and *The McNeil-Lehrer NewsHour*. Writes a nationally syndicated column. Born in 1955 in Berea, KY.

JOSEPH SOBRAN: Conservative writer and commentator. Served as senior editor and then critic at large of *National Review*. Generated controversy in the 1980s for several columns that were viewed by some as being anti-Semitic, and again in 1990 for his opposition to the Gulf War. Also generated controversy in academic and literary circles for his claim in his 1997 book *Alias Shakespeare: Solving the Greatest Literary Mystery of All Time* that the Earl of Oxford was the true author of the plays attributed to William Shakespeare. Born in 1946 in Detroit, MI.

DR. THOMAS SOWELL: Conservative African American economist, writer, and educator. His belief that individuals—not the government—are responsible for improving their lives and his opposition to such programs as affirmative action, busing, minimum wage, and welfare have generated criticism from liberals and other black leaders. Has written extensively on race issues as they relate to social and economic policy. Has taught at Amherst University, Brandeis University, Cornell University, Rutgers University, and the University of California at Los Angeles. Serves as a senior fellow at the Hoover Institution on War, Revolution and Peace. Born in 1930 in Gastonia, NC.

CAL THOMAS: Conservative columnist and commentator. Hosted his own interview program on CNBC and is a commentator for Fox News Channel and a panelist on *Fox News Watch*. One-time spokesperson for the Moral Majority. Author of several books, including *Blinded by Might: Can the Religious Right Save America?* and *The Wit and Wisdom of Cal Thomas*. Writes an internationally syndicated column.

R. EMMETT TYRRELL, JR.: Conservative writer. Founded *American Spectator*, a magazine taking an irreverent look at liberals and liberal causes. Has written several books of political commentary, including *Public Nuisances*, *The Liberal Crack-Up*, *The Conservative Crack-up*, and *Boy Clinton: The Political Biography*. Writes a nationally syndicated column. Born in 1943 in Chicago, IL.

BEN WATTENBERG: Demographer and writer. Beginning with the 1965 publication of *This U.S.A.: An Unexpected Family Portrait of 194,067,286 Americans Drawn from the Census*, coauthored with Richard M. Scammon, Wattenberg has used statistics to paint a generally optimistic picture of American life. Because he has challenged popularly held beliefs about American life—such as the divorce rate is increasing, a population explosion is underway, and the standard of living for African Americans is not improving—his writings have generated criticism. Is a senior fellow at the American Enterprise Institute, moderates the PBS program *Think Tank*, and writes a syndicated column. Born in 1933 in New York, NY.

GEORGE WILL: Conservative columnist, writer, and commentator. Columnist for the *Washington Post* and *Newsweek*, and a commentator on the television programs *This Week* and *World News Tonight*. Received the Pulitzer Prize for distinguished commentary in 1977. Has published several collections of his magazine and newspaper columns, and written other books on social and political topics. An avid baseball fan, wrote *Men* *at Work: The Craft of Baseball* and *Bunts, Curt Flood, Camden Yards, Pete Rose and Other Reflections on Baseball*. Born in 1941 in Champaign, IL.

BOB WOODWARD: Journalist and author. As a reporter for the *Washington Post*, Woodward and fellow *Post* reporter Carl Bernstein pursued the story surrounding the 1972 break-in at the Democratic National Party's offices in the Watergate Hotel and the subsequent cover-up by members of the Nixon administration. In 1974, Woodward and Bernstein published *All the President's Men*, which told the story of their efforts to uncover the scandal. Has written other books on the government and public figures, and continues to work at the *Post*. Born in 1943 in Geneva, IL.

Index

B

C

D

E

F

G

H

I

J

K

L

M

N

O

P

Q

R

S

T

U

V

W

Y

Z

About the Author

Gina Misiroglu is a fourteen-year veteran of the West Coast publishing industry, specializing in the development and editing of popular culture, reference, and history titles. Misiroglu is the author of *Girls Like Us: 40 Extraordinary Women Celebrate Girlhood in Story, Poetry, and Song*, winner of the New York Public Library's "Best Book for Teens" Award, and *Imagine: The Spirit of Twentieth-Century American Heroes* (both New World Library, 1999). Of the titles she has contributed to, she is particularly proud of her co-authorship of *Space Jammin': Bugs and Michael Hit the Big Screen* (Rutledge Hill Press, 1997), and her work as editor and contributing writer to *Lay Down Body: Living History in African-American Cemeteries*, a reference book on African American genealogy, history, and folklore (Visible Ink Press, 1996). Misiroglu resides in Los Angeles.